DATE DUE			

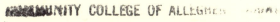

THE SHAPE OF FICTION

BRITISH
AND AMERICAN
SHORT
STORIES

THE SHAPE OF FICTION

BRITISH AND AMERICAN SHORT STORIES

LEO HAMALIAN

FREDERICK R. KARL

Both of The City College of New York

McGraw-Hill Book Company
New York
St. Louis
San Francisco
Toronto

THE SHAPE OF FICTION
British and American Short Stories

Library of Congress Catalog Card Number 67-12624

1234567890VB7432106987

Acknowledgments

Conrad Aiken, "Impulse" from *The Collected Short Stories of Conrad Aiken.* Copyright © 1933, 1960 by Conrad Aiken. Published by arrangement with The World Publishing Company, Cleveland and New York.

Sherwood Anderson, "The Teacher" from *Winesburg, Ohio* by Sherwood Anderson. Copyright 1919 by B. W. Huebsch, Inc., 1947 by Eleanor Copenhaver Anderson. Reprinted by permission of The Viking Press, Inc.

Saul Bellow, "Leaving the Yellow House" from *Esquire* (January, 1958), published by Esquire, Inc. Copyright © 1958 by Saul Bellow. Reprinted by permission of Saul Bellow.

Ambrose Bierce, "Killed at Resaca" from *In the Midst of Life, Tales of Soldiers and Civilians* by Ambrose Bierce, 1892.

Kay Boyle, "The Effigy of War," copyright 1940 by Kay Boyle. First published in *The New Yorker* (May 25, 1940).

Hortense Calisher, "Il Plœ:r Dã Mõ Kœ:r," copyright © 1956 by Hortense Calisher; originally appeared in *The New Yorker.* From *Extreme Magic* by Hortense Calisher, by permission of Little, Brown and Co.

Willa Cather, "Paul's Case" from *Youth and the Bright Medusa* by Willa Cather, 1904, courtesy of Alfred A. Knopf, Inc.

Joseph Conrad, "Il Conde" from *A Set of Six,* 1908. Reprinted by permission of J. M. Dent & Sons Ltd. and the Trustees of the Joseph Conrad Estate.

Stephen Crane, "The Upturned Face" from *Last Words* by Stephen Crane, 1902.

William Faulkner, "Dry September." Copyright 1930 and renewed 1958 by William Faulkner. Reprinted from *The Collected Stories of William Faulkner,* by permission of Random House, Inc.

Graham Greene, "Brother" from *Twenty-One Stories* by Graham Greene. Copyright 1947 by Graham Greene. Reprinted by permission of The Viking Press, Inc., and William Heinemann Limited.

Nathaniel Hawthorne, "Young Goodman Brown" from *Mosses from an Old Manse* by Nathaniel Hawthorne, 1846.

Lafcadio Hearn, "Mujina" from *Kwaidan: Stories and Studies of Strange Things* by Lafcadio Hearn, 1904.

Ernest Hemingway, "The Capital of the World," copyright 1936 Ernest Hemingway; renewal copyright © 1964 Mary Hemingway; first published in *Esquire* under the title "The Horns of the Bull." From *The Short Stories of Ernest Hemingway,* by permission of Charles Scribner's Sons.

Henry James, "Paste" from *The Soft Side* by Henry James, 1900.

James Joyce, "Counterparts" from *Dubliners* by James Joyce. Originally published by B. W. Huebsch in 1916. Reprinted by permission of The Viking Press, Inc.

D. H. Lawrence, "The Horse Dealer's Daughter" from *The Complete Short Stories of D. H. Lawrence,* Vol. II. Copyright 1922 by Thomas B. Seltzer, Inc., 1950 by Frieda Lawrence. Reprinted by permission of The Viking Press, Inc.

Jack London, "Love of Life" from *Love of Life and Other Stories* by Jack London, 1907.

Norman Mailer, "The Language of Men" from *Advertisements for Myself* by Norman Mailer. Copyright 1959 by Norman Mailer. Reprinted by permission of G. P. Putnam's Sons.

Bernard Malamud, "The Prison" from *The Magic Barrel* by Bernard Malamud. Copyright 1950 by Bernard Malamud. Reprinted by permission of Farrar, Straus & Giroux, Inc.

H. H. Munro (Saki), "The Mouse" (1910) from *The Complete Short Stories of Saki* (1930) by H. H. Munro. All Rights Reserved. Reprinted by permission of The Viking Press, Inc., and The Bodley Head Ltd., London.

Vladimir Nabokov, "That in Aleppo Once . . . ," copyright 1943 by Atlantic Monthly Company, from *Nabokov's Dozen* by Vladimir Nabokov. Reprinted by permission of Doubleday & Company, Inc.

Hugh Nissenson, "The Well" from *A Pile of Stones* by Hugh Nissenson. Copyright © 1960 Hugh Nissenson. Reprinted by permission of Charles Scribner's Sons.

Flannery O'Connor, "A Good Man Is Hard to Find" from *A Good Man Is Hard to Find and Other Stories,* copyright 1953 by Flannery O'Connor. Reprinted by permission of Harcourt, Brace & World, Inc.

Frank O'Connor, "First Confession." Copyright 1951 by Frank O'Connor. Reprinted from *Stories of Frank O'Connor,* by permission of Alfred A. Knopf, Inc.

Liam O'Flaherty, "The Touch" from *The Stories of Liam O'Flaherty,* published 1956 by The Devin-Adair Co.; copyright 1956 by The Devin-Adair Co. Reprinted by permission of the publisher.

Edgar Allan Poe, "The Cask of Amontillado," first published in *Godey's Lady Book* (November, 1846).

Katherine Anne Porter, "The Grave" from *The Leaning Tower and Other Stories,* copyright 1944 by Katherine Anne Porter. Reprinted by permission of Harcourt, Brace & World, Inc.

J. F. Powers, "The Eye" from *Prince of Darkness and Other Stories,* copyright 1947 by J. F. Powers. Reprinted by permission of Doubleday & Company, Inc.

James Purdy, "Don't Call Me by My Right Name" from *Color of Darkness,* copyright © 1957, 1956 by James Purdy. Reprinted by permission of the publisher, New Directions.

Florence Engel Randall, "The Watchers" from *Harper's* (March, 1965). Copyright © 1965 by Harper's Magazine, Inc. Reprinted by permission of the author and her agent, Theron Raines.

William Sansom, "The Boiler-room." Reprinted by permission of the author.

Irwin Shaw, "The Girls in Their Summer Dresses." Copyright 1939 by Irwin Shaw. Reprinted from *Selected Short Stories of Irwin Shaw,* by permission of Random House, Inc.

Jesse Stuart, "Fight Number Twenty-Five" from *Clearing in the Sky* by Jesse Stuart. Copyright 1950 by Jesse Stuart. Reprinted by permission of the publisher, McGraw-Hill Book Company.

Dylan Thomas, "One Warm Saturday" from *Portrait of the Artist As a Young Dog* by Dylan Thomas. Copyright 1940 by New Directions. Reprinted by permission of the publisher, New Directions, J. M. Dent & Sons Ltd., and the Literary Executors of the Dylan Thomas Estate.

John Updike, "Dear Alexandros." © Copyright 1962 by John Updike. Reprinted from *Pigeon Feathers and Other Stories,* by John Updike, by permission of Alfred A. Knopf, Inc.

Robert Penn Warren, "The Unvexed Isles" from *The Circus in the Attic and Other Stories,* copyright 1947 by Robert Penn Warren. Reprinted by permission of Harcourt, Brace & World, Inc.

H. G. Wells, "The Country of the Blind" from *The Short Stories of H. G. Wells,* 1911. Reprinted by permission of A. P. Watt & Son and the executors of the H. G. Wells Estate.

Eudora Welty, "A Visit of Charity" from *A Curtain of Green and Other Stories,* copyright 1941 by Eudora Welty. Reprinted by permission of Harcourt, Brace & World, Inc.

PREFACE

The Shape of Fiction: British and American Short Stories is essentially an analytical text; that is, it assumes that the development of individual critical judgment—the ability to read with sensitivity and understanding—constitutes one of the chief pleasures of fiction. And such understanding is, after all, a reader's right. To this end, we have included with each story, analysis and questions extensive and careful enough to lead the student toward valid critical conclusions without anticipating his responses or preempting his judgments. Brief introductions acquaint the student with each significant aspect of fiction. Specific questions following each story lead him step-by-step toward his own interpretation. There is, thus, ample guidance along with maximum freedom in the development of individual critical judgment which constitutes the pleasure of reading and the goal of education.

We have chosen to organize this material by means of the basic aspects of the genre: plot, character, mood, theme, style, and point of view. These simple distinctions seem to permit the greatest clarity and flexibility with little danger of overlapping and confusion. The emphasis in each section falls on the specific aspect to which that section is devoted; topics that have preceded, however, are discussed and amplified as the book progresses. Such interrelations, we hope, will tie all of the material together and enforce the sense of totality of the work. Our intention here is to lead the student toward comprehending how a whole story "works," toward recognizing the particular craft of the writer and an informed appreciation of the effects he achieves.

Any new story collection must base its claim to existence on a number of counts. The first, obviously, is quality of content. Each story should be the best of its kind, and as editors, we have labored to this end. In addition, the collection covers the full range of American fiction from the "classics" of Poe, Hawthorne, and James, through the naturalistic stories of London, Crane, and Anderson, to such "modern classics" as those of Hemingway, Faulkner, Katherine Anne Porter, and Flannery O'Connor. Contemporary writers, such as Updike, Purdy, Florence Engel Randall, and Hortense Calisher, also appear, along with the masters of English short fiction—Conrad, Joyce, Lawrence, and H. G. Wells. In brief, we have tried to blend the past with the present in pleasing and intelligent proportion.

An alternate table of contents lists the stories chronologically in case that approach is desired.

All the stories here were written originally in English. Thus we are presenting the student with fiction in his own tongue and idiom. More important, however, is the availability and, indeed, the validity of close textual reading and analysis. Everyone who has read a work in translation, from those of Sappho to those of Yevgeny Yevtushenko, no matter how skillful the translation may be, knows the frustration and final impossibility of any attempt to appreciate the language and, in the end, the total meaning of the piece. The stories here give the reader complete freedom of analysis and, what is more, access to ultimate understanding.

We hope we are presenting here an analytical text which provides such access and which leads, furthermore, to a critical understanding and an informed enjoyment of the art of the story. We could ask for little more.

Leo Hamalian
Frederick R. Karl

CONTENTS

CHRONOLOGICAL CONTENTS

INTRODUCTION

Despite the veritable blizzard of short story anthologies in recent years, few indeed have been created for both the instruction of the student and the pleasure of the instructor. Toward this end, we have divided the stories of this collection into what we consider to be meaningful categories in the order of their significance: Setting, Mood and Atmosphere, Plot, Character, Theme, and Style and Point of View, with lengthy comments and questions that spill over significantly into other categories as well. Thus, a story discussed under Plot will also be treated, for example, under Theme, Character, and Setting, if those categories are relevant. We have asked questions and made observations that should help the student to read and, we hope, to enjoy these stories. At the same time, our queries open up areas for further discussion and exploration. Everything is fluid; nothing is intended to be dogmatic.

One danger involved in asking questions is that they frequently assume an understanding of a story when such is not the fact. Very often the reader will go through a tale failing to catch the most important elements. When he finishes, his interpretation will naturally be a matter of guesswork—based on a faulty grasp of essentials and an inattention to relevant detail. We have attempted to remove much of the guesswork. Without forcing the reader into our own interpretations, we have guided him into meaningful areas, particularly where details may be overlooked or misunderstood. Many questions help him along before he can compound certain wrong assumptions. Such questions are also provocative enough to provide abundant classroom discussion. Although some are technical in nature—driving toward the whole problem of what a short story is—we have never avoided social, political, and personal implications. In every instance, we have followed the story wherever it has led.

By restricting this anthology to British and American stories, we have made it possible to ask questions about style. When stories appear in translation, there is little point in seriously discussing their style, since the original language has been lost or at least modified considerably. The style of a translation is the style of the translator, not that of the writer—no matter how careful the translation is. In nearly all the present stories, style is a considerable factor, and we have asked such questions whenever necessary. There is no doubt that analyses of style give the reader a greater awareness of what a short story is—how it is constructed, what choices are open to the writer, how he selects language and figures of speech, how he sees his material through. Such considerations not only "open up" the story but lend themselves to classroom exercises or to home themes, as the instructor may wish.

The reader of short stories, particularly the more modern ones, becomes increasingly aware of their fluidity. All categories or distinctions are temporary affairs of convenience, and the careful reader must be aware of the artificiality of all forms of "scientific" interpretation. A short story is like a poem or a piece of music: everything is connected. And yet in discussing one, we tear it to pieces and try to consume it raw. We must always remember that a story—especially a good one—is more than the total of our interpretations. A good piece of fiction will always contain mysteries that an analysis cannot reveal. Such a story—and we have included many here—will continue to yield ideas and sparks as long as we keep at it. Yet there are limits to our energies and interests. We stop analyzing and talking at a certain point. And that point is usually the brink of evaluation.

The careful reader evaluates everything he reads, and in the final analysis, it is the evaluation that counts with fiction. Yet we have tried to avoid the obvious or booby-trapped questions like "Did you like the story?" and "How would you rate this work?" and have instead buried the evaluative questions inside the analytical questions. However, once these questions are touched by the reader, the signposts to evaluation should spring up. If ever it seems that the questions do not probe and penetrate deeply enough, he should remember that he is seeing the limitations of the editors, not of the story.

Should several of these stories seem ugly and morbid in content, it is because of the nature of modern fiction. The very best of fiction is often morbid. But morbidity is not always an absolute term, and frequently such an atmosphere is transcended by other qualities. Many of the present stories are concerned with such a transcendence, with the whole range of human experience. At every point, we have attempted to probe these areas of experience, for better or worse. And while our discussions may lead the reader into painful regions, they will at the same time bring awareness of what the best writers in English are concerned with.

For the convenience of the reader, we have included two stories as front pieces with elaborate analyses of each. We have discussed Joseph Conrad's "Il Conde" primarily under the category of Plot and Plot Structure, to show how that classification can be handled fully. Then we have followed through the same story, discussing aspects of it also under Theme or Purpose, Characterization, Setting and Atmosphere, Style and Point of View, and Further Aspects—comprising nearly every way in which it can be analyzed. No other story in the collection receives such close attention. For Saul Bellow's "Leaving the Yellow House," we have provided an extensive treatment that cuts equally across all categories.

Fiction should not be the source of anxiety about its meaning nor the basis of indiscriminate guesswork. It is surely most pleasurable when the author reaches across to tell us something new and profitable and we fully understand him. The aim of this book is to promote such understanding. That is what reading is all about.

IL CONDE

Joseph Conrad

"Vedi Napoli e poi mori"

The first time we got into conversation was in the National Museum in Naples, in the rooms on the ground floor containing the famous collection of bronzes from Herculaneum and Pompeii: that marvelous legacy of antique art whose delicate perfection has been preserved for us by the catastrophic fury of a volcano.

He addressed me first, over the celebrated Resting Hermes which we had been looking at side by side. He said the right things about that wholly admirable piece. Nothing profound. His taste was natural rather than cultivated. He had obviously seen many fine things in his life and appreciated them; but he had no jargon of a dilettante or the connoisseur. A hateful tribe. He spoke like a fairly intelligent man of the world, a perfectly unaffected gentleman.

We had known each other by sight for some few days past. Staying in the same hotel—good, but not extravagantly up to date—I had noticed him in the vestibule going in and out. I judged he was an old and valued client. The bow of the hotel-keeper was cordial in its deference, and he acknowledged it with familiar courtesy. For the servants he was *Il Conde.* There was some squabble over a man's parasol—yellow silk with white lining sort of thing—the waiter had discovered abandoned outside the dining-room door. Our gold-laced doorkeeper recognized it and I heard him directing one of the lift boys to run after *Il Conde* with it. Perhaps he was the only count staying in the hotel, or perhaps he had the distinction of being *the* Count *par excellence,* conferred upon him because of his tried fidelity to the house.

Having conversed at the Museo—(and by the by he had expressed his dislike of the busts and statues of Roman emperors in the gallery of marbles: their faces were too vigorous, too pronounced for him)—having conversed already in the morning I did not think I was intruding when in the evening, finding the dining room very full, I proposed to share his little table. Judging by the quiet urbanity of his consent he did not think so either. His smile was very attractive.

He dined in an evening waistcoat and a "smoking" (he

called it so) with a black tie. All this of very good cut, not new—just as these things should be. He was, morning or evening, very correct in his dress. I have no doubt that his whole existence had been correct, well ordered and conventional, undisturbed by startling events. His white hair brushed upwards off a lofty forehead gave him the air of an idealist, of an imaginative man. His white mustache, heavy but carefully trimmed and arranged, was not unpleasantly tinted a golden yellow in the middle. The faint scent of some very good perfume, and of good cigars (that last an odor quite remarkable to come upon in Italy) reached me across the table. It was in his eyes that his age showed most. They were a little weary with creased eyelids. He must have been sixty or a couple of years more. And he was communicative. I would not go so far as to call it garrulous—but distinctly communicative.

He had tried various climates, of Abbazia, of the Riviera, of other places, too, he told me, but the only one which suited him was the climate of the Gulf of Naples. The ancient Romans, who, he pointed out to me were men expert in the art of living, knew very well what they were doing when they built their villas on these shores, in Baiæ, in Vico, in Capri. They came down to this seaside in search of health, bringing with them their trains of mimes and flute-players to amuse their leisure. He thought it extremely probable that the Romans of the higher classes were specially predisposed to painful rheumatic affections.

This was the only personal opinion I heard him express. It was based on no special erudition. He knew no more of the Romans than an average informed man of the world is expected to know. He argued from personal experience. He had suffered himself from a painful and dangerous rheumatic affection till he found relief in this particular spot of Southern Europe.

This was three years ago, and ever since he had taken up his quarters on the shores of the gulf, either in one of the hotels in Sorrento or hiring a small villa in Capri. He had a piano, a few books; picked up transient acquaintances of a day, week, or month in the stream of travelers from all Europe. One can imagine him going out for his walks in the streets and lanes, becoming known to beggars, shopkeepers, children, country people; talking amiably over the walls to the *contadini*—and coming back to his rooms or his villa to sit before the piano, with his white hair brushed up and his thick orderly mustache, "to make a little music for myself." And, of course, for a change there was Naples near by—life, movement, animation, opera. A little amusement, as he said, is necessary for health. Mimes and flute-players, in fact. Only unlike the magnates of ancient Rome, he had no affairs of the city to call him away from these moderate delights. He had no affairs at all. Probably he had never had any grave affairs to attend to in his life. It was a kindly existence, with its joys and sorrows regulated by the course of Nature—marriages, births, deaths—ruled by the prescribed usages of good society and protected by the State.

He was a widower; but in the months of July and August he ventured to cross the Alps for six weeks on a visit to his married daughter. He told me her name. It was that of a very aristocratic family. She had a castle—in Bohemia, I think. This is as near as I ever came to ascertaining his nationality. His own name, strangely enough, he never mentioned. Perhaps he thought I had seen in to the published list. Truth to say, I never looked. At any rate, he was a good European—he spoke four languages to my certain knowledge—and a man of fortune. Not of great fortune evidently and appropriately. I imagine that to be extremely rich would have appeared to him improper, *outré*—too blatant altogether. And obviously, too, the fortune was not of his making. The making of a fortune cannot be achieved without some roughness. It is a matter of temperament. His nature was too kindly for strife. In the course of conversation he mentioned his estate quite by the way, in reference to that painful and alarming rheumatic affection. One year, staying incautiously beyond the Alps as late as the middle of September, he had been laid up for three months in that lonely country house with no one but his valet and the caretaking couple to attend to him. Because, as he expressed it, he "kept no establishment there." He had only gone for a couple of days to confer with his land agent. He promised himself never to be so imprudent in the future. The first weeks of September would find him on the shores of his beloved gulf.

Sometimes in traveling one comes upon such lonely men, whose only business is to wait for the unavoidable. Deaths and marriages have made a solitude round them, and one really cannot blame their endeavors to make the waiting as easy as possible. As he remarked to me, "At my time of life freedom from physical pain is a very important matter."

It must not be imagined that he was a wearisome hypochondriac. He was really much too well bred to be a nuisance. He had an eye for the small weaknesses of humanity. But it was a good-natured eye. He made a restful, easy, pleasant companion for the hours between dinner and bedtime. We spent three evenings together, and then I had to leave Naples in a hurry to look after a friend who had fallen seriously ill in Taormina. Having nothing to do, *Il Conde* came to see me off at the station. I was somewhat upset, and his idleness was always ready to take a kindly form. He was by no means an indolent man.

He went along the train peering into the carriages for a good seat for me, and then remained talking cheerily from below. He declared he would miss me that evening very much and announced his intention of going after dinner to listen to the band in the public garden, the Villa Nazionale. He would amuse himself by hearing excellent music and looking at the best society. There would be a lot of people, as usual.

I seem to see him yet—his raised face with a friendly smile under the thick mustaches, and his kind, fatigued eyes. As the train began to move, he addressed me in two languages: first in French, saying "*Bon voyage*"; then in his very good, somewhat emphatic English, encouragingly, because he could see my concern: "All will—be—well—yet!"

My friend's illness having taken a decidedly favorable turn, I returned to Naples on the tenth day. I cannot say I had given much thought to *Il Conde* during my absence, but entering the dining room I looked for him in his habitual place. I had an idea he might have gone back to Sorrento to his piano and his books and his fishing. He was great friends with all the boatmen, and fished a good deal with lines from a boat. But I made out his white head in the crowd of heads, and even from a distance noticed something unusual in his attitude. Instead of sitting erect, gazing all round with alert urbanity, he drooped over his plate. I stood opposite him for some time before he looked up, a little wildly, if such a strong word can be used in connection with his correct appearance.

"Ah, my dear sir! Is it you?" he greeted me. "I hope all is well."

He was very nice about my friend. Indeed, he was always nice, with the niceness of people whose hearts are genuinely humane. But this time it cost him an effort. His attempts at general conversation broke down into dullness. It occurred to me he might have been indisposed. But before I could frame the inquiry he muttered:

"You find me here very sad."

"I am sorry for that," I said. "You haven't had bad news, I hope?"

It was very kind of me to take an interest. No. It was not that. No bad news, thank God. And he became very still as if holding his breath. Then, leaning forward a little, and in an odd tone of awed embarrassment, he took me into his confidence.

"The truth is that I have had a very—a very—how shall I say?—abominable adventure happen to me."

The energy of the epithet was sufficiently startling in that man of moderate feelings and toned-down vocabulary. The word unpleasant I should have thought would have fitted amply the worst experience likely to befall a man of his stamp. And an adventure, too. Incredible! But it is in human nature to believe the worst; and I confess I eyed him stealthily, wondering what he had been up to. In a moment, however, my unworthy suspicions vanished. There was a fundamental refinement of nature about the man which made me dismiss all idea of some more or less disreputable scrape.

"It is very serious. Very serious." He went on, nervously. "I will tell you after dinner, if you will allow me."

I expressed my perfect acquiescence by a little bow, nothing more. I wished him to understand that I was not likely to hold him to that offer, if he thought better of it later on. We talked of indifferent things, but with a sense of difficulty quite unlike our former easy gossipy intercourse. The hand raising a piece of bread to his lips, I noticed, trembled slightly. This symptom, in regard to my reading of the man, was no less than startling.

In the smoking room he did not hang back at all. Directly we had taken our usual seats he leaned sideways over the arm of his chair and looked straight into my eyes earnestly.

"You remember," he began, "that day you went away? I told you then I would go to the Villa Nazionale to hear some music in the evening."

I remembered. His handsome old face, so fresh for his age, unmarked by any trying experience, appeared haggard for an instant. It was like the passing of a shadow. Returning his steadfast gaze, I took a sip of my black coffee. He was systematically minute in his narrative, simply in order, I think, not to let his excitement get the better of him.

After leaving the railway station, he had an ice, and read the paper in a café. Then he went back to the hotel, dressed for dinner, and dined with a good appetite. After dinner he lingered in the hall (there were chairs and tables there) smoking his cigar; talked to the little girl of the Primo Tenore of the San Carlo Theater, and exchanged a few words with that "amiable lady,'' the wife of the Primo Tenore. There was no performance that evening, and these people were going to the Villa also. They went out of the hotel. Very well.

At the moment of following their example—it was half-past nine already—he remembered he had a rather large sum of money in his pocketbook. He entered, therefore, the office and deposited the greater part of it with the bookkeeper of the hotel. This done, he took a *carozella* and drove to the seashore. He got out of the cab and entered the Villa on foot from the Largo di Vittoria end.

He stared at me very hard. And I understood then how really impressionable he was. Every small fact and event of that evening stood out in his memory as if endowed with mystic significance. If he did not mention to me the color of the pony which drew the *carozella,* and the aspect of the man who drove, it was a mere oversight arising from his agitation, which he repressed manfully.

He had then entered the Villa Nazionale from the Largo di Vittoria end. The Villa Nazionale is a public pleasure-ground laid out in grass plots, bushes, and flowerbeds and between the houses of the Riviera di Chiaja and the waters of the bay. Alleys of trees, more or less parallel, stretch its whole length—which is considerable. On the Riviera di Chiaja side the electric tramcars run close to the railings. Between the garden and the sea is the fashionable drive, a broad road bordered by a low wall, beyond which the Mediterranean splashes with gentle murmurs when the weather is fine.

As life goes on late at night in Naples, the broad drive was all astir with a brilliant swarm of carriage lamps moving in pairs, some creeping slowly, others running rapidly under the thin, motionless line of electric lamps defining the shore. And a brilliant swarm of stars hung above the land humming with voices, piled up with houses, glittering with lights—and over the silent flat shadows of the sea.

The gardens themselves are not very well lit. Our friend went forward in the warm gloom, his eyes fixed upon a distant luminous region extending nearly across the whole width of the Villa, as if the air had glowed there with its own cold, bluish, and dazzling light. This magic spot, behind the black trunks of trees and masses of inky foliage, breathed out sweet sounds mingled with bursts of brassy roar, sudden clashes of metal, and grave, vibrating thuds.

As he walked on, all these noises combined together into a

piece of elaborate music whose harmonious phrases came persuasively through a great disorderly murmur of voices and shuffling of feet on the gravel of that open space. An enormous crowd immersed in the electric light, as if in a bath of some radiant and tenuous fluid shed upon their heads by luminous globes, drifted in hundreds round the band. Hundreds more sat on chairs in more or less concentric circles, receiving unflinchingly the great waves of sonority that ebbed out into the darkness. The Count penetrated the throng, drifted with it in tranquil enjoyment, listening and looking at the faces. All people of good society: mothers with their daughters, parents and children, young men and young women all talking, smiling, nodding to each other. Very many pretty faces, and very many pretty toilettes. There was, of course, a quantity of diverse types: showy old fellows with white mustaches, fat men, thin men, officers in uniform; but what predominated, he told me, was the South Italian type of young man, with a colorless, clear complexion, red lips, jet-black little mustache and liquid black eyes so wonderfully effective in leering or scowling.

Withdrawing from the throng, the Count shared a little table in front of the café with a young man of just such a type. Our friend had some lemonade. The young man was sitting moodily before an empty glass. He looked up once, and then looked down again. He also tilted his hat forward. Like this—

The Count made the gesture of a man pulling his hat down over his brow, and went on:

"I think to myself: he is sad; something is wrong with him; young men have their troubles. I take no notice of him, of course. I pay for my lemonade, and go away."

Strolling about in the neighborhood of the band, the Count thinks he saw twice that young man wandering alone in the crowd. Once their eyes met. It must have been the same young man, but there were so many there of that type that he could not be certain. Moreover, he was not very much concerned except in so far that he had been struck by the marked, peevish discontent of that face.

Presently, tired of the feeling of confinement one experiences in a crowd, the Count edged away from the band. An alley, very somber by contrast, presented itself invitingly with its promise of solitude and coolness. He entered it, walking slowly on till the sound of the orchestra became distinctly deadened. Then he walked back and turned about once more. He did this several times before he noticed that there was somebody occupying one of the benches.

The spot being midway between two lampposts the light was faint.

The man lolled back in the corner of the seat, his legs stretched out, his arms folded and his head drooping on his breast. He never stirred, as though he had fallen asleep there, but when the Count passed by next time he had changed his attitude. He sat leaning forward. His elbows were propped on his knees, and his hands were rolling a cigarette. He never looked up from that occupation.

The Count continued his stroll away from the band. He returned slowly, he said. I can imagine him enjoying to the full, but with his usual tranquility, the balminess of the southern night and the sounds of music softened delightfully by the distance.

Presently, he approached for the third time the man on the garden seat, still leaning forward with his elbows on his knees. It was a dejected pose. In the semiobscurity of the alley his high shirt collar and his cuffs made small patches of vivid whiteness. The Count said that he had noticed him getting up brusquely as if to walk away, but almost before he was aware of it the man stood before him asking in a low, gentle tone whether the signore would have the kindness to oblige him with a light.

The Count answered this request by a polite "Certainly," and dropped his hands with the intention of exploring both pockets of his trousers for the matches.

"I dropped my hands," he said, "but I never put them in my pockets. I felt a pressure there—"

He put the tip of his finger on a spot close under his breastbone, the very spot of the human body where a Japanese gentleman begins the operations of the hara-kiri, which is a form of suicide following upon dishonor, upon an intolerable outrage to the delicacy of one's feelings.

"I glance down," the Count continued in an awe-struck voice, "and what do I see? A knife! A long knife—"

"You don't mean to say," I exclaimed, amazed, "that you have been held up like this in the Villa at half-past ten o'clock, within a stone's throw of a thousand people!"

He nodded several times, staring at me with all his might.

"The clarinet," he declared, solemnly, "was finishing its solo, and I assure you I could hear every note. Then the band crashed *fortissimo,* and that creature rolled its eyes and gnashed its teeth hissing at me with the greatest ferocity, 'Be silent! No noise or—' "

I could not get over my astonishment.

"What sort of knife was it?" I asked, stupidly.

"A long blade. A stiletto—perhaps a kitchen knife. A long narrow blade. It gleamed. And his eyes gleamed. His white teeth, too. I could see them. He was very ferocious. I thought to myself: 'If I hit him he will kill me.' How could I fight with him? He had the knife and I had nothing. I am nearly seventy, you know, and that was a young man. I seemed even to recognize him. The moody young man of the café. The young man I met in the crowd. But I could not tell. There are so many like him in this country."

The distress of that moment was reflected in his face. I should think that physically he must have been paralyzed by surprise. His thoughts, however, remained extremely active. They ranged over every alarming possibility. The idea of setting up a vigorous shouting for help occurred to him, too. But he did nothing of the kind, and the reason why he refrained gave me a good opinion of his mental self-possession. He saw in a flash that nothing prevented the other from shouting, too.

"That young man might in an instant have thrown away his knife and pretended I was the aggressor. Why not? He might have said I attacked him. Why not? It was one incredible story against another! He might have said anything—bring some dishonoring charge against me—what do I know? By his dress he was no common robber. He seemed to belong to the better classes. What could I say? He was an Italian—I am a foreigner. Of course, I have my passport, and there is our consul—but to be arrested, dragged at night to the police office like a criminal!"

He shuddered. It was in his character to shrink from scandal much more than from mere death. And certainly for many people this would have always remained—considering certain peculiarities of Neapolitan manners—a deucedly queer story. The Count was no fool. His belief in the respectable placidity of life having received this rude shock, he thought that now anything might happen. But also a notion came into his head that this young man was perhaps merely an infuriated lunatic.

This was for me the first hint of his attitude towards this adventure. In his exaggerated delicacy of sentiment he felt that nobody's self-esteem need be affected by what a madman may choose to do to one. It became apparent, however, that the Count was to be denied that consolation. He enlarged upon the abominably savage way in which that young man rolled his glistening eyes and gnashed his white teeth. The band was going now through a slow movement of solemn braying by all the trombones. With deliberately repeated bangs of the big drum.

"But what did you do?" I asked, greatly excited.

"Nothing," answered the Count. "I let my hands hang down very still. I told him quietly I did not intend making a noise. He snarled like a dog, then said in an ordinary voice:

" '*Vostro portofolio.*'

"So I naturally," continued the Count—and from this point acted the whole thing in pantomime. Holding me with his eyes, he went through all the motions of reaching into his inside breast pocket, taking out a pocketbook, and handing it over. But that young man, still bearing steadily on the knife, refused to touch it.

He directed the Count to take the money out himself, received it into his left hand, motioned the pocketbook to be returned to the pocket, all this being done to the sweet trilling of flutes and clarinets sustained by the emotional drone of the hautboys. And the "young man," as the Count called him, said: "This seems very little."

"It was indeed, only 340 or 360 lire," the Count pursued. "I had left my money in the hotel, as you know. I told him this was all I had on me. He shook his head impatiently and said:

" '*Vostro orologio.*' "

The Count gave me the dumb show of pulling out his watch, detaching it. But, as it happened, the valuable gold half-chronometer he possessed had been left at a watchmaker's for cleaning. He wore that evening (on a leather guard) the Waterbury fifty-franc thing he used to take with him on his fishing expeditions. Perceiving the nature of this booty, the well-dressed robber made a contemptuous clicking sound with his tongue like this, "Tse-Ah!" and waved it away hastily. Then, as the Count was returning the disdained object to his pocket, he demanded with a threateningly increased pressure of the knife on the epigastrium, by the way of reminder:

"*Vostri anelli.*"

"One of the rings," went on the Count, "was given me many years ago by my wife; the other is the signet ring of my father. I said, 'No. *That* you shall not have!' "

Here the Count reproduced the gesture corresponding to that declaration by clapping one hand upon the other, and pressing both thus against his chest. It was touching in its resignation. "That you shall not have," he repeated, firmly, and closed his eyes, fully expecting—I don't know whether I am right in recording that such an unpleasant word had passed his lips—fully expecting to feel himself being—I really hesitate to say—being disemboweled by the push of the long, sharp blade resting murderously against the pit of his stomach—the very seat, in all human beings, of anguishing sensations.

Great waves of harmony went on flowing from the band.

Suddenly the Count felt the nightmarish pressure removed from the sensitive spot. He opened his eyes. He was alone. He had heard nothing. It is probable that "the young man" had departed, with light steps, some time before, but the sense of the horrid pressure had lingered even after the knife had gone. A feeling of weakness came over him. He had just time to stagger to the garden seat. He felt as though he had held his breath for a long time. He sat all in a heap, panting with the shock of the reaction.

The band was executing, with immense bravura, the complicated finale. It ended with a tremendous crash. He heard it, unreal and remote, as if his ears had been stopped, and then the hard clapping of a thousand, more or less, pairs of hands, like a sudden hail shower passing away. The profound silence which succeeded recalled him to himself.

A tramcar resembling a long glass box wherein people sat with their heads strongly lighted, ran along swiftly within sixty yards of the spot where he had been robbed. Then another rustled by, and yet another going the other way. The audience about the band had broken up, and were entering the alley in small conversing groups. The Count sat up straight and tried to think calmly of what had happened to him. The vileness of it took his breath away again. As far as I can make it out he was disgusted with himself. I do not mean to say with his behavior. Indeed, if his pantomimic rendering of it for my information was to be trusted, it was simply perfect. No, it was not that. He was not ashamed. He was shocked at being the selected victim, not of robbery so much as of contempt. His tranquillity had been wantonly desecrated. His lifelong, kindly nicety of outlook had been defaced.

Nevertheless, at that stage, before the iron had time to sink deep, he was able to argue himself into comparative equanimity. As his agitation calmed down somewhat, he became aware that he was frightfully hungry. Yes, hungry. The sheer emotion had made him simply ravenous. He left the seat and, after walking for some time, found himself outside the gardens and before an arrested tramcar, without knowing very well how he came there. He got in as if in a dream, by a sort of instinct. Fortunately he found in his trouser pocket a copper to satisfy the conductor. Then the car stopped, and as everybody was getting out he got out, too. He recognized the Piazza San Ferdinando, but apparently it did not occur to him to take a cab and drive to the hotel. He remained in distress on the Piazza like a lost dog, thinking vaguely of the best way of getting something to eat at once.

Suddenly he remembered his twenty-franc piece. He explained to me that he had that piece of French gold for something like three years. He used to carry it about with him as a sort of reserve in case of accident. Anybody is liable to have his pocket picked—a quite different thing from a brazen and insulting robbery.

The monumental arch of the Galleria Umberto faced him at the top of a noble flight of stairs. He climbed these without loss of time, and directed his steps towards the Café Umberto. All the tables outside were occupied by a lot of people who were drinking. But as he wanted something to eat, he went inside into the café, which is divided into aisles by square pillars set all round with long looking glasses. The Count sat down on a red plush bench against one of these pillars, waiting for his *risotto*. And his mind reverted to his abominable adventure.

He thought of the moody, well-dressed young man, with whom he had exchanged glances in the crowd around the bandstand, and who, he felt confident, was the robber. Would he recognize him again? Doubtless. But he did not want ever to see him again. The best thing was to forget this humiliating episode.

The Count looked round anxiously for the coming of his *risotto*, and, behold! to the left against the wall—there sat the young man. He was alone at a table, with a bottle of some sort of wine or syrup and a carafe of iced water before him. The smooth olive cheeks, the red lips, the little jet-black mustache turned up gallantly, the fine black eyes a little heavy and shaded by long eyelashes, that peculiar expression of cruel discontent to be seen only in the busts of some Roman emperors—it was he, no doubt at all. But that was a type. The Count looked away hastily. The young officer over there reading a paper was like that, too. Same type. Two young men farther away playing checkers also resembled—

The Count lowered his head with the fear in his heart of being everlastingly haunted by the vision of that young man. He began to eat his *risotto.* Presently he heard the young man on his left call the waiter in a bad-tempered tone.

At the call, not only his own waiter, but two other idle waiters belonging to a quite different row of tables, rushed towards him with obsequious alacrity, which is not the general characteristic of the waiters in the Café Umberto. The young man muttered something and one of the waiters walking rapidly to the nearest door called out into the Galleria: "Pasquale! O! Pasquale!"

Everybody knows Pasquale, the shabby old fellow who, shuffling between the tables, offers for sale cigars, cigarettes, picture postcards, and matches to the clients of the café. He is in many respects an engaging scoundrel. The Count saw the gray-haired, unshaven ruffian enter the café, the glass case hanging from his neck by a leather strap, and, at a word from the waiter, make his shuffling way with a sudden spurt to the young man's table. The young man was in need of a cigar with which Pasquale served him fawningly. The old peddler was going out, when the Count, on a sudden impulse, beckoned to him.

Pasquale approached, the smile of deferential recognition combining oddly with the cynical searching expression of his eyes. Leaning his case on the table, he lifted the glass lid without a word. The Count took a box of cigarettes and urged by a fearful curiosity, asked as casually as he could—

"Tell me, Pasquale, who is that young signore sitting over there?"

The other bent over his box confidentially.

"That, *Signor Conde,*" he said, beginning to rearrange his wares busily and without looking up, "that is a young *Cavaliere* of a very good family from Bari. He studies in the University here, and is the chief, *capo,* of an association of young men—of very nice young men."

He paused, and then, with mingled discretion and pride of knowledge, murmured the explanatory word "*Camorra*" and shut down the lid. "A very powerful *Camorra,*" he breathed out. "The professors themselves respect it greatly . . . *una lira e cinquanti centesimi, Signor Conde.*"

Our friend paid with the gold piece. While Pasquale was making up the change, he observed that the young man, of whom he had heard so much in a few words, was watching the transaction covertly. After the old vagabond had withdrawn with a bow, the Count settled with the waiter and sat still. A numbness, he told me, had come over him.

The young man paid, too, got up, and crossed over, apparently for the purpose of looking at himself in the mirror set in the pillar nearest to the Count's seat. He was dressed all in black with a dark green bow tie. The count looked round, and was startled by meeting a vicious glance out of the corners of the other's eyes. The young *Cavaliere* from Bari (according to Pasquale; but Pasquale is, of course, an accomplished liar) went on arranging his tie, settling his hat before the glass, and meantime he spoke just loud enough to be heard by the Count. He spoke through his teeth with the most insulting venom of contempt and gazing straight into the mirror.

"Ah! So you had some gold on you—you old liar—you old *birba*—you *furfante!* But you are not done with me yet."

The fiendishness of his expression vanished like lightning, and he lounged out of the café with a moody impassive face.

The poor Count, after telling me this last episode fell back trembling in his chair. His forehead broke into perspiration. There was a wanton insolence in the spirit of this outrage which appalled even me. What it was to the Count's delicacy I won't attempt to guess. I am sure that if he had been not too refined to do such a blatantly vulgar thing as dying from apoplexy in a café, he would have had a fatal stroke there and then. All irony apart, my difficulty was to keep him from seeing the full extent of my commiseration. He shrank from every excessive sentiment, and my commiseration was practically unbounded. It did not surprise me to hear that he had been in bed a week. He had got up to make his arrangements for leaving Southern Italy for good and all.

And the man was convinced that he could not live through a whole year in any other climate!

No argument of mine had any effect. It was not timidity, though he did say to me once: "You do not know what a *Camorra* is, my dear sir. I am a marked man." He was not afraid of what could be done to him. His delicate conception of his dignity was defiled by a degrading experience. He couldn't stand that. No Japanese gentleman, outraged in his exaggerated sense of honor, could have gone about his preparations for hara-kiri with greater resolution. To go home really amounted to suicide for the poor Count.

There is a saying of Neapolitan patriotism, intended for the information of foreigners, I presume: "See Naples and then die." *Vedi Napoli e poi mori.* It is a saying of excessive vanity, and everything excessive was abhorrent to the nice moderation of the poor Count. Yet, as I was seeing him off at the railway station, I thought he was behaving with singular fidelity to its conceited spirit. *Vedi Napoli!* . . . He had seen it! He had seen it with startling thoroughness—and now he was going to his grave. He was going to it by the *train de luxe* of the International Sleeping Car Company, via Trieste and Vienna. As the four long, somber coaches pulled out of the station I raised my hat with the solemn feeling of paying the last tribute of respect to a funeral cortège. *Il Conde's* profile, much aged already, glided away from me in stony immobility, behind the lighted pane of glass—*Vedi Napoli e poi mori!*

Plot (Events of the Story) and Plot Structure (How the Events Are Put Together)

1 Summarize the plot of "Il Conde." Does it sound like very much of a story? Why should you feel that so much is lost? Perhaps this sense of loss is connected with Conrad's method of plotting; that is, plot is not of primary importance, while other values are. Conrad uses what we might call a *bare plot*—one without an elaborate setting and with a limited number of characters. What does he gain by stripping his plot in this way? Does he lose anything?

2 A story frequently will proceed by counterpointing; through this method, the author will play off several forces against each other to create another dimension of reality. These contrasting forces may be of several types, taking the form of ideas, images, characters, values, even details of appearance. Such elements "carry" the plot, particularly in experimental and modern fiction. Usually such devices are of various kinds, for the author who uses only one type of contrast may become repetitious and obvious.

A good deal of the effectiveness of "Il Conde" depends on just such contrasts. The basic contrast is between the Count and the young man who accosts him in the gardens, although there are several other counterpointing elements as well. Try to describe as many differences between the young man and the Count as you can (see also question 4 under Theme or Purpose); exclude obvious difference of age, appearance, etc. Use their second encounter also as a source of information.

3 The author's use of music will often play a large part in the construction and development of a story. It is often there to indicate a dimension beyond the music itself. How does the music function in "Il Conde"? Is there any reason for it to be there beyond its decorative function? How does it become an element of the plot structure? Does the description of the museum at the beginning of the story, brief as it is, serve a similar purpose?

4 Conrad is careful to make the young man a member of the "better classes," as he calls them. The young man, in fact, comes from a class not very different from the Count's. What purpose does the emphasis on the young man's class serve? Does it really matter what class he comes from? Could he just as well be a member of the poorer, deprived class?

5 The young man seems intent on robbery, yet we suspect that robbery is not his entire intention. What clues does Conrad provide to establish the fact that his intention is not simply robbery? Would the Count be as disturbed if robbery were the sole motive? The question is speculative, but Conrad provides several clues for an answer. What does the Count suspect about the young man? What does the latter's physical appearance tell about him?

6 The young man points a stiletto at the Count's stomach, and this, understandably, causes terror and fear in the Count. Would a gun have created the same fear? Why does a knife serve Conrad's purpose better than a gun would?

7 In his second encounter with the young man, the Count recognizes that he must leave Naples. What forces seem to be operating that will drive him into exile, even though he knows his health needs Naples? Does his conviction to leave Naples seem within character? Why? Does Conrad lose any element of character (in the Count) for the sake of the plot?

Theme or Purpose

1 Conrad claimed, in his now-famous Preface to *The Nigger of the 'Narcissus,'* that the task of the writer is "to make you hear, to make you feel—it is, before all, to make you *see.*" Does he succeed in doing so? As you reread the story, indicate some of the ways in which Conrad makes you hear, feel, see; that is, indicate how he creates a tangible sense of reality.

2 Is Conrad's purpose limited to this attempt to make you hear, feel, and see, or does he aim for something else? How do you know?

3 Is there any connection between Conrad's way of presenting his material and what he wants to say? We can usually assume that an author will present his material in such a way as to bring out what he wants to say. As you read a story, try to extend its immediate matter into a larger frame of reference. Look for details, symbols, etc., as clues that the author wants you to read his story on several levels. In "Il Conde," Conrad's physical description of the Count is such a clue.

4 As suggested in question 3, Conrad is trying to indicate a vast clash of values which indicates that several important issues are at stake. This may seem to be a great deal of weight for a short, rather slow-moving story to bear, yet Conrad obviously has in mind a large social and political theme. We might say, in fact, that without the larger theme the story would fail to engage us deeply. Look for the values involved in the clash between the Count's generation and that of the young man's, between their respective tastes, their manners of dress, their appearances, their cultural attitudes. Ask yourself: Who is preferable, and why?

Characterization

1 The characters in this story are seen through the eyes of another personality. We see the Count through the narrator's eyes, and we see the young man through the Count's. Does this strengthen or weaken the reality of characterization? Perhaps it does both; yet an author must choose which manner of presentation suits his work best. Evidently Conrad felt that a first-person narrative was appropriate to this particular story, even though such a narrative device keeps the characters at arm's length. Does the character of the narrator serve any purpose beyond providing a filter for the story? Does he convince you that what he sees is really true, or does the story take on certain unreal qualities? Perhaps such unreal qualities—if they exist—are part of Conrad's intention, that is, to create a kind of fable rather than a strictly realistic story with entirely realistic characters. Comment on this point.

2 Very often authors reveal character indirectly—through surrounding objects, the use of place (setting), seemingly arbitrary details, even through climatic conditions (heat, cold, fog, sun, etc.). At the beginning of "Il Conde," how does Conrad suggest what type of person the Count is? Why is it important for the Count to be this kind of person? Again going through the story, pick out similar information which helps you to pinpoint the

Count as an individual. Then do the same with the young man, from his first introduction through each encounter with the Count. Is there consistency to each one's actions, and does each seem consistently motivated? Do not be afraid to be critical. A poor story often will show its weaknesses in the lack of consistency in its characters, whereas a good story will be strong in this very point.

3 Despite his fear, the Count refuses to hand over the signet ring that once belonged to his father. Is this burst of bravado in keeping with the Count's character? Or does it seem to be an action at odds with what we know about him? Is this detail of the ring simply an arbitrary element, or does it serve any function?

4 Does the Count lose our sympathy when he plans to run away from a situation temporarily out of control? Should he stay to confront the young man again just as he confronted him with the signet ring? Does Conrad make the Count's impending departure from Naples appear well motivated and sympathetic? Do you, at this point, feel sorry for him? If so, why? Do you think Conrad wants your sympathy for him? How do you know?

Setting and Atmosphere (Mood)

1 Note the epigraph at the beginning of the story: *"Vedi Napoli e poi mori"* ("See Naples and then die"). An epigraph is a short phrase or sentence which gives the reader some insight into the story (or essay, or novel) which follows. Conrad's use of this phrase is particularly relevant, for it gives a strong and immediate sense of place. Keep it in mind as you reread the story and then try to apply it.

2 Does Conrad mean the epigraph literally? If so, how? If not, what does he mean? Perhaps there are several meanings, just as the story itself has several meanings.

3 What other details about Naples and its surroundings help to "fill out" the setting and provide atmosphere? Are such details necessary? If so, why? Could the story move along just as well without them? Once again, be critical. A poor story will provide insufficient detail and then proceed as if it were there. This matter of detail is something that only a careful writer can gauge when he is writing. He must know how much to give, when to stop, when to move on. Such matters are elements of pace, and through them the writer manipulates us so that we read his story the way he wants us to.

Style and Point of View

1 Is the story presented with an excess of description, or is it stripped bare or lean? The style of a story, or the manner in which the author presents his material, is usually a good clue to what he is trying to say. In a Hemingway story, the style is short and clipped, the dialogue simple and repetitious, even mechanical. The result is a certain rhythm or beat—what every story has if it is successful. Hemingway's style is intended to create the atmosphere of defeat and negation which is ever present in and around his characters, and therefore his style is completely functional. In "Il Conde," the manner of narration and the use of detail are very different from Hemingway's style. Describe some aspects of Conrad's narrative method—note his use of words, his pacing of the story (the way he slows you up and then speeds you on), his choice of sounds (as in poetry). As you read the story, what effect does Conrad's style have upon you? Does it help or hinder the point he is trying to make about the Count and the world he lives in? Whenever you make a statement, give particular words, images, and phrases.

2 Through his tone an author indicates how he wishes the reader to accept his characters. Conrad is obviously sympathetic to this old man, who superficially may appear rather unimportant, even useless in social terms. But first, how does Conrad create a sympathetic attitude toward the old Count? What are his values? Are they worth preserving? Does Conrad think they are worth preserving? How do you know?

3 How important is the narrator in the story? Why? How would the story be changed if Il Conde himself were telling it? Would the story be improved in any way if he were the narrator? If the young man were the narrator? What would be lost or gained by either change?

Further Aspects

1 Every short story worth reading, whatever its origin or language, has some relevance to us, although its significance may be disguised. "Il Conde" may appear rather benign on the surface, but beneath it are suggested some very brutal events. What application, if any, does the theme of the story have to us at present?

2 Do you accept Conrad's interpretation of the values at stake in the modern world? Are these values, in your estimation, the values that really count (no pun intended), or are there others of greater significance? Be sure you know first what is at stake.

3 Do you feel that Conrad falls short in the story? Keep in mind that it is a short story, and do not judge it as you would a novel.

4 What can a story (like this) do that a novel cannot do? Contrariwise, what can a novel do that a short story can only begin to do? In your consideration, keep a proper perspective.

5 Did you find the story enjoyable to read? Does it add significantly to your scope of experience? Briefly summarize the reasons for your answers.

6 What is hara-kiri? What relation does it have to the story?

LEAVING THE YELLOW HOUSE

Saul Bellow

The neighbors—there were in all six white people who lived at Sego Desert Lake—told one another that old Hattie could no longer make it alone. The desert life, even with a forced-air furnace in the house and butane gas brought from town in a truck, was still too difficult for her. There were older women in the county. Twenty miles away was Amy Walters, the gold miner's widow. But she was a hardier old girl. Every day of the year she took a bath in the lake. And Amy was crazy about money and knew how to manage it, as Hattie did not. Hattie was not exactly a drunkard, but she hit the bottle pretty hard, and now she was in trouble and there was a limit to the help she could expect from even the best of neighbors.

They were fond of her, though. You couldn't help being fond of Hattie. She was big and cheerful, puffy, comic, boastful, with a big round back and stiff, rather long legs. Before the century began she had graduated from finishing school and studied the organ in Paris. But now she didn't know a note from a skillet; she had tantrums when she played canasta. And all that remained of her fine fair hair was frizzled along her forehead in small grey curls. Her forehead was not much wrinkled, but the skin was bluish, the color of skim milk. She walked with long strides in spite of the heaviness of her hips, pushing on, round-backed, with her shoulders and showing the flat rubber bottoms of her shoes.

Once a week, in the same cheerful, plugging but absent way, she took off her short skirt and the dirty aviator's jacket with the wool collar and but on a girdle, a dress and high-heeled shoes. When she stood on these heels her fat old body trembled. She wore a big brown Rembrandt-like tam with a ten-cent-store brooch, eyelike, carefully centered. She drew a straight line with lipstick on her mouth, leaving part of the upper lip pale. At the wheel of her old turret-shaped car, she drove, seemingly methodical but speeding dangerously, across forty miles of mountainous desert to buy frozen meat pies and whiskey. She went to the Laundromat and the hairdresser, and then had lunch with two Martinis at the Arlington. Afterwards she would often visit Marian Nabot's Silvermine Hotel at Miller Street near skid row and pass the rest of the day gossiping and drinking with her cronies, old divorcées like herself who had settled in the West. Hattie never gambled any more and she didn't care for the movies, and at five o'clock she drove back at the same speed, calmly, partly blinded by the smoke of her cigarette. She was a tough-looking smoker. The fixed cigarette gave her a watering eye.

The Rolfes and the Paces were her only white neighbors at Sego Desert Lake. There was Sam Jervis too, but he was only an old gandy walker who did odd jobs in her garden, and she did not count him. Nor did she count among her neighbors Darly, the dudes' cowboy who worked for the Paces, nor Swede, the telegrapher. Pace had a guest ranch, and Rolfe and his wife were rich and had retired. Thus there were three good houses at the lake, Hattie's yellow house, Pace's and the Rolfes'. All the rest of the population—Sam, Swede, Watchtah the section foreman, and the Mexicans and Indians and Negroes—lived in shacks and boxcars. You could count all the trees in a minute's time: cottonwoods and box elders. All the rest, down to the shores, was sagebrush and juniper. The lake was what remained of an old sea that had covered the volcanic mountains. To the north there were some tungsten mines; to the south, fifteen miles, was an Indian village built of railroad ties.

In this barren place Hattie had lived for more than twenty years. Her first summer was spent not in a house but in an Indian wikiup on the shore. She used to say that she had watched the stars from this almost roofless shelter. After her divorce she took up with a cowboy named Wicks. Neither of them had any money—it was the Depression—and they had lived on the range, trapping coyotes for a living. Once a month they would come into town and rent a room and go on a bender. Hattie told this sadly, but also gloatingly, and with many trimmings. A thing no sooner happened to her than it was transformed into something else. "We were caught in a storm," she said, "and we rode hard, down to the lake and knocked on the door of the yellow house"—now her house. "Alice Parmenter took us in and let us sleep on the floor." What had actually happened was that the wind was blowing—there had been no storm—and they were not far away from the house anyway; and Alice Parmenter, who knew that Hattie and Wicks were not married, offered them separate beds; but Hattie, swaggering, had said in a loud voice, "Why get two sets of sheets dirty?" And she and her cowboy had slept in Alice's double bed while Alice had taken the sofa.

Now Wicks was gone. There was never anybody like him in the

sack; he was brought up in a whorehouse and the girls taught him everything, said Hattie. She didn't really understand what she was saying, but believed that she was being Western, and more than anything else she wanted to be thought of as a rough, experienced woman of the West. Still, she was a lady, too. She had good silver and good china and engraved stationery, but she kept canned beans and A-1 sauce and tunafish and bottles of catsup and fruit salad on the library shelves of her living room. On the night table was the Bible her pious brother Angus—her other brother was a heller—had given her; but behind the little cabinet door was a bottle of bourbon. When she awoke in the night she tippled herself back to sleep. In the glove compartment of her old car she kept little sample bottles for emergencies on the road. Old Darly found them after her accident.

The accident did not happen far out in the desert as she had always feared, but near her home. She had had a few Martinis with the Rolfes one evening and as she was driving home over the railroad crossing she lost control of the car and drove off the crossing onto the tracks. The explanation she gave was that she had sneezed, and the sneeze had blinded her and made her twist the wheel. The motor was killed and all four wheels of the car sat smack on the rails. Hattie crept down from the door, high off the roadbed. A great fear took hold of her—for the car, for the future, and not only for the future but for the past—and she began to hurry on stiff legs through the sagebrush to Pace's ranch.

Now the Paces were away on a hunting trip and had left old Darly in charge; he was tending bar in the old cabin that went back to the days of the pony express when Hattie burst in. There were two customers, a tungsten miner and his girl.

"Darly, I'm in trouble. Help me. I've had an accident," said Hattie.

How the face of a man will alter when a woman has bad news to tell him! It happened now to lean old Darly; his eyes went flat and looked unwilling, his jaw moved in and out, his wrinkled cheeks began to flush, and he said, "What's the matter—what's happened to you now?"

"I'm stuck on the tracks. I sneezed. I lost control of the car. Tow me off, Darly, with the pickup before the train comes."

Darly threw down his towel and stamped his high-heeled boots with anger. "Now what have you gone and done?" he said. "I told you to stay home after dark."

"Where's Pace? Ring the fire bell and fetch Pace."

"There's nobody on the property but me," said the lean old man. "And I'm not supposed to close the bar and you know it as well as I do."

"Please, Darly. I can't leave my car on the tracks."

"Too bad!" he said. Nevertheless he moved from behind the bar. "How did you say it happened?"

"I told you, I sneezed," said Hattie.

Everyone, as she later told it, was as drunk as sixteen thousand dollars: Darly, the miner and the miner's girl.

Darly was limping as he locked the door of the bar. A year before, a kick from one of Pace's mares had broken his ribs as he was loading her into the trailer, and he hadn't recovered from it. He was too old. But he dissembled the pain. The high-heeled narrow boots helped, and his painful bending looked like the ordinary stooping posture of a cowboy on the ground. However, Darly was not a genuine cowboy, like Pace who had grown up in the saddle. He was a late-comer from the east and until the age of forty had never been on horseback. In this respect he and Hattie were alike. They were not the Westerners they seemed to be.

Hattie hurried after him through the ranch yard.

"Damn you!" he said to her. "I got thirty bucks out of that sucker and I would have skinned him out of his whole pay check if you minded your business. Pace is going to be sore as hell."

"You've got to help me. We're neighbors," said Hattie.

"You're not fit to be living out here. You can't do it any more. Besides, you're swacked all the time."

Hattie couldn't afford to talk back to him. The thought of her car on the tracks made her frantic. If a freight came now and smashed it, her life at Sego Desert Lake would be finished. And where would she go then? She was not fit to live in this place. She had never made the grade at all; she only seemed to have made it. And Darly—why did he say such hurtful things to her? Because he himself was sixty-eight years old, and he had no other place to go, either; he took bad treatment from Pace besides. Darly stayed because his only alternative was to go to the soldiers' home. Moreover, the dude women would crawl into his sack. They wanted a cowboy and they thought he was one. Why, he couldn't even raise himself out of his bunk in the morning. And where else would he get women? "After the season," she wanted to say to him, "you always have to go to the Veterans' Hospital to get yourself fixed up again." But she didn't dare offend him now.

The moon was due to rise. It appeared as they drove over the ungraded dirt road toward the crossing where Hattie's turret-shaped car was sitting on the rails. At great speed Darly wheeled the pickup around, spraying dirt on the miner and his girl who had followed in their car.

"You get behind the wheel and steer," Darly told Hattie.

She climbed into the seat. Waiting at the wheel she lifted up her face and said, "Please, God, I didn't bend the axle or crack the oil pan."

When Darly crawled under the bumper of Hattie's car the pain in his ribs suddenly cut off his breath, so instead of doubling the tow chain he fastened it at full length. He rose and trotted back to the truck on the narrow boots. Motion seemed the only remedy for the pain; not even booze did the trick any more. He put the pickup into towing gear and began to pull. One side of Hattie's car dropped into the roadbed with a heave of springs. She sat with a stormy, frightened, conscience-stricken face, racing the motor until she flooded it.

The tungsten miner yelled, "Your chain's too long."

Hattie was raised high in the air by the pitch of the wheels. She had to roll down the window to let herself out because the door handle had been jammed from inside for years. Hattie struggled out on the uplifted side crying, "I better call the Swede. I better have him signal. There's a train due."

"Go on, then," said Darly. "You're no good here."

"Darly, be careful with my car. Be careful."

The ancient sea bed at this place was flat and low and the lights of her car and of the truck and of the tungsten miner's Chevrolet were bright and big at twenty miles. Hattie was too frightened to think of this. All she could think was that she was a procrastinating old woman; she had lived by delays; she had meant to stop drinking, she had put off the time, and now she had smashed her car—a terrible end, a terrible judgment on her. She got to the ground and, drawing up her skirt, she started to get over the tow chain. To prove that the chain didn't have to be shortened, and to get the whole thing over with, Darly threw the pickup forward again. The chain jerked up and struck Hattie in the knee and she fell forward and broke her arm.

She cried, "Darly, Darly, I'm hurt. I fell."

"The old lady tripped on the chain," said the miner. "Back up here and I'll double it for you. You're getting nowheres."

Drunkenly the miner lay down on his back in the dark, soft red cinders of the roadbed. Darly had backed up to slacken the chain. Darly hurt the miner, too. He tore some skin from his fingers by racing ahead before the chain was secure. Uncomplainingly the miner wrapped his hand in his shirttail saying, "She'll do it now." The old car came down from the tracks and stood on the shoulder of the road.

"There's your goddam car," said Darly to Hattie.

"Is it all right?" she said. Her left side was covered with dirt, but she managed to pick herself up and stand, round-backed and heavy, on her stiff legs. "I'm hurt, Darly." She tried to convince him of it.

"Hell if you are," he said. He believed she was putting on an act to escape blame. The pain in his ribs made him especially impatient with her. "Christ, if you can't look after yourself any more you've got no business out here."

"You're old yourself," she said. "Look what you did to me. You can't hold your liquor."

This offended him greatly. He said, "I'll take you to the Rolfes. They let you tie this on in the first place, so let them worry about you. I'm tired of your bunk, Hattie."

He speeded up. Chains, spade and crowbar clashed on the sides of the truck. She was frightened and held her arm and cried. Rolfe's dogs jumped at her to lick her when she went through the gate. She shrank from them crying, "Down, down."

"Darly," she cried in the darkness, "take care of my car. Don't leave it standing there on the road. Darly, take care of it, please."

But Darly in his ten-gallon hat, his chin-bent face wrinkled, small and angry, a furious pain in his ribs, tore away at high speed.

"Oh, God, what will I do," she said.

The Rolfes were having a last drink before dinner, sitting at their fire of pitchy railroad ties, when Hattie opened the door. Her knee was bleeding, her eyes were tiny with shock, her face grey with dust.

"I'm hurt," she said desperately. "I had an accident. I sneezed and lost control of the wheel. Jerry, look after the car. It's on the road."

They bandaged her knee and took her home and put her to bed. Helen Rolfe wrapped a heating pad around her arm.

"I can't have the pad," Hattie complained. "The switch goes on and off and every time it does it starts my generator and uses up the gas."

"Ah, now, Hattie," Rolfe said, "this is not the time to be stingy. We'll take you to town in the morning and have you looked over. Helen will phone Doctor Stroud."

Hattie wanted to say, "Stingy! Why you're the stingy ones. I just haven't got anything. You and Helen are ready to hit each other over two bits in canasta." But the Rolfes were good to her; they were her only real friends here. Darly would have let her lie in the yard all night, and Pace would sell her to the bone man if he had an offer.

So she didn't talk back to the Rolfes, but as soon as they left the yellow house and walked through the super-clear moonlight under the great skirt of branch shadows to their new car, Hattie turned off the switch and the heavy swirling and battering of the generator stopped. Presently she began to have her first real taste of the pain in her arm, and she sat rigid and warmed the injured place with her hand. It seemed to her that she could feel the bone. Before leaving, Helen Rolfe had thrown over her a comforter that had belonged to Hattie's dead friend India, from whom she had inherited the small house and everything in it. Had the comforter lain on India's bed the night she died? Hattie tried to remember, but her thoughts were mixed up. She was fairly sure the death-bed pillow was in the loft, and she believed she had put the rest of the bedding in a trunk. Then how had this comforter got out? She couldn't do anything about it now but draw it away from contact with her skin. It kept her legs warm; this she accepted, but she didn't want it any nearer.

More and more Hattie saw her own life as though from birth to the present every moment had been filmed. Her fancy was that when she died she would see the film shown. Then she would know how she appeared from the back, watering the plants, in the bathroom, asleep, playing the organ, embracing—everything, even tonight, in pain, almost the last pain, perhaps, for she couldn't take much more. How many more turns had life to show her yet? There couldn't be a lot. To lie awake and think such thoughts was the worst thing in the world. Better death than insomnia. Hattie not only loved sleep, she believed in it.

The first attempt to set the bone was not successful. "Look what they've done to me," said Hattie and showed the discolored skin on her breast. After the second operation her mind wandered. The sides of her bed had to be raised, for in her delirium she roamed the wards. She cried at the nurses when they shut her in, "You can't make people prisoners in a democracy without a trial." She cursed them fiercely.

For several weeks her mind was not clear. Asleep, her face was lifeless; her cheeks were puffed out and her mouth, no longer wide and grinning, was drawn round and small. Helen sighed when she saw her.

"Shall we get in touch with her family?" she asked the doctor. "She has a brother in Maine who is very strait-laced. And another one down in Mexico, even older than Hattie."

"No younger relations?" asked the doctor. His skin was white and thick. He had chestnut hair, abundant but very dry. He sometimes explained to his patients, "I had a tropical disease during the war."

"Cousins' children," said Helen. She tried to think who would be called to her own bedside. Rolfe would see that she was cared for. He would hire a nurse. Hattie could not afford one. She had already gone beyond her means. A trust company in Philadelphia paid her eighty dollars a month. She had a small bank account.

"I suppose it will be up to us to get her out of hock," said Rolfe. "Unless the brother down in Mexico comes across."

In the end, no relations had to be called. Hattie began to recover. At last she could recognize some of her friends, though her mind was still in disorder; much that had happened she couldn't recall.

"How much blood did they have to give me," she kept asking. "I seem to remember five, six, eight different times. Daylight, electric light. . . ." She tried to smile, but she couldn't make a pleasant face as yet. "How am I going to pay?" she said. "At twenty-five bucks a quart. My little bit of money is just about wiped out."

Blood became her constant topic, her preoccupation. She told everyone who came to see her, "—have to replace all that blood. They poured gallons of the stuff into me. I hope it was all good." And, though very weak, she began to grin and laugh again. There was more of a hiss in her laughter than formerly; the illness had affected her chest.

"No cigarettes, no booze," the doctor told Helen.

"Doctor," Helen asked him, "do you expect her to change?"

"All the same, I am obliged to say it."

"Life may not be much of a temptation to her," said Helen.

Her husband laughed. When his laughter was intense it blinded one of his eyes and his short Irish face turned red except for the bridge of his small, sharp nose where the skin grew white.

"Hattie's like me," he said. "She'll be in business till she's cleaned out. And if Sego Lake was all whiskey she'd use her last strength to knock her old yellow house down and build a raft of it. So why talk temperance to her now?"

Hattie recognized the similarity between them. When he came to see her she said, "Jerry, you're the only one I can really talk to about my troubles. What am I going to do for money? I have Hotchkiss Insurance. I paid eight dollars a month."

"That won't do you much good, Hat. No Blue Cross?"

"I let it drop ten years ago. Maybe I could sell some of my valuables."

"What have you got?" he said. His eye began to droop with laughter.

"Why," she said defiantly, "there's plenty. First there's the beautiful, precious Persian rug that India left me."

"Coals from the fireplace have been burning it for years, Hat!"

"The rug is in perfect condition," she said with an angry sway of her shoulders. "A beautiful object like that never loses its value. And the oak table from the Spanish monastery is three hundred years old."

"With luck you could get twenty bucks for it. It would cost fifty to haul it out of here. It's the house you ought to sell."

"The house?" she said. Yes, that had been in her mind. "I'd have to get twenty thousand for it."

"Eight is a fair price."

"Fifteen. . . ." She was offended, and her voice recovered its strength. "India put eight into it in two years. And don't forget that Sego Lake is one of the most beautiful places in the world."

"But where is it? Five hundred and some miles to San Francisco and two hundred to Salt Lake City. Who wants to live way out here in Utah but a few eccentrics like you and India and me?"

"There are things you can't put a price tag on. Beautiful things."

"Oh bull, Hattie! You don't know what they are any more than I do. I live here because it figures for me, and you because India left you the house. And just in the nick of time, too. Without it you wouldn't have had a pot of your own."

His words offended Hattie; more than that, they frightened her. She was silent and then grew thoughtful, for she was fond of Jerry Rolfe and he of her. He had good sense and moreover he only spoke her own thoughts. He spoke no more than the truth about India's death and the house. But she told herself, *He doesn't know everything. You'd have to pay a San Francisco architect ten thousand just to* think *of such a house. Before he drew a line.*

"Jerry," the old woman said, "what am I going to do about replacing the blood in the blood bank?"

"Do you want a quart from me, Hat?" His eye began to fall shut.

"You won't do. You had that tumor, two years ago. I think Darly ought to give some."

"The old man?" Rolfe laughed at her. "You want to kill him?"

"Why," said Hattie with anger, lifting up her massive face with its fringe of curls which had become frayed by fever and perspiration; at the back of her head the hair had knotted and matted so that it had to be shaved, "he almost killed me. It's his fault that I'm in this condition. He must have blood in him. He runs after all the chicks—all of them—young and old."

"Come, you were drunk, too," said Rolfe.

"I've driven drunk for forty years. It was the sneeze. Oh, Jerry, I feel wrung out," said Hattie, haggard, sitting forward in bed. But her face was cleft by her nonsensically happy grin. She was not one to be miserable for long; she had the expression of a perennial survivor.

Every other day she went to the therapist. The young woman worked her arm for her; it was a pleasure and a comfort to Hattie, who would have been glad to leave the whole cure to her. However, she was given other exercises to do, and these were not so easy. They rigged a pulley for her and Hattie had to hold both ends of a rope and saw it back and forth through the scraping little wheel. She bent heavily from the hips and coughed over her cigarette. But the most important exercise of all she shirked. This required her to put the flat of her hand to the wall at the level of her hips and, by working her fingertips slowly, to make the hand ascend to the height of her shoulder. That was painful; she often forgot to do it, although the doctor warned her, "Hattie, you don't want adhesions, do you?"

A light of despair crossed Hattie's eyes. Then she said, "Oh, Dr. Stroud, buy my house from me."

"I'm a bachelor. What would I do with a house?"

"I know just the girl for you—my cousin's daughter. Perfectly charming and very brainy. Just about got her Ph.D."

"You must get quite a few proposals yourself," said the doctor.

"From crazy desert rats. They chase me. But," she said, "after I pay my bills I'll be in pretty punk shape. If at least I could replace that blood in the blood bank I'd feel easier."

"If you don't do as the therapist tells you, Hattie, you'll need another operation. Do you know what adhesions are?"

She knew. But Hattie thought, *How long must I go on taking care of myself?* It made her angry to hear him speak of another operation. She had a moment of panic, but she veiled it from him. With him, this young man whose skin was already as thick as buttermilk and whose chestnut hair was as dry as death, she always assumed the part of a small child. She said, "Yes, doctor." But her heart was in a fury.

Night and day, however, she repeated, "I was in the Valley of the Shadow. But I'm alive." She was weak, she was old, she couldn't follow a train of thought very easily, she felt faint in the head. But she was still here; here was her body, it filled space, a great body. And though she had worries and perplexities, and once in a while her arm felt as though it was about to give her the last stab of all; and though her hair was scrappy and old, like onion roots, and scattered like nothing under the comb, yet she sat and amused herself with visitors; her great grin split her face; her heart warmed with every kind word.

And she thought, "People will help me out. It never did me any good to worry. At the last minute something turned up, when I wasn't looking for it. Marian loves me. Helen and Jerry love me. Half Pint loves me. They would never let me go to the ground. And I love them. If it were the other way around, I'd never let them go down."

Above a horizon in a baggy vastness which Hattie by herself occasionally visited, the features of India, or her shade, sometimes rose. She was indignant and scolding. Not mean. Not really mean. Few people had ever really been mean to Hattie. But India was annoyed with her. "The garden is going to hell, Hattie," she said. "Those lilac bushes are all shriveled."

"But what can I do? The hose is rotten. It broke. It won't reach."

"Then dig a trench," said the phantom of India. "Have old Sam dig a trench. But save the bushes."

Am I thy servant still? said Hattie to herself. *No,* she thought, *let the dead bury their dead.*

But she didn't defy India now any more than she had done

when they lived together. Hattie was supposed to keep India off the bottle, but often both of them began to get drunk after breakfast. They forgot to dress, and in their slips the two of them wandered drunkenly around the house and blundered into each other, and they were in despair at having been so weak. Late in the afternoon they would be sitting in the living room, waiting for the sun to set. It shrank, burning itself out on the crumbling edges of the mountains. When the sun passed, the fury of the daylight ended and the mountain surfaces were more blue, broken, like cliffs of coal. They no longer suggested faces. The east began to look simple, and the lake less inhuman and haughty. At last India would say, "Hattie—it's time for the lights." And Hattie would pull the switch chains of the lamps, several of them, to give the generator a good shove. She would turn on some of the wobbling eighteenth-century-style lamps whose shades stood out from their slender bodies like dragonflies' wings. The little engine in the shed would shuffle, then spit, then charge and bang, and the first weak light would rise unevenly in the bulbs.

"Hettie!" cried India. After she drank she was penitent, but her penitence too was a hardship to Hattie, and the worse her temper the more English her accent became. *"Where the hell ah you Hettie!"* After India's death Hattie found some poems she had written in which she, Hattie, was affectionately and even touchingly mentioned. But Hattie's interest in ideas was very small, whereas India had been all over the world and was used to brilliant society. India wanted her to discuss Eastern religion, Bergson and Proust, and Hattie had no head for this, and so India blamed her drinking on Hattie. "I can't talk to you," she would say. "And I'm here because I'm not fit to be anywhere else. I can't live in New York any more. It's too dangerous for a woman my age to be drunk in the street at night."

And Hattie, talking to her Western friends about India, would say, "She is a lady" (implying that they made a pair). "She is a creative person" (this was why they found each other so congenial). "But helpless? Completely. Why she can't even get her own girdle on."

"Hettie! come here. Het-tie! Do you know what sloth is?"

Undressed, India sat on her bed and with the cigarette in her drunken, wrinkled, ringed hand she burned holes in the blankets. On Hattie's pride she left many small scars, too. She treated her like a servant.

Weeping, India begged her afterward to forgive her. *"Hattie, please, don't condemn me in your heart. Forgive me, dear, I know I am bad. But I hurt myself more in my evil than I hurt you.''*

Hattie would keep a stiff bearing. She would lift up her face with its incurved nose and puffy eyes, and say, ''I am a Christian person. I never bear a grudge.'' And by repeating this she actually brought herself to forgive India.

But of course she had no husband, no child, no skill, no savings. And what she would have done if India had not died and left her the yellow house, nobody knows.

Jerry Rolfe said privately to Marian, ''Hattie can't do anything for herself. If I hadn't been around during the '44 blizzard she and India both would have starved. She's always been careless and lazy and now she can't even chase a cow out of her yard. She's too feeble. The thing for her to do is go East to her brother. Hattie would have ended at the poor farm if it hadn't been for India. But India should have left her something besides the house. Some dough. India didn't use her head.''

When Hattie returned to the lake she stayed with the Rolfes. ''Well, old shellback,'' said Jerry, ''there's a little more life in you now.''

Indeed, with joyous eyes, the cigarette in her mouth and her hair newly frizzed and overhanging her forehead, she seemed to have triumphed again. She was pale, but she grinned, she chuckled, and she held a bourbon Old-Fashioned with a cherry and a slice of orange in it. She was on rations; the Rolfes allowed her two a day. Her back, Helen noted, was more bent than before. Her knees went outward a little weakly; her feet, however, came close together at the ankles.

''Oh, Helen dear and Jerry dear, I am so thankful, so glad to be back at the lake. I can look after my place again, and I'm here to see the spring. It's more gorgeous than ever.''

Heavy rains had fallen while Hattie was away. The sego lilies, which bloomed only after a wet winter, came up from the loose dust, especially around the marl pit; but even on the burnt granite they seemed to grow. Desert peach was beginning to appear and in Hattie's yard the rosebushes were filling out. The roses were yellow and abundant, and the odor they gave off was like that of damp tea leaves.

''Before it gets hot enough for the rattlesnakes,'' said Hattie to Helen, ''we ought to drive up to Marky's ranch to cut watercress.''

Hattie was going to attend to lots of things, but the heat came early that year and, as there was no television to keep her awake, she slept most of the day. She was now able to dress herself, though there was little more that she could do. Sam Jervis rigged the pulley for her on the porch and she remembered once in a while to use it. Mornings when she had her strength she rambled over to her own house, examining things, behaving importantly and giving orders to Sam Jervis and Wanda Gingham. At ninety, Wanda, a Shoshone, was still an excellent seamstress and housecleaner.

Hattie looked over the car, which was parked under a cottonwood tree. She tested the engine. Yes, the old pot would still go. Proudly, happily, she listened to the noise of tappets; the dry old pipe shook as the smoke went out at the rear. She tried to work the shift, turn the wheel. That, as yet, she couldn't do. But it would come soon, she was confident.

At the back of the house the soil had caved in a little over the cesspool and a few of the old railroad ties over the top had rotted. Otherwise things were in good shape. Sam had looked after the garden. He had fixed a new catch for the gate after Pace's horses—maybe because he never could afford to keep them in hay—had broken in and Sam found them grazing and drove them out. Luckily they hadn't damaged many of her plants. Hattie felt a moment of wild rage against Pace. He had brought the horses into her garden, she was sure. But her anger didn't last long. It was reabsorbed into the feeling of golden pleasure that enveloped her. She had little strength, but all that she had was a pleasure to her. So she forgave even Pace, who would have liked to do her out of the house, who had always used her, embarrassed her, cheated her at cards, passed the buck whenever he could. He was a fool about horses. They were ruining him. Breeding horses was a millionaire's amusement.

She saw the animals in the distance, feeding. Unsaddled, the mares appeared undressed; they reminded her of naked women walking with their glossy flanks in the sego lilies which curled on the ground. The flowers were yellowish, like winter wool, but fragrant; the mares, naked and gentle, walked through them. Their strolling, their perfect beauty, the sound of their hoofs on stone touched a deep place in Hattie's nature. Her love for horses, birds and dogs was well-known. Dogs led the list. And now a piece cut from a green blanket reminded her of Richie. The blanket was one he had torn, and she had cut it into strips and placed them under the doors to keep out the draughts. In the house she found more traces of him: hair he had shed on the furniture. Hattie was going to borrow Helen's vacuum cleaner, but there wasn't really enough current to make it pull as it should. On the doorknob of India's room hung the dog collar.

Hattie had decided to have herself moved into India's bed when she lay dying. Why use two beds? A perilous look came into her eyes while her lips pressed together forbiddingly. "I follow," she said, speaking to India with an inner voice, "so never mind." Presently—before long, she would have to leave the yellow house in her turn. And as she went into the parlor thinking of the will, she sighed. Pretty soon she would have to attend to it. India's lawyer, Claiborne, helped her with such things. She had phoned him in town, while she was staying with Marian, and talked matters over with him. He had promised to try to sell the house for her. Fifteen thousand was her bottom price, she said. If he couldn't find a buyer, perhaps he could find a tenant. Two hundred dollars a month was the rental she set. Rolfe laughed. But Hattie turned toward him one of those proud, dulled looks she always took on when he angered her and said haughtily, "For summer on Sego Lake?"

"You're competing with Pace's ranch."

"Why, the food is stinking down there. He cheats the dudes," said Hattie. "He really cheats them at cards. You'll never catch me playing blackjack with him again."

And what would she do, thought Hattie, if Claiborne could neither rent nor sell the house? This question she shook off as regularly as it returned. *I don't have to be a burden on anybody,* thought Hattie. *It's looked bad many a time before, but when push came to shove, I made it. Somehow I got by.* But she argued with herself. *How many times? How long, O God—an old thing, feeble, no use to anyone?* Who said she had any right to hold a piece of property?

She was sitting on her sofa which was very old, India's sofa, eight feet long, kidney-shaped, puffy and bald. An underlying pink shone through the green; the upholstered tufts were like the pads of dogs' paws; between them rose bunches of hair. Here Hattie slouched, resting, with her knees wide apart and a cigarette in her mouth, eyes half shut but far-seeing. The mountains seemed not fifteen miles but fifteen hundred yards away, the lake a blue band; the tea-like odor of the roses, though they were still unopened, was already in the air, for Sam was watering them in the heat. Gratefully Hattie yelled, "Sam!"

Sam was very old, and all shanks. His feet looked big. His old railroad jacket was made tight across his back by his stoop. A crooked finger with its great broad nail over the mouth of the hose made the water spray and sparkle. Happy to see Hattie he turned his long jaw, empty of teeth, and his blue eyes, which seemed to penetrate his temples with their length (it was his face that turned, not his body), and he said, "Oh, there, Hattie. You've made it back today? Welcome, Hattie."

"Have a beer, Sam. Come around the back and I'll give you a beer."

She never had Sam come in, owing to his skin disease. There were raw patches on his chin and the back of his ears. Hattie feared infection from his touch. She gave him the beer can, never a glass, and she put on gloves before she used the garden tools. Since he would take no money from her—she had to pay Wanda Gingham a dollar a day—she got Marian to find old clothes for him in town and she left food for him at the door of the damp-wood-smelling boxcar where he lived.

"How's the old wing, Hat?" he said.

"It's coming. I'll be driving again before you know it," she told him. "By the first of May I'll be driving again." Every week she moved the date forward. "By Decoration Day I expect to be on my own again," she said. In mid-June however she was still unable to drive. Helen Rolfe said to her, "Hattie, Jerry and I are due in Seattle the first week of July."

"Why, you never told me that," said Hattie.

"You don't mean to tell me this is the first you heard of it," said Helen. "You've known about it from the first—since Christmas."

It wasn't easy for Hattie to meet her eyes. She presently put her head down. Her face became very dry, especially the lips. "Well, don't you worry about me. I'll be all right here," she said.

"Who's going to look after you?" said Jerry. He evaded nothing himself and tolerated very little evasion in others. Except, as Hattie knew, he always indulged her. She couldn't count on her friend Half Pint, she couldn't really count on Marian either. Until now, this very moment, she had only the Rolfes to turn to. Helen, trying to be steady, gazed at her and made sad, involuntary movements with her head, sometimes nodding, sometimes seeming as if she disagreed. Hattie, with her inner voice, swore at her: *Bitch-eyes. I can't win because I'm old. Is that fair?* And yet she admired Helen's eyes. Even the skin about them, slightly wrinkled underneath, was touching, beautiful. There was a heaviness in her bust that went, as if by attachment, with the heaviness of her eyes. Her head, her hands and feet should have taken a more slender body. Helen, said Hattie, was the nearest thing she had on this earth to a sister. But there was no reason to go to Seattle—no genuine business. It was only idleness, only a holiday. The only reason was Hattie herself; this was their way of telling her that there was a limit to what she could expect them to do. Helen's head wavered, but her thoughts were steady; she knew what was passing through Hattie's mind. Like Hattie, she was an idle woman. Why was her right to idleness better?

Because of money? thought Hattie. Because of age? Because she has a husband? Because she had a daughter in Swarthmore College? But a funny thing occurred to her. Helen disliked being idle, whereas she herself never made any bones that an idle life was all she was ever good for. But for her it was uphill, all the way, because when Waggoner divorced her she didn't have a cent. She even had to support Wicks for seven or eight years. Except with horses, he had no sense. And then she had had to take a ton of dirt from India. *I am the one,* Hattie asserted to herself. *I would know what to do with Helen's advantages. She only suffers from them. And if she wants to stop being an idle woman why can't she start with me, her neighbor?* Her skin, for all its puffiness, burned with anger. She said to Rolfe and Helen: "Don't worry. I'll make out by myself. But if I have to leave the lake you'll be ten times more lonely than before. Now I'm going back to my house."

She lifted up her broad old face and her lips were childlike with suffering. She would never take back what she had said.

But the trouble was no ordinary trouble. Hattie was herself aware that she rambled, forgot names, and answered when no one spoke.

"We can't just take charge of her," Rolfe said. "What's more, she ought to be near a doctor. She keeps her shotgun loaded so she can fire it if anything happens to her in the house. But who knows what she'll do? I don't believe it was Jacamares who killed that Doberman of hers."

He drove into her yard the day after she returned to her house and said, "I'm going into town. I can bring you some chow if you like."

She couldn't afford to refuse his offer, angry though she was, and she said, "Yes, bring me some stuff from the Mountain Street Market. Charge it." She only had some frozen shrimp and a few cans of beer in the icebox. When Rolfe had gone she put out the shrimp to thaw.

People really used to stick by one another in the West. Hattie now saw herself as one of the pioneers. This modern race had come later. After all, she had lived on the range like an old-timer. Wicks had had to shoot their Christmas dinner and she had cooked it—venison. He killed it on the reservation, and if the Paiutes had caught them there would have been hell to pay.

The weather was hot, the clouds were heavy and calm in a large sky. The horizon was so huge that in it the lake must have seemed like a saucer of milk. *Some milk!* Hattie thought. Two thousand feet deep in the middle, so deep no body could ever be recovered. It went around with the currents, and there were rocks like eyeteeth, and hot springs, and colorless fish at the bottom which were never caught. Now that the white pelicans were nesting they patrolled the rocks for snakes and other egg thieves. They were so big and flew so slow you might imagine they were angels. Hattie no longer visited the lake shore; the walk exhausted her. She saved her strength to go to Pace's bar in the afternoon.

She took off her shoes and stockings and walked on bare feet from one end of her house to the other. On the land side she saw Wanda Gingham sitting near the tracks while her great-grandson played in the soft red gravel. Wanda wore a large purple shawl and her black head was bare. All about her was—was nothing, Hattie thought; for she had taken a drink, breaking her rule. Nothing but mountains, thrust out like men's bodies; the sagebrush was the hair on their chests.

The warm wind blew dust from the marl pit. This white powder made her sky less blue. On the water side were the pelicans, pure as spirits, slow as angels, blessing the air as they flew with great wings.

Should she or should she not have Sam do something about the vine on the chimney? Sparrows nested in it, and she was glad of that. But all summer long the king snakes were after them and she was afraid to walk in the garden. When the sparrows scratched the ground for seed they took a funny bound; they held their legs stiff and flung back the dust with both feet. Hattie sat down at her old Spanish table, watching them in the cloudy warmth of the day, clasping her hands, chuckling and sad. The bushes were crowded with yellow roses, half of them now rotted. The lizards scrambled from shadow to shadow. The water was smooth as air, gaudy as silk. The mountains succumbed, falling asleep in the heat. Drowsy, Hattie lay down on her sofa; its pads were like dogs' paws. She gave in to sleep and when she woke it was midnight; she did not want to alarm the Rolfes by putting on her lights, so took advantage of the moon to eat a few thawed shrimps and go to the bathroom. She undressed and lifted herself into bed and lay there feeling her sore arm. Now she knew how much she missed her dog. The whole matter of the dog weighed heavily on her soul; she came close to tears in thinking about him and she went to sleep, oppressed by her secret.

I suppose I had better try to pull myself together a little, thought Hattie nervously in the morning. *I can't just sleep my way through.* She knew what her difficulty was. Before any serious question her mind gave way; it became diffused. She said to herself, *I can see bright, but I feel dim. I guess I'm not so lively any more. Maybe I'm becoming a little touched in the head, as mother was.* But she was not so old as her mother was when she did those strange things. At eighty-five her mother had to be kept from going naked in the street. *I'm not as bad as that yet,* thought Hattie. *Thank God. I walked into the men's wards, but that was when I had a fever, and my nightie was on.*

She drank a cup of Nescafé and it strengthened her determination to do something for herself. In all the world she had only her brother Angus to go to. Her brother Will had led a rough life; he was an old heller, and now he drove everyone away. He was too crabby, thought Hattie. Besides he was angry because she had lived so long with Wicks. Angus would forgive her. But then he and his wife were not her kind. With them she couldn't drink, she couldn't smoke, she had to make herself small-mouthed, and she would have to wait while they read a chapter of the Bible before breakfast. Hattie could not bear to wait for meals. Besides, she had a house of her own at last; why should she have to leave it? She had never owned a thing before. And now she was not allowed to enjoy her yellow house. *But I'll keep it,* she said to herself rebelliously. *I swear to God I'll keep it. Why, I barely just got it. I haven't had time.* And she went out on the porch to work the pulley and do something about the adhesions in her arm. She was sure now that they were there. *And what will I do?* she cried to herself. *What will I do? Why did I ever go to Rolfe's that night—and why did I lose control on the crossing!* She couldn't say now "I sneezed." She couldn't even remember what had happened, except that she saw the boulders and the twisting blue rails and Darly. It was Darly's fault. He was sick and old himself, and couldn't make it. He envied her the house, and her woman's peaceful life. Since she returned from the hospital he hadn't even come to visit her. He only said, "Hell, I'm sorry for her, but it was her fault." What hurt him most was that she said he couldn't hold his liquor.

Her resolve to pull herself together did not last; she remained the same procrastinating old woman. She had a letter to answer from Hotchkiss Insurance, and it drifted out of sight. She was going to phone Claiborne the lawyer, and it slipped her mind. One morning she announced to Helen that she believed she would apply to an institution in Los Angeles that took over the property of old people and managed it for them. They gave you an apartment right on the ocean, and your meals and medical care. You had to sign over half of your estate. "It's fair enough," said Hattie. "They take a gamble. I may live to be a hundred."

"I wouldn't be surprised," said Helen.

However, Hattie never got around to sending to Los Angeles for the brochure. But Jerry Rolfe took it on himself to write a letter to her brother Angus about her condition. And he drove over also to have a talk with Amy Walters, the gold miner's widow at Fort Walters—as the ancient woman called it. One old tar-paper building was what she owned, plus the mine shafts, no longer in use since the death of her second husband. On a heap of stones near the road a crimson sign *Fort Walters* was placed, and over it a flagpole. The American flag was raised every day. Amy was working in the garden in one of dead Bill's shirts. He had brought water down from the mountains for her in a homemade aqueduct so she could raise her own peaches and vegetables.

"Amy," Rolfe said, "Hattie's back from the hospital and living all alone. You have no folks and neither has she. Not to beat around the bush about it, why don't you live together?"

Amy's face had great delicacy. Her winter baths in the lake and her soups and the waltzes she played for herself alone on the grand piano that stood beside her wood stove and the murder stories she read till darkness made her go to bed had made her remote. She looked delicate, yet her composure couldn't be touched. It was very strange.

"Hattie and me have different habits, Jerry," said Amy.

"And Hattie wouldn't like my company. I can't drink with her."

"That's true," said Rolfe, recalling that Hattie referred to Amy as though she were a ghost. He couldn't speak to Amy of the solitary death that was in store for her. There was not a cloud in the arid sky today, and there was not a shadow of death on Amy. She was tranquil, she seemed to be supplied with a sort of pure fluid that would feed her life slowly for years to come.

He said, "All kinds of things could happen to a woman like Hattie in that yellow house, and nobody would know."

"That's a fact. She doesn't know how to take care of herself."

"She can't. Her arm hasn't healed."

Amy didn't say that she was sorry to hear it. In the place of those words came a silence which could have meant that. Then she said, "I might go for a few hours a day, but she would have to pay me."

"Now, Amy, you must know as well as I do that Hattie has never had any money—not much more than her pension. Just the house."

At once Amy said, no pause coming between his words and hers, "I would take care of her if she'd agree to leave the house to me."

"Leave it in your hands, you mean?" said Rolfe. "To manage?"

"In her will. To belong to me."

"Why, Amy, what would you do with Hattie's house?" he said.

"It would be my property, that's all. I'd have it."

"Maybe you would leave Fort Walters to her in your will," he said.

"Oh, no," she answered quickly. "Why should I do that? I'm not asking Hattie for her help. I don't need it. Hattie is a city woman."

Rolfe could not carry this proposal back to Hattie. He was too wise ever to mention her will to her.

But Pace was not so careful of her feelings. By mid-June Hattie had begun to visit the bar regularly. She had so many things to think about she couldn't keep herself at home. When Pace came in from the yard one day—he had been packing the axles of his horsetrailer and was wiping grease from his fingers—he said with his usual bluntness, "How would you like it if I paid you fifty bucks a month for the rest of your life, Hat?"

Hattie was holding her second Old-Fashioned of the day. At the bar she made it appear that she observed the limit; but she had started drinking at home after lunch. She began to grin, expecting Pace to make one of his jokes. But he was wearing his scoop-shaped Western hat as level as a Quaker, and he had drawn down his chin, a sign that he was not fooling. She said, "That would be nice, but what's the catch?"

"No catch," he said. "This is what we'd do. I'd give you five hundred dollars cash, and fifty bucks a month for life, and you'd let me put some dudes in the yellow house, and you'd leave the house to me in your will."

"What kind of a deal is that?" said Hattie, her look changing. "I thought we were friends."

"It's the best deal you'll ever get," he said.

The day was sultry, but Hattie till now had thought that it was nice, that she was dreamy, but comfortable, about to begin to enjoy the cool of the day; but now she felt that such cruelty and injustice had been waiting to attack her, that it would have been better to die in the hospital than be so disillusioned.

She cried, "Everybody wants to push me out. You're a cheater, Pace. God! I know you. Pick on somebody else. Why do you have to pick on me? Just because I happen to be around?"

"Why, no, Hattie," he said, trying now to be careful. "It was just a business offer."

"Why don't you give me some blood for the bank if you're such a friend of mine?"

"Well, Hattie, you drink too much, and you oughtn't have been driving anyway."

"The whole thing happened because I sneezed. Everybody knows it. I wouldn't sell you my house. I'd give it away to the lepers first. You'd let me go and then never send me a cent. You never pay anybody. You can't even buy wholesale in town any more because nobody trusts you. It looks as though I'm stuck, that's all, just stuck. I keep on saying that this is my only home in all the world, this is where my friends are, and the weather is always perfect and the lake is beautiful. I wish the whole damn empty old place were in Hell. It's not human and neither are you. But I'll be here the day the sheriff takes your horses—you never mind."

He told her then that she was drunk again, and so she was, but she was more than that, and though her head was spinning she decided to go back to the house at once and take care of some things she had been putting off. This very day she was going to write to the lawyer, Claiborne, and make sure that Pace never got her property. She wouldn't put it past him to swear in court that India had promised him the yellow house.

She sat at the table with pen and paper, trying to think how to put it.

"I want this on record," she wrote. "I could kick myself in the head when I think how he's led me on. I have been his patsy ten thousand times. As when that drunk crashed his Cub plane on the lake shore. At the coroner's jury he let me take the whole blame. He had instructed me when I was working for him never to take in any drunks. And this flier was drunk. He had nothing on but a T shirt and Bermuda shorts and he was flying from Sacramento to Salt Lake City. At the inquest Pace denied he had ever given me such instructions. The same was true when the cook went haywire. She was a tramp. He never hires decent help. He cheated her on the bar bill and blamed me and she went after me with a meat cleaver. She disliked me because I criticized her for drinking at the bar in her one-piece white bathing suit with the dude guests. But he turned her loose on me. He hints that he did certain things for India. She would never have let him. He was too common for her. It can never be said about India that she was not a lady in every way. He thinks he is the greatest sack-artist in the world. He only loves horses, as a fact. He has no claims at all, oral or written, on this yellow house. I want you to have this over my signature. He was cruel to Pickle-Tits who was his first wife, and he's no better to the charming woman who is his present one. I don't know why she takes it. It must be despair." She said to herself, *I don't suppose I'd better send that.*

She was still angry. Her heart was knocking from within: the deep pulses, as after a hot bath, beat at the back of her thighs. The air outside was dotted with transparent particles. The mountains were red as clinkers. The iris leaves were fan sticks —they stuck out like Jiggs's hair.

She always ended by looking out of the window at the desert and the lake. *They drew you from yourself. But after they had drawn you what did they do with you? It was too late to find out. I'll never know. I wasn't meant to. I'm not the type,* Hattie reflected. *Maybe something too cruel for women or for any woman, young or old.*

So she stood up and, rising, she had the sensation that she had gradually become a container for herself. *You get old, your heart, your liver, your lungs seem to expand in size, and the walls of the body give way outward,* she thought, *and you take the shape of an old jug, wider and wider toward the top. You swell up with tears and fat.* She no longer even smelled to herself like a woman. Her face with its much-slept-upon skin was only faintly like her own—like a cloud that has changed. It was a face. It became a ball of yarn. It had drifted open. It had scattered.

I was never one single thing anyway, she thought. *Never my own. I was only loaned to myself.*

But the thing wasn't over yet. And in fact she didn't know for certain that it was ever going to be over; she had only had other people's word for it that death was such and such. *How do I know?* she asked herself challengingly. Her anger had sobered her for a little while. Now she was again drunk. *It was strange. It is strange. It may continue being strange.* She further thought, *I used to wish for death more than I do now. Because I didn't have anything at all. I changed when I got a roof of my own over me. And now? Do I have to go? I thought Marian loved me, but she has a sister. And I never thought Helen and Jerry would desert me. And now Pace insulted me. They think I'm not going to make it.*

She went to the cupboard—she kept the bourbon bottle there; she drank less if each time she had to rise and open the cupboard door. And, as if she were being watched, she poured a drink and swallowed it.

The notion that in this emptiness someone saw her was connected with the other fancy that she was being filmed from birth to death. That this was done for everyone. And afterward you could view your life.

Hattie wanted to see some of it now, and she sat down on the dogs' paw cushions of her sofa and, with her knees far apart and a smile of yearning and of fright, she bent her round back, burned a cigarette at the corner of her mouth and saw—the Church of Saint-Sulpice in Paris where her organ teacher used to bring her. It looked like country walls of stone, but rising high and leaning outward were towers. She was very young. She knew music. The sky was grey. After this she saw some entertaining things she liked to tell people about. She was a young wife. She was in Aix-les-Bains with her mother-in-law, and they played bridge in a mud bath with a British general and his aide. There were artifical waves in the swimming pool. She lost her bathing suit because it was a size too big. How did she get out? Ah, you got out of everything.

She saw her husband, James John Waggoner IV. They were snowbound together in New Hampshire. "Jimmy, Jimmy, how can you fling a wife away?" she asked him. "Have you forgotten love? Did I drink too much—did I bore you?" He had married again and had two children. He had gotten tired of her. And though he was a vain man with nothing to be vain about—no looks, not too much intelligence, nothing but an old Philadelphia family—she had loved him. She too had been a snob about her Philadelphia connections: Give up the name of Waggoner? How could she? For this reason she had never married Wicks. "How dare you," she had said to Wicks, "come without a shave in a dirty shirt and muck on you, come and ask me to marry! If you want to propose, go and clean up first." But his dirt was only a pretext. *Trade Waggoner for Wicks?* she asked herself again with a swing of her shoulders. She wouldn't think of it. Wicks was an excellent man. But he was a cowboy. He couldn't even read. But she saw this on her film. They were in Athens Canyon, in a cratelike house, and she was reading aloud to him from *The Count of Monte Cristo.* He wouldn't let her stop. While walking to stretch her legs, she read, and he followed her about to catch each word. After all, he was very dear to her. Such a man! Now she saw him jump from his horse. They were living on the range, trapping coyotes. It was just the second grey of evening, cloudy, moments after the sun had gone down. There was an animal in the trap, and he went toward it to kill it. He wouldn't waste a bullet on the creatures, but killed them with a kick of his boot. And then Hattie saw that this coyote was all white—snarling teeth, white cruff. "Wicks, he's white! White as a polar bear. You're not going to kill him, are you?" The animal flattened to the ground. He snarled and cried. He couldn't pull away because of the heavy trap. And Wicks killed him. What else could he have done? The white beast lay dead. The dust of Wicks' boots hardly showed on its head and jaws. Blood ran from the muzzle.

And now came something on Hattie's film she tried to shun. It was she herself who had killed her dog, Richie. Just as Rolfe and Pace had warned her, he was vicious, his brain was turned. She, because she was on the side of all dumb creatures, defended him when he bit the trashy woman Jacamares was living with. Perhaps if she had had Richie from a puppy he wouldn't have turned on her. When she got him he was already a year and a half old and she couldn't break him of his habits. But she thought only she understood him. And Rolfe had warned her, "You'll be sued, do you know it? The dog will take out after somebody smarter than that Jacamares' woman and you'll be in for it."

Hattie saw herself as she swayed her shoulders and said, "Nonsense."

But what fear she had felt when the dog went for her on the porch. Suddenly she could see by his skull, by his eyes that he was evil. She screamed at him, "Richie!" And what had she done to him? He had lain under the gas range all day growling and wouldn't come out. She tried to urge him out with the broom, and he snatched it in his teeth. She pulled him out and he left the stick and tore at her. Now, as the spectator of this, her eyes opened, beyond the pregnant curtain and the air wave of marl dust, summer's snow, drifting over the water. "Oh, my God! Richie!" Her thigh was snatched by his jaws. His teeth went through her skirt. She felt she would fall. Would she go down? Then the dog would rush at her throat—then black night, bad-odored mouth, the blood pouring from her torn veins. Her heart shriveled as the teeth went in her thigh, and she couldn't delay another second but took her kindling hatchet from the nail, strengthened her grip on the smooth wood and hit the dog. She saw the blow. She saw him die at once. And then in fear and shame she hid the body. And at night she buried him in the yard. Next day she accused Jacamares. On him she laid the blame for the disappearance of her dog.

She stood up; she spoke to herself in silence, as was her habit. *God, what shall I do? I have taken life. I have lied. I have borne false witness. I have stalled. And now what shall I do? Nobody will help me.*

And suddenly she made up her mind that she should go and do what she had been putting off for weeks, namely, test herself with the car, and she slipped on her shoes and went out. Lizards ran before her in the thirsty dust. She opened the hot, broad door of the car. She lifted her lame hand onto the wheel. Her right hand she reached far to the left and turned the wheel with all her might. Then she started the motor and tried to drive out of the yard. But she could not release the emergency brake with its rasplike rod. She reached with her good hand, the right, under the steering wheel and pressed her bosom on it and strained. No, she could not shift the gears and steer. She couldn't even reach the hand brake. The sweat broke out on her skin. Her efforts were too much. She was deeply wounded by the pain in her arm. The door of the car fell open again and she turned from the wheel and with her stiff legs outside the door she wept. What could she do now? And when she had wept over the ruin of her life she got out of the old car and went back to the house. She took the bottle of bourbon from the cupboard and picked up the ink bottle and a pad of paper and sat down to write her will.

My Will, she wrote, and sobbed to herself.

Since the death of India she had numberless times asked the question, To Whom? Who will get this when I die? she had unconsciously put people to the test to find out whether they were worthy. It made her more severe than before.

Now she wrote, "I, Harriet Simmons Waggoner, being of sound mind and not knowing what may be in store for me at the age of seventy-two (born 1885), living alone at Sego Desert Lake, instruct my lawyer, Harold Claiborne, Paiute County Court Building, to draw my last will and testament upon the following terms."

She sat perfectly still now to hear from within who would be the lucky one, who would inherit the yellow house. For which she had waited. Yes, waited for India's death, choking on her bread because she was a rich woman's servant and whipping girl. But who had done for her, Hattie, what she had done for India? And who, apart from India, had ever held out a hand to her? Kindness, yes. Here and there people had been kind. But the word in her head was not kindness, it was succor. And who had given her that? Only India. If at least next best after succor, someone had given her a shake and said, "Stop stalling. Don't be such a slow, old, procrastinating sit-stiller." Again, it was only India who had done her good. She had offered her succor. *"Het-tie!"* said that drunken mask. *"Do you know what sloth is? Damn your poky old life!"*

But I was waiting, Hattie realized. *I was waiting, thinking, "Youth is terrible, frightening. I will wait it out. And men? Men are cruel and strong. They want things I haven't got to give." There were no kids in me,* thought Hattie. *Not that I wouldn't have loved them, but such my nature was. And who can blame me for having it? My nature?*

She drank from an Old-Fashioned glass. There was no orange in it, no ice, no bitters or sugar, only the stinging, clear bourbon.

So then, she continued looking at the dry sun-stamped dust and the last freckled flowers of red wild peach, *to live with*

Angus and his wife, and have to hear a chapter from the Bible before breakfast; once more in the house—not of a stranger, perhaps, but not far from it either. In other houses, in someone else's house, to wait for mealtimes was her lifelong punishment. She always felt it in the throat and stomach. And so she would again, and to the very end. However, she must think of someone to leave the house to.

And first of all she wanted to do right by her family. None of them had ever dreamed that she, Hattie, would ever have something to bequeath. Until a few years ago it had certainly looked as if she would die a pauper. So now she could keep her head up with the proudest of them. And, as this occurred to her, she actually lifted up her face with its broad nose and victorious eyes; if her hair had become shabby as onion roots, if at the back her head was round and bald as a newel post, what did that matter? Her heart experienced a childish glory, not yet tired of it after seventy-two years. She, too, had amounted to something. *I'll do some good by going,* she thought. *Now I believe I should leave it to, to. . . .* She returned to the old point of struggle. She had decided many times and many times changed her mind. She tried to think, *Who would get the most out of it?* It was a tearing thing to go through. If it had not been the yellow house but instead some brittle thing she could hold in her hand, then the last thing she would do would be to throw and smash it, and so the thing and she herself would be demolished together. But it was vain to think such thoughts. To whom should she leave it? Her brothers? Not they. Nephews? One was a submarine commander. The other was a bachelor in the State Department. Then began the roll call of cousins. Merton? He owned an estate in Connecticut. Anna? She had a face like a hot-water bottle. That left Joyce, the orphaned daughter of her cousin Wilfred. Joyce was the most likely heiress. Hattie had already written to her and had her out to the lake at Thanksgiving, two years ago. But this Joyce was another odd one; over thirty, good, yes, but placid, running to fat, a scholar—ten years in Eugene, Oregon, working for her degree. In Hattie's opinion this was only another form of sloth. Nevertheless, Joyce yet hoped to marry. Whom? Not Dr. Stroud. He wouldn't. And still she had vague hope. Hattie knew how that could be. At least have a man she could argue with.

She was now more drunk than at any time since her accident. Again she filled her glass. *Have ye eyes and see not? Sleepers, awake!*

Knees wide apart she sat in the twilight, thinking. Marian? Marian didn't need another house. Half Pint? She wouldn't know what to do with it. Brother Louis came up for consideration next. He was an old actor who had a church for the Indians at Athens Canyon. Hollywood stars of the silent days sent him their negligées; he altered them and wore them in the pulpit. The Indians loved his show. But when Billy Shawah blew his brains out after his two-week bender, they still tore his shack down and turned it inside out to get rid of his ghost. They had their old religion. No, not Brother Louis. He'd show movies in the yellow house to the tribe or make a nursery of it.

And now she began to consider Wicks. When last heard from he was south of Bishop, California, a handy man in a saloon off toward Death Valley. It wasn't she who heard from him but Pace. Herself, she hadn't actually seen Wicks since—how low she had sunk then!—she had kept the hamburger stand on Route 158. The little lunchroom had supported them both. Wicks hung around on the end stool, rolling cigarettes (she saw it on the film). Then there was a quarrel. Things had been going from bad to worse. He'd begun to grouse now about this and now about that. He complained about the food, at last. She saw and heard him. "Hat," he said, "I'm good and tired of hamburger." "Well, what do you think I eat?" she said with that round, defiant movement of her shoulders which she herself recognized as characteristic (*me all over,* she thought). But he opened the cash register and took out thirty cents and crossed the street to the butcher's and brought back a steak. He threw it on the griddle. "Fry it," he said. She did and watched him eat.

And when he was through she could bear her rage no longer. "Now," she said, "you've had your meat. Get out. Never come back." She kept a pistol under the counter. She picked it up, cocked it, pointed it at his heart. "If you ever come in that door again, I'll kill you," she said.

She saw it all. *I couldn't bear to fall so low,* she thought, *to be slave to a shiftless cowboy.*

Wicks said, "Don't do that, Hat. Guess I went too far. You're right."

"You'll never have a chance to make it up," she cried. "Get out!"

On that cry he disappeared, and since then she had never seen him.

"Wicks, dear," she said. "Please! I'm sorry. Don't condemn

me in your heart. Forgive me. I hurt myself in my evil. I always had a thick idiot head. I was born with a thick head.''

Again she wept, for Wicks. She was too proud. A snob. Now they might have lived together in this house, old friends, simple and plain.

She thought, *He really was my good friend.*

But what would Wicks do with a house like this, alone, if he was alive and survived her? He was too wiry for soft beds or easy chairs.

And she was the one who had said stiffly to India, ''I'm a Christian person. I do not bear a grudge.''

Ah, yes, she said to herself. *I have caught myself out too often. How long can this go on?* And she began to think, or try to think of Joyce, her cousin's daughter. Joyce was like herself, a woman alone, getting on, clumsy. She would have given much, now, to succor Joyce.

But it seemed to her now that that too had been a story. First you heard the pure story. Then you heard the impure story. Both stories. She had paid out years, now to one shadow, now to another shadow.

Joyce would come here to the house. She had a little income and could manage. She would live as Hattie had lived, alone. Here she would rot, start to drink, maybe, and day after day read, day after day sleep. See how beautiful it was here? It burned you out. How empty? It turned you into ash.

''How can I doom a young person to the same life?'' asked Hattie. ''It's for somebody like me. When I was younger it wasn't right. But now it is. Only I fit in here. It was made for my old age, to spend my last years peacefully. If I hadn't let Jerry make me drunk that night—if I hadn't sneezed! My arm! I'll have to live with Angus. My heart will break there away from my only home.''

She now was very drunk, and she said to herself, *Take what God brings. He gives no gifts unmixed. He makes loans.*

She resumed her letter of instructions to lawyer Claiborne: ''Upon the following terms,'' she wrote a second time. ''Because I have suffered much. Because I only lately received what I have to give away, I can't bear it.'' The drunken blood was soaring to her head. But her hand was clear enough. She wrote, ''It is too soon! Too soon! Because I do not find it in my heart to care for anyone as I would wish. Being cast off and lonely, and doing no harm where I am. Why should it be? This breaks my heart. In addition to everything else, why must I worry about this, which I must leave? I am tormented out of my mind. Even though by my own fault I have put myself into this position. And am not ready to give up on this. No, not yet. And so I'll tell you what, I leave this property, land, house, garden and water rights, to Hattie Simmons Waggoner. Me! I realize this is bad and wrong. It cannot happen. Yet it is the only thing I really wish to do, so may God have mercy on my soul."

"How can that be?" She studied what she had written and finally she acknowledged that she was drunk. "I'm drunk," she said, "and don't know what I'm doing. I'll die, and end. Like India. Dead as that lilac bush. Only tonight I can't give the house away. I'm drunk and so I need it. But I won't be selfish from the grave. I'll think again tomorrow," she promised herself. She went to sleep then.

Theme

Very frequently an author will use a central image or symbol to suggest his theme. In Saul Bellow's story, the yellow house, which is mentioned in the title and thereafter on nearly every page, is such a symbol. The house is a fixed element which draws toward itself everything else in the story and from which emanate nearly all events of interest. Thus, its centrality.

1 As you read the story, consider the ways in which the house gains significance. What does it mean to each character? Principally, what does it mean to Hattie Waggoner? Why does she overrate the value of the house? Why does she hold on to it with such stubbornness? Why does even Amy Walters, who owns her own house, want it to the extent that she would live with Hattie in order to gain it?

2 Can you recall—from your reading or your own experience—other possessions which take on such a magical or supernatural quality that the owner attaches a value to them far beyond their real value? What does this say about human nature? What point is Bellow making?

3 Having determined some of the meaning of the house, we can move further, to Hattie herself. She is an isolated woman, unsuited to a hard life, unattractive, old and fat, almost crippled, virtually a drunkard, self-centered, largely helpless. Yet she dominates the story, and Bellow makes her a sympathetic creature despite her unattractiveness as a heroine. The conventional heroine, if an older woman, is clean, of good habits, thrifty, capable, independent, and a do-gooder. Hattie is none of these things, obviously—in fact, she is the very opposite. Why then does Bellow make her so important? What point does he make through her? In his eyes, what does she stand for?

4 How does Bellow's vision of Hattie coincide with his presentation of the house? Are she and the house united in some mystical fashion? How? On what grounds understandable to you?

Character

1 As mentioned in question 3 under Theme, Hattie is unconventional in nearly every way. Yet she throbs with life. Possibly she lives so strongly as a character because of her own views of herself, many of them expressed in the italicized portions. What is meant by the following:

a "*I was never one single thing anyway,* she thought. *Never my own. I was only loaned to myself.*"
b "*They* [desert and lake] *drew you from yourself. But after they had drawn you, what did they do with you? It was too late to find out. I'll never know.*"
c "*. . . and the walls of the body give way outward,* she thought, *and you take the shape of an old jug, wider and wider toward the top.*"

2 Bellow provides a counterpointing or contrasting character to Hattie in the form of Amy Walters, who lives in Fort Walters, as she calls her home. Amy is a very different type of woman, as evidenced by her entire way of life. How would you characterize Amy? What significance do you attach to the name of her home? Why does she find Hattie distasteful? Can you understand her position? In what way is she a contrast to Hattie? What does Bellow gain, if anything, from juxtaposing the two women, from having them cross each other's paths without making substantial contact?

3 A further contrast to Hattie comes in the form of India, her now dead friend and the former owner of the yellow house. India is not too clearly drawn, perhaps because we chiefly see her through the drunken haze of Hattie's eyes. India, however, was a woman of wide tastes, well traveled, drawn to ideas; she was even a poetess. What is Bellow's purpose in making such a woman Hattie's companion? How does this set off Hattie?

4 India is mentioned as showing an interest in Eastern religion, Bergson, and Proust. Why these particular interests, especially Eastern religion? How do such tastes characterize India? What do they mean to Hattie? Does Hattie gain or lose by the contrast?

5 Hattie is shown as a woman with a great sympathy for horses and dogs. There are, in fact, several references to dogs, especially to her own doberman, Richie. What, then, is the purpose of having her kill Richie, beyond the fact, of course, that he attacked her? Why is she ashamed of having done it? After all, her act was one of self-defense. What does this episode mean to her? Is it a meaningful episode, or simply a decorative addition to the story?

Setting and Atmosphere (Mood)

Part of Bellow's purpose is to create a sense of the West, that is, to give the feel of what it is like to live in the open West without too many resources. Even though the year is 1957 and there are cars and other modern conveniences, the time seems much earlier, much more primitive. It is this quality that Bellow is attempting to capture.

1 Since this "feel" for the West is necessary if you are to understand Hattie and her situation, try to find clues as to how Bellow conveys this sense. Is it merely a matter of the description of the land? of the house? of the dude ranch? of the people living in relative isolation? What other qualities are involved?

2 How would you know that this is the West and not the rural South, for example, or rural New England, leaving aside the fact that Bellow names the place?

3 Is the setting important? What dimensions does it give to the story?

Tone (Style)

Despite several unsympathetic traits and actions, Hattie comes to us as a sympathetic creation. We tend to like her as we see her in the story. Her presentation is a triumph of *tone:* that is, the author has made us accept his attitude, which prevails over our own. It prevails, at least, as long as we read the story.

The tone of a story is central, for it is tone which tells us how to read. If a story or novel lacked tone altogether—which is virtually impossible—we would not know how we were to accept the characters or the tale. It is through tone that the author presents his view of his material, and it is through tone that he influences us. Thus in Joyce's "Counterparts," the tone conveys frustration and dinginess; in Purdy's "Don't Call Me by My Right Name," the tone is flippant and satiric, suggesting a brittle existence in which nothing seems to matter. For Bellow, many things matter—one of them Hattie Waggoner.

1 What are some of the devices Bellow uses to make Hattie sympathetic? Is she merely pitiful? If so, would the story descend into sentimentality? What, then, is she? How is it that we tolerate her shameful dependence on others, her constant drinking, her monstrous egotism, her moments of greed?

2 How would the tone of the story change if it were told from the point of view of Hattie (i.e., in her own words or through her eyes exclusively)? Would the danger of sentimentality be increased or decreased?

3 What impact would first-person narration (in the words of Hattie) have upon mood and atmosphere? Upon characterization? What unquestionably would be lost?

ONE

SETTING

Of all the categories under which we may analyze a short story, setting is possibly the most easily accessible. In older stories—those of the nineteenth century and the turn of the twentieth—setting is almost always apparent. Frequently it was regional, explicitly stated, and directly applicable to the events of the narrative. Within the first paragraph, more often than not, the author told the reader where his tale was taking place. For many of us, that constitutes setting. Recall, for example, the Hudson River Valley background of Washington Irving's stories.

Some of that directness of setting still exists, but it has become intertwined with other elements—particularly with mood and atmosphere—and it has become less clear an element. We still know generally where a story takes place, but our views of setting, of place itself, have become more sophisticated. Merely knowing *where* is not enough. Setting often generates more complex ideas and becomes diffuse, leading into several other elements—such as theme, character, and plot. Frequently, it is theme to which setting is attached, as we see in Faulkner's "Dry September." There, the setting is not only a particular time and a particular place but the very substance of a region, down to its dust—how the people think, how they react, their prejudices, their insanities, their very life style—with all elements suggested indirectly.

Obviously, the fragmentation of setting is one of the key changes in modern short stories. Setting is there, but we must look hard to pin it down, unless the writer specifies a place, a time. If more is designated, as in Faulkner, Kay Boyle, Crane, and to a lesser extent O'Flaherty, then we must begin the process of disentanglement. Stories have changed and our way of reading them has also changed. At one time we put our finger on setting and said, "There it is." We were then ready to move to other forms of identification. Now we hover over our categories; in fact, we recognize just how frail rigid categories can be. When we think we have finally cornered *setting* we find little pieces of other things embedded in it.

For safety's sake, we can say that setting encompasses not only the usual quantities of time and place, as well as the element loosely called background, but also aspects of atmosphere, a series of details, nuances, and gestures, which give a certain shape to theme and plot. Possibly you can search for setting best by keeping in mind a number of questions, some of which may at first appear negative:

1 Could the setting be transferred elsewhere without changing the matter and manner of the story?
2 What does setting contribute, if anything? Could it possibly be altogether eliminated as an element?
3 To what extent is setting embedded in the other elements, particularly in plot and theme?
4 What qualities do the characters have that seem to derive from that setting and no other?
5 How does setting help you to come to some conclusions about the story?
6 Would the story have been as effective if setting had been decreased, or if you had been unaware of it?

Such questions are obviously artificial; yet we ask them, and we find answers. Sometimes they help.

EFFIGY OF WAR

Kay Boyle

The barman at the big hotel on the sea front had been an officer in the Italian army during the last war, and somehow or other the rumor began to get around. Whether it was that he said too much to people who spoke his own language with him, saying late at night that the vines in Italy were like no other vines and the voices more musical and the soldiers as good as any others, no matter what history had to say about them, or whether it got around in some other way, it was impossible to know. But the story came to the director of the hotel (Cannes, it was, and the people just as gaudily dressed as other years, and the shops on the Croisette as fancy), and because of the feeling that ran high against the foreigner and against the name of Italy, the director stepped into the lounge bar about eleven one morning to tell the barman what he'd better do. He was a dressy, expensive-looking little man, the director, who could speak four languages with ease, and he had been a Russian once, a White Russian, so that France was the only country left to him now. He came into the bar at a quiet hour, just before the idle would begin wandering in out of the eternally springtime sun, and he jerked his cuffs inside his morning coat and screwed the soft, sagging folds of his throat from his collar wings and started speaking quietly over the mahogany-colored bar.

"Maestro," he said to the barman who had been ten years with them, "with all this trouble going on the management would quite understand your wanting to go back to Italy."

"Italy?" the barman said, and it might have been Siberia he was pronouncing as a destination and the look in his eyes was as startled. He stopped whatever it was he had been doing, setting the glasses straight or putting the ash trays out or the olives, and he looked at the director. He was a slight, dark man and his face was as delicate-boned as a monkey's, and the hair was oiled down flat upon his monkey-fragile skull.

"A lot of Italians are going back," the director said, and he swung himself up onto the stool as elegantly and lightly as a dwarf dressed up for a public appearance, the flesh hairless and pink, and the hand on the wood of the bar as plump as a child's. "Give me a glass of milk," he said, and he went on saying in a lower voice: "In times like these everyone wants to avoid all the trouble they can. Everybody likes to feel he's in his own country." He said it with a slight Russian accent, and the barman waited while the director took the cigarette out of the silver case, and then the barman snapped the lighter open and held the flame to the end of the cigarette in his dark, monkey-nervous hand. "We're perfectly willing to discuss things with you," the director said, and as the first bluish breath of smoke drifted between them, their eyes met for a moment across it, and the director was the first to look away.

"Ah, if we should all go back to the places we belong to!" the barman said as he put the lighter into the pocket of his starched white coat. He turned aside to take the bottle of milk off the ice, and he went on saying in strangely poetic sorrow: "If we all returned to the waters of our own seas and the words of our own languages, France would be left a wilderness—"

"Of course, there are some national exceptions," the director added quickly. "There are some nationalities which cannot go back." He took a swallow of milk and looked rather severely at the barman. "In countries where there have been revolutions, economic upheavals," he went on, his hand with the cigarette in it making the vague, comprehensive gestures of unrest. "But with Italians," he said, and the barman suddenly leaned forward and laid his small bony hands down flat upon the bar.

"Well, me," he said, "I've been fifteen years in this country. I'm too old to go back now. For me, Mussolini was an economic upheaval," he said. He picked up the bottle of milk again and filled the director's glass, pouring it out a little too quickly. "I've never gone back, not since fifteen years," he said, the words spoken sharply and rapidly, almost breathlessly across the bar. "I'm like a refugee, like a political refugee," he said. "I haven't the right to go back."

"That can be taken care of," the director said, and he took out his folded handkerchief and dabbed at the drops of milk on his upper lip. "The management would advance you what you needed to get back, write you a good testimonial—"

"I haven't done military service for them," the barman said, and he was smiling in something like pain at the director, the grin pulled queer and ancient as a monkey's across his face. "I can't go back," he said. "This is my country by now. If I can't go on working here I can't work anywhere. I wouldn't leave this country no matter what anybody said to me or no matter what they did to me."

"You never did very much about getting any papers out," said the director. He was looking straight ahead at the small silk flags of all the nations and at his own immaculately preserved reflection in the glass. "You never did much about trying to change your nationality," he said, and he took another discreet swallow of milk. "You should have thought of that before."

"I might have been a Frenchman today if it hadn't been for my wife," the barman said, and his tongue ran eagerly out along his lip. "My wife—" he said, and he leaned closer, the starched sleeves, with the hairy, bony little wrists showing, laid on the bar. "I haven't seen her for fifteen years," he said, and the director looked at the glass of milk and shrugged his shoulders. "She's in Italy, and she wouldn't sign the papers. She wouldn't do that one thing," he said, the eyes dark and bright, and the face lit suddenly, like a poet's with eagerness and pain. "Not that she wanted me," he said. "It wasn't that. But women like that, Italian women, they're as soft and beautiful as flowers and as stubborn as weeds." He said it in abrupt poetic violence, and the director stirred a little uneasily and finished the milk in his glass.

"Now, you take a run up to the Italian Consul this afternoon and have a talk with him," he said, and he wiped his upper lip with his folded handkerchief again. "Tell him you're thinking of going back. Put Raymond on duty for the afternoon. And another thing, Maestro," he said as he got down off the bar stool, "Don't keep that *Corriere della Sera* out there where everybody can see it. Put it in your pocket and read it when you get home," he said.

It might have passed off quietly enough like that if the Dane hadn't come into it. He was a snub-nosed, sun-blacked, blond-headed little man who gave swimming lessons in one of the bathing establishments on the beach. He had been a long time there, walking season after season tough and cocky up and down the beach with his chest high and his thumbs hooked into the white belt of his bathing trunks. He wore a bright clean linen cap down to his yellow brows, and royal-blue swimming shorts, and the muscles in his shoulders and arms were as thick and smooth as taffy. But after the war came, he didn't parade up and down the esplanade in the same way in the sun, but stayed hour after hour in the water or else in a corner of the beach café. He still gave lessons, but he let the pupils seek him out in the shade of the café, as if the eyes of the mobilized and the uniformed and the envious could see him less distinctly there.

The one who started it all was the Greek waiter in the big hotel who had got his French naturalization papers eight months before and was leaving for training camp in a week or two. He'd lean over the diners—what was left of the English and the American colony, and the dukes and duchesses, and the Spanish who had got their jewels and their pelts and their money out of Spain—and he'd say:

"What nationality do you think I am, eh? What country would you say I come from?" showing his teeth in pride and pleasure at them as he slipped the dishes of *filets de soles bonne femme* or *champignons à la Reine d'Angleterre* down before them, provided the maître d'hôtel was looking the other way. Sometimes the guests would say he looked one thing, and sometimes another: Italian, Rumanian, or even Argentine, and he'd smile like a prima donna at them, leaning almost on their shoulders, with his eyes shining and the serviette flung rather wildly over his arm.

"No, no, oh, *mon dieu,* no!" he'd say. "I'm pure French. What do you think of that? In another two or three months you'll see me coming in here with gold stripes on my sleeve, ordering everything like everybody else has to eat." And then he'd take out his mobilization order and show it to them, balancing the *homard à l'américaine* on its platter in the other hand as he opened out the stamped, signed paper. "I'm French," he'd say, with the garlic hanging on his breath. "I'm going right into the French army to fight. I'm going to fight for everybody sitting here having dinner tonight," he'd say, and he'd give the people at the next table their salad, holding his mobilization order open in his hand.

The Greek waiter had never liked the look of the Dane, and now that he had his military orders he couldn't so much as stand the sight of the cold-eyed, golden little man. In the hours he had off in the afternoons, he took the habit of walking out on the esplanade and stopping just above the bathing place to call the names down to him. There he would be, the Dane, with his white cap on and his royal-blue bathing trunks, talking half naked to the half naked girls or women on the beach, war or no war, and going on making money just the same.

"*Sale étranger!*" the Greek would call down, with a fine Greek accent to it, and "*Crepule!,*" with his voice ringing out like an opera singer's across the sand and the striped bathing houses and the sea. "France for the French!" he'd roar over the railing, and the little Dane in his bathing suit would go quietly on with his swimming lessons, or if he were alone he'd turn and go into the beach café and sit down out of sight in the shade. There was a week ahead still before the Greek waiter would go, and all those days in the afternoons he'd stand on the esplanade and call the names down. In the end he appealed to the French themselves, exhorting them to rise. "The French for the French!" he'd shout down through the funnel of his hands. "Don't employ foreigners! Give a Frenchman the job!"

The last night of the week the little Dane came into the lounge bar for a drink before he went to bed; coming late, in discretion, when no one else was there. The two of them were talking there together, the Dane sitting on the stool with the glass of beer before him, and the Italian on the other side with his starched jacket on and the wisps of his monkey hair slicked flat across his skull, and in a few minutes the barman would have taken the bottles down and locked the safes and turned the lights out, and then nothing would have occurred. But now the barman was leaning on the counter, speaking the French tongue in a low, rather grievous voice to the swimming teacher, his thin hand rocking from side to side like a little boat as he talked.

"Drinking has ceased," he was saying in faultless pentameter, "in the old way it has ceased. Even before September there was a difference, as if the thirst of man had been slaked at last. To any sensitive eye, the marks of death were to be seen for years on the façades of casinos, palace hotels, luxury restaurants, and on the terraces of country clubs and vast private estates. Even the life of the big bars has been dying," he said. "For years now that I can remember, the lounge bar has been passing through the agonies of death." He made a tragic and noble gesture toward the empty leather armchairs in the half-darkened room, and he said in a low, dreamy voice: "All this is finished. There is no more place in the hearts of men for this kind of thing. The race that insisted on this atmosphere of redundance for its pleasure, that demanded this futility, is vanishing, dying—"

"War levels the ranks," the Dane said quietly. His sun-blacked, sun-withered face under the bright light thatch of hair was as immobile as if carved from wood.

"Ah, before the war even," the barman said softly, and then he stopped, for the men had come into the bar. The Greek waiter walked a little ahead of the others, wearing a gray jersey and a cap pulled down, and they both of them knew him; it was the others behind him they had never seen before.

"Get that one, the one on the stool," the Greek waiter said, and one of the other men stepped past him and walked toward the bar. Just before he got there he lifted his right arm and hit the swimming teacher on the chin. The little, light-crowned head and the strong, small body rose clear of the stool an instant, like a piece of paper lifted and spun sidewise by the wind, and then it sailed into the corner and collapsed there, bent double, by the leather chair. "That's the kind of language he understands," the Greek said, and he crossed the length of thick, soft carpet, jerking his cap up on his forehead. He was smiling with delight when he kicked the swimming teacher's body into another shape. "Walking up and down out there on the beach," the Greek said, and he turned back to the others and the Italian barman behind the bar. "Giving lessons just like men weren't bleeding their guts out for him and people like him—"

"He volunteered. I tell you that man volunteered," the barman began saying, and his bones were shaking like a monkey's in his skin. "I've seen the paper he got. I know he volunteered to fight like anybody else would—" And when he jumped for the bell the Greek waiter reached over and took him by the collar of his starched white coat and dragged him out across the plates of potato chips and the empty beer bottle and the glass the Dane had been drinking and slung him across the elegant little glass-topped tables into the other corner of the room.

"Pick him up and take him along too," the Greek said. "I know all about him I need to know. He was an officer last war, officer in the Italian army, so you'll know what side he'll fight on this time. Take them both out," he said. "This country's not good enough for them, not good enough for either of them."

They did it by moonlight, taking the two men's clothes off on the sand and shingles by the Mediterranean water, and giving it to them in fiercely accelerating violence. They broke the swimming teacher's jaw, and they snapped the arms of the barman behind him like firewood, beating the breath and the life from them with whatever fell under their hands. The Greek carried over an armful of folding iron chairs from the bathing establishment's darkened, abandoned porch and, with these as weapons, they battered the two men's heads down and drove their mouths into the sand.

"So now repeat this after me, foreigners," the Greek began saying in wild holy passion as he kneeled beside them. He had taken the flag out of his jersey and was shaking out its folds. "So now repeat what I'm going to tell you," he said in violent religious fervor against the pulsing and murmuring of the water, and his hands were trembling as he laid the flag out where their mouths could bleed upon the tricolor emblem, the cotton stuff transformed now to the exigencies of a nation and a universe.

Setting

The setting of a story can mean many things besides the obvious "where it takes place." Of course it means that—the locale, the background, the regional aspect. It can also designate a particular time, an historical era, a political situation. In an effective story, the setting is usually integrated into other aspects—into plot or theme, into character, into philosophical implication. Only rarely can setting be isolated, and then only momentarily. In Kay Boyle's story, setting is certainly integrated, but we temporarily isolate it to indicate its significance. Here setting is the focal point for character, theme, plot, even style. The setting is Cannes, the jewel of the French Riviera during World War II, while France was still fighting Nazi Germany. With a background of tangled political fortunes, refugees and escaped nationals, violent hatreds and feelings of revenge, assumptions of power on one hand, inadequacy on the other, the setting reminds us of all the dislocation that war brings.

It is this atmosphere of dislocation, alienation, revenge, hatred, and self-pity that dominates the story. In wartime, people feel free to indulge passions that they would ordinarily suppress, or be obliged to suppress. This is, of course, one of the many horrors of war—the fact that it opens a way for man's savagery to come out, that it virtually forces man to become a savage in order to survive. These values form the setting and the theme of Kay Boyle's short story. Each element helps contribute to this overall effect.

1 Why does the author choose Cannes? What do you know of the place? of the location? Wouldn't any other place have done as well?

2 Why is the barman an Italian? Would any other nationality do as well? Why is he described as having the aspect of a monkey? How does Miss Boyle create sympathy for him despite his obvious weaknesses?

3 Characterize the director of the hotel. Even though he argues reasonably, we dislike him. How does Miss Boyle manipulate our feelings so that he appears distasteful? Look for details of language, background, description.

4 The story seems to divide into two parts with the introduction of the Danish swimming teacher. How does the Dane fit? Is he sympathetic despite the fact that he seems to be getting rich and enjoying himself while others are fighting and dying?

5 Why does Miss Boyle make a point of mentioning some of the lavish dishes that the Greek waiter serves? Is this simply to indicate that Cannes is for the very rich?

6 Is the point of view of the Greek waiter sympathetic? Treat him carefully and remember that the wartime setting creates a passionate involvement in which emotion chokes reason.

7 How are our feelings directed? Ordinarily we could expect to be sympathetic to the man who fights for his country and feel only distaste for the man who avoids commitment. But are these the feeling generated here? What, instead, does Miss Boyle seem to be saying?

Theme, or Purpose

Throughout the story, Miss Boyle makes comments about war and about wartime experiences. Most of us are accustomed to hearing that war is horrible, that war is subhuman, and so forth, but when we see it focused in the lives of a few individuals, we are reminded anew of man's inhumanity to man.

1 Consider the title of the story, "Effigy of War." What does this mean? What or who is the effigy?

2 What is the significance of the symbolic (and actual) mouths bleeding on the French flag at the end of the story?

3 Why is the Greek described as speaking in a "wild holy passion"?

4 What is the meaning of "the exigencies of a nation and a universe"?

5 How does the particularity of the setting, Cannes, contribute to the statement Miss Boyle is making about war? Consider in terms of contrasts, opposing elements.

6 Finally, is anyone to blame for what happens? Is there a moral element in the story? Is the naturalized Greek a villain? Can individuals be held to task when countries cannot be?

DRY SEPTEMBER

William Faulkner

I

Through the bloody September twilight, aftermath of sixty-two rainless days, it had gone like a fire in dry grass—the rumor, the story, whatever it was. Something about Miss Minnie Cooper and a Negro. Attacked, insulted, frightened: none of them, gathered in the barber shop on that Saturday evening where the ceiling fan stirred, without freshening it, the vitiated air, sending back upon them, in recurrent surges of stale pomade and lotion, their own stale breath and odors, knew exactly what had happened.

"Except it wasn't Will Mayes," a barber said. He was a man of middle age; a thin, sand-colored man with a mild face, who was shaving a client. "I know Will Mayes. He's a good nigger. And I know Miss Minnie Cooper, too."

"What do you know about her?" a second barber said.

"Who is she?" the client said. "A young girl?"

"No," the barber said. "She's about forty, I reckon. She aint married. That's why I dont believe—"

"Believe, hell!" a hulking youth in a sweat-stained silk shirt said. "Wont you take a white woman's word before a nigger's?

"I dont believe Will Mayes did it," the barber said. "I know Will Mayes."

"Maybe you know who did it, then. Maybe you already got him out of town, you damn niggerlover."

"I dont believe anybody did anything. I dont believe anything happened. I leave it to you fellows if them ladies that get old without getting married dont have notions that a man cant—"

"Then you are a hell of a white man," the client said. He moved under the cloth. The youth had sprung to his feet.

"You dont?" he said. "Do you accuse a white woman of lying?"

The barber held the razor poised about the half-risen client. He did not look around.

"It's this durn weather," another said. "It's enough to make a man do anything. Even to her."

Nobody laughed. The barber said in his mild, stubborn tone: "I aint accusing nobody of nothing. I just know and you fellows know how a woman that never—"

"You damn niggerlover!" the youth said.

"Shut up, Butch," another said. "We'll get the facts in plenty of time to act."

"Who is? Who's getting them?" the youth said. "Facts, hell! I—"

"You're a fine white man," the client said. "Aint you?" In his frothy beard he looked like a desert rat in the moving pictures. "You tell them, Jack," he said to the youth. "If there aint any white men in this town, you can count on me, even if I aint only a drummer and a stranger."

"That's right, boys," the barber said. "Find out the truth first. I know Will Mayes."

"Well, by God!" the youth shouted. "To think that a white man in this town—"

"Shut up, Butch," the second speaker said. "We got plenty of time."

The client sat up. He looked at the speaker. "Do you claim that anything excuses a nigger attacking a white woman? Do you mean to tell me you are a white man and you'll stand for it? You better go back North where you came from. The South dont want your kind here."

"North what?" the second youth said. "I was born and raised in this town."

"Well, by God!" the youth said. He looked about with a strained, baffled gaze, as if he was trying to remember what it was he wanted to say or to do. He drew his sleeve across his sweating face. "Damn if I'm going to let a white woman—"

"You tell them, Jack," the drummer said. "By God, if they—"

The screen door crashed open. A man stood in the floor, his feet apart and his heavy-set body poised easily. His white shirt was open at the throat; he wore a felt hat. His hot, bold glance swept the group. His name was McLendon. He had commanded troops at the front in France and had been decorated for valor.

"Well," he said, "are you going to sit there and let a black son rape a white woman of the streets of Jefferson?"

Butch sprang up again. The silk of his shirt clung flat to his heavy shoulders. At each armpit was a dark halfmoon. "That's what I been telling them! That's what I—"

"Did it really happen?" a third said. "This aint the first man scare she ever had, like Hawkshaw says. Wasn't there something about a man on the kitchen roof, watching her undress, about a year ago?"

"What?" the client said. "What's that?" The barber had

been slowly forcing him back into the chair; he arrested himself reclining, his head lifted, the barber still pressing him down.

McLendon whirled on the third speaker. "Happen? What the hell difference does it make? Are you going to let the black sons get away with it until one really does it?"

"That's what I'm telling them!" Butch shouted. He cursed, long and steady, pointless.

"Here, here," a fourth said. "Not so loud. Dont talk so loud."

"Sure," McLendon said; "no talking necessary at all. I've done my talking. Who's with me?" He poised on the balls of his feet, roving his gaze.

The barber held the drummer's face down, the razor poised. "Find out the facts first, boys. I know Willy Mayes. It wasn't him. Let's get the sheriff and do this thing right."

McLendon whirled upon him his furious, rigid face. The barber did not look away. They looked like men of different races. The other barbers had ceased also above their prone clients. "You mean to tell me," McLendon said, "that you'd take a nigger's word before a white woman's? Why, you damn nigger-loving—"

The third speaker rose and grasped McLendon's arm; he too had been a soldier. "Now, now. Let's figure this thing out. Who knows anything about what really happened?"

"Figure out hell!" McLendon jerked his arm free. "All that're with me get up from there. The ones that aint—" He roved his gaze, dragging his sleeve across his face.

Three men rose. The drummer in the chair sat up. "Here," he said, jerking at the cloth about his neck; "get this rag off me. I'm with him. I dont live here, but by God, if our mothers and wives and sisters—" He smeared the cloth over his face and flung it to the floor. McLendon stood in the floor and cursed the others. Another rose and moved toward him. The remainder sat uncomfortable, not looking at one another, then one by one they rose and joined him.

The barber picked the cloth from the floor. He began to fold it neatly. "Boys, dont do that. Will Mayes never done it. I know."

"Come on," McLendon said. He whirled. From his hip pocket protruded the butt of a heavy automatic pistol. They went out. The screen door crashed behind them reverberant in the dead air.

The barber wiped the razor carefully and swiftly, and put it away, and ran to the rear, and took his hat from the wall. "I'll be back as soon as I can," he said to the other barbers. "I cant let—" He went out, running. The two other barbers followed him to the door and caught it on the rebound, leaning out and looking up the street after him. The air was flat and dead. It had a metallic taste at the base of the tongue.

"What can he do?" the first said. The second one was saying "Jees Christ, Jees Christ" under his breath. "I'd just as lief be Will Mayes as Hawk, if he gets McLendon riled."

"Jees Christ, Jees Christ," the second whispered.

"You reckon he really done it to her?" the first said.

II

She was thirty-eight or thirty-nine. She lived in a small frame house with her invalid mother and a thin, sallow, unflagging aunt, where each morning between ten and eleven she would appear on the porch in a lace-trimmed boudoir cap, to sit swinging in the porch swing until noon. After dinner she lay down for a while, until the afternoon began to cool. Then, in one of the three or four new voile dresses which she had each summer, she would go downtown to spend the afternoon in the stores with the other ladies, where they would handle the goods and haggle over the prices in cold, immediate voices, without any intention of buying.

She was of comfortable people—not the best in Jefferson, but good people enough—and she was still on the slender side of ordinary looking, with a bright, faintly haggard manner and dress. When she was young she had had a slender, nervous body and a sort of hard vivacity which had enabled her for a time to ride upon the crest of the town's social life as exemplified by the high school party and church social period of her contemporaries while still children enough to be unclassconscious.

She was the last to realize that she was losing ground; that those among whom she had been a little brighter and louder flame than any other were beginning to learn the pleasure of snobbery—male—and retaliation—female. That was when her face began to wear that bright, haggard look. She still carried it to parties on shadowy porticoes and summer lawns, like a mask or a flag, with that bafflement of furious repudiation of truth in her eyes. One evening at a party she heard a boy and two girls, all schoolmates, talking. She never accepted another invitation.

She watched the girls with whom she had grown up as they married and got homes and children, but no man ever called on her steadily until the children of the other girls had been calling her "aunty" for several years, the while their mothers told them in bright voices about how popular Aunt Minnie had been as a girl. Then the town began to see her driving on Sunday afternoons with the cashier in the bank. He was a widower of about forty—a high-colored man, smelling always faintly of the barber shop or of whiskey. He owned the first automobile in town, a red runabout; Minnie had the first motoring bonnet and veil the town ever saw. Then the town began to say: "Poor Minnie." "But she is old enough to take care of herself," others said. That was when she began to ask her old schoolmates that their children call her "cousin" instead of "aunty."

It was twelve years now since she had been relegated into adultery by public opinion, and eight years since the cashier had gone to a Memphis bank, returning for one day each Christmas, which he spent at an annual bachelors' party at a hunting club on the river. From behind their curtains the neighbors would see the party pass, and during the over-the-way Christmas day visiting they would tell her about him, about how well he looked, and how they heard that he was prospering in the city, watching with bright, secret eyes her haggard, bright face. Usually by that hour there would be the scent of whiskey on her breath. It was supplied her by a youth, a clerk at the soda fountain: "Sure; I buy it for the old gal. I reckon she's entitled to a little fun."

Her mother kept to her room altogether now; the gaunt aunt ran the house. Against that background Minnie's bright dresses, her idle and empty days, had a quality of furious unreality. She went out in the evenings only with women now, neighbors, to the moving pictures. Each afternoon she dressed in one of the new dresses and went downtown alone, where her young "cousins" were already strolling in the late afternoons with their delicate, silken heads and thin, awkward arms and conscious hips, clinging to one another or shrieking and giggling with paired boys in the soda fountain when she passed and went on along the serried store fronts, in the doors of which the sitting and lounging men did not even follow her with their eyes any more.

III

The barber went swiftly up the street where the sparse lights, insect-swirled, glared in rigid and violent suspension in the lifeless air. The day had died in a pall of dust; above the darkened square, shrouded by the spent dust, the sky was as clear as the inside of a brass bell. Below the east was a rumor of the twice-waxed moon.

When he overtook them McLendon and three others were getting into a car parked in an alley. McLendon stooped his thick head, peering out beneath the top. "Changed your mind, did you?" he said. "Damn good thing; by God, tomorrow when this town hears about how you talked tonight—"

"Now, now," the other ex-soldier said. "Hawkshaw's all right. Come on, Hawk; jump in."

"Will Mayes never done it, boys," the barber said. "If anybody done it. Why, you all know well as I do there aint any town where they got better niggers than us. And you know how a lady will kind of think things about men when there aint any reason to, and Miss Minnie anyway—"

"Sure, sure," the soldier said. "We're just going to talk to him a little; that's all."

"Talk hell!" Butch said. "When we're through with the—"

"Shut up, for God's sake!" the soldier said. "Do you want everybody in town—"

"Tell them, by God!" McLendon said. "Tell every one of the sons that'll let a white woman—"

"Let's go; let's go: here's the other car." The second car slid squealing out of a cloud of dust at the alley mouth. McLendon started his car and took the lead. Dust lay like fog in the street. The street lights hung nimbused as in water. They drove on out of town.

A rutted lane turned at right angles. Dust hung above it too, and above all the land. The dark bulk of the ice plant, where the Negro Mayes was night watchman, rose against the sky. "Better stop here, hadn't we?" the soldier said. McLendon did not reply. He hurled the car up and slammed to a stop, the headlights glaring on the blank wall.

"Listen here, boys," the barber said; "if he's here, dont that prove he never done it? Dont it? If it was him, he would run. Dont you see he would?" The second car came up and stopped. McLendon got down; Butch sprang down beside him. "Listen boys," the barber said.

"Cut the lights off!" McLendon said. The breathless dark rushed down. There was no sound in it save their lungs as they sought air in the parched dust in which for two months they had lived; then the diminishing crunch of McLendon's and Butch's feet, and a moment later McLendon's voice:

"Will! . . . Will!"

Below the east the wan hemorrhage of the moon increased. It heaved above the ridge, silvering the air, the dust, so that they seemed to breathe, live, in a bowl of molten lead. There was no sound of nightbird nor insect, no sound save their breathing and the faint ticking of contracting metal about the cars. Where their bodies touched one another they seemed to sweat dryly, for no more moisture came. "Christ!" a voice said; "let's get out of here."

But they didn't move until vague noises began to grow out of the darkness ahead; then they got out and waited tensely in the breathless dark. There was another sound: a blow, a hissing expulsion of breath and McLendon cursing in undertone. They stood a moment longer, then they ran forward. They ran in a stumbling clump, as though they were fleeing something. "Kill him, kill the son," a voice whispered. McLendon flung them back.

"Not here," he said. "Get him into the car." "Kill him, kill the black son!" the voice murmured. They dragged the Negro to the car. The barber had waited beside the car. He could feel himself sweating and he knew he was going to be sick at the stomach.

"What is it, captain?" the Negro said. "I aint done nothing. 'Fore God, Mr John." Someone produced handcuffs. They worked busily about the Negro as though he were a post, quiet, intent, getting in one another's way. He submitted to the handcuffs, looking swiftly and constantly from dim face to dim face. "Who's here, captains?" he said, leaning to peer into the faces until they could feel his breath and smell his sweaty reek. He spoke a name or two. "What you all say I done, Mr John?"

McLendon jerked the car door open. "Get in!" he said.

The Negro did not move. "What you all going to do with me, Mr John? I aint done nothing. White folks, captains, I aint done nothing: I swear 'fore God." He called another name.

"Get in!" McLendon said. He struck the Negro. The others expelled their breath in a dry hissing and struck him with random blows and he whirled and cursed them, and swept his manacled hands across their faces and slashed the barber upon the mouth, and the barber struck him also. "Get him in there," McLendon said. They pushed at him. He ceased struggling and got in and sat quietly as the others took their places. He sat between the barber and the soldier, drawing his limbs in so as not to touch them, his eyes going swiftly and constantly from face to face. Butch clung to the running board. The car moved on. The barber nursed his mouth with his handkerchief.

"What's the matter, Hawk?" the soldier said.

"Nothing," the barber said. They regained the highroad and turned away from town. The second car dropped back out of the dust. They went on, gaining speed; the final fringe of houses dropped behind.

"Goddamn, he stinks!" the soldier said.

"We'll fix that," the drummer in front beside McLendon said. On the running board Butch cursed into the hot rush of air. The barber leaned suddenly forward and touched McLendon's arm.

"Let me out, John," he said.

"Jump out, niggerlover," McLendon said without turning his head. He drove swiftly. Behind them the sourceless lights of the second car glared in the dust. Presently McLendon turned into a narrow road. It was rutted with disuse. It led back to an abandoned brick kiln—a series of reddish mounds and weed- and vine-choked vats without bottom. It had been used for pasture once, until one day the owner missed one of his mules. Although he prodded carefully in the vats with a long pole, he could not even find the bottom of them.

"John," the barber said.

"Jump out, then," McLendon said, hurling the car along the ruts. Beside the barber the Negro spoke:

"Mr Henry."

The barber sat forward. The narrow tunnel of the road rushed up and past. Their motion was like an extinct furnace blast: cooler, but utterly dead. The car bounded from rut to rut.

"Mr Henry," the Negro said.

The barber began to tug furiously at the door. "Look out, there!" the soldier said, but the barber had already kicked the door open and swung onto the running board. The soldier leaned across the Negro and grasped at him, but he had already jumped. The car went on without checking speed.

The impetus hurled him crashing through dust-sheathed weeds, into the ditch. Dust puffed about him, and in a thin, vicious crackling of sapless stems he lay choking and retching until the second car passed and died away. Then he rose and limped on until he reached the highroad and turned toward town, brushing at his clothes with his hands. The moon was higher, riding high and clear of the dust at last, and after a while the town began to glare beneath the dust. He went on, limping. Presently he heard cars and the glow of them grew in the dust behind him and he left the road and crouched again in the weeds until they passed. McLendon's car came last now. There were four people in it and Butch was not on the running board.

They went on; the dust swallowed them; the glare and the sound died away. The dust of them hung for a while, but soon the eternal dust absorbed it again. The barber climbed back onto the road and limped on toward town.

IV

As she dressed for supper on that Saturday evening, her own flesh felt like fever. Her hands trembled among the hooks and eyes, and her eyes had a feverish look, and her hair swirled crisp and crackling under the comb. While she was still dressing the friends called for her and sat while she donned her sheerest underthings and stockings and a new voile dress. "Do you feel strong enough to go out?" they said, their eyes bright too, with a dark glitter. "When you have time to get over the shock, you must tell us what happened. What he said and did; everything."

In the leafed darkness, as they walked toward the square, she began to breathe deeply, something like a swimmer preparing to dive, until she ceased trembling, the four of them walking slowly because of the terrible heat and out of solicitude for her. But as they neared the square she began to tremble again, walking with her head up, her hands clenched at her sides, their voices about her murmurous, also with that feverish, glittering quality of their eyes.

They entered the square, she in the center of the group, fragile in her fresh dress. She was trembling worse. She walked slower and slower, as children eat ice cream, her head up and her eyes bright in the haggard banner of her face, passing the hotel and the coatless drummers in chairs along the curb looking around at her. "That's the one: see? The one in pink in the middle." "Is that her? What did they do with the nigger? Did they—?" "Sure. He's all right." "All right, is he?" "Sure. He went on a little trip." Then the drug store, where even the young men lounging in the doorway tipped their hats and followed with their eyes the motion of her hips and legs when she passed.

They went on, passing the lifted hats of the gentlemen, the suddenly ceased voices, deferent, protective. "Do you see?" the friends said. Their voices sounded like long, hovering sighs of hissing exultation. "There's not a Negro on the square. Not one."

They reached the picture show. It was like a miniature fairyland with its lighted lobby and colored lithographs of life caught in its terrible and beautiful mutations. Her lips began to tingle. In the dark, when the picture began, it would be all right; she could hold back the laughing so it would not waste away so fast and so soon. So she hurried on before the turning faces, the undertones of low astonishment, and they took their accustomed places where she could see the aisle against the silver glare and the young men and girls coming in two and two against it.

The lights flicked away; the screen glowed silver, and soon life began to unfold, beautiful and passionate and sad, while still the young men and girls entered, scented and sibilant in the half dark, their paired backs in silhouette delicate and sleek, their slim, quick bodies awkward, divinely young, while beyond them the silver dream accumulated, inevitably on and on. She began to laugh. In trying to suppress it, it made more noise than ever; heads began to turn. Still laughing, her friends raised her and led her out, and she stood at the curb, laughing on a high, sustained note, until the taxi came up and they helped her in.

They removed the pink voile and the sheer underthings and the stockings, and put her to bed, and cracked ice for her temples, and sent for the doctor. He was hard to locate, so they ministered to her with hushed ejaculations, renewing the ice and fanning her. While the ice was fresh and cold she stopped laughing and lay still for a time, moaning only a little. But soon the laughing welled again and her voice rose screaming.

"Shhhhhhhhhhh! Shhhhhhhhhhhhhh!" they said, freshening the icepack, smoothing her hair, examining it for gray; "poor girl!" Then to one another: "Do you suppose anything really happened?" their eyes darkly aglitter, secret and passionate. "Shhhhhhhhh! Poor girl! Poor Minnie!"

V

It was midnight when McLendon drove up to his neat new house. It was trim and fresh as a birdcage and almost as small, with its clean, green-and-white paint. He locked the car and mounted the porch and entered. His wife rose from a chair beside the reading lamp. McLendon stopped in the floor and stared at her until she looked down.

"Look at that clock," he said, lifting his arm, pointing. She stood before him, her face lowered, a magazine in her hands. Her face was pale, strained, and weary-looking. "Haven't I told you about sitting up like this, waiting to see when I come in?"

"John," she said. She laid the magazine down. Poised on the balls of his feet, he glared at her with his hot eyes, his sweating face.

"Didn't I tell you?" He went toward her. She looked up then. He caught her shoulder. She stood passive, looking at him.

"Don't, John. I couldn't sleep . . . The heat; something. Please, John. You're hurting me."

"Didn't I tell you?" He released her and half struck, half flung her across the chair, and she lay there and watched him quietly as he left the room.

He went on through the house, ripping off his shirt, and on the dark, screened porch at the rear he stood and mopped his head and shoulders with the shirt and flung it away. He took the pistol from his hip and laid it on the table beside the bed, and sat on the bed and removed his shoes, and rose and slipped his trousers off. He was sweating again already, and he stooped and hunted furiously for the shirt. At last he found it and wiped his body again, and, with his body pressed against the dusty screen, he stood panting. There was no movement, no sound, not even an insect. The dark world seemed to lie stricken beneath the cold moon and the lidless stars.

Setting and Atmosphere

As mentioned in the comments on Kay Boyle's "Effigy of War," setting can mean many things: locale, natural background, region, political situation, historical era, particular time. When we say that setting predominates in a story, we mean that the story derives completely from that locale, time, and historical era.

1 Such a story is Faulkner's "Dry September," which grows out of the South in the twentieth century, out of the rural South, to be more exact. The story has particularity of time and place. So overwhelming is the setting that Faulkner makes the very dust (together with dryness) into an important symbol. Whenever the word "dust" or something similar to it appears, a whole cluster of meanings arises. As you read through the story, look for descriptions of dust and try to analyze its function as a symbol. Keep in mind that a symbol is some concrete object or some idea which embodies several possible meanings. Often such a symbol serves as the cohesive force in a story or novel, from which the author projects his various meanings. Once you see how dust is used in a particular passage, trace its meaning throughout the story.

2 Why does the weather become of such importance to the story? How does Faulkner attach weather to theme or meaning?

3 Examine the first paragraph of the story, especially the first words. Why does Faulkner use the word "bloody" in describing a September twilight? Does the word become symbolic?

4 As you analyze the first paragraph for atmospheric and mood words, consider smells, stillness, torpor. See how many words convey these feelings.

5 Consider also the title, "Dry September." What does the word "dry" signify, besides its obvious meaning of "no rain"? How does the dryness of the weather, the dust of the earth, the redness of the sun contribute to the mental state of the characters?

Characterization

William Faulkner was a creator of memorable characters. He peopled his section of the South—in and around Oxford, Mississippi—with a whole gallery of types and individuals. Miss Minnie Cooper and McLendon are in themselves not particularly memorable, but they are miniatures of larger Faulkner creations and as such are typical of his world.

1 As Faulkner depicts her, Miss Minnie represents one aspect of Southern womanhood, though by no means all aspects. Try to reconstruct her past and present life from what Faulkner provides. Does he convince you that she is the type of person who would imagine the rape? Does he suggest that she even furthers the idea of the rape in order to make herself appear more attractive?

2 Discuss why she begins to laugh hysterically in the theater. Why there and not elsewhere?

3 McLendon presents himself as the defender of Miss Minnie's purity, and he kills the Negro in order to be sure that women like Miss Minnie will never be threatened by attack. This, of course, is McLendon's own version of what he does. Faulkner's interpretation is quite different. He moves outside McLendon and shows us a character who acts from his own personal needs. What are these needs?

4 In connection with question 3, why does Faulkner make McLendon a man who "had been decorated for valor" during World War I? Discuss the physical descriptions of McLendon throughout the story. What does his physique indicate?

5 How does Faulkner connect the weather to McLendon's murder of the Negro?

6 Near the end of the story, McLendon gains the focus of the story. Why? How do you account for his action in striking and pushing his wife? Analyze the final paragraph in terms of how it helps to explain McLendon.

Further Aspects

This is a powerful and horrifying story of man's inhumanity to man. It is particularly horrifying because Faulkner presents rational motives as lost amidst mob behavior, obsessive psychological needs, and individual insanity. The story, accordingly, offers many possibilities for ripe discussion.

1 The barber seems to resist the mob action, yet at the same time he strikes the Negro, Mayes. Why? Why does Faulkner even introduce the barber? Why do the others turn on him so fiercely?

2 What is really behind the murder of the Negro?

3 Does the mob gain what it wished from the murder?

4 Faulkner suggests that boredom and discomfort can lead to the most hideous of crimes. Do you agree? Are other factors needed? Such as?

5 Is everyone at some time or another pulled along into a mob reaction that runs counter to his own feelings? How do you explain the ease with which people can be manipulated into committing irrational acts?

THE TOUCH

Liam O'Flaherty

A white mare galloped west along the strand against the fierce Spring wind. Her tail was stretched out stiff and motionless. Flecks of foam dropped from her jaws with each outrush of her breath. Her wide-open nostrils were blood red. Hailstones, carried slantwise at a great speed by the wind's power, struck with a loud noise against the canvas of her straddle. Two horsehair ropes trailed low from the holed bottoms of her wicker panniers which flapped with her heaving gait, their halters whining as they shifted round the pegs of the straddle's wooden yoke. The wind tore loose wisps from the layer of straw that cushioned her back against the rough canvas. The wisps were maintained afloat upon the air by the sweeping blast. They sailed away to the east, in a straggling line, frolicking like butterflies at dance.

Cáit Paudeen Pheadair, a girl of eighteen, sat sideways on the mare's haunches, crouching forward over the straddle yoke. She gripped one of the upright pegs with her mittened left hand. A can of hot tea bundled up in a woolen cloth, was held aloft in her right hand. She wore a heavy dress of purple frieze, a sheepskin jacket, rawhide shoes and a head shawl that was knotted under her chin. Her blue eyes were half-closed for protection against the stinging hail. She rode with skill, in complete union with the movement of the mare.

Over at the western end of the strand, the people of the district had been gathering drift weed from the surf since a long time before dawn. Now there were many cocks of the red weed scattered over the gray sand, up from the curving limit of the breaking waves.

Nearly all the men stopped working when they saw the girl come riding towards them on the white mare at a fierce gallop.

"There is a virgin that is fit partner for a king," one man said.

"By the blade of the lance!" said a second man. "If I were single today, it would be on her finger I'd want to put my ring."

"Aye," said the third, "and in her womb my son."

A young man named Bartla Choilm Brighde was working for Cáit's father as a day laborer that Spring. He flushed with anger on hearing these remarks. He was in love with the girl.

"Loose-mouthed devils!" he muttered under his breath, as he came out of the tide with a load of seaweed on his pitchfork.

"May the swine be maimed and gouged! I'd like to choke them all."

He glanced towards the girl furtively as he threw the weed from his pitchfork onto the cock. Then he hurried back into the sea for another load. He was anxious to conceal his emotion from the other men. He was chilled to the marrow of his bones after wading back and forth through the icy water for many hours. His hands and feet were numbed. His thighs were scalded. Yet the intensity of his love for the girl made him feel there was a warm fire burning within him. His blood was coursing madly through his veins.

The girl deftly brought the mare to an abrupt halt near her father's gathered weed. Then she leaped to the sand, still holding aloft her can of hot tea.

"God bless the work," she called out gaily to the people.

"You, too," they answered her.

Her father, Paudeen Pheadair Reamoinn, came over in a state of great anger. He was a stooped little man. His crabbed features were distorted by the cold. He was about sixty. His wife had given him no sons. His daughters, with the exception of Cáit, had all emigrated in search of a livelihood. That was why he was obliged to take a laboring man to help him with the sowing that Spring.

"Are you crazy?" he said, catching the mare by the head.

"Why so?" said Cáit.

"For racing this one west along the strand," he said. "That's the reason."

Cáit laughed. She was much taller than her father, a splendid supple girl with the exuberance of health in her wild countenance.

"I couldn't hold her," she said. "It must have been the Spring she felt in her blood. She wanted no part of quick-walking or trotting. She only wanted to gallop. There is no end to her courage, even though she is only a little one."

"You are sillier than your mother," Paudeen said. "God help me, having to deal with the two of ye."

He loosened the bellyband and put his hand in between the straw and the mare's back.

"Aie!" he said. "She's half drowned in her own sweat."

The mare shuddered when she felt the coldness of his hand touching her heated skin.

"Aie!" Paudeen said again. "A silly girl racing this poor creature that's as fat as a pig after her winter's idleness."

Cáit laughed again as she walked over to a big granite rock.

"Ara! That's fool's talk," she said. "That race will only do her good."

Paudeen put the padded tailpiece outside the mare's tail. Then he moved the straddle from side to side, in order to air her heated back. When she began to shiver violently he returned the tailpiece and half-tightened the bellyband.

"Aie!" he said mournfully. "Woe to him who is without a son to tend horses."

He put a small basketful of hay to the mare's head. He took a handful of straw from the straddle and began to rub her legs.

"Aie!" he repeated. "A man is cursed truly, when he has only a female to guide his horses."

Cáit took shelter under the rock and loosened her sheepskin jacket. Her apron was wound around her waist beneath it. She loosened the apron also and spread the bundle it contained upon the sand. There were large slices of buttered griddle cake, boiled eggs, salt, two spoons and two mugs. When she had everything arranged she unwound a cloth from the can of tea. She opened the can and poured hot tea into the mugs.

"Come on over now," she shouted at the two men. "Drink this warm sup. Don't let it get cold."

Bartla hurried over to the rock. He sat down on his heels, took off his cap and made the sign of the cross on his forehead. Cáit handed him a mug.

"God increase you," he said as he accepted it.

"Same to you," she said.

They looked one another in the eyes. They blushed. Even though the few words they had spoken were those of common courtesy, they got as shy as if they had disclosed the secret of their love. Cáit looked away suddenly. Bartla bent over his food.

Paudeen came over to the rock blowing on his cupped hands.

"Go on over and catch hold of her head," he said to Cáit, "for fear she might take fright. She's as wild as the devil on account of the cold."

He sat down on the sand and put his legs crosswise under him. He blessed himself hurriedly and began to eat. He bolted his food like a person half-dead from hunger.

"Lord God!" Cáit said as she handed him a mug of tea. "Why don't you have patience with your bite?"

"Bad cess to you!" Paudeen said. "Clear off over there."

Cáit went to the mare and began to rub her forehead. Another shower of hailstones was now falling. The mare was trying to pull her halter. She was very excited.

"Easy now, treasure," Cáit whispered to her. "Take it easy, darling. Preoil! My little hag!"

The mare soon lowered her snout to the hay once more, as she grew quiet under the touch of the girl's gentle hand.

"Hurry up there," Paudeen said to Bartla. "Poor people can't take the whole day with their meal. Hurry, I say. We have a lot to do and the day is nearly spent already."

The young man did not speak. Although he had felt faint from hunger for two hours previously, he was unable to eat more than a few morsels. He found difficulty in swallowing even that little. Hunger left him when he saw the holy light of love in Cáit's eyes as they looked at one another.

Every other time she looked at him he had only seen the gay light of mockery in her eyes. Every other time, her lips smiled when she looked at him. This time her lips did not smile. They had frowned in wonder and awe.

That was why his hunger left him. That was why his throat contracted, making it difficult to swallow. So that, instead of eating, he kept looking back furtively over his shoulder in her direction.

The father soon noticed these furtive glances that the young laborer cast in the direction of his daughter. His anger blazed.

"They say a cat is entitled to look at a princess," he said. "That may be, but it is certain that a boorish land-slave has no such right. The worthless land-slave has no right in the world to look at the daughter of an honorable freeman. Do you understand what I'm saying, son of Choilm Brighde?"

The young man's anger blazed. He looked sharply at Paudeen. There was no outward sign of his anger in any part of his countenance except in his eyes, which shone fiercely. He did not speak.

"Watch out for yourself, I say," the old man continued. "You have only a small garden by the door of your cottage, two goats and an ass. You have neither father, nor brother, nor sister. You have only your mother, and she is sick for the past ten years and she is depending on you like a newborn infant for every little service. Nobody belonging to you ever had land or foreshore in this district. They were only rogues and vagrants, stray people that were driven to our place by the famine long ago."

Bartla jumped to his feet. His hands were trembling with rage.

"You have said enough, son of Pheadair Reomoinn," he cried. "There was never a rogue of my kindred. Only honest, God-fearing people belong to my kindred."

"Devil a bit I care," said Paudeen. "Stay clear of my daughter. It's not on a girl that was born in a house of two cows that a man of two goats should cast eyes."

"You have said enough, old man," Bartla repeated.

"Clear off, then," Paudeen said. "If you have eaten, go on over and be loading weed."

Bartla rushed over to the mare. He pushed aside one of the baskets with his shoulder and tightened the bellyband fiercely. Then he began to load seaweed into the two baskets. When they were full to overflowing, he picked up his fork and continued to load the weed onto the top of the straddle.

Cáit's heart now beat wildly as she watched the young man. The fierce movement of his laboring strength made her intoxicated. She had to lean against the mare's shoulder, with dazed eyes and open lips. Even though hailstones were still falling and striking sharply against the side of her face, she was unaware of their bitter touch. She was only aware of the desire that possessed her heart and soul.

Paudeen noticed her prepossession as he came over from the rock. He understood at once. He halted with his back to the shower. He rubbed his chin with his thumb and forefinger.

"There now!" said he to himself. "That young scoundrel has got hold of her. There now!"

He looked at Bartla. Now he hated the young man bitterly. He hated the young back that was as straight as an oar. He hated the fair hair and the shining blue eyes that were able to drive women to folly with desire.

"Damn him," he said with venom. "The beggar! The devil of a beggar! Without a penny-piece in his pocket! The beggar! I'll soon put an end to his shaping. The stinking fellow!"

He went to the mare and caught up his pitchfork. He began to load seaweed. The two men worked fiercely, one on each side of the mare. The weed was soon heaped high above the straddle in a tower. It was time to throw the first rope.

"Look out for the rope," Paudeen said.

"Let me have it," said Bartla.

Paudeen threw the rope across the top of the load.

"Got it?" he said to Bartla.

The wind blew the rope-end out ahead. It fell across Cáit's bosom. She caught it and handed it to Bartla.

"Did you get it?" Paudeen called again.

Bartla made no answer. When he was taking the rope-end from Cáit, his fingers touched the back of her hand. The two of them started as a result of the touch. They became dizzy.

They let go their hold of the rope-end. They seized one another by the hands. They stood breast to breast. They trembled from head to foot. Their faces were ablaze.

They remained standing breast to breast like that, touching, for several moments. Then Paudeen screamed.

"What the devil ails you, scoundrel?" he yelled. "Why don't you speak?"

Bartla started. He dropped Cáit's hands, picked up the rope end and tied it around a tooth that projected from the bottom of the basket. Then he threw across the second rope.

"Here it comes," he cried.

Paudeen caught the second rope and tied it around the tooth. When he had his knee against the side of the basket, tightening the rope, the mare let one of her hind legs go dead. The load became unbalanced. It almost fell on top of the old man.

"Stand!" Bartla yelled, as he kicked the mare in the shin.

She returned her weight to the defaulting leg and the load righted itself at once.

"You're all right now," Bartla said to Paudeen. "You can fasten."

Paudeen secured the rope and then he ran over to Bartla's side, his teeth chattering with rage.

"You devil!" he cried. "Were you trying to kill me?"

"It wasn't my fault," Bartla said. "It was how she let her foot go dead."

"You're a dirty scoundrel. There was a day when I'd. . . ."

"You've said enough," Bartla said.

"Scoundrel!" Paudeen said. "Rogue!"

"Shut up," Bartla said. "Don't say anything you might regret, if I were to lose patience with you."

Paudeen went over to his own side of the mare, boasting as he went.

"There was a day," he cried, "when I'd chastise the best men in the place, if they dared insult me."

"I don't hear you," Bartla said.

The young man and Cáit looked at one another. Now there was terror in their eyes and despair. They both understood there was a chasm which could not be bridged standing between them and their love. Bartla stretched out his hand and touched her lightly on the shoulder. Overcome with emotion, she turned away from him and sobbed. She hid her face in the mare's white mane and her whole body shook as she wept. Bartla took his pitchfork and began to work fiercely once more.

The two men loaded seaweed and threw ropes and tightened until there was as much seaweed above the straddle as the mare could carry. The load was like a wet red tower.

"Be off now," Paudeen said sharply to the young man. "Hurry. We have at least ten loads to bring to the potato garden."

Bartla took the halter from Cáit. Now they did not look at one another. He twisted the halter around his left hand, with which he then took hold of the load. He picked up a sea-rod from the cock.

"Go on!" he cried to the mare, flashing the sea-rod by her head. "Twous!"

The mare went forward slowly, up the strand through the cocks of gathered weed, her feet sinking deep into the soft sand, under the heavy load.

"Go on!" Bartla kept shouting angrily, as he shook the sea-rod at her head.

They mounted the slope onto the sand bank that bound the road, a red tower walking on long white feet and a young man guiding it.

Cáit went over to the rock and knelt beside the remains of the meal. Then she watched Bartla with longing until he went from sight. Darkness fell upon her soul when he disappeared beyond the sand bank, just as if she would never see him again. Indeed, she knew that she had just suffered an eternal loss. When she tried to pick up the gear she discovered that she was unable to lift the lightest object. She had to lower her head on her bosom and give way once more to her tears.

Paudeen also stood looking after the young man until he was out of sight. The old man was talking to himself and there was an evil expression on his countenance.

"There, now!" he was saying. "Nice kettle of fish. A dirty beggar planning to come into my house as son-in-law. I'll soon put an end to his foolish ideas. The beggar!"

He went east along the strand to the place where Marcus Joyce was working.

"Listen," he said to Marcus.

Marcus was a big strong man with a head of red hair. He and Paudeen took shelter under a cock of weed, both of them sitting on their heels. They lighted a pipe.

"You were talking of a match a short while ago," Paudeen said.

"I was," said Marcus. "I was thinking of that second son I have, Red Mike."

"A good man, God bless him," Paudeen said. "I've no fault with him at all, but with the amount of money you intended to give him and he getting a lovely girl as well as two-fourths of land."

" 'Faith two hundred and fifty is no trifle," Marcus said.

"Put another hundred with it," Paudeen said, "and that makings of a bull you have. The yearling."

"Oh! You devil!" Marcus said. "Where would I get that riches?"

"Listen, Marcus," Paudeen said. "Whisper. You have half a score of Roscommon sheep and . . ."

When Cáit had wept a little she was able to gather up her belongings. She tied the bundle under her jacket and then looked round for her father. When she saw him in earnest conversation with Marcus Joyce under the cock of seaweed she took great fright. She made the sign of the cross on her lips.

"God between me and misfortune!" she said earnestly.

She knew well that they spoke of a match between her and Red Mike. She also knew that the match was practically settled, judging by their gestures. The two men were striking one another's palms forcefully and shouldering one another and passing the pipe after every few words. These were indications that the bargain was already concluded, except for the minor details.

"Oh! Lord God!" Cáit said to herself, as she hurried east along the strand towards her home. "The damage is done. He has sold me to Red Mike Joyce, just as if I were a cow or a sheep."

She mounted the sand bank and then went south along the narrow road that led to her village. Another great shower of hailstones came. She took shelter under the fence that bound the road. She sat on the ground with her back to the fence, a finger between her teeth, staring at the ground, with her mind a blank. Then she suddenly thought of Bartla. She started just as if she had been struck. Her eyes opened wide and she stared at the opposite fence.

At first she thought of his hands touching her hands and of his bosom touching her bosom. She thought of the intoxication produced in her being by that touch.

Then the suffering of eternal hell came upon her with the memory of that touch, for it was manifest to her that this first touch of love would be her last.

A wail of despair came to her throat but it went no farther up into her mouth. She only stared in silence at the far fence and at the cold hailstones that lashed against the cold gray stones.

Aie! Aie! Hailstones! Cold hailstones and a young girl staring without tears at her stillborn love.

Setting

Sometimes the setting can be of great significance even when its exact location is indefinite to the foreign reader. In this story, all other elements of the story—plot, narrative, style, characterization, mood—are secondary to the importance of setting. As in Faulkner's "Dry September," the people are creatures of their locale and behave as they are conditioned to behave.

1 From the names of the characters, can you figure out the country involved? What else can you tell about the location? A strand is mentioned—what does that tell you? What else can you add about the setting even if you cannot determine the exact locale?

2 Examine the language and pick out those words which help create the setting. How would you characterize the descriptive words?

3 How does this particular locale condition the people? Can you think of several places where this type of life is still common at the present time? When do you think this story takes place?

4 Why is so much made of the mare?

5 What is a "house of two cows"? What values are involved?

6 From the father's point of view, is Cáit really anything more than a cow or a sheep?

7 How does O'Flaherty create a dramatic situation from the material of the setting?

8 Cáit is eighteen years old, lovely, and romantic, but would life itself defeat her if she allowed her dreams to predominate? Is there any room for dreams?

9 Does the storm of hailstones serve any function, or is it extraneous? Do you see any connection between it and the main subject of the story?

10 What do the religious references mean in terms of the main idea? Are these simply decorative touches, or are they significant?

11 The tone of the author creates sympathy for Cáit and her plight in this bleak region, but at the same time it indicates that her wishes can never come to pass. How does O'Flaherty convince us of both points of view?

12 Why does Cáit stare "without tears at her stillborn love"? Why are the hailstones introduced at this point?

THE UPTURNED FACE

Stephen Crane

"What will we do now?" said the adjutant, troubled and excited.

"Bury him," said Timothy Lean.

The two officers looked down close to their toes where lay the body of their comrade. The face was chalk-blue; gleaming eyes stared at the sky. Over the two upright figures was a windy sound of bullets, and on top of the hill Lean's prostrate company of Spitzbergen infantry was firing measured volleys.

"Don't you think it would be better—" began the adjutant. "We might leave him until to-morrow."

"No," said Lean. "I can't hold that post an hour longer. I've got to fall back, and we've got to bury old Bill."

"Of course," said the adjutant, at once. "Your men got entrenching tools?"

Lean shouted back to his little line, and two men came slowly, one with a pick, one with a shovel. They started in the direction of the Rostina sharpshooters. Bullets cracked near their ears. "Dig here," said Lean gruffly. The men, thus caused to lower their glances to the turf, became hurried and frightened, merely because they could not look to see whence the bullets came. The dull beat of the pick striking the earth sounded amid the swift snap of close bullets. Presently the other private began to shovel.

"I suppose," said the adjutant, slowly, "we'd better search his clothes for—things."

Lean nodded. Together in curious abstraction they looked at the body. Then Lean stirred his shoulders suddenly, arousing himself.

"Yes," he said, "we'd better see what he's got." He dropped to his knees, and his hands approached the body of the dead officer. But his hands wavered over the buttons of the tunic. The first button was brick-red with drying blood, and he did not seem to dare touch it.

"Go on," said the adjutant, hoarsely.

Lean stretched his wooden hand, and his fingers fumbled the bloodstained buttons. At last he rose with ghastly face. He had gathered a watch, a whistle, a pipe, a tobacco-pouch, a handkerchief, a little case of cards and papers. He looked at the adjutant. There was a silence. The adjutant was feeling that he had been a coward to make Lean do all the grisly business.

"Well," said Lean, "that's all, I think. You have his sword and revolver?"

"Yes," said the adjutant, his face working, and then he burst out in a sudden strange fury at the two privates. "Why don't you hurry up with that grave? What are you doing, anyhow? Hurry, do you hear? I never saw such stupid—"

Even as he cried out in his passion the two men were labouring for their lives. Ever overhead the bullets were spitting.

The grave was finished. It was not a masterpiece—a poor little shallow thing. Lean and the adjutant again looked at each other in a curious silent communication.

Suddenly the adjutant croaked out a weird laugh. It was a terrible laugh, which had its origin in that part of the mind which is first moved by the singing of the nerves. "Well," he said humorously to Lean, "I suppose we had best tumble him in."

"Yes," said Lean. The two privates stood waiting, bent over their implements. "I suppose," said Lean, "it would be better if we laid him in ourselves."

"Yes," said the adjutant. Then, apparently remembering that he had made Lean search the body, he stooped with great fortitude and took hold of the dead officer's clothing. Lean joined him. Both were particular that their fingers should not feel the corpse. They tugged away; the corpse lifted, heaved, toppled, flopped into the grave, and the two officers, straightening, looked again at each other—they were always looking at each other. They sighed with relief.

The adjutant said, "I suppose we should—we should say something. Do you know the service, Tim?"

"They don't read the service until the grave is filled in," said Lean, pressing his lips to an academic expression.

"Don't they?" said the adjutant, shocked that he had made the mistake. "Oh, well," he cried, suddenly, "let us—let us say something—while he can hear us."

"All right," said Lean. "Do you know the service?"

"I can't remember a line of it," said the adjutant.

Lean was extremely dubious. "I can repeat two lines, but—"

"Well, do it," said the adjutant. "Go as far as you can. That's better than nothing. And the beasts have got our range exactly."

Lean looked at his two men. "Attention," he barked. The privates came to attention with a click, looking much aggrieved. The adjutant lowered his helmet to his knee. Lean, bareheaded, stood over the grave. The Rostina sharpshooters fired briskly.

"O Father, our friend has sunk in the deep waters of death, but his spirit has leaped toward Thee as the bubble arises from the lips of the drowning. Perceive, we beseech, O Father, the little flying bubble, and—"

Lean, although husky and ashamed, had suffered no hesitation up to this point, but he stopped with a hopeless feeling and looked at the corpse.

The adjutant moved uneasily. "And from Thy superb heights—" he began, and then he too came to an end.

"And from Thy superb heights," said Lean.

The adjutant suddenly remembered a phrase in the back of the Spitzbergen burial service, and he exploited it with the triumphant manner of a man who has recalled everything, and can go on.

"O God, have mercy—"

"O God, have mercy—" said Lean.

"Mercy," repeated the adjutant, in quick failure.

"Mercy," said Lean. And then he was moved by some violence of feeling, for he turned upon his two men and tigerishly said, "Throw the dirt in."

The fire of the Rostina sharpshooters was accurate and continuous.

One of the aggrieved privates came forward with his shovel. He lifted his first shovel-load of earth, and for a moment of inexplicable hesitation it was held poised above this corpse, which from its chalk-blue face looked keenly out from the grave. Then the soldier emptied his shovel on—on the feet.

Timothy Lean felt as if tons had been swiftly lifted from off his forehead. He had felt that perhaps the private might empty the shovel on—on the face. It had been emptied on the feet. There was a great point gained there—ha, ha!—the first shovelful had been emptied on the feet. How satisfactory!

The adjutant began to babble. "Well, of course—a man we've messed with all these years—impossible—you can't, you know, leave your intimate friends rotting on the field. Go on, for God's sake, and shovel, you."

The man with the shovel suddenly ducked, grabbed his left arm with his right hand, and looked at his officer for orders. Lean picked the shovel from the ground. "Go to the rear," he said to the wounded man. He also addressed the other private.

"You get under cover, too; I'll finish this business."

The wounded man scrambled hard still for the top of the ridge without devoting any glances to the direction from whence the bullets came, and the other man followed at an equal pace; but he was different, in that he looked back anxiously three times.

This is merely the way—often—of the hit and unhit.

Timothy Lean filled the shovel, hesitated, and then, in a movement which was like a gesture of abhorrence, he flung the dirt into the grave, and as it landed it made a sound—plop. Lean suddenly stopped and mopped his brow—a tired labourer.

"Perhaps we have been wrong," said the adjutant. His glance wavered stupidly. "It might have been better if we hadn't buried him just at this time. Of course, if we advance tomorrow the body would have been—"

"Damn you," said Lean, "shut your mouth." He was not the senior officer.

He again filled the shovel and flung the earth. Always the earth made the sound—plop. For a space Lean worked frantically, like a man digging himself out of danger.

Soon there was nothing to be seen but the chalk-blue face. Lean filled the shovel. "Good God," he cried to the adjutant. "Why didn't you turn him somehow when you put him in? This—" Then Lean began to stutter.

The adjutant understood. He was pale to the lips. "Go on, man," he cried, beseechingly, almost in a shout.

Lean swung back the shovel. It went forward in a pendulum curve. When the earth landed it made a sound—plop.

Setting

In Crane's story, setting takes on a meaning different from what it is in Faulkner's "Dry September," Kay Boyle's "Effigy of War," or O'Flaherty's "The Touch," although our discussions there are also relevant here. Crane uses setting to provide a situation for a feeling or an idea of how the living respond to the dead. Since war—whether big or little—always seems to be with us, the relationship between the living and the violently dead remains of significance. The setting, then, of "The Upturned Face" is less importantly a battle during the Civil War than it is a situation in which those who might soon be dead must react to someone, like themselves, who recently died.

The setting is established through interspersed dialogue and explanatory passages which set up the next dialogue. In this device, there is a short exchange followed by a description of the corpse. Thus the corpse and the burial squad, two elements, which are so close together in reality, are brought together technically in the narrative scheme. Characterization, plot, narrative, theme or purpose, style—all these are secondary to the burial, in which the living must inter the dead.

1 Why do the two officers hesitate to search Bill's body? They are, after all, used to blood and death. Why is this special?

2 Once Bill's possessions are spread out, what effect does their appearance have on the burial squad?

3 Why should there be a silence? Why does the adjutant suddenly burst out in fury at the two privates?

4 The service that is haltingly said over Bill fills a good part, almost one-fifth, of the story. Why do you think Crane stressed the service? Why are the two officers so unsure about it? Certainly during their war careers, or even before, they must have heard many services. What does their uncertainty indicate about them? about the situation?

5 During the burial itself, why do the two officers tug at the body instead of making the privates do it? Why should the adjutant feel that he must make the first move? What relationship does his behavior have to the "setting" of the story?

6 When the time comes to throw in the dirt, why is the first shovel emptied on the feet? Why does Crane stress the sound "plop" of the dirt falling into the grave? In fact, why does he end the story with the word "plop"?

7 What is there about Bill's face that makes the squad so nervous? Keep in mind that as soon as the burial is completed, they will return to killing other men just like Bill.

Further Aspects

Implied in the setting is Crane's attitude toward war. The Civil War was, for many young men, a romantic chance to don a uniform, handle a gun, and face danger. They idealized their role, and they idealized the war itself. Crane's view of the war is actuality stripped of romanticism. This is, as he presents it, the daily give-and-take of war—watching one's comrades fall, digging their graves, and covering them forever with dirt, thrown by one's own shovel. What other details and hints about Crane's view of war do you find in the story? Gather as many as you can, and see how they help fill out what we here call "setting."

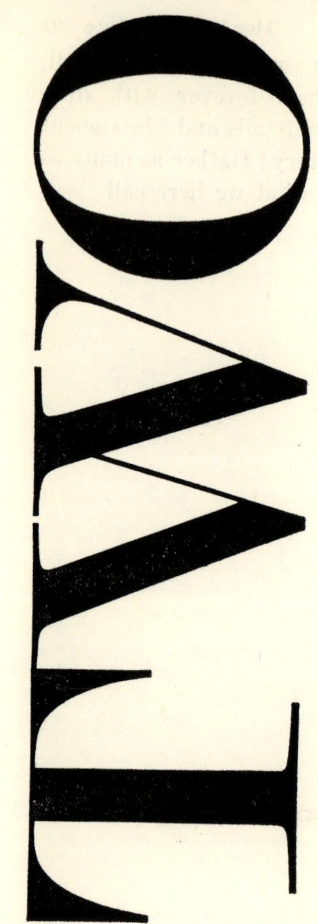
TWO

MOOD AND ATMOSPHERE

In many collections of stories, mood and atmosphere are considered under a single heading with setting, as though all are the same. Obviously they are not—we may well sense mood and atmosphere without being aware of any specific or even general setting. In Florence Randall's "The Watcher," there is a tense atmosphere of impending doom, and yet we have no knowledge of time or place. In Hemingway's "The Capital of the World," the setting is Madrid, but the setting only gains meaning from the atmosphere that Hemingway generated; he defines Madrid, as it were, by its atmosphere, not by specifics of setting.

As the short story has developed in the present century, mood and atmosphere have taken on considerable significance. Atmosphere now does not mean "atmospheric," as in the days when one spoke of a piece as having "atmosphere." The quality now is more elusive, much more closely attached to character and theme, an integrated element in any good short story. To extract the essence of atmosphere, or mood, is really impossible.

Atmosphere and mood are not fixed qualities. They can mean many different things in different stories. In Nabokov's "That in Aleppo Once . . ." the atmosphere is one of disruption, and thus the bizarre language follows the line of breakup and fragmentation. In "The Grave," Katherine Anne Porter foreshadows her theme of the grave by creating an atmosphere filled with deathlike images. Lafcadio Hearn's use of atmosphere is entirely different from any other writer's; he uses mood to give another dimension to life, one akin to a fantasy or nightmare in which real things seem to happen senselessly.

Thus, atmosphere and mood are connected with the meaning of a story possibly even more than setting is. Any division we make of these interconnected elements is like wrenching child from mother. However, when we read a story, we do separate it into pieces—even while claiming that we shouldn't. Atmosphere is possibly closest to the main character—*he* generates it, *he* controls it. Farrington in Joyce's story is the atmospheric center of the narrative line; what he is, so is Dublin. Thus, we read the story.

Always remember that mood and atmosphere help us to understand. Like the other categories which we use to analyze stories, they are tools. They work only momentarily, but in that moment of insight into atmosphere, you might grasp the point.

As you read, keep the following questions in mind:

1 Can you sense or feel an atmosphere that is capable of definition? How much can you put into words? What do you lose in the restatement?

2 Does the atmosphere, or mood, help you to understand the characters? Does it generate ideas about the theme?

3 In what ways does the author create what we call the atmosphere of the story? Through language, images, symbols, motifs? Analyze his language for the quality of his verbs, adverbs, adjectives—their kind and quantity.

4 Is the atmosphere integrated into the story, or is it seemingly a separate element? Does it help or hurt the story, or is it simply a neutral force?

THE WATCHERS

Florence Engel Randall

From the moment Althea awoke that morning, she knew their building had been chosen. She knew it even before she saw the excitement in her husband's eyes as he handed her the official notice that had been put under their door.

"Well," he said, smiling at her while she read it, "what do you think of that?"

"I had a feeling, George," she said, "even before I opened my eyes, I had a feeling that this would happen today."

"We were due to be next," George said. "The setup here is about perfect for it."

"Will you be home early?" She watched him while he sipped his coffee.

"It won't start until late," he said. "It won't start until it gets dark. You know how these things are."

"Just the same," she said, "I couldn't bear it just sitting around and waiting for you. We have so much to do. We have to have dinner first and then change our clothes and find seats. We want to have good seats," she reminded him. "They won't reserve any for us, you know."

"Don't worry about it." He touched her cheek lightly with the back of his hand. "I'll be home in plenty of time."

"Do you have everything? I was never so scared in my life yesterday when I found your gun on the top of the dresser. I just couldn't believe my eyes. I wanted to run after you but I didn't know which route you had taken."

"I always carry a spare," he said. "You know that. I always keep a spare in my coat pocket. Why don't you trust me?"

"I know I'm being foolish," Althea said, kissing him goodbye. "Just be careful, that's all. I don't want you to be so sure of yourself that you'll get careless."

"You be careful," he said. "Do you have to go out today?"

She frowned. "I have to go marketing, and then I thought I'd go downtown and buy a new dress for tonight. All the women will be dressed up and I don't want to go looking like a frump."

"Watch out for the department stores," he reminded her. "They can be dangerous. Don't take any crowded elevators and check the dressing room before you try anything on."

She locked and double-locked the door after him, then fastened the chain before she had her own breakfast. Standing at the window while she drank her coffee, she thought how ridiculous it was the way they went through the same routine each morning as if the very fact that they had to take precautions was making them nervous. When they were first married two years ago, it would never have occurred to either of them that there was any reason for worry.

It must be because we're so much in love, she told herself, stacking the dishes in the washer. Love breeds its own vulnerability, its own fear.

When the signal flashed on the wall, Althea had just finished dressing. She watched it for a moment. It was their code, all right. Three lights in a row, the flickering pause, and then the slow, deliberate hold. She pressed the button that buzzed downstairs.

"Who is it?" she said, her mouth against the intercom.

"It's all right," said a woman's voice, clear and high and a bit too shrill. "I've already shown my identification to your doorman. I'm Sally Milford—Cary Milford's wife. My husband works in your husband's office."

"What do you want?" said Althea cautiously. "I'm much too busy to see anyone this morning. Besides, I'm on my way out." She bit her lip. George would be right if he scolded her for being careless. Why had she told this woman she was going out?

"I'll only take a moment of your time. It's important."

"Can't you tell me what it is over the intercom?"

"If I wanted to talk this way, I could have called you on the phone. I must see you. Please."

"All right," said Althea, reluctantly, knowing she was being foolish, "you can come up."

She checked her own gun even though she knew it was loaded and she palmed the small dagger—the one her mother had given her as a wedding present—the one with the jeweled handle.

"Things are so different now," her mother had said, sighing. She had lifted the dagger from the tissue paper and had studied it for a moment before she handed it to Althea. "In my day we could walk the streets without this sort of thing."

"That's not true," Althea reminded her. "You told me you used to wear stilt-like heels and you always carried a whistle in your purse."

"But that's not the same. It still wasn't like this," said her mother. "Did you know we weren't allowed to carry weapons?"

"You weren't?" said Althea, startled.

"That was before everyone realized that our laws were lagging behind our customs and public opinion. That was before the Citizen's Defense Act was passed."

"There is only one crime," Althea said firmly, "and that is to be a victim. Nothing makes sense otherwise."

"I suppose not." Her mother shook her head. "I guess I'm just being sentimental," she added wistfully. "Sometimes I miss the policemen we used to have. They would wear blue uniforms and they would drive around with sirens blaring and lights flashing. It seems a shame they became obsolete. Why I can even remember the time when we could take a walk in the park."

"In the park?" said Althea, incredulous. "You could actually do that?"

Now Althea bit her lip. There was no point in daydreaming. She stationed herself at the oneway peephole. The woman who now came within her range of vision was thin of face and well-dressed. She blinked her eyes nervously and hesitated before she knocked.

"Just a moment," said Althea. She unfastened the chain and the two locks, and then stepped back so that when the door opened she would be behind it. "Come in," she said.

"Where are you?"

"Right behind you," said Althea, her hand on her gun. "You're not very smart to walk right in like that, are you?"

"But I know who you are," said Sally Milford, her eyes wide with fright. "My husband and your husband are good friends."

"The first thing you have to learn," said Althea, "is not to trust anyone." She kicked the door shut. "Hold up your hands." She found a small acid gun in Sally's purse and a knife in the pocket of her jacket. "Just put them on the table," Althea directed, "and then sit down. Would you like some coffee?"

Sally shook her head, "Look," she said, her mouth trembling, "I wouldn't trouble you like this—I wouldn't have come at all if I didn't, in a way, know you. You see that, don't you?"

"No," said Althea firmly, "I don't see anything. Suppose you tell me what you want."

Sally clasped her hands on the edge of the table. "I have a

brother-in-law who knows someone on the Board of Commissioners," she said, leaning forward in her eagerness, "and we heard that your apartment house has been chosen."

"These things are supposed to be a secret," Althea said sharply. "No one except the people involved is supposed to know. Don't you realize what can happen to you if they find out? And what can happen to me?"

"I'm sorry but I just couldn't help it. When I heard about it—all I could think was that I simply had to go. I have never been to a performance and, the way things look, I'll never have a chance."

"Where do you live?" Althea asked, putting the gun away.

"On the East Side. You know how safe it's getting to be over there. We haven't had an incident in months."

"That doesn't mean they won't choose your building eventually."

"Do you really think they will?"

"Why not?" said Althea.

"Then, in that case, why can't you make believe that we're visiting you or something? They do have special passes for visitors and then, when we're finally chosen, we could reciprocate. Cary and I could invite you and George. That way we could each see two performances."

"It wouldn't work," said Althea. "In the first place, we have the perfect setting for this sort of thing. That's why we picked this particular apartment building. We could have had a much better place to live but both George and I agreed that our best chance was being here. We had to wait two years for this day, and if they ever suspect that this was a put-up thing, you know what would happen to us."

"I suppose I was foolish to even hope." Sally stood up. "I thought it would work out."

"It won't," said Althea, feeling a sudden pity for her. "Believe me, Sally, it won't. I happen to know that Mrs. Tremont, who lives on the third floor, has her sister-in-law staying with her; that, of course, makes it possible for her sister-in-law to go tonight, but if she had just arrived today someone would be sure to report it and Mrs. Tremont would get into trouble."

"You said you were going out," said Sally. "Do you want a ride with me?"

"I'm going downtown," said Althea. "I thought I'd buy a new dress for tonight."

"I haven't been shopping in ages," said Sally. "Cary won't

let me go without him and he's been much too busy on Saturdays. We could shop together and maybe have lunch."

"Just remember one thing," Althea warned as she reached for her coat and hat. "No matter what you say, I won't change my mind. You can spend the whole day with me if you like but I still won't change my mind."

"I know you're right," said Sally as they pressed the button for the elevator. "It's just that I'm glad to have some company on the subway."

"Are you still taking the subway?" Althea stared at her, amazed. "George insists that I take the bus. Not taxis—they're not too reliable anymore but a bus is still fine."

"It takes too long," said Sally. "The subway is much quicker. I have my own system. I never wait on a platform if I'm alone and I usually ride in the first car where the motorman is and, just in case anyone is following me, I change at every other stop."

"Now," said Althea, watching as the elevator stopped at their floor, "run!"

They pounded through the corridor and down one flight of steps. Then they rang for the elevator again. When it arrived, it was empty and they rode it the rest of the way down.

It turned out to be, Althea told George later, a rather pleasant day. With the two of them together, the shopping proved much easier. Sally stood watch while Althea tried on dresses and Althea stood guard while Sally shopped. When they finally parted, it was after four.

Althea took a bus uptown again and got off three blocks before her destination. She glanced behind to make sure she wasn't being followed; then she bought a steak at the meat market. Steak would be the quickest thing to cook for dinner and she didn't want to load her arms with too many packages. It was difficult enough carrying the dress, although she had insisted that the clerk put it in a shopping bag instead of a box. With a shopping bag she would feel less clumsy and have one hand free.

The doorman beamed at her when she entered the lobby.

"This is a great day for us," he said.

Althea nodded. "I bought a new dress," she told him happily, "a black sheath."

"I'll ride the elevator with you if you like," he offered generously. "Most of the tenants are home by now."

"You're not supposed to leave your post," Althea reminded him. "Anyone could come in while you were away. You know what happened to the last doorman we had?"

"You're right," he admitted. "For a moment I forgot."

"By the way," she whispered, "do you know who will be giving the performance?"

He shook his head. "No one knows," he said. "I've been asking but no one knows for sure. I think it's a young one. They usually are."

"You'd think those kids could learn," said Althea, ringing for the elevator. "My parents were pretty strict with me—I can tell you that."

"That's the best way," the doorman said. "You have to be firm with them. I always say that from the time they can walk, they can be taught. Now, you take that kid of Mrs. Hammond. You know the Hammonds on the fifth floor? He got his first slash today and was sent home from school in disgrace."

"Oh, no," said Althea, in horror. "He's only eleven. He's only allowed two more mistakes."

"The way Mrs. Hammond spanked him, he'll learn," the doorman said. "That'll never happen to him again, I can tell you that."

"Who was the other boy?"

"It was a girl," said the doorman. "A pretty little thing, I understand. Well, she'll get her first gold star for that."

"I got a gold star when I was twelve," said Althea, stepping into the elevator.

She rode it to the fourth floor and got out. She took the stairs the rest of the way, then stood before her own front door for a moment, listening. When she was positive it was safe, she inserted her key in the lock.

At precisely six o'clock George came home and, by seven thirty, they had finished dinner and were dressed.

"I'd like to go now," said Althea, impatiently.

"It won't get dark until eight," George said. "You know how it is this time of year. Even then, we'll have to wait a while."

"I can see the stands from here," said Althea, craning her neck as she peered out of the window. "People are beginning to arrive now. Please, darling, let's go."

"You're like a child," he said, hugging her. "Just an anxious little kid."

"I can't help it," she said. "I'm excited. Aren't you thrilled, George?"

"Come on," he said, indulgently. He looked at her, chic and lovely in her new black sheath. "No pockets," he said, shaking his head. "What made you buy a dress without any pockets? I didn't know they made them that way anymore."

"I'll only wear it when I'm with you," she said. "Besides, I have a knife in my purse."

"Just see that you keep it handy." He held the door for her. "I'm glad you used your head this morning."

"For a moment I was tempted," Althea confessed. "Sally seems like a sweet person and it might be fun if we could go there sometimes, but then I realized we'd be taking a chance."

"It doesn't pay to take chances," said George. "Otherwise you can end up giving the performance instead of watching it."

"The doorman told me it was a young one. Probably a girl."

"It usually is," said George.

"Do you know what she did?" Althea asked as they walked through the back of the lobby and out into the courtyard. "No one seems to know what she did."

"Probably something stupid," said George, looking around and waving to their neighbors. "You know, honey, you were right. The stands are filling up."

The stands had been placed next to their building. They were permanent, sturdily built of brick and stone, and erected when the building itself had been new. Optimistically every building had its stands ready for the day when it would be chosen, and Althea looked around proudly as she and George found seats in the second row.

Mr. and Mrs. Hammond were there and seated between them was their son, Timmy. Timmy's right arm was bandaged and he huddled close to his mother.

"I heard about it," said Althea, with sympathy. "I'm sure Timmy will never let it happen again."

"Because she was pretty. Because it was a girl," said Mrs. Hammond bitterly. "She called to him and he ran right over, leaving his knife in his pocket as if a knife ever did anybody any good in a pocket. Just because it was a little girl, he trusted her. But he's learned his lesson, haven't you, Timmy?" she said, slapping him across the face.

"No more," Timmy wept, putting his bandaged arm across his eyes. "Please, Mommy, don't hit me anymore."

He'll never amount to anything, Althea thought, staring at him in dismay. Only three chances and he's used up one already. He's too soft. When I have a child—

She thought about it for a moment, longing for a child but the apartment they were in was too small and they hadn't wanted to move until they had a chance at a performance. Maybe now—maybe now that they were finally spectators—perhaps now that the longed-for, dreamed-about moment had finally arrived, they could move to a larger place and she would have a child.

"You have to train them from the beginning," she whispered to George.

"Sure," he said, knowing what she meant. "It won't happen to us."

"It won't happen to us," she agreed, seeing the way George, even now, even at this moment of pleasure and relaxation, kept his hand in his pocket; George's hand curled over the bulge of his gun.

Althea leaned back. She had known, of course, what the stage setting would be but, just the same, sitting there, part of the expectant, eager audience, she had to admire its reality.

It represented a street scene. It could have been Althea's own street with its middle-class, red-brick buildings, the old-fashioned canopies extending from wide entrances to the edge of the curb. Behind the lighted windows of the buildings, Althea could see the people, all the families together, having dinner, watching television, reading, talking, laughing—all the people of the city settling down for the night.

In the center of the stage was a street lamp, still unlit although it was twilight now; on the far right, there was a fire hydrant. The first floor of the center building was occupied by a shop. The sign said, "ANTIQUES," and Althea could see the lovely things in the window—the paintings in the carved, ornate frames, the delicate crystal goblets, a curved brass bowl. Suddenly the street light went on, dominating the center of the stage with its soft, gentle glow.

The curtain is rising, thought Althea, taking a deep breath. She always loved that moment in the theatre, that magic moment when all the murmuring and the movement and the whispering stopped, the hush and wonder when the curtain rose and the stage lay there before them, the play ready to begin.

Someone somewhere in the back coughed and Althea drew a deep, sighing gasp of impatience.

The stage became alive. From the center building a man emerged, a nondescript man walking his dog at night. The dog tugged and the man whistled softly between his teeth as the two of them walked down the street. The stage became empty again and Althea clasped her hands in her lap, amazed to discover that they were shaking.

At the far right two shadows blurred, moved, took form. Now a girl and a boy strolled down the street. His arm was flung around her shoulders and, from the way she smiled at him, Althea knew they were in love. They moved slowly across the stage. They stopped before the antique shop and the girl pointed to the brass bowl and the boy nodded and gestured expansively, showing her there was nothing in the world he wouldn't get for her. They disappeared on the far left and the stage was empty again.

Althea unclasped her hands and, because her palms were wet, she rubbed them furtively together. Beside her she could hear the sound of George's breathing, slow, heavy, as if each breath were an effort.

Onstage, in the lighted backdrop, in the center building, some of the windows began to darken as if the occupants were retiring for the night.

It's getting late, thought Althea, watching. The lights are dimming all over the city. People are yawning and stretching and getting into bed and even the sounds of the distant traffic seem muted as if someone had muffled all the rolling wheels.

A shadow, part of the shadow of the building, almost part of the square shape of the center building, took on form, and Althea saw that it was a man, a man who had been there all the time, hiding there without her being conscious of his presence.

From the far right she could hear the clicking of high heels on the pavement. Someone else, she thought, will walk down this street this night.

There was a rustle and a stir in the stands.

"Please, Mommy," Timmy whispered. "I don't want to stay here."

"Oh, you'll stay all right," said Mrs. Hammond grimly. "You just open your eyes wide. You watch everything, Timmy Hammond, if you know what's good for you."

"Be quiet down there," someone hissed. "Do you want to spoil everything?"

Althea gripped George's arm.

The footsteps grew louder and a girl came into view, entering downstage from the right. The shadow that was the man moved, and then became very still, waiting.

The girl moved across the stage. She paused under the street light. She touched the lamppost as if the feel of it under her fingers gave her some sort of reassurance. She hesitated, reluctant to leave the light.

Althea could see her clearly now. She was very young. She could be no more than nineteen—perhaps twenty. She wore a red suit and a little red beret with a feather stuck jauntily in it and her handbag was tucked under her arm. Her hair was blond and it tumbled loose over her shoulders.

Althea watched absorbed as the second figure moved again, the man crouching and then straightening as he ran toward the light, toward the girl in the red suit. At the clear view of his black-jacketed, black-clad figure, there was a sudden roar of applause. Althea clapped until her hands ached.

Out of the dark, into the light, he moved. The girl had her back toward him, not seeing him as the watchers saw him—sinuous, beautiful in his grace, tall, broad of shoulder, his hair allowed to grow long in back and his black cap set on the back of his head. The knife in his hand caught the light and sparkled.

He ran and then stopped. Deliberately, he stalked her. Professional that he was, he began to move slowly, coming down light on the balls of his feet.

The girl whirled around and, at the sight of him, she made a little whimpering sound in her throat. Her back now to the audience, she darted to the left and, as if they were part of a rigid dance pattern, the man stepped after her. She turned and ran to the right, her heels clicking frantically but he was there before her.

"Please," said the girl in the red suit. She darted back to the lamppost, back where the light was the brightest, where she could be seen most clearly. She turned and faced the backdrop, faced the buildings, the windows where the people were. Her right hand still clutched her purse, her left was now at her throat.

"Oh, please." Her voice rose to a keening wail of terror and anguish.

"Please," she screamed, her voice begging, her body begging. Then blindly she turned again and ran.

This cry in the night had awakened the sleepers. It had roused the dreamers. The darkened windows in the backdrop were illuminated again. Figures moved; there were silhouettes framed in the windows. The sleepers were awake. The dreamers had stopped dreaming and the city was alert and watching.

"Help me."

The city held its breath and listened.

"Please, help me."

But, Althea saw, she couldn't run far enough. She couldn't run fast enough. The man had her pinned against the wall now, pinned against the lighted, listening backdrop of the building and her handbag fell to the ground.

"I beg you." She was almost hidden by the man's bulk as he bent over her. "Won't someone help me?"

The man in the black jacket raised his arm and the knife flashed. The girl screamed in agony, her cheek now as crimson as her suit. Dodging under his arm, she ran again, the slowing rhythm of her clicking heels the only sound to be heard.

The man watched her for a moment. The quiet, lighted windows watched and the filled stands watched. The man stood very still as if he were resting and then, gracefully, quickly, easily, he caught her again.

That does it, thought Althea, her heart pounding; that does it.

The knife gleamed and Althea held her breath. The arm lifted. The black-draped arm lifted and fell, lifted and fell. The red suit crumpled, falling as if it were empty, the red suit only a splotch now on the pavement. Then the man moved toward the hushed, absorbed watchers.

And there he stood, bowing and smiling, the knife dripping red at his side. Over and over again he took his bow while they all gave him the ultimate, the supreme tribute of their silence.

Mood and Atmosphere

As we shall see in "That in Aleppo Once . . ." by Nabokov, "The Watchers" lacks what we can loosely call plot, normal characterization, even setting. Instead, it appears to project, almost allegorically, a state of mind or a set of conditions suitable for some future era. Mrs. Randall envisages a new kind of society in which people must be ever watchful and careful. By asking a number of questions and attempting specific answers, perhaps we can come close to an understanding of this society and the type of people in it. Nothing, remember, is stated; everything is part of an atmosphere of fear, a nightmarish mood of vigils and precautions.

1 Are these normal people, or figures in an allegory—that is, are they stylized to function as ideas rather than as people?
2 What is the point of having them function normally in their everyday jobs—working, shopping, cooking dinner? How do such activities contribute to the mood and atmosphere?
3 As you reread the story, examine the use of language. Do you notice any figurative devices, such as metaphors or similes? Can you find any images or allusions? What about the diction? Is it flat and hard, or soft, descriptive, flexible? Compare Mrs. Randall's diction with the language of Nabokov's story. What conclusions can you draw? How does her use of language contribute to atmosphere, in effect, create a particular atmosphere? Could her story have been as ornate and exotic (in language) as Nabokov's?
4 Now we can move into more specific areas. Why are Althea and George so pleased that their building has been chosen for the evening's performance? What does it really mean that "their building had been chosen"? What prestige is attached to "being chosen"?
5 Why do Althea and George carry guns?
6 Why are they constantly taking precautions—with the door, the elevator, the various codes and signals, the bus, the trip back from the store?
7 What does Althea mean by "There is only one crime . . . and that is to be a victim"?
8 Why is there so much excitement over the "performance" that evening? Why is Sally anxious to attend? Does Mrs. Randall's use of calculated suspense add to the excitement? How does she create suspense?
9 What is involved in the slash that the Hammond child received at school? Why are the Hammonds so upset, when the slash itself seems minor? What does Althea mean when she says

that "He's only allowed two more mistakes"? And then the doorman says that the slasher will "get her first gold star for that." What does he mean? Why does Mrs. Hammond repeatedly strike Timmy and then later make him watch the performance?

10 The performance itself becomes the climax of the story, just as it climaxes the events of the day for the chief characters. Try to retell exactly what happens from the moment you see the stage setting of a street scene. What does the setting represent? Who are the first people on the stage? For what purpose? Why is the key man at first hidden, then made barely visible? Who is he? Who is the girl who appears on the stage? Why does she hesitate at the light? Does she seem to suspect her fate? Why does the man stalk the girl, in full sight of the watchful audience? Why doesn't anyone help her? How can you explain the murderer's bow at the end of the performance? Is there any question that he actually killed the girl? What was his motive?

11 Why does the audience react with silence, its "supreme tribute"? Why not applause or gasps of horror?

Tone

1 What evidence is there that the tone of the story is satiric? Or is it straightforward and to be taken literally?

2 If the tone is satiric, what is Mrs. Randall satirizing?

3 How is her tone demonstrated in her descriptions of Althea and George and their daily environment?

4 Does she indicate how we are to accept her characters?

Further Aspects

1 In a story reminiscent of this one, "The Lottery" by Shirley Jackson, the townspeople every year reenact a ritual in which they stone to death one of their number chosen by lottery. Mrs. Randall's story starts from this point, but her victims are not chosen by lottery. How are they chosen? Who is the victim for the evening performance? How does this differ from a lottery? Does Mrs. Randall's system make more sense?

2 What kind of society is Mrs. Randall projecting? Is it something recognizable, or does it appear to be the setting for a fantasy, like an H. G. Wells's world of the future?

3 Do you think that we, in America, are becoming like the people in "The Watchers"? From where, then, does Mrs. Randall obtain her types? Is her society totalitarian or free?

4 What forces are operating to create such a society? Do you believe that such forces can make us like Althea and George? What is Mrs. Randall really attacking with her satire? Are we immune to it?

"THAT IN ALEPPO ONCE . . ."

Vladimir Nabokov

Dear V.—Among other things, this is to tell you that at last I am here, in the country whither so many sunsets have led. One of the first persons I saw was our good old Gleb Alexandrovich Gekko gloomily crossing Columbus Avenue in quest of the *petit café du coin* which none of us three will ever visit again. He seemed to think that somehow or other you were betraying our national literature, and he gave me your address with a deprecatory shake of his gray head, as if you did not deserve the treat of hearing from me.

I have a story for you. Which reminds me—I mean putting it like this reminds me—of the days when we wrote our first udder-warm bubbling verse, and all things, a rose, a puddle, a lighted window, cried out to us: "I'm a rhyme!" Yes, this is a most useful universe. We play, we die, *ig-rhyme, umi-rhyme*. And the sonorous souls of Russian verbs lend a meaning to the wild gesticulation of trees or to some discarded newspaper sliding and pausing, and shuffling again, with abortive flaps and apterous jerks along an endless wind-swept embankment. But just now I am not a poet. I come to you like that gushing lady in Chekhov who was dying to be described.

I married, let me see, about a month after you left France and a few weeks before the gentle Germans roared into Paris. Although I can produce documentary proofs of matrimony, I am positive now that my wife never existed. You may know her name from some other source, but that does not matter: it is the name of an illusion. Therefore, I am able to speak of her with as much detachment as I would of a character in a story (one of your stories, to be precise).

It was love at first touch rather than at first sight, for I had met her several times before without experiencing any special emotions; but one night, as I was seeing her home, something quaint she had said made me stoop with a laugh and lightly kiss her on the hair—and of course we all know of that blinding blast which is caused by merely picking up a small doll from the floor of a carefully abandoned house: the soldier involved hears nothing; for him it is but an ecstatic soundless and boundless expansion of what had been during his life a pin point of light in the dark center of his being. And really, the reason we think of death in celestial terms is that the visible firmament, especially at night (above our blacked-out Paris with the gaunt arches of its Boulevard Exelmans and the ceaseless Alpine gurgle of desolate latrines), is the most adequate and ever-present symbol of that vast silent explosion.

But I cannot discern her. She remains as nebulous as my best poem—the one you made such gruesome fun of in the *Literaturnïe Zapiski.* When I want to imagine her, I have to cling mentally to a tiny brown birthmark on her downy forearm, as one concentrates upon a punctuation mark in an illegible sentence. Perhaps, had she used a greater amount of make-up or used it more constantly, I might have visualized her face today, or at least the delicate transverse furrows of dry, hot rouged lips; but I fail, I fail—although I still feel their elusive touch now and then in the blindman's buff of my senses, in that sobbing sort of dream when she and I clumsily clutch at each other through a heartbreaking mist and I cannot see the color of her eyes for the blank luster of brimming tears drowning their irises.

She was much younger than I—not as much younger as was Nathalie of the lovely bare shoulders and long earrings in relation to swarthy Pushkin; but still there was a sufficient margin for that kind of retrospective romanticism which finds pleasure in imitating the destiny of a unique genius (down to the jealousy, down to the filth, down to the stab of seeing her almond-shaped eyes turn to her blond Cassio behind her peacock-feathered fan) even if one cannot imitate his verse. She liked mine though, and would scarcely have yawned as the other was wont to do every time her husband's poem happened to exceed the length of a sonnet. If she has remained a phantom to me, I may have been one to her: I suppose she had been solely attracted by the obscurity of my poetry; then tore a hole through its veil and saw a stranger's unlovable face.

As you know, I had been for some time planning to follow the example of your fortunate flight. She described to me an uncle of hers who lived, she said, in New York: he had taught riding at a Southern college and had wound up by marrying a wealthy American woman; they had a little daughter born deaf. She said she had lost their address long ago, but a few days later it miraculously turned up, and we wrote a dramatic letter to which we never received any reply. This did not much matter, as I had already obtained a sound affidavit from Professor Lomchenko of Chicago; but little else had been done in the way of getting the necessary papers, when the invasion began, whereas I foresaw that if we stayed on in Paris some helpful compatriot of mine would sooner or later point out to the interested party sundry passages in one of my books where I argued that, with all her many black sins, Germany was still bound to remain forever and ever the laughing stock of the world.

So we started upon our disastrous honeymoon. Crushed and jolted amid the apocalyptic exodus, waiting for unscheduled trains that were bound for unknown destinations, walking through the stale stage setting of abstract towns, living in a permanent twilight of physical exhaustion, we fled; and the farther we fled, the clearer it became that what was driving us on was something more than a booted and buckled fool with his assortment of variously propelled junk—something of which he was a mere symbol, something monstrous and impalpable, a timeless and faceless mass of immemorial horror that still keeps coming at me from behind even here, in the green vacuum of Central Park.

Oh, she bore it gamely enough—with a kind of dazed cheerfulness. Once, however, quite suddenly she started to sob in a sympathetic railway carriage. "The dog," she said, "the dog we left. I cannot forget the poor dog." The honesty of her grief shocked me, as we had never had any dog. "I know," she said, "But I tried to imagine we had actually bought that setter. And just think, he would be now whining behind a locked door." There had never been any talk of buying a setter.

I should also not like to forget a certain stretch of highroad and the sight of a family of refugees (two women, a child) whose old father, or grandfather, had died on the way. The sky was a chaos of black and flesh-colored clouds with an ugly sunburst beyond a hooded hill, and the dead man was lying on his back under a dusty plane tree. With a stick and their hands the women had tried to dig a roadside grave, but the soil was too hard; they had given it up and were sitting side by side, among the anemic poppies, a little apart from the corpse and its upturned beard. But the little boy was still scratching and scraping and tugging until he tumbled a flat stone and forgot the object of his solemn exertions as he crouched on his haunches, his thin, eloquent neck showing all its vertebrae to the headsman, and watched with surprise and delight thousands of minute brown ants seething, zigzagging, dispersing, heading for places of safety in the Gard, and the Aude, and the Drome, and the Var, and the Basses-Pyrénées—we two paused only in Pau.

Spain proved too difficult and we decided to move on to Nice. At a place called Faugères (a ten-minute stop) I squeezed out of the train to buy some food. When a couple of minutes later I came back, the train was gone, and the muddled old man responsible for the atrocious void that faced me (coal dust glittering in the heat between naked indifferent rails, and a lone piece of orange peel) brutally told me that, anyway, I had had no right to get out.

In a better world I could have had my wife located and told what to do (I had both tickets and most of the money); as it was, my nightmare struggle with the telephone proved futile, so I dismissed the whole series of diminutive voices barking at me from afar, sent two or three telegrams which are probably on their way only now, and late in the evening took the next local to Montpellier, farther than which her train would not stumble. Not finding her there, I had to choose between two alternatives: going on because she might have boarded the Marseilles train which I had just missed, or going back because she might have returned to Faugères. I forgot now what tangle of reasoning led me to Marseilles and Nice.

Beyond such routine action as forwarding false data to a few unlikely places, the police did nothing to help: one man bellowed at me for being a nuisance; another sidetracked the question by doubting the authenticity of my marriage certificate because it was stamped on what he contended to be the wrong side; a third, a fat *commissaire* with liquid brown eyes confessed that he wrote poetry in his spare time. I looked up various acquaintances among the numerous Russians domiciled or stranded in Nice. I heard those among them who chanced to have Jewish blood talk of their doomed kinsmen crammed into hell-bound trains; and my own plight, by contrast, acquired a commonplace air of irreality while I sat in some crowded café with the milky blue sea in front of me and a shell-hollow murmur behind telling and retelling the tale of massacre and misery, and the gray paradise beyond the ocean, and the ways and whims of harsh consuls.

A week after my arrival an indolent plain-clothes man called upon me and took me down a crooked and smelly street to a black-stained house with the word "hotel" almost erased by dirt and time; there, he said, my wife had been found. The girl he produced was an absolute stranger, of course; but my friend Holmes kept on trying for some time to make her and me confess we were married, while her taciturn and muscular bedfellow stood by and listened, his bare arms crossed on his striped chest.

When at length I got rid of those people and had wandered back to my neighborhood, I happened to pass by a compact queue waiting at the entrance of a food store; and there, at the very end, was my wife, straining on tiptoe to catch a glimpse of what exactly was being sold. I think the first thing she said to me was that she hoped it was oranges.

Her tale seemed a trifle hazy, but perfectly banal. She had returned to Faugères and gone straight to the Commissariat instead of making inquiries at the station, where I had left a message for her. A party of refugees suggested that she join them; she spent the night in a bicycle shop with no bicycles, on the floor, together with three elderly women who lay, she said, like three logs in a row. Next day she realized that she had not enough money to reach Nice. Eventually she borrowed some from one of the log-women. She got into the wrong train, however, and traveled to a town the name of which she could not remember. She had arrived at Nice two days ago and had found some friends at the Russian church. They had told her I was somewhere around, looking for her, and would surely turn up soon.

Some time later, as I sat on the edge of the only chair in my garret and held her by her slender young hips (she was combing her soft hair and tossing her head back with every stroke), her dim smile changed all at once into an odd quiver and she placed one hand on my shoulder, staring down at me as if I were a reflection in a pool, which she had noticed for the first time.

"I've been lying to you, dear," she said. "*Ya lgunia.* I stayed for several nights in Montpellier with a brute of a man I met on the train. I did not want it at all. He sold hair lotions."

The time, the place, the torture. Her fan, her gloves, her mask. I spent that night and many others getting it out of her bit by bit, but not getting it all. I was under the strange delusion that first I must find out every detail, reconstruct every minute, and only then decide whether I could bear it. But the limit of desired knowledge was unattainable, nor could I ever foretell the approximate point after which I might imagine myself satiated, because of course the denominator of every fraction of knowledge was potentially as infinite as the number of intervals between the fractions themselves.

Oh, the first time she had been too tired to mind, and the next had not minded because she was sure I had deserted her; and she apparently considered that such explanations ought to be a kind of consolation prize for me instead of the nonsense and agony they really were. It went on like that for eons, she breaking down every now and then, but soon rallying again, answering my unprintable questions in a breathless whisper or trying with a pitiful smile to wriggle into the semisecurity of irrelevant commentaries, and I crushing and crushing the mad molar till my jaw almost burst with pain, a flaming pain which seemed somehow preferable to the dull, humming ache of humble endurance.

And mark, in between the periods of this inquest, we were trying to get from reluctant authorities certain papers which in their turn would make it lawful to apply for a third kind which would serve as a steppingstone towards a permit enabling the holder to apply for yet other papers which might or might not give him the means of discovering how and why it had happened. For even if I could imagine the accursed recurrent scene, I failed to link up its sharp-angled grotesque shadows with the dim limbs of my wife as she shook and rattled and dissolved in my violent grasp.

So nothing remained but to torture each other, to wait for hours on end in the Prefecture, filling forms, conferring with friends who had already probed the innermost viscera of all visas, pleading with secretaries, and filling forms again, with the result that her lusty and versatile traveling salesman became blended in a ghastly mix-up with rat-whiskered snarling officials, rotting bundles of obsolete records, the reek of violet ink, bribes slipped under gangrenous blotting paper, fat flies tickling moist necks with their rapid cold padded feet, new-laid clumsy concave photographs of your six subhuman doubles, the tragic eyes and patient politeness of petitioners born in Slutzk, Starodub, or Bobruisk, the funnels and pulleys of the Holy Inquisition, the awful smile of the bald man with the glasses, who had been told that his passport could not be found.

I confess that one evening, after a particularly abominable day, I sank down on a stone bench weeping and cursing a mock world where millions of lives were being juggled by the clammy hands of consuls and *commissaires.* I noticed she was crying too, and then I told her that nothing would really have mattered the way it mattered now, had she not gone and done what she did.

"You will think me crazy," she said with a vehemence that, for a second, almost made a real person of her, "but I didn't—I swear that I didn't. Perhaps I live several lives at once. Perhaps I wanted to test you. Perhaps this bench is a dream and we are in Saratov or on some star."

It would be tedious to niggle the different stages through which I passed before accepting finally the first version of her delay. I did not talk to her and was a good deal alone. She would glimmer and fade, and reappear with some trifle she thought I would appreciate—a handful of cherries, three precious cigarettes or the like—treating me with the unruffled mute sweetness of a nurse that trips from and to a gruff convalescent. I ceased visiting most of our mutual friends because they had lost all interest in my passport affairs and seemed to have turned vaguely inimical. I composed several poems. I drank all the wine I could get. I clasped her one day to my groaning breast, and we went for a week to Caboule and lay on the round pink pebbles of the narrow beach. Strange to say, the happier our new relations seemed, the stronger I felt an undercurrent of poignant sadness, but I kept telling myself that this was an intrinsic feature of all true bliss.

In the meantime, something had shifted in the moving pattern of our fates and at last I emerged from a dark and hot office with a couple of plump *visas de sortie* cupped in my trembling hands. Into these the U.S.A. serum was duly injected, and I dashed to Marseilles and managed to get tickets for the very next boat. I returned and tramped up the stairs. I saw a rose in a glass on the table—the sugar pink of its obvious beauty, the parasitic air bubbles clinging to its stem. Her two spare dresses were gone, her comb was gone, her checkered coat was gone, and so was the mauve hairband with a mauve bow that had been her hat. There was no note pinned to the pillow, nothing at all in the room to enlighten me, for of course the rose was merely what French rhymsters call *une cheville.*

I went to the Veretennikovs, who could tell me nothing; to the Hellmans, who refused to say anything; and to the Elagins, who were not sure whether to tell me or not. Finally the old lady—and you know what Anna Vladimirovna is like at crucial moments—asked for her rubber-tipped cane, heavily but energetically dislodged her bulk from her favorite armchair, and took me into the garden. There she informed me that, being twice my age, she had the right to say I was a bully and a cad.

You must imagine the scene: the tiny graveled garden with its blue Arabian Nights jar and solitary cypress; the cracked terrace where the old lady's father had dozed with a rug on his knees when he retired from his Novgorod governorship to spend a few last evenings in Nice; the pale-green sky; a whiff of vanilla in the deepening dusk; the crickets emitting their metallic trill pitched at two octaves above middle C; and Anna Vladimirovna, the folds of her cheeks jerkily dangling as she flung at me a motherly but quite undeserved insult.

During several preceding weeks, my dear V., every time she had visited by herself the three or four families we both knew, my ghostly wife had filled the eager ears of all those kind people with an extraordinary story. To wit: that she had madly fallen in love with a young Frenchman who could give her a turreted home and a crested name; that she had implored me for a divorce and I had refused; that in fact I had said I would rather shoot her and myself than sail to New York alone; that she had said her father in a similar case had acted like a gentleman; that I had answered I did not give a hoot for her *cocu de père.*

There were loads of other preposterous details of the kind—but they all hung together in such a remarkable fashion that no wonder the old lady made me swear I would not seek to pursue the lovers with a cocked pistol. They had gone, she said, to a château in Lozère. I inquired whether she had ever set eyes upon the man. No, but she had been shown his picture. As I was about to leave, Anna Vladimirovna, who had slightly relaxed and had even given me her five fingers to kiss, suddenly flared up again, struck the gravel with her cane, and said in her deep strong voice: "But one thing I shall never forgive you—her dog, that poor beast which you hanged with your own hands before leaving Paris."

Whether the gentleman of leisure had changed into a traveling salesman, or whether the metamorphosis had been reversed, or whether again he was neither the one nor the other, but the nondescript Russian who had courted her before our marriage—all this was absolutely inessential. She had gone. That was the end. I should have been a fool had I begun the nightmare business of searching and waiting for her all over again.

On the fourth morning of a long and dismal sea voyage, I met on the deck a solemn but pleasant old doctor with whom I had played chess in Paris. He asked me whether my wife was very much incommoded by the rough seas. I answered that I had sailed alone; whereupon he looked taken aback and then said he had seen her a couple of days before going on board, namely in Marseilles, walking, rather aimlessly he thought, along the embankment. She said that I would presently join her with bag and tickets.

This is I gather, the point of the whole story—although if you write it, you had better not make him a doctor, as that kind of thing has been overdone. It was at that moment that I suddenly knew for certain that she had never existed at all. I shall tell you another thing. When I arrived I hastened to satisfy a certain morbid curiosity: I went to the address she had given me once; it proved to be an anonymous gap between two office buildings; I looked for her uncle's name in the directory; it was not there; I made some inquiries, and Gekko, who knows everything, informed me that the man and his horsey wife existed all right, but had moved to San Francisco after their deaf little girl had died.

Viewing the past graphically, I see our mangled romance engulfed in a deep valley of mist between the crags of two matter-of-fact mountains: life had been real before, life will be real from now on, I hope. Not tomorrow, though. Perhaps after tomorrow. You, happy mortal, with your lovely family (how is Ines? how are the twins?) and your diversified work (how are the lichens?), can hardly be expected to puzzle out my misfortune in terms of human communion, but you may clarify things for me through the prism of your art.

Yet the pity of it. Curse your art, I am hideously unhappy. She keeps on walking to and fro where the brown nets are spread to dry on the hot stone slabs and the dappled light of the water plays on the side of a moored fishing boat. Somewhere, somehow, I have made some fatal mistake. There are tiny pale bits of broken fish scales glistening here and there in the brown meshes. It may all end in *Aleppo* if I am not careful. Spare me, V.: you would load your dice with an unbearable implication if you took that for a title.

Mood and Atmosphere

This story is lacking almost completely in anything we can call a plot. In fact, the form is that of a letter, which further removes it from the area of plot. It also lacks credible characterization, and possibly a theme. It does not even have the definiteness of setting of Joyce's story or Thomas's wild tale. Rather it is a series of blending and melting images, of exotic language overlapping with dreamlike sequences, of unreal people occasionally doing real things. The general atmosphere is one of mad fantasy, but it is a madness pursued by the author toward some general purpose.

1 Since the atmosphere is one of a state of lunacy and disruption, you should be able to find numerous words, phrases, entire scenes which reflect this kind of world. Start with words—

Nabokov is a master of the odd and eccentric word, which he uses for its obscurity as well as its wittiness. Then move into phrases and scenes.

2 Explain phrases like "'I'm a rhyme!'", "apterous jerks," ". . . we all know of that blinding blast which is caused by merely picking up a small doll from the floor of a carefully abandoned house," "Alpine gurgle of desolate latrines," the reference to Pushkin and Nathalie, the narrator's attitude toward Germany, "the semisecurity of irrelevant commentaries," ". . . the denominator of every fraction of knowledge was potentially as infinite as the number of intervals between the fractions themselves," "the innermost viscera of all visas," "the funnels and pulleys of the Holy Inquisition," "Spare me, V.: you would load the dice with an unbearable implication if you took that for a title."

The more phrases and sentences you can explain, the deeper you will enter into the spirit of the story. Most of these phrases and sentences are witty, marked by an obscure learning which is reflected in the obscure wording. The sum total of such language is the mood and atmosphere of the story.

Characterization

1 Even though character is not stressed, the narrator comes through somewhat strongly. What can you say about him? Remember that Nabokov gives us nothing from his own point of view; we only know what the narrator himself reveals.

2 Similarly, what do we know of the narrator's wife? Can you characterize her from the clues the narrator provides? Is there any purpose in not giving her a name? Why does she seem so mysterious? Is there any question of her real existence, or does the narrator simply play with the idea that she is an illusion for the sake of fun?

3 Can you explain why character becomes so murky and submerged in this kind of story?

4 Is the fantasy so strong that these characters seem to derive from a fairy tale? What kind of fairy tale?

5 Does the fact that the title is a quotation from the Moor's final speech in "Othello" give any significance to the story?

Style

What can you say about Nabokov's style? Relate him to the other stylists in this collection: James, Thomas, Purdy, Mansfield, and Powers. To whom does he appear closest? In what ways can you classify him as a stylist, that is, as a writer who is forging a unique form of expression? Is such a unique quality true of all the stylists in this book? Of all writers?

Further Aspects

1 Does Nabokov appear to be driving toward any larger point, or is he satisfied with a witty fantasy set during World War II?

2 Can you see any pattern or patterns in his fantasy by which a consistent point of view emerges?

3 Does the fantasy take on allegorical significance? Do you sense that the surface is just a facade for Nabokov's real purpose? If you do, what then is his real purpose?

4 Is the story, finally, about World War II? Or is it about human beings at any time?

5 Where is Aleppo and why does Nabokov use that particular name place in his title?

THE GIRLS IN THEIR SUMMER DRESSES

Irwin Shaw

Fifth Avenue was shining in the sun when they left the Brevoort. The sun was warm, even though it was February, and everything looked like Sunday morning—the buses and the well-dressed people walking slowly in couples and the quiet buildings with the windows closed.

Michael held Frances' arm tightly as they walked toward Washington Square in the sunlight. They walked lightly, almost smiling, because they had slept late and had a good breakfast and it was Sunday. Michael unbuttoned his coat and let it flap around him in the mild wind.

"Look out," Frances said as they crossed Eighth Street. "You'll break your neck." Michael laughed and Frances laughed with him.

"She's not so pretty," Frances said. "Anyway, not pretty enough to take a chance of breaking your neck."

Michael laughed again. "How did you know I was looking at her?"

Frances cocked her head to one side and smiled at her husband under the brim of her hat. "Mike, darling," she said.

"O.K.," he said. "Excuse me."

Frances patted his arm lightly and pulled him along a little faster toward Washington Square. "Let's not see anybody all day," she said. "Let's just hang around with each other. You and me. We're always up to our neck in people, drinking their Scotch or drinking our Scotch; we only see each other in bed. I want to go out with my husband all day long. I want him to talk only to me and listen only to me."

"What's to stop us?" Michael asked.

"The Stevensons. They want us to drop by around one o'clock and they'll drive us into the country."

"The cunning Stevensons," Mike said. "Transparent. They can whistle. They can go driving in the country by themselves."

"Is it a date?"

"It's a date."

Frances leaned over and kissed him on the tip of the ear. "Darling," Michael said, "this is Fifth Avenue."

"Let me arrange a program," Frances said. "A planned Sunday in New York for a young couple with money to throw away."

"Go easy."

"First let's go to the Metropolitan Museum of Art," Frances suggested, because Michael had said during the week he wanted to go. "I haven't been there in three years and there're at least ten pictures I want to see again. Then we can take the bus down to Radio City and watch them skate. And later we'll go down to Cavanagh's and get a steak as big as a blacksmith's apron, with a bottle of wine, and after that there's a French picture at the Filmarte that everybody says—say, are you listening to me?"

"Sure," he said. He took his eyes off the hatless girl with the dark hair, cut dancer-style like a helmet, who was walking past him.

"That's the program for the day," Frances said flatly. "Or maybe you'd just rather walk up and down Fifth Avenue."

"No," Michael said. "Not at all."

"You always look at other women," Frances said. "Everywhere. Every damned place we go."

"No, darling," Michael said, "I look at everything. God gave me eyes and I look at women and men in subway excavations and moving pictures and the little flowers of the field. I casually inspect the universe."

"You ought to see the look in your eye," Frances said, "as you casually inspect the universe on Fifth Avenue."

"I'm a happily married man." Michael pressed her elbow tenderly. "Example for the whole twentieth century—Mr. and Mrs. Mike Loomis. Hey, let's have a drink," he said, stopping.

"We just had breakfast."

"Now listen, darling," Mike said, choosing his words with care, "it's a nice day and we both feel good and there's no reason why we have to break it up. Let's have a nice Sunday."

"All right. I don't know why I started this. Let's drop it. Let's have a good time."

They joined hands consciously and walked without talking among the baby carriages and the old Italian men in their Sunday clothes and the young women with Scotties in Washington Square Park.

"At least once a year everyone should go to the Metropolitan Museum of Art," Frances said after a while, her tone a good imitation of the tone she had used at breakfast and at the beginning of their walk. "And it's nice on Sunday. There're a lot of people looking at the pictures and you get the feeling maybe Art isn't on the decline in New York City, after all—"

"I want to tell you something," Michael said very seriously. "I have not touched another woman. Not once. In all the five years."

"All right," Frances said.

"You believe that, don't you?"

"All right."

They walked between the crowded benches, under the scrubby city-park trees.

"I try not to notice it," Frances said, "but I feel rotten inside, in my stomach, when we pass a woman and you look at her and I see that look in your eye and that's the way you looked at me the first time. In Alice Maxwell's house. Standing there in the living room, next to the radio, with a green hat on and all those people."

"I remember the hat," Michael said.

"The same look," Frances said. "And it makes me feel bad. It makes me feel terrible."

"Sh-h-h, please, darling, sh-h-h."

"I think I would like a drink now," Frances said.

They walked over to a bar on Eighth Street, not saying anything, Michael automatically helping her over curbstones and guiding her past automobiles. They sat near a window in the bar and the sun streamed in and there was a small, cheerful fire in the fireplace. A little Japanese waiter came over and put down some pretzels and smiled happily at them.

"What do you order after breakfast?" Michael asked.

"Brandy, I suppose," Frances said.

"Courvoisier," Michael told the waiter. "Two Courvoisiers."

The waiter came with the glasses and they sat drinking the brandy in the sunlight. Michael finished half his and drank a little water.

"I look at women," he said. "Correct. I don't say it's wrong or right. I look at them. If I pass them on the street and I don't look at them, I'm fooling you, I'm fooling myself."

"You look at them as though you want them," Frances said, playing with her brandy glass. "Every one of them."

"In a way," Michael said, speaking softly and not to his wife, "in a way that's true. I don't do anything about it, but it's true."

"I know it. That's why I feel bad."

"Another brandy," Michael called. "Waiter, two more brandies."

He sighed and closed his eyes and rubbed them gently with his fingertips. "I love the way women look. One of the things I like best about New York is the battalions of women. When I first came to New York from Ohio that was the first thing I noticed, the million wonderful women, all over the city. I walked around with my heart in my throat."

"A kid," Frances said. "That's a kid's feeling."

"Guess again," Michael said. "Guess again. I'm older now. I'm a man getting near middle age, putting on a little fat, and I still love to walk along Fifth Avenue at three o'clock on the east side of the street between Fiftieth and Fifty-seventh Streets. They're all out then, shopping, in their furs and their crazy hats, everything all concentrated from all over the world into seven blocks—the best furs, the best clothes, the handsomest women, out to spend money and feeling good about it."

The Japanese waiter put the two drinks down, smiling with great happiness.

"Everything is all right?" he asked.

"Everything is wonderful," Michael said.

"If it's just a couple of fur coats," Frances said, "and forty-five dollar hats—"

"It's not the fur coats. Or the hats. That's just the scenery for that particular kind of woman. Understand," he said, "you don't have to listen to this."

"I want to listen."

"I like the girls in the offices. Neat, with their eyeglasses, smart, chipper, knowing what everything is about. I like the girls on Forty-fourth Street at lunchtime, the actresses, all dressed up on nothing a week. I like the salesgirls in the stores, paying attention to you first because you're a man, leaving lady customers waiting. I got all this stuff accumulated in me because I've been thinking about it for ten years and now you've asked for it and here it is."

"Go ahead," Frances said.

"When I think of New York City, I think of all the girls on parade in the city. I don't know whether it's something special with me or whether every man in the city walks around with the same feeling inside him, but I feel as though I'm at a picnic in this city. I like to sit near the women in the theatres, the famous beauties who've taken six hours to get ready and look it. And the young girls at the football games, with the red cheeks, and when the warm weather comes, the girls in their summer dresses.'' He finished his drink. ''That's the story.''

Frances finished her drink and swallowed two or three times extra. ''You say you love me?''

''I love you.''

''I'm pretty, too,'' Frances said. ''As pretty as any of them.''

''You're beautiful,'' Michael said.

''I'm good for you,'' Frances said, pleading. ''I've made a good wife, a good housekeeper, a good friend. I'd do any damn thing for you.''

''I know,'' Michael said. He put his hand out and grasped hers.

''You'd like to be free to—'' Frances said.

''Sh-h-h.''

''Tell the truth.'' She took her hand away from under his.

Michael flicked the edge of his glass with his finger. ''O.K.,'' he said gently. ''Sometimes I feel I would like to be free.''

''Well,'' Frances said, ''any time you say.''

''Don't be foolish.'' Michael swung his chair around to her side of the table and patted her thigh.

She began to cry silently into her handkerchief, bent over just enough so that nobody else in the bar would notice. ''Someday,'' she said, crying, ''you're going to make a move.''

Michael didn't say anything. He sat watching the bartender slowly peel a lemon.

''Aren't you?'' Frances asked harshly. ''Come on, tell me. Talk. Aren't you?''

''Maybe,'' Michael said. He moved his chair back again. ''How the hell do I know?''

''You know,'' Frances persisted. ''Don't you know?''

''Yes,'' Michael said after a while, ''I know.''

Frances stopped crying then. Two or three snuffles into the handkerchief and she put it away and her face didn't tell anything to anybody. ''At least do me one favor,'' she said.

''Sure.''

''Stop talking about how pretty this woman is or that one. Nice eyes, nice breasts, a pretty figure, good voice.'' She mimicked his voice. ''Keep it to yourself. I'm not interested.''

Michael waved to the waiter. ''I'll keep it to myself,'' he said.

Frances flicked the corners of her eyes. ''Another brandy,'' she told the waiter.

"Two," Michael said.

"Yes, Ma'am, yes, sir," said the waiter, backing away.

Frances regarded Michael coolly across the table. "Do you want me to call the Stevensons?" she asked. "It'll be nice in the country."

"Sure," Michael said. "Call them."

She got up from the table and walked across the room toward the telephone. Michael watched her walk, thinking what a pretty girl, what nice legs.

Mood and Atmosphere

Just as Joyce in "Counterparts" suggests the particular mood and atmosphere of Dublin, so Shaw in this story tries to convey the feel of New York. This is a big-city story, specifically a New York City story. Its success depends on Shaw's success in communicating the feel of New York City within a certain milieu.

1 Indicate, first, some of the images that help fix the setting and atmosphere as "big city." Are these images soft and warm or cold and hard? Justify Shaw's use of either kind of image.

2 Michael and Frances are obviously not like all New Yorkers in their activities and freedom. What do they typify? Can you characterize them? How does their type contribute to the mood and atmosphere?

3 Why does Shaw set the story on Sunday? Could it be any other day? Why not?

4 What do the Stevensons mean in the lives of Michael and Frances? Why do they wish to avoid the Stevensons on this particular day? Why then do they finally agree to go driving in the country with them? Why does Shaw present it as a surrender to something they wish to avoid?

5 If we say that the atmosphere is one of disillusionment and frustration, what would we mean? List as many points as you can to indicate such disillusionment, first with Frances and then with Michael.

6 Shaw creates atmosphere through carefully placed details. Consider the phrase, "They joined hands consciously. . . ." Why the word "consciously"? In "Frances said flatly," what does "flatly" signify? How do these two adverbs typify the predominant atmosphere of the story?

7 Shaw keeps the Japanese waiter carefully before our eyes. How does the waiter contribute to the atmosphere? Why is he always smiling? Is his smile depressing or cheerful to the couple?

8 Is Frances's attitude toward Michael simply jealousy of his attention to other girls or is it something more? Where does Shaw place the fault? To answer this question, you must understand the nature of these people, their weaknesses, their outlook, their feelings about themselves and each other. All this is directly or indirectly connected with the atmosphere of the big city.

9 What is behind Michael's desire for other girls? Is it solely sexual attraction? Or does it indicate other directions as well? This point is also connected with the atmosphere of New York.

10 What does the ending mean? Why does Michael make this comment? Is he in love with life itself, or do his feelings indicate something else about him? At one point, Frances accuses him of having a "kid's feelings." Is she right that Michael is simply immature?

11 What is Shaw saying about the relationship between the sexes? Does the point extend into something more than a big-city story? Or are these people so clearly of one time and one place that their lives have no further significance?

12 The title itself: Is it to be taken ironically or literally? What does it mean and how does it help establish atmosphere?

13 Compare the atmosphere generated by this story with that generated by Joyce's "Counterparts." Which comes through more strongly, Shaw's New York or Joyce's Dublin? Which writer seems the more profound? Judge on the basis of how deeply you feel the experience each one is communicating. One way to approach their works is through language: Compare Shaw's use of words with Joyce's, and then note how words become images, ideas, and feelings.

THE CAPITAL OF THE WORLD

Ernest Hemingway

Madrid is full of boys named Paco, which is the diminutive of the name Francisco, and there is a Madrid joke about a father who came to Madrid and inserted an advertisement in the personal columns of *El Liberal* which said: PACO MEET ME AT HOTEL MONTANA NOON TUESDAY ALL IS FORGIVEN PAPA and how a squadron of Guardia Civil had to be called out to disperse the eight hundred young men who answered the advertisement. But this Paco, who waited on table at the Pension Luarca, had no father to forgive him, nor anything for the father to forgive. He had two older sisters who were chambermaids at the Luarca, who had gotten their place through coming from the same small village as a former Luarca chambermaid who had proven hardworking and honest and hence given her village and its products a good name; and these sisters had paid his way on the auto-bus to Madrid and gotten him his job as an apprentice waiter. He came from a village in a part of Extramadura where conditions were incredibly primitive, food scarce, and comforts unknown and he had worked hard ever since he could remember.

He was a well built boy with very black, rather curly hair, good teeth and a skin that his sisters envied, and he had a ready and unpuzzled smile. He was fast on his feet and did his work well and he loved his sisters, who seemed beautiful and sophisticated; he loved Madrid, which was still an unbelievable place, and he loved his work which, done under bright lights, with clean linen, the wearing of evening clothes, and abundant food in the kitchen, seemed romantically beautiful.

There were from eight to a dozen other people who lived at the Luarca and ate in the dining room but for Paco, the youngest of the three waiters who served at table, the only ones who really existed were the bull fighters.

Second-rate matadors lived at that pension because the address in the Calle San Jeronimo was good, the food was excellent and the room and board was cheap. It is necessary for a bull fighter to give the appearance, if not of prosperity, at least of respectability, since decorum and dignity rank above courage as the virtues most highly prized in Spain, and bull fighters stayed at the Luarca until their last pesetas were gone. There is no record of any bull fighter having left the Luarca for a better or more expensive hotel; second-rate bull fighters never became first rate; but the descent from the Luarca was swift since any one could stay there who was making anything at all and a bill was never presented to a guest unasked until the woman who ran the place knew that the case was hopeless.

At this time there were three full matadors living at the Luarca as well as two very good picadors, and one excellent banderillero. The Luarca was luxury for the picadors and the banderilleros who, with their families in Seville, required lodging in Madrid during the Spring season; but they were well paid and in the fixed employ of fighters who were heavily contracted during the coming season and the three of these subalterns would probably make much more apiece than any of the three matadors. Of the three matadors one was ill and trying to conceal it; one had passed his short vogue as a novelty; and the third was a coward.

The coward had at one time, until he had received a peculiarly atrocious horn wound in the lower abdomen at the start of his first season as a full matador, been exceptionally brave and remarkably skillful and he still had many of the hearty mannerisms of his days of success. He was jovial to excess and laughed constantly with and without provocation. He had, when successful, been very addicted to practical jokes but he had given them up now. They took an assurance that he did not feel. This matador had an intelligent, very open face and he carried himself with much style.

The matador who was ill was careful never to show it and was meticulous about eating a little of all the dishes that were presented at the table. He had a great many handkerchiefs which he laundered himself in his room and, lately, he had been selling his fighting suits. He had sold one, cheaply, before Christmas and another in the first week of April. They had been very expensive suits, had always been well kept and he had one more. Before he had become ill he had been a very promising, even a sensational, fighter and, while he himself could not read, he had clippings which said that in his debut in Madrid he had been better than Belmonte. He ate alone at a small table and looked up very little.

The matador who had once been a novelty was very short and brown and very dignified. He also ate alone at a separate table and he smiled very rarely and never laughed. He came from Valladolid, where the people are extremely serious, and he was a capable matador; but his style had become old-fashioned before he had ever succeeded in endearing himself to the public through his virtues, which were courage and a calm capability, and his name on a poster would draw no one to a bull ring. His novelty had been that he was so short that he could barely see over the bull's withers, but there were other short fighters, and he had never succeeded in imposing himself on the public's fancy.

Of the picadors one was a thin, hawk-faced, gray-haired man, lightly built but with legs and arms like iron, who always wore cattle-men's boots under his trousers, drank too much every evening and gazed amorously at any woman in the pension. The other was huge, dark, brown-faced, good-looking, with black hair like an Indian and enormous hands. Both were great picadors although the first was reputed to have lost much of his ability through drink and dissipation, and the second was said to be too headstrong and quarrelsome to stay with any matador more than a single season.

The banderillero was middle-aged, gray, cat-quick in spite of his years and, sitting at the table he looked a moderately prosperous business man. His legs were still good for this season, and when they should go he was intelligent and experienced enough to keep regularly employed for a long time. The difference would be that when his speed of foot would be gone he would always be frightened where now he was assured and calm in the ring and out of it.

On this evening every one had left the dining room except the hawk-faced picador who drank too much, the birthmarked-faced auctioneer of watches at the fairs and festivals of Spain, who also drank too much, and two priests from Galicia who were sitting at a corner table and drinking if not too much certainly enough. At that time wine was included in the price of the room and board at the Luarca and the waiters had just brought fresh bottles of Valdepeñas to the tables of the auctioneer, then to the picador and, finally, to the two priests.

The three waiters stood at the end of the room. It was the rule of the house that they should all remain on duty until the diners whose tables they were responsible for should all have left, but the one who served the table of the two priests had an appointment to go to an Anarcho-Syndicalist meeting and Paco had agreed to take over his table for him.

Upstairs the matador who was ill was lying face down on his bed alone. The matador who was no longer a novelty was sitting looking out of his window preparatory to walking out to the café. The matador who was a coward had the older sister of Paco in his room with him and trying to get her to do something which she was laughingly refusing to do. This matador was saying "Come on, little savage."

"No," said the sister. "Why should I?"

"For a favor."

"You've eaten and now you want me for dessert."

"Just once. What harm can it do?"

"Leave me alone. Leave me alone, I tell you."

"It is a very little thing to do."

"Leave me alone, I tell you."

Down in the dining room the tallest of the waiters, who was overdue at the meeting, said "Look at those black pigs drink."

"That's no way to speak," said the second waiter. "They are decent clients. They do not drink too much."

"For me it is a good way to speak," said the tall one. "There are the two curses of Spain, the bulls and the priests."

"Certainly not the individual bull and the individual priest," said the second waiter.

"Yes," said the tall waiter. "Only through the individual can you attack the class. It is necessary to kill the individual bull and the individual priest. All of them. Then there are no more."

"Save it for the meeting," said the other waiter.

"Look at the barbarity of Madrid," said the tall waiter. "It is now half-past eleven o'clock and these are still guzzling."

"They only started to eat at ten," said the other waiter. "As you know there are many dishes. That wine is cheap and these have paid for it. It is not a strong wine."

"How can there be solidarity of workers with fools like you?" asked the tall waiter.

"Look," said the second waiter who was a man of fifty. "I have worked all my life. In all that remains of my life I must work. I have no complaints against work. To work is normal."

"Yes, but the lack of work kills."

"I have always worked," said the older waiter. "Go on to the meeting. There is no necessity to stay."

"You are a good comrade," said the tall waiter. "But you lack all ideology."

"*Mejor si me falta eso que el otro,*" said the older waiter (meaning it is better to lack that than work). "Go on to the *mitin.*"

Paco had said nothing. He did not yet understand politics but it always gave him a thrill to hear the tall waiter speak of the necessity for killing the priests and the Guardia Civil. The tall waiter represented to him revolution and revolution also was romantic. He himself would like to be a good catholic, a revolutionary, and have a steady job like this, while, at the same time, being a bullfighter.

"Go on to the meeting, Ignacio," he said. "I will respond for your work."

"The two of us," said the older waiter.

"There isn't enough for one," said Paco. "Go on to the meeting."

"*Pues, me voy,*" said the tall waiter. "And thanks."

In the meantime, upstairs, the sister of Paco had gotten out of the embrace of the matador as skilfully as a wrestler breaking a hold and said, now angry, "These are the hungry people. A failed bullfighter. With your ton-load of fear. If you have so much of that, use it in the ring."

"That is the way a whore talks."

"A whore is also a woman, but I am not a whore."

"You'll be one."

"Not through you."

"Leave me," said the matador who, now, repulsed and refused, felt the nakedness of his cowardice returning.

"Leave you? What hasn't left you?" said the sister. "Don't you want me to make up the bed? I'm paid to do that."

"Leave me," said the matador, his broad good-looking face wrinkled into a contortion that was like crying. "You whore. You dirty little whore."

"Matador," she said, shutting the door. "My Matador."

Inside the room the matador sat on the bed. His face still had the contortion which, in the ring, he made into a constant smile which frightened those people in the first rows of seats who knew what they were watching. "And this," he was saying aloud. "And this. And this."

He could remember when he had been good and it had only been three years before. He could remember the weight of the heavy gold-brocaded fighting jacket on his shoulders on that hot afternoon in May when his voice had still been the same in the ring as in the café, and now he sighed along the point-dripping blade at the place in the top of the shoulders where it was dusty in the short-haired black hump of muscle above the wide, wood-knocking, splintered-tipped horns that lowered as he went in to kill, and how the sword pushed in as easy as into a mound of stiff butter with the palm of his hand pushing the pommel, his left arm crossed low, his left shoulder forward, his weight on his left leg, and then his weight wasn't on his leg. His weight was on his lower belly and as the bull raised his head the horn was out of sight in him and he swung over on it twice before they pulled him off it. So now when he went in to kill, and it was seldom, he could not look at the horns and what did any whore know about what he went through before he fought? And what had they been through that laughed at him? They were all whores and they knew what they could do with it.

Down in the dining room the picador sat looking at the priests. If there were women in the room he stared at them. If there were no women he would stare with enjoyment at a foreigner, *un inglés,* but lacking women or strangers, he now stared with enjoyment and insolence at the two priests. While he stared the birth-marked auctioneer rose and folding his napkin went out, leaving over half the wine in the last bottle he had ordered. If his accounts had been paid up at the Luarca he would have finished the bottle.

The two priests did not stare back at the picador. One of them was saying, "It is ten days since I have been here waiting to see him and all day I sit in the ante-chamber and he will not receive me."

"What is there to do?"

"Nothing. What can one do? One cannot go against authority."

"I have been here for two weeks and nothing. I wait and they will not see me."

"We are from the abandoned country. When the money runs out we can return."

"To the abandoned country. What does Madrid care about Galicia? We are a poor province."

"One understands the action of our brother Basilio."

"Still I have no real confidence in the integrity of Basilio Alvarez."

"Madrid is where one learns to understand. Madrid kills Spain."

"If they would simply see one and refuse."

"No. You must be broken and worn out by waiting."

"Well, we shall see. I can wait as well as another."

At this moment the picador got to his feet, walked over to the priests' table and stood, gray-headed and hawk-faced, staring at them and smiling.

"A torero," said one priest to the other.

"And a good one," said the picador and walked out of the dining room, gray-jacketed, trim-waisted, bow-legged, in tight breeches over his high-heeled cattleman's boots that clicked on the floor as he swaggered quite steadily, smiling to himself. He lived in a small, tight, professional world of personal efficiency, nightly alcoholic triumph, and insolence. Now he lit a cigar and tilting his hat at an angle in the hallway went out to the café.

The priests left immediately after the picador, hurriedly conscious of being the last people in the dining room, and there was no one in the room now but Paco and the middle-aged waiter. They cleared the tables and carried the bottles into the kitchen.

In the kitchen was the boy who washed the dishes. He was three years older than Paco and was very cynical and bitter.

"Take this," the middle-aged waiter said, and poured out a glass of the Valdepeñas and handed it to him.

"Why not?" the boy took the glass.

"Tu, Paco?" the older waiter asked.

"Thank you," said Paco. The three of them drank.

"I will be going," said the middle-aged waiter.

"Good night," they told him.

He went out and they were alone. Paco took a napkin one of the priests had used and standing straight, his heels planted, lowered the napkin and with head following the movement, swung his arms in the motion of a slow sweeping veronica. He turned and advancing his right foot slightly, made the second pass, gained a little terrain on the imaginary bull and made a third pass, slow, perfectly timed and suave, then gathered the napkin to his waist and swung his hips away from the bull in a media-veronica.

The dishwasher, whose name was Enrique, watched him critically and sneeringly.

"How is the bull?" he said.

"Very brave," said Paco. "Look."

Standing slim and straight he made four more perfect passes, smooth, elegant and graceful.

"And the bull?" asked Enrique standing against the sink, holding his wine glass and wearing his apron.

"Still has lots of gas," said Paco.

"You make me sick," said Enrique.

"Why?"

"Look."

Enrique removed his apron and citing the imaginary bull he sculptured four perfect, languid gypsy veronicas and ended up with a rebolera that made the apron swing in a stiff arc past the bull's nose as he walked away from him.

"Look at that," he said. "And I wash dishes."

"Why?"

"Fear," said Enrique. "*Miedo.* The same fear you would have in a ring with a bull."

"No," said Paco. "I wouldn't be afraid."

"*Leche!*" said Enrique. "Every one is afraid. But a torero can control his fear so that he can work the bull. I went in an amateur fight and I was so afraid I couldn't keep from running. Every one thought it was very funny. So would you be afraid. If it wasn't for fear every bootblack in Spain would be a bull-fighter. You, a country boy, would be frightened worse than I was."

"No," said Paco.

He had done it too many times in his imagination. Too many times he had seen the horns, seen the bull's wet muzzle, the ear twitching, then the head go down and the charge, the hoofs thudding and the hot bull pass him as he swung the cape, to re-charge as he swung the cape again, then again, and again, and again, to end winding the bull around him in his great media-veronica, and walk swingingly away, with bull hairs caught in the gold ornaments of his jacket from the close passes; the bull standing hypnotized and the crowd applauding. No, he would not be afraid. Others, yes. Not he. He knew he would not be afraid. Even if he ever was afraid he knew that he could do it anyway. He had confidence. "I wouldn't be afraid," he said.

Enrique said, "*Leche,*" again.

Then he said, "If we should try it?"

"How?"

"Look," said Enrique. "You think of the bull but you do not think of the horns. The bull has such force that the horns rip like a knife, they stab like a bayonet, and they kill like a club. Look," he opened a table drawer and took out two meat knives. "I will bind these to the legs of a chair. Then I will play bull for you with the chair held before my head. The knives are the horns. If you make those passes then they mean something."

"Lend me your apron," said Paco. "We'll do it in the dining room."

"No," said Enrique, suddenly not bitter. "Don't do it, Paco."

"Yes," said Paco. "I'm not afraid."

"You will be when you see the knives come."

"We'll see," said Paco. "Give me the apron."

At this time, while Enrique was binding the two heavy-bladed razor-sharp meat knives fast to the legs of the chair with two soiled napkins holding the half of each knife, wrapping them tight and then knotting them, the two chambermaids, Paco's sisters, were on their way to the cinema to see Greta Garbo in "Anna Christie." Of the two priests, one was sitting in his underwear reading his breviary and the other was wearing a nightshirt and saying the rosary. All the bullfighters except the one who was ill had made their evening appearance at the Café Fornos, where the big, dark-haired picador was playing billiards, the short serious matador was sitting at a crowded table before a coffee and milk, along with the middle-aged banderillero and other serious workmen.

The drinking, gray-headed picador was sitting with a glass of cazalas brandy before him staring with pleasure at a table where the matador whose courage was gone sat with another matador who had renounced the sword to become a banderillero again, and two very houseworn-looking prostitutes.

The auctioneer stood on the street corner talking with friends. The tall waiter was at the Anarcho-Syndicalist meeting waiting for an opportunity to speak. The middle-aged waiter was seated on the terrace of the Café Alvarez drinking a small beer. The woman who owned the Luarca was already asleep in her bed, where she lay on her back with the bolster between her legs; big, fat, honest, clean, easy-going, very religious and never having ceased to miss or pray daily for her husband, dead, now, twenty years. In his room, alone, the matador who was ill lay face down on his bed with his mouth against a handkerchief.

Now, in the deserted dining room, Enrique tied the last knot in the napkins that bound the knives to the chair legs and lifted the chair. He pointed the legs with the knives on them forward and held the chair over his head with the two knives pointing straight ahead, one on each side of his head.

"It's heavy," he said. "Look, Paco. It is very dangerous. Don't do it." He was sweating.

Paca stood facing him, holding the apron spread, holding a fold of it bunched in each hand, thumbs up, first finger down, spread to catch the eye of the bull.

"Charge straight," he said. "Turn like a bull. Charge as many times as you want."

"How will you know when to cut the pass?" asked Enrique. "It's better to do three and then a media."

"All right," said Paco. "But come straight. Huh, torito! Come on, little bull!"

Running with head down Enrique came toward him and Paco swung the apron just ahead of the knife blade as it passed close in front of his belly and as it went by it was, to him, the real horn, white-tipped, black, smooth, and as Enrique passed him and turned to rush again it was the hot, blood-flanked mass of the bull that thudded by, then turned like a cat and came again as he swung the cape slowly. Then the bull turned and came again and, as he watched the onrushing point, he stepped his left foot two inches too far forward and the knife did not pass, but had slipped in as easily as into a wineskin and there was a hot scalding rush above and around the sudden inner rigidity of steel and Enrique shouting. "Ay! Ay! Let me get it out! Let me get it out!" and Paco slipped forward on the chair, the apron cap still held, Enrique pulling on the chair as the knife turned in him, in him, Paco.

The knife was out now and he sat on the floor in the widening warm pool.

"Put the napkin over it. Hold it!" said Enrique. "Hold it tight. I will run for the doctor. You must hold in the hemorrhage."

"There should be a rubber cup," said Paco. He had seen that used in the ring.

"I came straight," said Enrique, crying. "All I wanted was to show the danger."

"Don't worry," said Paco, his voice sounding far away. "But bring the doctor."

In the ring they lifted you and carried you, running with you, to the operating room. If the femoral artery emptied itself before you reached there they called the priest.

"Advise one of the priests," said Paco, holding the napkin tight against his lower abdomen. He could not believe that this had happened to him.

But Enrique was running down the Carrera San Jeromino to the all-night first-aid station and Paco was alone, first sitting up, then huddled over, then slumped on the floor, until it was over, feeling his life go out of him as dirty water empties from a bathtub when the plug is drawn. He was frightened and he felt faint and he tried to say an act of contrition and he remembered how it started but before he had said, as fast as he could, "Oh, my God, I am heartily sorry for having offended Thee who art worthy of all my love and I firmly resolve . . . ," he felt too faint and he was lying face down on the floor and it was over very quickly. A severed femoral artery empties itself faster than you can believe.

As the doctor from the first-aid station came up the stairs accompanied by a policeman who held on to Enrique by the arm, the two sisters of Paco were still in the moving picture palace of the Gran Via, where they were intensely disappointed in the Garbo film, which showed the great star in miserable low surroundings when they had been accustomed to see her surrounded by great luxury and brilliance. The audience disliked the film thoroughly and were protesting by whistling and stamping their feet. All the other people from the hotel were doing almost what they had been doing when the accident happened, except that the two priests had finished their devotions and were preparing for sleep, and the gray-haired picador had moved his drink over to the table with the two houseworn prostitutes. A little later he went out of the café with one of them. It was the one for whom the matador who had lost his nerve had been buying drinks.

The boy Paco had never known about any of this nor about what all these people would be doing on the next day and on other days to come. He had no idea how they really lived nor how they ended. He did not even realize they ended. He died, as the Spanish phrase has it, full of illusions. He had not had time in his life to lose any of them, nor even, at the end, to complete an act of contrition.

He had not even had time to be disappointed in the Garbo picture which disappointed all Madrid for a week.

Mood and Atmosphere

Hemingway's story has something in common with Joyce's "Counterparts" in that both use large cities as background for frustration, defeat, and spiritual or actual death. In a more limited respect, Shaw in "The Girls in Their Summer Dresses" uses New York as Hemingway uses Madrid and as Joyce uses Dublin. Joyce and Hemingway are obviously greater artists than Shaw, and therefore their very choice of language, as well as their selection of narrative details, becomes relevant.

1 Find instances of words and images which convey Hemingway's sense of despair and bitterness. Look in particular for the repetition of words and for rhythms which "create" mood.

2 How do the three matadors function as part of the atmosphere? Although they are only sketched in, does Hemingway convey enough of their flavor to give them reality? Is it necessary to know more about them, or is Hemingway's economy of description effective?

3 Why should Hemingway characterize the two picadors and the banderillero as being very good, even excellent, in the ring, while he makes the matadors defeated or cowardly?

4 Characterize the pension where they live. Why is the Luarca so depressing a place even though the food and lodgings are considered excellent?

5 Is the title of the story ironic or literal? What about the function of the opening paragraph on boys named Paco?

6 How does Paco fit into this world of defeat and despair? Is he an intrinsic part of it or does he rise above it? Does Paco have assumptions and beliefs that are any different from those of the others? Does Hemingway sufficiently differentiate him, or does he blend in with the Luarca and the defeated matadors and waiters?

7 Why does Hemingway introduce the priests? Is it simply for the sake of anti-Catholic sentiment on the part of one of the waiters? What are the priests waiting for? Are they any different from the matadors? And the waiters—what role do they play?

8 How does the idea of the bulls and bullfighting fit into this general atmosphere? Is bullfighting an escape from the world of the Luarca, or is it part of the atmosphere of defeat? Why does it appeal to Paco and to Enrique?

9 What is the purpose of the episode between Paco's sister and the cowardly matador? Is it simply to show the cowardice of the matador and the chastity of Paco's sister? How do all the sexual references contribute to the atmosphere?

10 What purposes do the references to Garbo in "Anna Christie" serve? If you know something about the play by O'Neill or the motion picture itself, the reference will become more significant.

11 What sense of the outside world do we obtain? Is there, in fact, any outside world beyond the restaurant? What is the point of the self-enclosed nature of Hemingway's material?

12 If we say that Hemingway presents Spain as a country of death and the dead, what do we mean?

Characterization

1 Although Paco is the chief character, we actually see relatively little of him. Yet we sense a good deal about him. How does Hemingway give us this "feel" for Paco?

2 How do the other characters and the atmosphere of the Luarca contribute to our sense of Paco?

3 What does bullfighting mean to the young boy?

4 Why is the element of fear introduced so often, and what connection does it have to Paco?

5 Is Paco's death in any way a sacrificial death? That is, does he die to serve any purpose (whether good or bad) beyond the fact itself? Why does Hemingway have him die in this particular way? Is it a heroic or sordid death? Does it matter that Paco should die (beyond, of course, what it means to him)?

6 In terms of Paco, what is the function of the ironical ending of the story?

7 What were Paco's illusions that Hemingway mentions near the end? Is it better that he die with illusions than live disillusioned?

Theme

The surface of a Hemingway story is usually very deceptive in its simplicity. He seems chiefly concerned with an interesting, adventurous narrative and with little else. Yet throughout this story and several of his other stories there is a view of life that transcends the storytelling.

1 What are some of Hemingway's attitudes as they poke through "The Capital of the World"?

2 What does he say about men? How does he evaluate them?

3 Is Paco a hero for him? A fool?

4 Do you feel that he has objectively presented despair, or that he himself is involved in the quality?

5 Does his view of Madrid and that particular world say anything further about men elsewhere? Is the Luarca a miniature world that can be projected anywhere at any time? How do you know?

COUNTERPARTS

James Joyce

The bell rang furiously and, when Miss Parker went to the tube, a furious voice called out in a piercing North of Ireland accent:

"Send Farrington here!"

Miss Parker returned to her machine, saying to a man who was writing at a desk:

"Mr. Alleyne wants you upstairs."

The man muttered "*Blast* him!" under his breath and pushed back his chair to stand up. When he stood up he was tall and of great bulk. He had a hanging face, dark wine-coloured, with fair eyebrows and moustache: his eyes bulged forward slightly and the whites of them were dirty. He lifted up the counter and, passing by the clients, went out of the office with a heavy step.

He went heavily upstairs until he came to the second landing, where a door bore a brass plate with the inscription *Mr. Alleyne.* Here he halted, puffing with labour and vexation, and knocked. The shrill voice cried:

"Come in!"

The man entered Mr. Alleyne's room. Simultaneously Mr. Alleyne, a little man wearing gold-rimmed glasses on a clean-shaven face, shot his head up over a pile of documents. The head itself was so pink and hairless it seemed like a large egg reposing on the papers. Mr. Alleyne did not lose a moment:

"Farrington? What is the meaning of this? Why have I always to complain of you? May I ask you why you haven't made a copy of that contract between Bodley and Kirwan? I told you it must be ready by four o'clock."

"But Mr. Shelley said, sir—"

"*Mr. Shelley said, sir.* . . . Kindly attend to what I say and not to what *Mr. Shelley says, sir.* You have always some excuse or another for shirking work. Let me tell you that if the contract is not copied before this evening I'll lay the matter before Mr. Crosbie. . . . Do you hear me now?"

"Yes, sir."

"Do you hear me now? . . . Ay and another little matter! I might as well be talking to the wall as talking to you. Understand once for all that you get a half an hour for your lunch and not an hour and a half. How many courses do you want, I'd like to know. . . . Do you mind me now?"

"Yes, sir."

Mr. Alleyne bent his head again upon his pile of papers. The man stared fixedly at the polished skull which directed the affairs of Crosbie & Alleyne, gauging its fragility. A spasm of rage gripped his throat for a few moments and then passed, leaving after it a sharp sensation of thirst. The man recognised the sensation and felt that he must have a good night's drinking. The middle of the month was passed and, if he could get the copy done in time, Mr. Alleyne might give him an order on the cashier. He stood still, gazing fixedly at the head upon the pile of papers. Suddenly Mr. Alleyne began to upset all the papers, searching for something. Then, as if he had been unaware of the man's presence till that moment, he shot up his head again, saying:

"Eh? Are you going to stand there all day? Upon my word, Farrington, you take things easy!"

"I was waiting to see . . ."

"Very good, you needn't wait to see. Go downstairs and do your work."

The man walked heavily towards the door and, as he went out of the room, he heard Mr. Alleyne cry after him that if the contract was not copied by evening Mr. Crosbie would hear of the matter.

He returned to his desk in the lower office and counted the sheets which remained to be copied. He took up his pen and dipped it in the ink but he continued to stare stupidly at the last words he had written: *In no case shall the said Bernard Bodley be* . . . The evening was falling and in a few minutes they would be lighting the gas: then he could write. He felt that he must slake the thirst in his throat. He stood up from his desk and, lifting the counter as before, passed out of the office. As he was passing out the chief clerk looked at him inquiringly.

"It's all right, Mr. Shelley," said the man, pointing with his finger to indicate the objective of his journey.

The chief clerk glanced at the hat-rack, but, seeing the row complete, offered no remark. As soon as he was on the landing the man pulled a shepherd's plaid cap out of his pocket, put it on his head and ran quickly down the rickety stairs. From the street door he walked on furtively on the inner side of the path towards the corner and all at once dived into a doorway. He was now safe in the dark snug of O'Neill's shop, and, filling up the little window that looked into the bar with his inflamed face, the colour of dark wine or dark meat, he called out:

"Here, Pat, give us a g.p., like a good fellow."

The curate brought him a glass of plain porter. The man drank it at a gulp and asked for a caraway seed. He put his penny on the counter and, leaving the curate to grope for it in the gloom, retreated out of the snug as furtively as he had entered it.

Darkness, accompanied by a thick fog, was gaining upon the dusk of February and the lamps in Eustace Street had been lit. The man went up by the houses until he reached the door of the office, wondering whether he could finish his copy in time. On the stairs a moist pungent odour of perfumes saluted his nose: evidently Miss Delacour had come while he was out in O'Neill's. He crammed his cap back again into his pocket and re-entered the office, assuming an air of absent-mindedness.

"Mr. Alleyne has been calling for you," said the chief clerk severely. "Where were you?"

The man glanced at the two clients who were standing at the counter as if to intimate that their presence prevented him from answering. As the clients were both male the chief clerk allowed himself a laugh.

"I know that game," he said. "Five times in one day is a little bit. . . . Well, you better look sharp and get a copy of our correspondence in the Delacour case for Mr. Alleyne."

This address in the presence of the public, his run upstairs and the porter he had gulped down so hastily confused the man and, as he sat down at his desk to get what was required, he realised how hopeless was the task of finishing his copy of the contract before half past five. The dark damp night was coming and he longed to spend it in the bars, drinking with his friends amid the glare of gas and the clatter of glasses. He got out the Delacour correspondence and passed out of the office. He hoped Mr. Alleyne would not discover that the last two letters were missing.

The moist pungent perfume lay all the way up to Mr. Alleyne's room. Miss Delacour was a middle-aged woman of Jewish appearance. Mr. Alleyne was said to be sweet on her or on her money. She came to the office often and stayed a long time when she came. She was sitting beside his desk now in an aroma of perfumes, smoothing the handle of her umbrella and nodding the great black feather in her hat. Mr. Alleyne had swivelled his chair round to face her and thrown his right foot jauntily upon his left knee. The man put the correspondence on the desk and bowed respectfully but neither Mr. Alleyne nor Miss Delacour took any notice of his bow. Mr. Alleyne tapped a finger on the correspondence and then flicked it towards him as if to say: "*That's all right: you can go.*"

The man returned to the lower office and sat down again at his desk. He stared intently at the incomplete phrase: *In no case shall the said Bernard Bodley be* . . . and thought how strange it was that the last three words began with the same letter. The chief clerk began to hurry Miss Parker, saying she would never have the letters typed in time for post. The man listened to the clicking of the machine for a few minutes and then set to work to finish his copy. But his head was not clear and his mind wandered away to the glare and rattle of the public-house. It was a night for hot punches. He struggled on with his copy, but when the clock struck five he had still fourteen pages to write. Blast it! He couldn't finish it in time. He longed to execrate aloud, to bring his fist down on something violently. He was so enraged that he wrote *Bernard Bernard* instead of *Bernard Bodley* and had to begin again on a clean sheet.

He felt strong enough to clear out the whole office single-handed. His body ached to do something, to rush out and revel in violence. All the indignities of his life enraged him. . . . Could he ask the cashier privately for an advance? No, the cashier was no good, no damn good: he wouldn't give an advance. . . . He knew where he would meet the boys: Leonard and O'Halloran and Nosey Flynn. The barometer of his emotional nature was set for a spell of riot.

His imagination had so abstracted him that his name was called twice before he answered. Mr. Alleyne and Miss Delacour were standing outside the counter and all the clerks had turned round in anticipation of something. The man got up from his desk. Mr. Alleyne began a tirade of abuse, saying that two letters were missing. The man answered that he knew nothing about them, that he had made a faithful copy. The tirade continued: it was so bitter and violent that the man could hardly restrain his fist from descending upon the head of the manikin before him:

"I know nothing about any other two letters," he said stupidly.

"*You—know—nothing.* Of course you know nothing," said Mr. Alleyne. "Tell me," he added, glancing first for approval to the lady beside him, "do you take me for a fool? Do you think me an utter fool?"

The man glanced from the lady's face to the little egg-shaped head and back again; and, almost before he was aware of it, his tongue had found a felicitous moment:

"I don't think, sir," he said, "that that's a fair question to put to me."

There was a pause in the very breathing of the clerks. Everyone was astounded (the author of the witticism no less than his neighbours) and Miss Delacour, who was a stout amiable person, began to smile broadly. Mr. Alleyne flushed to the hue of a wild rose and his mouth twitched with a dwarf's passion. He shook his fist in the man's face till it seemed to vibrate like the knob of some electric machine:

"You impertinent ruffian! You impertinent ruffian! I'll make short work of you! Wait till you see! You'll apologise to me for your impertinence or you'll quit the office instanter! You'll quit this, I'm telling you, or you'll apologise to me!"

He stood in a doorway opposite the office watching to see if the cashier would come out alone. All the clerks passed out and finally the cashier came out with the chief clerk. It was no use trying to say a word to him when he was with the chief clerk. The man felt that his position was bad enough. He had been obliged to offer an abject apology to Mr. Alleyne for his impertinence but he knew what a hornet's nest the office would be for him. He could remember the way in which Mr. Alleyne had hounded little Peake out of the office in order to make room for his own nephew. He felt savage and thirsty and revengeful, annoyed with himself and with everyone else. Mr. Alleyne would never give him an hour's rest; his life would be a hell to him. He had made a proper fool of himself this time. Could he not keep his tongue in his cheek? But they had never pulled together from the first, he and Mr. Alleyne, ever since the day Mr. Alleyne had overheard him mimicking his North of Ireland accent to amuse Higgins and Miss Parker; that had been the beginning of it. He might have tried Higgins for the money, but sure Higgins never had anything for himself. A man with two establishments to keep up, of course he couldn't. . . .

He felt his great body again aching for the comfort of the public-house. The fog had begun to chill him and he wondered could he touch Pat in O'Neill's. He could not touch him for more than a bob—and a bob was no use. Yet he must get money somewhere or other: he had spent his last penny for the g.p. and soon it would be too late for getting money anywhere. Suddenly, as he was fingering his watch-chain, he thought of Terry Kelly's pawn-office in Fleet Street. That was the dart! Why didn't he think of it sooner?

He went through the narrow alley of Temple Bar quickly, muttering to himself that they could all go to hell because he was going to have a good night of it. The clerk in Terry Kelly's said *A crown!* but the consignor held out for six shillings; and in the end the six shillings was allowed him literally. He came out of the pawn-office joyfully, making a little cylinder of the coins between his thumb and fingers. In Westmoreland Street the footpaths were crowded with young men and women returning from business and ragged urchins ran here and there yelling out the names of the evening editions. The man passed through the crowd, looking on the spectacle generally with proud satisfaction and staring masterfully at the office-girls. His head was full of the noises of tram-gongs and swishing trolleys and his nose already sniffed the curling fumes of punch. As he walked on he preconsidered the terms in which he would narrate the incident to the boys:

"So, I just looked at him—coolly, you know, and looked at her. Then I looked back at him again—taking my time, you know. 'I don't think that that's a fair question to put to me,' says I."

Nosey Flynn was sitting up in his usual corner of Davy Byrne's and, when he heard the story, he stood Farrington a half-one, saying it was as smart a thing as ever he heard. Farrington stood a drink in his turn. After a while O'Halloran and Paddy Leonard came in and the story was repeated to them. O'Halloran stood tailors of malt hot all round and told the story of the retort he had made to the chief clerk when he was in Callan's of Fownes's Street; but, as the retort was after the manner of the liberal shepherds in the eclogues, he had to admit that it was not as clever as Farrington's retort. At this Farrington told the boys to polish off that and have another.

Just as they were naming their poisons who should come in but Higgins! Of course he had to join in with the others. The men asked him to give his version of it, and he did so with great vivacity for the sight of five small hot whiskies was very exhilarating. Everyone roared laughing when he showed the way in which Mr. Alleyne shook his fist in Farrington's face. Then he imitated Farrington, saying, *"And here was my nabs, as cool as you please,"* while Farrington looked at the company out of his heavy dirty eyes, smiling and at times drawing forth stray drops of liquor from his moustache with the aid of his lower lip.

When that round was over there was a pause. O'Halloran had money but neither of the other two seemed to have any; so the whole party left the shop somewhat regretfully. At the corner of Duke Street Higgins and Nosey Flynn bevelled off to the left while the other three turned back towards the city. Rain was drizzling down on the cold streets and, when they reached the Ballast Office, Farrington suggested the Scotch House. The bar was full of men and loud with the noise of tongues and glasses. The three men pushed past the whining match-sellers at the door and formed a little party at the corner of the counter. They began to exchange stories. Leonard introduced them to a young fellow named Weathers who was performing at the Tivoli as an acrobat and knockabout *artiste.* Farrington stood a drink all round. Weathers said he would take a small Irish and Apollinaris. Farrington, who had definite notions of what was what, asked the boys would they have an Apollinaris too; but the boys told Tim to make theirs hot. The talk became theatrical. O'Halloran stood a round and then Farrington stood another round, Weathers protesting that the hospitality was too Irish. He promised to get them in behind the scenes and introduce them to some nice girls. O'Halloran said that he and Leonard would go, but that Farrington wouldn't go because he was a married man; and Farrington's heavy dirty eyes leered at the company in token that he understood he was being chaffed. Weathers made them all have just one little tincture at his expense and promised to meet them later on at Mulligan's in Poolbeg Street.

When the Scotch House closed they went round to Mulligan's. They went into the parlour at the back and O'Halloran ordered small hot specials all around. They were all beginning to feel mellow. Farrington was just standing another round when Weathers came back. Much to Farrington's relief he drank a glass of bitter this time. Funds were getting low but they had enough to keep them going. Presently two young women with big hats and a young man in a check suit came in and sat at a table close by. Weathers saluted them and told the company that they were out of the Tivoli. Farrington's eyes wandered at every moment in the direction of one of the young women. There was something striking in her appearance. An immense scarf of peacock-blue muslin was wound round her hat and knotted in a great bow under her chin; and she wore bright yellow gloves, reaching to the elbow. Farrington gazed admiringly at the plump arm which she moved very often and with much grace;

and when, after a little time, she answered his gaze he admired still more her large dark brown eyes. The oblique staring expression in them fascinated him. She glanced at him once or twice and, when the party was leaving the room, she brushed against his chair and said *"O, pardon!"* in a London accent. He watched her leave the room in the hope that she would look back at him, but he was disappointed. He cursed his want of money and cursed all the rounds he had stood, particularly all the whiskies and Apollinaris which he had stood to Weathers. If there was one thing that he hated it was a sponge. He was so angry that he lost count of the conversation of his friends.

When Paddy Leonard called him he found that they were talking about feats of strength. Weathers was showing his biceps muscle to the company and boasting so much that the other two had called on Farrington to uphold the national honour. Farrington pulled up his sleeve accordingly and showed his biceps muscle to the company. The two arms were examined and compared and finally it was agreed to have a trial of strength. The table was cleared and the two men rested their elbows on it, clasping hands. When Paddy Leonard said *"Go!"* each was to try to bring down the other's hand on to the table. Farrington looked very serious and determined.

The trial began. After about thirty seconds Weathers brought his opponent's hand slowly down on to the table. Farrington's dark wine-coloured face flushed darker still with anger and humiliation at having been defeated by such a stripling.

"You're not to put the weight of your body behind it. Play fair," he said.

"Who's not playing fair?" said the other.

"Come on again. The two best out of three."

The trial began again. The veins stood out on Farrington's forehead, and the pallor of Weathers' complexion changed to peony. Their hands and arms trembled under the stress. After a long struggle Weathers again brought his opponent's hand slowly on to the table. There was a murmur of applause from the spectators. The curate, who was standing beside the table, nodded his red head towards the victor and said with stupid familiarity:

"Ah! that's the knack!"

"What the hell do you know about it?" said Farrington fiercely, turning on the man. "What do you put in your gab for?"

"Sh, sh!" said O'Halloran, observing the violent expression

of Farrington's face. "Pony up, boys. We'll have just one little smahan more and then we'll be off."

A very sullen-faced man stood at the corner of O'Connell Bridge waiting for the little Sandymount tram to take him home. He was full of smouldering anger and revengefulness. He felt humiliated and discontented; he did not even feel drunk; and he had only two-pence in his pocket. He cursed everything. He had done for himself in the office, pawned his watch, spent all his money; and he had not even got drunk. He began to feel thirsty again and he longed to be back again in the hot reeking public-house. He had lost his reputation as a strong man, having been defeated twice by a mere boy. His heart swelled with fury and, when he thought of the woman in the big hat who had brushed against him and said *Pardon!* his fury nearly choked him.

His tram let him down at Shelbourne Road and he steered his great body along the shadow of the wall of the barracks. He loathed returning to his home. When he went in by the side-door he found the kitchen empty and the kitchen fire nearly out. He bawled upstairs:

"Ada! Ada!"

His wife was a little sharp-faced woman who bullied her husband when he was sober and was bullied by him when he was drunk. They had five children. A little boy came running down the stairs.

"Who is that?" said the man, peering through the darkness.

"Me, pa."

"Who are you? Charlie?"

"No, pa. Tom."

"Where's your mother?"

"She's out at the chapel."

"That's right. . . . Did she think of leaving any dinner for me?"

"Yes, pa. I—"

"Light the lamp. What do you mean by having the place in darkness? Are the other children in bed?"

The man sat down heavily on one of the chairs while the little boy lit the lamp. He began to mimic his son's flat accent, saying half to himself: *"At the chapel. At the chapel, if you please!"* When the lamp was lit he banged his fist on the table and shouted:

"What's for my dinner?"

"I'm going . . . to cook it, pa," said the little boy.

The man jumped up furiously and pointed to the fire.

"On that fire! You let the fire out! By God, I'll teach you to do that again!"

He took a step to the door and seized the walking-stick which was standing behind it.

"I'll teach you to let the fire out!" he said, rolling up his sleeve in order to give his arm free play.

The little boy cried *"O, pa!"* and ran whimpering round the table, but the man followed him and caught him by the coat. The little boy looked about him wildly but, seeing no way to escape, fell upon his knees.

"Now, you'll let the fire out the next time!" said the man, striking at him vigorously with the stick. "Take that, you little whelp!"

The boy uttered a squeal of pain as the stick cut his thigh. He clasped his hands together in the air and his voice shook with fright.

"O, pa!" he cried. "Don't beat me, pa! And I'll . . . I'll say a *Hail Mary* for you. . . . I'll say a *Hail Mary* for you, pa, if you don't beat me. . . . I'll say a *Hail Mary*. . . ."

Mood and Atmosphere

The mood and atmosphere of a story are generally elusive qualities, not nearly so well defined as plot, theme, setting, or characterization. To a large extent, mood and atmosphere depend on hints, suggestions, small changes of pace, tiny variations in the narrative. They determine—along with "tone"—how we feel about a story, what attitude we carry away from a reading.

After a reading of "Counterparts," we retain an image of men whose frustrated lives are nurtured amid gray desolation. The story appears to take place against a darkened background, the kind of mixture of grays and blacks we find in a Rembrandt painting: what is called *chiaroscuro,* a contrast of darks and lights. Out of these half tints Farrington emerges. He himself prefers the gaslit, somber colors of the pub and identifies with its atmosphere. He is not a man for light: light stands for success, and Farrington is made for defeat.

1 An author may suggest mood or atmosphere through description, through contrasts of characters, through conflicts (major or minor), through carefully wrought dialogue. Indicate from the first page or two some of Joyce's descriptive terms as he builds mood.

2 Indicate also some of the contrasts as they begin to develop —both within the chief character and outside of him. After two or three pages, do we know him and his situation? Be careful and accept him as Joyce presents him, not as a victim of drink or as someone lacking the will to do better. Do not intrude your own moral views.

3 How does Joyce's description of Farrington establish him as an outsider in his profession? What does he seem better suited for? Why does he hate Mr. Alleyne?

4 What kind of conflicts are raging within Farrington? Is there any solution to them?

5 Suppose Farrington worked harder and set a good example. Would he move ahead in the firm? How do his feelings about his future contribute to the mood of the story?

6 What does the name "Miss Delacour" suggest to you? Why does Farrington break out with his witticism in front of her?

7 What is the nature of his job and how does it contribute to the mood? Can you see any reason why he should write "*Bernard Bernard*" instead of "*Bernard Bodley*"? Is his doing so contributory to mood and atmosphere?

8 What role does the dialogue play? Can you characterize it? What attitudes does it generate in you?

Plot and Narrative

1 The story is structured on the series of defeats which Farrington suffers. List as many defeats as you can and show how each is slightly different from the others. Try to explain what their effects might be on Farrington.

2 After these defeats, can you understand a little better his treatment of his son at the end of the story? Why is the ending so shocking?

3 Compare this story with others in this collection and you will see that Joyce, like many of today's writers, had dispensed with a regular plot and narrative. How does he proceed instead? Are there any really high points or low points? Is there any change of fortune? Is there a desirable character?

Characterization

1 Joyce deftly creates character so that we know as much about each person as is necessary—no more, no less. Re-create what you know of Farrington. Can he be any different? Can he strive for a better life? What is Joyce's attitude toward him?

2 Do you feel that Farrington is trapped in something he can never understand? Are the inadequacies within him? Within his society? Or where? Do values keep shifting in the story so that internal and external elements are in continual movement?

3 Could the sense of entrapment be the crucial element in the story?

4 Characterize Mr. Alleyne. Is he also trapped, or has he "beaten" the system?

5 How about Farrington's cronies? Have they found a niche denied to Farrington?

Further Aspects

1 Where does the story gain its power? How can such a deceptively simple surface create a sense of depth?

2 Is Joyce saying something that extends beyond Dublin? What is he suggesting?

3 Characterize this type of short story. How does it differ from the stories of London, Cather, and Stuart, for example?

THE GRAVE

Katherine Anne Porter

The grandfather, dead for more than thirty years, had been twice disturbed in his long repose by the constancy and possessiveness of his widow. She removed his bones first to Louisiana and then to Texas as if she had set out to find her own burial place, knowing well she would never return to the places she had left. In Texas she set up a small cemetery in a corner of her first farm, and as the family connection grew, and oddments of relations came over from Kentucky to settle, it contained at last about twenty graves. After the grandmother's death, part of her land was to be sold for the benefit of certain of her children, and the cemetery happened to lie in the part set aside for sale. It was necessary to take up the bodies and bury them again in the family plot in the big new public cemetery, where the grandmother had been buried. At last her husband was to lie beside her for eternity, as she had planned.

The family cemetery had been a pleasant small neglected garden of tangled rose bushes and ragged cedar trees and cypress, the simple flat stones rising out of uncropped sweet-smelling wild grass. The graves were lying open and empty one burning day when Miranda and her brother Paul, who often went together to hunt rabbits and doves, propped their twenty-two Winchester rifles carefully against the rail fence, climbed over and explored among the graves. She was nine years old and he was twelve.

They peered into the pits all shaped alike with such purposeful accuracy, and looking at each other with pleased adventurous eyes, they said in solemn tones: "These were graves!" trying by words to shape a special, suitable emotion in their minds, but they felt nothing except an agreeable thrill of wonder: they were seeing a new sight, doing something they had not done before. In them both there was also a small disappointment at the entire commonplaceness of the actual spectacle. Even if it had once contained a coffin for years upon years, when the coffin was gone a grave was just a hole in the ground. Miranda leaped into the pit that had held her grandfather's bones. Scratching around aimlessly and pleasurably as any young animal, she scooped up a lump of earth and weighed it in her palm. It had a pleasantly sweet, corrupt smell, being mixed with cedar needles and small leaves, and as the crumbs fell apart, she saw a silver dove no larger than a hazel nut, with spread wings and a neat fan-shaped tail. The breast had a deep round hollow in it. Turning it up to the fierce sunlight, she saw that the inside of the hollow was cut in little whorls. She scrambled out, over the pile of loose earth that had fallen back into one end of the grave, calling to Paul that she had found something, he must guess what . . . His head appeared smiling over the rim of another grave. He waved a closed hand at her. "I've got something too!" They ran to compare treasures, making a game of it, so many guesses each, all wrong, and a final showdown with opened palms. Paul had found a thin wide gold ring carved with intricate flowers and leaves. Miranda was smitten at sight of the ring and wished to have it. Paul seemed more impressed by the dove. They made a trade, with some little bickering. After he had got the dove in his hand, Paul said, "Don't you know what this is? This is a screw head for a *coffin!* . . . I'll bet nobody else in the world has one like this!"

Miranda glanced at it without covetousness. She had the gold ring on her thumb; it fitted perfectly. "Maybe we ought to go now," she said, "maybe one of the niggers 'll see us and tell somebody." They knew the land had been sold, the cemetery was no longer theirs, and they felt like trespassers. They climbed back over the fence, slung their rifles loosely under their arms—they had been shooting at targets with various kinds of firearms since they were seven years old—and set out to look for the rabbits and doves or whatever small game might happen along. On these expeditions Miranda always followed at Paul's heels along the path, obeying instructions about handling her gun when going through fences; learning how to stand it up properly so it would not slip and fire unexpectedly; how to wait her time for a shot and not just bang away in the air without looking, spoiling shots for Paul, who really could hit things if given a chance. Now and then, in her excitement at seeing birds whizz up suddenly before her face, or a rabbit leap across her very toes, she lost her head, and almost without sighting she flung her rifle up and pulled the trigger. She hardly ever hit any sort of mark. She had no proper sense of hunting at all. Her brother would be often completely disgusted with her. "You don't care whether you get your bird or not," he said. "That's no way to hunt." Miranda could not understand his indignation. She had seen him smash his hat and yell with fury when he had missed his aim. "What I like about shooting," said Miranda, with exasperating inconsequence, "is pulling the trigger and hearing the noise."

"Then, by golly," said Paul, "whyn't you go back to the range and shoot at bulls-eyes?"

"I'd just as soon," said Miranda, "only like this, we walk around more."

"Well, you just stay behind and stop spoiling my shots," said Paul, who, when he made a kill, wanted to be certain he had made it. Miranda, who alone brought down a bird once in twenty rounds, always claimed as her own any game they got when they fired at the same moment. It was tiresome and unfair and her brother was sick of it.

"Now, the first dove we see, or the first rabbit, is mine," he told her. "And the next will be yours. Remember that and don't get smarty."

"What about snakes?" asked Miranda idly. "Can I have the first snake?"

Waving her thumb gently and watching her gold ring glitter, Miranda lost interest in shooting. She was wearing her summer roughing outfit: dark blue overalls, a light blue shirt, a hired-man's straw hat and thick brown sandals. Her brother had the same outfit except his was a sober hickory-nut color. Ordinarily Miranda preferred her overalls to any other dress, though it was making rather a scandal in the countryside, for the year was 1903, and in the back country the law of female decorum had teeth in it. Her father had been criticized for letting his girls dress like boys and go careering around astride barebacked horses. Big sister Maria, the really independent and fearless one, in spite of her rather affected ways, rode at a dead run with only a rope knotted around her horse's nose. It was said the motherless family was running down, with the grandmother no longer there to hold it together. It was known that she had discriminated against her son Harry in her will, and that he was in straits about money. Some of his old neighbors reflected with vicious satisfaction that now he would probably not be so stiff-necked, nor have any more high-stepping horses either. Miranda knew this, though she could not say how. She had met along the road old women of the kind who smoked corn-cob pipes, who had treated her grandmother with most sincere respect. They slanted their gummy old eyes side-ways at the granddaughter and said, "Ain't you ashamed of yoself, Missy? It's aginst the Scriptures to dress like that. Whut yo Pappy thinkin about?" Miranda, with her powerful social sense, which was like a fine set of antennae radiating from every pore of her skin, would feel ashamed because she knew well it was rude and ill-bred to shock anybody, even bad-tempered old crones, though she had faith in her father's judgment and was perfectly comfortable in the clothes. Her father had said, "They're just what you need, and they'll save your dresses for school . . ." This sounded quite simple and natural to her. She had been brought up in rigorous economy. Wastefulness was vulgar. It was also a sin. These were truths; she had heard them repeated many times and never once disputed.

Now the ring, shining with the serene purity of fine gold on her rather grubby thumb, turned her feelings against her overalls and sockless feet, toes sticking through the thick brown leather straps. She wanted to go back to the farmhouse, take a good cold bath, dust herself with plenty of Maria's violet talcum powder—provided Maria was not present to object, of course—put on the thinnest, most becoming dress she owned, with a big sash, and sit in a wicker chair under the trees . . . These things were not all she wanted, of course; she had vague stirrings of desire for luxury and a grand way of living which could not take precise form in her imagination but were founded on family legend of past wealth and leisure. These immediate comforts were what she could have, and she wanted them at once. She lagged rather far behind Paul, and once she thought of just turning back without a word and going home. She stopped, thinking that Paul would never do that to her, and so she would have to tell him. When a rabbit leaped, she let Paul have it without dispute. He killed it with one shot.

When she came up with him, he was already kneeling, examining the wound, the rabbit trailing from his hands. "Right through the head," he said complacently, as if he had aimed for it. He took out his sharp, competent bowie knife and started to skin the body. He did it very cleanly and quickly. Uncle Jimbilly knew how to prepare the skins so that Miranda always had fur coats for her dolls, for though she never cared much for her dolls she liked seeing them in fur coats. The children knelt facing each other over the dead animal. Miranda watched admiringly while her brother stripped the skin away as if he were taking off a glove. The flayed flesh emerged dark scarlet, sleek, firm; Miranda with thumb and finger felt the long fine muscles with the silvery flat strips binding them to the joints. Brother lifted the oddly bloated belly. "Look," he said, in a low amazed voice. "It was going to have young ones."

Very carefully he slit the thin flesh from the center ribs to the flanks, and a scarlet bag appeared. He slit again and pulled the bag open, and there lay a bundle of tiny rabbits, each wrapped in a thin scarlet veil. The brother pulled these off and there they were, dark gray, their sleek wet down lying in minute even ripples, like a baby's head just washed, their unbelievably small delicate ears folded close, their little blind faces almost featureless.

Miranda said, "Oh, I want to see," under her breath. She looked and looked—excited but not frightened, for she was accustomed to the sight of animals killed in hunting—filled with pity and astonishment and a kind of shocked delight in the wonderful little creatures for their own sakes, they were so pretty. She touched one of them ever so carefully. "Ah, there's blood running over them," she said and began to tremble without knowing why. Yet she wanted most deeply to see and to know. Having seen, she felt at once as if she had known all along. The very memory of her former ignorance faded, she had always known just this. No one had ever told her anything outright, she had been rather unobservant of the animal life around her because she was so accustomed to animals. They seemed simply disorderly and unaccountably rude in their habits, but altogether natural and not very interesting. Her brother had spoken as if he had known about everything all along. He may have seen all this before. He had never said a word to her, but she knew now a part at least of what he knew. She understood a little of the secret, formless intuitions in her own mind and body, which had been clearing up, taking form, so gradually and so steadily she had not realized that she was learning what she had to know. Paul said cautiously, as if he were talking about something forbidden: "They were just about ready to be born." His voice dropped on the last word. "I know," said Miranda, "like kittens. I know, like babies." She was quietly and terribly agitated, standing again with her rifle under her arm, looking down at the bloody heap. "I don't want the skin," she said, "I won't have it." Paul buried the young rabbits again in their mother's body, wrapped the skin around her, carried her to a clump of sage bushes, and hid her away. He came out again at once and said to Miranda, with an eager friendliness, a confidential tone quite unusual in him, as if he were taking her into an important secret on equal terms: "Listen now. Now you listen to me, and don't ever forget. Don't you ever tell a living soul that you saw this. Don't tell a soul. Don't tell Dad because I'll get into trouble. He'll say I'm leading you into things you ought not to do. He's always saying that. So now don't you go and forget and blab out sometime the way you're always doing . . . Now, that's a secret. Don't you tell."

Miranda never told, she did not even wish to tell anybody. She thought about the whole worrisome affair with confused unhappiness for a few days. Then it sank quietly into her mind and was heaped over by accumulated thousands of impressions, for nearly twenty years. One day she was picking her path among the puddles and crushed refuse of a market street in a strange city of a strange country, when without warning, plain and clear in its true colors as if she looked through a frame upon a scene that had not stirred nor changed since the moment it happened, the episode of that far-off day leaped from its burial place before her mind's eye. She was so reasonlessly horrified she halted suddenly staring, the scene before her eyes dimmed by the vision back of them. An Indian vendor had held up before her a tray of dyed sugar sweets, in the shapes of all kinds of small creatures: birds, baby chicks, baby rabbits, lambs, baby pigs. They were in gay colors and smelled of vanilla, maybe. . . . It was a very hot day and the smell in the market, with its piles of raw flesh and wilting flowers, was like the mingled sweetness and corruption she had smelled that other day in the empty cemetery at home: the day she had remembered always until now vaguely as the time she and her brother had found treasure in the opened graves. Instantly upon this thought the dreadful vision faded, and she saw clearly her brother, whose childhood face she had forgotten, standing again in the blazing sunshine, again twelve years old, a pleased sober smile in his eyes, turning the silver dove over and over in his hands.

Mood and Atmosphere

Mood and atmosphere in a story can be generated by a particular place, such as the Dublin of Joyce's "Counterparts," or result more vaguely from an idea or a view of life, as in Katherine Anne Porter's story. The mood of "The Grave," an outgrowth of the relationship between youth and death, is something intangible, indefinite, and mysterious. It contains no outlines, no substance, and its possibilities are almost infinite. All we know is that Miss Porter has generated a certain feeling in her material, what we loosely call mood or atmosphere.

1 The dominant image in this very short story is the grave. As the image is repeated in various forms and contexts, it takes on symbolic importance; in effect, it helps create the "mood" of the story.

How does the image of the grave operate at the beginning of the story in connection with the grandparents?

2 What is the function in the graveyard scene of the gold ring and the screw head for the coffin?

3 Does the stress on the gun, the shooting habits of the children, and their manner of dress have any relevance to the symbol of the grave? If not, are they irrelevant?

If you feel they are irrelevant, then a good deal of the story becomes ineffective and you should be ready to back up that opinion with solid argument. If you feel that the story is effective, then each part should contribute to the whole, and you must be prepared to see the various relationships.

4 The scene with the dead rabbit is the culmination of the "grave" image. This scene, symbolic as well as tangible, brings together the substance of the story, for here the two children realize things they had hardly thought about before.

What kind of change do you sense in the children? What do they recognize? Why does the presence of rabbit fetuses so impress them? As the author says, Miranda, and surely her brother, knew about animals. Yet Miranda "began to tremble without knowing why." Do you know why? What relevance does all this have to the image of the grave at the beginning of the story?

5 Why should Paul warn Miranda to keep the episode with the rabbit a secret? And why does Miranda reject the rabbit skin for her dolls?

6 The final paragraph, all narrative, rounds off the idea of the grave. Why did Miss Porter include this section at all? Couldn't the story have ended with the rabbit episode? Why is the now-grown Miranda momentarily horrified by the vision from the past, a memory intact in all its details? Why is the memory described in terms of "sweetness and corruption"?

7 The final lines, in which the dreadful vision fades, would appear to contradict what comes earlier in the paragraph. Is the ending contradictory, or is it a new development? Does the sunny nature of the ending (full of words like "childhood," "blazing sunshine," "smile," "the silver dove") destroy the image of the grave, or give it a further dimension?

Characterization

1 In a story where one aspect dominates, as mood does here, often characterization is not sharply defined; frequently, the character or characters take on general qualities. Miranda, for example, may seem to stand for all young girls rather than one particular girl. Do you think that this is true? Or do you think that Miss Porter has created enough details to make Miranda substantial in her own right? If so, supply some of these details and show how they add to her particularity.

2 Consider that possibly both arguments are correct, that Miranda is at the same time both an individual and a type. Try to supply details and hints that would support such duality. Can the same thing be said of Paul, or is he too generalized?

THREE

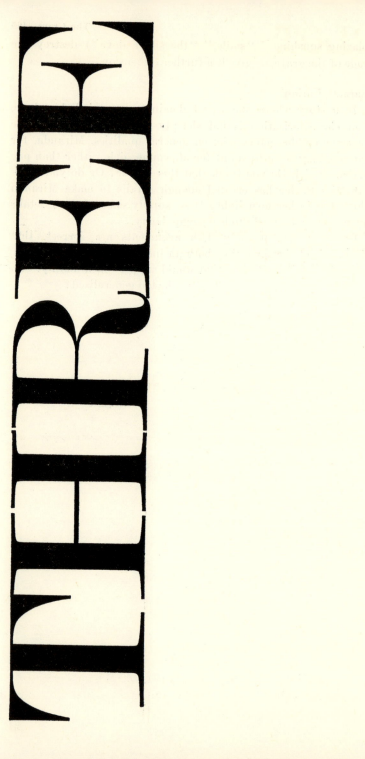

PLOT

At one time in the development of the short story, plot predominated. Stories were often thought of as forms of pure entertainment, and one spoke of a good plot or a compelling plot. One read the story, often enough, for the plot; and if the plot flagged, so did interest.

This conception of a story has changed. Plot has, as it were, suffered a downfall. In fact, critics now hardly speak of plot as such—it has become a component of other elements, to such an extent that it is difficult to find modern stories featuring plot. In Conrad's use of plot, for example, any discussion immediately carries the reader off into character, theme, even setting and atmosphere. Like climax and denouement, plot can barely be identified; and although this may be a good thing for the development of the short story, it is often frustrating for the reader.

Perhaps it is best to start with some old-fashioned questions about plot and see if they apply. First, try to begin with a plot summary. That is, try to put into words what the story says (not its meaning, for that comes closer to theme). You will probably find that it doesn't say very much. Don't be discouraged. Plot is only one element. Is the story bare (that is, limited in events), or is it crowded (panoramic)? How are the parts connected? Can you see where one element of plot ends and the other begins? Or does the author disguise his "seams" so well that elements blend imperceptibly?

You may also ask yourself about the logic of the plot—do events occur naturally on the basis of cause and effect, or do events seem to arise without any basis in fact? Whatever the case, does it appear to be part of the author's purpose; that is, does he want consistency or fragmentation? Can you discern any artificiality in the writer's attitude; that is, does he contrive any event solely to gain an effect, without regard for the realities of human nature?

Can you also discern any rising action in the plot toward some climax, however vague and indirect it may be? How does the author build toward this climax, if it does exist? Some of the author's devices may be atmosphere, the use of symbols, recurring motifs, contrasts, ironies—all these can help achieve unity of plot and make it alive. Language itself may be the means: through the rise and fall of intense and slack words, the author may manipulate both you and the plot.

In the long run, does the plot convey a sense of totality? Or is it fragmented into splinter groups unconnected to each other? Have the characters been sufficiently dramatized so that they contribute to the overall plot?

Many of these questions may be difficult to answer. In fact, with many short stories, you cannot begin to answer several of these questions. The stories work by other means, and the plot is like an iceberg, seven-eighths submerged and hardly discernible to the most practiced eye. Do not feel too frustrated at first—you may be looking for something that doesn't exist. Plot and plotting are no longer so important. The question now is one of *meaning,* and meaning often comes to us through devious methods, chiefly through atmosphere and character.

MUJINA

Lafcadio Hearn

On the Akasaka Road, in Tōkyō, there is a slope called Kii-no-kuni-zaka,—which means the Slope of the Province of Kii. I do not know why it is called the Slope of the Province of Kii. On one side of this slope you see an ancient moat, deep and very wide, with high green banks rising up to some place of gardens;—and on the other side of the road extend the long and lofty walls of an imperial palace. Before the era of street-lamps and jinrikishas, this neighborhood was very lonesome after dark; and belated pedestrians would go miles out of their way rather than mount the Kii-no-kuni-zaka, alone, after sunset.

All because of a Mujina that used to walk there.

The last man who saw the Mujina was an old merchant of the Kyōbashi quarter, who died about thirty years ago. This is the story, as he told it:—

One night, at a late hour, he was hurrying up the Kii-no-kuni-zaka, when he perceived a woman crouching by the moat, all alone, and weeping bitterly. Fearing that she intended to drown herself, he stopped to offer her any assistance or consolation in his power. She appeared to be a slight and graceful person, handsomely dressed; and her hair was arranged like that of a young girl of good family. "O-jochū,"[1] he exclaimed, approaching her,—"O-jochū, do not cry like that! . . . Tell me what the trouble is; and if there be any way to help you, I shall be glad to help you." (He really meant what he said; for he was a very kind man.) But she continued to weep,—hiding her face from him with one of her long sleeves. "O-jochū," he said again, as gently as he could,—"please, please listen to me! . . . This is no place for a young lady at night! Do not cry, I implore you!—only tell me how I may be of some help to you!" Slowly she rose up, but turned her back to him, and continued to moan and sob behind her sleeve. He laid his hand lightly upon her shoulder, and pleaded:—"O-jochū!—O-jochū!—O-jochū! . . . Listen to me, just for one little moment! . . . O-jochū!—O-jochū!" . . . Then that O-jochū turned round, and dropped her sleeve, and stroked her face with her hand;—and the man saw that she had no eyes or nose or mouth,—and he screamed and ran away.

[1] O-jochū ("honorable damsel"),—a polite form of address used in speaking to a young lady whom one does not know.

Up Kii-no-kuni-zaka he ran and ran; and all was black and empty before him. On and on he ran, never daring to look back; and at last he saw a lantern, so far away that it looked like the gleam of a firefly; and he made for it. It proved to be only the lantern of an itinerant *soba*-seller,[2] who had set down his stand by the road-side; but any light and any human companionship was good after that experience; and he flung himself down at the feet of the *soba*-seller, crying out, "Aa!—aa!!—*aa!!!*" . . . "*Koré! Koré!*" roughly exclaimed the *soba*-man. "Here! what is the matter with you? Anybody hurt you?"

"No—nobody hurt me," panted the other,—"only . . . *Aa! —aa!*"

"Only scared you?" queried the peddler, unsympathetically. "Robbers?"

"Not robbers,—not robbers," gasped the terrified man. . . . "I saw . . . I saw a woman—by the moat—and she showed me . . . *Aa!* I cannot tell you what she showed me!" . . .

"Hé! Was it anything like this she showed you?" cried the *soba*-man, stroking his own face—which therewith became like unto an Egg— And simultaneously, the light went out.

Obviously this story differs from any of the others in this volume and possibly from any other short story you have ever read. There is, indeed, a question of whether it can strictly be called a short story. But the story form is large and embraces a multitude of types.

"Mujina" falls into the general type which embraces fantasy, fairy tale, tall tale, legend, and folk tale. It is perhaps closest to the fantasy or fairy tale in that its form is so fluid that character, theme, plot, and narrative are all interchangeable. Also, its final effect involves a feeling, an attitude, an inexpressible substance. And the very recessiveness of plot is related to this effect.

Plot

1 By comparison with the other stories in this section, "Mujina" is almost totally lacking in plot elements. There are two brief actions but hardly anything that qualifies as plot. Does this bareness render the story ineffective? Can a story be very

[2] *Soba* is a preparation of buckwheat, somewhat resembling vermicelli.

slight in plot and yet exhibit the quality essential to all successful fiction—significant order, or coherence? Would you say "Mujina" has this quality?

2 To answer question 1 in any detail, you must ask yourself: What is the relation of the plot to mood, theme, and character? For mood and theme the relation can be worked out, but the characterization is as slight as the plot itself. Is this second slightness a failure on the part of Hearn? Or is "Mujina" a story that depends upon other elements for its effect?

3 What possible meaning does the ending—with the light going out—have? Does it turn us back toward some basic quality in the story itself, a quality that modifies feeling or attitude in the reader? That is, does the ending leave us liberated or chilled or saddened or enlarged in our sympathies?

4 This is known as a *framework* plot; that is, the first-person narrator tells us a story that he has heard from someone else, without himself ever entering into the story. Is the framework approach appropriate for this type of story? Why?

Mood

1 How does the first paragraph contribute to the mood of fantasy?

2 Even before that, what does the title suggest? What is the "Mujina"? Does Hearn ever define it? How do you know what it is supposed to be? Does this indefiniteness hurt or hinder the story? Does it fit into the recessiveness of the plot?

3 Before the woman turns and shows her face, do you expect something strange? Through what clues are you led to such an expectation (if you are)? Are they sufficiently obvious? Or are they subtle?

4 What function does the *soba*-seller's lantern play in creating atmosphere?

5 Is the old merchant-narrator going insane? Is the tale possibly a dream? Does he imagine these sights? Turn back to the beginning of the tale for clues concerning the nature of his experience.

6 As a fantasy, this tale leaves us with a sense of wonderment—we recognize that there are dimensions to the world beyond ordinary comprehension. Eastern religions, of course, stress just this part of the human experience. What are some of the possibilities of this extrasensory vision of a twilight world? Can you think of anything in your own experience to approximate it?

7 How does the style of this tale relate to the mood? Is it decorative, clean, slow, rapid? Does the style add to the extrasensory dimension or distract us from it?

8 Dylan Thomas's "One Warm Saturday" is also a fantasy. How does it differ from "Mujina"? What conclusions can you draw about the type of story we loosely call fantasy?

A GOOD MAN IS HARD TO FIND

Flannery O'Connor

The grandmother didn't want to go to Florida. She wanted to visit some of her connections in east Tennessee and she was seizing at every chance to change Bailey's mind. Bailey was the son she lived with, her only boy. He was sitting on the edge of his chair at the table, bent over the orange sports section of the *Journal.* "Now look here, Bailey," she said, "see here, read this," and she stood with one hand on her thin hip and the other rattling the newspaper at his bald head. "Here this fellow that calls himself The Misfit is aloose from the Federal Pen and headed toward Florida and you read here what it says he did to these people. Just you read it. I wouldn't take my children in any direction with a criminal like that aloose in it. I couldn't answer to my conscience if I did."

Bailey didn't look up from his reading so she wheeled around then and faced the children's mother, a young woman in slacks, whose face was as broad and innocent as a cabbage and was tied around with a green head-kerchief that had two points on the top like rabbit's ears. She was sitting on the sofa, feeding the baby his apricots out of a jar. "The children have been to Florida before," the old lady said. "You all ought to take them somewhere else for a change so they would see different parts of the world and be broad. They never have been to east Tennessee."

The children's mother didn't seem to hear her but the eight-year-old boy, John Wesley, a stocky child with glasses, said, "If you don't want to go to Florida, why dontcha stay at home?" He and the little girl, June Star, were reading the funny papers on the floor.

"She wouldn't stay at home to be queen for a day," June Star said without raising her yellow head.

"Yes and what would you do if this fellow, The Misfit, caught you?" the grandmother asked.

"I'd smack his face," John Wesley said.

"She wouldn't stay at home for a million bucks," June Star said. "Afraid she'd miss something. She has to go everywhere we go."

"All right, Miss," the grandmother said. "Just remember that the next time you want me to curl your hair."

June Star said her hair was naturally curly.

The next morning the grandmother was the first one in the car, ready to go. She had her big black valise that looked like the head of a hippopotamus in one corner, and underneath it she was hiding a basket with Pitty Sing, the cat, in it. She didn't intend for the cat to be left alone in the house for three days because he would miss her too much and she was afraid he might brush against one of the gas burners and accidentally asphyxiate himself. Her son, Bailey, didn't like to arrive at a motel with a cat.

She sat in the middle of the back seat with John Wesley and June Star on either side of her. Bailey and the children's mother and the baby sat in front and they left Atlanta at eight forty-five with the mileage on the car at 55890. The grandmother wrote this down because she thought it would be interesting to say how many miles they had been when they got back. It took them twenty minutes to reach the outskirts of the city.

The old lady settled herself comfortably, removing her white cotton gloves and putting them up with her purse on the shelf in front of the back window. The children's mother still had on slacks and still had her head tied up in a green kerchief, but the grandmother had on a navy blue straw sailor hat with a bunch of white violets on the brim and a navy blue dress with a small white dot in the print. Her collars and cuffs were white organdy trimmed with lace and at her neckline she had pinned a purple spray of cloth violets containing a sachet. In case of an accident, anyone seeing her dead on the highway would know at once that she was a lady.

She said she thought it was going to be a good day for driving, neither too hot nor too cold, and she cautioned Bailey that the speed limit was fifty-five miles an hour and that the patrolmen hid themselves behind billboards and small clumps of trees and sped out after you before you had a chance to slow down. She pointed out interesting details of the scenery: Stone Mountain; the blue granite that in some places came up to both sides of the highway; the brilliant red clay banks slightly streaked with purple; and the various crops that made rows of green lace-work on the ground. The trees were full of silver-white sunlight and the meanest of them sparkled. The children were reading comic magazines and their mother had gone back to sleep.

"Let's go through Georgia fast so we won't have to look at it much," John Wesley said.

"If I were a little boy," said the grandmother, "I wouldn't talk about my native state that way. Tennessee has the mountains and Georgia has the hills."

"Tennessee is just a hillbilly dumping ground," John Wesley said, "and Georgia is a lousy state too."

"You said it," June Star said.

"In my time," said the grandmother, folding her thin veined fingers, "children were more respectful of their native states and their parents and everything else. People did right then. Oh look at the cute little pickaninny!" she said and pointed to a Negro child standing in the door of a shack. "Wouldn't that make a picture, now?" she asked and they all turned and looked at the little Negro out of the back window. He waved.

"He didn't have any britches on," June Star said.

"He probably didn't have any," the grandmother explained. "Little niggers in the country don't have things like we do. If I could paint, I'd paint that picture," she said.

The children exchanged comic books.

The grandmother offered to hold the baby and the children's mother passed him over the front seat to her. She set him on her knee and bounced him and told him about the things they were passing. She rolled her eyes and screwed up her mouth and stuck her leathery thin face into his smooth bland one. Occasionally he gave her a faraway smile. They passed a large cotton field with five or six graves fenced in the middle of it, like a small island. "Look at the graveyard!" the grandmother said, pointing it out. "That was the old family burying ground. That belonged to the plantation."

"Where's the plantation?" John Wesley asked.

"Gone With the Wind," said the grandmother. "Ha. Ha."

When the children finished all the comic books they had brought, they opened the lunch and ate it. The grandmother ate a peanut butter sandwich and an olive and would not let the children throw the box and the paper napkins out the window. When there was nothing else to do they played a game by choosing a cloud and making the other two guess what shape it suggested. John Wesley took one the shape of a cow and June Star guessed a cow and John Wesley said, no, an automobile, and June Star said he didn't play fair, and they began to slap each other over the grandmother.

The grandmother said she would tell them a story if they would keep quiet. When she told a story, she rolled her eyes and waved her head and was very dramatic. She said once when she was a maiden lady she had been courted by a Mr. Edgar Atkins Teagarden from Jasper, Georgia. She said he was a very good-looking man and a gentleman and that he brought her a watermelon every Saturday afternoon with his initials cut in it, E. A. T. Well, one Saturday, she said, Mr. Teagarden brought the watermelon and there was nobody at home and he left it on the front porch and returned in his buggy to Jasper, but she never got the watermelon, she said, because a nigger boy ate it when he saw the initials, E. A. T.! This story tickled John Wesley's funny bone and he giggled and giggled but June Star didn't think it was any good. She said she wouldn't marry a man that just brought her a watermelon on Saturday. The grandmother said she would have done well to marry Mr. Teagarden because he was a gentleman and had bought Coca-Cola stock when it first came out and that he had died only a few years ago, a very wealthy man.

They stopped at The Tower for barbecued sandwiches. The Tower was a part stucco and part wood filling station and dance hall set in a clearing outside of Timothy. A fat man named Red Sammy Butts ran it and there were signs stuck here and there on the building and for miles up and down the highway saying, TRY RED SAMMY'S FAMOUS BARBECUE. NONE LIKE FAMOUS RED SAMMY'S! RED SAM! THE FAT BOY WITH THE HAPPY LAUGH. A VETERAN! RED SAMMY'S YOUR MAN!

Red Sammy was lying on the bare ground outside The Tower with his head under a truck while a gray monkey about a foot high, chained to a small chinaberry tree, chattered nearby. The monkey sprang back into the tree and got on the highest limb as soon as he saw the children jump out of the car and run toward him.

Inside, The Tower was a long dark room with a counter at one end and tables at the other and dancing space in the middle. They all sat down at a board table next to the nickelodeon and Red Sam's wife, a tall burnt-brown woman with hair and eyes lighter than her skin, came and took their order. The children's mother put a dime in the machine and played "The Tennessee Waltz," and the grandmother said that tune always made her want to dance. She asked Bailey if he would like to dance but he only glared at her. He didn't have a naturally sunny disposition like she did and trips made him nervous. The grandmother's brown eyes were very bright. She swayed her head from side to side and pretended she was dancing in her chair. June Star said play something she could tap to so the children's mother put in another dime and played a fast number and June Star stepped out onto the dance floor and did her tap routine.

"Ain't she cute?" Red Sam's wife said, leaning over the counter. "Would you like to come be my little girl?"

"No I certainly wouldn't," June Star said. "I wouldn't live in a broken-down place like this for a million bucks!" and she ran back to the table.

"Ain't she cute?" the woman repeated, stretching her mouth politely.

"Arn't you ashamed?" hissed the grandmother.

Red Sam came in and told his wife to quit lounging on the counter and hurry up with these people's order. His khaki trousers reached just to his hip bones and his stomach hung over them like a sack of meal swaying under his shirt. He came over and sat down at a table nearby and let out a combination sigh and yodel. "You can't win," he said. "You can't win," and he wiped his sweating red face off with a gray handkerchief. "These days you don't know who to trust," he said. "Ain't that the truth?"

"People are certainly not nice like they used to be," said the grandmother.

"Two fellers come in here last week," Red Sammy said, "driving a Chrysler. It was a old beat-up car but it was a good one and these boys looked all right to me. Said they worked at the mill and you know I let them fellers charge the gas they bought? Now why did I do that?"

"Because you're a good man!" the grandmother said at once.

"Yes'm, I suppose so," Red Sam said as if he were struck with this answer.

His wife brought the orders, carrying the five plates all at once without a tray, two in each hand and one balanced on her arm. "It isn't a soul in this green world of God's that you can trust," she said. "And I don't count nobody out of that, not nobody," she repeated, looking at Red Sammy.

"Did you read about that criminal, The Misfit, that's escaped?" asked the grandmother.

"I wouldn't be a bit surprised if he didn't attact this place right here," said the woman. "If he hears about it being here, I wouldn't be none surprised to see him. If he hears it's two cent in the cash register, I wouldn't be a tall surprised if he . . ."

"That'll do," Red Sam said. "Go bring these people their Co'-Colas," and the woman went off to get the rest of the order.

"A good man is hard to find," Red Sammy said. "Everything is getting terrible. I remember the day you could go off and leave your screen door unlatched. Not no more."

He and the grandmother discussed better times. The old lady said that in her opinion Europe was entirely to blame for the way things were now. She said the way Europe acted you would think we were made of money and Red Sam said it was no use talking about it, she was exactly right. The children ran outside into the white sunlight and looked at the monkey in the lacy chinaberry tree. He was busy catching fleas on himself and biting each one carefully between his teeth as if it were a delicacy.

They drove off again into the hot afternoon. The grandmother took cat naps and woke up every few minutes with her own snoring. Outside of Toombsboro she woke up and recalled an old plantation that she had visited in this neighborhood once when she was a young lady. She said the house had six white columns across the front and that there was an avenue of oaks leading up to it and two little wooden trellis arbors on either side in front where you sat down with your suitor after a stroll in the garden. She recalled exactly which road to turn off to get to it. She knew that Bailey would not be willing to lose any time looking at an old house, but the more she talked about it, the more she wanted to see it once again and find out if the little twin arbors were still standing. "There was a secret panel in this house," she said craftily, not telling the truth but wishing that she were, "and the story went that all the family silver was hidden in it when Sherman came through but it was never found . . ."

"Hey!" John Wesley said. "Let's go see it! We'll find it! We'll poke all the woodwork and find it! Who lives there? Where do you turn off at? Hey Pop, can't we turn off there?"

"We never have seen a house with a secret panel!" June Star shrieked. "Let's go to the house with the secret panel! Hey Pop, can't we go see the house with the secret panel!"

"It's not far from here, I know," the grandmother said. "It wouldn't take over twenty minutes."

Bailey was looking straight ahead. His jaw was as rigid as a horseshoe. "No," he said.

The children began to yell and scream that they wanted to see the house with the secret panel. John Wesley kicked the back of the front seat and June Star hung over her mother's shoulder and whined desperately into her ear that they never had any fun even on their vacation, that they could never do what THEY wanted to do. The baby began to scream and John Wesley kicked the back of the seat so hard that his father could feel the blows in his kidney.

"All right!" he shouted and drew the car to a stop at the side of the road. "Will you all shut up? Will you all just shut up for one second? If you don't shut up, we won't go anywhere."

"It would be very educational for them," the grandmother murmured.

"All right," Bailey said, "but get this: this is the only time we're going to stop for anything like this. This is the one and only time."

"The dirt road that you have to turn down is about a mile back," the grandmother directed. "I marked it when we passed."

"A dirt road," Bailey groaned.

After they had turned around and were headed toward the dirt road, the grandmother recalled other points about the house, the beautiful glass over the front doorway and the candle-lamp in the hall. John Wesley said that the secret panel was probably in the fireplace.

"You can't go inside this house," Bailey said. "You don't know who lives there."

"While you all talk to the people in front, I'll run around behind and get in a window," John Wesley suggested.

"We'll all stay in the car," his mother said.

They turned onto the dirt road and the car raced roughly along in a swirl of pink dust. The grandmother recalled the times when there were no paved roads and thirty miles was a day's journey. The dirt road was hilly and there were sudden washes in it and sharp curves on dangerous embankments. All at once they would be on a hill, looking down over the blue tops of trees for miles around, then the next minute, they would be in a red depression with the dust-coated trees looking down on them.

"This place had better turn up in a minute," Bailey said, "or I'm going to turn around."

The road looked as if no one had traveled on it in months.

"It's not much farther," the grandmother said and just as she said it, a horrible thought came to her. The thought was so embarrassing that she turned red in the face and her eyes dilated and her feet jumped up, upsetting her valise in the corner. The instant the valise moved, the newspaper top she had over the basket under it rose with a snarl and Pitty Sing, the cat, sprang onto Bailey's shoulder.

The children were thrown to the floor and their mother, clutching the baby, was thrown out the door onto the ground; the old lady was thrown into the front seat. The car turned over once and landed right-side-up in a gulch off the side of the road. Bailey remained in the driver's seat with the cat—gray-striped with a broad white face and an orange nose—clinging to his neck like a caterpillar.

As soon as the children saw they could move their arms and legs, they scrambled out of the car, shouting, "We've had an ACCIDENT!" The grandmother was curled up under the dashboard, hoping she was injured so that Bailey's wrath would not come down on her all at once. The horrible thought she had had before the accident was that the house she had remembered so vividly was not in Georgia but in Tennessee.

Bailey removed the cat from his neck with both hands and flung it out the window against the side of a pine tree. Then he got out of the car and started looking for the children's mother. She was sitting against the side of the red gutted ditch, holding the screaming baby, but she only had a cut down her face and a broken shoulder. "We've had an ACCIDENT!" the children screamed in a frenzy of delight.

"But nobody's killed," June Star said with disappointment as the grandmother limped out of the car, her hat still pinned to her head but the broken front brim standing up at a jaunty angle and the violet spray hanging off the side. They all sat down in the ditch, except the children, to recover from the shock. They were all shaking.

"Maybe a car will come along," said the children's mother hoarsely.

"I believe I have injured an organ," said the grandmother, pressing her side, but no one answered her. Bailey's teeth were clattering. He had on a yellow sport shirt with bright blue parrots designed in it and his face was as yellow as the shirt. The grandmother decided that she would not mention that the house was in Tennessee.

The road was about ten feet above and they could see only the tops of the trees on the other side of it. Behind the ditch they were sitting in there were more woods, tall and dark and deep. In a few minutes they saw a car some distance away on top of a hill, coming slowly as if the occupants were watching them. The grandmother stood up and waved both arms dramatically to attract their attention. The car continued to come on slowly, disappeared around a bend and appeared again, moving even slower, on top of the hill they had gone over. It was a big black battered hearse-like automobile. There were three men in it.

It came to a stop just over them and for some minutes, the driver looked down with a steady expressionless gaze to where they were sitting, and didn't speak. Then he turned his head and muttered something to the other two and they got out. One was a fat boy in black trousers and a red sweat shirt with a silver stallion embossed on the front of it. He moved around on the right side of them and stood staring, his mouth partly open in a kind of loose grin. The other had on khaki pants and a blue striped coat and a gray hat pulled down very low, hiding most of his face. He came around slowly on the left side. Neither spoke.

The driver got out of the car and stood by the side of it, looking down at them. He was an older man than the other two. His hair was just beginning to gray and he wore silver-rimmed spectacles that give him a scholarly look. He had a long creased face and didn't have on any shirt or undershirt. He had on blue jeans that were too tight for him and was holding a black hat and a gun. The two boys also had guns.

"We've had an ACCIDENT!" the children screamed.

The grandmother had the peculiar feeling that the bespectacled man was someone she knew. His face was as familiar to her as if she had known him all her life but she could not recall who he was. He moved away from the car and began to come down the embankment, placing his feet carefully so that he wouldn't slip. He had on tan and white shoes and no socks, and his ankles were red and thin. "Good afternoon," he said. "I see you all had you a little spill."

"We turned over twice!" said the grandmother.

"Oncet," he corrected. "We seen it happen. Try their car and see will it run, Hiram," he said quietly to the boy with the gray hat.

"What you got that gun for?" John Wesley asked. "Whatcha gonna do with that gun?"

"Lady," the man said to the children's mother, "would you mind calling them children to sit down by you? Children make me nervous. I want all you all to sit down right together there where you're at."

"What are you telling US what to do for?" June Star asked.

Behind them the line of woods gaped like a dark open mouth. "Come here," said their mother.

"Look here now," Bailey began suddenly, "we're in a predicament! We're in . . ."

The grandmother shrieked. She scrambled to her feet and stood staring. "You're The Misfit!" she said. "I recognized you at once!"

"Yes'm," the man said, smiling slightly as if he were pleased in spite of himself to be known, "but it would have been better for all of you, lady, if you hadn't of reckernized me."

Bailey turned his head sharply and said something to his mother that shocked even the children. The old lady began to cry and The Misfit reddened.

"Lady," he said, "don't you get upset. Sometimes a man says things he don't mean. I don't reckon he meant to talk to you thataway."

"You wouldn't shoot a lady, would you?" the grandmother said and removed a clean handkerchief from her cuff and began to slap at her eyes with it.

The Misfit pointed the toe of his shoe into the ground and made a little hole and then covered it up again. "I would hate to have to," he said.

"Listen," the grandmother almost screamed, "I know you're a good man. You don't look a bit like you have common blood. I know you must come from nice people!"

"Yes mam," he said, "finest people in the world." When he smiled he showed a row of strong white teeth. "God never made a finer woman than my mother and my daddy's heart was pure gold," he said. The boy with the red sweat shirt had come around behind them and was standing with his gun at his hip. The Misfit squatted down on the ground. "Watch them children, Bobby Lee," he said. "You know they make me nervous." He looked at the six of them huddled together in front of him and he seemed to be embarrassed as if he couldn't think of anything to say. "Ain't a cloud in the sky," he remarked, looking up at it. "Don't see no sun but don't see no cloud neither."

"Yes, it's a beautiful day," said the grandmother. "Listen," she said, "you shouldn't call yourself The Misfit because I know you're a good man at heart. I can just look at you and tell."

"Hush!" Bailey yelled. "Hush! Everybody shut up and let me handle this!" He was squatting in the position of a runner about to sprint forward but he didn't move.

"I pre-chate that, lady," The Misfit said and drew a little circle in the ground with the butt of his gun.

"It'll take a half a hour to fix this here car," Hiram called, looking over the raised hood of it.

"Well, first you and Bobby Lee get him and that little boy to step over yonder with you," The Misfit said, pointing to Bailey and John Wesley. "The boys want to ast you something," he said to Bailey. "Would you mind stepping back in them woods there with them?"

"Listen," Bailey began, "we're in a terrible predicament! Nobody realizes what this is," and his voice cracked. His eyes were as blue and intense as the parrots in his shirt and he remained perfectly still.

The grandmother reached up to adjust her hat brim as if she were going to the woods with him but it came off in her hand. She stood staring at it and after a second she let it fall on the ground. Hiram pulled Bailey up by the arm as if he were assisting an old man. John Wesley caught hold of his father's hand and Bobby Lee followed. They went off toward the woods and just as they reached the dark edge, Bailey turned and supporting himself against a gray naked pine trunk, he shouted, "I'll be back in a minute, Mamma, wait on me!"

"Come back this instant!" his mother shrilled but they all disappeared into the woods.

"Bailey Boy!" the grandmother called in a tragic voice but she found she was looking at The Misfit squatting on the ground in front of her. "I just know you're a good man," she said desperately. "You're not a bit common!"

"Nome, I ain't a good man," The Misfit said after a second as if he had considered her statement carefully, "but I ain't the worst in the world neither. My daddy said I was a different breed of dog from my brothers and sisters. 'You know,' Daddy said, 'it's some that can live their whole life out without asking about it and it's others has to know why it is, and this boy is one of the latters. He's going to be into everything!' " He put on his black hat and looked up suddenly and then away deep into the woods as if he were embarrassed again. "I'm sorry I don't have on a shirt before you ladies," he said, hunching his shoulders slightly. "We buried our clothes that we had on when we escaped and we're just making do until we can get better. We borrowed these from some folks we met," he explained.

"That's perfectly all right," the grandmother said. "Maybe Bailey has an extra shirt in his suitcase."

"I'll look and see terrectly," The Misfit said.

"Where are they taking him?" the children's mother screamed.

"Daddy was a card himself," The Misfit said. "You couldn't

put anything over on him. He never got in trouble with the Authorities though. Just had the knack of handling them.''

''You could be honest too if you'd only try,'' said the grandmother. ''Think how wonderful it would be to settle down and live a comfortable life and not have to think about somebody chasing you all the time.''

The Misfit kept scratching in the ground with the butt of his gun as if he were thinking about it. ''Yes'm, somebody is always after you,'' he murmured.

The grandmother noticed how thin his shoulder blades were just behind his hat because she was standing up looking down on him. ''Do you ever pray?'' she asked.

He shook his head. All she saw was the black hat wiggle between his shoulder blades. ''Nome,'' he said.

There was a pistol shot from the woods, followed closely by another. Then silence. The old lady's head jerked around. She could hear the wind move through the tree tops like a long satisfied insuck of breath. ''Bailey Boy!'' she called.

''I was a gospel singer for a while,'' The Misfit said. ''I been most everything. Been in the arm service, both land and sea, at home and abroad, been twict married, been an undertaker, been with the railroads, plowed Mother Earth, been in a tornado, seen a man burnt alive oncet,'' and he looked up at the children's mother and the little girl who were sitting close together, their faces white and their eyes glassy; ''I even seen a woman flogged,'' he said.

''Pray, pray,'' the grandmother began, ''pray, pray . . .''

''I never was a bad boy that I remember of,'' The Misfit said in an almost dreamy voice, ''but somewheres along the line I done something wrong and got sent to the penitentiary. I was buried alive,'' and he looked up and held her attention to him by a steady stare.

''That's when you should have started to pray,'' she said. ''What did you do to get sent to the penitentiary that first time?''

''Turn to the right, it was a wall,'' The Misfit said, looking up again at the cloudless sky. ''Turn to the left, it was a wall. Look up it was a ceiling, look down it was a floor. I forget what I done, lady. I set there and set there, trying to remember what it was I done and I ain't recalled it to this day. Oncet in a while, I would think it was coming to me, but it never come.''

''Maybe they put you in by mistake,'' the old lady said vaguely.

"Nome," he said. "It wasn't no mistake. They had the papers on me."

"You must have stolen something," she said.

The Misfit sneered slightly. "Nobody had nothing I wanted," he said. "It was a head-doctor at the penitentiary said what I had done was kill my daddy but I known that for a lie. My daddy died in nineteen ought nineteen of the epidemic flu and I never had a thing to do with it. He was buried in the Mount Hopewell Baptist churchyard and you can go there and see for yourself."

"If you would pray," the old lady said, "Jesus would help you."

"That's right," The Misfit said.

"Well then, why don't you pray?" she asked trembling with delight suddenly.

"I don't want no hep," he said. "I'm doing all right by myself."

Bobby Lee and Hiram came ambling back from the woods. Bobby Lee was dragging a yellow shirt with bright blue parrots in it.

"Thow me that shirt, Bobby Lee," The Misfit said. The shirt came flying at him and landed on his shoulder and he put it on. The grandmother couldn't name what the shirt reminded her of. "No, lady," The Misfit said while he was buttoning it up, "I found out the crime don't matter. You can do one thing or you can do another, kill a man or take a tire off his car, because sooner or later you're going to forget what it was you done and just be punished for it."

The children's mother had begun to make heaving noises as if she couldn't get her breath. "Lady," he asked, "would you and that little girl like to step off yonder with Bobby Lee and Hiram and join your husband?"

"Yes, thank you," the mother said faintly. Her left arm dangled helplessly and she was holding the baby, who had gone to sleep, in the other. "Hep that lady up, Hiram," The Misfit said as she struggled to climb out of the ditch, "and Bobby Lee, you hold onto that little girl's hand."

"I don't want to hold hands with him," June Star said. "He reminds me of a pig."

The fat boy blushed and laughed and caught her by the arm and pulled her off into the woods after Hiram and her mother.

Alone with The Misfit, the grandmother found that she had lost her voice. There was not a cloud in the sky nor any sun.

There was nothing around her but woods. She wanted to tell him that he must pray. She opened and closed her mouth several times before anything came out. Finally she found herself saying, "Jesus. Jesus," meaning, Jesus will help you, but the way she was saying it, it sounded as if she might be cursing.

"Yes'm," The Misfit said as if he agreed. "Jesus thown everything off balance. It was the same case with Him as with me except He hadn't committed any crime and they could prove I had committed one because they had the papers on me. Of course," he said, "they never shown me my papers. That's why I sign myself now. I said long ago, you get you a signature and sign everything you do and keep a copy of it. Then you'll know what you done and you can hold up the crime to the punishment and see do they match and in the end you'll have something to prove you ain't been treated right. I call myself The Misfit," he said, "because I can't make what all I done wrong fit what all I gone through in punishment."

There was a piercing scream from the woods, followed closely by a pistol report. "Does it seem right to you, lady, that one is punished a heap and another ain't punished at all?"

"Jesus!" the old lady cried. "You've got good blood! I know you wouldn't shoot a lady! I know you come from nice people! Pray! Jesus, you ought not to shoot a lady. I'll give you all the money I've got!"

"Lady," The Misfit said, looking beyond her far into the woods, "there never was a body that give the undertaker a tip."

There were two more pistol reports and the grandmother raised her head like a parched old turkey hen crying for water and called, "Bailey Boy, Bailey Boy!" as if her heart would break.

"Jesus was the only One that ever raised the dead," The Misfit continued, "and He shouldn't have done it. He thown everything off balance. If He did what He said, then it's nothing for you to do but thow away everything and follow Him, and if He didn't, then it's nothing for you to do but enjoy the few minutes you got left the best way you can—by killing somebody or burning down his house or doing some other meanness to him. No pleasure but meanness," he said and his voice had become almost a snarl.

"Maybe He didn't raise the dead," the old lady mumbled, not knowing what she was saying and feeling so dizzy that she sank down in the ditch with her legs twisted under her.

"I wasn't there so I can't say He didn't," The Misfit said. "I wisht I had of been there," he said, hitting the ground with his fist. "It ain't right I wasn't there because if I had of been there I would of known. Listen lady," he said in a high voice, "if I had of been there I would of known and I wouldn't be like I am now." His voice seemed about to crack and the grandmother's head cleared for an instant. She saw the man's face twisted close to her own as if he were going to cry and she murmured, "Why you're one of my babies. You're one of my own children!" She reached out and touched him on the shoulder. The Misfit sprang back as if a snake had bitten him and shot her three times through the chest. Then he put his gun down on the ground and took off his glasses and began to clean them.

Hiram and Bobby Lee returned from the woods and stood over the ditch, looking down at the grandmother who half sat and half lay in a puddle of blood with her legs crossed under her like a child's and her face smiling up at the cloudless sky.

Without his glasses, The Misfit's eyes were red-rimmed and pale and defenseless-looking. "Take her off and thow her where you thown the others," he said, picking up the cat that was rubbing itself against his leg.

"She was a talker, wasn't she?" Bobby Lee said, sliding down the ditch with a yodel.

"She would of been a good woman," The Misfit said, "if it had been somebody there to shoot her every minute of her life."

"Some fun!" Bobby Lee said.

"Shut up, Bobby Lee," The Misfit said. "It's no real pleasure in life."

Plot

Obviously the plot structure here has a weight different from the plot in Poe's "The Cask of Amontillado." It is, in fact, closer to Conrad's complex use of plot in "Il Conde," where plot is inextricably wedded to all other elements. In Poe's tale, plot is virtually exclusive—that is, plot is almost the sole element that keeps the story moving toward its conclusion. In "A Good Man Is Hard to Find," it is difficult to separate plot from the other components, especially character and theme. This is a story with a very powerful theme, one full of ironies and satirical intent.

Nevertheless, plot and plot structure, the working out of a given situation to its inevitable settlement, would appear to predominate.

1 How is character used to create elements of plot? That is, how does Miss O'Connor manipulate her characters so that their desires, even their errors, are translated into plot terms?
2 How does she prepare us for the appearance of The Misfit? Do you suspect early in the story that he will appear?
3 Does the method the author uses to confront the family with The Misfit seem forced or natural?
4 How much of the plot structure depends on coincidence? Are we prepared to believe the plot, or does its lack of probability detract from the value of the story?
5 How would you characterize the plotting? Is it linear (straightforward) or circular? How does this plot compare with the plots of the stories in this collection by Hearn, Wells, Stuart?
6 List some of the details that help contribute to the plot and plot structure. Consider all hints, gestures, foreshadowings.

Theme

A good deal of the theme revolves around the grandmother and her values; that is why the author filters so much of the trip through her eyes and mind. Not only is she the sole character in the family developed at any length, but she is also the one who makes the journey real for the reader. The trip is begun, the landscape is seen, stories are told—all through the grandmother as the medium of expression.

1 Describe in detail the type of person the grandmother is. Does she remind you of Saul Bellow's Hattie Waggoner in "Leaving the Yellow House"? Both are tenacious creatures with a hold upon life that far transcends their paltry social status. How does the grandmother begin to set the theme? Keep in mind that the theme, or purpose, comes out in the eventual confrontation between the family and The Misfit.
2 What is Miss O'Connor's attitude toward the grandmother? What does she find hollow in her? How does she show up her pretenses, her artificiality, her falseness without losing her as a character?
3 Why is there such a stress upon a "good man," from the title itself to the repeated comments of the grandmother to The Misfit? Is there irony in the title and the remark? Does the

grandmother really know anything about a "good man," or is she just parroting religious beliefs she has never examined?

4 What values does The Misfit live by? What does he mean when he says that "Jesus thown everything off balance"? And then, shortly afterward, he says that if Jesus did raise the dead, then one must follow Him; but if He didn't, then anything goes—killing, burning, any kind of meanness. What is The Misfit saying here? And why does the grandmother suddenly change her line of argument and agree that maybe Jesus didn't raise the dead? What does this imply about her?

5 Why does The Misfit shoot her when she touches him? Why at that moment?

6 Why is Miss O'Connor's conception of The Misfit as central to the theme as her conception of the grandmother? In the meeting of the two—as it were, a kind of uneven duel—the theme is suggested.

Style

1 Does the manner of presentation create a sense of artificiality or even fantasy? Give examples.

2 How does Miss O'Connor convey a sense of impending doom?

3 Does it seem unreal that the characters go to their death so easily, or does the stylization of the material remove this as a serious problem?

4 How does the style remove the shock of the brutal murders?

5 Do you see a type of mordant wit operating in this story? How is it possible that an author can treat such brutality and inhumanity wittily? If there is satire, what is Miss O'Connor satirizing?

THE COUNTRY OF THE BLIND

H. G. Wells

Three hundred miles and more from Chimborazo, one hundred from the snows of Cotopaxi, in the wildest wastes of Ecuador's Andes, there lies that mysterious mountain valley, cut off from the world of men, the Country of the Blind. Long years ago that valley lay so far open to the world that men might come at last through frightful gorges and over an icy pass into its equable meadows; and thither indeed men came, a family or so of Peruvian half-breeds fleeing from the lust and tyranny of an evil Spanish ruler. Then came the stupendous outbreak of Mindobamba, when it was night in Quito for seventeen days, and the water was boiling at Yaguachi and all the fish floating dying even as far as Guayaquil; everywhere along the Pacific slopes there were landslips and swift thawings and sudden floods, and one whole side of the Arauca crest slipped and came down in thunder, and cut off the Country of the Blind for ever from the exploring feet of men. But one of these early settlers had chanced to be on the hither side of the gorges when the world had so terribly shaken itself, and he perforce had to forget his wife and his child and all the friends and possessions he had left up there, and start life over again in the lower world. He started it again but ill, blindness overtook him, and he died of punishment in the mines; but the story he told begot a legend that lingers along the length of the Cordilleras of the Andes to this day.

He told of his reason for venturing back from that fastness, into which he had first been carried lashed to a llama, beside a vast bale of gear, when he was a child. The valley, he said, had in it all that the heart of man could desire—sweet water, pasture, and even climate, slopes of rich brown soil with tangles of a shrub that bore an excellent fruit, and on one side great hanging forests of pine that held the avalanches high. Far overhead, on three sides, vast cliffs of grey-green rock were capped by cliffs of ice; but the glacier stream came not to them but flowed away by the farther slopes, and only now and then huge ice masses fell on the valley side. In this valley it neither rained nor snowed, but the abundant springs gave a rich green pasture, that irrigation would spread over all the valley space. The settlers did well indeed there. Their beasts did well and multiplied, and but one thing marred their happiness. Yet it was enough to mar it greatly. A strange disease had come upon them, and had made all the children born to them there—and indeed, several older children also—blind. It was to seek some charm or antidote against this plague of blindness that he had with fatigue and danger and difficulty returned down the gorge. In those days, in such cases, men did not think of germs and infections but of sins; and it seemed to him that the reason of this affliction must lie in the negligence of these priestless immigrants to set up a shrine so soon as they entered the valley. He wanted a shrine—a handsome, cheap, effectual shrine—to be erected in the valley; he wanted relics and such-like potent things of faith, blessed objects and mysterious medals and prayers. In his wallet he had a bar of native silver for which he would not account; he insisted there was none in the valley with something of the insistence of an inexpert liar. They had all clubbed their money and ornaments together, having little need for such treasure up there, he said, to buy them holy help against their ill. I figure this dim-eyed young mountaineer, sunburnt, gaunt, and anxious, hat-brim clutched feverishly, a man all unused to the ways of the lower world, telling this story to some keen-eyed, attentive priest before the great convulsion; I can picture him presently seeking to return with pious and infallible remedies against that trouble, and the infinite dismay with which he must have faced the tumbled vastness where the gorge had once come out. But the rest of his story of mischances is lost to me, save that I know of his evil death after several years. Poor stray from that remoteness! The stream that had once made the gorge now bursts from the mouth of a rocky cave, and the legend his poor, ill-told story set going developed into the legend of a race of blind men somewhere "over there" one may still hear to-day.

And amidst the little population of that now isolated and forgotten valley the disease ran its course. The old became groping and purblind, the young saw but dimly, and the children that were born to them saw never at all. But life was very easy in that snow-rimmed basin, lost to all the world, with neither thorns nor briars, with no evil insects nor any beasts save the gentle breed of llamas they had lugged and thrust and followed up the beds of the shrunken rivers in the gorges up which they had come. The seeing had become purblind so gradually that they scarcely noted their loss. They guided the sightless youngsters hither and thither until they knew the whole valley marvellously, and when at last sight died out among them the race lived on. They had even time to adapt themselves to the blind control of fire, which they made carefully in stoves of stone. They were a simple strain of people at the first, unlettered, only slightly touched with the Spanish civilisation, but with something of a tradition of the arts of old Peru and of its lost philosophy. Generation followed generation. They forgot many things; they devised many things. Their tradition of the greater world they came from became mythical in colour and uncertain. In all things save sight they were strong and able; and presently the chance of birth and heredity sent one who had an original mind and who could talk and persuade among them, and then afterwards another. These two passed, leaving their effects, and the little community grew in numbers and in understanding, and met and settled social and economic problems that arose. Generation followed generation. Generation followed generation. There came a time when a child was born who was fifteen generations from that ancestor who went out of the valley with a bar of silver to seek God's aid, and who never returned. Thereabouts it chanced that a man came into this community from the outer world. And this is the story of that man.

He was a mountaineer from the country near Quito, a man who had been down to the sea and had seen the world, a reader of books in an original way, an acute and enterprising man, and he was taken on by a party of Englishmen who had come out to Ecuador to climb mountains, to replace one of their three Swiss guides who had fallen ill. He climbed here and he climbed there, and then came the attempt on Parascotopetl, the Matterhorn of the Andes, in which he was lost to the outer world. The story of the accident has been written a dozen times. Pointer's narrative is the best. He tells how the party worked their difficult and almost vertical way up to the very foot of the last and greatest precipice, and how they built a night shelter amidst the snow upon a little shelf of rock, and, with a touch of real dramatic power, how presently they found Nunez had gone from them. They shouted, and there was no reply, shouted and whistled, and for the rest of that night they slept no more.

As the morning broke they saw the traces of his fall. It seems impossible he could have uttered a sound. He had slipped eastward towards the unknown side of the mountain; far below he had struck a steep slope of snow, and ploughed his way down it in the midst of a snow avalanche. His track went straight to the edge of a frightful precipice, and beyond that everything was hidden. Far, far below, and hazy with distance, they could see trees rising out of a narrow, shut-in valley—the lost Country of the Blind. But they did not know it was the lost Country of the Blind, nor distinguish it in any way from any other narrow streak of upland valley. Unnerved by this disaster, they abandoned their attempt in the afternoon, and Pointer was called away to the war before he could make another attack. To this day Parascotopetl lifts an unconquered crest, and Pointer's shelter crumbles unvisited amidst the snows.

And the man who fell survived.

At the end of the slope he fell a thousand feet, and came down in the midst of a cloud of snow upon a snow slope even steeper than the one above. Down this he was whirled, stunned and insensible, but without a bone broken in his body; and then at last came to gentler slopes, and at last rolled out and lay still, buried amidst a softening heap of the white masses that had accompanied and saved him. He came to himself with a dim fancy that he was ill in bed; then realised his position with a mountaineer's intelligence, and worked himself loose and, after a rest or so, out until he saw the stars. He rested flat upon his chest for a space, wondering where he was and what had happened to him. He explored his limbs, and discovered that several of his buttons were gone and his coat turned over his head. His knife had gone from his pocket and his hat was lost, though he had tied it under his chin. He recalled that he had been looking for loose stones to raise his piece of the shelter wall. His ice-axe had disappeared.

He decided he must have fallen, and looked up to see, exaggerated by the ghastly light of the rising moon, the tremendous flight he had taken. For a while he lay, gazing blankly at that vast pale cliff towering above, rising moment by moment out of a subsiding tide of darkness. Its phantasmal, mysterious beauty held him for a space, and then he was seized with a paroxysm of sobbing laughter. . . .

After a great interval of time he became aware that he was near the lower edge of the snow. Below, down what was now a moonlit and practicable slope, he saw the dark and broken appearance of rock-strewn turf. He struggled to his feet, aching in every joint and limb, got down painfully from the heaped loose snow about him, went downward until he was on the turf, and there dropped rather than lay beside a boulder, drank deep from the flask in his inner pocket, and instantly fell asleep.

He was awakened by the singing of birds in the trees far below.

He sat up and perceived he was on a little alp at the foot of a vast precipice, that was grooved by the gully down which he and his snow had come. Over against him another wall of rock reared itself against the sky. The gorge between these precipices ran east and west and was full of the morning sunlight, which lit to the westward the mass of fallen mountain that closed the descending gorge. Below him it seemed there was a precipice equally steep, but behind the snow in the gully he found a sort of chimney-cleft dripping with snow-water down which a desperate man might venture. He found it easier than it seemed, and came at last to another desolate alp, and then after a rock climb of no particular difficulty to a steep slope of trees. He took his bearings and turned his face up the gorge, for he saw it opened out above upon green meadows, among which he now glimpsed quite distinctly a cluster of stone huts of unfamiliar fashion. At times his progress was like clambering along the face of a wall, and after a time the rising sun ceased to strike along the gorge, the voices of the singing birds died away, and the air grew cold and dark about him. But the distant valley with its houses was all the brighter for that. He came presently to talus, and among the rocks he noted—for he was an observant man—an unfamiliar fern that seemed to clutch out of the crevices with intense green hands. He picked a frond or so and gnawed its stalk and found it helpful.

About midday he came at last out of the throat of the gorge into the plain and the sunlight. He was stiff and weary; he sat down in the shadow of a rock, filled up his flask with water from a spring and drank it down, and remained for a time resting before he went on to the houses.

They were very strange to his eyes, and indeed the whole aspect of that valley became, as he regarded it, queerer and more unfamiliar. The greater part of its surface was lush green meadow, starred with many beautiful flowers, irrigated with extraordinary care, and bearing evidence of systematic cropping piece by piece. High up and ringing the valley about was a wall, and what appeared to be a circumferential water-channel, from which the little trickles of water that fed the meadow plants came, and on the higher slopes above this flocks of llamas cropped the scanty herbage. Sheds, apparently shelters or feeding-places for the llamas, stood against the boundary wall here and there. The irrigation streams ran together into a main channel down the centre of the valley, and this was enclosed on either side by a wall breast high. This gave a singularly urban quality to this secluded place, a quality that was greatly enhanced by the fact that a number of paths paved with black and white stones, and each with a curious little kerb at the side, ran hither and thither in an orderly manner. The houses of the central village were quite unlike the casual and higgledy-piggledy agglomeration of the mountain villages he knew; they stood in a continuous row on either side of a central street of astonishing cleanness; here and there their parti-coloured façade was pierced by a door, and not a solitary window broke their even frontage. They were parti-coloured with extraordinary irregularity; smeared with a sort of plaster that was sometimes grey, sometimes drab, sometimes slate-coloured or dark brown; and it was the sight of this wild plastering first brought the word "blind" into the thoughts of the explorer. "The good man who did that," he thought, "must have been as blind as a bat."

He descended a steep place, and so came to the wall and channel that ran about the valley, near where the latter spouted out its surplus contents into the deeps of the gorge in a thin and wavering thread of cascade. He could now see a number of men and women resting on piled heaps of grass, as if taking a siesta, in the remoter part of the meadow, and nearer the village a number of recumbent children, and then nearer at hand three men carrying pails on yokes along a little path that ran from the encircling wall towards the houses. These latter were clad in garments of llama cloth and boots and belts of leather, and they wore caps of cloth with back and ear flaps. They followed one another in single file, walking slowly and yawning as they walked, like men who have been up all night. There was something so reassuringly prosperous and respectable in their bearing that after a moment's hesitation Nunez stood forward as conspicuously as possible upon his rock, and gave vent to a mighty shout that echoed round the valley.

The three men stopped, and moved their heads as though they were looking about them. They turned their faces this way and that, and Nunez gesticulated with freedom. But they did not appear to see him for all his gestures, and after a time, directing themselves towards the mountains far away to the right, they shouted as if in answer. Nunez bawled again, and then once more, and as he gestured ineffectually the word "blind" came up to the top of his thoughts. "The fools must be blind," he said.

When at last, after much shouting and wrath, Nunez crossed

the stream by a little bridge, came through a gate in the wall, and approached them, he was sure that they were blind. He was sure that this was the Country of the Blind of which the legends told. Conviction had sprung upon him, and a sense of great and rather enviable adventure. The three stood side by side, not looking at him, but with their ears directed towards him, judging him by his unfamiliar steps. They stood close together like men a little afraid, and he could see their eyelids closed and sunken, as though the very balls beneath had shrunk away. There was an expression near awe on their faces.

"A man," one said, in hardly recognisable Spanish—"a man it is—a man or a spirit—coming down from the rocks."

But Nunez advanced with the confident steps of a youth who enters upon life. All the old stories of the lost valley and the Country of the Blind had come back to his mind, and through his thoughts ran this old proverb, as if it were a refrain—

"In the Country of the Blind the One-eyed Man is King."

"In the Country of the Blind the One-eyed Man is King."

And very civilly he gave them greeting. He talked to them and used his eyes.

"Where does he come from, brother Pedro?" asked one.

"Down out of the rocks."

"Over the mountains I come," said Nunez, "out of the country beyond there—where men can see. From near Bogota, where there are a hundred thousands of people, and where the city passes out of sight."

"Sight?" muttered Pedro. "Sight?"

"He comes," said the second blind man, "out of the rocks."

The cloth of their coats Nunez saw was curiously fashioned, each with a different sort of stitching.

They startled him by a simultaneous movement towards him, each with a hand outstretched. He stepped back from the advance of these spread fingers.

"Come hither," said the third blind man, following his motion and clutching him neatly.

And they held Nunez and felt him over, saying no word further until they had done so.

"Carefully," he cried, with a finger in his eye, and found they thought that organ, with its fluttering lids, a queer thing in him. They went over it again.

"A strange creature, Correa," said the one called Pedro. "Feel the coarseness of his hair. Like a llama's hair."

"Rough he is as the rocks that begot him," said Correa, investigating Nunez's unshaven chin with a soft and slightly moist hand. "Perhaps he will grow finer." Nunez struggled a little under their examination, but they gripped him firm.

"Carefully," he said again.

"He speaks," said the third man. "Certainly he is a man."

"Ugh!" said Pedro, at the roughness of his coat.

"And you have come into the world?" asked Pedro.

"Out of the world. Over mountains and glaciers; right over above there, half-way to the sun. Out of the great big world that goes down, twelve days' journey to the sea."

They scarcely seemed to heed him. "Our fathers have told us men may be made by the forces of Nature," said Correa. "It is the warmth of things and moisture, and rottenness—rottenness."

"Let us lead him to the elders," said Pedro.

"Shout first," said Correa, "lest the children be afraid. This is a marvellous occasion."

So they shouted, and Pedro went first and took Nunez by the hand to lead him to the houses.

He drew his hand away. "I can see," he said.

"See?" said Correa.

"Yes, see," said Nunez, turning towards him, and stumbled against Pedro's pail.

"His senses are still imperfect," said the third blind man. "He stumbles, and talks unmeaning words. Lead him by the hand."

"As you will," said Nunez, and was led along, laughing.

It seemed they knew nothing of sight.

Well, all in good time, he would teach them.

He heard people shouting, and saw a number of figures gathering together in the middle roadway of the village.

He found it taxed his nerve and patience more than he had anticipated, that first encounter with the population of the Country of the Blind. The place seemed larger as he drew near to it, and the smeared plasterings queerer, and a crowd of children and men and women (the women and girls, he was pleased to note, had some of them quite sweet faces, for all that their eyes were shut and sunken) came about him, holding on to him, touching him with soft, sensitive hands, smelling at him, and listening at every word he spoke. Some of the maidens and children, however, kept aloof as if afraid, and indeed his voice seemed coarse and rude beside their softer notes. They mobbed him. His three guides kept close to him with an effect of proprietorship, and said again and again, "A wild man out of the rocks."

"Bogota," he said. "Bogota. Over the mountain crests."

"A wild man—using wild words," said Pedro. "Did you hear that—*Bogota?* His mind is hardly formed yet. He has only the beginnings of speech."

A little boy nipped his hand. "Bogota!" he said mockingly.

"Ay! A city to your village. I come from the great world—where men have eyes and see."

"His name's Bogota," they said.

"He stumbled," said Correa, "stumbled twice as we came hither."

"Bring him to the elders."

And they thrust him suddenly through a doorway into a room as black as pitch, save at the end there faintly glowed a fire. The crowd closed in behind him and shut out all but the faintest glimmer of day, and before he could arrest himself he had fallen headlong over the feet of a seated man. His arm, outflung, struck the face of someone else as he went down; he felt the soft impact of features and heard a cry of anger, and for a moment he struggled against a number of hands that clutched him. It was a one-sided fight. An inkling of the situation came to him, and he lay quiet.

"I fell down," he said; "I couldn't see in this pitchy darkness."

There was a pause as if the unseen persons about him tried to understand his words. Then the voice of Correa said: "He is but newly formed. He stumbles as he walks and mingles words that mean nothing with his speech."

Others also said things about him that he heard or understood imperfectly.

"May I sit up?" he asked, in a pause. "I will not struggle against you again."

They consulted and let him rise.

The voice of an older man began to question him, and Nunez found himself trying to explain the great world out of which he had fallen, and the sky and mountains and sight and such-like marvels, to these elders who sat in darkness in the Country of the Blind. And they would believe and understand nothing whatever he told them, a thing quite outside his expectation. They would not even understand many of his words. For fourteen generations these people had been blind and cut off from all the seeing world; the names for all the things of sight had faded and changed; the story of the outer world was faded and changed to a child's story; and they had ceased to concern themselves with anything beyond the rocky slopes above their circling wall. Blind men of genius had arisen among them and questioned the shreds of belief and tradition they had brought with them from their seeing days, and had dismissed all these things as idle fancies, and replaced them with new and saner explanations. Much of their imagination had shrivelled with their eyes, and they had made for themselves new imaginations with their ever more sensitive ears and finger-tips. Slowly Nunez realised this; that his expectation of wonder and reverence at his origin and his gifts was not to be borne out; and after his poor attempt to explain sight to them had been set aside as the confused version of a new-made being describing the marvels of his incoherent sensations, he subsided, a little dashed, into listening to their instruction. And the eldest of the blind men explained to him life and philosophy and religion, how that the world (meaning their valley) had been first an empty hollow in the rocks, and then had come, first, inanimate things without the gift of touch, and llamas and a few other creatures that had little sense, and then men, and at last angels, whom one could hear singing and making fluttering sounds, but whom no one could touch at all, which puzzled Nunez greatly until he thought of the birds.

He went on to tell Nunez how this time had been divided into the warm and the cold, which are the blind equivalents of day and night, and how it was good to sleep in the warm and work during the cold, so that now, but for his advent, the whole town of the blind would have been asleep. He said Nunez must have been specially created to learn and serve the wisdom they had acquired, and for that all his mental incoherency and stumbling behaviour he must have courage, and do his best to learn, and at that all the people in the doorway murmured encouragingly. He said the night—for the blind call their day night—was now far gone, and it behooved every one to go back to sleep. He asked Nunez if he knew how to sleep, and Nunez said he did, but that before sleep he wanted food.

They brought him food—llama's milk in a bowl, and rough salted bread—and led him into a lonely place to eat out of their hearing, and afterwards to slumber until the chill of the mountain evening roused them to begin their day again. But Nunez slumbered not at all.

Instead, he sat up in the place where they had left him, resting his limbs and turning the unanticipated circumstances of his arrival over and over in his mind.

Every now and then he laughed, sometimes with amusement, and sometimes with indignation.

"Unformed mind!" he said. "Got no senses yet! They little know they've been insulting their heaven-sent king and master. I see I must bring them to reason. Let me think—let me think."

He was still thinking when the sun set.

Nunez had an eye for all beautiful things, and it seemed to him that the glow upon the snowfields and glaciers that rose about the valley on every side was the most beautiful thing he had ever seen. His eyes went from that inaccessible glory to the village and irrigated fields, fast sinking into the twilight, and suddenly a wave of emotion took him, and he thanked God from the bottom of his heart that the power of sight had been given him.

He heard a voice calling to him from out of the village.

"Ya ho there, Bogota! Come hither!"

At that he stood up smiling. He would show these people once and for all what sight would do for a man. They would seek him, but not find him.

"You move not, Bogota," said the voice.

He laughed noiselessly, and made two stealthy steps aside from the path.

"Trample not on the grass, Bogota; that is not allowed."

Nunez had scarcely heard the sound he made himself. He stopped amazed.

The owner of the voice came running up the piebald path towards him.

He stepped back into the pathway. "Here I am," he said.

"Why did you not come when I called you?" said the blind man. "Must you be led like a child? Cannot you hear the path as you walk?"

Nunez laughed. "I can see it," he said.

"There is no such word as *see*," said the blind man, after a pause. "Cease this folly, and follow the sound of my feet."

Nunez followed, a little annoyed.

"My time will come," he said.

"You'll learn," the blind man answered. "There is much to learn in the world."

"Has no one told you, 'In the Country of the Blind the One-eyed Man is King'?"

"What is blind?" asked the blind man carelessly over his shoulder.

Four days passed, and the fifth found the King of the Blind still incognito, as a clumsy and useless stranger among his subjects.

It was, he found, much more difficult to proclaim himself than he had supposed, and in the meantime, while he meditated his *coup d'état,* he did what he was told and learned the manners and customs of the Country of the Blind. He found working and going about at night a particularly irksome thing, and he decided that that should be the first thing he would change.

They led a simple, laborious life, these people, with all the elements of virtue and happiness, as these things can be understood by men. They toiled, but not oppressively; they had food and clothing sufficient for their needs; they had days and seasons of rest; they made much of music and singing, and there was love among them, and little children.

It was marvellous with what confidence and precision they went about their ordered world. Everything, you see, had been made to fit their needs; each of the radiating paths of the valley area had a constant angle to the others, and was distinguished by a special notch upon its kerbing; all obstacles and irregularities of path or meadow had long since been cleared away; all their methods and procedure arose naturally from their special needs. Their senses had become marvellously acute; they could hear and judge the slightest gesture of a man a dozen paces away—could hear the very beating of his heart. Intonation had long replaced expression with them, and touches gesture, and their work with hoe and spade and fork was as free and confident as garden work can be. Their sense of smell was extraordinarily fine; they could distinguish individual differences as readily as a dog can, and they went about the tending of the llamas, who lived among the rocks above and came to the wall for food and shelter, with ease and confidence. It was only when at last Nunez sought to assert himself that he found how easy and confident their movements could be.

He rebelled only after he had tried persuasion.

He tried at first on several occasions to tell them of sight. "Look you here, you people," he said. "There are things you do not understand in me."

Once or twice one or two of them attended to him; they sat with faces downcast and ears turned intelligently towards him, and he did his best to tell them what it was to see. Among his hearers was a girl, with eyelids less red and sunken than the others, so that one could almost fancy she was hiding eyes, whom especially he hoped to persuade. He spoke of the beauties of sight, of watching the mountains, of the sky and the sunrise, and they heard him with amused incredulity that presently became condemnatory. They told him there were indeed no mountains at all, but that the end of the rocks where the llamas grazed was indeed the end of the world; thence sprang a cavernous roof of the universe, from which the dew and the avalanches fell; and when he maintained stoutly the world had neither end nor roof such as they supposed, they said his thoughts were wicked. So far as he could describe sky and clouds and stars to them it seemed to them a hideous void, a terrible blankness in the place of the smooth roof to things in which they believed—it was an article of faith with them that the cavern roof was exquisitely smooth to the touch. He saw that in some manner he shocked them, and gave up that aspect of the matter altogether, and tried to show them the practical value of sight. One morning he saw Pedro in the path called Seventeen and coming towards the central houses, but still too far off for hearing or scent, and he told them as much. "In a little while," he prophesied, "Pedro will be here." An old man remarked that Pedro had no business on path Seventeen, and then, as if in confirmation, that individual as he drew near turned and went transversely into Path Ten, and so back with nimble paces towards the outer wall. They mocked Nunez when Pedro did not arrive, and afterwards, when he asked Pedro questions to clear his character, Pedro denied and outfaced him, and was afterwards hostile to him.

Then he induced them to let him go a long way up the sloping meadows towards the wall with one complacent individual, and to him he promised to describe all that happened among the houses. He noted certain goings and comings, but the things that really seemed to signify to these people happened inside of or behind the windowless houses—the only things they took note of to test him by—and of these he could see or tell nothing; and it was after the failure of this attempt, and the ridicule they could not repress, that he resorted to force. He thought of seizing a spade and suddenly smiting one or two of them to earth, and so in fair combat showing the advantage of eyes. He went so far with that resolution as to seize his spade, and then he discovered a new thing about himself, and that was that it was impossible for him to hit a blind man in cold blood.

He hesitated, and found them all aware that he snatched up the spade. They stood alert, with their heads on one side, and bent ears towards him for what he would do next.

"Put that spade down," said one, and he felt a sort of helpless horror. He came near obedience.

Then he thrust one backwards against a house wall, and fled past him and out of the village.

He went athwart one of their meadows, leaving a track of trampled grass behind his feet, and presently sat down by the side of one of their ways. He felt something of the buoyancy that comes to all men in the beginning of a fight, but more perplexity. He began to realise that you cannot even fight happily with creatures who stand upon a different mental basis to yourself. Far away he saw a number of men carrying spades and sticks come out of the street of houses, and advance in a spreading line along the several paths towards him. They advanced slowly, speaking frequently to one another, and ever and again the whole cordon would halt and sniff the air and listen.

The first time they did this Nunez laughed. But afterwards he did not laugh.

One struck his trail in the meadow grass, and came stooping and feeling his way along it.

For five minutes he watched the slow extension of the cordon, and then his vague disposition to do something forthwith became frantic. He stood up, went a pace or so towards the circumferential wall, turned, and went back a little way. There they all stood in a crescent, still and listening.

He also stood still, gripping his spade very tightly in both hands. Should he charge them?

The pulse in his ears ran into the rhythm of "In the Country of the Blind the One-eyed Man is King!"

Should he charge them?

He looked back at the high and unclimbable wall behind—unclimbable because of its smooth plastering, but withal pierced with many little doors, and at the approaching line of seekers. Behind these, others were now coming out of the street of houses.

Should he charge them?

"Bogota!" called one. "Bogota! where are you?"

He gripped his spade still tighter, and advanced down the meadows towards the place of habitations, and directly he moved they converged upon him. "I'll hit them if they touch me," he swore; "by Heaven, I will. I'll hit." He called aloud, "Look here, I'm going to do what I like in this valley. Do you hear? I'm going to do what I like and go where I like!"

They were moving in upon him quickly, groping, yet moving rapidly. It was like playing blind man's buff, with everyone blindfolded except one. "Get hold of him!" cried one. He found himself in the arc of a loose curve of pursuers. He felt suddenly he must be active and resolute.

"You don't understand," he cried in a voice that was meant to be great and resolute, and which broke. "You are blind, and I can see. Leave me alone!"

"Bogota! Put down that spade, and come off the grass!"

The last order, grotesque in its urban familiarity, produced a gust of anger.

"I'll hurt you," he said, sobbing with emotion. "By Heaven, I'll hurt you. Leave me alone!"

He began to run, not knowing clearly where to run. He ran from the nearest blind man, because it was a horror to hit him. He stopped, and then made a dash to escape from their closing ranks. He made for where a gap was wide, and the men on either side, with a quick perception of the approach of his paces, rushed in on one another. He sprang forward, and then saw he must be caught, and *swish!* the spade had struck. He felt the soft thud of hand and arm, and the man was down with a yell of pain, and he was through.

Through! And then he was close to the street of houses again, and blind men, whirling spades and stakes, were running with a sort of reasoned swiftness hither and thither.

He heard steps behind him just in time, and found a tall man rushing forward and swiping at the sound of him. He lost his nerve, hurled his spade a yard wide at his antagonist, and whirled about and fled, fairly yelling as he dodged another.

He was panic-stricken. He ran furiously to and fro, dodging when there was no need to dodge, and in his anxiety to see on every side of him at once, stumbling. For a moment he was down and they heard his fall. Far away in the circumferential wall a little doorway looked like heaven, and he set off in a wild rush for it. He did not even look round at his pursuers until it was gained, and he had stumbled across the bridge, clambered a little way among the rocks, to the surprise and dismay of a young llama, who went leaping out of sight, and lay down sobbing for breath.

And so his *coup d'état* came to an end.

He stayed outside the wall of the valley of the Blind for two nights and days without food or shelter, and meditated upon the unexpected. During these meditations he repeated very frequently and always with a profounder note of derision the exploded proverb: "In the Country of the Blind the One-eyed Man is King." He thought chiefly of ways of fighting and conquering these people, and it grew clear that for him no practicable way was possible. He had no weapons, and now it would be hard to get one.

The canker of civilisation had got to him even in Bogota, and he could not find it in himself to go down and assassinate a blind man. Of course, if he did that, he might then dictate terms on the threat of assassinating them all. But—sooner or later he must sleep! . . .

He tried also to find food among the pine trees, to be comfortable under pine boughs while the frost fell at night, and—with less confidence—to catch a llama by artifice in order to try to kill it—perhaps by hammering it with a stone—and so finally, perhaps, to eat some of it. But the llamas had a doubt of him and regarded him with distrustful brown eyes, and spat when he drew near. Fear came on him the second day and fits of shivering. Finally he crawled down to the wall of the Country of the Blind and tried to make terms. He crawled along by the stream, shouting, until two blind men came out to the gate and talked to him.

"I was mad," he said. "But I was only newly made."

They said that was better.

He told them he was wiser now, and repented of all he had done.

Then he wept without intention, for he was very weak and ill now, and they took that as a favourable sign.

They asked him if he still thought he could *"see."*

"No," he said. "That was folly. The word means nothing—less than nothing!"

They asked him what was overhead.

"About ten times ten the height of a man there is a roof above the world—of rock—and very, very smooth." . . . He burst again into hysterical tears. "Before you ask me any more, give me some food or I shall die."

He expected dire punishments, but these blind people were capable of toleration. They regarded his rebellion as but one more proof of his general idiocy and inferiority; and after they had whipped him they appointed him to do the simplest and heaviest work they had for anyone to do, and he, seeing no other way of living, did submissively what he was told.

He was ill for some days, and they nursed him kindly. That refined his submission. But they insisted on his lying in the dark, and that was a great misery. And blind philosophers came and talked to him of the wicked levity of his mind, and reproved him so impressively for his doubts about the lid of rock that covered their cosmic casserole that he almost doubted whether indeed he was not the victim of hallucination in not seeing it overhead.

So Nunez became a citizen of the Country of the Blind, and these people ceased to be a generalised people and became individualities and familiar to him, while the world beyond the mountains became more and more remote and unreal. There was Yacob, his master, a kindly man when not annoyed; there was Pedro, Yacob's nephew; and there was Medina-saroté, who was the youngest daughter of Yacob. She was little esteemed in the world of the blind, because she had a clear-cut face, and lacked that satisfying, glossy smoothness that is the blind man's ideal of feminine beauty; but Nunez thought her beautiful at first, and presently the most beautiful thing in the whole creation. Her closed eyelids were not sunken and red after the common way of the valley, but lay as though they might open again at any moment; and she had long eyelashes, which were considered a grave disfigurement. And her voice was strong, and did not satisfy the acute hearing of the valley swains. So that she had no lover.

There came a time when Nunez thought that, could he win her, he would be resigned to live in the valley for all the rest of his days.

He watched her; he sought opportunities of doing her little services, and presently he found that she observed him. Once at a rest-day gathering they sat side by side in the dim starlight, and the music was sweet. His hand came upon hers and he dared to clasp it. Then very tenderly she returned his pressure. And one day, as they were at their meal in the darkness, he felt her hand very softly seeking him, and as it chanced the fire leaped then and he saw the tenderness of her face.

He sought to speak to her.

He went to her one day when she was sitting in the summer moonlight spinning. The light made her a thing of silver and mystery. He sat down at her feet and told her he loved her, and told her how beautiful she seemed to him. He had a lover's voice, he spoke with a tender reverence that came near to awe, and she had never before been touched by adoration. She made him no definite answer, but it was clear his words pleased her.

After that he talked to her whenever he could make an opportunity. The valley became the world for him, and the world beyond the mountains where men lived in sunlight seemed no more than a fairy tale he would some day pour into her ears. Very tentatively and timidly he spoke to her of sight.

Sight seemed to her the most poetical of fancies, and she listened to his description of the stars and the mountains and her own sweet white-lit beauty as though it was a guilty indulgence. She did not believe, she could only half understand, but she was mysteriously delighted, and it seemed to him that she completely understood.

His love lost its awe and took courage. Presently he was for demanding her of Yacob and the elders in marriage, but she became fearful and delayed. And it was one of her elder sisters who first told Yacob that Medina-saroté and Nunez were in love.

There was from the first very great opposition to the marriage of Nunez and Medina-saroté; not so much because they valued her as because they held him as a being apart, an idiot, an incompetent thing below the permissible level of a man. Her sisters opposed it bitterly as bringing discredit on them all; and old Yacob, though he had formed a sort of liking for his clumsy, obedient serf, shook his head and said the thing could not be. The young men were all angry at the idea of corrupting the race, and one went so far as to revile and strike Nunez. He struck back. Then for the first time he found an advantage in seeing, even by twilight, and after that fight was over no one was disposed to raise a hand against him. But they still found his marriage impossible.

Old Yacob had a tenderness for his last little daughter, and was grieved to have her weep upon his shoulder.

"You see, my dear, he's an idiot. He has delusions; he can't do anything right."

"I know," wept Medina-saroté. "But he's better than he was. He's getting better. And he's strong, dear father, and kind—stronger and kinder than any other man in the world. And he loves me—and, father, I love him."

Old Yacob was greatly distressed to find her inconsolable, and, besides—what made it more distressing—he liked Nunez for many things. So he went and sat in the windowless council-chamber with the other elders and watched the trend of the talk, and said, at the proper time, "He's better than he was. Very likely, some day, we shall find him as sane as ourselves."

Then afterwards one of the elders, who thought deeply, had an idea. He was the great doctor among these people, their medicine-man, and he had a very philosophical and inventive mind, and the idea of curing Nunez of his peculiarities appealed to him. One day when Yacob was present he returned to the topic of Nunez.

"I have examined Bogota," he said, "and the case is clearer to me. I think very probably he might be cured."

"That is what I have always hoped," said old Yacob.

"His brain is affected," said the blind doctor.

The elders murmured assent.

"Now, *what* affects it?"

"Ah!" said old Yacob.

"*This*," said the doctor, answering his own question. "Those queer things that are called the eyes, and which exist to make an agreeable soft depression in the face, are diseased, in the case of Bogota, in such a way as to affect his brain. They are greatly distended, he has eyelashes, and his eyelids move, and consequently his brain is in a state of constant irritation and distraction."

"Yes?" said old Yacob. "Yes?"

"And I think I may say with reasonable certainty that, in order to cure him completely, all that we need do is a simple and easy surgical operation—namely, to remove these irritant bodies."

"And then he will be sane?"

"Then he will be perfectly sane, and a quite admirable citizen."

"Thank Heaven for science!" said old Yacob, and went forth at once to tell Nunez of his happy hopes.

But Nunez's manner of receiving the good news struck him as being cold and disappointing.

"One might think," he said, "from the tone you take, that you did not care for my daughter."

It was Medina-saroté who persuaded Nunez to face the blind surgeons.

"*You* do not want me," he said, "to lose my gift of sight?"

She shook her head.

"My world is sight."

Her head drooped lower.

"There are the beautiful things, the beautiful little things—the flowers, the lichens among the rocks, the lightness and softness on a piece of fur, the far sky with its drifting down of clouds, the sunsets and the stars. And there is *you*. For you alone it is good to have sight, to see your sweet, serene face, your kindly lips, your dear, beautiful hands folded together. . . . It is these eyes of mine you won, these eyes that hold me to you, that these idiots seek. Instead, I must touch you, hear you, and never see you again. I must come under that roof of rock and stone and darkness, that horrible roof under which your imagination stoops. . . . No; you would not have me do that?"

A disagreeable doubt had risen in him. He stopped, and left the thing a question.

"I wish," she said, "sometimes—" She paused.

"Yes?" said he, a little apprehensively.

"I wish sometimes—you would not talk like that."

"Like what?"

"I know it's pretty—it's your imagination. I love it, but *now*—"

He felt cold. "*Now?*" he said faintly.

She sat quite still.

"You mean—you think—I should be better, better perhaps—"

He was realising things very swiftly. He felt anger, indeed, anger at the dull course of fate, but also sympathy for her lack of understanding—a sympathy near akin to pity.

"Dear," he said, and he could see by her whiteness how intensely her spirit pressed against the things she could not say. He put his arms about her, he kissed her ear, and they sat for a time in silence.

"If I were to consent to this?" he said at last, in a voice that was very gentle.

She flung her arms about him, weeping wildly. "Oh, if you would," she sobbed, "if only you would!"

For a week before the operation that was to raise him from the servitude and inferiority to the level of a blind citizen, Nunez knew nothing of sleep, and all through the warm sunlit hours, while the others slumbered happily, he sat brooding or wandered aimlessly, trying to bring his mind to bear on his dilemma. He had given his answer, he had given his consent, and still he was not sure. And at last work-time was over, the sun rose in splendour over the golden crests, and his last day of vision began for him. He had a few minutes with Medina-saroté before she went apart to sleep.

"To-morrow," he said, "I shall see no more."

"Dear heart!" she answered, and pressed his hands with all her strength.

"They will hurt you but little," she said; "and you are going through this pain—you are going through it, dear lover, for *me*. . . . Dear, if a woman's heart and life can do it, I will repay you. My dearest one, my dearest with the tender voice, I will repay."

He was drenched in pity for himself and her.

He held her in his arms, and pressed his lips to hers, and looked on her sweet face for the last time. "Good-bye!" he whispered at that dear sight, "good-bye!"

And then in silence he turned away from her.

She could hear his slow retreating footsteps, and something in the rhythm of them threw her into a passion of weeping.

He had fully meant to go to a lonely place where the meadows were beautiful with white narcissus, and there remain until the hour of his sacrifice should come, but as he went he lifted up his eyes and saw the morning, the morning like an angel in golden armour, marching down the steeps. . . .

It seemed to him that before this splendour he, and this blind world in the valley, and his love, and all, were no more than a pit of sin.

He did not turn aside as he had meant to do, but went on, and passed through the wall of the circumference and out upon the rocks, and his eyes were always upon the sunlit ice and snow.

He saw their infinite beauty, and his imagination soared over them to the things beyond he was now to resign for ever.

He thought of that great free world he was parted from, the world that was his own, and he had a vision of those further slopes, distance beyond distance, with Bogota, a place of multitudinous stirring beauty, a glory by day, a luminous mystery by night, a place of palaces and fountains and statues and white houses, lying beautifully in the middle distance. He thought how for a day or so one might come down through passes, drawing ever nearer and nearer to its busy streets and ways. He thought of the river journey, day by day, from great Bogota to the still vaster world beyond, through towns and villages, forest and desert places, the rushing river day by day, until its banks receded and the big steamers came splashing by, and one had reached the sea—the limitless sea, with its thousand islands, its thousands of islands, and its ships seen dimly far away in their incessant journeyings round and about that greater world. And there, unpent by mountains, one saw the sky—the sky, not such a disc as one saw it here, but an arch of immeasurable blue, a deep of deeps in which the circling stars were floating. . . .

His eyes scrutinised the great curtain of the mountains with a keener inquiry.

For example, if one went so, up that gully and to that chimney there, then one might come out high among those stunted pines that ran round in a sort of shelf and rose still higher and higher as it passed above the gorge. And then? That talus might be managed. Thence perhaps a climb might be found to take him up to the precipice that came below the snow; and if that chimney failed, then another farther to the east might serve his purpose better. And then? Then one would be out upon the amber-lit snow there, and halfway up to the crest of those beautiful desolations.

He glanced back at the village, then turned right round and regarded it steadfastly.

He thought of Medina-saroté, and she had become small and remote.

He turned again towards the mountain wall, down which the day had come to him.

Then very circumspectly he began to climb.

When sunset came he was no longer climbing, but he was far and high. He had been higher, but he was still very high. His clothes were torn, his limbs were blood-stained, he was bruised in many places, but he lay as if he were at his ease, and there was a smile on his face.

From where he rested the valley seemed as if it were in a pit and nearly a mile below. Already it was dim with haze and shadow, though the mountain summits around him were things of light and fire. The little details of the rocks near at hand were drenched with subtle beauty—a vein of green mineral piercing the grey, the flash of crystal faces here and there, a minute, minutely beautiful orange lichen close beside his face. There were deep mysterious shadows in the gorge, blue deepening into purple, and purple into a luminous darkness, and overhead was the illimitable vastness of the sky. But he heeded these things no longer, but lay quite inactive there, smiling as if he were satisfied merely to have escaped from the valley of the Blind in which he had thought to be King.

The glow of the sunset passed, and the night came, and still he lay peacefully contented under the cold stars.

Theme

This story fits into the general category of allegory, like Swift's *Gulliver's Travels,* Orwell's *1984,* and Huxley's *Brave New World.* Allegory can be very complex, but at its simplest it involves at least two levels. The first is the narrative line itself; the second is the real meaning which follows closely upon each turn in the narrative. Allegory differs from other fictional types in that the meaning hugs the story line at every point: there is almost a direct one-to-one relationship between the progress of the narrative and its true significance. In most other fiction, such a relationship is looser, much less categorical. When a story or poem is allegorical, usually all other elements are sacrificed to theme or idea: characterization may be weak or unimportant; plot is full of unbelievable details; setting becomes fantastic, as in a fairy tale.

1 Find all the examples you can of allegory in this story. The beginning itself would be a good instance—the narration of events in the past which relate to something in the present. Also consider the title.

2 How does the legend of the first two paragraphs relate to the later plot development? Be sure to determine whether the legend is necessary at all. Technically, couldn't Wells have plunged directly into his story of Nunez?

3 How does Nunez's entrance into the Country of the Blind fit into the allegory?

4 What is the purpose of the refrain? Is this refrain—"In the Country of the Blind, the One-eyed Man is King"—borne out? What point does Wells make with this adage?

5 Why does Wells present the Country of the Blind as a kind of paradise? Usually lack of sight is equated to misery, frustration, personal anguish. Why is it so different here? Can you see any point that Wells is making?

6 What expectation does Nunez have in this country where only he has sight? Why is he frustrated?

7 Which becomes normal, sight or blindness? For what purpose does Wells reverse the usual values?

8 Is the blind "philosopher's" explanation of the world logical, that is, as logical as any? What is Wells's point here?

9 Does Nunez react expectedly to each situation? For what reason does he reject violence? Why does he allow the blind men to gain their own terms?

10 What does the episode with Medina-saroté mean? What are the temptations which Nunez must face? Why does he reject them?

Further Aspects

We are now ready to tackle the underlying meaning of the story, to probe what lies below the narrative line, that is, to understand the allegory.

1 If we say that the story is about freedom, what do we mean? Whose freedom? Whose bondage? What does Nunez's escape at the end signify? Even if he dies, is he free?

2 What political and social significance do you see in the story? Who are the blind? Who are the One-eyed? Who has full vision? How far does the allegory carry this point?

3 Is blindness really a paradise, while sight involves pain and anguish, or are the values reversed? At whom is Wells's irony directed? Or can we accept the story literally, without irony?

4 What good is sight when the blind are kings?

5 What does Nunez stand for in Wells's scale of values?

6 What does Wells ask of the reader? And we must assume that he asks for much.

7 Are there any hints that Nunez, as one who *sees*, the *seer*, may be a poet among peasants?

THE CASK OF AMONTILLADO

Edgar Allan Poe

The thousand injuries of Fortunato I had borne as I best could, but when he ventured upon insult I vowed revenge. You, who so well know the nature of my soul, will not suppose, however, that I gave utterance to a threat. *At length* I would be avenged; this was a point definitely settled—but the very definitiveness with which it was resolved precluded the idea of risk. I must not only punish but punish with impunity. A wrong is unredressed when retribution overtakes its redresser. It is equally unredressed when the avenger fails to make himself felt as such to him who has done the wrong.

It must be understood that neither by word nor deed had I given Fortunato cause to doubt my good will. I continued, as was my wont, to smile in his face, and he did not perceive that my smile *now* was at the thought of his immolation.

He had a weak point—this Fortunato—although in other regards he was a man to be respected and even feared. He prided himself on his connoisseurship in wine. Few Italians have the true virtuoso spirit. For the most part their enthusiasm is adopted to suit the time and opportunity, to practise imposture upon the British and Austrian *millionnaires*. In painting and gemmary, Fortunato, like his countrymen, was a quack, but in the matter of old wines he was sincere. In this respect I did not differ from him materially;—I was skilful in the Italian vintages myself, and bought largely whenever I could.

It was about dusk, one evening during the supreme madness of the carnival season, that I encountered my friend. He accosted me with excessive warmth, for he had been drinking much. The man wore motley. He had on a tight-fitting parti-striped dress, and his head was surmounted by the conical cap and bells. I was so pleased to see him that I thought I should never have done wringing his hand.

I said to him—"My dear Fortunato, you are luckily met. How remarkably well you are looking to-day. But I have received a pipe of what passes for Amontillado, and I have my doubts."

"How?" said he. "Amontillado? A pipe? Impossible! And in the middle of the carnival!"

"I have my doubts," I replied; "and I was silly enough to pay the full Amontillado price without consulting you in the matter. You were not to be found, and I was fearful of losing a bargain."

"Amontillado!"

"I have my doubts."

"Amontillado!"

"And I must satisfy them."

"Amontillado!"

"As you are engaged, I am on my way to Luchresi. If any one has a critical turn, it is he. He will tell me—"

"Luchresi cannot tell Amontillado from Sherry."

"And yet some fools will have it that his taste is a match for your own."

"Come, let us go."

"Thither?"

"To your vaults."

"My friend, no; I will not impose upon your good nature. I perceive you have an engagement. Luchresi—"

"I have no engagement;—come."

"My friend, no. It is not the engagement, but the severe cold with which I perceive you are afflicted. The vaults are insufferably damp. They are encrusted with nitre."

"Let us go, nevertheless. The cold is merely nothing. Amontillado! You have been imposed upon. And as for Luchresi, he cannot distinguish Sherry from Amontillado."

Thus speaking, Fortunato possessed himself of my arm; and putting on a mask of black silk and drawing a *roquelaire* closely about my person, I suffered him to hurry me to my palazzo.

There were no attendants at home; they had absconded to make merry in honour of the time. I had told them that I should not return until the morning, and had given them explicit orders not to stir from the house. These orders were sufficient, I well knew, to insure their immediate disappearance, one and all, as soon as my back was turned.

I took from their sconces two flambeaux, and giving one to Fortunato, bowed him through several suites of rooms to the archway that led into the vaults. I passed down a long and winding staircase, requesting him to be cautious as he followed. We came at length to the foot of the descent, and stood together on the damp ground of the catacombs of the Montresors.

The gait of my friend was unsteady, and the bells upon his cap jingled as he strode.

"The pipe?" said he.

"It is farther on," said I; "but observe the white web-work which gleams from these cavern walls."

He turned towards me, and looked into my eyes with two filmy orbs that distilled the rheum of intoxication.

"Nitre?" he asked, at length.

"Nitre," I replied. "How long have you had that cough?"

"Ugh! ugh! ugh!—ugh! ugh! ugh!—ugh! ugh! ugh!—ugh! ugh! ugh!—ugh! ugh! ugh!"

My poor friend found it impossible to reply for many minutes.

"It is nothing," he said, at last.

"Come," I said, with decision, "we will go back; your health is precious. You are rich, respected, admired, beloved; you are happy, as once I was. You are a man to be missed. For me it is no matter. We will go back; you will be ill, and I cannot be responsible. Besides, there is Luchresi—"

"Enough," he said; "the cough is a mere nothing; it will not kill me. I shall not die of a cough."

"True—true," I replied; "and, indeed, I had no intention of alarming you unnecessarily—but you should use all proper caution. A draught of this Medoc will defend us from the damps."

Here I knocked off the neck of a bottle which I drew from a long row of its fellows that lay upon the mould.

"Drink," I said, presenting him the wine.

He raised it to his lips with a leer. He paused and nodded to me familiarly, while his bells jingled.

"I drink," he said, "to the buried that repose around us."

"And I to your long life."

He again took my arm, and we proceeded.

"These vaults," he said, "are extensive."

"The Montresors," I replied, "were a great and numerous family."

"I forget your arms."

"A huge human foot d'or, in a field azure; the foot crushes a serpent rampant whose fangs are imbedded in the heel."

"And the motto?"

"*Nemo me impune lacessit.*"[1]

"Good!" he said.

The wine sparkled in his eyes and the bells jingled. My own fancy grew warm with the Medoc. We had passed through long walls of piled skeletons, with casks and puncheons intermingling,

[1] "No one hurts me with impunity." [Editors' translation.]

into the inmost recesses of the catacombs. I paused again, and this time I made bold to seize Fortunato by an arm above the elbow.

"The nitre!" I said; "see, it increases. It hangs like moss upon the vaults. We are below the river's bed. The drops of moisture trickle among the bones. Come, we will go back ere it is too late. Your cough—"

"It is nothing," he said; "let us go on. But first, another draught of the Medoc."

I broke and reached him a flagon of De Grâve. He emptied it at a breath. His eyes flashed with a fierce light. He laughed and threw the bottle upward with a gesticulation I did not understand.

I looked at him in surprise. He repeated the movement—a grotesque one.

"You do not comprehend?" he said.

"Not I," I replied.

"Then you are not of the brotherhood."

"How?"

"You are not of the masons."

"Yes, yes," I said; "yes, yes."

"You? Impossible! A mason?"

"A mason," I replied.

"A sign," he said, "a sign."

"It is this," I answered, producing from beneath the folds of my *roquelaire* a trowel.

"You jest," he exclaimed, recoiling a few paces. "But let us proceed to the Amontillado."

"Be it so," I said, replacing the tool beneath the cloak and again offering him my arm. He leaned upon it heavily. We continued our route in search of the Amontillado. We passed through a range of low arches, descended, passed on, and descending again, arrived at a deep crypt, in which the foulness of the air caused our flambeaux rather to glow than flame.

At the most remote end of the crypt there appeared another less spacious. Its walls had been lined with human remains, piled to the vault overhead, in the fashion of the great catacombs of Paris. Three sides of this interior crypt were still ornamented in this manner. From the fourth the bones had been thrown down, and lay promiscuously upon the earth, forming at one point a mound of some size. Within the wall thus exposed by the displacing of the bones, we perceived a still interior crypt or recess, in depth about four feet, in width three, in height six or seven. It seemed to have been constructed for no especial use within itself, but formed merely the interval between two of the colossal supports of the roof of the catacombs, and was backed by one of their circumscribing walls of solid granite.

It was in vain that Fortunato, uplifting his dull torch, endeavoured to pry into the depth of the recess. Its termination the feeble light did not enable us to see.

"Proceed," I said; "herein is the Amontillado. As for Luchresi—"

"He is an ignoramus," interrupted my friend, as he stepped unsteadily forward, while I followed immediately at his heels. In an instant he had reached the extremity of the niche, and finding his progress arrested by the rock, stood stupidly bewildered. A moment more and I had fettered him to the granite. In its surface were two iron staples, distant from each other about two feet, horizontally. From one of these depended a short chain, from the other a padlock. Throwing the links about his waist, it was but the work of a few seconds to secure it. He was too much astounded to resist. Withdrawing the key I stepped back from the recess.

"Pass your hand," I said, "over the wall; you cannot help feeling the nitre. Indeed it is *very* damp. Once more let me *implore* you to return. No? Then I must positively leave you. But I must first render you all the little attentions in my power."

"The Amontillado!" ejaculated my friend, not yet recovered from his astonishment.

"True," I replied; "the Amontillado."

As I said these words I busied myself among the pile of bones of which I have before spoken. Throwing them aside, I soon uncovered a quantity of building stone and mortar. With these materials and with the aid of my trowel, I began vigorously to wall up the entrance of the niche.

I had scarcely laid the first tier of the masonry when I discovered that the intoxication of Fortunato had in a great measure worn off. The earliest indication I had of this was a low moaning cry from the depth of the recess. It was *not* the cry of a drunken man. There was then a long and obstinate silence. I laid the second tier, and the third, and the fourth; and then I heard the furious vibrations of the chain. The noise lasted for several minutes, during which, that I might hearken to it with the more satisfaction, I ceased my labours and sat down upon the bones.

When at last the clanking subsided, I resumed the trowel, and finished without interruption the fifth, the sixth, and the seventh tier. The wall was now nearly upon a level with my breast. I again paused, and holding the flambeaux over the mason-work, threw a few feeble rays upon the figure within.

A succession of loud and shrill screams, bursting suddenly from the throat of the chained form, seemed to thrust me violently back. For a brief moment I hesitated, I trembled. Unsheathing my rapier, I began to grope with it about the recess; but the thought of an instant reassured me. I placed my hand upon the solid fabric of the catacombs, and felt satisfied. I reapproached the wall. I replied to the yells of him who clamoured. I re-echoed, I aided, I surpassed them in volume and in strength. I did this, and the clamourer grew still.

It was now midnight, and my task was drawing to a close. I had completed the eighth, the ninth and the tenth tier. I had finished a portion of the last and the eleventh; there remained but a single stone to be fitted and plastered in. I struggled with its weight; I placed it partially in its destined position. But now there came from out the niche a low laugh that erected the hairs upon my head. It was succeeded by a sad voice, which I had difficulty in recognizing as that of the noble Fortunato. The voice said—

"Ha! ha! ha!—he! he! he!—a very good joke, indeed—an excellent jest. We will have many a rich laugh about it at the palazzo—he! he! he!—over our wine—he! he! he!"

"The Amontillado!" I said.

"He! he! he!—he! he he!—yes, the Amontillado. But is it not getting late? Will not they be awaiting us at the palazzo, the Lady Fortunato and the rest? Let us be gone."

"Yes," I said, "let us be gone."

"For the love of God, Montresor!"

"Yes," I said, "for the love of God!"

But to these words I hearkened in vain for a reply. I grew impatient. I called aloud—

"Fortunato!"

No answer. I called again—

"Fortunato!"

No answer still. I thrust a torch through the remaining aperture and let it fall within. There came forth in return only a jingling of the bells. My heart grew sick; on account of the dampness of the catacombs. I hastened to make an end of my labour. I forced the last stone into its position; I plastered it up.

Against the new masonry I re-erected the old rampart of bones. For the half of a century no mortal has disturbed them. *In pace requiescat!*

Plot

The main element of this story by Poe is its plot, that is, the working out of a particular set of events directed toward a preconceived end. In Poe's hands, the plot is fairly simple, without the complications that one often finds in a more modern short story. The narrative line is simple and unencumbered, and we know that Poe attempted certain direct effects rather than great profundity. In a contemporary short story, plot is ordinarily a component of character. We are usually made aware of plot as it is sifted through the eyes of a character or characters, or even as it is revealed by means of a sum of events which occur within a set of characters, as in Conrad's "Il Conde." This shift from plot to character is possibly the chief development in modern fiction. Nevertheless, Poe demonstrates that plot in its old-fashioned sense can create excitement, even in a story as well worn as "The Cask of Amontillado."

1 No matter how simplified his plot or plot structure, an author must use certain devices to carry the story forward. Poe has several of these devices embedded in his story. Explain the following as elements of plot:

a The motley that Fortunato wears
b The carnival season
c The character Luchresi, who never appears
d The Montresors' coat of arms
e The ever-present nitre
f The setting of the catacombs
g The flagon of De Grâve
h The pun on masons and masonry
i The presence of human bones
j Fortunato's cough
k The screams of the narrator in reply to Fortunato's yells
l The Amontillado as the source of greed and vanity
m The jingling of the bells
n The significance of "In pace requiescat"

o The character of the narrator

p The character of Fortunato

2 How does the plot of this story grow out of the setting and the atmosphere? If either were changed, what elements of the plot would have to be changed as well? Does integration of setting, atmosphere, and plot seem to be a valid criterion for judging the worth of a story?

FIGHT NUMBER TWENTY-FIVE

Jesse Stuart

I'd just taken my first shipment of hides to the Greenwood express office when Hade Stableton saw me.

"Eddie—hey, you Eddie Battlestrife—just a minute," Hade hollered at me. "I want to see you!"

"Make it snappy," I yelled. "I want to get this batch of hides on Number Three."

I didn't want to fool with Hade. For every time he'd ever stopped me in his life, he wanted to borrow something from me or he wanted me to do something for him.

"Eddie, I had bad luck last night," Hade grunted soon as he reached me.

"What happened?" I asked.

"Lost my good tree dog, old Rags, and a hundred dollars to boot," he sighed. "You caused it, Eddie!"

"How did I cause it?" I asked him.

"Remember that big wildcat you catched out on Seaton Ridge?" he asked me.

"But what does that have to do with your losin' your best tree dog and a hundred dollars?" I asked. "That wildcat went to West Virginia."

"West Virginia, hell," Hade said. "That wildcat's right up here at Auckland in a cage. I wish that wildcat's hide was among this batch of fur you're expressin'. I'd be a lot better off."

"How'd that wildcat get to Auckland?" I said. "I sold 'im to Elmer Pratt."

"You know who's got the wildcat now?"

"No, I don't."

"Jason Radnor's got 'im," Hade told me.

"Jason Radnor?" I said.

"Yep, Jason Radnor's got 'im," Hade said, shaking his head sadly. "He's got 'im in a big cage. And you pay a dollar to get in to see the cat fight a dog. If you fight a dog against the cat, you pay five dollars! And there's plenty of betting a-goin' on. Old Jason will cover any bet that the cat will whip a dog. Now he's even giving odds. Last night bets went up to five hundred dollars. Jason covered everything that the men bet against his cat!"

"I sold that wildcat to Elmer Pratt for fifty dollars," I said. "I don't need a cat. I didn't want to keep 'im. I could get more for 'im that way than I could for his pelt."

"I know it's bad, Eddie," Hade said. "But I thought I'd tell you! I thought you ought to know about it."

"Yes, I'm glad you told me," I said, as I began thinking about what the wildcat had done to Hade's dog. "I need to know about it. Where do they have that cage?"

"Over the hill from the slaughterhouse where we used to fight our game roosters. But listen, Eddie," Hade went on to warn me, "if you're thinkin' about a-takin' old Buck up there and fightin' that cat you'd better be keerful! I'm a-tellin' you, Eddie! It looked like easy money to me. And I went atter it. Old Scout kilt many a wildcat too. But he never fit one like this cat! He'll never fight another cat! Scout was the nineteenth dog the wildcat's kilt. Boys told me up there last night that old Jason was a-feedin' the wildcat beef blood to make 'im mean. Never saw a meaner cat in my life! Didn't hardly get old Scout in the cage until the cat sprang on him and laid open his side until you could see a whole panel of his ribs!"

"But that didn't kill 'im?" I said.

"Nope, but the old cat spat 'im with the other paw," Hade said. "That finished the best dog I ever had! Had to give a man five dollars to take Scout out behind the house and shoot 'im to put 'im outen his misery. Guns barked all the time I was there. Had to take the dogs that fit the cat out behind the house and polish 'em off."

"I'd fight that wildcat myself," I said, as I thought about the poor dogs the cat had mangled. "I'll go in the cage with it!"

"Somebody'd haf to polish you off, too," Hade said. "Now don't get riled. Don't get worked up and lose your head. If I'd a-knowed it would've upset you like this I wouldn't have told you!"

I stood a minute looking down at the toe of my shoe. I thought about the October night when old Buck put the cat up a tree and the way he ran it, full speed like he's after a fox. That was the way Buck had put many a coon up a tree. And just as soon as he treed, I hurried to the tree, thinking he'd got me a coon. But when I reached the place where he was barkin' up a great saw-timber-sized oak with branches big enough for crossties sprangled out from its bushy top, I knew it wasn't any coon. I hardly had to use my lamp, for the big wagon wheel of an October moon was as bright as day and flooded the fields and woods with light.

And the wind had whipped enough of the rich wine-colored leaves from the tree so that I could about see over every limb. I walked around the tree looking up and spied the old cat, stretched out, his belly against a big flat limb. He didn't look worried to me. He looked like a cat that was full of confidence. He was a pretty thing a-layin' up there on the limb with his head a-stickin' over and his eyes shining like wind-whipped embers on a pitch-black night.

"Buck, you won't fight 'im," I said to myself. "I'll take care of him, myself." So I went up the tree with my lasso rope. The old cat didn't mind my climbing up there. He laid perfectly still. He was a-takin' himself a good rest. Buck had crowded him pretty hard in the chase. He didn't let him get to the Artner rock cliffs. That was where the wildcats denned. I climbed up at about the right distance and hung my lamp on a twig. I looked for the right opening to throw my rope so I wouldn't hit a limb and scare the cat and make him jump from the tree. I didn't want Buck to fight this cat; I wanted to take 'im alive. I found the right opening. I steadied myself and I threw my lasso.

Guess I was lucky. It went around his neck and I jerked the slack as the cat jumped. But I had him. The more he jumped the tighter the rope drew around his neck. And when his long red tongue popped outen his mouth, I drew him up to me, some weight at the end of the rope. I took him from the tree and released the lasso enough to give him enough breath to keep him alive. I tied his feet with the cords, good and tight. I kept the lasso tight enough not to give him too much wind. I put the wildcat under my arm and carried him to Blakesburg.

Old Buck wasn't satisfied because he didn't get to fight the cat, and he trailed along at my heels a little disappointed. But I knew this was a good catch for one night. It was more than a coffee sack full of dead possums, coons, polecats, minks, weasels, and foxes. If you hunt in these woods, fifty dollars for one night is not to be sneezed at. And it made me the most respected hunter in Blake County, for I was the only man that had ever gone up a tree and took a wildcat with my hands and carried him home in my arms. People knew that I did it, for I'd done it many times before. Older hunters than I was had seen me do it. I took the wildcat home, put him in a cage, and when people passed along the street, they'd come to look at him. And it pleased me when they walked over to see what kind of a looking man I was, just a little, slender, beanpole-sized man with a scraggly beard, that could go up a tree and catch a wildcat.

"Eddie, I'm a-tellin' you not to fight old Buck against that cat," Hade said. "If you'd see that thing cut a dog all to pieces once, you'd never go up in the tree and take him down any more. You'd lose your nerve. The way my poor old Scout run to the side of the cage, looked at me, and cried like a baby," Hade's voice changed until I thought he was crying, "I'll never be able to forget."

I couldn't stand to see that, I thought. I love dogs too well. But I didn't say another word to Hade. Thoughts were running through my mind. I walked into the express office and left Hade standing.

"Remember, Eddie, that my dog was the nineteenth dog that cat had kilt," Hade warned me. "Remember, Radnor'll take your money and—"

I didn't hear the rest of his words. I knew what I was going to do. I knew Buck or I, one, would fight the cat. I didn't want it a-killin' any more dogs. And I knew that I'd like to fight Jason Radnor to even up an old score. I didn't care if he did weigh two hundred and ninety. I hardly knew what I was doin' when I expressed my batch of hides. I went to the First and Peoples Bank and drew out every dollar I'd ever saved. When I got home, I went over to the corner of the house where I had old Buck tied.

"Buck, one of us has to kill a wildcat tonight," I said. "Do you think you can do it?"

Old Buck looked up at me with his big, soft, brown eyes. Then I unsnapped his chain and started across the yard. I was on my way.

"You're not a-goin' a-huntin' this early," Mollie said when she saw me leading Buck across the yard.

"Yep, I am," I said. "There's a wildcat that's a-killin' a lot of dogs and we want to get 'im."

"Do be careful, Eddie," Mollie warned me. "If it's that dangerous and old Buck trees it, don't you go up and take it from the tree."

"I'll promise you I won't take it from a tree," I said.

I wonder if old Jason will remember me, I thought, as I walked toward Auckland, a distance of twelve miles.

When I reached the shack down the hill from the slaughterhouse there was a man ahead of me with a big English bull.

"There's the dog that'll kill that damned wildcat," a beardy-faced man said, pointing to the big broad bulldog.

The beardy-faced man looked at old Buck, then he looked at

me. Buck wasn't a big dog. And he looked pinched in two, for I hadn't fed him anything. I didn't want to feed 'im anything before a fight. Buck smelled blood and trouble. He held his tail down as if he were about to spring at something. Then I heard a pistol go off behind the house and I knew another dog was finished. Buck was on his mettle, for he didn't know exactly what was taking place. I pulled my hat down low and got my six-hundred-odd dollars ready.

Soon as the big red-faced man ahead of me had paid the five dollars to fight his bulldog, I stepped up to the entrance.

"Say, feller," said the tall, hatchet-faced man at the door, "you don't aim to fight that old dog against this wildcat, do you? He's not as big as the wildcat!"

"I want to fight the dog or fight the wildcat myself," I said, and then I gave a wild laugh.

The man looked at me with his black, beady eyes like he thought I was crazy. But he let me inside the shack.

It was a big room filled with men and a few dogs. Over at the far end of the room was a big wire cage. And inside the cage lay the same old wildcat that I had taken from the oak tree on Seaton Ridge. He was a-layin' there as peaceful-like, just like any cat, with his head across his paws, as if he wanted to sleep and the men and dogs wouldn't let him. He looked just as mean as he did the night I carried him back to Blakesburg. His big tushes hung out over his lips. And his whiskers looked like old Davey Burton's handle-bar mustache. Beardy-faced men, with mean-looking eyes, stood back and looked at the cat. I led Buck up to the cage where he could get a whiff of the cat. I looked down to see what Buck thought. All he did was jerk his tail. He never even growled.

When the big, clean-shaven, well-dressed man led his bulldog up to the cage, the bull tried to break through to the cat. He trembled all over, growled, and scratched the floor. When he barked, the slobbers flew from his big mouth.

"I'm a-puttin' up a hundred dollars on that dog," a man said. "What odds you givin'?"

And then the bets started. I looked over against the wall and there sat big Jason Radnor behind a table, counting out money to cover the bet. Since the cat belonged to Jason, no one but him was allowed to bet on the cat. Jason covered all the money that was hot on the dog, giving three-to-two odds. It was a funny way to bet, and we'd never bet that way at rooster fighting. And I guess that's why everybody wanted to see the cat killed. Jason was raking in the money. But I wanted to see the cat killed because it was killin' the dogs.

"Jason's got a gold mine with that cat," said a tall lantern-jawed man who was standing beside me.

And while the greenbacks were shelled out on top of the table, for the bulldog was a good bet, Jason pulled money from a drawer and covered each bet. I watched Jason to see if he was looking at me and if he recognized me. But he was too busy betting and making money to recognize anybody. He was sitting there with all that money around him, and I knew this kind of betting was better than playing poker on Sundays or spitting at cracks. Jason was in the money.

"Say, mister, what have you been a-feedin' that bulldog?" asked a short, dark-complexioned man.

"Beef blood and beef bones," the owner said. "I've been a-feedin' 'im that and getting 'im ready for this fight ever since Radnor first brought the cat here!"

"I'll bet a hundred then," the man said.

Jason covered his hundred while the bulldog charged at the chain.

"All bets in?" Jason asked.

There wasn't any answer.

"Let 'im in the gate, Little Man," Jason said.

A little man with a scattered, heavy beard on his weather-beaten face unlocked the cage door. And the big man patted his dog on the back.

He's a good-lookin' bull to be slaughtered by that cat, I thought.

"Take 'im, Buck, and good luck!" the man spoke with a trembling voice as he unsnapped the collar and the bulldog charged full force toward the cat. As the bulldog charged at its throat, the cat leaped high in the air, and when it came down on the dog's back, it raked a paw around his slats, his big claws, longer than a tack hammer, sinking deeper and deeper as the bulldog groaned.

"There goes my money," a man shouted.

"There goes all our money," the tall man said. "Damn, I wish we'd get a dog that could kill that hellcat. I've lost over a thousand dollars in this dang hole."

I didn't listen to all the men said. I looked down at my Buck. He was moving his tail like a cat does when it sees a mouse and gets ready for the crouch. When the poor bulldog got the cat's claws from his ribs, he came over to the wire and cried like a baby. I never heard more pitiful crying. It hurt me through and through to hear it.

"He's through," a man said. "When they do that, they've had enough. Take him from the cage."

He didn't look like he was clawed up too badly until he came from the cage.

"Mister, you'll have to have Sherman to polish 'im off," Little Man said. "He's through. If you don't have 'im finished, he'll die by degrees."

When the well-dressed man led his bulldog out behind the house to have Sherman polish him off, another tall lanky man from Culp Creek came up with a big mountain cur. He was a long dog with a mean black eye.

You might not get to fight the cat, Buck, I thought. If I were betting, I'd bet on this dog.

"What have you been a-feedin' this dog, mister?" a little stooped-shouldered man asked.

"Corndodger," the cur's owner said. "Just what you feed a good dog."

"I was raised on it, mister," another man said. "I'm bettin' fifty on your dog!"

"Looks like a good bet to me," a tall lanky man with fuzzy chin whiskers said. "I like his build. Listen to his growlin' at that cat! Sounds like low thunder!"

But the bets didn't go as high as they did on the English bull. I looked over at Jason's table and I didn't see the stacks of greenbacks like I'd seen there a few minutes before. And just as the last money was in and Jason was covering it, we heard a pistol fire twice. The English bull had been polished off. And the big mountain cur, with his bristles raised on his back like jutted rocks along the top of a winter-bleak mountain, charged against the chain to get to the cat.

"Ready to go, Little Man," Jason said. "Turn 'im in."

The beard-scant, weathered-looking little man who tended to the cage unlocked the door, and the tall man let the big cur inside and unsnapped the collar. When the cat saw this big black mountain cur, he never rose to his feet but laid flat on his back as the dog charged, and just as the dog started over for the cat's throat, he ripped into him from beneath with both hind feet. The cur whined, fell over, got up again, and whined as pitifully as a small baby crying. He walked slowly to a corner of the cage—I couldn't bear to look at him. I wanted to get into that cage so bad I could hardly stand it.

"It's a shame," one of the men said, "to fight good dogs against that murdering wildcat. You can feed 'em beef, beef's blood, corndodger, and anything you want to feed 'em, but that doesn't make any difference when it comes to a fight. Not one dog has stayed with that cat three minutes!"

"Lost again," another man said, not paying any attention to the poor cur that had lost his life. "Lost another fifty bucks."

Sighs went up from among the mean-eyed men when Little Man pulled the cur through the door. He was awful to look at, and to think of him now makes me mad. Old Buck looked at the poor cut-to-pieces cur disgustedly.

"Get 'im to Sherman quick," Little Man said. "Let 'im polish 'im off soon as he can, to put 'im outen his misery."

We saw two more fights. We saw the cat lay on his back and cut a pretty shepherd to pieces. There wasn't much betting on this fight although the shepherd came the nearest getting to the cat's throat of any of the dogs. And there was a big brindle bulldog that the cat seemed to hate more than any dog that had been turned in. That bull never even got close to the wildcat. He had him cut to pieces before he got halfway across the cage. What was left of him was dragged outside by his master, a well-dressed city man from Auckland.

"I'm glad it's over," said a big fat man with a handle-bar mustache. "I'd rather see cockfighting, a boxing bout, or a wrestling match any old time as to see these good-looking dogs go in there and get ripped up."

"Yep, I'd rather go with my wife to the movies as to slip out here to this unlawful place and see this," said the tall man who had bet heavily on every fight against the cat.

"It's a wonder this place ain't raided by the law!"

"But it's not over yet," I said loud enough so the men could hear me.

They were mixing around and intermingling in the crowded room, getting ready to leave. And I couldn't blame them for that. I'd smelled enough and I'd seen enough for one evening. The smell in the shack was awful. The crowd was awful, too.

I couldn't understand how anybody could enjoy seein' dogs cut to pieces by a wildcat.

"But that dog can't do anything," one man said. "That cat'd kill 'im before Little Man got 'im inside."

"Little Man ain't a-puttin' this dog in," I said. "I'm goin' in the cage with 'im myself."

"What's that I hear?" Jason said from over in the corner, as he stacked his money away.

"I'm going to take old Buck in myself," I said.

"Are you crazy, feller?" Jason said. "Don't you know if a man gets ripped up here, we can't have Sherman to polish 'im off, and this place will be raided shore enough."

"I wouldn't be afraid to fight that cat," I said. "Give me a piece of rope fourteen feet long and I'll fight 'im."

"Don't be foolish," Jason said. "You don't seem to know much about the power of a wildcat!"

Then I heard a lot of whispers in the crowd. I heard men saying that I was off in the head.

"How much are you willing to bet that my wildcat won't kill your dog?" Jason said. "You'll be the only one to bet on your dog. No one else will!"

"I think I got about six hundred and fifty-three dollars," I said. "It's my life savings and I don't want to bet it all."

"Well, I've got ten times that," Jason said. "I'll put my pile against yours!"

Then the men who'd been moving toward the door stopped. They were surprised at the money I had. And they were surprised when Jason said he'd put up all he had against what I had. They knew he had a pile, for he had taken their money on twenty-four fights. My dog was Number Twenty-five for the cat to fight. And I knew all the men except Sherman, Little Man, Jason, and the fellow who took our money at the door would be for me. They'd want to see my dog win.

"Mister Radnor, I hate to bet all my money," I said. "If I lose, I won't have a dollar in the world left and my dog will be gone."

"Well, that's what you come here for, to fight that old mongrel, wasn't it?" Jason said gruffly as he put the last roll of bills back in the table drawer. "And I'd as soon have your money as anybody else's."

"Yes, but I didn't know you had such a big wildcat," I said. "And I can't stand to see it a-killin' all these fine-looking dogs."

"Come on or get out," Jason said. "After all, we bet here. This isn't a playhouse. It's a fightin' house."

"Will you let me take my dog inside? If you will, I'll put my pile up against yours!"

"I'm afraid of it," Jason said.

"Let 'im learn," one of the men shouted. "We've seen about everything now. Let's see something new!"

"I'm willin' to run the risk," Jason said thoughtfully, as he arose from the table and looked me over.

Then I went over to the table and counted out my money. Jason brought his from the drawer and I made him let me look inside to see that the drawer was clean.

"You watch the money, men," I said to the fellows gathered around me. "I want this to be square and honest."

"We'll see to that," said the fellow that had lost the big English bull.

"Sure we will," said the one that had lost the cur.

"Then open the door, Little Man," I said.

Old Buck didn't growl and he didn't charge against the chain. He just looked at the cat and jerked his tail.

"He's a funny dog," said one of the men behind me.

But I didn't look back to see who had said it. I had my eye on the cat. Buck had his eye on the cat. Then I reached down and rubbed his back. I patted his head as I reached midway of the cage. The cat laid perfectly still. He planned to work on Buck like he did the big mountain cur. Then I unsnapped Buck's chain. Buck crouched halfway. But he didn't take his eye off the cat. And he never growled, but he crept slowly toward the cat as I stepped to one side. Men rushed up and stood on their toes around the cage, like something was going to happen.

Buck went close. But he wouldn't go farther.

"Watch 'im, Buck," I said. "Let 'im make the first move."

Buck held like an Irish setter—he didn't go a step. The cat looked at him with his shiny green eyes, and Buck looked back at the cat. Then all at once the cat began to crouch. Buck held his position. Then the cat made a flying charge and Buck flattened on the cage floor. As the cat went over, Buck whirled and sprang from behind like April lightning. He caught the cat across the skull and the sound went plunk. It was a light crash but the cat sprawled senseless on the floor, its legs quivering and drawing up to its body then out again, each time a little weaker.

"What did that dog do?" a man asked me.

"What about that?" another man said.

"Leave that money or there'll be another death," I heard a voice growl.

"That dog knows how to tree wildcats," I said. "And he knows how to kill them. It's been suicide on the dogs to put them in here, dogs that never fought a wildcat. Buck knows that a wildcat's skull is as easy to crush as a rabbit's. It's a little bit easier—a wildcat's skull is thinner."

"Good boy, Buck." I patted his head.

I snapped the chain into his collar and we left the cage. The wildcat had breathed his last.

"There's your cat, Jason Radnor," I said. "He'll never kill another dog. And the money you made by clawin' dogs to pieces won't do you any good."

"Who are you, anyway?" Jason said, his voice trembling. He was shaking all over.

"Jason, I'm the man that caught that wildcat," I said. "My dog treed it and I went up in the tree and brought it down with my hands. I'm Eddie Battlestrife. You remember my dad, don't you—remember, you tried to kill him? Shot 'im not four feet away between the eyes but you didn't kill him. The bullet parted his hair. He was taking a few quarters from you in a poker game that Sunday afternoon. Now don't shake, Jason, I'm not a-goin' to hurt you. I just want all that money. It's good money and I like money and I like to see old Buck kill a wildcat that's kilt twenty-four dogs."

"Easy, Radnor," said the tall man that owned the cur. "Don't move. Keep your hands up! He took your money and he took it fair."

"Fairer than the way you got it from us," the bulldog's owner said.

"Nice bank account now," I said as I picked up the rolls of greenbacks and put them back in my hunting coat.

"It's a fraud," Jason wept. "It's a stick-up!"

"Easy, Mr. Radnor," the tall man said, as I walked from the shack with old Buck. "Keep your hands up!"

"You won't have to polish this dog off, Sherman," I said as I went through the door. "You can bury your cat."

Plot

This story differs from most others in this collection in its stress upon plot. In fact, the somewhat old-fashioned appearance of the material is a consequence of an emphasis upon plot and plot structure. Yet the nature of Stuart's material calls for just this emphasis.

1 If you outline the events of the story in chronological order, do you find that the story loses much? How much? Does it lose as much as a story like Bellow's "Leaving the Yellow House" or Joyce's "Counterparts"?

2 Notice that much of the point of view is the narrator's, the "I" of the first line, Eddie Battlestrife. Do you think the plot gains from this personal involvement, or would you prefer a third-person narrative for such material? How about a narrative from the owner of the wildcat? Or a combination of points of view?

3 Is the plotting satisfactory in all places, or do you find it improbable? Does the story lose anything? Or can you justify any improbabilities you might discover?

4 Does the revenge motif at the end deflect our interest from the main plot? Is that motif necessary at all, or could the story have ended with the triumph of Buck and the settlement of the bet?

Characterization

1 Are the men characterized in any depth? Does this type of story require greater characterization? Why or why not?

2 Can we consider Buck a character in this story? Do you find the unity and the credibility of the story violated by raising an animal to this level of importance? Why does Stuart have the dog take on certain qualities while the wildcat remains simply a wild animal?

3 Are there distinctions that the author makes among the animals, as between the English bull and Buck, as between the big mountain cur and Buck?

4 Are there several distinctions among the men themselves? What kind of men does Stuart present? Do they all fit into types, or are they individualized?

Setting

1 Try to reconstruct the setting from what Stuart tells us. Is the information sufficient, or do we need more background for the story? How would you characterize this setting? What does it have in common with the setting of Faulkner's "Dry September" or Powers' "The Eye"?

2 Do the sums of money seem unbelievably high for this type of setting? If they do, do you think Stuart had any purpose in making them so high?

3 Given the setting, wouldn't Eddie have claimed the cat's hide and sold it along with his other hides? Does his sarcastic line at the end seem inconsistent with his character, or is there some reason for his remark?

Theme

Many of us are familiar with the "tall tale" and the folk legends popular in many parts of rural America. Some of these tales and legends also go back further to ancient myths dealing with monsters which terrorized the countryside until the "savior" came along and slew them.

1 What elements of this story fit such tales and legends?

2 Where does the name of the narrator fit into this scheme?

3 Does Stuart make the story realistic within the framework of a legend or myth? If so, how does he do it? Do you think the story loses anything by straining your credulity in places?

FOUR

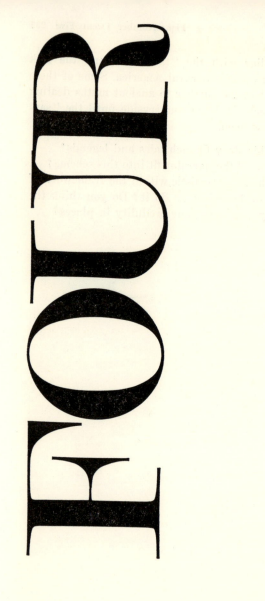

CHARACTER

As indicated in several of our story analyses, one of the chief developments in modern fiction has been in the increasing emphasis upon characterization. Many of the stories set in other categories in this collection could as easily have been stressed here, with slight shifts in tone and attitude. The reasons for the emergence of character are complex, but not the least is the discovery and development of psychoanalysis. As psychoanalysts have revealed more and more about the inner reserves of the individual, authors have naturally enough found new areas to probe. Speculation about the psychological nature of man now has a firmer foundation than it ever had.

This is not to state, of course, that character was not an important element in earlier fiction. Obviously it was, and many nineteenth-century novelists are remembered chiefly as creators of great characters. What the above comment does mean is that character development has become, in most instances, more subtle. New developments have meant that character as such is less clear, more of it below the surface or merged with other elements. Thus, a "modern" character fits into no neat pigeonholes (not that he ever really did); often, he is completely different from what he seems, and the author's attitude toward him must be recognized as ironical or ambiguous.

Begin to understand a literary character by attempting a description in your own terms. Carry this description as far as it will go, into the psychological makeup of the character, into questions of his individual and social nature, into areas of his normality or (relative) insanity. Attempt to see what he is—whether he is socially motivated or whether his actions and words derive from some inner mystery. Whenever possible, attempt to probe the mystery, the ambiguous ego that constitutes a human being. Most modern writers are attempting to do this very thing themselves.

After this, examine the consistency of the character, but only after you have determined if he should be consistent. Consistency might be a fault in a character intended to demonstrate the opposite. Then, see whether the character is an individual or a type—and which better serves the author's purpose. If the story is allegorical, that is, concerned only with meaning, the character may well be a type, a general representation of the message the author wishes to impart.

From a purely technical point of view, consider how the author develops his characters. Does he probe internally or describe externally? Does he work through contrast and comparison? Does the character become identified with a symbol, and for what purpose? Are the conflicts, such as they are, the result of the character's struggle with inner demons or with social forces? Is there sufficient motivation and does it seem well placed?

Further, you should ask yourself how the author's view of character reveals his view of the world. That is, how do the characters and the author's attitude toward them demonstrate his theme? Only rarely will a writer state any special point of view, but often he will incorporate what he means in a particular character or in a confrontation between characters. Many of the stories in this section, indeed in this entire collection, are "opened up" through the author's use of character. If you fail to understand that, you miss the import of the story.

Finally, character is of interest for the very personal reason that we want to see how other people live, how they make decisions and react to responsibility, how they pursue their goals. We measure ourselves by them. Think of characters in stories and novels as real people, and then let your imagination go.

THE PRISON

Bernard Malamud

Though he tried not to think of it, at twenty-nine Tommy Castelli's life was a screaming bore. It wasn't just Rosa or the store they tended for profits counted in pennies, or the unendurably slow hours and endless drivel that went with selling candy, cigarettes, and soda water; it was this sick-in-the-stomach feeling of being trapped in old mistakes, even some he had made before Rosa changed Tony into Tommy. He had been as Tony a kid of many dreams and schemes, especially getting out of this tenement-crowded, kid-squawking neighborhood, with its lousy poverty, but everything had fouled up against him before he could. When he was sixteen he quit the vocational school where they were making him into a shoemaker, and began to hang out with the gray-hatted, thick-soled-shoe boys, who had the spare time and the mazuma and showed it in fat wonderful rolls down in the cellar clubs to all who would look, and everybody did, popeyed. They were the ones who had bought the silver caffe espresso urn and later the television, and they arranged the pizza parties and had the girls down; but it was getting in with them and their cars, leading to the holdup of a liquor store, that had started all the present trouble. Lucky for him the coal-and-ice man who was their landlord knew the leader in the district, and they arranged something so nobody bothered him after that. Then before he knew what was going on—he had been frightened sick by the whole mess—there was his father cooking up a deal with Rosa Agnello's old man that Tony would marry her and the father-in-law would, out of his savings, open a candy store for him to make an honest living. He wouldn't spit on a candy store, and Rosa was too plain and lank a chick for his personal taste, so he beat it off to Texas and bummed around in too much space, and when he came back everybody said it was for Rosa and the candy store, and it was all arranged again and he, without saying no, was in it.

That was how he had landed on Prince Street in the Village, working from eight in the morning to almost midnight every day, except for an hour off each afternoon when he went upstairs to sleep, and on Tuesdays, when the store was closed and he slept some more and went at night alone to the movies. He was too tired always for schemes now, but once he tried to make a little cash on the side by secretly taking in punchboards some syndicate was distributing in the neighborhood, on which he collected a nice cut and in this way saved fifty-five bucks that Rosa didn't know about; but then the syndicate was written up by a newspaper, and the punchboards all disappeared. Another time, when Rosa was at her mother's house, he took a chance and let them put in a slot machine that could guarantee a nice piece of change if he kept it long enough. He knew of course he couldn't hide it from her, so when she came and screamed when she saw it, he was ready and patient, for once not yelling back when she yelled, and he explained it was not the same as gambling because anybody who played it got a roll of mints every time he put in a nickel. Also the machine would supply them a few extra dollars cash they could use to buy television so he could see the fights without going to a bar; but Rosa wouldn't let up screaming, and later her father came in shouting that he was a criminal and chopped the machine apart with a plumber's hammer. The next day the cops raided for slot machines and gave out summonses wherever they found them, and though Tommy's place was practically the only candy store in the neighborhood that didn't have one, he felt bad about the machine for a long time.

Mornings had been his best time of day because Rosa stayed upstairs cleaning, and since few people came into the store till noon, he could sit around alone, a toothpick in his teeth, looking over the *News* and *Mirror* on the fountain counter, or maybe gab with one of the old cellar-club guys who had happened to come by for a pack of butts, about a horse that was running that day or how the numbers were paying lately; or just sit there, drinking coffee and thinking how far away he could get on the fifty-five he had stashed away in the cellar. Generally the mornings were this way, but after the slot machine, usually the whole day stank and he along with it. Time rotted in him, and all he could think of the whole morning, was going to sleep in the afternoon, and he would wake up with the sour remembrance of the long night in the store ahead of him, while everybody else was doing as he damn pleased. He cursed the candy store and Rosa, and cursed, from its beginning, his unhappy life.

It was on one of these bad mornings that a ten-year-old girl from around the block came in and asked for two rolls of colored tissue paper, one red and one yellow. He wanted to tell her to go to hell and stop bothering, but instead went with bad grace to the rear, where Rosa, whose bright idea it was to keep the stuff, had put it. He went from force of habit, for the girl had been coming in every Monday since the summer for the same thing, because her rock-faced mother, who looked as if she arranged her own widowhood, took care of some small kids after school and gave them the paper to cut out dolls and such things. The girl, whose name he didn't know, resembled her mother, except her features were not quite so sharp and she had very light skin with dark eyes; but she was a plain kid and would be more so at twenty. He had noticed, when he went to get the paper, that she always hung back as if afraid to go where it was dark, though he kept the comics there and most of the other kids had to be slapped away from them; and that when he brought her the tissue paper her skin seemed to grow whiter and her eyes shone. She always handed him two hot dimes and went out without glancing back.

It happened that Rosa, who trusted nobody, had just hung a mirror on the back wall, and as Tommy opened the drawer to get the girl her paper this Monday morning that he felt so bad, he looked up and saw in the glass something that made it seem as if he were dreaming. The girl had disappeared, but he saw a white hand reach into the candy case for a chocolate bar and for another, then she came forth from behind the counter and stood there, innocently waiting for him. He felt at first like grabbing her by the neck and socking till she threw up, but he had been caught, as he sometimes was, by this thought of how his Uncle Dom, years ago before he went away, used to take with him Tony alone of all the kids, when he went crabbing to Sheepshead Bay. Once they went at night and threw the baited wire traps into the water and after a while pulled them up and they had this green lobster in one, and just then this fat-faced cop came along and said they had to throw it back unless it was nine inches. Dom said it was nine inches, but the cop said not to be a wise guy so Dom measured it and it was ten, and they laughed about that lobster all night. Then he remembered how he had felt after Dom was gone, and tears filled his eyes. He found himself thinking about the way his life had turned out, and then about this girl, moved that she was so young and a thief. He felt he ought to do something for her, warn her to cut it out before she got trapped and fouled up her life before it got started. His urge to do this was strong, but when he went forward she looked up frightened because he had taken so long. The fear in her eyes bothered him and he didn't say anything. She thrust out the dimes, grabbed at the tissue rolls and ran out of the store.

He had to sit down. He kept trying to make the desire to speak to her go away, but it came back stronger than ever. He asked himself what difference does it make if she swipes candy—so she swipes it; and the role of reformer was strange and distasteful to him, yet he could not convince himself that what he felt he must do was unimportant. But he worried he would not know what to say to her. Always he had trouble speaking right, stumbled over words, especially in new situations. He was afraid he would sound like a jerk and she would not take him seriously. He had to tell her in a sure way so that even if it scared her, she would understand he had done it to set her straight. He mentioned her to no one but often thought about her, always looking around whenever he went outside to raise the awning or wash the window, to see if any of the girls playing in the street was her, but they never were. The following Monday, an hour after opening the store he had smoked a full pack of butts. He thought he had found what he wanted to say but was afraid for some reason she wouldn't come in, or if she did, this time she would be afraid to take the candy. He wasn't sure he wanted that to happen until he had said what he had to say. But at about eleven, while he was reading the *News*, she appeared, asking for the tissue paper, her eyes shining so he had to look away. He knew she meant to steal. Going to the rear he slowly opened the drawer, keeping his head lowered as he sneaked a look into the glass and saw her slide behind the counter. His heart beat hard and his feet felt nailed to the floor. He tried to remember what he had intended to do, but his mind was like a dark, empty room so he let her, in the end, slip away and stood tongue-tied, the dimes burning his palm.

Afterwards, he told himself that he hadn't spoken to her because it was while she still had the candy on her, and she would have been scared worse than he wanted. When he went upstairs, instead of sleeping, he sat at the kitchen window, looking out into the back yard. He blamed himself for being too soft, too chicken, but then he thought, no there was a better way to do it. He would do it indirectly, slip her a hint he knew, and he was pretty sure that would stop her. Sometime after, he would explain to her why it was good she had stopped. So next time he cleaned out this candy platter she helped herself from, thinking she might get wise he was on to her, but she seemed not to, only hesitated with her hand before she took two candy bars from the next plate and dropped them into the black patent leather purse she always had with her. The time after that he cleaned out the whole top shelf, and still she was not suspicious, and reached down to the next and took something different. One Monday he put some loose change, nickels and dimes, on the candy plate, but she left them there, only taking the candy, which bothered him a little. Rosa asked him what he was mooning about so much and why was he eating chocolate lately. He didn't answer her, and she began to look suspiciously at the women who came in, not excluding the little girls; and he would have been glad to rap her in the teeth, but it didn't matter as long as she didn't know what he had on his mind. At the same time he figured he would have to do something sure soon, or it would get harder for the girl to stop her stealing. He had to be strong about it. Then he thought of a plan that satisfied him. He would leave two bars on the plate and put in the wrapper of one a note she could read when she was alone. He tried out on paper many messages to her, and the one that seemed best he cleanly printed on a strip of cardboard and slipped it under the wrapper of one chocolate bar. It said, "Don't do this any more or you will suffer your whole life." He puzzled whether to sign it A Friend or Your Friend and finally chose Your Friend.

This was Friday, and he could not hold his impatience for Monday. But on Monday she did not appear. He waited for a long time, until Rosa came down, then he had to go up and the girl still hadn't come. He was greatly disappointed because she had never failed to come before. He lay on the bed, his shoes on, staring at the ceiling. He felt hurt, the sucker she had played him for and was now finished with because she probably had another on her hook. The more he thought about it the worse he felt. He worked up a splitting headache that kept him from sleeping, then he suddenly slept and woke without it. But he had awaked depressed, saddened. He thought about Dom getting out of jail and going away God knows where. He wondered whether he would ever meet up with him somewhere, if he took the fifty-five bucks and left. Then he remembered Dom was a pretty old guy now, and he might not know him if they did meet. He thought about life. You never really got what you wanted. No matter how hard you tried you made mistakes and couldn't get past them. You could never see the sky outside or the ocean because you were in a prison, except nobody called it a prison, and if you did they didn't know what you were talking about, or they said they didn't. A pall settled on him. He lay motionless, without thought or sympathy for himself or anybody.

But when he finally went downstairs, ironically amused that Rosa had allowed him so long a time without bitching, there were people in the store and he could hear her screeching. Shoving his way through the crowd he saw in one sickening look that she had caught the girl with the candy bars and was shaking her so hard the kid's head bounced back and forth like a balloon on a stick. With a curse he tore her away from the girl, whose sickly face showed the depth of her fright.

"Whatsamatter," he shouted at Rosa, "you want her blood?"

"She's a thief," cried Rosa.

"Shut your face."

To stop her yowling he slapped her across her mouth, but it was a harder crack than he had intended. Rosa fell back with a gasp. She did not cry but looked around dazedly at everybody, and tried to smile, and everybody there could see her teeth were flecked with blood.

"Go home," Tommy ordered the girl, but then there was a movement near the door and her mother came into the store.

"What happened?" she said.

"She stole my candy," Rosa cried.

"I let her take it," said Tommy.

Rosa stared at him as if she had been hit again, then with mouth distorted began to sob.

"One was for you, Mother," said the girl.

Her mother socked her hard across the face. "You little thief, this time you'll get your hands burned good."

She pawed at the girl, grabbed her arm and yanked it. The girl, like a grotesque dancer, half ran, half fell forward, but at the door she managed to turn her white face and thrust out at him her red tongue.

Character

Although this story might be considered under plot or even setting as well as under character, Malamud seems to emphasize Tommy Castelli over the other elements. By filtering all the events of the narrative through Tommy's eyes and mind, Malamud indicates that these events are colored by the way Tommy sees them. Often this distinction is the sole one between character and plot, so intertwined are they with each other. If the main character appears weak, then plot appears stronger; and, conversely, with a strong character, the plot becomes secondary. In Poe's "The Cask of Amontillado," for example, the same problem might arise. But there the background of Fortunato is so shadowy and vague that we are carried along almost solely by the plot.

1 Does Malamud give you enough information about Tommy Castelli so that he is "created" in your mind? How does Malamud force the reader to create and reconstruct the character? An image of Tommy is necessary if you are to understand why he behaves the way he does toward the young girl. If Malamud has failed to suggest sufficient motivation, then Tommy's desire to help the girl becomes meaningless.
2 How does the title of the story contribute to your understanding of Tommy?
3 What are some of the things frustrating him? Does he feel cut out for better things? Such as?
4 Are his desires dishonest, or do we sympathize with them? How does Malamud create sympathy for Tommy, even though many of his actions are illegal or bordering on illegality? Give specific instances of how Malamud presents Tommy favorably even as he runs afoul of the law or of propriety.
5 How does Malamud turn us against Tommy's wife, Rosa, even though she is upright, honest, and hard working? What values are accepted by Tommy that are lacking in Rosa?
6 When we turn to the young girl, we know even less of her than we know of Tommy. How much of her past can you reconstruct from the hints Malamud provides? Can her thefts be explained by her background, such as it is?
7 Now that you have tried to make some order of the young girl's life, can you understand her behavior at the very end, when she thrusts out her red tongue at Tommy? Why this act of defiance when he has tried to help her? What does this say about her? Is she simply ungrateful, or is Malamud driving at a deeper consistency in her character?
8 Even though the story ends with the girl being dragged away by her mother, what effect do you think the girl's defiance will have on Tommy? Can he understand her lack of gratitude? Or will he attribute her act to the general cynicism of people, simply another aspect of his prison? There is of course no fixed answer, but Malamud does provide enough information about Tommy so that you can speculate with some certainty.

Setting

1 To what extent does the setting of the candy store contribute to character and theme? Why does Malamud use a candy store?

Could he have equally chosen a bakeshop, a grocery store, or something similar?

2 How does the setting contribute to the mood of frustration and depression?

3 Is it ironical that someone like Tommy should find himself the proprietor of a candy store? Why?

Theme

"Il Conde" and "A Visit of Charity" are also concerned with the confrontation between an older person and a younger one, with sharp results in each case. Do you find "The Prison" similar to either of these stories? If so, what added dimension of theme do you then find in the Malamud story? That is, after comparison, do you find that this story extends beyond its borders into something more universal?

YOUNG GOODMAN BROWN

Nathaniel Hawthorne

Young Goodman Brown came forth at sunset into the street at Salem village; but put his head back, after crossing the threshold, to exchange a parting kiss with his young wife. And Faith, as the wife was aptly named, thrust her own pretty head into the street, letting the wind play with the pink ribbons of her cap while she called to Goodman Brown.

"Dearest heart," whispered she, softly and rather sadly, when her lips were close to his ear, "prithee put off your journey until sunrise and sleep in your own bed to-night. A lone woman is troubled with such dreams and such thoughts that she's afeared of herself sometimes. Pray tarry with me this night, dear husband, of all nights in the year."

"My love and my Faith," replied young Goodman Brown, "of all nights in the year, this one night must I tarry away from thee. My journey, as thou callest it, forth and back again, must needs be done 'twixt now and sunrise. What, my sweet, pretty wife, dost thou doubt me already, and we but three months married?"

"Then God bless you!" said Faith, with the pink ribbons; "and may you find all well when you come back."

"Amen!" cried Goodman Brown. "Say thy prayers, dear Faith, and go to bed at dusk, and no harm will come to thee."

So they parted; and the young man pursued his way until, being about to turn the corner by the meeting-house, he looked back and saw the head of Faith still peeping after him with a melancholy air, in spite of her pink ribbons.

"Poor little Faith!" thought he, for his heart smote him. "What a wretch am I to leave her on such an errand! She talks of dreams, too. Methought as she spoke there was trouble in her face, as if a dream had warned her what work is to be done to-night. But no, no; 't would kill her to think it. Well, she's a blessed angel on earth; and after this one night I'll cling to her skirts and follow her to heaven."

With this excellent resolve for the future, Goodman Brown felt himself justified in making more haste on his present evil purpose. He had taken a dreary road, darkened by all the gloomiest trees of the forest, which barely stood aside to let the narrow path creep through, and closed immediately behind. It was all as lonely as could be; and there is this peculiarity in such a solitude, that the traveller knows not who may be concealed by the innumerable trunks and the thick boughs overhead; so that with lonely footsteps he may yet be passing through an unseen multitude.

"There may be a devilish Indian behind every tree," said Goodman Brown to himself; and he glanced fearfully behind him as he added, "What if the devil himself should be at my very elbow!"

His head being turned back, he passed a crook of the road, and, looking forward again, beheld the figure of a man, in grave and decent attire, seated at the foot of an old tree. He arose at Goodman Brown's approach and walked onward side by side with him.

"You are late, Goodman Brown," said he. "The clock of the Old South was striking as I came through Boston, and that is full fifteen minutes agone."

"Faith kept me back a while," replied the young man, with a tremor in his voice, caused by the sudden appearance of his companion, though not wholly unexpected.

It was now deep dusk in the forest, and deepest in that part of it where these two were journeying. As nearly as could be discerned, the second traveller was about fifty years old, apparently in the same rank of life as Goodman Brown, and bearing a considerable resemblance to him, though perhaps more in expression than features. Still they might have been taken for father and son. And yet, though the elder person was as simply clad as the younger, and as simple in manner too, he had an indescribable air of one who knew the world, and who would not have felt abashed at the governor's dinner table or in King William's court, were it possible that his affairs should call him thither. But the only thing about him that could be fixed upon as remarkable was his staff, which bore the likeness of a great black snake, so curiously wrought that it might almost be seen to twist and wriggle itself like a living serpent. This, of course, must have been an ocular deception, assisted by the uncertain light.

"Come, Goodman Brown," cried his fellow-traveller, "this is a dull pace for the beginning of a journey. Take my staff, if you are so soon weary."

"Friend," said the other, exchanging his slow pace for a full stop, "having kept covenant by meeting thee here, it is my purpose now to return whence I came. I have scruples touching the matter thou wot'st of."

"Sayest thou so?" replied he of the serpent, smiling apart. "Let us walk on, nevertheless, reasoning as we go; and if I convince thee not thou shalt turn back. We are but a little way in the forest yet."

"Too far! too far!" exclaimed the goodman, unconsciously resuming his walk. "My father never went into the woods on such an errand, nor his father before him. We have been a race of honest men and good Christians since the days of the martyrs; and shall I be the first of the name of Brown that ever took this path and kept"—

"Such company, thou wouldst say," observed the elder person, interpreting his pause. "Well said, Goodman Brown! I have been as well acquainted with your family as with ever a one among the Puritans; and that's no trifle to say. I helped your grandfather, the constable, when he lashed the Quaker woman so smartly through the streets of Salem; and it was I that brought your father a pitch-pine knot, kindled at my own heart, to set fire to an Indian village, in King Philip's war. They were my good friends, both; and many a pleasant walk have we had along this path, and returned merrily after midnight. I would fain be friends with you for their sake."

"If it be as thou sayest," replied Goodman Brown, "I marvel they never spoke of these matters; or, verily, I marvel not, seeing that the least rumor of the sort would have driven them from New England. We are a people of prayer, and good works to boot, and abide no such wickedness."

"Wickedness or not," said the traveller with the twisted staff, "I have a very general acquaintance here in New England. The deacons of many a church have drunk the communion wine with me; the selectmen of divers towns make me their chairman; and a majority of the Great and General Court are firm supporters of my interest. The governor and I, too— But these are state secrets."

"Can this be so?" cried Goodman Brown, with a stare of amazement at his undisturbed companion. "Howbeit, I have nothing to do with the governor and council; they have their own ways, and are no rule for a simple husbandman like me. But, were I to go on with thee, how should I meet the eye of that good old man, our minister, at Salem village? Oh, his voice would make me tremble both Sabbath day and lecture day."

Thus far the elder traveller had listened with due gravity; but now burst into a fit of irrepressible mirth, shaking himself so violently that his snake-like staff actually seemed to wriggle in sympathy.

"Ha! ha! ha!" shouted he again and again, then composing himself, "Well, go on, Goodman Brown, go on; but, prithee, don't kill me with laughing."

"Well, then, to end the matter at once," said Goodman Brown, considerably nettled, "there is my wife, Faith. It would break her dear little heart, and I'd rather break my own."

"Nay, if that be the case," answered the other, "even go thy ways, Goodman Brown. I would not for twenty old women like that one hobbling before us that Faith should come to any harm."

As he spoke he pointed his staff at a female figure on the path, in whom Goodman Brown recognized a very pious and exemplary dame, who had taught him his catechism in youth, and was still his moral and spiritual adviser, jointly with the minister and Deacon Gookin.

"A marvel, truly, that Goody Cloyse should be so far in the wilderness at nightfall," said he. "But with your leave, friend, I shall take a cut through the woods until we have left this Christian woman behind. Being a stranger to you, she might ask whom I was consorting with and whither I was going."

"Be it so," said his fellow-traveller. "Betake you to the woods, and let me keep the path."

Accordingly the young man turned aside, but took care to watch his companion, who advanced softly along the road until he had come within a staff's length of the old dame. She, meanwhile, was making the best of her way, with singular speed for so aged a woman, and mumbling some indistinct words—a prayer, doubtless—as she went. The traveller put forth his staff and touched her withered neck with what seemed the serpent's tail.

"The devil!" screamed the pious old lady.

"Then Goody Cloyse knows her old friend?" observed the traveller, confronting her and leaning on his writhing stick.

"Ah, forsooth, and is it your worship indeed?" cried the good dame. "Yea, truly is it, and in the very image of my old gossip, Goodman Brown, the grandfather of the silly fellow that now is. But—would your worship believe it?—my broomstick hath strangely disappeared, stolen, as I suspect, by that unhanged witch, Goody Cory, and that, too, when I was all anointed with the juice of smallage, and cinquefoil, and wolf's bane"—

"Mingled with fine wheat and the fat of a new-born babe," said the shape of old Goodman Brown.

"Ah, your worship knows the recipe," cried the old lady,

cackling aloud. "So, as I was saying, being all ready for the meeting, and no horse to ride on, I made up my mind to foot it; for they tell me there is a nice young man to be taken into communion to-night. But now your good worship will lend me your arm, and we shall be there in a twinkling."

"That can hardly be," answered her friend. "I may not spare you my arm, Goody Cloyse; but here is my staff, if you will."

So saying, he threw it down at her feet, where, perhaps, it assumed life, being one of the rods which its owner had formerly lent to the Egyptian magi. Of this fact, however, Goodman Brown could not take cognizance. He had cast up his eyes in astonishment, and, looking down again, beheld neither Goody Cloyse nor the serpentine staff, but his fellow-traveller alone, who waited for him as calmly as if nothing had happened.

"That old woman taught me my catechism," said the young man; and there was a world of meaning in this simple comment.

They continued to walk onward, while the elder traveller exhorted his companion to make good speed and persevere in the path, discoursing so aptly that his arguments seemed rather to spring up in the bosom of his auditor than to be suggested by himself. As they went, he plucked a branch of maple to serve for a walking stick, and began to strip it of the twigs and little boughs, which were wet with evening dew. The moment his fingers touched them they became strangely withered and dried up as with a week's sunshine. Thus the pair proceeded, at a good free pace, until suddenly, in a gloomy hollow of the road, Goodman Brown sat himself down on the stump of a tree and refused to go any farther.

"Friend," said he, stubbornly, "my mind is made up. Not another step will I budge on this errand. What if a wretched old woman do choose to go to the devil when I thought she was going to heaven: is that any reason why I should quit my dear Faith and go after her?"

"You will think better of this by and by," said his acquaintance, composedly. "Sit here and rest yourself a while; and when you feel like moving again, there is my staff to help you along."

Without more words, he threw his companion the maple stick, and was as speedily out of sight as if he had vanished into the deepening gloom. The young man sat a few moments by the roadside, applauding himself greatly, and thinking with how clear a conscience he should meet the minister in his morning walk, nor shrink from the eye of good old Deacon Gookin. And what calm sleep would be his that very night, which was to have been spent so wickedly, but so purely and sweetly now, in the arms of Faith! Amidst these pleasant and praiseworthy meditations, Goodman Brown heard the tramp of horses along the road, and deemed it advisable to conceal himself within the verge of the forest, conscious of the guilty purpose that had brought him thither, though now so happily turned from it.

On came the hoof tramps and the voices of the riders, two grave old voices, conversing soberly as they drew near. These mingled sounds appeared to pass along the road, within a few yards of the young man's hiding-place; but, owing doubtless to the depth of the gloom at that particular spot, neither the travellers nor their steeds were visible. Though their figures brushed the small boughs by the wayside, it could not be seen that they intercepted, even for a moment, the faint gleam from the strip of bright sky athwart which they must have passed. Goodman Brown alternately crouched and stood on tiptoe, pulling aside the branches and thrusting forth his head as far as he durst without discerning so much as a shadow. It vexed him the more, because he could have sworn, were such a thing possible, that he recognized the voices of the minister and Deacon Gookin, jogging along quietly, as they were wont to do, when bound to some ordination or ecclesiastical council. While yet within hearing, one of the riders stopped to pluck a switch.

"Of the two, reverend sir," said the voice like the deacon's, "I had rather miss an ordination dinner than to-night's meeting. They tell me that some of our community are to be here from Falmouth and beyond, and others from Connecticut and Rhode Island, besides several of the Indian powwows, who, after their fashion, know almost as much deviltry as the best of us. Moreover, there is a goodly young woman to be taken into communion."

"Mighty well, Deacon Gookin!" replied the solemn old tones of the minister. "Spur up, or we shall be late. Nothing can be done, you know, until I get on the ground."

The hoofs clattered again; and the voices, talking so strangely in the empty air, passed on through the forest, where no church had ever been gathered or solitary Christian prayed. Whither, then, could these holy men be journeying so deep into the heathen wilderness? Young Goodman Brown caught hold of a tree for support, being ready to sink down on the ground, faint and overburdened with the heavy sickness of his heart. He looked up to the sky, doubting whether there really was a heaven above him. Yet there was the blue arch, and the stars brightening in it.

"With heaven above and Faith below, I will yet stand firm against the devil!" cried Goodman Brown.

While he still gazed upward into the deep arch of the firmament and had lifted his hands to pray, a cloud, though no wind was stirring, hurried across the zenith and hid the brightening stars. The blue sky was still visible, except directly overhead, where this black mass of cloud was sweeping swiftly northward. Aloft in the air, as if from the depths of the cloud, came a confused and doubtful sound of voices. Once the listener fancied that he could distinguish the accents of towns-people of his own, men and women, both pious and ungodly, many of whom he had met at the communion table, and had seen others rioting at the tavern. The next moment, so indistinct were the sounds, he doubted whether he had heard aught but the murmur of the old forest, whispering without a wind. Then came a stronger swell of those familiar tones, heard daily in the sunshine at Salem village, but never until now from a cloud of night. There was one voice, of a young woman, uttering lamentations, yet with an uncertain sorrow, and entreating for some favor, which, perhaps, it would grieve her to obtain; and all the unseen multitude, both saints and sinners, seemed to encourage her onward.

"Faith!" shouted Goodman Brown, in a voice of agony and desperation; and the echoes of the forest mocked him, crying, "Faith! Faith!" as if bewildered wretches were seeking her all through the wilderness.

The cry of grief, rage, and terror was yet piercing the night, when the unhappy husband held his breath for a response. There was a scream, drowned immediately in a louder murmur of voices, fading into far-off laughter, as the dark cloud swept away, leaving the clear and silent sky above Goodman Brown. But something fluttered lightly down through the air and caught on the branch of a tree. The young man seized it, and beheld a pink ribbon.

"My Faith is gone!" cried he, after one stupefied moment. "There is no good on earth; and sin is but a name. Come, devil; for to thee is this world given."

And, maddened with despair, so that he laughed loud and long, did Goodman Brown grasp his staff and set forth again, at such a rate that he seemed to fly along the forest path rather than to walk or run. The road grew wilder and drearier and more faintly traced, and vanished at length, leaving him in the heart of the dark wilderness, still rushing onward with the instinct that guides mortal man to evil. The whole forest was peopled with frightful sounds—the creaking of the trees, the howling of wild beasts, and the yell of Indians; while sometimes the wind tolled like a distant church bell, and sometimes gave a broad roar around the traveller, as if all Nature were laughing him to scorn. But he was himself the chief horror of the scene, and shrank not from its other horrors.

"Ha! ha! ha!" roared Goodman Brown when the wind laughed at him. "Let us hear which will laugh loudest. Think not to frighten me with your deviltry. Come witch, come wizard, come Indian powwow, come devil himself, and here comes Goodman Brown. You may as well fear him as he fear you."

In truth, all through the haunted forest there could be nothing more frightful than the figure of Goodman Brown. On he flew among the black pines, brandishing his staff with frenzied gestures, now giving vent to an inspiration of horrid blasphemy, and now shouting forth such laughter as set all the echoes of the forest laughing like demons around him. The fiend in his own shape is less hideous than when he rages in the breast of man. Thus sped the demoniac on his course, until, quivering among the trees, he saw a red light before him, as when the felled trunks and branches of a clearing have been set on fire, and throw up their lurid blaze against the sky, at the hour of midnight. He paused, in a lull of the tempest that had driven him onward, and heard the swell of what seemed a hymn, rolling solemnly from a distance with the weight of many voices. He knew the tune; it was a familiar one in the choir of the village meeting-house. The verse died heavily away, and was lengthened by a chorus, not of human voices, but of all the sounds of the benighted wilderness pealing in awful harmony together. Goodman Brown cried out, and his cry was lost to his own ear by its unison with the cry of the desert.

In the interval of silence he stole forward until the light glared full upon his eyes. At one extremity of an open space, hemmed in by the dark wall of the forest, arose a rock, bearing some rude, natural resemblance either to an altar or a pulpit, and surrounded by four blazing pines, their tops aflame, their stems untouched, like candles at an evening meeting. The mass of foliage that had overgrown the summit of the rock was all on fire, blazing high into the night and fitfully illuminating the whole field. Each pendent twig and leafy festoon was in a blaze. As the red light arose and fell, a numerous congregation alternately shone forth, then disappeared in shadow, and again grew, as it were, out of the darkness, peopling the heart of the solitary woods at once.

"A grave and dark-clad company," quoth Goodman Brown.

In truth they were such. Among them, quivering to and fro between gloom and splendor, appeared faces that would be seen next day at the council board of the province, and others which, Sabbath after Sabbath, looked devoutly heavenward, and benignantly over the crowded pews, from the holiest pulpits in the land. Some affirm that the lady of the governor was there. At least there were high dames well known to her, and wives of honored husbands, and widows, a great multitude, and ancient maidens, all of excellent repute, and fair young girls, who trembled lest their mothers should espy them. Either the sudden gleams of light flashing over the obscure field bedazzled Goodman Brown, or he recognized a score of the church members of Salem village famous for their especial sanctity. Good old Deacon Gookin had arrived, and waited at the skirts of that venerable saint, his revered pastor. But, irreverently consorting with these grave, reputable, and pious people, these elders of the church, these chaste dames and dewy virgins, there were men of dissolute lives and women of spotted fame, wretches given over to all mean and filthy vice, and suspected even of horrid crimes. It was strange to see that the good shrank not from the wicked, nor were the sinners abashed by the saints. Scattered also among their pale-faced enemies were the Indian priests, or powwows, who had often scared their native forest with more hideous incantations than any known to English witchcraft.

"But where is Faith?" thought Goodman Brown: and as hope came into his heart, he trembled.

Another verse of the hymn arose, a slow and mournful strain, such as the pious love, but joined to words which expressed all that our nature can conceive of sin, and darkly hinted at far more. Unfathomable to mere mortals is the lore of fiends. Verse after verse was sung; and still the chorus of the desert swelled between like the deepest tone of a mighty organ; and with the final peal of that dreadful anthem there came a sound, as if the roaring wind, the rushing streams, the howling beasts, and every other voice of the unconcerted wilderness were mingling and according with the voice of guilty man in homage to the prince of all. The four blazing pines threw up a loftier flame, and obscurely discovered shapes and visages of horror on the smoke wreaths above the impious assembly. At the same moment the fire on the rock shot redly forth and formed a glowing arch above its base, where now appeared a figure. With reverence be it spoken, the figure bore no slight similitude, both in garb and manner, to some grave divine of the New England churches.

"Bring forth the converts!" cried a voice that echoed through the field and rolled into the forest.

At the word, Goodman Brown stepped forth from the shadow of the trees and approached the congregation, with whom he felt a loathful brotherhood by the sympathy of all that was wicked in his heart. He could have well-nigh sworn that the shape of his own dead father beckoned him to advance, looking downward from a smoke wreath, while a woman, with dim features of despair, threw out her hand to warn him back. Was it his mother? But he had no power to retreat one step, nor to resist, even in thought, when the minister and good old Deacon Gookin seized his arms and led him to the blazing rock. Thither came also the slender form of a veiled female, led between Goody Cloyse, that pious teacher of the catechism, and Martha Carrier, who had received the devil's promise to be queen of hell. A rampant hag was she. And there stood the proselytes beneath the canopy of fire.

"Welcome, my children," said the dark figure, "to the communion of your race. Ye have found thus young your nature and your destiny. My children, look behind you!"

They turned; and flashing forth, as it were, in a sheet of flame, the fiend worshippers were seen; the smile of welcome gleamed darkly on every visage.

"There," resumed the sable form, "are all whom ye have reverenced from youth. Ye deemed them holier than yourselves and shrank from your own sin, contrasting it with their lives of righteousness and prayerful aspirations heavenward. Yet here are they all in my worshipping assembly. This night it shall be granted you to know their secret deeds: how hoary-bearded elders of the church have whispered wanton words to the young maids of their households; how many a woman, eager for widows' weeds, has given her husband a drink at bedtime and let him sleep his last sleep in her bosom; how beardless youths have made haste to inherit their fathers' wealth; and how fair damsels —blush not, sweet ones—have dug little graves in the garden, and bidden me, the sole guest, to an infant's funeral. By the sympathy of your human hearts for sin ye shall scent out all the places—whether in church, bedchamber, street, field, or forest —where crime has been committed, and shall exult to behold the whole earth one stain of guilt, one mighty blood spot. Far more than this. It shall be yours to penetrate, in every bosom, the deep mystery of sin, the fountain of all wicked arts, and which inexhaustibly supplies more evil impulses than human power—than my power at its utmost—can make manifest in deeds. And now, my children, look upon each other."

They did so; and, by the blaze of the hell-kindled torches, the wretched man beheld his Faith, and the wife her husband, trembling before that unhallowed altar.

"Lo, there ye stand, my children," said the figure, in a deep and solemn tone, almost sad with its despairing awfulness, as if his once angelic nature could yet mourn for our miserable race. "Depending upon one another's hearts, ye had still hoped that virtue were not all a dream. Now are ye undeceived. Evil is the nature of mankind. Evil must be your only happiness. Welcome again, my children, to the communion of your race."

"Welcome," repeated the fiend worshippers, in one cry of despair and triumph.

And there they stood, the only pair, as it seemed, who were yet hesitating on the verge of wickedness in this dark world. A basin was hollowed, naturally, in the rock. Did it contain water, reddened by the lurid light? or was it blood? or, perchance, a liquid flame? Herein did the shape of evil dip his hand and prepare to lay the mark of baptism upon their foreheads, that they might be partakers of the mystery of sin, more conscious of the secret guilt of others, both in deed and thought, than they could now be of their own. The husband cast one look at his pale wife, and Faith at him. What polluted wretches would the next glance show them to each other, shuddering alike at what they disclosed and what they saw!

"Faith! Faith!" cried the husband, "look up to heaven, and resist the wicked one."

Whether Faith obeyed he knew not. Hardly had he spoken when he found himself amid calm night and solitude, listening to a roar of the wind which died heavily away through the forest. He staggered against the rock, and felt it chill and damp; while a hanging twig, that had been all on fire, besprinkled his cheek with the coldest dew.

The next morning young Goodman Brown came slowly into the street of Salem village, staring around him like a bewildered man. The good old minister was taking a walk along the graveyard to get an appetite for breakfast and meditate his sermon, and bestowed a blessing, as he passed, on Goodman Brown. He shrank from the venerable saint as if to avoid an anathema. Old Deacon Gookin was at domestic worship, and the holy words of his prayer were heard through the open window. "What God doth the wizard pray to?" quoth Goodman Brown. Goody Cloyse, that excellent old Christian, stood in the early sunshine at her own lattice, catechizing a little girl who had brought her a pint of morning's milk. Goodman Brown snatched away the child as from the grasp of the fiend himself. Turning the corner by the meeting-house, he spied the head of Faith, with the pink ribbons, gazing anxiously forth, and bursting into such joy at sight of him that she skipped along the street and almost kissed her husband before the whole village. But Goodman Brown looked sternly and sadly into her face, and passed on without a greeting.

Had Goodman Brown fallen asleep in the forest and only dreamed a wild dream of a witch-meeting?

Be it so if you will; but, alas! it was a dream of evil omen for young Goodman Brown. A stern, a sad, a darkly meditative, a distrustful, if not a desperate man did he become from the night of that fearful dream. On the Sabbath day, when the congregation were singing a holy psalm, he could not listen because an anthem of sin rushed loudly upon his ear and drowned all the blessed strain. When the minister spoke from the pulpit with power and fervid eloquence, and, with his hand on the open Bible, of the sacred truths of our religion, and of saint-like lives and triumphant deaths, and of future bliss or misery unutterable, then did Goodman Brown turn pale, dreading lest the roof should thunder down upon the gray blasphemer and his hearers. Often, awaking suddenly at midnight, he shrank from the bosom of Faith; and at morning or eventide, when the family knelt down at prayer, he scowled and muttered to himself, and gazed sternly at his wife, and turned away. And when he had lived long, and was borne to his grave a hoary corpse, followed by Faith, an aged woman, and children and grandchildren, a goodly procession, besides neighbors not a few, they carved no hopeful verse upon his tombstone, for his dying hour was gloom.

Character

Although all elements in this story are virtually indistinguishable from each other, character appears to predominate. Clearly, the changes that take place are brought about through Brown's character, and Hawthorne has titled the story so that this emphasis should not be missed. In reading "Young Goodman Brown," however, we should always be aware that character here is not isolated; it is a tightly structured component of plot, theme, setting, and even mood.

1 An understanding of the story must obviously start with an understanding of Goodman Brown. What is a "goodman"? What information does Hawthorne supply about his parents and grandparents? How long has he been married? When we first meet him, where is he going? What is his frame of mind? Do you know what his "secret mission" is?

2 Now that you have collected some information about Brown, how would you characterize him from the first page or two? Does the "young" before his name have any meaning? Can you see any way in which his mental state would influence what happens to him during the night?

3 Who is the old man Brown meets in the forest? What clues does Hawthorne provide about the old man's identity? What does this meeting with the old man say about Brown?

4 Brown has married a girl named Faith. What significance does this name have? What is Hawthorne's point in giving Brown's wife such a name? What does this say about Brown himself?

5 Consider the setting of Brown's secret mission. How would you describe it? List some of the adjectives that Hawthorne uses to establish the atmosphere. What relationship between setting and character can you see?

6 What psychological effect would this setting have on Brown? Is it possible that the atmosphere is of his own making—that he is in a state of mind which "creates" such a setting?

7 In *The Scarlet Letter,* Hawthorne's masterpiece, he contrasts lights and darks throughout the novel in an ever-shifting pattern of values. Can you see any of that practice here as it relates to character? What is the first example of light or fire? For what purposes does Hawthorne use the light of the gathering in the forest? Do the pink ribbons at the beginning and later have any "color" significance?

8 What effect do Deacon Gookin, the minister, and Goody Cloyse have upon Brown? Do they help unsettle him? In what direction is their influence? Why does Hawthorne even introduce them?

9 How would you characterize the gathering in the forest? In this scene, Hawthorne uses setting for powerful effects. This scene is, in fact, the central one of the story. Who is present? Why these people? What is Brown's reaction to seeing them? What is the speaker saying?

10 How does Hawthorne present this scene as the epitome of wickedness? Describe some of his techniques. Stress particularly his use of lights and darks. Since we are concerned chiefly with Brown's reaction to the scene, what does it mean to him? Why is he appalled at seeing Faith there, when he is there himself? What does he really see in the forest?

11 What is Brown's attitude to Faith when he sees her at the edge of the forest gathering? Why doesn't he seize her and drag her away?

12 How do you explain the fact that Brown suddenly finds himself alone when he calls out loudly to Faith?

13 The theme of the story as it works out in the development of Brown's character appears in the final paragraph. What kind of person is Brown now? Compare him with the Brown of the first paragraph or two. Why does he "turn pale" when the minister speaks from the pulpit? Why does he shrink from Faith's side? How do you explain the pervading gloom that falls over him?

14 A good deal of the meaning of the story turns on the question of whether or not Brown really saw anything in the forest. That is, was the vision an internal condition or something he actually saw? Take each possibility and develop Hawthorne's evidence for that position. Where does it leave you? In the final accounting, does it really matter if Brown saw what he thinks he saw?

15 Why does Hawthorne make Brown's behavior revolve around his wife Faith? She was, after all, only one of many at the forest gathering. What does this say about Brown? About his possible feelings for his wife? About his possible faith?

16 From Brown's experience and reaction to it, Hawthorne draws a moral point, one that he makes many times in his stories and novels. It is concerned with man's relationship to good and evil and his further relationship to the rest of mankind. Can you see how this moral point works out in Brown's experience? Does Hawthorne look favorably upon Brown at the end of the story?

Further Aspects

What larger conclusions, if any, can you draw from the story? Be careful not to read in any simple views of good and evil, such as the point that one should not attend strange forest meetings at night. Hawthorne's point is considerably more subtle and sophisticated. He senses a human tragedy in Brown's experience, one that extends to every person in every age. In what ways do we all share in Brown's "night journey"?

THE TEACHER

Sherwood Anderson

Snow lay deep in the streets of Winesburg. It had begun to snow about ten o'clock in the morning and a wind sprang up and blew the snow in clouds along Main Street. The frozen mud roads that led into town were fairly smooth and in places ice covered the mud. "There will be good sleighing," said Will Henderson, standing by the bar in Ed Griffith's saloon. Out of the saloon he went and met Sylvester West the druggist stumbling along in the kind of heavy overshoes called arctics. "Snow will bring the people into town on Saturday," said the druggist. The two men stopped and discussed their affairs. Will Henderson, who had on a light overcoat and no overshoes, kicked the heel of his left foot with the toe of the right. "Snow will be good for the wheat," observed the druggist sagely.

Young George Willard, who had nothing to do, was glad because he did not feel like working that day. The weekly paper had been printed and taken to the post office on Wednesday evening and the snow began to fall on Thursday. At eight o'clock, after the morning train had passed, he put a pair of skates in his pocket and went up to Waterworks Pond but did not go skating. Past the pond and along a path that followed Wine Creek he went until he came to a grove of beech trees. There he built a fire against the side of a log and sat down at the end of the log to think. When the snow began to fall and the wind to blow he hurried about getting fuel for the fire.

The young reporter was thinking of Kate Swift who had once been his school teacher. On the evening before he had gone to her house to get a book she wanted him to read and had been alone with her for an hour. For the fourth or fifth time the woman had talked to him with great earnestness and he could not make out what she meant by her talk. He began to believe she might be in love with him and the thought was both pleasing and annoying.

Up from the log he sprang and began to pile sticks on the fire. Looking about to be sure he was alone he talked aloud pretending he was in the presence of the woman. "Oh, you're just letting on, you know you are," he declared. "I am going to find out about you. You wait and see."

The young man got up and went back along the path toward

town leaving the fire blazing in the wood. As he went through the streets the skates clanked in his pocket. In his own room in the New Willard House he built a fire in the stove and lay down on top of the bed. He began to have lustful thoughts and pulling down the shade of the window closed his eyes and turned his face to the wall. He took a pillow into his arms and embraced it thinking first of the school teacher, who by her words had stirred something within him and later of Helen White, the slim daughter of the town banker, with whom he had been for a long time half in love.

By nine o'clock of that evening snow lay deep in the streets and the weather had become bitter cold. It was difficult to walk about. The stores were dark and the people had crawled away to their houses. The evening train from Cleveland was very late but nobody was interested in its arrival. By ten o'clock all but four of the eighteen hundred citizens of the town were in bed.

Hop Higgins, the night watchman, was partially awake. He was lame and carried a heavy stick. On dark nights he carried a lantern. Between nine and ten o'clock he went his rounds. Up and down Main Street he stumbled through the drifts trying the doors of the stores. Then he went into alleyways and tried the back doors. Finding all tight he hurried around the corner to the New Willard House and beat on the door. Through the rest of the night he intended to stay by the stove. "You go to bed. I'll keep the stove going," he said to the boy who slept on a cot in the hotel office.

Hop Higgins sat down by the stove and took off his shoes. When the boy had gone to sleep he began to think of his own affairs. He intended to paint his house in the spring and sat by the stove calculating the cost of paint and labor. That led him into other calculations. The night watchman was sixty years old and wanted to retire. He had been a soldier in the Civil War and drew a small pension. He hoped to find some new method of making a living and aspired to become a professional breeder of ferrets. Already he had four of the strangely shaped savage little creatures, that are used by sportsmen in the pursuit of rabbits, in the cellar of his house. "Now I have one male and three females," he mused. "If I am lucky by spring I shall have twelve or fifteen. In another year I shall be able to begin advertising ferrets for sale in the sporting papers."

The night watchman settled into his chair and his mind became a blank. He did not sleep. By years of practice he had trained himself to sit for hours through the long nights neither asleep nor awake. In the morning he was almost as refreshed as though he had slept.

With Hop Higgins safely stowed away in the chair behind the stove only three people were awake in Winesburg. George Willard was in the office of the *Eagle* pretending to be at work on the writing of a story but in reality continuing the mood of the morning by the fire in the wood. In the bell tower of the Presbyterian Church the Reverend Curtis Hartman was sitting in the darkness preparing himself for a revelation from God, and Kate Swift, the school teacher, was leaving her house for a walk in the storm.

It was past ten o'clock when Kate Swift set out and the walk was unpremeditated. It was as though the man and the boy, by thinking of her, had driven her forth into the wintry streets. Aunt Elizabeth Swift had gone to the county seat concerning some business in connection with mortgages in which she had money invested and would not be back until the next day. By a huge stove, called a base burner, in the living room of the house sat the daughter reading a book. Suddenly she sprang to her feet and, snatching a cloak from a rack by the front door, ran out of the house.

At the age of thirty Kate Swift was not known in Winesburg as a pretty woman. Her complexion was not good and her face was covered with blotches that indicated ill health. Alone in the night in the winter streets she was lovely. Her back was straight, her shoulders square and her features were as the features of a tiny goddess on a pedestal in a garden in the dim light of a summer evening.

During the afternoon the school teacher had been to see Dr. Welling concerning her health. The doctor had scolded her and had declared she was in danger of losing her hearing. It was foolish for Kate Swift to be abroad in the storm, foolish and perhaps dangerous.

The woman in the streets did not remember the words of the doctor and would not have turned back had she remembered. She was very cold but after walking for five minutes no longer minded the cold. First she went to the end of her own street and then across a pair of hay scales set in the ground before a feed barn and into Trunion Pike. Along Trunion Pike she went to Ned Winter's barn and turning east followed a street of low frame houses that led over Gospel Hill and into Sucker Road that ran down a shallow valley past Ike Smead's chicken farm to Waterworks Pond. As she went along, the bold, excited mood that had driven her out of doors passed and then returned again.

There was something biting and forbidding in the character of Kate Swift. Everyone felt it. In the schoolroom she was silent, cold, and stern, and yet in an odd way very close to her pupils. Once in a long while something seemed to have come over her and she was happy. All of the children in the schoolroom felt the effect of her happiness. For a time they did not work but sat back in their chairs and looked at her.

With hands clasped behind her back the school teacher walked up and down in the schoolroom and talked very rapidly. It did not seem to matter what subject came into her mind. Once she talked to the children of Charles Lamb and made up strange intimate little stories concerning the life of the dead writer. The stories were told with the air of one who had lived in a house with Charles Lamb and knew all the secrets of his private life. The children were somewhat confused, thinking Charles Lamb must be someone who had once lived in Winesburg.

On another occasion the teacher talked to the children of Benvenuto Cellini. That time they laughed. What a bragging, blustering, brave, lovable fellow she made of the old artist! Concerning him also she invented anecdotes. There was one of a German music teacher who had a room above Cellini's lodgings in the city of Milan that made the boys guffaw. Sugars McNutts, a fat boy with red cheeks, laughed so hard that he became dizzy and fell off his seat and Kate Swift laughed with him. Then suddenly she became again cold and stern.

On the winter night when she walked through the deserted snow-covered streets, a crisis had come into the life of the school teacher. Although no one in Winesburg would have suspected it, her life had been very adventurous. It was still adventurous. Day by day as she worked in the schoolroom or walked in the streets, grief, hope, and desire fought within her. Behind a cold exterior the most extraordinary events transpired in her mind. The people of the town thought of her as a confirmed old maid and because she spoke sharply and went her own way thought her lacking in all the human feeling that did so much to make and mar their own lives. In reality she was the most eagerly passionate soul among them, and more than once, in the five years since she had come back from her travels to settle in Winesburg and become a school teacher, had been compelled to go out of the house and walk half through the night fighting out some battle raging within. Once on a night when it rained she had stayed out six hours and when she came home had a quarrel with Aunt Elizabeth Swift. "I am glad you're not a man," said the mother sharply. "More than once I've waited for your father to come home, not knowing what new mess he had got into. I've had my share of uncertainty and you cannot blame me if I do not want to see the worst side of him reproduced in you."

Kate Swift's mind was ablaze with thoughts of George Willard. In something he had written as a school boy she thought she had recognized the spark of genius and wanted to blow on the spark. One day in the summer she had gone to the *Eagle* office and finding the boy unoccupied had taken him out Main Street to the fair ground, where the two sat on a grassy bank and talked. The school teacher tried to bring home to the mind of the boy some conception of the difficulties he would have to face as a writer. "You will have to know life," she declared, and her voice trembled with earnestness. She took hold of George Willard's shoulders and turned him about so that she could look into his eyes. A passer-by might have thought them about to embrace. "If you are to become a writer you'll have to stop fooling with words," she explained. "It would be better to give up the notion of writing until you are better prepared. Now it's time to be living. I don't want to frighten you, but I would like to make you understand the import of what you think of attempting. You must not become a mere peddler of words. The thing to learn is to know what people are thinking about, not what they say."

On the evening before that stormy Thursday night, when the Reverend Curtis Hartman sat in the bell tower of the church waiting to look at her body, young Willard had gone to visit the teacher and to borrow a book. It was then the thing happened that confused and puzzled the boy. He had the book under his arm and was preparing to depart. Again Kate Swift talked with great earnestness. Night was coming on and the light in the room grew dim. As he turned to go she spoke his name softly and with an impulsive movement took hold of his hand. Because the reporter was rapidly becoming a man something of his man's appeal, combined with the winsomeness of the boy, stirred the heart of the lonely woman. A passionate desire to have him understand the import of life, to learn to interpret it truly and honestly, swept over her. Leaning forward, her lips brushed his cheek. At the same moment he for the first time became aware of the marked beauty of her features. They were both embarrassed, and to relieve her feeling she became harsh and domineering.

"What's the use? It will be ten years before you begin to understand what I mean when I talk to you," she cried passionately.

On the night of the storm and while the minister sat in the church waiting for her, Kate Swift went to the office of the *Winesburg Eagle,* intending to have another talk with the boy. After the long walk in the snow she was cold, lonely, and tired. As she came through Main Street she saw the light from the print shop window shining on the snow and on an impulse opened the door and went in. For an hour she sat by the stove in the office talking of life. She talked with passionate earnestness. The impulse that had driven her out into the snow poured itself out into talk. She became inspired as she sometimes did in the presence of the children in school. A great eagerness to open the door of life to the boy, who had been her pupil and whom she thought might possess a talent for the understanding of life, had possession of her. So strong was her passion that it became something physical. Again her hands took hold of his shoulders and she turned him about. In the dim light her eyes blazed. She arose and laughed, not sharply as was customary with her, but in a queer, hesitating way. "I must be going," she said. "In a moment, if I stay, I'll be wanting to kiss you."

In the newspaper office a confusion arose. Kate Swift turned and walked to the door. She was a teacher but she was also a woman. As she looked at George Willard, the passionate desire to be loved by a man, that had a thousand times before swept like a storm over her body, took possession of her. In the lamplight George Willard looked no longer a boy, but a man ready to play the part of a man.

The school teacher let George Willard take her into his arms. In the warm little office the air became suddenly heavy and the strength went out of her body. Leaning against a low counter by the door she waited. When he came and put a hand on her shoulder she turned and let her body fall heavily against him. For George Willard the confusion was immediately increased. For a moment he held the body of the woman tightly against his body and then it stiffened. Two sharp little fists began to beat on his face. When the school teacher had run away and left him alone, he walked up and down in the office swearing furiously.

It was into this confusion that the Reverend Curtis Hartman protruded himself. When he came in George Willard thought the town had gone mad. Shaking a bleeding fist in the air, the minister proclaimed the woman George had only a moment before held in his arms an instrument of God bearing a message of truth.

George blew out the lamp by the window and locking the door of the print shop went home. Through the hotel office, past Hop Higgins lost in his dream of the raising of ferrets, he went and up into his own room. The fire in the stove had gone out and he undressed in the cold. When he got into bed the sheets were like blankets of dry snow.

George Willard rolled about in the bed on which he had lain in the afternoon hugging the pillow and thinking thoughts of Kate Swift. The words of the minister, who he thought had gone suddenly insane, rang in his ears. His eyes stared about the room. The resentment, natural to the baffled male, passed and he tried to understand what had happened. He could not make it out. Over and over he turned the matter in his mind. Hours passed and he began to think it must be time for another day to come. At four o'clock he pulled the covers up about his neck and tried to sleep. When he became drowsy and closed his eyes, he raised a hand and with it groped about in the darkness. "I have missed something. I have missed something Kate Swift was trying to tell me," he muttered sleepily. Then he slept and in all Winesburg he was the last soul on that winter night to go to sleep.

Character

All the stories in Anderson's *Winesburg, Ohio,* are concerned with aspects of loneliness and isolation. Around the central character, George Willard, the townspeople play out their lives separated from him and from one another by an impassable gulf. Forced back on themselves, they develop characteristics peculiar to small-town life in America. One of these stories and one of these characters is the teacher, Kate Swift.

1 Why is the profession of teacher particularly relevant to a study of loneliness in a small town? Does Kate Swift fill the stereotype that most of you have about small-town schoolteachers? Just what is that stereotype?

2 Anderson has Kate move through the town in the dark. In

the key scene in the story, she visits George in his newspaper office at night; she frequently walks in the dark and often roams the black, deserted countryside. What does this movement indicate about her? Is there any reason for her connection with the night and the dark?

3 To complete the play of lights and darks in this story, Kate is also connected with the snow and with the image of snow. The technique is a common one. An author will use the elements of rain, wind, and snow to bring out certain traits in his characters or to intensify certain scenes. Can you see any relationship between Kate and the snow? What properties do they have in common? Does the snow help increase her isolation? Or decrease it?

4 George Willard, as the "bright student," takes on the hopes of a teacher who finds herself frustrated by her sex and her limitations. Keep this in mind as you read the advice she gives him: "The thing to learn is to know what people are thinking about, not what they say." Does this statement apply to her as well as to him? In what way? What does this advice say about her?

5 Below the surface of this moody, morose woman there is a passionate being, Anderson tells us. Just what is this passion that burns so strongly? What is the point of making her a passionate woman? And if passion does dominate her, why does she beat on George's face with her fists when he tries to embrace her? Why does she run away from him?

6 As you answer these questions, you will find that a character has been created. Is Kate now the stereotype that you originally thought she was, or has she taken on the elements of individuality? Is her role now sympathetic as well as pitiful? Incidentally, is pity the only feeling we are expected to have for her?

Further Aspects

1 *Winesburg, Ohio,* is also about George Willard, his growth and development—really the development of his sensibility. There is a good deal that he does not as yet understand about Kate Swift. Because he partly sees her as a woman who wants to make love to him, when she withdraws he is confused and upset. At this point, the Reverend Curtis Hartman enters and says that Kate, whom he has just met, is like an angel, "bearing a message of truth." Is this the Kate whom George has just known? What does this reveal about her?

2 What limitations in George would make him miss "something Kate Swift was trying to tell him"? What does he miss about her? About himself?

3 The bafflement George experiences before these questions is the natural bafflement of a youth confronting adult experiences. This is, surely, the theme of the story. Does Anderson make this aspect of the story plausible? Do you sense the quality of George's confusion? Can you define it?

THE LANGUAGE OF MEN

Norman Mailer

In the beginning, Sanford Carter was ashamed of becoming an Army cook. This was not from snobbery, at least not from snobbery of the most direct sort. During the two and a half years Carter had been in the Army he had come to hate cooks more and more. They existed for him as a symbol of all that was corrupt, overbearing, stupid, and privileged in Army life. The image which came to mind was a fat cook with an enormous sandwich in one hand, and a bottle of beer in the other, sweat pouring down a porcine face, foot on a flour barrel, shouting at the K.P.'s, "Hurry up, you men, I ain't got all day." More than once in those two and a half years, driven to exasperation, Carter had been on the verge of throwing his food into a cook's face as he passed on the serving line. His anger often derived from nothing: the set of a pair of fat lips, the casual heavy thump of the serving spoon into his plate, or the resentful conviction that the cook was not serving him enough. Since life in the Army was in most aspects a marriage, this rage over apparently harmless details was not a sign of unbalance. Every soldier found some particular habit of the Army spouse impossible to support.

Yet Sanford Carter became a cook and, to elaborate the irony, did better as a cook than he had done as anything else. In a few months he rose from a Private to a first cook with the rank of Sergeant, Technician. After the fact, it was easy to understand. He had suffered through all his Army career from an excess of eagerness. He had cared too much, he had wanted to do well, and so he had often been tense at moments when he would better have been relaxed. He was very young, twenty-one, had lived the comparatively gentle life of a middle-class boy, and needed some success in the Army to prove to himself that he was not completely worthless.

In succession, he had failed as a surveyor in Field Artillery, a clerk in an Infantry headquarters, a telephone wireman, and finally a rifleman. When the war ended, and his regiment went to Japan, Carter was still a rifleman; he had been a rifleman for eight months. What was more to the point, he had been in the platoon as long as any of its members; the skilled hard-bitten nucleus of veterans who had run his squad had gone home one by one, and it seemed to him that through seniority he was entitled to at least a corporal's rating. Through seniority he was so entitled, but on no other ground. Whenever responsibility had been handed to him, he had discharged it miserably, tensely, overconscientiously. He had always asked too many questions, he had worried the task too severely, he had conveyed his nervousness to the men he was supposed to lead. Since he was also sensitive enough and proud enough never to curry favor with the noncoms in the platoons, he was in no position to sit in on their occasional discussions about who was to succeed them. In a vacuum of ignorance, he had allowed himself to dream that he would be given a squad to lead, and his hurt was sharp when the squad was given to a replacement who had joined the platoon months after him.

The war was over, Carter had a bride in the States (he had lived with her for only two months), he was lonely, he was obsessed with going home. As one week dragged into the next, and the regiment, the company, and his own platoon continued the same sort of training which they had been doing ever since he had entered the Army, he thought he would snap. There were months to wait until he would be discharged and meanwhile it was intolerable to him to be taught for the fifth time the nomenclature of the machine gun, to stand a retreat parade three evenings a week. He wanted some niche where he could lick his wounds, some Army job with so many hours of work and so many hours of complete freedom, where he could be alone by himself. He hated the Army, the huge Army which had proved to him that he was good at no work, and incapable of succeeding at anything. He wrote long, aching letters to his wife, he talked less and less to the men around him and he was close to violent attacks of anger during the most casual phases of training—during close-order drill or cleaning his rifle for inspection. He knew that if he did not find his niche it was possible that he would crack.

So he took an opening in the kitchen. It promised him nothing except a day of work, and a day of leisure which would be completely at his disposal. He found that he liked it. He was given at first the job of baking the bread for the company, and every other night he worked till early in the morning, kneading and shaping his fifty-pound mix of dough. At two or three he would be done, and for his work there would be the tangible reward of fifty loaves of bread, all fresh from the oven, all clean and smelling of fertile accomplished creativity. He had the rare and therefore intensely satisfying emotion of seeing at the end of an Army chore the product of his labor.

A month after he became cook the regiment was disbanded, and those men who did not have enough points to go home were sent to other outfits. Carter ended at an ordnance company in another Japanese city. He had by now given up all thought of getting a noncom's rating before he was discharged, and was merely content to work each alternate day. He took his work for granted and so he succeeded at it. He had begun as a baker in the new company kitchen; before long he was the first cook. It all happened quickly. One cook went home on points, another caught a skin disease, a third was transferred from the kitchen after contracting a venereal infection. On the shift which Carter worked there were left only himself and a man who was illiterate. Carter was put nominally in charge, and was soon actively in charge. He looked up each menu in an Army recipe book, collected the items, combined them in the order indicated, and after the proper time had elapsed, took them from the stove. His product tasted neither better nor worse than the product of all other Army cooks. But the mess sergeant was impressed. Carter had filled a gap. The next time ratings were given out Carter jumped at a bound from Private to Sergeant T/4.

On the surface he was happy; beneath the surface he was overjoyed. It took him several weeks to realize how grateful and delighted he felt. The promotion coincided with his assignment to a detachment working in a small seaport up the coast. Carter arrived there to discover that he was in charge of cooking for thirty men, and would act as mess sergeant. There was another cook, and there were four permanent Japanese K.P.'s, all of them good workers. He still cooked every other day, but there was always time between meals to take a break of at least an hour and often two; he shared a room with the other cook and lived in comparative privacy for the first time in several years; the seaport was beautiful; there was only one officer, and he left the men alone; supplies were plentiful due to a clerical error which assigned rations for forty men rather than thirty; and in general everything was fine. The niche had become a sinecure.

This was the happiest period of Carter's life in the Army. He came to like his Japanese K.P.'s. He studied their language, he visited their homes, he gave them gifts of food from time to time. They worshiped him because he was kind to them and generous, because he never shouted, because his good humor bubbled over into games, and made the work of the kitchen seem pleasant. All the while he grew in confidence. He was not a big man, but his body filled out from the heavy work; he was likely to sing a great deal, he cracked jokes with the men on the chow line. The kitchen became his property, it became his domain, and since it was a warm room, filled with sunlight, he came to take pleasure in the very sight of it. Before long his good humor expanded into a series of efforts to improve the food. He began to take little pains and make little extra efforts which would have been impossible if he had been obliged to cook for more than thirty men. In the morning he would serve the men fresh eggs scrambled or fried to their desire in fresh butter. Instead of cooking sixty eggs in one large pot he cooked two eggs at a time in a frying pan, turning them to the taste of each soldier. He baked like a housewife satisfying her young husband; at lunch and dinner there was pie or cake, and often both. He went to great lengths. He taught the K.P.'s how to make the toast come out right. He traded excess food for spices in Japanese stores. He rubbed paprika and garlic on the chickens. He even made pastries to cover such staples as corn beef hash and meat and vegetable stew.

It all seemed to be wasted. In the beginning the men might have noticed these improvements, but after a period they took them for granted. It did not matter how he worked to satisfy them; they trudged through the chow line with their heads down, nodding coolly at him, and they ate without comment. He would hang around the tables after the meal, noticing how much they consumed, and what they discarded; he would wait for compliments, but the soldiers seemed indifferent. They seemed to eat without tasting the food. In their faces he saw mirrored the distaste with which he had once stared at cooks.

The honeymoon was ended. The pleasure he took in the kitchen and himself curdled. He became aware again of his painful desire to please people, to discharge responsibility, to be a man. When he had been a child, tears had come into his eyes at a cross word, and he had lived in an atmosphere where his smallest accomplishment was warmly praised. He was the sort of young man, he often thought bitterly, who was accustomed to the attention and the protection of women. He would have thrown away all he possessed—the love of his wife, the love of his mother, the benefits of his education, the assured financial security of entering his father's business—if he had been able just once to dig a ditch as well as the most ignorant farmer.

Instead, he was back in the painful unprotected days of his

first entrance into the Army. Once again the most casual actions became the most painful, the events which were most to be taken for granted grew into the most significant, and the feeding of the men at each meal turned progressively more unbearable.

So Sanford Carter came full circle. If he had once hated the cooks, he now hated the troops. At mealtimes his face soured into the belligerent scowl with which he had once believed cooks to be born. And to himself he muttered the age-old laments of the housewife: how little they appreciated what he did.

Finally there was an explosion. He was approached one day by Corporal Taylor, and he had come to hate Taylor, because Taylor was the natural leader of the detachment and kept the other men endlessly amused with his jokes. Taylor had the ability to present himself as inefficient, shiftless, and incapable, in such a manner as to convey that really the opposite was true. He had the lightest touch, he had the greatest facility, he could charm a geisha in two minutes and obtain anything he wanted from a supply sergeant in five. Carter envied him, envied his grace, his charmed indifference; then grew to hate him.

Taylor teased Carter about the cooking, and he had the knack of knowing where to put the knife. "Hey, Carter," he would shout across the mess hall while breakfast was being served, "you turned my eggs twice, and I asked for them raw." The men would shout with laughter. Somehow Taylor had succeeded in conveying all of the situation, or so it seemed to Carter, insinuating everything, how Carter worked and how it meant nothing, how Carter labored to gain their affection and earned their contempt. Carter would scowl, Carter would answer in a rough voice, "Next time I'll crack them over your head." "You crack 'em, I'll eat 'em," Taylor would pipe back, "but just don't put your fingers in 'em." And there would be another laugh. He hated the sight of Taylor.

It was Taylor who came to him to get the salad oil. About twenty of the soldiers were going to have a fish fry at the geisha house; they had bought the fish at the local market, but they could not buy oil, so Taylor was sent as the deputy to Carter. He was charming to Carter, he complimented him on the meal, he clapped him on the back, he dissolved Carter to warmth, to private delight in the attention, and the thought that he had misjudged Taylor. Then Taylor asked for the oil.

Carter was sick with anger. Twenty men out of the thirty in the detachment were going on the fish fry. It meant only that Carter was considered one of the ten undesirables. It was something he had known, but the proof of knowledge is always more painful than the acquisition of it. If he had been alone his eyes would have clouded. And he was outraged at Taylor's deception. He could imagine Taylor saying ten minutes later, "You should have seen the grease job I gave to Carter. I'm dumb, but man, he's dumber."

Carter was close enough to giving him the oil. He had a sense of what it would mean to refuse Taylor, he was on the very edge of mild acquiescence. But he also had a sense of how he would despise himself afterward.

"No," he said abruptly, his teeth gritted, "you can't have it."

"What do you mean we can't have it?"

"I won't give it to you." Carter could almost feel the rage which Taylor generated at being refused.

"You won't give away a lousy five gallons of oil to a bunch of G.I.'s having a party?"

"I'm sick and tired," Carter began.

"So am I." Taylor walked away.

Carter knew he would pay for it. He left the K.P.'s and went to change his sweat-soaked work shirt, and as he passed the large dormitory in which most of the detachment slept he could hear Taylor's high-pitched voice. Carter did not bother to take off his shirt. He returned instead to the kitchen, and listened to the sound of men going back and forth through the hall and of a man shouting with rage. That was Hobbs, a Southerner, a big man with a big bellowing voice.

There was a formal knock on the kitchen door. Taylor came in. His face was pale and his eyes showed a cold satisfaction. "Carter," he said, "the men want to see you in the big room."

Carter heard his voice answer huskily. "If they want to see me, they can come into the kitchen."

He knew he would conduct himself with more courage in his own kitchen than anywhere else. "I'll be here for a while."

Taylor closed the door, and Carter picked up a writing board to which was clamped the menu for the following day. Then he made a pretense of examining the food supplies in the pantry closet. It was his habit to check the stocks before deciding what to serve the next day, but on this night his eyes ranged thoughtlessly over the canned goods. In a corner were seven five-gallon tins of salad oil, easily enough cooking oil to last a month. Carter came out of the pantry and shut the door behind him.

He kept his head down and pretended to be writing the menu

when the soldiers came in. Somehow there were even more of them than he had expected. Out of the twenty men who were going to the party, all but two or three had crowded through the door.

Carter took his time, looked up slowly. "You men want to see me?" he asked flatly.

They were angry. For the first time in his life he faced the hostile expressions of many men. It was the most painful and anxious moment he had ever known.

"Taylor says you won't give us the oil," someone burst out.

"That's right, I won't," said Carter. He tapped his pencil against the scratchboard, tapping it slowly and, he hoped, with an appearance of calm.

"What a stink deal," said Porfirio, a little Cuban whom Carter had always considered his friend.

Hobbs, the big Southerner, stared down at Carter. "Would you mind telling the men why you've decided not to give us the oil?" he asked quietly.

" 'Cause I'm blowed if I'm going to cater to you men. I've catered enough," Carter said. His voice was close to cracking with the outrage he had suppressed for so long, and he knew that if he continued he might cry. "I'm the acting mess sergeant," he said as coldly as he could, "and I decide what goes out of this kitchen." He stared at each one in turn, trying to stare them down, feeling mired in the rut of his own failure. They would never have dared this approach to another mess sergeant.

"What crud," someone muttered.

"You won't give a lousy five-gallon can of oil for a G.I. party," Hobbs said more loudly.

"I won't. That's definite. You men can get out of here."

"Why, you lousy little snot," Hobbs burst out, "how many five-gallon cans of oil have you sold on the black market?"

"I've never sold any." Carter might have been slapped with the flat of a sword. He told himself bitterly, numbly, that this was the reward he received for being perhaps the single honest cook in the whole United States Army. And he even had time to wonder at the obscure prejudice which had kept him from selling food for his own profit.

"Man, I've seen you take it out," Hobbs exclaimed. "I've seen you take it to the market."

"I took food to trade for spices," Carter said hotly.

There was an ugly snicker from the men.

"I don't mind if a cook sells," Hobbs said, "every man has

his own deal in this Army. But a cook ought to give a little food to a G.I. if he wants it."

"Tell him," someone said.

"It's bull," Taylor screeched. "I've seen Carter take butter, eggs, every damn thing to the market."

Their faces were red, they circled him.

"I never sold a thing," Carter said doggedly.

"And I'm telling you," Hobbs said, "that you're a two-bit crook. You been raiding that kitchen, and that's why you don't give to us now."

Carter knew there was only one way he could possibly answer if he hoped to live among these men again. "That's a goddam lie," Carter said to Hobbs. He laid down the scratchboard, he flipped his pencil slowly and deliberately to one corner of the room, and with his heart aching he lunged toward Hobbs. He had no hope of beating him. He merely intended to fight until he was pounded unconscious, advancing the pain and bruises he would collect as collateral for his self-respect.

To his indescribable relief Porfirio darted between them, held them apart with the pleased ferocity of a small man breaking up a fight. "Now, stop this! Now, stop this!" he cried out.

Carter allowed himself to be pushed back, and he knew that he had gained a point. He even glimpsed a solution with some honor.

He shrugged violently to free himself from Porfirio. He was in a rage, and yet it was a rage he could have ended at any instant. "All right, you men," he swore, "I'll give you the oil, but now that we're at it, I'm going to tell you a thing or two." His face red, his body perspiring, he was in the pantry and out again with a five gallon tin. "Here," he said, "you better have a good fish fry, 'cause it's the last good meal you're going to have for quite a while. I'm sick of trying to please you. You think I have to work—" he was about to say, my fingers to the bone—"well, I don't. From now on, you'll see what chow in the Army is supposed to be like." He was almost hysterical. "Take that oil. Have your fish fry." The fact that they wanted to cook for themselves was the greatest insult of all. "Tomorrow I'll give you real Army cooking."

His voice was so intense that they backed away from him. "Get out of this kitchen," he said. "None of you has any business here."

They filed out quietly, and they looked a little sheepish.

Carter felt weary, he felt ashamed of himself, he knew he had not meant what he said. But half an hour later, when he left the kitchen and passed the large dormitory, he heard shouts of raucous laughter, and he heard his name mentioned and then more laughter.

He slept badly that night, he was awake at four, he was in the kitchen by five, and stood there white-faced and nervous, waiting for the K.P.'s to arrive. Breakfast that morning landed on the men like a lead bomb. Carter rummaged in the back of the pantry and found a tin of dehydrated eggs covered with dust, memento of a time when fresh eggs were never on the ration list. The K.P.'s looked at him in amazement as he stirred the lumpy powder into a pan of water. While it was still half-dissolved he put it on the fire. While it was still wet, he took it off. The coffee was cold, the toast was burned, the oatmeal stuck to the pot. The men dipped forks into their food, took cautious sips of their coffee, and spoke in whispers. Sullenness drifted like vapors through the kitchen.

At noontime Carter opened cans of meat-and-vegetable stew. He dumped them into a pan and heated them slightly. He served the stew with burned string beans and dehydrated potatoes which tasted like straw. For dessert the men had a single lukewarm canned peach and cold coffee.

So the meals continued. For three days Carter cooked slop, and suffered even more than the men. When mealtime came he left the chow line to the K.P.'s and sat in his room, perspiring with shame, determined not to yield and sick with the determination.

Carter won. On the fourth day a delegation of men came to see him. They told him that indeed they had appreciated his cooking in the past, they told him that they were sorry they had hurt his feelings, they listened to his remonstrances, they listened to his grievances, and with delight Carter forgave them. That night, for supper, the detachment celebrated. There was roast chicken with stuffing, lemon meringue pie and chocolate cake. The coffee burned their lips. More than half the men made it a point to compliment Carter on the meal.

In the weeks which followed the compliments diminished, but they never stopped completely. Carter became ashamed at last. He realized the men were trying to humor him, and he wished to tell them it was no longer necessary.

Harmony settled over the kitchen. Carter even became friends with Hobbs, the big Southerner. Hobbs approached him one day, and in the manner of a farmer talked obliquely for an hour. He spoke about his father, he spoke about his girl friends, he alluded indirectly to the night they had almost fought, and finally with the courtesy of a Southerner he said to Carter, "You know, I'm sorry about shooting off my mouth. You were right to want to fight me, and if you're still mad I'll fight you to give you the satisfaction, although I just as soon would not."

"No, I don't want to fight with you now," Carter said warmly. They smiled at each other. They were friends.

Carter knew he had gained Hobbs' respect. Hobbs respected him because he had been willing to fight. That made sense to a man like Hobbs. Carter liked him so much at this moment that he wished the friendship to be more intimate.

"You know," he said to Hobbs, "it's a funny thing. You know I really never did sell anything on the black market. Not that I'm proud of it, but I just didn't."

Hobbs frowned. He seemed to be saying that Carter did not have to lie. "I don't hold it against a man," Hobbs said, "if he makes a little money in something that's his own proper work. Hell, I sell gas from the motor pool. It's just I also give gas if one of the G.I.'s wants to take the jeep out for a joy ride, kind of."

"No, but I never did sell anything." Carter had to explain. "If I ever had sold on the black market, I would have given the salad oil without question."

Hobbs frowned again, and Carter realized he still did not believe him. Carter did not want to lose the friendship which was forming. He thought he could save it only by some further admission. "You know," he said again, "remember when Porfirio broke up our fight? I was awful glad when I didn't have to fight you." Carter laughed, expecting Hobbs to laugh with him, but a shadow passed across Hobbs' face.

"Funny way of putting it," Hobbs said.

He was always friendly thereafter, but Carter knew that Hobbs would never consider him a friend. Carter thought about it often, and began to wonder about the things which made him different. He was no longer so worried about becoming a man; he felt that to an extent he had become one. But in his heart he wondered if he would ever learn the language of men.

Character

This short story by one of America's leading contemporary novelists falls loosely under the heading of the apprenticeship-to-life type of fiction. It has dominated literature in the twentieth century and various aspects of it continue to appear. As the category suggests, it is a literature concerned with the development of a young man, or woman, as he or she confronts various situations, internal and external. During the course of the story or novel, the young person learns what life is and usually learns how to handle what happens to him. At the end, he is more experienced, and definitely more mature, than he was at the beginning. He is a "man," or she is a "woman," although not all his problems—such as they are—are definitely resolved. Often his problems are only partially solved, with these partial resolutions leading into new areas of experience. Nevertheless, we have a feeling when we close such a story or novel that the chief character is ready to live in the world, whether happily or not.

1 Sanford Carter, in "The Language of Men," is of this type. Try to fill out what kind of person he is. From Mailer's hints, what do we know of Carter's background and tastes? Are these details important? Why? Is he a big-city or country boy? How do you know? Does this make any difference to him?

2 How does Mailer convey sympathy for Carter, even though he is not a hero, certainly not entirely pleasant? Or do you fail to sympathize with him? Do you identify with his anguish and failure before he becomes a cook, or do you feel that the failure is his fault and none of our concern? How does Mailer tip the scales in Carter's favor at this stage of the story?

3 Once Carter is developed as a character, can you understand his refusal of the salad oil? What issues are involved? Make the decision for yourself, giving yourself Carter's "problems" at this point. How does Taylor enter into Carter's refusal—that is, what part does Taylor play in it?

4 Mailer suggests that Carter becomes a man when he denies the oil to the men. Do you understand what Mailer means?

5 Once you have resolved this point, can you see the mixed nature of Carter's success? To some extent, he has matured by refusing to back down on the oil until he can make his own decision to offer it. But at the same time, what has he lost?

6 Part of Mailer's success with the story is his ability to give a little to Carter while taking away a little. Does Carter himself recognize that he loses ground every time he gains something? How do you know?

Setting

1 How does the Army setting intensify whatever problems Carter has?

2 How does the setting bring home to Carter his difference from other men?

3 Characterize the setting. Is this your view of Army life, or did you expect something different? What, for example?

4 One further point: Does Mailer gain anything by making Carter into a cook? That is, could he be anything else, or would the story suffer?

Narrative

The first paragraph of this story is a good example of the narrative art practiced skillfully. The author begins with a general statement: "In the beginning, Sanford Carter was ashamed of becoming an Army cook." Then the rest of the paragraph, indeed the entire story, is a variation of this point. The succeeding lines of the paragraph create images of hatred—why Army cooks have become symbols to Carter "of all that was corrupt," etc. Then, to put his character in a more general focus, Mailer tells us that everyone in the Army has his pet hatred. Thus, the paragraph has a classic development: the idea, followed by particulars, concluded by a statement that projects the initial statement into a more general truth.

1 There are, of course, many other forms of narrative art, but this method is one of the most common. Can you find other paragraphs in this story that have a similar arrangement?

2 What happens to this kind of development when there is a good deal of dialogue?

Further Aspects

Besides saying something about character in this story, Mailer is also saying something about the Army. The Army is based on power, not only the obvious power of the mass of men but also the power of the individuals making it up. In this respect, Hobbs, the big Southerner, along with Taylor, represents the

Army. Hobbs is strong, capable, he can fight, he knows how to survive easily in an impersonal organization, he understands the ways of men and speaks their language; he is without question a "man." To be like Hobbs, then, is to be an integral part of the Army. To be different from Hobbs is to be outside or isolated from the general run of men.

1 Despite his sheltered background, Carter wants to be like Hobbs, speak like Hobbs, act like Hobbs. What point is Mailer making about people? About the Army?

2 Is Hobbs voicing something we all accept when he says that everyone is expected to have "his own deal in this Army"? Is this the sole way to survive? If it is, what point is Mailer making?

3 What is the language of men? Where does Carter fail in his attempt to learn how men talk? When a "shadow passed across Hobbs' face," what kind of shadow was it? What did Hobbs have in mind?

4 Does Mailer's point about the Army expand into a more general point? That is, are his remarks applicable to any large impersonal organization which swallows individuals and makes them behave as a mass? If so, what larger point is Mailer making about life? Do his remarks concern you even if you never enter the Army?

KILLED AT RESACA

Ambrose Bierce

The best soldier of our staff was Lieutenant Herman Brayle, one of the two aides-de-camp. I don't remember where the general picked him up; from some Ohio regiment, I think; none of us had previously known him, and it would have been strange if we had, for no two of us came from the same State, nor even from adjoining States. The general seemed to think that a position on his staff was a distinction that should be so judiciously conferred as not to beget any sectional jealousies and imperil the integrity of that part of the country which was still an integer. He would not even choose officers from his own command, but by some jugglery at department headquarters obtained them from other brigades. Under such circumstances, a man's services had to be very distinguished indeed to be heard of by his family and the friends of his youth; and "the speaking trump of fame" was a trifle hoarse from loquacity, anyhow.

Lieutenant Brayle was more than six feet in height and of splendid proportions, with the light hair and gray-blue eyes which men so gifted usually find associated with a high order of courage. As he was commonly in full uniform, especially in action, when most officers are content to be less flamboyantly attired, he was a very striking and conspicuous figure. As to the rest, he had a gentleman's manners, a scholar's head, and a lion's heart. His age was about thirty.

We all soon came to like Brayle as much as we admired him, and it was with sincere concern that in the engagement at Stone's River—our first action after he joined us—we observed that he had one most objectionable and unsoldierly quality: he was vain of his courage. During all the vicissitudes and mutations of that hideous encounter, whether our troops were fighting in the open cotton fields, in the cedar thickets or behind the railway embankment, he did not once take cover, except when sternly commanded to do so by the general, who usually had other things to think of than the lives of his staff officers—or those of his men, for that matter.

In every later engagement while Brayle was with us it was the same way. He would sit his horse like an equestrian statue, in a storm of bullets and grape, in the most exposed places—wherever, in fact, duty, requiring him to go, permitted him to remain—

when, without trouble and with distinct advantage to his reputation for common sense, he might have been in such security as is possible on a battlefield in the brief intervals of personal inaction.

On foot, from necessity or in deference to his dismounted commander or associates, his conduct was the same. He would stand like a rock in the open when officers and men alike had taken to cover; while men older in service and years, higher in rank and of unquestionable intrepidity, were loyally preserving behind the crest of a hill lives infinitely precious to their country, this fellow would stand, equally idle, on the ridge, facing in the direction of the sharpest fire.

When battles are going on in open ground it frequently occurs that the opposing lines, confronting each other within a stone's throw for hours, hug the earth as closely as if they loved it. The line officers in their proper places flatten themselves no less, and the field officers, their horses all killed or sent to the rear, crouch beneath the infernal canopy of hissing lead and screaming iron without a thought of personal dignity.

In such circumstances the life of a staff officer of a brigade is distinctly "not a happy one," mainly because of its precarious tenure and the unnerving alternations of emotion to which he is exposed. From a position of that comparative security from which a civilian would ascribe his escape to a "miracle," he may be despatched with an order to some commander of a prone regiment in the front line—a person for the moment inconspicuous and not always easy to find without a deal of search among men somewhat preoccupied, and in a din in which question and answer alike must be imparted in the sign language. It is customary in such cases to duck the head and scuttle away on a keen run, an object of lively interest to some thousands of admiring marksmen. In returning—well, it is not customary to return.

Brayle's practice was different. He would consign his horse to the care of an orderly,—he loved his horse,—and walk quietly away on his perilous errand with never a stoop of the back, his splendid figure, accentuated by his uniform, holding the eye with a strange fascination. We watched him with suspended breath, our hearts in our mouths. On one occasion of this kind, indeed, one of our number, an impetuous stammerer, was so possessed by his emotion that he shouted at me:

"I'll b-b-bet you t-two d-d-dollars they d-drop him b-b-before he g-gets to that d-d-ditch!"

I did not accept the brutal wager; I thought they would.

Let me do justice to a brave man's memory; in all these needless exposures of life there was no visible bravado nor subsequent narration. In the few instances when some of us had ventured to remonstrate, Brayle had smiled pleasantly and made some light reply, which, however, had not encouraged a further pursuit of the subject. Once he said:

"Captain, if ever I come to grief by forgetting your advice, I hope my last moments will be cheered by the sound of your beloved voice breathing into my ear the blessed words, 'I told you so.' "

We laughed at the captain—just why we could probably not have explained—and that afternoon when he was shot to rags from an ambuscade Brayle remained by the body for some time, adjusting the limbs with needless care—there in the middle of a road swept by gusts of grape and canister! It is easy to condemn this kind of thing, and not very difficult to refrain from imitation, but it is impossible not to respect, and Brayle was liked none the less for the weakness which had so heroic an expression. We wished he were not a fool, but he went on that way to the end, sometimes hard hit, but always returning to duty about as good as new.

Of course, it came at last; he who ignores the law of probabilities challenges an adversary that is seldom beaten. It was at Resaca, in Georgia, during the movement that resulted in the taking of Atlanta. In front of our brigade the enemy's line of earthworks ran through open fields along a slight crest. At each end of this open ground we were close up to him in the woods, but the clear ground we could not hope to occupy until night, when darkness would enable us to burrow like moles and throw up earth. At this point our line was a quarter-mile away in the edge of a wood. Roughly, we formed a semicircle, the enemy's fortified line being the chord of the arc.

"Lieutenant, go tell Colonel Ward to work up as close as he can get cover, and not to waste much ammunition in unnecessary firing. You may leave your horse."

When the general gave his direction we were in the fringe of the forest, near the right extremity of the arc. Colonel Ward was at the left. The suggestion to leave the horse obviously enough meant that Brayle was to take the longer line, through the woods and among the men. Indeed, the suggestion was needless; to go by the short route meant absolutely certain failure to deliver the message. Before anybody could interpose, Brayle had cantered lightly into the field and the enemy's works were in crackling conflagration.

"Stop that damned fool!" shouted the general.

A private of the escort, with more ambition than brains, spurred forward to obey, and within ten yards left himself and his horse dead on the field of honor.

Brayle was beyond recall, galloping easily along, parallel to the enemy and less than two hundred yards distant. He was a picture to see! His hat had been blown or shot from his head, and his long, blond hair rose and fell with the motion of his horse. He sat erect in the saddle, holding the reins lightly in his left hand, his right hanging carelessly at his side. An occasional glimpse of his handsome profile as he turned his head one way or the other proved that the interest which he took in what was going on was natural and without affectation.

The picture was intensely dramatic, but in no degree theatrical. Successive scores of rifles spat at him viciously as he came within range, and our own line in the edge of the timber broke out in visible and audible defense. No longer regardful of themselves or their orders, our fellows sprang to their feet, and swarming into the open sent broad sheets of bullets against the blazing crest of the offending works, which poured an answering fire into their unprotected groups with deadly effect. The artillery on both sides joined the battle, punctuating the rattle and roar with deep, earth-shaking explosions and tearing the air with storms of screaming grape, which from the enemy's side splintered the trees and spattered them with blood, and from ours defiled the smoke of his arms with banks and clouds of dust from his parapet.

My attention had been for a moment drawn to the general combat, but now, glancing down the unobscured avenue between these two thunderclouds, I saw Brayle, the cause of the carnage. Invisible now from either side, and equally doomed by friend and foe, he stood in the shot-swept space, motionless, his face toward the enemy. At some little distance lay his horse. I instantly saw what had stopped him.

As topographical engineer I had, early in the day, made a hasty examination of the ground, and now remembered that at that point was a deep and sinuous gully, crossing half the field from the enemy's line, its general course at right angles to it. From where we now were it was invisible, and Brayle had evidently not known about it. Clearly, it was impassable. Its salient angles would have afforded him absolute security if he had chosen to be satisfied with the miracle already wrought in his favor and leapt into it. He could not go forward, he would not turn back; he stood awaiting death. It did not keep him long waiting.

By some mysterious coincidence, almost instantaneously as he fell, the firing ceased, a few desultory shots at long intervals serving rather to accentuate than break the silence. It was as if both sides had suddenly repented of their profitless crime. Four stretcher-bearers of ours, following a sergeant with a white flag, soon afterward moved unmolested into the field, and made straight for Brayle's body. Several Confederate officers and men came out to meet them, and with uncovered heads assisted them to take up their sacred burden. As it was borne toward us we heard beyond the hostile works fifes and a muffled drum—a dirge. A generous enemy honored the fallen brave.

Amongst the dead man's effects was a soiled Russia-leather pocketbook. In the distribution of mementoes of our friend, which the general, as administrator, decreed, this fell to me.

A year after the close of the war, on my way to California, I opened and idly inspected it. Out of an overlooked compartment fell a letter without envelope or address. It was in a woman's handwriting, and began with words of endearment, but no name.

It had the following date line: "San Francisco, Cal., July 9, 1862." The signature was "Darling," in marks of quotation. Incidentally, in the body of the text, the writer's full name was given—Marian Mendenhall.

The letter showed evidence of cultivation and good breeding, but it was an ordinary love letter, if a love letter can be ordinary. There was not much in it, but there was something. It was this:

"Mr. Winters, whom I shall always hate for it, has been telling that at some battle in Virginia, where he got his hurt, you were seen crouching behind a tree. I think he wants to injure you in my regard, which he knows the story would do if I believed it. I could bear to hear of my soldier lover's death, but not of his cowardice."

These were the words which on that sunny afternoon, in a distant region, had slain a hundred men. Is woman weak?

One evening I called on Miss Mendenhall to return the letter to her. I intended, also, to tell her what she had done—but not that she did it. I found her in a handsome dwelling on Rincon Hill. She was beautiful, well bred—in a word, charming.

"You knew Lieutenant Herman Brayle," I said, rather abruptly. "You know, doubtless, that he fell in battle. Among his effects was found this letter from you. My errand here is to place it in your hands."

She mechanically took the letter, glanced through it with deepening color, and then, looking at me with a smile, said:

"It is very good of you, though I am sure it was hardly worth while." She started suddenly and changed color. "This stain," she said, "is it—surely it is not—"

"Madam," I said, "pardon me, but that is the blood of the truest and bravest heart that ever beat."

She hastily flung the letter on the blazing coals. "Uh! I cannot bear the sight of blood!" she said. "How did he die?"

I had involuntarily risen to rescue that scrap of paper, sacred even to me, and now stood partly behind her. As she asked the question she turned her face about and slightly upward. The light of the burning letter was reflected in her eyes and touched her cheek with a tinge of crimson like the stain upon its page. I had never seen anything so beautiful as this detestable creature.

"He was bitten by a snake," I replied.

Theme

1 Bierce is concerned with the nature of honor and courage, a theme that is particularly relevant during wartime. He embodies this theme in the figure of Lieutenant Brayle. Does he make the idea convincing as it appears in Brayle? We may ask: Is there any value to this kind of honor? Or is Brayle a fool for holding such standards?

2 What function does the first paragraph, concerning the dissimilarity of the men on the general's staff, play in the story? Ask yourself, first, why men show courage and display a sense of honor. Is it for themselves, for others, or for what?

3 Does the introduction of the girl at the end of the story serve any thematic function? Could the story end with Brayle's death, or must it continue through Bierce's cynical ending?

4 What is Bierce's attitude toward the girl? Why does he take such an attitude? Can her reaction to the death of the lieutenant be projected further, beyond her?

5 At what point does the story begin to assume importance beyond simply the foolish death of a daring and foolish young man out to display his courage? Or does the story, in your opinion, fail to go beyond this particular event into something more generally true?

Character

1 The story is obviously caught between character and theme. That is, the character of the one chief figure becomes, ultimately, the theme of the short story. What clues does Bierce provide that Brayle's character must be projected into theme? Note the following example, and then see if you can find others. When Brayle is calmly picking his way through the lines, both sides throw everything they have at each other. He remains calm, almost oblivious, while the men themselves become very agitated. Why does Bierce present the incident in this particular way? Remember that a writer has several choices open to him. Bierce might have had both sides remain silent, watchful; he might have had Brayle come through alive; he might have had him wounded; he might have had him break and run, or hide in the gulley that crossed the field.

2 Although terms like honor, courage, and chivalry have become old-fashioned for many people, during the Civil War these qualities found a high place in most men's scale of values. How do we feel when we see a life like Brayle's thrown away? Can we understand him, or is he a dim, noncomprehensible figure from the past?

3 Would it have been better for such a man to save himself to fight another day? What is Bierce's attitude?

4 Brayle's deed gains meaning and value in the scene between the girl and the narrator. Do you think Bierce included this scene for that reason—that is, to strengthen the value of what the lieutenant did on the field of battle?

Plot and Plot Structure

1 "Killed at Resaca" obviously does not have any thickness of plot nor density of event. If you tell the plot of this short story in a few words, is much lost? If so, what? Compare it in this respect with a short story like Conrad's "Il Conde" or Lawrence's "The Horse Dealer's Daughter" in order to gain a perspective.

2 If the plot here is somewhat thin, what carries Bierce through? It is certainly not the writing, which is careful and precise but hardly ambitious. What does work?

Setting

1 On first reading, the story seems to minimize setting. But Bierce has neatly placed many details along the way which give us a meaningful setting. Can you indicate some of these details?
2 How can you tell from these details that the war in question is the Civil War? Three obvious leads are the use of the word "Confederate," the date on the letter, "July 9, 1862," and the indication of Resaca, Georgia. But there are other signs if you read carefully.

FIRST CONFESSION

Frank O'Connor

It was a Saturday afternoon in early spring. A small boy whose face looked as though it had been but newly scrubbed was being led by the hand by his sister through a crowded street. The little boy showed a marked reluctance to proceed; he affected to be very interested in the shop-windows. Equally, his sister seemed to pay no attention to them. She tried to hurry him; he resisted. When she dragged him he bagan to bawl. The hatred with which she viewed him was almost diabolical, but when she spoke her words and tone were full of passionate sympathy.

"Ah, sha, God help us!" she intoned into his ear in a whine of commiseration.

"Leave me go!" he said, digging his heels into the pavement. "I don't want to go. I want to go home."

"But, sure, you can't go home, Jackie. You'll have to go. The parish priest will be up to the house with a stick."

"I don't care. I won't go."

"Oh, Sacred Heart, isn't it a terrible pity you weren't a good boy? Oh Jackie, me heart bleeds for you! I don't know what they'll do to you at all, Jackie, me poor child. And all the trouble you caused your poor old nanny, and the way you wouldn't eat in the same room with her, and the time you kicked her on the shins, and the time you went for me with the bread knife under the table. I don't know will he ever listen to you at all, Jackie. I think meself he might sind you to the bishop. Oh, Jackie, how will you think of all your sins?"

Half stupefied with terror, Jackie allowed himself to be led through the sunny streets to the very gates of the church. It was an old one with two grim iron gates and a long, low, shapeless stone front. At the gates he stuck, but it was already too late. She dragged him behind her across the yard, and the commiserating whine with which she had tried to madden him gave place to a yelp of triumph.

"Now you're caught! Now, you're caught. And I hope he'll give you the pinitintial psalms! That'll cure you, you suppurating little caffler!"

Jackie gave himself up for lost. Within the old church there was no stained glass; it was cold and dark and desolate, and in the silence, the trees in the yard knocked hollowly at the tall windows. He allowed himself to be led through the vaulted silence, the intense and magical silence which seemed to have frozen within the ancient walls, buttressing them and shouldering the high wooden roof. In the street outside, yet seeming a million miles away, a ballad singer was drawling a ballad.

Nora sat in front of him beside the confession box. There were a few old women before her, and later a thin, sad-looking man with long hair came and sat beside Jackie. In the intense silence of the church that seemed to grow deeper from the plaintive moaning of the ballad singer, he could hear the buzz-buzz-buzz of a woman's voice in the box, and then the husky ba-ba-ba of the priest's. Lastly the soft thud of something that signalled the end of the confession, and out came the woman, head lowered, hands joined, looking neither to right nor left, and tiptoed up to the altar to say her penance.

It seemed only a matter of seconds till Nora rose and with a whispered injunction disappeared from his sight. He was all alone. Alone and next to be heard and the fear of damnation in his soul. He looked at the sad-faced man. He was gazing at the roof, his hands joined in prayer. A woman in a red blouse and black shawl had taken her place below him. She uncovered her head, fluffed her hair out roughly with her hand, brushed it sharply back, then, bowing, caught it in a knot and pinned it on her neck. Nora emerged. Jackie rose and looked at her with a hatred which was inappropriate to the occasion and the place. Her hands were joined on her stomach, her eyes modestly lowered, and her face had an expression of the most rapt and tender recollection. With death in his heart he crept into the compartment she left open and drew the door shut behind him.

He was in pitch darkness. He could see no priest nor anything else. And anything he had heard of confession got all muddled up in his mind. He knelt to the right-hand wall and said: "Bless me, father, for I have sinned. This is my first confession." Nothing happened. He repeated it louder. Still it gave no answer. He turned to the opposite wall, genuflected first, then again went on his knees and repeated the charm. This time he was certain he would receive a reply, but none came. He repeated the process with the remaining wall without effect. He had the feeling of someone with an unfamiliar machine, of pressing buttons at random. And finally the thought struck him that God knew.

God knew about the bad confession he intended to make and had made him deaf and blind so that he could neither hear nor see the priest.

Then as his eyes grew accustomed to the blackness, he perceived something he had not noticed previously: a sort of shelf at about the height of his head. The purpose of this eluded him for a moment. Then he understood. It was for kneeling on.

He had always prided himself upon his powers of climbing, but this took it out of him. There was no foothold. He slipped twice before he succeeded in getting his knee on it; and the strain of drawing the rest of his body up was almost more than he was capable of. However, he did at last get his two knees on it, there was just room for those, but his legs hung down uncomfortably and the edge of the shelf bruised his shins. He joined his hands and pressed the last remaining button. "Bless me, father, for I have sinned. This is my first confession."

At the same moment the slide was pushed back and a dim light streamed into the little box. There was an uncomfortable silence, and then an alarmed voice asked, "Who's there?" Jackie found it almost impossible to speak into the grille which was on the level with his knees, but he got a firm grip of the molding above it, bent his head down and sideways, and as though he were hanging by his feet like a monkey found himself looking almost upside down at the priest. But the priest was looking sideways at him, and Jackie, whose knees were being tortured by this new position, felt it was a queer way to hear confessions.

" 'Tis me, father," he piped, and then, running all his words together in excitement, he rattled off, "Bless me, father, for I have sinned. This is my first confession."

"What?" exclaimed a deep and angry voice, and the sombre soutaned figure stood bolt upright, disappearing almost entirely from Jackie's view. "What does this mean? What are you doing there? Who are you?"

And with the shock Jackie felt his hands lose their grip and his legs their balance. He discovered himself tumbling into space, and, falling, he knocked his head against the door, which shot open and permitted him to thump right into the center of the aisle. Straight on this came a small, dark-haired priest with a biretta well forward on his head. At the same time Nora came skeltering madly down the church.

"Lord God!" she cried. "The snivelling little caffler! I knew he'd do it! I knew he'd disgrace me!"

Jackie received a clout over the ear which reminded him that for some strange reason he had not yet begun to cry and that people might possibly think he wasn't hurt at all. Nora slapped him again.

"What's this? What's this?" cried the priest. "Don't attempt to beat the child, you little vixen!"

"I can't do me pinance with him," cried Nora shrilly, cocking a shocked eye on the priest. "He have me driven mad. Stop your crying, you dirty scut! Stop it now or I'll make you cry at the other side of your ugly puss!"

"Run away out of this, you little jade!" growled the priest. He suddenly began to laugh, took out a pocket handkerchief, and wiped Jackie's nose. "You're not hurt, sure you're not. Show us the ould head. . . . Ah, 'tis nothing. 'Twill be better before you're twice married. . . . So you were coming to confession?"

"I was, father."

"A big fellow like you should have terrible sins. Is it your first?"

" 'Tis, father."

"Oh, my, worse and worse! Here, sit down there and wait till I get rid of these ould ones and we'll have a long chat. Never mind that sister of yours."

With a feeling of importance that glowed through his tears Jackie waited. Nora stuck out her tongue at him, but he didn't even bother to reply. A great feeling of relief was welling up in him. The sense of oppression that had been weighing him down for a week, the knowledge that he was about to make a bad confession, disappeared. Bad confession, indeed! He had made friends, made friends with the priest, and the priest expected, even demanded terrible sins. Oh, women! Women! It was all women and girls and their silly talk. They had no real knowledge of the world!

And when the time came for him to make his confession he did not beat about the bush. He may have clenched his hands and lowered his eyes, but wouldn't anyone?

"Father," he said huskily, "I made it up to kill me grandmother."

There was a moment's pause. Jackie did not dare to look up, but he could feel the priest's eyes on him. The priest's voice also seemed a trifle husky.

"Your grandmother?" he asked, but he didn't after all sound very angry.

"Yes, father."

"Does she live with you?"

"She do, father."

"And why did you want to kill her?"

"Oh, God, father, she's a horrible woman!"

"Is she now?"

"She is, father."

"What way is she horrible?"

Jackie paused to think. It was hard to explain.

"She takes snuff, father."

"Oh, my!"

"And she goes round in her bare feet, father."

"Tut-tut-tut!"

"She's a horrible woman, father," said Jackie with sudden earnestness. "She takes porter. And she ates the potatoes off the table with her hands. And me mother do be out working most days, and since that one came 'tis she gives us our dinner and I can't ate the dinner." He found himself sniffling. "And she gives pinnies to Nora and she doesn't give no pinnies to me because she knows I can't stand her. And me father sides with her, father, and he bates me, and me heart is broken and wan night in bed I made it up the way I'd kill her."

Jackie began to sob again, rubbing his nose with his sleeve, as he remembered his wrongs.

"And what way were you going to kill her?" asked the priest smoothly.

"With a hatchet, father."

"When she was in bed?"

"No, father."

"How, so?"

"When she ates the potatoes and drinks the porter she falls asleep, father."

"And you'd hit her then?"

"Yes, father."

"Wouldn't a knife be better?"

" 'Twould, father, only I'd be afraid of the blood."

"Oh, of course, I never thought of the blood."

"I'd be afraid of that, father. I was near hitting Nora with the bread knife one time she came after me under the table, only I was afraid."

"You're a terrible child," said the priest with awe.

"I am, father," said Jackie noncommittally, sniffling back his tears.

"And what would you do with the body?"

"How, father?"

"Wouldn't someone see her and tell?"

"I was going to cut her up with a knife and take away the pieces and bury them. I could get an orange box for threepence and make a cart to take them away."

"My, my," said the priest. "You had it all well planned."

"Ah, I tried that," said Jackie with mounting confidence. "I borrowed a cart and practised it by meself one night after dark."

"And weren't you afraid?"

"Ah, no," said Jackie half-heartedly. "Only a bit."

"You have terrible courage," said the priest. "There's a lot of people I want to get rid of, but I'm not like you. I'd never have the courage. And hanging is an awful death."

"Is it?" asked Jackie, responding to the brightness of a new theme.

"Oh, an awful blooming death!"

"Did you ever see a fellow hanged?"

"Dozens of them, and they all died roaring."

"Jay!" said Jackie.

"They do be swinging out of them for hours and the poor fellows lepping and roaring, like bells in a belfry, and then they put lime on them to burn them up. Of course, they pretend they're dead but sure, they don't be dead at all."

"Jay!" said Jackie again.

"So if I were you I'd take my time and think about it. In my opinion 'tisn't worth it, not even to get rid of a grandmother. I asked dozens of fellows like you that killed their grandmothers about it, and they all said, no, 'twasn't worth it. . . ."

Nora was waiting in the yard. The sunlight struck down on her across the high wall and its brightness made his eyes dazzle. "Well?" she asked. "What did he give you?"

"Three Hail Marys."

"You mustn't have told him anything."

"I told him everything," said Jackie confidently.

"What did you tell him?"

"Things you don't know."

"Bah! He gave you three Hail Marys because you were a cry baby!"

Jackie didn't mind. He felt the world was very good. He began to whistle as well as the hindrance in his jaw permitted.

"What are you sucking?"

"Bull's eyes."

"Was it he gave them to you?"

" 'Twas."

"Almighty God!" said Nora. "Some people have all the luck. I might as well be a sinner like you. There's no use in being good."

Characterization

The literature of the last hundred years is full of stories and novels in which a young boy or man is faced by a test or an obstacle. Whatever it is usually creates apprehension and fear. We think almost immediately of young boys as different as Huckleberry Finn, David Copperfield, and Stephen Dedalus (in Joyce's *A Portrait of the Artist as a Young Man*), all of whom are faced by people and situations which seem too much for their limited experience. Yet all are able to summon up whatever is necessary to come through.

The authors of such novels and stories see childhood as a time of constant struggle against obstacles. This type of literature of course rings true, for it presents a universal situation—the fear of the unknown, whether in childhood or later.

Frank O'Connor captures this note of anxiety and fear in a young boy facing confession. First confession is, of course, a great unknown, comprising the darkness of the confessional, the coldness of the church, the sense of one's own frailty, the fear of a drastic penitence, the larger fear of permanent damnation if one is not honest.

1 Why does O'Connor have the story take place on a Saturday afternoon in early spring? Is the particular time of any significance in young Jackie's mind?

2 What effect does his relationship with his sister have upon him? Is it a typical relationship? What is her attitude? What kind of child does he appear to be from her comments? What do you learn about her?

3 The confrontation with the priest in the confessional box is, in miniature, the confrontation of the child's world with the world of the adult. The child's world is full of activity and climbing, mischievous pranks, little acts of naughtiness without much thought of consequences. The world of the adult is darker, full of responsibilities, and fraught with retribution—at least as it is seen by the child. Why, then does O'Connor make this confrontation so funny?

4 Jackie's attempt to confess is a fiasco, although most serious to him. He is appalled by the consequences of his earnest action. Yet the priest sees it humorously. What does this say about the priest? Is he on good ground? How does he know that Jackie's feelings won't be hurt?

5 How would you characterize the priest? Are his responses the ones usually expected of a religious man? What is revealed about O'Connor's view of the priesthood and its functions?

6 Is the comedy in keeping with a solemn occasion like a first confession? How does the comedy work together with setting and atmosphere to create character?

Further Aspects

1 What is the significance of the description of the church as Jackie first sees it: "Within the old church there was no stained glass; it was cold and dark and desolate, and in the silence, the trees in the yard knocked hollowly at the tall windows. He allowed himself to be led through the vaulted silence, the intense and magical silence which seemed to have frozen within the ancient walls, buttressing them and shouldering the high wooden roof."

2 What is the purpose of the "ballad singer" in the distance?

3 Why are Jackie's eyes dazzled when he meets Nora in the yard at the end of the story?

4 Why does Jackie's attempt at confession take place in the total darkness? That is, besides the physical fact, how does it serve O'Connor's purpose?

5 Does the story expand beyond this singular event to a more universal experience? Is there a "first confession" in everyone's background? What are some of the equivalent experiences you can think of—assuming you have not made a first confession?

PAUL'S CASE

Willa Cather

It was Paul's afternoon to appear before the faculty of the Pittsburgh High School to account for his various misdemeanours. He had been suspended a week ago, and his father had called at the Principal's office and confessed his perplexity about his son. Paul entered the faculty room suave and smiling. His clothes were a trifle outgrown, and the tan velvet on the collar of his overcoat was frayed and worn; but for all that there was something of the dandy about him, and he wore an opal pin in his neatly knotted black four-in-hand, and a red carnation in his buttonhole. This later adornment the faculty somehow felt was not properly significant of the contrite spirit befitting a boy under the ban of suspension.

Paul was tall for his age and very thin, with high, cramped shoulders and a narrow chest. His eyes were remarkable for a certain hysterical brilliancy, and he continually used them in a conscious, theatrical sort of way, peculiarly offensive in a boy. The pupils were abnormally large, as though he were addicted to belladonna, but there was a glassy glitter about them which that drug does not produce.

When questioned by the Principal as to why he was there, Paul stated, politely enough, that he wanted to come back to school. This was a lie, but Paul was quite accustomed to lying; found it, indeed, indispensable for overcoming friction. His teachers were asked to state their respective charges against him, which they did with such a rancour and aggrievedness as evinced that this was not a usual case. Disorder and impertinence were among the offences named, yet each of his instructors felt that it was scarcely possible to put into words the real cause of the trouble, which lay in a sort of hysterically defiant manner of the boy's; in the contempt which they all knew he felt for them, and which he seemingly made not the least effort to conceal. Once, when he had been making a synopsis of a paragraph at the blackboard, his English teacher had stepped to his side and attempted to guide his hand. Paul had started back with a shudder and thrust his hands violently behind him. The astonished woman could scarcely have been more hurt and embarrassed had he struck at her. The insult was so involuntary and definitely personal as to be unforgettable. In one way and another, he had made all his teachers, men and women alike, conscious of the same feeling of physical aversion. In one class he habitually sat with his hand shading his eyes; in another he always looked out of the window during the recitation; in another he made a running commentary on the lecture, with humorous intent.

His teachers felt this afternoon that his whole attitude was symbolized by his shrug and his flippantly red carnation flower, and they fell upon him without mercy, his English teacher leading the pack. He stood through it smiling, his pale lips parted over his white teeth. (His lips were continually twitching, and he had a habit of raising his eyebrows that was contemptuous and irritating to the last degree.) Older boys than Paul had broken down and shed tears under that ordeal, but his set smile did not once desert him, and his only sign of discomfort was the nervous trembling of the fingers that toyed with the buttons of his overcoat, and an occasional jerking of the other hand which held his hat. Paul was always smiling, always glancing about him, seeming to feel that people might be watching him and trying to detect something. This conscious expression, since it was as far as possible from boyish mirthfulness, was usually attributed to insolence or "smartness."

As the inquisition proceeded, one of his instructors repeated an impertinent remark of the boy's, and the Principal asked him whether he thought that a courteous speech to make to a woman. Paul shrugged his shoulders slightly and his eyebrows twitched.

"I don't know," he replied. "I didn't mean to be polite or impolite, either. I guess it's a sort of way I have, of saying things regardless."

The Principal asked him whether he didn't think that a way it would be well to get rid of. Paul grinned and said he guessed so. When he was told that he could go, he bowed gracefully and went out. His bow was like a repetition of the scandalous red carnation.

His teachers were in despair, and his drawing master voiced the feeling of them all when he declared there was something about the boy which none of them understood. He added: "I don't really believe that smile of his comes altogether from insolence; there's something sort of haunted about it. The boy is not strong, for one thing. There is something wrong about the fellow."

The drawing master had come to realize that, in looking at Paul, one saw only his white teeth and the forced animation of his eyes. One warm afternoon the boy had gone to sleep at his drawing-board, and his master had noted with amazement what a white, blue-veined face it was; drawn and wrinkled like an old man's about the eyes, the lips twitching even in his sleep.

His teachers left the building dissatisfied and unhappy; humiliated to have felt so vindictive toward a mere boy, to have uttered this feeling in cutting terms, and to have set each other on, as it were, in the gruesome game of intemperate reproach. One of them remembered having seen a miserable street cat set at bay by a ring of tormentors.

As for Paul, he ran down the hill whistling the Soldiers' Chorus from *Faust*, looking wildly behind him now and then to see whether some of his teachers were not there to witness his light-heartedness. As it was now late in the afternoon and Paul was on duty that evening as usher at Carnegie Hall, he decided that he would not go home to supper.

When he reached the concert hall the doors were not yet open. It was chilly outside, and he decided to go up into the picture gallery—always deserted at this hour—where there were some of Raffelli's gay studies of Paris streets and an airy blue Venetian scene or two that always exhilarated him. He was delighted to find no one in the gallery but the old guard, who sat in the corner, a newspaper on his knee, a black patch over one eye and the other closed. Paul possessed himself of the place and walked confidently up and down, whistling under his breath. After a while he sat down before a blue Rico and lost himself. When he bethought him to look at his watch, it was after seven o'clock, and he rose with a start and ran downstairs, making a face at Augustus Caesar, peering out from the cast-room, and an evil gesture at the Venus of Milo as he passed her on the stairway.

When Paul reached the ushers' dressing-room half-a-dozen boys were there already, and he began excitedly to tumble into his uniform. It was one of the few that at all approached fitting, and Paul thought it very becoming—though he knew the tight, straight coat accentuated his narrow chest, about which he was exceedingly sensitive. He was always excited while he dressed, twanging all over to the tuning of the strings and the preliminary flourishes of the horns in the music-room; but tonight he seemed quite beside himself, and he teased and plagued the boys until, telling him that he was crazy, they put him down on the floor and sat on him.

Somewhat calmed by his suppression, Paul dashed out to the front of the house to seat the early comers. He was a model usher. Gracious and smiling he ran up and down the aisles. Nothing was too much trouble for him; he carried messages and brought programs as though it were his greatest pleasure in life, and all the people in his section thought him a charming boy, feeling that he remembered and admired them. As the house filled, he grew more and more vivacious and animated, and the colour came to his cheeks and lips. It was very much as though this were a great reception and Paul were the host. Just as the musicians came out to take their places, his English teacher arrived with checks for the seats which a prominent manufacturer had taken for the season. She betrayed some embarrassment when she handed Paul the tickets, and a *hauteur* which subsequently made her feel very foolish. Paul was startled for a moment, and had the feeling of wanting to put her out; what business had she here among all these fine people and gay colours? He looked her over and decided that she was not appropriately dressed and must be a fool to sit downstairs in such togs. The tickets had probably been sent her out of kindness, he reflected, as he put down a seat for her, and she had about as much right to sit there as he had.

When the symphony began Paul sank into one of the rear seats with a long sigh of relief, and lost himself as he had done before the Rico. It was not that symphonies, as such, meant anything in particular to Paul, but the first sigh of the instruments seemed to free some hilarious spirit within him; something that struggled there like the Genius in the bottle found by the Arab fisherman. He felt a sudden zest of life; the lights danced before his eyes and the concert hall blazed into unimaginable splendour. When the soprano soloist came on, Paul forgot even the nastiness of his teacher's being there, and gave himself up to the peculiar intoxication such personages always had for him. The soloist chanced to be a German woman, by no means in her first youth, and the mother of many children; but she wore a satin gown and a tiara, and she had that indefinable air of achievement, that world-shine upon her, which always blinded Paul to any possible defects.

After a concert was over, Paul was often irritable and wretched until he got to sleep, and tonight he was even more than usually restless. He had this feeling of not being able to let down; of its being impossible to give up this delicious excitement which was the only thing that could be called living at all. During the last number he withdrew and, after hastily changing his clothes in the dressing-room, slipped out to the side door where the singer's carriage stood. Here he began pacing rapidly up and down the walk, waiting to see her come out.

Over yonder the Schenley, in its vacant stretch, loomed big

and square through the fine rain, the windows of its twelve stories glowing like those of a lighted card-board house under a Christmas tree. All the actors and singers of any importance stayed there when they were in the city, and a number of the big manufacturers of the place lived there in the winter. Paul had often hung about the hotel, watching the people go in and out, longing to enter and leave school-masters and dull care behind him forever.

At last the singer came out, accompanied by the conductor, who helped her into her carriage and closed the door with a cordial *auf wiedersehen,*—which set Paul to wondering whether she were not an old sweetheart of his. Paul followed the carriage over to the hotel, walking so rapidly as not to be far from the entrance when the singer alighted and disappeared behind the swinging glass doors which were opened by a negro in a tall hat and a long coat. In the moment that the door was ajar, it seemed to Paul that he, too, entered. He seemed to feel himself go after her up the steps, into the warm, lighted building, into an exotic, a tropical world of shiny, glistening surfaces and basking ease. He reflected upon the mysterious dishes that were brought into the dining-room, the green bottles in buckets of ice, as he had seen them in the supper party pictures of the Sunday supplement. A quick gust of wind brought the rain down with sudden vehemence, and Paul was startled to find that he was still outside in the slush of the gravel driveway; that his boots were letting in the water and his scanty overcoat was clinging wet about him; that the lights in front of the concert hall were out, and that the rain was driving in sheets between him and the orange glow of the windows above him. There it was, what he wanted—tangibly before him, like the fairy world of a Christmas pantomime; as the rain beat in his face, Paul wondered whether he were destined always to shiver in the black night outside, looking up at it.

He turned and walked reluctantly toward the car tracks. The end had to come sometime; his father in his nightclothes at the top of the stairs, explanations that did not explain, hastily improvised fictions that were forever tripping him up, his upstairs room and its horrible yellow wallpaper, the creaking bureau with the greasy plush collar-box, and over his painted wooden bed the pictures of George Washington and John Calvin, and the framed motto, "Feed my Lambs," which had been worked in red worsted by his mother, whom Paul could not remember.

Half an hour later, Paul alighted from the Negley Avenue car and went slowly down one of the side streets off the main thoroughfare. It was a highly respectable street, where all the houses were exactly alike, and where business men of moderate means begot and reared large families of children, all of whom went to Sabbath-school and learned the shorter catechism, and were interested in arithmetic; all of whom were as exactly alike as their homes, and of a piece with the monotony in which they lived. Paul never went up Cordelia Street without a shudder of loathing. His home was next the house of the Cumberland minister. He approached it tonight with the nerveless sense of defeat, the hopeless feeling of sinking back forever into ugliness and commonness that he had always had when he came home. The moment he turned into Cordelia Street he felt the waters close above his head. After each of these orgies of living, he experienced all the physical depression which follows a debauch; the loathing of respectable beds, of common food, of a house permeated by kitchen odours; a shuddering repulsion for the flavourless, colourless mass of every-day existence; a morbid desire for cool things and soft lights and fresh flowers.

The nearer he approached the house, the more absolutely unequal Paul felt to the sight of it all; his ugly sleeping chamber; the cold bath-room with the grimy zinc tub, the cracked mirror, the dripping spiggots; his father, at the top of the stairs, his hairy legs sticking out from his nightshirt, his feet thrust into carpet slippers. He was so much later than usual that there would certainly be inquiries and reproaches. Paul stopped short before the door. He felt that he could not be accosted by his father tonight; that he could not toss again on that miserable bed. He would not go in. He would tell his father that he had no car fare, and it was raining so hard he had gone home with one of the boys and stayed all night.

Meanwhile, he was wet and cold. He went around to the back of the house and tried one of the basement windows, found it open, raised it cautiously, and scrambled down the cellar wall to the floor. There he stood, holding his breath, terrified by the noise he had made; but the floor above him was silent, and there was no creak on the stairs. He found a soap-box, and carried it over to the soft ring of light that streamed from the furnace door, and sat down. He was horribly afraid of rats, so he did not try to sleep, but sat looking distrustfully at the dark, still terrified lest he might have awakened his father. In such reactions, after one of the experiences which made days and nights out of the dreary blanks of the calendar, when his senses were deadened, Paul's head was always singularly clear. Suppose his father had heard him getting in at the window and had come down and shot him for a burglar? Then, again, suppose his father had come down, pistol in hand, and he had cried out in time to save himself, and his father had been horrified to think how nearly he had killed him? Then, again, suppose a day should come when his father would remember that night, and wish there had been no warning cry to stay his hand? With this last supposition Paul entertained himself until daybreak.

The following Sunday was fine; the sodden November chill was broken by the last flash of autumnal summer. In the morning Paul had to go to church and Sabbath-school, as always. On seasonable Sunday afternoons the burghers of Cordelia Street usually sat out on their front "stoops," and talked to their neighbours on the next stoop, or called to those across the street in neighbourly fashion. The men sat placidly on gay cushions placed upon the steps that led down to the sidewalk, while the women, in their Sunday "waists," sat in rockers on the cramped porches, pretending to be greatly at their ease. The children played in the streets; there were so many of them that the place resembled the recreation grounds of a kindergarten. The men on the steps—all in their shirt sleeves, their vests unbuttoned—sat with their legs well apart, their stomachs comfortably protruding, and talked of the prices of things, or told anecdotes of the sagacity of their various chiefs and overlords. They occasionally looked over the multitude of squabbling children, listened affectionately to their high-pitched, nasal voices, smiling to see their own proclivities reproduced in their offspring, and interspersed their legends of the iron kings with remarks about their sons' progress at school, their grades in arithmetic, and the amounts they had saved in their toy banks.

On this last Sunday of November, Paul sat all the afternoon on the lowest step of his "stoop," staring into the street, while his sisters, in their rockers, were talking to the minister's daughters next door about how many shirt-waists they had made in the last week, and how many waffles some one had eaten at the last church supper. When the weather was warm, and his father was in a particularly jovial frame of mind, the girls made lemonade, which was always brought out in a red-glass pitcher, ornamented with forget-me-knots in blue enamel. This the girls thought very fine, and the neighbours joked about the suspicious colour of the pitcher.

Today Paul's father, on the top step, was talking to a young man who shifted a restless baby from knee to knee. He happened to be the young man who was daily held up to Paul as a model, and after whom it was his father's dearest hope that he would pattern. This young man was of a ruddy complexion, with a compressed, red mouth, and faded, near-sighted eyes, over which he wore thick spectacles, with gold bows that curved about his ears. He was clerk to one of the magnates of a great steel corporation, and was looked upon in Cordelia Street as a young man with a future. There was a story that, some five years ago—he was now barely twenty-six—he had been a trifle "dissipated," but in order to curb his appetites and save the loss of time and strength that a sowing of wild oats might have entailed, he had taken his chief's advice, oft reiterated to his employés, and at twenty-one had married the first woman whom he could persuade to share his fortunes. She happened to be an angular school-mistress, much older than he, who also wore thick glasses, and who had now borne him four children, all near-sighted, like herself.

The young man was relating how his chief, now cruising in the Mediterranean, kept in touch with all the details of the business, arranging his office hours on his yacht just as though he were at home, and "knocking off work enough to keep two stenographers busy." His father told, in turn, the plan his corporation was considering, of putting in an electric railway plant at Cairo. Paul snapped his teeth; he had an awful apprehension that they might spoil it all before he got there. Yet he rather liked to hear these legends of the iron kings, that were told and retold on Sundays and holidays; these stories of palaces in Venice, yachts on the Mediterranean, and high play at Monte Carlo appealed to his fancy, and he was interested in the triumphs of cash boys who had become famous, though he had no mind for the cash-boy stage.

After supper was over, and he had helped to dry the dishes, Paul nervously asked his father whether he could go to George's to get some help in his geometry, and still more nervously asked for car-fare. This latter request he had to repeat, as his father, on principle, did not like to hear requests for money, whether much or little. He asked Paul whether he could not go to some boy who lived nearer, and told him that he ought not to leave his school work until Sunday; but he gave him the dime. He was not a poor man, but he had a worthy ambition to come up in the world. His only reason for allowing Paul to usher was that he thought a boy ought to be earning a little.

Paul bounded upstairs, scrubbed the greasy odour of the dishwater from his hands with the ill-smelling soap he hated, and then shook over his fingers a few drops of violet water from the bottle he kept hidden in his drawer. He left the house with his geometry conspicuously under his arm, and the moment he got out of Cordelia Street and boarded a downtown car, he shook off the lethargy of two deadening days, and began to live again.

The leading juvenile of the permanent stock company which played at one of the downtown theatres was an acquaintance of Paul's, and the boy had been invited to drop in at the Sunday-night rehearsals whenever he could. For more than a year Paul had spent every available moment loitering about Charley Edwards's dressing-room. He had won a place among Edwards's following not only because the young actor, who could not afford to employ a dresser, often found him useful, but because he recognized in Paul something akin to what churchmen term "vocation."

It was at the theatre and at Carnegie Hall that Paul really lived; the rest was but a sleep and a forgetting. This was Paul's fairy tale, and it had for him all the allurement of a secret love. The moment he inhaled the gassy, painty, dusty odour behind the scenes, he breathed like a prisoner set free, and felt within him the possibility of doing or saying splendid, brilliant things. The moment the cracked orchestra beat out the overture from *Martha,* or jerked at the serenade from *Rigoletto,* all stupid and ugly things slid from him, and his senses were deliciously, yet delicately fired.

Perhaps it was because, in Paul's world, the natural nearly always wore the guise of ugliness, that a certain element of artificiality seemed to him necessary in beauty. Perhaps it was because his experience of life elsewhere was so full of Sabbath-school picnics, petty economies, wholesome advice as to how to succeed in life, and the unescapable odours of cooking, that he found this existence so alluring, these smartly-clad men and women so attractive, that he was so moved by these starry apple orchards that bloomed perennially under the lime-light.

It would be difficult to put it strongly enough how convincingly the stage entrance of that theatre was for Paul the actual portal of Romance. Certainly none of the company ever suspected it, least of all Charley Edwards. It was very like the old stories that used to float about London of fabulously rich Jews, who had subterranean halls, with palms, and fountains, and soft lamps and richly apparelled women who never saw the disenchanting light of London day. So, in the midst of that smoke-palled city, enamoured of figures and grimy toil, Paul had his secret temple, his wishing-carpet, this bit of blue-and-white Mediterranean shore bathed in perpetual sunshine.

Several of Paul's teachers had a theory that his imagination had been perverted by garish fiction; but the truth was, he scarcely ever read at all. The books at home were not such as would either tempt or corrupt a youthful mind, and as for reading the novels that some of his friends urged upon him—well, he got what he wanted much more quickly from music; any sort of music, from an orchestra to a barrel organ. He needed only the spark, the indescribable thrill that made his imagination master of his senses, and he could make plots and pictures enough of his own. It was equally true that he was not stagestruck—not, at any rate, in the usual acceptation of that expression. He had no desire to become an actor, any more than he had to become a musician. He felt no necessity to do any of these things; what he wanted was to see, to be in the atmosphere, float on the wave of it, to be carried out, blue league after blue league, away from everything.

After a night behind the scenes, Paul found the schoolroom more than ever repulsive; the bare floors and naked walls; the prosy men who never wore frock coats, or violets in their buttonholes; the women with their dull gowns, shrill voices, and pitiful seriousness about prepositions that govern the dative. He could not bear to have the other pupils think, for a moment, that he took these people seriously; he must convey to them that he considered it all trivial, and was there only by way of a joke, anyway. He had autograph pictures of all the members of the stock company which he showed his classmates, telling them the most incredible stories of his familiarity with these people, of his acquaintance with the soloists who came to Carnegie Hall, his suppers with them and the flowers he sent them. When these stories lost their effect, and his audience grew listless, he would bid all the boys good-bye, announcing that he was going to travel for awhile; going to Naples, to California, to Egypt. Then, next Monday, he would slip back, conscious and nervously smiling; his sister was ill, and he would have to defer his voyage until spring.

Matters went steadily worse with Paul at school. In the itch to let his instructors know how heartily he despised them, and how thoroughly he was appreciated elsewhere, he mentioned once or twice that he had no time to fool with theorems; adding—with a twitch of the eyebrows and a touch of that nervous bravado which so perplexed them—that he was helping the people down at the stock company; they were old friends of his.

The upshot of the matter was, that the Principal went to Paul's father, and Paul was taken out of school and put to work. The manager at Carnegie Hall was told to get another usher in his stead; the doorkeeper at the theatre was warned not to admit him to the house; and Charley Edwards remorsefully promised the boy's father not to see him again.

The members of the stock company were vastly amused when some of Paul's stories reached them—especially the women. They were hard-working women, most of them supporting indolent husbands or brothers, and they laughed rather bitterly at having stirred the boy to such fervid and florid inventions. They agreed with the faculty and with his father, that Paul's was a bad case.

The east-bound train was ploughing through a January snowstorm; the dull dawn was beginning to show grey when the engine whistled a mile out of Newark. Paul started up from the seat where he had lain curled in uneasy slumber, rubbed the breath-misted window glass with his hand, and peered out. The snow was whirling in curling eddies above the white bottom lands, and the drifts lay already deep in the fields and along the fences, while here and there the long dead grass and dried weed stalks protruded black above it. Lights shone from the scattered houses, and a gang of labourers who stood beside the track waved their lanterns.

Paul had slept very little, and he felt grimy and uncomfortable. He had made the all-night journey in a day coach because he was afraid if he took a Pullman he might be seen by some Pittsburgh business man who had noticed him in Denny & Carson's office. When the whistle woke him, he clutched quickly at his breast pocket, glancing about him with an uncertain smile. But the little, clay-bespattered Italians were still sleeping, the slatternly women across the aisle were in open-mouthed oblivion, and even the crumby, crying babies were for the nonce stilled. Paul settled back to struggle with his impatience as best he could.

When he arrived at the Jersey City station, he hurried through his breakfast, manifestly ill at ease and keeping a sharp eye about him. After he reached the Twenty-third Street station, he consulted a cabman, and had himself driven to a men's furnishing establishment which was just opening for the day. He spent upward of two hours there, buying with endless reconsidering and great care. His new street suit he put on in the fitting-room; the frock coat and dress clothes he had bundled into the cab with his new shirts. Then he drove to a hatter's and a shoe house. His next errand was at Tiffany's, where he selected silver mounted brushes and a scarf-pin. He would not wait to have his silver marked, he said. Lastly, he stopped at a trunk shop on Broadway, and had his purchases packed into various travelling bags.

It was a little after one o'clock when he drove up to the Waldorf, and, after settling with the cabman, went into the office. He registered from Washington; said his mother and father had been abroad, and that he had come down to await the arrival of their steamer. He told his story plausibly and had no trouble, since he offered to pay for them in advance, in engaging his rooms; a sleeping-room, sitting-room and bath.

Not once, but a hundred times Paul had planned this entry into New York. He had gone over every detail of it with Charley Edwards, and in his scrap book at home there were pages of description about New York hotels, cut from the Sunday papers.

When he was shown to his sitting-room on the eighth floor, he saw at a glance that everything was as it should be; there was but one detail in his mental picture that the place did not realize, so he rang for the bell boy and sent him down for flowers. He moved about nervously until the boy returned, putting away his new linen and fingering it delightedly as he did so. When the flowers came, he put them hastily into water, and then tumbled into a hot bath. Presently he came out of his white bath-room, resplendent in his new silk underwear, and playing with the tassels of his red robe. The snow was whirling so fiercely outside his windows that he could scarcely see across the street; but within, the air was deliciously soft and fragrant. He put the violets and jonquils on the tabouret beside the couch, and threw himself down with a long sigh, covering himself with a Roman blanket. He was thoroughly tired; he had been in such haste, he had stood up to such a strain, covered so much ground in the last twenty-four hours, that he wanted to think how it had all come about. Lulled by the sound of the wind, the warm air, and the cool fragrance of the flowers, he sank into deep, drowsy retrospection.

It had been wonderfully simple; when they had shut him out of the theatre and concert hall, when they had taken away his bone, the whole thing was virtually determined. The rest was a mere matter of opportunity. The only thing that at all surprised him was his own courage—for he realized well enough that he had always been tormented by fear, a sort of apprehensive dread that, of late years, as the meshes of the lies he had told closed about him, had been pulling the muscles of his body tighter and tighter. Until now, he could not remember a time when he had not been dreading something. Even when he was a little boy, it was always there—behind him, or before, or on either side. There had always been the shadowed corner, the dark place into which he dared not look, but from which something seemed always to be watching him—and Paul had done things that were not pretty to watch, he knew.

But now he had a curious sense of relief, as though he had at last thrown down the gauntlet to the thing in the corner.

Yet it was but a day since he had been sulking in the traces; but yesterday afternoon that he had been sent to the bank with Denny & Carson's deposit, as usual—but this time he was instructed to leave the book to be balanced. There was about two thousand dollars in checks, and nearly a thousand in the bank notes which he had taken from the book and quietly transferred to his pocket. At the bank he had made out a new deposit slip. His nerves had been steady enough to permit of his returning to the office, where he had finished his work and asked for a full day's holiday tomorrow, Saturday, giving a perfectly reasonable pretext. The bank book, he knew, would not be returned before Monday or Tuesday, and his father would be out of town for the next week. From the time he slipped the bank notes into his pocket until he boarded the night train for New York, he had not known a moment's hesitation. How astonishingly easy it had all been; here he was, the thing done; and this time there would be an awakening, no figure at the top of the stairs. He watched the snow flakes whirling by his window until he fell asleep.

When he awoke, it was four o'clock in the afternoon. He bounded up with a start; one of his precious days gone already! He spent nearly an hour in dressing, watching every stage of his toilet carefully in the mirror. Everything was quite perfect; he was exactly the kind of boy he had always wanted to be.

When he went downstairs, Paul took a carraige and drove up Fifth Avenue toward the Park. The snow had somewhat abated; carriages and tradesmen's wagons were hurrying soundlessly to and fro in the winter twilight; boys in woollen mufflers were shovelling off the doorsteps; the avenue stages made fine spots of colour against the white street. Here and there on the corners whole flower gardens blooming behind glass windows, against which the snow flakes stuck and melted; violets, roses, carnations, lilies of the valley—somehow vastly more lovely and alluring that they blossomed thus unnaturally in the snow. The Park itself was a wonderful stage winter-piece.

When he returned, the pause of the twilight had ceased, and the tune of the streets had changed. The snow was falling faster, lights streamed from the hotels that reared their many stories fearlessly up into the storm, defying the raging Atlantic winds. A long, black stream of carriages poured down the avenue, intersected here and there by other streams, tending horizontally. There were a score of cabs about the entrance of his hotel, and his driver had to wait. Boys in livery were running in and out of the awning stretched across the sidewalk, up and down the red velvet carpet laid from the door to the street. Above, about, within it all, was the rumble and roar, the hurry and toss of thousands of human beings as hot for pleasure as himself, and on every side of him towered the glaring affirmation of the omnipotence of wealth.

The boy set his teeth and drew his shoulders together in a spasm of realization; the plot of all dramas, the text of all romances, the nerve-stuff of all sensations was whirling about him like the snow flakes. He burnt like a faggot in a tempest.

When Paul came down to dinner, the music of the orchestra floated up the elevator shaft to greet him. As he stepped into the thronged corridor, he sank back into one of the chairs against the wall to get his breath. The lights, the chatter, the perfumes, the bewildering medley of colour—he had, for a moment, the feeling of not being able to stand it. But only for a moment; these were his own people, he told himself. He went slowly about the corridors, through the writing-rooms, smoking-rooms, reception-rooms, as though he were exploring the chambers of an enchanted palace, built and peopled for him alone.

When he reached the dining-room he sat down at a table near a window. The flowers, the white linen, the many-coloured wine glasses, the gay toilettes of the women, the low popping of corks, the undulating repetitions of the *Blue Danube* from the orchestra, all flooded Paul's dream with bewildering radiance. When the roseate tinge of his champagne was added—that cold, precious, bubbling stuff that creamed and foamed in his glass—Paul wondered that there were honest men in the world at all. This was what all the world was fighting for, he reflected; this was what all the struggle was about. He doubted the reality of his past. Had he ever known a place called Cordelia Street, a place where fagged looking business men boarded the early car? Mere rivets in a machine they seemed to Paul,—sickening men, with combings of children's hair always hanging to their coats, and the smell of cooking in their clothes. Cordelia Street—Ah, that belonged to another time and country! Had he not always been thus, had he not sat here night after night, from as far back as he could remember, looking pensively over just such shimmering textures, and slowly twirling the stem of a glass like this one between his thumb and middle finger? He rather thought he had.

He was not in the least abashed or lonely. He had no especial desire to meet or to know any of these people; all he demanded was the right to look on and conjecture, to watch the pageant. The mere stage properties were all he contended for. Nor was he lonely later in the evening, in his loge at the Opera. He was entirely rid of his nervous misgivings, of his forced aggressiveness, of the imperative desire to show himself different from his surroundings. He felt now that his surroundings explained him. Nobody questioned the purple; he had only to wear it passively. He had only to glance down at his dress coat to reassure himself that here it would be impossible for anyone to humiliate him.

He found it hard to leave his beautiful sitting-room to go to bed that night, and sat long watching the raging storm from his turret window. When he went to sleep, it was with the lights turned on in his bedroom; partly because of his old timidity, and partly so that, if he should wake in the night, there would be no wretched moment of doubt, no horrible suspicion of yellow wall-paper, or of Washington and Calvin above his bed.

On Sunday morning the city was practically snowbound. Paul breakfasted late, and in the afternoon he fell in with a wild San Francisco boy, a freshman at Yale, who said he had run down for a "little flyer" over Sunday. The young man offered to show Paul the night side of the town, and the two boys went off together after dinner, not returning to the hotel until seven o'clock the next morning. They had started out in the confiding warmth of a champagne friendship, but their parting in the elevator was singularly cool. The freshman pulled himself together to make his train, and Paul went to bed. He awoke at two o'clock in the afternoon, very thirsty and dizzy, and rang for ice-water, coffee, and the Pittsburgh papers.

On the part of the hotel management, Paul excited no suspicion. There was this to be said for him, that he wore his spoils with dignity and in no way made himself conspicuous. His chief greediness lay in his ears and eyes, and his excesses were not offensive ones. His dearest pleasures were the grey winter twilights in his sitting-room; his quiet enjoyment of his flowers, his clothes, his wide divan, his cigarette and his sense of power. He could not remember a time when he had felt so at peace with himself. The mere release from the necessity of petty lying, lying every day and every day, restored his self-respect. He had never lied for pleasure, even at school; but to make himself noticed and admired, to assert his difference from other Cordelia Street boys; and he felt a good deal more manly, more honest, even, now that he had no need for boastful pretensions, now that he could, as his actor friends used to say, "dress the part." It was characteristic that remorse did not occur to him. His golden days went by without a shadow, and he made each as perfect as he could.

On the eighth day after his arrival in New York, he found the whole affair exploited in the Pittsburgh papers, exploited with a wealth of detail which indicated that local news of a sensational nature was at a low ebb. The firm of Denny & Carson announced that the boy's father had refunded the full amount of his theft. and that they had no intention of prosecuting. The Cumberland minister had been interviewed, and expressed his hope of yet reclaiming the motherless lad, and Paul's Sabbath-school teacher declared that she would spare no effort to that end. The rumour had reached Pittsburgh that the boy had been seen in a New York hotel, and his father had gone East to find him and bring him home.

Paul had just come in to dress for dinner; he sank into a chair, weak in the knees, and clasped his head in his hands. It was to be worse than jail, even; the tepid waters of Cordelia Street were to close over him finally and forever. The grey monotony stretched before him in hopeless, unrelieved years; Sabbath-school, Young People's Meeting, the yellow-papered room, the damp dish-towels; it all rushed back upon him with sickening vividness. He had the old feeling that the orchestra had suddenly stopped, the sinking sensation that the play was over. The sweat broke out on his face, and he sprang to his feet, looking about him with his white, conscious smile, and winked at himself in the mirror. With something of the childish belief in miracles with which he had so often gone to class, all his lessons unlearned, Paul dressed and dashed whistling down the corridor to the elevator.

He had no sooner entered the dining-room and caught the measure of the music, than his remembrance was lightened by his old elastic power of claiming the moment, mounting with it, and finding it all sufficient. The glare and glitter about him, the mere scenic accessories had again, and for the last time, their old potency. He would show himself that he was game, he would finish the thing splendidly. He doubted, more than ever, the existence of Cordelia Street, and for the first time he drank his wine recklessly. Was he not, after all, one of these fortunate beings? Was he not still himself, and in his own place? He drummed a nervous accompaniment to the music and looked about him, telling himself over and over that it had paid.

He reflected drowsily, to the swell of the violin and the chill sweetness of his wine, that he might have done it more wisely. He might have caught an outbound steamer and been well out of their clutches before now. But the other side of the world had seemed too far away and too uncertain then; he could not have waited for it; his need had been too sharp. If he had to choose over again, he would do the same thing tomorrow. He looked affectionately about the dining-room, now gilded with a soft mist. Ah, it had paid indeed!

Paul was awakened next morning by a painful throbbing in his head and feet. He had thrown himself across the bed without undressing, and had slept with his shoes on. His limbs and hands were lead heavy, and his tongue and throat were parched. There came upon him one of those fateful attacks of clear-headedness that never occurred except when he was physically exhausted and his nerves hung loose. He lay still and closed his eyes and let the tide of realities wash over him.

His father was in New York; "stopping at some joint or other," he told himself. The memory of successive summers on the front stoop fell upon him like a weight of black water. He had not a hundred dollars left; and he knew now, more than ever, that money was everything, the wall that stood between all he loathed and all he wanted. The thing was winding itself up; he had thought of that on his first glorious day in New York, and had even provided a way to snap the thread. It lay on his dressing-table now; he had got it out last night when he came blindly up from dinner,—but the shiny metal hurt his eyes, and he disliked the look of it, anyway.

He rose and moved about with a painful effort, succumbing now and again to attacks of nausea. It was the old depression exaggerated; all the world had become Cordelia Street. Yet somehow he was not afraid of anything, was absolutely calm; perhaps because he had looked into the dark corner at last, and knew. It was bad enough, what he saw there; but somehow not so bad as his long fear of it had been. He saw everything clearly now. He had a feeling that he had made the best of it, that he had lived the sort of life he was meant to live, and for half an hour he sat staring at the revolver. But he told himself that was not the way, so he went downstairs and took a cab to the ferry.

When Paul arrived at Newark, he got off the train and took another cab, directing the driver to follow the Pennsylvania tracks out of the town. The snow lay heavy on the roadways and had drifted deep in the open fields. Only here and there the dead grass or dried weed stalks projected, singularly black, above it. Once well into the country, Paul dismissed the carriage and walked, floundering along the tracks, his mind a medley of irrelevant things. He seemed to hold in his brain an actual picture of everything he had seen that morning. He remembered every feature of both his drivers, the toothless old woman from whom he had bought the red flowers in his coat, the agent from whom he had got his ticket, and all of his fellow-passengers on the ferry. His mind, unable to cope with vital matters near at hand, worked feverishly and deftly at sorting and grouping these images. They made for him a part of the ugliness of the world, of the ache in his head, and the bitter burning on his tongue. He stooped and put a handful of snow into his mouth as he walked, but that, too, seemed hot. When he reached a little hillside, where the tracks ran through a cut some twenty feet below him, he stopped and sat down.

The carnations in his coat were drooping with the cold, he noticed; all their red glory over. It occurred to him that all the flowers he had seen in the show windows that first night must have gone the same way, long before this. It was only one splendid breath they had, in spite of their brave mockery at the winter outside the glass. It was a losing game in the end, it seemed, this revolt against the homilies by which the world is run. Paul took one of the blossoms carefully from his coat and scooped a little hole in the snow, where he covered it up. Then he dozed a while, from his weak condition, seeming insensible to the cold.

The sound of an approaching train woke him, and he started to his feet, remembering only his resolution, and afraid lest he should be too late. He stood watching the approaching locomotive, his teeth chattering, his lips drawn away from them in a frightened smile; once or twice he glanced nervously sidewise, as though he were being watched. When the right moment came, he jumped. As he fell, the folly of his haste occurred to him with merciless clearness, the vastness of what he had left undone. There flashed through his brain, clearer than ever before, the blue of Adriatic water, the yellow of Algerian sands.

He felt something strike his chest,—his body was being thrown swiftly through the air, on and on, immeasurably far and fast, while his limbs gently relaxed. Then, because the picture making mechanism was crushed, the disturbing visions flashed into black, and Paul dropped back into the immense design of things.

Character

In a sense, Willa Cather's story was a pioneering attempt among American writers to probe sympathetically the nature of a disordered personality. The enduring fame of the story points to her success in saying something universally meaningful. To some extent, the world that Paul is reacting against is part of each one of us: Cordelia Street is the street and atmosphere we wish to put behind us.

1 Do you feel that it is fair to say that everyone must reject Cordelia Street or its equivalent? Or do you feel that Paul's case is a special pathological one inapplicable to others?
2 What clues does Willa Cather provide to counter the argument that Paul is unique?
3 What about the things that Paul likes? Name some of them. Do they form a pattern so that his personality begins to emerge?
4 Try to re-create what Paul must have been like. If you were his teacher, neighbor, or parent, what would you have thought of him before he stole the money? Would you have sympathized with him or come down hard on his vagaries?

5 In the atmosphere of Cordelia Street could Paul have reconciled his tastes with his environment? If so, how? Should he have worked hard to obtain what he wanted? Does Miss Cather indicate that he might have followed that course?

6 Does the very name of Cordelia Street have any significance?

7 Were the things that Paul wanted worthwhile, or was he merely a parasite who deserved no consideration?

8 Very often a writer will use a character to illustrate a criticism of life. Can you see where Paul fits into this criticism? Does Miss Cather appear sympathetic to his tastes? Which ones? Are such tastes worth cultivating?

9 What happens if one has certain tastes without any talent for cultivating or developing them?

10 Ultimately, we must ask ourselves basic questions, for the story forces a real commitment to ideas. Is Paul sane or are his actions those of an unbalanced youth? Is Miss Cather concerned with the fastidious tastes of a normal boy or with the tastes of a boy whose looks and manners indicate a perverted mind?

11 Why does he elicit such loathing in the people who must deal with him?

12 Is urban America as destestable as it seems to Paul? Are most American ideals as hateful as they appear to Paul?

Plot

The plot structure of "Paul's Case" is very carefully wrought. Yet the plot itself is simple—a boy, finding that he can't bear his home and school, steals money to live well; and when his money is exhausted and he is about to be discovered, he kills himself.

1 But the structure consists of a rising crescendo of action. The first body of material concerns Paul and his school. Then counterpointed (or contrasted) to this atmosphere is that of the music hall (Carnegie Hall). The story then proceeds by further contrasts and counterpoints to another body of material. Try to work out the development employed by Miss Cather. Place the material in boxes and connect one to the other until you see the care she has taken to present a coherent and unified tale.

2 Do you feel that the coherence of the tale adds to or detracts from the main character who is himself often irrational and emotionally unstable?

3 Another part of the plot, though not concerned with structure itself, involves the use of tangible objects. These objects help to define the main character and to give texture to the scenes; they provide coherence to the various elements. One of these objects is "snow." Try to explain how the snow works—it appears to interact with Paul's entire New York experience, outside his hotel room and then at his death. It is obviously of great significance and helps suggest many important points. After you have analyzed snow, do the same with flowers and then try to think of any other like objects.

Further Aspects

1 Does Miss Cather take a moral attitude toward Paul's theft of the money?

2 When we first see Paul, he is wearing a neatly knotted black four-in-hand and a red carnation in his buttonhole. What is the reason for stressing this aspect of his appearance, particularly the carnation?

3 Did you notice that carnations, and flowers in general, appear repeatedly throughout the story? Why? At the end, Paul spends some of his final moments thinking of his carnation and placing one in the snow. What is the purpose of this touch? Do the carnations take on the quality of a symbol, that is, an object that acquires several meanings as a piece of fiction is developed?

4 Why does Paul resent his teacher's entrance into the exclusive section of Carnegie Hall? Are his feelings justified?

5 When Paul steals the money, does he lose our sympathy for failing to think of his father and his father's position back in Pittsburgh?

6 Paul considers shooting himself with a revolver, but doesn't do so. Why is shooting unsuitable, when jumping in front of the train is acceptable?

7 What does Miss Cather mean when she says that there "flashed through his brain, clearer than ever before, the blue of Adriatic water, the yellow of Algerian sands"? What does she mean by the "vastness of what he had left undone"? What is the "picture making mechanism" of the final paragraph?

8 Does Miss Cather make you feel any sense of loss with Paul's suicide? If so, what is lost? Do you feel that a part of every individual has been crushed with the crushing of Paul in front of the train?

FIVE

THEME

Now that you have reached the category of theme, you have done most of your work. All stories have a theme or purpose, no matter how deviously the author chooses to present it. At one time authors stated their purpose, but such a procedure has become old-fashioned; no self-respecting writer at present will do more than imply his theme. He suggests it through character, atmosphere, setting, plot, and style—thus theme is a kind of composite statement which requires our comprehension of numerous other elements.

For many students, an understanding of the theme requires a lot of guesswork. The instructor will start out by asking what a particular story is about, a question which usually leads to a great deal of speculation. Often the student will guess nearly anything; occasionally, he will come close. The whole process should not of course be a matter of hit or miss, unless we assume —as at times we might—that the author himself was confused by his creation. A safer assumption, however, is that the author knew what he was doing and that his work is consistent and meaningful. We take part of that on faith and part of it based on the author's reputation with experienced readers.

We should, therefore, take the guesswork out of the theme. We have tried to do this by bringing you along step by step, by asking you relevant questions, so that you, as reader, are led into certain conclusions before you go on. Once you have answered one set of questions, you are then guided into a new group. The end result should be that glimmer of light which indicates revelation.

Obviously, no system is foolproof and many guesses will remain. Often, the author is himself so ambiguous and subtle that even the experienced reader will have to speculate. For consolation, remember that every major work of literature has provoked an endless stream of varying interpretations. But there should be *general* agreement concerning the theme of a story—the theme can't be anything you choose to make it. Every interpretation must be consistent with what the author has provided. If you defend a particular meaning that you feel deeply about, remember that it must coincide with every element of the story. You can't impose yourself; you must expose the story.

In addition to the various helps provided in the analyses, you might ask yourself these questions:

1 Is a clear, unambiguous thematic statement the chief purpose of the author?

2 Does the story present a social, moral, individual, political, or spiritual theme? Possibly it will be a composite of many or all of these.

3 How does the author suggest his theme? Does he use symbols, allegory, satire, irony? Is he straightforward and realistic? Does he seem to state his theme in a given character, or in the confrontation of two or more characters?

4 Does the theme have any significance? That is, does it say something worthwhile to us, or does it have only temporary meaning within the writer's own world?

5 How is that particular theme the end result of plot, character, atmosphere, setting, and style?

Remember that theme hunting is possibly the most enjoyable, and rewarding, part of a short story, but it is also the most dangerous, the most open to wild error. If you want to find meaning, you must put yourself in the writer's hands and efface part of yourself. Otherwise every story, regrettably, will sound exactly like you.

A VISIT OF CHARITY

Eudora Welty

It was mid-morning—a very cold, bright day. Holding a potted plant before her, a girl of fourteen jumped off the bus in front of the Old Ladies' Home, on the outskirts of town. She wore a red coat, and her straight yellow hair was hanging down loose from the pointed white cap all the little girls were wearing that year. She stopped for a moment beside one of the prickly dark shrubs with which the city had beautified the Home, and then proceeded slowly toward the building, which was of whitewashed brick and reflected the winter sunlight like a block of ice. As she walked vaguely up the steps she shifted the small pot from hand to hand; then she had to set it down and remove her mittens before she could open the heavy door.

"I'm a Campfire Girl. . . . I have to pay a visit to some old lady," she told the nurse at the desk. This was a woman in a white uniform who looked as if she were cold; she had close-cut hair which stood up on the very top of her head exactly like a sea wave. Marian, the little girl, did not tell her that this visit would give her a minimum of only three points in her score.

"Acquainted with any of our residents?" asked the nurse. She lifted one eyebrow and spoke like a man.

"With any old ladies? No—but—that is, any of them will do," Marian stammered. With her free hand she pushed her hair behind her ears, as she did when it was time to study Science.

The nurse shrugged and rose. "You have a nice *multiflora cineraria* there," she remarked as she walked ahead down the hall of closed doors to pick out an old lady.

There was loose, bulging linoleum on the floor. Marian felt as if she were walking on the waves, but the nurse paid no attention to it. There was a smell in the hall like the interior of a clock. Everything was silent until, behind one of the doors, an old lady of some kind cleared her throat like a sheep bleating. This decided the nurse. Stopping in her tracks, she first extended her arm, bent her elbow, and leaned forward from the hips—all to examine the watch strapped to her wrist; then she gave a loud double-rap on the door.

"There are two in each room," the nurse remarked over her shoulder.

"Two what?" asked Marian without thinking. The sound like a sheep's bleating almost made her turn around and run back.

One old woman was pulling the door open in short, gradual jerks, and when she saw the nurse a strange smile forced her old face dangerously awry. Marian, suddenly propelled by the strong, impatient arm of the nurse, saw next the side-face of another old woman, even older, who was lying flat in bed with a cap on and a counterpane drawn up to her chin.

"Visitor," said the nurse, and after one more shove she was off up the hall.

Marian stood tongue-tied; both hands held the potted plant. The old woman, still with that terrible, square smile (which was a smile of welcome) stamped on her bony face, was waiting. . . . Perhaps she said something. The old woman in bed said nothing at all, and she did not look around.

Suddenly Marian saw a hand, quick as a bird claw, reach up in the air and pluck the white cap off her head. At the same time, another claw to match drew her all the way into the room, and the next moment the door closed behind her.

"My, my, my," said the old lady at her side.

Marian stood enclosed by a bed, a washstand, and a chair; the tiny room had altogether too much furniture. Everything smelled wet—even the bare floor. She held onto the back of the chair, which was wicker and felt soft and damp. Her heart beat more and more slowly, her hands got colder and colder, and she could not hear whether the old woman was saying anything or not. She could not see them very clearly. How dark it was! The window shade was down, and the only door was shut. Marian looked at the ceiling. . . . It was like being caught in a robber's cave, just before one was murdered.

"Did you come to be our little girl for a while?" the first robber asked.

Then something was snatched from Marian's hand—the little potted plant.

"Flowers!" screamed the old woman. She stood holding the pot in an undecided way. "Pretty flowers," she added.

Then the old woman in bed cleared her throat and spoke. "They are not pretty," she said, still without looking around, but very distinctly.

Marian suddenly pitched against the chair and sat down in it.

"Pretty flowers," the first old woman insisted. "Pretty—pretty. . . ."

Marian wished she had the little pot back for just a moment—she had forgotten to look at the plant herself before giving it away. What did it look like?

"Stinkweeds," said the other old woman sharply. She had a bunchy white forehead and red eyes like a sheep. Now she turned them toward Marian. The fogginess seemed to rise in her throat again, and she bleated, "Who—are—you?"

To her surprise, Marian could not remember her name. "I'm a Campfire Girl," she said finally.

"Watch out for the germs," said the old woman like a sheep, not addressing anyone.

"One came out last month to see us," said the first old woman.

A sheep or a germ? wondered Marian dreamily, holding onto the chair.

"Did not!" cried the other old woman.

"Did so! Read to us out of the Bible, and we enjoyed it!" screamed the first.

"Who enjoyed it!" said the woman in bed. Her mouth was unexpectedly small and sorrowful, like a pet's.

"We enjoyed it," insisted the other. "You enjoyed it—I enjoyed it."

"We all enjoyed it," said Marian, without realizing that she had said a word.

The first old woman had just finished putting the potted plant high, high on the top of the wardrobe, where it could hardly be seen from below. Marian wondered how she had ever succeeded in placing it there, how she could ever have reached so high.

"You mustn't pay any attention to old Addie," she now said to the little girl. "She's ailing today."

"Will you shut your mouth?" said the woman in bed. "I am not."

"You're a story."

"I can't stay but a minute—really, I can't," said Marian suddenly. She looked down at the wet floor and thought that if she were sick in here they would have to let her go.

With much to-do the first old woman sat down in a rocking chair—still another piece of furniture!—and began to rock. With the fingers of one hand she touched a very dirty cameo pin on her chest. "What do you do at school?" she asked.

"I don't know . . ." said Marian. She tried to think but she could not.

"Oh, but the flowers are beautiful," the old woman whispered. She seemed to rock faster and faster; Marian did not see how anyone could rock so fast.

"Ugly," said the woman in bed.

"If we bring flowers—" Marian began, and then fell silent. She had almost said that if Campfire Girls brought flowers to the Old Ladies' Home, the visit would count one extra point, and if they took a Bible with them on the bus and read it to the old ladies, it counted double. But the old woman had not listened, anyway; she was rocking and watching the other one, who watched back from the bed.

"Poor Addie is ailing. She has to take medicine—see?" she said, pointing a horny finger at a row of bottles on the table, and rocking so high that her black comfort shoes lifted off the floor like a little child's.

"I am no more sick than you are," said the woman in bed.

"Oh yes you are!"

"I just got more sense than you have, that's all," said the other old woman, nodding her head.

"That's only the contrary way she talks when *you all* come," said the first old lady with sudden intimacy. She stopped the rocker with a neat pat of her feet and leaned toward Marian. Her hand reached over—it felt like a petunia leaf, clinging and just a little sticky.

"Will you hush! Will you hush!" cried the other one.

Marian leaned back rigidly in her chair.

"When I was a little girl like you, I went to school and all," said the old woman in the same intimate, menacing voice. "Not here—another town. . . ."

"Hush!" said the sick woman. "You never went to school. You never came and you never went. You never were anywhere—only here. You never were born! You don't know anything. Your head is empty, your heart and hands and your old black purse are all empty, even that little old box that you brought with you, you brought empty—you showed it to me. And yet you talk, talk, talk, talk, talk all the time until I think I'm losing my mind. Who are you? You're a stranger—a perfect stranger! Don't you know you're a stranger? Is it possible that they have actually done a thing like this to anyone—sent them in a stranger to talk, and rock, and tell away her whole long rigmarole? Do they seriously suppose that I'll be able to keep it up, day in, day out, night in, night out, living in the same room with a terrible old woman—forever?"

Marian saw the old woman's eyes grow bright and turn toward her. This old woman was looking at her with despair and calculation in her face. Her small lips suddenly dropped apart, and exposed a half circle of false teeth with tan gums.

"Come here, I want to tell you something," she whispered. "Come here!"

Marian was trembling, and her heart nearly stopped beating altogether for a moment.

"Now, now, Addie," said the first old woman. "That's not polite. Do you know what's really the matter with old Addie today?" She, too, looked at Marian; one of her eyelids drooped low.

"The matter?" the child repeated stupidly. "What's the matter with her?"

"Why, she's mad because it's her birthday!" said the first old woman, beginning to rock again and giving a little crow as though she had answered her own riddle.

"It is not, it is not!" screamed the old woman in bed. "It is not my birthday, no one knows when that is but myself, and will you please be quiet and say nothing more, or I'll go straight out of my mind!" She turned her eyes toward Marian again, and presently she said in the soft, foggy voice, "When the worst comes to the worst, I ring this bell, and the nurse comes." One of her hands was drawn out from under the patched counterpane—a thin little hand with enormous black freckles. With a finger which would not hold still she pointed to a little bell on the table among the bottles.

"How old are you?" Marian breathed. Now she could see the old woman in bed very closely and plainly, and very abruptly, from all sides, as in dreams. She wondered about her—she wondered for a moment as though there was nothing else in the world to wonder about. It was the first time such a thing had happened to Marian.

"I won't tell!"

The old face on the pillow, where Marian was bending over it, slowly gathered and collapsed. Soft whimpers came out of the small open mouth. It was a sheep that she sounded like—a little lamb. Marian's face drew very close, the yellow hair hung forward.

"She's crying!" She turned a bright, burning face up to the first old woman.

"That's Addie for you," the old woman said spitefully.

Marian jumped up and moved toward the door. For the second

time, the claw almost touched her hair, but it was not quick enough. The little girl put her cap on.

"Well, it was a real visit," said the old woman, following Marian through the doorway and all the way out into the hall. Then from behind she suddenly clutched the child with her sharp little fingers. In an affected, high-pitched whine she cried, "Oh, little girl, have you a penny to spare for a poor old woman that's not got anything of her own? We don't have a thing in the world—not a penny for candy—not a thing! Little girl, just a nickel—a penny—"

Marian pulled violently against the old hands for a moment before she was free. Then she ran down the hall, without looking behind her and without looking at the nurse, who was reading *Field & Stream* at her desk. The nurse, after another triple motion to consult her wrist watch, asked automatically the question put to visitors in all institutions: "Won't you stay and have dinner with *us?*"

Marian never replied. She pushed the heavy door open into the cold air and ran down the steps.

Under the prickly shrub she stopped and quickly, without being seen, retrieved a red apple she had hidden there.

Her yellow hair under the white cap, her scarlet coat, her bare knees all flashed in the sunlight as she ran to meet the big bus rocketing through the street.

"Wait for me!" she shouted. As though at an imperial command, the bus ground to a stop.

She jumped on and took a big bite out of the apple.

Theme

Like several other stories in this collection, "A Visit of Charity" is concerned with a confrontation, here the confrontation of youth and extreme old age. In "Il Conde," "Miss Brill," and "The Prison," such encounters ostensibly took more violent form. And yet even here, below the apparently calm surface, a good deal occurs, a form of violent change which Miss Welty shrewdly underplays.

1 In "A Visit of Charity," we have an example of a skilled writer taking the simplest of stories and extracting from it a complex and subtle theme, putting the most into the least space. What is the theme? Is it about old age? Adolescence? About organized charity? About isolation? Can you bring all these possibilities together into a single statement of theme?

2 Many details of the setting contribute to the underlying purpose. Consider, for example, how the following convey a sense of the theme: Marian's pointed white cap, the whitewashed brick of the building, the loose, bulging linoleum, the strong odor of the hall, the potted plant, the wet smell of the room, the darkness of the room, the possibility of germs, the rocking back and forth of one old woman, the talk about a birthday.

3 Much of the theme hinges on what you make of the apple that Marian suddenly takes out and munches. Can you see any reason for this short episode? Why should Miss Welty end the story with this? What does an apple signify? Does it have any dimensions beyond the fact of the story? How far is Miss Welty carrying the story through the use of this detail?

Character

1 What kind of youngster is Marian? What are her feelings and attitudes about the Home? Do they change during the course of her adventure? Is she the same Campfire Girl at the end that she was at the beginning? What, if anything, is different?

2 How is the nurse characterized? Is she a type, or is she sufficiently individualized? What are her feelings about her work and the people she deals with?

3 The old women themselves: How does Miss Welty present them? Do they warrant sympathy? Do we react to them with the same revulsion and fear that Marian does, or do we sense a dimension that Marian misses?

Plot

1 The plot is relatively simple, but Miss Welty develops it chiefly through a series of contrasts. These contrasts not only keep the narrative line moving, but they also provide a subtle form of irony. Give several examples of contrast; that is, describe the contrast between the characters themselves, as well as between their ideas, basic assumptions, etc.

2 Why does Miss Welty need these contrasts? Could the theme have been as well developed in a straight line?

3 Why are there two old women and not one?

4 Is the nurse necessary to the development of the plot and theme?

Style

1 How does Miss Welty avoid sentimentality in areas where it is particularly dangerous?
2 How does she keep her tone fresh and brisk?

BROTHER

Graham Greene

The Communists were the first to appear. They walked quickly, a group of about a dozen, up the boulevard which runs from Combat to Ménilmontant; a young man and a girl lagged a little way behind because the man's leg was hurt and the girl was helping him along. They looked impatient, harassed, hopeless, as if they were trying to catch a train which they knew already in their hearts they were too late to catch.

The proprietor of the café saw them coming when they were still a long way off; the lamps at that time were still alight (it was later that the bullets broke the bulbs and dropped darkness all over that quarter of Paris), and the group showed up plainly in the wide barren boulevard. Since sunset only one customer had entered the café, and very soon after sunset firing could be heard from the direction of Combat; the Métro station had closed hours ago. And yet something obstinate and undefeatable in the proprietor's character prevented him from putting up the shutters; it might have been avarice; he could not himself have told what it was as he pressed his broad yellow forehead against the glass and stared this way and that, up the boulevard and down the boulevard.

But when he saw the group and their air of hurry he began immediately to close his café. First he went and warned his only customer, who was practising billiard shots, walking round and round the table, frowning and stroking a thin moustache between shots, a little green in the face under the low diffused lights.

"The Reds are coming," the proprietor said, "you'd better be off. I'm putting up the shutters."

"Don't interrupt. They won't harm me," the customer said. "This is a tricky shot. Red's in baulk. Off the cushion. Screw on spot." He shot his ball straight into a pocket.

"I knew you couldn't do anything with that," the proprietor said, nodding his bald head. "You might just as well go home. Give me a hand with the shutters first. I've sent my wife away." The customer turned on him maliciously, rattling the cue between his fingers. "It was your talking that spoilt the shot. You've cause to be frightened, I dare say. But I'm a poor man. I'm safe. I'm not going to stir." He went across to his coat and took out a dry cigar. "Bring me a bock." He walked round the table on his toes and the balls clicked and the proprietor padded back into the bar, elderly and irritated. He did not fetch the beer but began to close the shutters; every move he made was slow and clumsy. Long before he had finished the group of Communists was outside.

He stopped what he was doing and watched them with furtive dislike. He was afraid that the rattle of the shutters would attract their attention. If I am very quiet and still, he thought, they may go on, and he remembered with malicious pleasure the police barricade across the Place de la République. That will finish them. In the meanwhile I must be very quiet, very still, and he felt a kind of warm satisfaction at the idea that worldly wisdom dictated the very attitude most suited to his nature. So he stared through the edge of a shutter, yellow, plump, cautious, hearing the billiard balls crackle in the other room, seeing the young man come limping up the pavement on the girl's arm, watching them stand and stare with dubious faces up the boulevard towards Combat.

But when they came into the café he was already behind the bar, smiling and bowing and missing nothing, noticing how they had divided forces, how six of them had begun to run back the way they had come.

The young man sat down in a dark corner above the cellar stairs and the others stood round the door waiting for something to happen. It gave the proprietor an odd feeling that they should stand there in his café not asking for a drink, knowing what to expect, when he, the owner, knew nothing, understood nothing. At last the girl said "Cognac," leaving the others and coming to the bar, but when he had poured it out for her, very careful to give a fair and not a generous measure, she simply took it to the man sitting in the dark and held it to his mouth.

"Three francs," the proprietor said. She took the glass and sipped a little and turned it so that the man's lips might touch the same spot. Then she knelt down and rested her forehead against the man's forehead and so they stayed.

"Three francs," the proprietor said, but he could not make his voice bold. The man was no longer visible in his corner, only the girl's back, thin and shabby in a black cotton frock, as she knelt, leaning forward to find the man's face. The proprietor was daunted by the four men at the door, by the knowledge that they were Reds who had no respect for private property, who would drink his wine and go away without paying, who would rape his women (but there was only his wife, and she was not there), who would rob his bank, who would murder him as soon as look at him. So with fear in his heart he gave up the three francs as lost rather than attract any more attention.

Then the worst that he contemplated happened.

One of the men at the door came up to the bar and told him to pour out four glasses of cognac. "Yes, yes," the proprietor said, fumbling with the cork, praying secretly to the Virgin to send an angel, to send the police, to send the Gardes Mobiles, now, immediately, before the cork came out, "that will be twelve francs."

"Oh, no," the man said, "we are all comrades here. Share and share alike. Listen," he said, with earnest mockery, leaning across the bar, "all we have is yours just as much as it's ours, comrade," and stepping back a pace he presented himself to the proprietor, so that he might take his choice of stringy tie, of threadbare trousers, of starved features. "And it follows from that, comrade, that all you have is ours. So four cognacs. Share and share alike."

"Of course," the proprietor said, "I was only joking." Then he stood with bottle poised, and the four glasses tingled upon the counter. "A machine-gun," he said, "up by Combat," and smiled to see how for the moment the men forgot their brandy as they fidgeted near the door. Very soon now, he thought, and I shall be quit of them.

"A machine-gun," the Red said incredulously, "they're using machine-guns?"

"Well," the proprietor said, encouraged by this sign that the Gardes Mobiles were not very far away, "you can't pretend that you aren't armed yourselves." He leant across the bar in a way that was almost paternal. "After all, you know, your ideas—they wouldn't do in France. Free love."

"Who's talking of free love?" the Red said.

The proprietor shrugged and smiled and nodded at the corner. The girl knelt with her head on the man's shoulder, her back to the room. They were quite silent and the glass of brandy stood on the floor beside them. The girl's beret was pushed back on her head and one stocking was laddered and darned from knee to ankle.

"What, those two? They aren't lovers."

"I," the proprietor said, "with my bourgeois notions would have thought . . ."

"He's her brother," the Red said.

The men came clustering round the bar and laughed at him, but softly as if a sleeper or a sick person were in the house. All the time they were listening for something. Between their shoulders the proprietor could look out across the boulevard; he could see the corner of the Faubourg du Temple.

"What are you waiting for?"

"For friends," the Red said. He made a gesture with open palm as if to say, You see, we share and share alike. We have no secrets.

Something moved at the corner of the Faubourg du Temple.

"Four more cognacs," the Red said.

"What about those two?" the proprietor asked.

"Leave them alone. They'll look after themselves. They're tired."

How tired they were. No walk up the boulevard from Ménilmontant could explain the tiredness. They seemed to have come farther and fared a great deal worse than their companions. They were more starved; they were infinitely more hopeless, sitting in their dark corner away from the friendly gossip, the amicable desperate voices which now confused the proprietor's brain, until for a moment he believed himself to be a host entertaining friends.

He laughed and made a broad joke directed at the two of them; but they made no sign of understanding. Perhaps they were to be pitied, cut off from the camaraderie round the counter; perhaps they were to be envied for their deeper comradeship. The proprietor thought for no reason at all of the bare grey trees of the Tuileries like a series of exclamation marks drawn against the winter sky. Puzzled, disintegrated, with all his bearings lost, he stared out through the door towards the Faubourg.

It was as if they had not seen each other for a long while and would soon again be saying good-bye. Hardly aware of what he was doing he filled the four glasses with brandy. They stretched out worn blunted fingers for them.

"Wait," he said. "I've got something better than this"; then paused, conscious of what was happening across the boulevard. The lamplight splashed down on blue steel helmets; the Gardes Mobiles were lining out across the entrance to the Faubourg, and a machine-gun pointed directly at the café windows.

So, the proprietor thought, my prayers are answered. Now I must do my part, not look, not warn them, save myself. Have they covered the side door? I will get the other bottle. Real Napoleon brandy. Share and share alike.

He felt a curious lack of triumph as he opened the trap of the bar and came out. He tried not to walk quickly back towards the billiard room. Nothing that he did must warn these men; he tried to spur himself with the thought that every slow casual step he took was a blow for France, for his café, for his savings. He had to step over the girl's feet to pass her; she was asleep. He noted the sharp shoulder blades thrusting through the cotton, and raised his eyes and met her brother's, filled with pain and despair.

He stopped. He found he could not pass without a word. It was as if he needed to explain something, as if he belonged to the wrong party. With false bonhomie he waved the corkscrew he carried in the other's face. "Another cognac, eh?"

"It's no good talking to them," the Red said. They're German. They don't understand a word."

"German?"

"That's what's wrong with his leg. A concentration camp."

The proprietor told himself that he must be quick, that he must put a door between him and them, that the end was very close, but he was bewildered by the hopelessness in the man's gaze. "What's he doing here?" Nobody answered him. It was as if his question were too foolish to need a reply. With his head sunk upon his breast the proprietor went past, and the girl slept on. He was like a stranger leaving a room where all the rest are friends. A German. They don't understand a word; and up, up through the heavy darkness of his mind, through the avarice and the dubious triumph, a few German words remembered from very old days climbed like spies into the light: a line from the *Lorelei* learnt at school, *Kamerad* with its war-time suggestion of fear and surrender, and oddly from nowhere the phrase *mein Bruder.* He opened the door of the billiard room and closed it behind him and softly turned the key.

"Spot in baulk," the customer explained and leant across the great green table, but while he took aim, wrinkling his narrow peevish eyes, the firing started. It came in two bursts with a rip of glass between. The girl cried out something, but it was not one of the words he knew. Then feet ran across the floor, the trap of the bar slammed. The proprietor sat back against the table and listened and listened for any further sound; but silence came in under the door and silence through the keyhole.

"The cloth. My God, the cloth," the customer said, and the proprietor looked down at his own hand which was working the corkscrew into the table.

"Will this absurdity ever end?" the customer said. "I shall go home."

"Wait," the proprietor said. "Wait." He was listening to voices and footsteps in the other room. These were voices he did not recognize. Then a car drove up and presently drove away again. Somebody rattled the handle of the door.

"Who is it?" the proprietor called.

"Who are you? Open that door."

"Ah," the customer said with relief, "the police. Where was I now? Spot in baulk." He began to chalk his cue. The proprietor opened the door. Yes, the Gardes Mobiles had arrived; he was safe again, though his windows were smashed. The Reds had vanished as if they had never been. He looked at the raised trap, at the smashed electric bulbs, at the broken bottle which dripped behind the bar. The café was full of men, and he remembered with odd relief that he had not had time to lock the side door.

"Are you the owner?" the officer asked. "A bock for each of these men and a cognac for myself. Be quick about it."

The proprietor calculated: "Nine francs fifty," and watched closely with bent head the coins rattle down upon the counter.

"You see," the officer said with significance, "we pay." He nodded towards the side door. "Those others: did they pay?"

No, the proprietor admitted, they had not paid, but as he counted the coins and slipped them into the till, he caught himself silently repeating the officer's order—"A bock for each of these men." Those others, he thought, one's got to say that for them, they weren't mean about the drink. It was four cognacs with them. But, of course, they did not pay. "And my windows," he complained aloud with sudden asperity, "what about my windows?"

"Never you mind," the officer said, "the government will pay. You have only to send in your bill. Hurry up now with my cognac. I have no time for gossip."

"You can see for yourself," the proprietor said, "how the bottles have been broken. Who will pay for that?"

"Everything will be paid for," the officer said.

"And now I must go to the cellar to fetch more."

He was angry at the reiteration of the word pay. They enter my café, he thought, they smash my windows, they order me about and think that all is well if they pay, pay, pay. It occurred to him that these men were intruders.

"Step to it," the officer said and turned and rebuked one of the men who had leant his rifle against the bar.

At the top of the cellar stairs the proprietor stopped. They were in darkness, but by the light from the bar he could just make out a body half-way down. He began to tremble violently, and it was some seconds before he could strike a match. The young German lay head downwards, and the blood from his head had dropped on to the step below. His eyes were open and stared back at the proprietor with the old despairing expression of life. The proprietor would not believe that he was dead. "Kamerad," he said bending down, while the match singed his fingers and went out, trying to recall some phase in German, but he could only remember, as he bent lower still, "mein Bruder." Then suddenly he turned and ran up the steps, waved the match-box in the officer's face, and called out in a low hysterical voice to him and his men and to the customer stooping under the low green shade, "Cochons. Cochons."

"What was that? What was that?" the officer exclaimed. "Did you say that he was your brother? It's impossible," and he frowned incredulously at the proprietor and rattled the coins in his pocket.

Theme

In the space of only a few pages, Graham Greene suggests many searching questions, none of them easy to answer. In many ways, he reverses values, twists sympathies, and forces confrontations we often refuse to make. In brief, he makes us think.

1 Repeatedly he asks: Should common humanity prevail over political differences?

2 Are we human beings first or political creatures to the core? Can the two be disentangled?

3 Should we extend our sympathies to the underdog even if we disapprove of him?

4 Can we recognize and approve heroic action in people who otherwise don't gain our sympathies?

5 Are we capable of political change when our interests obviously call for conformity to the existing order?

6 What does brotherhood mean? Can it exist in a vacuum? Or must it be tested? What does the title mean to people like us?

7 Does the proprietor represent the interests of the majority of readers? Would they (you) act and feel the same way? Could they (you) permit a shift in their (your) values, political or otherwise?

8 Who are the heroes, and who are the villains? Does Green present the groups honestly?

9 What is Greene saying about people? Events? Sympathies? Life styles?

Character

1 What is there "obstinate and undefeatable" about the proprietor?

2 When does he begin to change his mind about his "guests"?

3 Why does the proprietor, who depends upon payment to survive, become sympathetic to the men who do not pay for their drinks and hostile to the men who do? What does the last paragraph mean in terms of the proprietor?

4 What kind of man owns the café? Try to characterize him from the details Greene provides. Does he react to the presence of the Communists as you would expect him to? Does the change that takes place in him seem possible, given the type of man he is? Or does Greene appear to be manipulating the proprietor to suit his own ideas without giving sufficient basis for change?

Setting

1 Could the action have taken place equally as well in a restaurant as in a café?

2 What is the function of the man practicing billiards in the background?

3 Could any country serve as well, or is it significant that the story should take place in France?

Tone

1 What effect does Greene gain from the hard-boiled, somewhat Hemingway-like tone? Find examples of clipped, broken-off words, phrases, and images.

2 Does the tough sound of the language clash with the tenderness of the theme, or do they complement each other?

3 Does the fact that no one is named, neither the proprietor nor the Communists, have any significance in terms of the tone? Does the namelessness harden or soften the tone? Is there any reason for the lack of names?

THE UNVEXED ISLES

Robert Penn Warren

The whisky—the best whisky in Russell Hill—sloshed with unthrifty golden opulence into the third and last of the glasses that stood on the lacquered tray. Professor Dalrymple, something of the crystal-gazer's pious abstraction in his regard, watched the spill and whirl of the liquor in the orbit of bright glass. Professor Dalrymple did not relish whisky, even the best whisky in Russell Hill, which, indeed, he dispensed. But he never entered the warm pantry on a Sunday evening, hearing the competent rustle of the electric refrigerator and the murmur of voices from a farther room, without feeling, as he lifted the decanter, a sense of decorous liberation. It was the same sense of liberation he sometimes felt when, looking at his own fine white hands, he recalled that one visit home and the sight of his brother's hands lying inert on the tablecloth in the lamplight: burned by sun, chapped by wind like rotten leather, grained irrevocably with black dirt from the prairie.

Sacramentally, the whisky sloshed into the glass. Bubbles of air streamed upward, and at the surface minutely exploded.

Professor Dalrymple set the silver-mounted siphon on the tray beside the silver bucket of ice, picked up the tray, squared his shoulders as he did these days when he detected that unconscious droop, and proceeded through the door, across the dining room, where articles of silver discreetly glimmered in the dimness, across the hall, and into the room where they sat, waiting.

"Not the true, the blushing Hippocrene," he uttered, and approached the bright fire where they sat, "but 'twill serve."

"It'll serve all right, Doctor," Phil Alburt said. "It's as much of a beaker full of the warm South as I ask, even on as lousy cold a night as tonight." His voice filled the room with authority, a kind of aimless vitality that seemed to make the fire burn up brighter and the bulbs behind their parchment shades glow with more assurance. "It was snowing again when I came in."

"So that's what you got out of my English 40, sir?" the Professor demanded.

"Not exactly." His laughter was like his voice.

"Well, Phil, if you didn't get more than that, nobody did. I'll wager on that."

"Don't loiter, George," Mrs. Dalrymple commanded, a tinge

of asperity licking along the edge of the pleasantry. ''Mr. Alburt can wait for his compliment, but I don't want to wait for my toddy.''

''Pardon me, Alice,'' he said, and with some formality presented the tray.

Looking at the ready tray, she commanded, ''Squirt it for me.''

Her husband set the tray on the little table, placed his long white thumb with its chalky nail on the siphon lever, and pressed. The liquor swirled, paled in the soft light, rose toward the brim.

''Ice,'' she said.

''On a night like this,'' Phil Alburt deplored.

''We always take ice back home in Baltimore,'' she said.

Professor Dalrymple handed his wife the glass.

''No ice for me,'' Phil Alburt said, ''and not much water.''

''I remember,'' the Professor said. ''No ice. Result of your English visits, I suppose.''

''Perhaps,'' Phil Alburt said, and laughed the vital, vacant laugh.

''Not the only result, I'm sure,'' the Professor said, and carried the tray across to him. The young man laid his cigarette on the receptacle beside him, looked up at his host with a smile of affable toleration, and reached for the siphon. ''Thank you, sir,'' he said.

The Professor regarded the head with its dark hair which lay in neat gleaming curly folds as though carved. As the water hissed peremptorily into the glass, the smoke lifted from the idle cigarette on the tray under the Professor's eyes and swayed in its delicate substance. The Professor's glance rested on the cigarette. *It is most singular,* he thought, *that the tip of that cigarette should be stained with lipstick.* The words came through his head with such emphatic clarity and distinctness that, rattling the glasses, he started as though the sentence had been spoken by an unseen observer.

''That's fine. Thank you,'' the young man was saying.

Professor Dalrymple, with effort, disengaged his eyes from the cigarette to meet the large features turned up at him in the contortion of amiability. The features were large and suddenly naked: the strong lips, the even white teeth unbared, the thrust of the nose, the wide brown eyes in which swam flecks of gold, the heavy eyebrows where hairs arched sleekly out from some vigor at the root.

"You're welcome," Professor Dalrymple rejoined mechanically, then, aware of his words, flushed. As he turned about and traversed the excessive distance across the blue carpet, he felt that all these objects accumulated around him—table, chair, chair, blue carpet, rug, lamp—were unfamiliar to him, and now for the first time might, if he so chose, be construed in their unique and rich unities. After he had adjusted the tray, with special care, on the stand, he gave to its obscure design a lingering and analytic regard. Lingering, as if he were a schoolboy unwilling at the last moment to lay aside the book before entering the examination room, or as if his attention to the intricacies of the design might postpone the need to inspect those people whose voices, somewhat remotely, impinged upon him.

The liquid was cold and sweetish in his mouth. He set the glass back, and as he did so discovered with some surprise that the muscles of his cheek were warped upward in an attentive smile. He might have caught sight of himself in a random mirror, so surely did he see, not feel, the thin, long, over-sensitive lips lift and recede beneath the accurate line of black bristle in the ambassadorial mustache. *I am making a great fool of myself,* he reflected, *grinning like that.*

Alice Dalrymple had just said, "I guess old Prexy would turn over in his truckle bed if he knew we were plying one of his charges with toddy."

Professor Dalrymple, yet smiling, cleared his throat slightly. "You know, Phil, we are not able to follow the dictates of hospitality as a general thing. Offering refreshment to our undergraduates is, as a general thing, shall I say, tabu. But I feel, we feel, that we are at liberty to do so in certain cases where the undergraduate's background is more liberal—when the undergraduate is more mature, more, shall I say, a man of the world." The words slipped precisely over his lips, and he was aware, at their conclusion, of the lips still warped upward in the smile. He was aware of having uttered the words at some time in the past, of some quality and inflection that implied rehearsal. But as he said "A man of the world," he did not experience that feeling of inner security and relish which customarily was his on like occasions.

Phil Alburt lolled in dark well-tailored mass behind a glass, a look of bland inattention on his features. When he spoke, it was, likewise, with an accent of rehearsal. "I must say I'm mature enough to appreciate the quality of this hospitality," he said, and significantly fingered the glass.

Professor Dalrymple thought, *A man of the world.* He slipped the phrase about in his mind as a child sucks candy, but the words were hard and savorless like marbles. Quite suddenly it occurred to him that the young man opposite, who nodded his head in amused approbation at some remark from the pretty woman fancied himself as a man of the world. *Because he is rich,* it occurred to him, *because he lives in New York and wears tailor-made clothes and goes to Europe and drinks whisky, and, in fact, has kissed Alice Bogan Dalrymple in my house, he fancies himself a man of the world. I was born in Nebraska in a house that stood on the bare ground with no trees.* Then with a feeling of distant fatality, his sense of warmth for Phil Alburt, somewhat modified but real enough, came back within him. In all perversity, it came back.

Alice Dalrymple gave her gaze to the fire, where flames scrolled ornamentally upward to the black chimney throat. The brass dogs gleamed, the hearth was swept to a sharp border, the flames sprouted upward like flowers from an accurate parterre. *She turns her head so,* Professor Dalrymple observed, *because she knows she looks best in profile. She is thinner these days, she looks tired.* Alice Dalrymple held her head at right angles to the young man's chair: her profile was clean and delicate, with a careful dyspeptic beauty. The young man himself was looking into the fire.

"So you are leaving Tuesday?" she said.

"Tuesday," Phil Alburt said with the air of one gently engrossed in the collaboration of fireside and toddy. "Tuesday, and I get home the next night just in time to hang up my stocking."

"And up early next morning," Professor Dalrymple said, "to see your new velocipede."

"Not to see my new velocipede, to take some Mother Sill's. You see, I've got to hang my stocking up over the wash basin on a boat to Bermuda. Mother is dragging me off down there."

Mrs. Dalrymple laughed, a quick accurate modulation. "And Old Santy comes down the hot water pipe and fills it with little guest cakes of Palmolive and Dr. West toothbrushes." She laughed. "Instead of ashes and switches."

"I won't care if it's full of horsewhips, I'll be feeling so bad that first morning. I'm a rotten sailor."

"Not horsewhips for a good little boy," Professor Dalrymple echoed, and, quite unexpectedly, laughed too.

"I've been planning to go East," Mrs. Dalrymple said in a tone of mild frustration. "To Baltimore."

"Home?" Phil Alburt said.

Home, Professor Dalrymple thought, *Mrs. George Dalrymple lives in Russell Hill in Illinois.* He tabulated the items of her address in his mind. *Mrs. George Dalrymple, 429 Poplar Street, Russell Hill, Illinois, U. S. A.*

"But George here can't go," she said, " and I'm going to be sweet and dutiful and stay right here."

"You ought to go, Alice," Professor Dalrymple said. And he said to himself, *She can't go because she can't buy a ticket on a train to Baltimore. Because she married a poor man.*

"George, you see, wants to finish up some research this vacation. He gets so little time during the year."

"What is it, Doctor?"

"Just a little Chaucer note I've been working on," the Professor answered, and thought for a minute that he might, after all, write a paper. Satisfaction and meaning filled him and velleities slipped away as he lifted his glass to his lips.

"So I'll stay here with him, a martyr to the noble cause of scholarship."

"A mild martyrdom, I would call it, to sit with my heels on the fender," the young man said.

"We used to have some pretty good Christmases in Baltimore, didn't we?" Mrs. Dalrymple gave her husband a full intimate glance, and he noted how the flesh dropped thinly away from the base of her nostrils. "I believe Father made the best eggnog I ever tasted. Everybody used to come in for eggnog on Christmas. Everybody. You ought to let your old research go hang this Christmas, George—"

"Yes, indeed," her husband said. He was conscious of the rhythm of forgotten voices, forgotten excitements, like the sea sound in empty whorls of a shell. Old Mr. Bogan's voice saying, "Gentlemen, gentlemen." Old Mrs. Bogan's voice with the shrillness all drained away in time. Form of voices with no sound.

"—but instead we'll just sit this Christmas."

Eggs. Dozens of eggs. Baskets of eggs. Whisky, sweetish and gold. Hams. Arrogant turkeys. Wine. A steaming mess heaped and poured on the altar of Lucile Bogan's and Alice Bogan's need for a man to share the bed and pay the bills. A steaming, sweating altar, while smoke ascended from twenty-five cent cigars. *Ah,* he thought, and old Mr. Bogan's ritualistic white shirt front obtruded, a-glitter with starch and studs, in the midst of his fancy. *Ah, they spent a lot of money and the best they got was me. But that was when Alice wrote her little verses for the Junior League magazine and showed an English professor to her friends.* Then he concluded with a flat feeling in his head like a run-down clock: *She would know better now.*

"Well," Phil Alburt said, "just sitting has its points. I'm going to do a good deal of sitting myself this vacation. Taking my little school satchel along."

"To Bermuda," Professor Dalrymple said, dryly he hoped, and realized on the instant that he hated Phil Alburt, not because lipstick stained a dead cigarette butt in the ash tray across the hearth, but because Phil Alburt had said those precise words in that precise accent of comfort.

"To Bermuda," Phil Alburt agreed, and laughed without embarrassment.

Mrs. Dalrymple laughed, again in quick accurate modulation. Her husband stonily inspected her mirth: *She has no more self-respect than to laugh after what he just said to her. When she laughs now she holds her head up so the skin won't sag in her neck. Craning her neck like that, she looks like a cigarette advertisement.* He looked guiltily across at the tray by Phil Alburt, as if it were necessary to assure himself that the dead butt reposed there in its matrix of ash.

"However, I can't just sit any more right now," the young man said. "I've got to go now and do a little work before bedtime. I just came to say good-bye." He stood in front of his chair, not really tall but erect, broad shoulders appearing broader by the cut of his coat, his hair with a dark waxen gleam in the light, the double-breasted coat buttoned sleek and flat over his hips and belly.

Professor Dalrymple rose.

"Must you go," Mrs. Dalrymple asked, and likewise stood.

"Must," he said.

"Off to the happy isles," Professor Dalrymple said cheerfully. Then: "I'm thinking about a trip myself. I think I'll go home this Christmas." With a certain pleasure he noted his wife's faint movement of surprise—or was it annoyance?

"Fine," Phil Alburt said.

"You see," he continued, "I haven't been home in a long

time. Not for nine years. I was born and reared out in Nebraska.''

''On a ranch, I bet,'' the young man said hopefully.

''No. On a dirt farm, that's what they call them. Near a place named Sinking Fork Station. Just a wheat elevator and a siding. Did you ever hear of the place?''

Phil Alburt looked quickly at Mrs. Dalrymple, a glance of appeal for support or enlightenment. Then he managed a smile. ''I can't say that I have,'' he said.

''I didn't really imagine that you had. My brother out there is still running the farm, I believe, unless they have foreclosed his various mortgages.''

''Recent times have been difficult for the agriculturist,'' Phil Alburt said, somehow with a touch of piety.

''Indeed,'' Professor Dalrymple said, an ambiguous inflection to the word which he himself, for the flicker of an instant, tried in his mind to decipher. But he could scarcely decide what he had intended. He stood passively while his guest, a perturbed peevish light in his brown eyes, hesitated before taking comfort in the circumstance of farewell. Phil Alburt and Mrs. Dalrymple said good-bye. Good-bye and Merry Christmas.

In the hall, while he held Phil Alburt's coat, he felt like a fool. At the door, he shook, cordially as one trying to make amends, the hand offered him, refrained from looking at the face of the parting guest for fear he might find a smile on it, and said, several times, ''Good-bye.''

After Phil Alburt had gone down the steps, he yet stood in the open doorway, while the cold wind blew down the street and a few small flakes whipped past, and watched the figure proceed the length of the walk and climb into an automobile. He called once, ''Merry Christmas,'' but his voice, he knew immediately, was lost in the easy, vicious whir of gears.

The wind which blew down the street tossed the decorative conifers by the walk so that they looked like two old women in tattered black shawls begging at his doorstep. He straightened his shoulders and experienced again, though but faintly, the accustomed sense of Sunday night complacency. Then his wife called, ''Shut the door!''

He knew exactly how she would be when he entered the room. She would be standing before the fireplace, very still, as though spent by agitations of the evening; the black chiffon, in contrast to pale skin and pale hair, would hang to her slender figure with that extravagant flimsiness which once had made him suspect that a dress was borrowed for the occasion; and her breasts, defined but flattish, would lift, then decline, in a movement of disturbing, finicky respiration.

He closed the heavy door, took three paces down the hall, and entered the room.

There she stood.

"I think, Alice," he announced with a premonitory clearing of the throat, "I think that I shall do that paper. The subject has never been approached from precisely—"

She fixed her eyes on him; said, "What paper? . . . Oh, of course"; and relapsed into her stillness. The cigarette which hung, almost artificially, from her thin nervous fingers surrendered its trail of smoke to the air.

As he approached her across the carpet, warily as though he trod a treacherous surface on which he might slip and lose dignity, desire, an irritable but profound desire, took him. "Alice," he said, unsure of what words were to follow.

She again looked at him. "You were very rude to Phil," she said.

"Rude?" he echoed.

"What ever made you so rude to him?" Her voice was the voice of dutiful catechism.

He almost said: "Under the circumstances I had a right to be rude to him"; but did not. Then he thought: *She is angry because I said what I did to that fool. She doesn't believe I am really going home. I am going home.*

"What made you so rude?" she patiently demanded.

He was conscious of a small kernel of blind, blank rage deep in him. Its tentacles dumbly, blindly, groped within him.

"I never saw you act like that before."

"If I was rude to Mr. Alburt, I am sorry." He framed his words with care. "I assure you that my intentions were of the kindest."

The desire came back, profound and dangerous, but he preserved from it a strange detachment. He felt like a man about to pick a scab: that perverse curiosity, that impulse to view the object, to test his own pain. "Alice," he said, hearing the syllables distantly, and put his arm round her shoulder. His kiss did not reach her mouth; he felt the bristles of his mustache press into the yielding flesh of her cheek.

He did not know whether she had disengaged herself, or

whether, in fact, his arm had simply fallen from her shoulders. There she stood, and she lifted one hand, palm against the temple, in that fatalistic gesture which now, as ever, filled him with a sense of insufficiency.

"I am very tired," she said.

"Yes," he agreed, "you look tired." And he felt with gratification that by not having said a moment before, "I love you," he had maintained his self-respect.

"Good night," she said.

She withdrew from him, past the chair where she had sat that evening, past the table where his own drained glass stood, and toward the door. With her movement the black chiffon fluttered and waggled.

He looked at the door through which she had just passed. Words took form in his mind with such special satisfaction that he was tempted to speak them aloud. *I would be doing my friend, Mr. Alburt, a favor if I should tell him that Alice Dalrymple is cold as a snake.* Then, as he surveyed the room, whose articles, now that she had gone, seemed out of focus, he could not help but wonder what she would have said, how she would have taken it, if, after all, he had said, "I love you."

He drifted toward the hall door, and out into the hall. Somewhere on the upper floor a light burned, splaying shadow and angular patches of illumination into the lower section like a gigantic, ghostly pack of cards. Without looking up, he passed down the hall to his study door, opened it, and threw the electric switch. The big bronze lamp on the desk in the center of the room released its steady flooding light over the appointed objects: over the tray of pens which lay in meticulous intimacy side by side, the bronze inkstand, the leather spectacle case. In shadow, just beyond the rim of light, the books, tier on tier, mounted like masonry of some blank, eyeless structure.

He seated himself before the desk; removed the spectacles from the case; dutifully wiped them with a white handkerchief; hooked them over his ears. He opened the book in front of him. He was scarcely aware that he had performed that set of actions, so habitual to him; it was, indeed, with a subdued surprise that to him came recognition of the words on the printed page. It was as if, on relaxing his attention at the end of each sentence, he should say, "Well, well, here I am."

He tried to follow the words that marched cleanly from margin to margin, line by line; but the faces persistently came. He perceived Phil Alburt's naked face set in the rich flaring fur of an overcoat collar, and beyond it another face, undefined, unknown, anonymous, the face of a girl whose body, reclining, was lapped in silk and fur: faces fixed above the dash lamp and the little white unwinking dials that said all was well, all was well, while the bold-flung beams of headlights ripped the snowy road and the dark that whirled toward the faces.

Between the words on the page, between the sentences, he saw the faces appear and reappear as between the spokes of a slowly revolving wheel. *Necking,* he thought, *out necking.* He suddenly discovered as though he had been searching for it, that word he had heard the students use. *And he is going to Bermuda,* he thought, and into his mind crowded the pictures he had seen in travel advertisements, the man and woman on horseback, in bright coats, riding along the white beach by blue water. *To Bermuda,* he thought, *but I am going home. Even if Alice doesn't believe me, I am going home.* That satisfied him and he felt, somehow surprised at his emotion, a deep homesickness.

He tried to comprehend the words on the page, but his mind, like nervous fingers, dropped them. While the wind sweeping down the great valley of the Mississippi beat the town, beat the house, and hurled the sparse lost flakes through the upper reaches of darkness, he sat in the ring of steady light from the bronze lamp on his desk. At length before he possessed the calm, sufficient meaning of the words under his eye, he knew that he would stay here forever in Russell Hill, Illinois, at this sad, pretentious little college on the plain, in this house with the rustling electric refrigerator and the tiers of books; that this Christmas, or any other, he would not go home; that the woman now sleeping upstairs where the single light burned was perfectly his own; and that Phil Alburt, who had, really, nothing to do with them, with George Dalrymple and Alice Bogan Dalrymple, would ride away, forever, on horseback, his naked face smiling as he rode down the white beaches beside the blue water of the unvexed isles.

Theme

There is an entire genre of literature, both story and novel, in which a somewhat settled couple is confronted by a third person who creates new dimensions in their lives. Usually such fiction proceeds by a series of ironies and contrasts. Frequently each person comes to see himself in a new way, or else the situation develops new aspects of his character. By the end of the story, the characters are different from what they were at the beginning—or at least their lives have been ruffled.

This type of story has also spilled over into the drama, one of the best recent examples being Edward Albee's "Who's Afraid of Virginia Woolf?" This work, too, involves a professor and his wife, and the intruders consist of a young couple who throw the older people's tortured lives into high relief. The substance of the play—like that of Warren's "The Unvexed Isles"—involves a subtle and strategic war of existence, a constant fencing for position, a sexual undertone that is often very unpleasant, and a fierce underlying animosity among all the characters. Of course these qualities are more open in Albee's play than they are in Warren's story, but nevertheless "The Unvexed Isles" contains a great number of issues below a seemingly "unvexed" surface.

1 Characterize the professor and his situation in Russell Hill, Illinois. Is he satisfied with his work, with himself? What does the article on Chaucer mean to him? What is his relationship with his wife? Cite examples of their dialogue that indicate their relationship. Is it in any danger of splitting into fragments? What holds it together?

2 From what you see of Mrs. Dalrymple, would you consider her satisfied with her present life? What do you learn of her past? Why did she marry George? Which of her remarks indicates that their marriage has settled into something neither one bargained for? Why does she assume so many poses in order to appear physically young and attractive? Does her attitudinizing go beyond the natural desire of an aging woman to remain youthful and appealing?

3 Phil Alburt appears as the "intruder," even though he is extended the hospitality of the Dalrymple household. On the surface he is the welcome guest, but beneath the surface he is a subtle threat. How does Phil's appearance type him as a menace? Cite some descriptive adjectives Warren employs to this effect. What does Phil threaten? Do you see any significance in the lipstick on the cigarette? What gives Phil his condescending superiority over the professor? Is it something in Phil or in the professor that creates the imbalance? Who condescends to whom? How does all this contribute to the theme?

4 Warren makes a great deal of places: Illinois, Nebraska,

Baltimore, Bermuda. Each place is important to one of the characters, and yet each finds the other's place somehow distasteful. Thus the mention of Bermuda, "the unvexed isles," forces the professor to mention his dirt-farm home in Nebraska. Why should he react this way? And why should Mrs. Dalrymple bring in Baltimore, her former base of operations? As for Illinois—how does Warren characterize Russell Hill? Does the name itself indicate anything about the Dalrymples?

5 The words "the unvexed isles" are the first we read in the story (as the title) and also the last. Obviously they are of importance. The title comes from Shakespeare's "The Tempest," where the Bermudas are referred to as "still-vex'd," that is, always stormy. Warren switches the original meaning and makes them "unvexed," but is he being ironical or literal? For whom are they unvexed? By working with the various plays on this word, you can come close to the theme of the story.

Characterization

No single character has a firm shape. What counts in this story is the relationship among the three central figures. Each character reveals himself in his connection with the others.

1 What is the ostensible relationship among the three central figures? Why has the professor invited Phil to his home? What does this say about the professor?

2 What is Mrs. Dalrymple's attitude toward Phil? Toward the professor? What does this say about her?

3 How does Phil feel toward his former professor in English 40?

4 Cite all the details you notice that show a disparity between the ostensible relationship and the real one. An example might help you. Very near the beginning, Professor Dalrymple, while serving the drinks, enters the room with the remark: " 'Not the true, the blushing Hippocrene . . . but 'twill serve.' " The reference to Hippocrene is a classical one to a sacred fountain on Mt. Helicon whose waters were reputed to inspire poets. The remark cuts several ways: it serves as disparagement for the professor's own serving set; it "wittily" cuts down all of them as less than divine and sacred, and certainly not as creatures turning into poets as a result of drinking whisky; and, most important, it sets a professorial tone to the evening—it demonstrates to Phil that the professor is a learned fellow, ever ready with a classical allusion whether accurately quoted or not. In effect, it is a way for the professor to keep his uneasy superiority over Phil even while he fears him. The small kernel of dialogue suggests the true, as opposed to the superficial, relationship.

Further Aspects

1 If we claim that the entire story concerns sex—its potency or its lack—what do we mean?

2 What does the professor mean when he says that he would be doing Phil a favor if "I should tell him that Alice Dalrymple is cold as a snake"? Does the remark cut more than one way?

3 The story is also about different kinds of power—who has it, who lacks it, who covets it. Explain this as a statement of the theme.

THE HORSE DEALER'S DAUGHTER

D. H. Lawrence

"Well, Mabel, and what are you going to do with yourself?" asked Joe, with foolish flippancy. He felt quite safe himself. Without listening for an answer, he turned aside, worked a grain of tobacco to the tip of his tongue, and spat it out. He did not care about anything, since he felt safe himself.

The three brothers and the sister sat round the desolate breakfast table, attempting some sort of desultory consultation. The morning's post had given the final tap to the family fortune, and all was over. The dreary dining-room itself, with its heavy mahogany furniture, looked as if it were waiting to be done away with.

But the consultation amounted to nothing. There was a strange air of ineffectuality about the three men, as they sprawled at table, smoking and reflecting vaguely on their own condition. The girl was alone, a rather short, sullen-looking young woman of twenty-seven. She did not share the same life as her brothers. She would have been good-looking, save for the impassive fixity of her face, "bulldog," as her brothers called it.

There was a confused tramping of horses' feet outside. The three men all sprawled round in their chairs to watch. Beyond the dark holly-bushes that separated the strip of lawn from the highroad, they could see a cavalcade of shire horses swinging out of their own yard, being taken for exercise. This was the last time. These were the last horses that would go through their hands. The young men watched with critical, callous look. They were all frightened at the collapse of their lives, and the sense of disaster in which they were involved left them no inner freedom.

Yet they were three fine, well-set fellows enough. Joe, the eldest, was a man of thirty-three, broad and handsome in a hot, flushed way. His face was red, he twisted his black moustache over a thick finger, his eyes were shallow and restless. He had a sensual way of uncovering his teeth when he laughed, and his bearing was stupid. Now he watched the horses with a glazed look of helplessness in his eyes, a certain stupor of downfall.

The great draught-horses swung past. They were tied head to

tail, four of them, and they heaved along to where a lane branched off from the highroad, planting their great hoofs floutingly in the fine black mud, swinging their great rounded haunches sumptuously, and trotting a few sudden steps as they were led into the lane, round the corner. Every movement showed a massive, slumbrous strength, and a stupidity which held them in subjection. The groom at the head looked back, jerking the leading rope. And the cavalcade moved out of sight up the lane, the tail of the last horse, bobbed up tight and stiff, held out taut from the swinging great haunches as they rocked behind the hedges in a motion like sleep.

Joe watched with glazed hopeless eyes. The horses were almost like his own body to him. He felt he was done for now. Luckily he was engaged to a woman as old as himself, and therefore her father, who was steward of a neighbouring estate, would provide him with a job. He would marry and go into harness. His life was over, he would be a subject animal now.

He turned uneasily aside, the retreating steps of the horses echoing in his ears. Then, with foolish restlessness, he reached for the scraps of bacon-rind from the plates, and making a faint whistling sound, flung them to the terrier that lay against the fender. He watched the dog swallow them, and waited till the creature looked into his eyes. Then a faint grin came on his face, and in a high, foolish voice he said:

"You won't get much more bacon, shall you, you little bitch?"

The dog faintly and dismally wagged its tail, then lowered its haunches, circled round, and lay down again.

There was another helpless silence at the table. Joe sprawled uneasily in his seat, not willing to go till the family conclave was dissolved. Fred Henry, the second brother, was erect, clean-limbed, alert. He had watched the passing of the horses with more sang-froid. If he was an animal, like Joe, he was an animal which controls, not one which is controlled. He was master of any horse, and he carried himself with a well-tempered air of mastery. But he was not master of the situations of life. He pushed his coarse brown moustache upwards, off his lip, and glanced irritably at his sister, who sat impassive and inscrutable.

"You'll go and stop with Lucy for a bit, shan't you?" he asked. The girl did not answer.

"I don't see what else you can do," persisted Fred Henry.

"Go as a skivvy," Joe interpolated laconically.

The girl did not move a muscle.

"If I was her, I should go in for training for a nurse," said Malcolm, the youngest of them all. He was the baby of the family, a young man of twenty-two, with a fresh, jaunty *museau*.

But Mabel did not take any notice of him. They had talked at her and round her for so many years, that she hardly heard them at all.

The marble clock on the mantelpiece softly chimed the half-hour, the dog rose uneasily from the hearthrug and looked at the party at the breakfast table. But still they sat on in ineffectual conclave.

"Oh, all right," said Joe suddenly, apropos of nothing. "I'll get a move on."

He pushed back his chair, straddled his knees with a downward jerk, to get them free, in horsey fashion, and went to the fire. Still he did not go out of the room; he was curious to know what the others would do or say. He began to charge his pipe, looking down at the dog and saying, in a high, affected voice:

"Going wi' me? Going wi' me are ter? Tha'rt goin' further tha that counts on just now, dost hear?"

The dog faintly wagged its tail, the man stuck out his jaw and covered his pipe with his hands, and puffed intently, losing himself in the tobacco, looking down all the while at the dog with an absent brown eye. The dog looked up at him in mournful distrust. Joe stood with his knees stuck out, in real horsey fashion.

"Have you had a letter from Lucy?" Fred Henry asked of his sister.

"Last week," came the neutral reply.

"And what does she say?"

There was no answer.

"Does she *ask* you to go and stop there?" persisted Fred Henry.

"She says I can if I like."

"Well, then, you'd better. Tell her you'll come on Monday."

This was received in silence.

"That's what you'll do then, is it?" said Fred Henry, in some exasperation.

But she made no answer. There was a silence of futility and irritation in the room. Malcolm grinned fatuously.

"You'll have to make up your mind between now and next Wednesday," said Joe loudly, "or else find yourself lodgings on the kerbstone."

The face of the young woman darkened, but she sat on immutable.

"Here's Jack Fergusson!" exclaimed Malcolm, who was looking aimlessly out of the window.

"Where?" exclaimed Joe, loudly.

"Just gone past."

"Coming in?"

Malcolm craned his neck to see the gate.

"Yes," he said.

There was a silence. Mabel sat on like one condemned, at the head of the table. Then a whistle was heard from the kitchen. The dog got up and barked sharply. Joe opened the door and shouted:

"Come on."

After a moment a young man entered. He was muffled up in overcoat and a purple woollen scarf, and his tweed cap, which he did not remove, was pulled down on his head. He was of medium height, his face was rather long and pale, his eyes looked tired.

"Hello, Jack! Well, Jack!" exclaimed Malcolm and Joe. Fred Henry merely said, "Jack."

"What's doing?" asked the newcomer, evidently addressing Fred Henry.

"Same. We've to to be out by Wednesday. Got a cold?"

"I have—got it bad, too."

"Why don't you stop in?"

"*Me* stop in? When I can't stand on my legs, perhaps I shall have a chance." The young man spoke huskily. He had a slight Scotch accent.

"It's a knock-out, isn't it," said Joe, boisterously, "if a doctor goes round croaking with a cold. Looks bad for the patients, doesn't it?"

The young doctor looked at him slowly.

"Anything the matter with *you,* then?" he asked sarcastically.

"Not as I know of. Damn your eyes, I hope not. Why?"

"I thought you were very concerned about the patients, wondered if you might be one yourself."

"Damn it, no, I've never been patient to no flaming doctor, and hope I never shall be," returned Joe.

At this point Mabel rose from the table, and they all seemed to become aware of her existence. She began putting the dishes together. The young doctor looked at her, but did not address her. He had not greeted her. She went out of the room with the tray, her face impassive and unchanged.

"When are you off then, all of you?" asked the doctor.

"I'm catching the eleven-forty," replied Malcolm. "Are you goin' down wi' th' trap, Joe?"

"Yes, I've told you I'm going down wi' th' trap, haven't I?"

"We'd better be getting her in then. So long, Jack, if I don't see you before I go," said Malcolm, shaking hands.

He went out, followed by Joe, who seemed to have his tail between his legs.

"Well, this is the devil's own," exclaimed the doctor, when he was left alone with Fred Henry. "Going before Wednesday, are you?"

"That's the orders," replied the other.

"Where, to Northampton?"

"That's it."

"The devil!" exclaimed Fergusson, with quiet chagrin.

And there was silence between the two.

"All settled up, are you?" asked Fergusson.

"About."

There was another pause.

"Well, I shall miss yer, Freddy, boy," said the young doctor.

"And I shall miss thee, Jack," returned the other.

"Miss you like hell," mused the doctor.

Fred Henry turned aside. There was nothing to say. Mabel came in again, to finish clearing the table.

"What are *you* going to do, then, Miss Pervin?" asked Fergusson. "Going to your sister's, are you?"

Mabel looked at him with her steady, dangerous eyes, that always made him uncomfortable, unsettling his superficial ease.

"No," she said.

"Well, what in the name of fortune *are* you going to do? Say what you mean to do," cried Fred Henry, with futile intensity.

But she only averted her head, and continued her work. She folded the white table-cloth, and put on the chenille cloth.

"The sulkiest bitch that ever trod!" muttered her brother.

But she finished her task with perfectly impassive face, the young doctor watching her interestedly all the while. Then she went out.

Fred Henry stared after her, clenching his lips, his blue eyes fixing in sharp antagonism, as he made a grimace of sour exasperation.

"You could bray her into bits, and that's all you'd get out of her," he said in a small, narrowed tone.

The doctor smiled faintly.

"What's she *going* to do, then?" he asked.

"Strike me if *I* know!" returned the other.

There was a pause. Then the doctor stirred.

"I'll be seeing you to-night, shall I?" he said to his friend.

"Ay—where's it to be? Are we going over to Jessdale?"

"I don't know. I've got a cold on me. I'll come round to the Moon and Stars, anyway."

"Let Lizzie and May miss their night for once, eh?"

"That's it—if I feel as I do now."

"All's one—"

The two young men went through the passage and down to the back door together. The house was large, but it was servantless now, and desolate. At the back was a small bricked house-yard, and beyond that a big square, gravelled fine and red, and having stables on two sides. Sloping, dank, winter-dark fields stretched away on the open sides.

But the stables were empty. Joseph Pervin, the father of the family, had been a man of no education, who had become a fairly large horse dealer. The stables had been full of horses, there was a great turmoil and come-and-go of horses and of dealers and grooms. Then the kitchen was full of servants. But of late things had declined. The old man had married a second time, to retrieve his fortunes. Now he was dead and everything was gone to the dogs, there was nothing but debt and threatening.

For months, Mabel had been servantless in the big house, keeping the home together in penury for her ineffectual brothers. She had kept house for ten years. But previously it was with unstinted means. Then, however brutal and coarse everything was, the sense of money had kept her proud, confident. The men might be foulmouthed, the women in the kitchen might have bad reputations, her brothers might have illegitimate children. But so long as there was money, the girl felt herself established, and brutally proud, reserved.

No company came to the house, save dealers and coarse men. Mabel had no associates of her own sex, after her sister went away. But she did not mind. She went regularly to church, she attended to her father. And she lived in the memory of her mother, who had died when she was fourteen, and whom she had loved. She had loved her father, too, in a different way, depending upon him, and feeling secure in him, until at the age of fifty-four he married again. And then she had set hard against him. Now he had died and left them all hopelessly in debt.

She had suffered badly during the period of poverty. Nothing, however, could shake the curious sullen, animal pride that dominated each member of the family. Now, for Mabel, the end had come. Still she would not cast about her. She would follow her own way just the same. She would always hold the keys of her own situation. Mindless and persistent, she endured from day to day. Why should she think? Why should she answer anybody? It was enough that this was the end, and there was no way out. She need not pass any more darkly along the main street of the small town, avoiding every eye. She need not demean herself any more, going into the shops and buying the cheapest food. This was at an end. She thought of nobody, not even of herself. Mindless and persistent, she seemed in a sort of ecstasy to be coming nearer to her fulfilment, her own glorification, approaching her dead mother, who was glorified.

In the afternoon she took a little bag, with shears and sponge and a small scrubbing brush, and went out. It was a grey, wintry day, with saddened, dark green fields and an atmosphere blackened by the smoke of foundries not far off. She went quickly, darkly along the causeway, heeding nobody, through the town to the churchyard.

There she always felt secure, as if no one could see her, although as a matter of fact she was exposed to the stare of every one who passed along under the churchyard wall. Nevertheless, once under the shadow of the great looming church, among the graves, she felt immune from the world, reserved within the thick churchyard wall as in another country.

Carefully she clipped the grass from the grave, and arranged the pinky white, small chrysanthemums in the tin cross. When this was done, she took an empty jar from a neighbouring grave, brought water, and carefully, most scrupulously sponged the marble headstone and the copingstone.

It gave her sincere satisfaction to do this. She felt in immediate contact with the world of her mother. She took minute pains, went through the park in a state bordering on pure happiness, as if in performing this task she came into a subtle, intimate connection with her mother. For the life she followed here in the world was far less real than the world of death she inherited from her mother.

The doctor's house was just by the church. Fergusson, being a mere hired assistant, was slave to the country-side. As he hurried now to attend to the outpatient in the surgery, glancing across the graveyard with his quick eye, he saw the girl at her task at the grave. She seemed so intent and remote, it was like looking into another world. Some mystical element was touched in him. He slowed down as he walked, watching her as if spell-bound.

She lifted her eyes, feeling him looking. Their eyes met. And each looked away again at once, each feeling, in some way, found out by the other. He lifted his cap and passed on down the road. There remained distinct in his consciousness, like a vision, the memory of her face, lifted from the tombstone in the churchyard, and looking at him with slow, large, portentous eyes. It *was* portentous, her face. It seemed to mesmerize him. There was a heavy power in her eyes which laid hold of his whole being, as if he had drunk some powerful drug. He had been feeling weak and done before. Now the life came back into him, he felt delivered from his own fretted, daily self.

He finished his duties at the surgery as quickly as might be, hastily filling up the bottle of the waiting people with cheap drugs. Then, in perpetual haste, he set off again to visit several cases in another part of his round, before teatime. At all times he preferred to walk if he could, but particularly when he was not well. He fancied the motion restored him.

The afternoon was falling. It was grey, deadened, and wintry, with a slow, moist, heavy coldness sinking in and deadening all the faculties. But why should he think or notice? He hastily climbed the hill and turned across the dark green fields, following the black cinder-track. In the distance, across a shallow dip in the country, the small town was clustered like smouldering ash, a tower, a spire, a heap of low, raw extinct houses. And on the nearest fringe of the town, sloping into the dip, was Oldmeadow, the Pervins' house. He could see the stables and the outbuildings distinctly, as they lay towards him on the slope. Well, he would not go there many more times! Another resource would be lost to him, another place gone: the only company he cared for in the alien, ugly little town he was losing. Nothing but work, drudgery, constant hastening from dwelling to dwelling among the colliers and the iron-workers. It wore him out, but at the same time he had a craving for it. It was a stimulant to him to be in the homes of the working people, moving as it were through the innermost body of their life. His nerves were excited and gratified. He could come so near, into the very lives of the rough, inarticulate, powerfully emotional men and women. He grumbled, he said he hated the hellish hole. But as a matter of fact it excited him, the contact with the rough, strongly-feeling people was a stimulant applied direct to his nerves.

Below Oldmeadow, in the green, shallow, soddened hollow of fields, lay a square, deep pond. Roving across the landscape, the doctor's quick eye detected a figure in black passing through the gate of the field, down towards the pond. He looked again. It would be Mabel Pervin. His mind suddenly became alive and attentive.

Why was she going down there? He pulled up on the path on the slope above, and stood staring. He could just make sure of the small black figure moving in the hollow of the failing day. He seemed to see her in the midst of such obscurity, that he was like a clairvoyant, seeing rather with the mind's eye than with ordinary sight. Yet he could see her positively enough, whilst he kept his eye attentive. He felt, if he looked away from her, in the thick, ugly falling dusk, he would lose her altogether.

He followed her minutely as she moved, direct and intent, like something transmitted rather than stirring in voluntary activity, straight down the field towards the pond. There she stood on the bank for a moment. She never raised her head. Then she waded slowly into the water.

He stood motionless as the small black figure walked slowly and deliberately towards the centre of the pond, very slowly, gradually moving deeper into the motionless water, and still moving forward as the water got up to her breast. Then he could see her no more in the dusk of the dead afternoon.

"There!" he exclaimed. "Would you believe it?"

And he hastened straight down, running over the wet, soddened fields, pushing through the hedges, down into the depression of callous wintry obscurity. It took him several minutes to come to the pond. He stood on the bank, breathing heavily. He could see nothing. His eyes seemed to penetrate the dead water. Yes, perhaps that was the dark shadow of her black clothing beneath the surface of the water.

He slowly ventured into the pond. The bottom was deep, soft clay, he sank in, and the water clasped dead cold round his legs. As he stirred he could smell the cold, rotten clay that fouled up into the water. It was objectionable in his lungs. Still, repelled and yet not heeding, he moved deeper into the pond. The cold water rose over his thighs, over his loins, upon his abdomen. The lower part of his body was all sunk in the hideous cold element. And the bottom was so deeply soft and uncertain he was afraid of pitching with his mouth underneath. He could not swim, and was afraid.

He crouched a little, spreading his hands under the water and moving them round, trying to feel for her. The dead cold pond swayed upon his chest. He moved again, a little deeper, and again, with his hands underneath, he felt all around under the water. And he touched her clothing. But it evaded his fingers. He made a desperate effort to grasp it.

And so doing he lost his balance and went under, horribly, suffocating in the foul earthy water, struggling madly for a few moments. At last, after what seemed an eternity, he got his footing, rose again into the air and looked around. He gasped, and knew he was in the world. Then he looked at the water. She had risen near him. He grasped her clothing, and drawing her nearer, turned to take his way to land again.

He went very slowly, carefully, absorbed in the slow progress. He rose higher, climbing out of the pond. The water was now only about his legs; he was thankful, full of relief to be out of the clutches of the pond. He lifted her and staggered on to the bank, out of the horror of wet, grey clay.

He laid her down on the bank. She was quite unconscious and running with water. He made the water come from her mouth, he worked to restore her. He did not have to work very long before he could feel the breathing begin again in her; she was breathing naturally. He worked a little longer. He could feel her live beneath his hands; she was coming back. He wiped her face, wrapped her in his overcoat, looked round into the dim, dark grey world, then lifted her and staggered down the bank and across the fields.

It seemed an unthinkably long way, and his burden so heavy he felt he would never get to the house. But at last he was in the stable-yard, and then in the house-yard. He opened the door and went into the house. In the kitchen he laid her down on the hearthrug, and called. The house was empty. But the fire was burning in the grate.

Then again he kneeled to attend to her. She was breathing regularly, her eyes were wide open and as if conscious, but there seemed something missing in her look. She was conscious in herself, but unconscious of her surroundings.

He ran upstairs, took blankets from a bed, and put them before the fire to warm. Then he removed her saturated, earthy-smelling clothing, rubbed her dry with a towel, and wrapped her naked in the blankets. Then he went into the dining-room, to look for spirits. There was a little whisky. He drank a gulp himself, and put some into her mouth.

The effect was instantaneous. She looked full into his face, as if she had been seeing him for some time, and yet had only just become conscious of him.

"Dr. Fergusson?" she said.

"What?" he answered.

He was divesting himself of his coat, intending to find some dry clothing upstairs. He could not bear the smell of the dead, clayey water, and he was mortally afraid for his own health.

"What did I do?" she asked.

"Walked into the pond," he replied. He had begun to shudder like one sick, and could hardly attend to her. Her eyes remained full on him, he seemed to be going dark in his mind, looking back at her helplessly. The shuddering became quieter in him, his life came back in him, dark and unknowing, but strong again.

"Was I out of my mind?" she asked, while her eyes were fixed on him all the time.

"Maybe, for the moment," he replied. He felt quiet, because his strength had come back. The strange fretful strain had left him.

"Am I out of my mind now?" she asked.

"Are you?" he reflected a moment. "No," he answered truthfully, "I don't see that you are." He turned his face aside. He was afraid now, because he felt dazed, and felt dimly that her power was stronger than his, in this issue. And she continued to look at him fixedly all the time. "Can you tell me where I shall find some dry things to put on?" he asked.

"Did you dive into the pond for me?" she asked.

"No," he answered. "I walked in. But I went in overhead as well."

There was silence for a moment. He hesitated. He very much wanted to go upstairs to get into dry clothing. But there was another desire in him. And she seemed to hold him. His will seemed to have gone to sleep, and left him, standing there slack before her. But he felt warm inside himself. He did not shudder at all, though his clothes were sodden on him.

"Why did you?" she asked.

"Because I didn't want you to do such a foolish thing," he said.

"It wasn't foolish," she said, still gazing at him as she lay on the floor, with a sofa cushion under her head. "It was the right thing to do. I knew best, then."

"I'll go and shift these wet things," he said. But still he had not the power to move out of her presence, until she sent him. It was as if she had the life of his body in her hands, and he could not extricate himself. Or perhaps he did not want to.

Suddenly she sat up. Then she became aware of her own immediate condition. She felt the blankets about her, she knew her own limbs. For a moment it seemed as if her reason were going. She looked round, with wild eye, as if seeking something. He stood still with fear. She saw her clothing lying scattered.

"Who undressed me?" she asked, her eyes resting full and inevitable on his face.

"I did," he replied, "to bring you round."

For some moments she sat and gazed at him awfully, her lips parted.

"Do you love me, then?" she asked.

He only stood and stared at her, fascinated. His soul seemed to melt.

She shuffled forward on her knees, and put her arms round him, round his legs, as he stood there, pressing her breasts against his knees and thighs, clutching him with strange, convulsive certainty, pressing his thighs against her, drawing him to her face, her throat, as she looked up at him with flaring, humble eyes of transfiguration, triumphant in first possession.

"You love me," she murmured, in strange transport, yearning and triumphant and confident. "You love me. I know you love me. I know."

And she was passionately kissing his knees, through the wet clothing, passionately and indiscriminately kissing his knees, his legs, as if unaware of everything.

He looked down at the tangled wet hair, the wild, bare, animal shoulders. He was amazed, bewildered, and afraid. He had never thought of loving her. He had never wanted to love her. When he rescued her and restored her, he was a doctor, and she was a patient. He had no single personal thought of her. Nay, this introduction of the personal element was very distasteful to him, a violation of his professional honour. It was horrible to have her there embracing his knees. It was horrible. He revolted from it, violently. And yet—and yet—he had not the power to break away.

She looked at him again, with the same supplication of powerful love, and that same transcendent, frightening light of triumph. In view of the delicate flame which seemed to come from her face like a light, he was powerless. And yet he had never intended to love her. He had never intended. And something stubborn in him could not give way.

"You love me," she repeated, in a murmur of deep, rhapsodic assurance. "You love me."

Her hands were drawing him, drawing him down to her. He

was afraid, even a little horrified. For he had, really, no intention of loving her. Yet her hands were drawing him towards her. He put out his hand quickly to steady himself, and grasped her bare shoulder. A flame seemed to burn the hand that grasped her soft shoulder. He had no intention of loving her: his whole will was against his yielding. It was horrible. And yet wonderful was the touch of her shoulders, beautiful the shining of her face. Was she perhaps mad? He had a horror of yielding to her. Yet something in him ached also.

He had been staring away at the door, away from her. But his hand remained on her shoulder. She had gone suddenly very still. He looked down at her. Her eyes were now wide with fear, with doubt, the light was dying from her face, a shadow of terrible greyness was returning. He could not bear the touch of her eyes' question upon him, and the look of death behind the question.

With an inward groan he gave way, and let his heart yield towards her. A sudden gentle smile came on his face. And her eyes, which never left his face, slowly, slowly filled with tears. He watched the strange water rise in her eyes, like some slow fountain coming up. And his heart seemed to burn and melt away in his breast.

He could not bear to look at her any more. He dropped on his knees and caught her head with his arms and pressed her face against his throat. She was very still. His heart, which seemed to have broken, was burning with a kind of agony in his breast. And he felt her slow, hot tears wetting his throat. But he could not move.

He felt the hot tears wet his neck and the hollows of his neck, and he remained motionless, suspended through one of man's eternities. Only now it had become indispensable to him to have her face pressed close to him; he could never let her go again. He could never let her head go away from the close clutch of his arm. He wanted to remain like that for ever, with his heart hurting him in a pain that was also life to him. Without knowing, he was looking down on her damp, soft brown hair.

Then, as it were suddenly, he smelt the horrid stagnant smell of that water. And at the same moment she drew away from him and looked at him. Her eyes were wistful and unfathomable. He was afraid of them, and he fell to kissing her, not knowing what he was doing. He wanted her eyes not to have that terrible, wistful, unfathomable look.

When she turned her face to him again, a faint delicate flush was glowing, and there was again dawning that terrible shining of joy in her eyes, which really terrified him, and yet which he now wanted to see, because he feared the look of doubt still more.

"You love me?" she said, rather faltering.

"Yes." The word cost him a painful effort. Not because it wasn't true. But because it was too newly true, the *saying* seemed to tear open again his newly-torn heart. And he hardly wanted it to be true, even now.

She lifted her face to him, and he bent forward and kissed her on the mouth, gently, with the one kiss that is an eternal pledge. And as he kissed her his heart strained again in his breast. He never intended to love her. But now it was over. He had crossed over the gulf to her, and all that he had left behind had shrivelled and become void.

After the kiss, her eyes again slowly filled with tears. She sat still, away from him, with her face drooped aside, and her hands folded in her lap. The tears fell very slowly. There was complete silence. He too sat there motionless and silent on the hearthrug. The strange pain of his heart that was broken seemed to consume him. That he should love her? That this was love! That he should be ripped open in this way! Him, a doctor! How they would all jeer if they knew! It was agony to him to think they might know.

In the curious naked pain of the thought he looked again to her. She was sitting there drooped into a muse. He saw a tear fall, and his heart flared hot. He saw for the first time that one of her shoulders was quite uncovered, one arm bare, he could see one of her small breasts; dimly, because it had become almost dark in the room.

"Why are you crying?" he asked, in an altered voice.

She looked up at him, and behind her tears the consciousness of her situation for the first time brought a dark look of shame to her eyes.

"I'm not crying, really," she said, watching him half frightened.

He reached his hand, and softly closed it on her bare arm.

"I love you! I love you!" he said in a soft, low vibrating voice, unlike himself.

She shrank, and dropped her head. The soft, penetrating grip of his hand on her arm distressed her. She looked up at him.

"I want to go," she said. "I want to go and get you some dry things."

"Why?" he said. "I'm all right."

"But I want to go," she said. "And I want you to change your things."

He released her arm, and she wrapped herself in the blanket, looking at him rather frightened. And still she did not rise.

"Kiss me," she said wistfully.

He kissed her, but briefly, half in anger.

Then, after a second, she rose nervously, all mixed up in the blanket. He watched her in her confusion, as she tried to extricate herself and wrap herself up so that she could walk. He watched her relentlessly, as she knew. And as she went, the blanket trailing, and as he saw a glimpse of her feet and her white leg, he tried to remember her as she was when he had wrapped her in the blanket. But then he didn't want to remember, because she had been nothing to him then, and his nature revolted from remembering her as she was when she was nothing to him.

A tumbling, muffled noise from within the dark house startled him. Then he heard her voice:—"There are clothes." He rose and went to the foot of the stairs, and gathered up the garments she had thrown down. Then he came back to the fire, to rub himself down and dress. He grinned at his own appearance when he had finished.

The fire was sinking, so he put on coal. The house was now quite dark, save for the light of a street-lamp that shone in faintly from beyond the holly trees. He lit the gas with matches he found on the mantelpiece. Then he emptied the pockets of his own clothes, and threw all his wet things in a heap into the scullery. After which he gathered up her sodden clothes, gently, and put them in a separate heap on the copper-top in the scullery.

It was six o'clock on the clock. His own watch had stopped. He ought to go back to the surgery. He waited, and still she did not come down. So he went to the foot of the stairs and called:

"I shall have to go."

Almost immediately he heard her coming down. She had on her best dress of black voile, and her hair was tidy, but still damp. She looked at him—and in spite of herself, smiled.

"I don't like you in those clothes," she said.

"Do I look a sight?" he answered.

They were shy of one another.

"I'll make you some tea," she said.

"No, I must go."

"Must you?" And she looked at him again with the wide, strained, doubtful eyes. And again, from the pain of his breast, he knew how he loved her. He went and bent to kiss her, gently, passionately, with his heart's painful kiss.

"And my hair smells so horrible," she murmured in distraction. "And I'm so awful, I'm so awful! Oh, no, I'm too awful." And she broke into bitter, heart-broken sobbing. "You can't want to love me, I'm horrible."

"Don't be silly, don't be silly," he said, trying to comfort her, kissing her, holding her in his arms. "I want you, I want to marry you, we're going to be married, quickly, quickly—tomorrow if I can."

But she only sobbed terribly, and cried:

"I feel awful. I feel awful. I feel I'm horrible to you."

"No, I want you, I want you," was all he answered, blindly, with that terrible intonation which frightened her almost more than her horror lest he should *not* want her.

Theme

Superficially, the theme of a story or longer work of fiction should be fairly clear to the reader. The careful reader should be able to say to himself, "The author is saying this or that." In fact, in much fiction of past eras, the author would himself state his theme, often in a summing up, occasionally along the way, so that there was no chance of misinterpretation.

In modern fiction, the theme is less readily available. It is, like the other elements of modern fiction, often hinted, suggested, found in a gesture, or embedded in a cluster of images. The theme of "The Horse Dealer's Daughter," for example, is never clarified by Lawrence. It is certainly not to be confused with the plot or the events of the narrative, which is very simple and straightforward. A young woman is isolated when the family disintegrates and, recognizing that she has no future, tries to drown herself. A young doctor rescues her and they fall in love. Stated simply, the plot would appear to be old-fashioned, hardly startling. Yet the theme is something else. Let us look for clues.

1 A good deal of the action is intermixed with movement of horses, with the sound of hoofs, the swaying of haunches. What function do the horses serve? Are they simply decorative, or are they an integral part of the story?

2 What kind of atmosphere do Mabel's brothers generate? How would you characterize them? Start with Joe, then Fred Henry, and finally Malcolm, stressing the two older ones.

3 What is the point of having Jack Fergusson a doctor? Could he be anything else? Why not a lawyer or bookkeeper?

4 What was the situation in the house as long as the father lived? What kind of men came to the house? Describe the atmosphere.

5 How is the water in which Mabel tries to drown herself described? What is the point of making the water thick and smelly?

6 Why does Mabel clasp the doctor so possessively when he tells her that he undressed her? What connection is there between his act and hers?

7 At this point, you should be ready to discuss the theme of the short story. What is the relationship between Mabel and the doctor? Are they in love? Do they like each other? Why does the young doctor seem to hold back? Why does the girl become so demanding of his love? Do you sense reservations on his part? If so, why does he succumb completely—"blindly," as Lawrence puts it?

Further Aspects

1 This story is a miniature of many of Lawrence's ideas, principally those on the relationship between the sexes. As you see the development of the attraction between the doctor and Mabel, what attitudes become important?

2 Lawrence smashed traditional notions of the male-female relationship. Can you see any of that iconoclasm operating here? Is his a typically romantic view? Does it appear harsh? Why?

LOVE OF LIFE

Jack London

This out of all will remain—
They have lived and have tossed:
So much of the game will be gain,
Though the gold of the dice has been lost.

They limped painfully down the bank, and once the foremost of the two men staggered among the rough-strewn rocks. They were tired and weak, and their faces had the drawn expression of patience which comes of hardship long endured. They were heavily burdened with blanket packs which were strapped to their shoulders. Head-straps passing across the forehead, helped support these packs. Each man carried a rifle. They walked in a stooped posture, the shoulders well forward, the head still farther forward, the eyes bent upon the ground.

"I wish we had just about two of them cartridges that's layin' in that cache of ourn," said the second man.

His voice was utterly and drearily expressionless. He spoke without enthusiasm; and the first man, limping into the milky stream that foamed over the rocks, vouchsafed no reply.

The other man followed at his heels. They did not remove their footgear, though the water was icy cold—so cold that their ankles ached and their feet went numb. In places the water dashed against their knees, and both men staggered for footing.

The man who followed slipped on a smooth boulder, nearly fell, but recovered himself with a violent effort, at the same time uttering a sharp exclamation of pain. He seemed faint and dizzy and put out his free hand while he reeled, as though seeking support against the air. When he had steadied himself he stepped forward, but reeled again and nearly fell. Then he stood still and looked at the other man, who had never turned his head.

The man stood still for fully a minute, as though debating with himself. Then he called out:

"I say, Bill, I've sprained my ankle."

Bill staggered on through the milky water. He did not look around. The man watched him go, and though his face was expressionless as ever, his eyes were like the eyes of a wounded deer.

The other man limped up the farther bank and continued

straight on without looking back. The man in the stream watched him. His lips trembled a little, so that the rough thatch of brown hair which covered them was visibly agitated. His tongue even strayed out to moisten them.

"Bill!" he cried out.

It was the pleading cry of a strong man in distress, but Bill's head did not turn. The man watched him go, limping grotesquely and lurching forward with stammering gait up the slow slope toward the soft sky line of the low-lying hill. He watched him go till he passed over the crest and disappeared. Then he turned his gaze and slowly took in the circle of the world that remained to him now that Bill was gone.

Near the horizon the sun was smoldering dimly, almost obscured by formless mists and vapors, which gave an impression of mass and density without outline or tangibility. The man pulled out his watch, the while resting his weight on one leg. It was four o'clock, and as the season was near the last of July or first of August—he did not know the precise date within a week or two—he knew that the sun roughly marked the northwest. He looked to the south and knew that somewhere beyond those bleak hills lay the Great Bear Lake; also, he knew that in that direction the Arctic Circle cut its forbidding way across the Canadian Barrens. This stream in which he stood was a feeder to the Coppermine River, which in turn flowed north and emptied into Coronation Gulf and the Arctic Ocean. He had never been there, but he had seen it, once, on a Hudson Bay Company chart.

Again his gaze completed the circle of the world about him. It was not a heartening spectacle. Everywhere was soft sky line. The hills were all low lying. There were no trees, no shrubs, no grasses—naught but a tremendous and terrible desolation that sent fear swiftly dawning into his eyes.

"Bill!" he whispered, once and twice, "Bill!"

He cowered in the midst of the milky water, as though the vastness were pressing in upon him with overwhelming force, brutally crushing him with its complacent awfulness. He began to shake as with an ague fit, till the gun fell from his hand with a splash. This served to rouse him. He fought with his fear and pulled himself together, groping in the water and recovering the weapon. He hitched his pack farther over on his left shoulder, so as to take a portion of its weight from off the injured ankle. Then he proceeded, slowly and carefully, wincing with pain, to the bank.

He did not stop. With a desperation that was madness, unmindful of the pain, he hurried up the slope to the crest of the hill over which his comrade had disappeared—more grotesque and comical by far than that limping, jerking comrade. But at the crest he saw a shallow valley, empty of life. He fought with his fear again, overcame it, hitched the pack still farther over on his left shoulder, and lurched on down the slope.

The bottom of the valley was soggy with water, which the thick moss held, spongelike, close to the surface. This water squirted out from under his feet at every step, and each time he lifted a foot the action culminated in a sucking sound as the wet moss reluctantly released its grip. He picked his way from muskeg to muskeg, and followed the other man's footsteps along and across the rocky ledges which thrust like islets through the sea of moss.

Though alone, he was not lost. Farther on he knew he would come to where dead spruce and fir, very small and weazened, bordered the shore of a little lake, the *titchin-nichilie,* in the tongue of the country, the "land of little sticks." And into that lake flowed a small stream, the water of which was not milky. There was rush grass on that stream—this he remembered well—but no timber, and he would follow it till its first trickle ceased at a divide. He would cross this divide to the first trickle of another stream, flowing to the west, which he would follow until it emptied into the river Dease, and here he would find a cache under an upturned canoe and piled over with many rocks. And in this cache would be ammunition for his empty gun, fishhooks and lines, a small net—all the utilities for the killing and snaring of food. Also, he would find flour—not much—a piece of bacon, and some beans.

Bill would be waiting for him there, and they would paddle away south down the Dease to the Great Bear Lake. And south across the lake they would go, ever south, till they gained the Mackenzie. And south, still south, they would go, while the winter raced vainly after them, and the ice formed in the eddies, and the days grew chill and crisp, south to some warm Hudson Bay Company post, where timber grew tall and generous and there was grub without end.

These were the thoughts of the man as he strove onward. But hard as he strove with his body, he strove equally hard with his mind, trying to think that Bill had not deserted him, that Bill would surely wait for him at the cache. He was compelled to think this thought, or else there would not be any use to strive, and he would have lain down and died. And as the dim ball of the sun sank slowly into the northwest he covered every inch—and many times—of his and Bill's flight south before the down-coming winter. And he conned the grub of the cache and the grub of the Hudson Bay Company post over and over again. He had not eaten for two days; for a far longer time he had not had all he wanted to eat. Often he stooped and picked pale muskeg berries, put them into his mouth, and chewed and swallowed them. A muskeg berry is a bit of seed enclosed in a bit of water. In the mouth the water melts away and the seed chews sharp and bitter. The man knew there was no nourishment in the berries, but he chewed them patiently with a hope greater than knowledge and defying experience.

At nine o'clock he stubbed his toe on a rocky ledge, and from sheer weariness and weakness staggered and fell. He lay for some time, without movement, on his side. Then he slipped out of the pack straps and clumsily dragged himself into a sitting posture. It was not yet dark, and in the lingering twilight he groped about among the rocks for shreds of dry moss. When he had gathered a heap he built a fire—a smoldering, smudgy fire—and put a tin pot of water on to boil.

He unwrapped his pack and the first thing he did was to count his matches. There were sixty-seven. He counted them three times to make sure. He divided them into several portions, wrapping them in oil paper, disposing of one bunch in his empty tobacco pouch, of another bunch in the inside band of his battered hat, of a third bunch under his shirt on the chest. This accomplished, a panic came upon him, and he unwrapped them all and counted them again. There were still sixty-seven.

He dried his wet footgear by the fire. The moccasins were in soggy shreds. The blanket socks were worn through in places, and his feet were raw and bleeding. His ankle was throbbing, and he gave it an examination. It had swollen to the size of his knee. He tore a long strip from one of his two blankets and bound the ankle tightly. He tore other strips and bound them about his feet to serve for both moccasins and socks. Then he drank the pot of water, steaming hot, wound his watch, and crawled between his blankets.

He slept like a dead man. The brief darkness around midnight came and went. The sun arose in the northeast—at least the day dawned in that quarter, for the sun was hidden by gray clouds.

At six o'clock he awoke, quietly lying on his back. He gazed straight up into the gray sky and knew that he was hungry. As he rolled over on his elbow he was startled by a loud snort, and saw a bull caribou regarding him with alert curiosity. The animal was not more than fifty feet away, and instantly into the man's mind leaped the vision and the savor of a caribou steak sizzling and frying over a fire. Mechanically he reached for the empty gun, drew a bead, and pulled the trigger. The bull snorted and leaped away, his hoofs rattling and clattering as he fled across the ledges.

The man cursed and flung the empty gun from him. He groaned aloud as he started to drag himself to his feet. It was a slow and arduous task. His joints were like rusty hinges. They worked harshly in their sockets, with much friction, and each bending or unbending was accomplished only through a sheer exertion of will. When he finally gained his feet, another minute or so was consumed in straightening up, so that he could stand erect as a man should stand.

He crawled up a small knoll and surveyed the prospect. There were no trees, no bushes, nothing but a gray sea of moss scarcely diversified by gray rocks, gray lakelets, and gray streamlets. The sky was gray. There was no sun nor hint of sun. He had no idea of north, and he had forgotten the way he had come to this spot the night before. But he was not lost. He knew that. Soon he would come to the land of the little sticks. He felt that it lay off to the left somewhere, not far—possibly just over the next low hill.

He went back to put his pack into shape for traveling. He assured himself of the existence of his three separate parcels of matches, though he did not stop to count them. But he did linger, debating, over a squat moose-hide sack. It was not large. He could hide it under his two hands. He knew that it weighed fifteen pounds—as much as all the rest of the pack—and it worried him. He finally set it to one side and proceeded to roll the pack. He paused to gaze at the squat moose-hide sack. He picked it up hastily with a defiant glance about him, as though the desolation were trying to rob him of it; and when he rose to his feet to stagger on into the day, it was included in the pack on his back.

He bore away to the left, stopping now and again to eat muskeg berries. His ankle had stiffened, his limp was more pronounced, but the pain of it was as nothing compared with the pain of his stomach. The hunger pangs were sharp. They gnawed and gnawed until he could not keep his mind steady on the course he must pursue to gain the land of little sticks. The muskeg berries did not allay this gnawing, while they made his tongue and the roof of his mouth sore with their irritating bite.

He came upon a valley where rock ptarmigan rose on whirring wings from the ledges and muskegs. Ker—ker—ker was the cry they made. He threw stones at them, but could not hit them. He placed his pack on the ground and stalked them as a cat stalks a sparrow. The sharp rocks cut through his pants legs till his knees left a trail of blood; but the hurt was lost in the hurt of his hunger. He squirmed over the wet moss, saturating his clothes and chilling his body; but he was not aware of it, so great was his fever for food. And always the ptarmigan rose, whirring, before him, till their ker—ker—ker became a mock to him, and he cursed them and cried aloud at them with their own cry.

Once he crawled upon one that must have been asleep. He did not see it till it shot up in his face from its rocky nook. He made a clutch as startled as was the rise of the ptarmigan, and there remained in his hand three tail feathers. As he watched its flight he hated it, as though it had done him some terrible wrong. Then he returned and shouldered his pack.

As the day wore along he came into valleys or swales where game was more plentiful. A band of caribou passed by, twenty and odd animals, tantalizingly within rifle range. He felt a wild desire to run after them, a certitude that he could run them down. A black fox came toward him, carrying a ptarmigan in his mouth. The man shouted. It was a fearful cry, but the fox, leaping away in fright, did not drop the ptarmigan.

Late in the afternoon he followed a stream, milky with lime, which ran through sparse patches of rush grass. Grasping these rushes firmly near the root, he pulled up what resembled a young onion sprout no larger than a shingle nail. It was tender, and his teeth sank into it with a crunch that promised deliciously of food. But its fibers were tough. It was composed of stringy filaments saturated with water, like the berries, and devoid of nourishment. He threw off his pack and went into the rush grass on hands and knees, crunching and munching, like some bovine creature.

He was very weary and often wished to rest, to lie down and sleep; but he was continually driven on, not so much by his desire to gain the land of little sticks as by his hunger. He searched little ponds for frogs and dug up the earth with his nails for worms, though he knew in spite that neither frogs nor worms existed so far north.

He looked into every pool of water vainly until, as the long twilight came on, he discovered a solitary fish, the size of a minnow, in such a pool. He plunged his arm in up to the shoulder, but it eluded him. He reached for it with both hands and stirred up the milky mud at the bottom. In his excitement he fell in, wetting himself to the waist. Then the water was too muddy to admit of his seeing the fish, and he was compelled to wait until the sediment had settled.

The pursuit was renewed, till the water was again muddied. But he could not wait. He unstrapped the tin bucket and began to bail the pool. He bailed wildly at first, splashing himself and flinging the water so short a distance that it ran back into the pool. He worked more carefully, striving to be cool, though his heart was pounding against his chest and his hands were trembling. At the end of half an hour the pool was nearly dry. Not a cupful of water remained. And there was no fish. He found a hidden crevice among the stones through which it had escaped to the adjoining and larger pool—a pool which he could not empty in a night and a day. Had he known of the crevice, he could have closed it with a rock at the beginning and the fish would have been his.

Thus he thought, and crumpled up and sank down upon the wet earth. At first he cried softly to himself, then he cried loudly to the pitiless desolation that ringed him around; and for a long time after he was shaken by great dry sobs.

He built a fire and warmed himself by drinking quarts of hot water, and made camp on a rocky ledge in the same fashion he had the night before. The last thing he did was to see that his matches were dry and to wind his watch. The blankets were wet and clammy. His ankle pulsed with pain. But he knew only that he was hungry, and through his restless sleep he dreamed of feasts and banquets and of food served and spread in all imaginable ways.

He awoke chilled and sick. There was no sun. The gray of earth and sky had become deeper, more profound. A raw wind was blowing, and the first flurries of snow were whitening the hilltops. The air about him thickened and grew white while he made a fire and boiled more water. It was wet snow, half rain, and the flakes were large and soggy. At first they melted as soon as they came in contact with the earth, but ever more fell, covering the ground, putting out the fire, spoiling his supply of moss fuel.

This was a signal for him to strap on his pack and stumble onward, he knew not where. He was not concerned with the land of little sticks, nor with Bill and the cache under the upturned canoe by the river Dease. He was mastered by the verb "to eat." He was hunger-mad. He took no heed of the course he pursued, so long as that course led him through the swale bottoms. He felt his way through the wet snow to the watery muskeg berries, and went by feel as he pulled up the rush grass by the roots. But it was tasteless stuff and did not satisfy. He found a weed that tasted sour and he ate all he could find of it, which was not much, for it was a creeping growth, easily hidden under the several inches of snow.

He had no fire that night, nor hot water, and crawled under his blanket to sleep the broken hunger-sleep. The snow turned into a cold rain. He awakened many times to feel it falling on his upturned face. Day came—a gray day and no sun. It had ceased raining. The keenness of his hunger had departed. Sensibility, as far as concerned the yearning for food, had been exhausted. There was a dull, heavy ache in his stomach, but it did not bother him so much. He was more rational, and once more he was chiefly interested in the land of little sticks and the cache by the river Dease.

He ripped the remnant of one of his blankets into strips and bound his bleeding feet. Also, he recinched the injured ankle and prepared himself for a day of travel. When he came to his pack, he paused long over the squat moose-hide sack, but in the end it went with him.

The snow had melted under the rain, and only the hilltops showed white. The sun came out, and he succeeded in locating the points of the compass, though he knew now that he was lost. Perhaps, in his previous days' wanderings, he had edged away too far to the left. He now bore off to the right to counteract the possible deviation from his true course.

Though the hunger pangs were no longer so exquisite, he realized that he was weak. He was compelled to pause for frequent rests, when he attacked the muskeg berries and rush-grass patches. His tongue felt dry and large, as though covered with a fine hairy growth, and it tasted bitter in his mouth. His heart gave him a great deal of trouble. When he had traveled a few minutes it would begin a remorseless thump, thump, thump, and then leap up and away in a painful flutter of beats that choked him and made him go faint and dizzy.

In the middle of the day he found two minnows in a large pool. It was impossible to bail it, but he was calmer now and managed to catch them in his tin bucket. They were no longer than his little finger, but he was not particularly hungry. The dull ache in his stomach had been growing duller and fainter. It seemed almost that his stomach was dozing. He ate the fish raw, masticating with painstaking care, for the eating was an act of pure reason. While he had no desire to eat, he knew that he must eat to live.

In the evening he caught three more minnows, eating two and saving the third for breakfast. The sun had dried stray shreds of moss, and he was able to warm himself with hot water. He had not covered more than ten miles that day; and the next day, traveling whenever his heart permitted him, he covered no more than five miles. But his stomach did not give him the slightest uneasiness. It had gone to sleep. He was in a strange country, too, and the caribou were growing more plentiful, also the wolves. Often their yelps drifted across the desolation, and once he saw three of them slinking away before his path.

Another night; and in the morning, being more rational, he untied the leather string that fastened the squat moose-hide sack. From its open mouth poured a yellow stream of coarse gold dust and nuggets. He roughly divided the gold in halves, caching one half on a prominent ledge, wrapped in a piece of blanket, and returning the other half to the sack. He also began to use strips of the one remaining blanket for his feet. He still clung to his gun, for there were cartridges in that cache by the river Dease.

This was a day of fog, and this day hunger awoke in him again. He was very weak and was afflicted with a giddiness which at times blinded him. It was no uncommon thing now for him to stumble and fall; and stumbling once, he fell squarely into a ptarmigan nest. There were four newly hatched chicks, a day old—little specks of pulsating life no more than a mouthful; and he ate them ravenously, thrusting them alive into his mouth and crunching them like eggshells between his teeth. The mother ptarmigan beat about him with great outcry. He used his gun as a club with which to knock her over, but she dodged out of reach. He threw stones at her and with one chance shot broke a wing. Then she fluttered away, running, trailing the broken wing, with him in pursuit.

The little chicks had no more than whetted his appetite. He hopped and bobbed clumsily along on his injured ankle, throwing stones and screaming hoarsely at times; at other times hopping and bobbing silently along, picking himself up grimly and patiently when he fell, or rubbing his eyes with his hand when the giddiness threatened to overpower him.

The chase led him across swampy ground in the bottom of the

valley, and he came upon footprints in the soggy moss. They were not his own—he could see that. They must be Bill's. But he could not stop, for the mother ptarmigan was running on. He would catch her first, then he would return and investigate.

He exhausted the mother ptarmigan; but he exhausted himself. She lay panting on her side. He lay panting on his side, a dozen feet away, unable to crawl to her. And as he recovered she recovered, fluttering out of reach as his hungry hand went out to her. The chase was resumed. Night settled down and she escaped. He stumbled from weakness and pitched head foremost on his face, cutting his cheek, his pack upon his back. He did not move for a long while, then he rolled over on his side, wound his watch, and lay there until morning.

Another day of fog. Half of his last blanket had gone into foot wrappings. He failed to pick up Bill's trail. It did not matter. His hunger was driving him too compellingly—only—only he wondered if Bill, too, were lost. By midday the irk of his pack became too oppressive. Again he divided the gold, this time merely spilling half of it on the ground. In the afternoon he threw the rest of it away, there remaining to him only the half blanket, the tin bucket, and the rifle.

An hallucination began to trouble him. He felt confident that one cartridge remained to him. It was in the chamber of the rifle and he had overlooked it. On the other hand, he knew all the time that the chamber was empty. But the hallucination persisted. He fought it off for hours, then threw his rifle open and was confronted with emptiness. The disappointment was as bitter as though he had really expected to find the cartridge.

He plodded on for half an hour, when the hallucination arose again. Again he fought it, and still it persisted, till for very relief he opened his rifle to unconvince himself. At times his mind wandered farther afield, and he plodded on, a mere automaton, strange conceits and whimsicalities gnawing at his brain like worms. But these excursions out of the real were of brief duration, for ever the pangs of the hunger-bite called him back. He was jerked back abruptly once from such an excursion by a sight that caused him nearly to faint. He reeled and swayed, doddering like a drunken man to keep from falling. Before him stood a horse. A horse! He could not believe his eyes. A thick mist was in them, intershot with sparkling points of light. He rubbed his eyes savagely to clear his vision, and beheld, not a horse, but a great brown bear. The animal was studying him with bellicose curiosity.

The man had brought his gun halfway to his shoulder before he realized. He lowered it and drew his hunting knife from its beaded sheath at his hip. Before him was meat and life. He ran his thumb along the edge of his knife. It was sharp. The point was sharp. He would fling himself upon the bear and kill it. But his heart began its warning thump, thump, thump. Then followed the wild upward leap and tattoo of flutters, the pressing as of an iron band about his forehead, the creeping of the dizziness into his brain.

His desperate courage was evicted by a great surge of fear. In his weakness, what if the animal attacked him? He drew himself up to his most imposing stature, gripping the knife and staring hard at the bear. The bear advanced clumsily a couple of steps, reared up, and gave vent to a tentative growl. If the man ran, he would run after him; but the man did not run. He was animated now with the courage of fear. He, too, growled, savagely, terribly, voicing the fear that is to life germane and that lies twisted about life's deepest roots.

The bear edged away to one side, growling menacingly, himself appalled by this mysterious creature that appeared upright and unafraid. But the man did not move. He stood like a statue till the danger was past, when he yielded to a fit of trembling and sank down into the wet moss.

He pulled himself together and went on, afraid now in a new way. It was not the fear that he should die passively from lack of food, but that he should be destroyed violently before starvation had exhausted the last particle of the endeavor in him that made toward surviving. There were the wolves. Back and forth across the desolation drifted their howls, weaving the very air into a fabric of menace that was so tangible that he found himself, arms in the air, pressing it back from him as it might be the walls of a wind-blown tent.

Now and again the wolves, in packs of two and three, crossed his path. But they sheered clear of him. They were not in sufficient numbers, and besides they were hunting the caribou, which did not battle, while this strange creature that walked erect might scratch and bite.

In the late afternoon he came upon scattered bones where the wolves had made a kill. The debris had been a caribou calf an hour before, squawking and running and very much alive. He contemplated the bones, clean-picked and polished, pink with the cell life in them which had not yet died. Could it possibly be that he might be that ere the day was done! Such was life, eh? A vain and fleeting thing. It was only life that pained. There was no hurt in death. To die was to sleep. It meant cessation, rest. Then why was he not content to die?

But he did not moralize long. He was squatting in the moss, a bone in his mouth, sucking at the shreds of life that still dyed it faintly pink. The sweet meaty taste, thin and elusive almost as a memory, maddened him. He closed his jaws on the bones and crunched. Sometimes it was the bone that broke, sometimes his teeth. Then he crushed the bones between rocks, pounded them to a pulp, and swallowed them. He pounded his fingers, too, in his haste, and yet found a moment in which to feel surprise at the fact that his fingers did not hurt much when caught under the descending rock.

Came frightful days of snow and rain. He did not know when he made camp, when he broke camp. He traveled in the night as much as in the day. He rested wherever he fell, crawled on whenever the dying life in him flickered up and burned less dimly. He, as a man, no longer strove. It was the life in him, unwilling to die, that drove him on. He did not suffer. His nerves had become blunted, numb, while his mind was filled with weird visions and delicious dreams.

But ever he sucked and chewed on the crushed bones of the caribou calf, the least remnants of which he had gathered up and carried with him. He crossed no more hills or divides, but automatically followed a large stream which flowed through a wide and shallow valley. He did not see this stream nor this valley. He saw nothing save visions. Soul and body walked or crawled side by side, yet apart, so slender was the thread that bound them.

He awoke in his right mind, lying on his back on a rocky ledge. The sun was shining bright and warm. Afar off he heard the squawking of caribou calves. He was aware of vague memories of rain and wind and snow, but whether he had been beaten by the storm for two days or two weeks he did not know.

For some time he lay without movement, the genial sunshine pouring upon him and saturating his miserable body with its warmth. A fine day, he thought. Perhaps he could manage to locate himself. By a painful effort he rolled over on his side. Below him flowed a wide and sluggish river. Its unfamiliarity puzzled him. Slowly he followed it with his eyes, winding in wide sweeps among the bleak, bare hills, bleaker and barer and lower lying than any hills he had yet encountered. Slowly, deliberately, without excitement or more than the most casual interest, he followed the course of the strange stream toward the sky line and saw it emptying into a bright and shining sea. He was still unexcited. Most unusual, he thought, a vision or a mirage—more likely a vision, a trick of his disordered mind. He was confirmed in this by sight of a ship lying at anchor in the midst of the shining sea. He closed his eyes for a while, then opened them. Strange how the vision persisted! Yet not strange. He knew there were no seas or ships in the heart of the barren lands, just as he had known there was no cartridge in the empty rifle.

He heard a snuffle behind him—a half-choking gasp or cough. Very slowly, because of his exceeding weakness and stiffness, he rolled over on his other side. He could see nothing near at hand, but he waited patiently. Again came the snuffle and cough, and outlined between two jagged rocks not a score of feet away he made out the gray head of a wolf. The sharp ears were not pricked so sharply as he had seen them on other wolves; the eyes were bleared and bloodshot, the head seemed to droop limply and forlornly. The animal blinked continually in the sunshine. It seemed sick. As he looked it snuffled and coughed again.

This, at least, was real, he thought, and turned on the other side so that he might see the reality of the world which had been veiled from him before by the vision. But the sea still shone in the distance and the ship was plainly discernible. Was it reality, after all? He closed his eyes for a long while and thought, and then it came to him. He had been making north by east, away from the Dease Divide and into the Coppermine Valley. This wide and sluggish river was the Coppermine. That shining sea was the Arctic Ocean. That ship was a whaler, strayed east, far east, from the mouth of the Mackenzie, and it was lying at anchor in Coronation Gulf. He remembered the Hudson Bay Company chart he had seen long ago, and it was all clear and reasonable to him.

He sat up and turned his attention to immediate affairs. He had worn through the blanket wrappings, and his feet were shapeless lumps of raw meat. His last blanket was gone. Rifle and knife were both missing. He had lost his hat somewhere, with the bunch of matches in the band, but the matches against his chest were safe and dry inside the tobacco pouch and oil paper. He looked at his watch. It marked eleven o'clock and was still running. Evidently he had kept it wound.

He was calm and collected. Though extremely weak, he had no

sensation of pain. He was not hungry. The thought of food was not even pleasant to him, and whatever he did was done by his reason alone. He ripped off his pants legs to the knees and bound them about his feet. Somehow he had succeeded in retaining the tin bucket. He would have some hot water before he began what he foresaw was to be a terrible journey to the ship.

His movements were slow. He shook as with a palsy. When he started to collect dry moss, he found he could not rise to his feet. He tried again and again, then contented himself with crawling about on hands and knees. Once he crawled near to the sick wolf. The animal dragged itself reluctantly out of his way, licking its chops with a tongue which seemed hardly to have the strength to curl. The man noticed that the tongue was not the customary healthy red. It was a yellowish brown and seemed coated with a rough and half-dry mucus.

After he had drunk a quart of hot water the man found he was able to stand, and even to walk as well as a dying man might be supposed to walk. Every minute or so he was compelled to rest. His steps were feeble and uncertain, just as the wolf's that trailed him were feeble and uncertain; and that night, when the shining sea was blotted out by blackness, he knew he was nearer to it by no more than four miles.

Throughout the night he heard the cough of the sick wolf, and now and then the squawking of the caribou calves. There was life all around him, but it was strong life, very much alive and well, and he knew the sick wolf clung to the sick man's trail in the hope that the man would die first. In the morning, on opening his eyes, he beheld it regarding him with a wistful and hungry stare. It stood crouched, with tail between its legs, like a miserable and woebegone dog. It shivered in the chill morning wind, and grinned dispiritedly when the man spoke to it in a voice that achieved no more than a hoarse whisper.

The sun rose brightly, and all morning the man tottered and fell toward the ship on the shining sea. The weather was perfect. It was the brief Indian Summer of the high latitudes. It might last a week. Tomorrow or next day it might be gone.

In the afternoon the man came upon a trail. It was of another man, who did not walk, but who dragged himself on all fours. The man thought it might be Bill, but he thought in a dull, uninterested way. He had no curiosity. In fact, sensation and emotion had left him. He was no longer susceptible to pain. Stomach and nerves had gone to sleep. Yet the life that was in him drove him on. He was very weary, but it refused to die. It was because it refused to die that he still ate muskeg berries and minnows, drank his hot water, and kept a wary eye on the sick wolf.

He followed the trail of the other man who dragged himself along, and soon came to the end of it—a few fresh-picked bones where the soggy moss was marked by the footpads of many wolves. He saw a squat moose-hide sack, mate to his own, which had been torn by sharp teeth. He picked it up, though its weight was almost too much for his feeble fingers. Bill had carried it to the last. Ha! ha! He would have the laugh on Bill. He would survive and carry it to the ship in the shining sea. His mirth was hoarse and ghastly, like a raven's croak, and the sick wolf joined him, howling lugubriously. The man ceased suddenly. How could he have the laugh on Bill if that were Bill; if those bones, so pinky-white and clean, were Bill?

He turned away. Well, Bill had deserted him; but he would not take the gold, nor would he suck Bill's bones. Bill would have, though, had it been the other way around, he mused as he staggered on.

He came to a pool of water. Stooping over in quest of minnows, he jerked his head back as though he had been stung. He had caught sight of his reflected face. So horrible was it that sensibility awoke long enough to be shocked. There were three minnows in the pool, which was too large to drain; and after several ineffectual attempts to catch them in the tin bucket he forbore. He was afraid, because of his great weakness, that he might fall in and drown. It was for this reason that he did not trust himself to the river astride one of the many drift logs which lined its sandpits.

That day he decreased the distance between him and the ship by three miles; the next day by two—for he was crawling now as Bill had crawled; and the end of the fifth day found the ship still seven miles away and him unable to make even a mile a day. Still the Indian Summer held on, and he continued to crawl and faint, turn and turn about; and ever the sick wolf laughed and wheezed at his heels. His knees had become raw meat like his feet, and though he padded them with the shirt from his back it was a red track he left behind him on the moss and stones. Once, glancing back, he saw the wolf licking hungrily his bleeding trail, and he saw sharply what his own end might be—unless—unless he could get the wolf. Then began as grim a tragedy of existence as was ever played—a sick man that crawled, a sick wolf that limped, two creatures dragging their dying carcasses across the desolation, and hunting each other's lives.

Had it been a well wolf, it would not have mattered so much to the man; but the thought of going to feed the maw of that loathsome and all but dead thing was repugnant to him. He was finicky. His mind had begun to wander again, and to be perplexed by hallucinations, while his lucid intervals grew rarer and shorter.

He was awakened once from a faint by a wheeze close in his ear. The wolf leaped lamely back, losing its footing and falling in its weakness. It was ludicrous, but he was not amused. Nor was he even afraid. He was too far gone for that. But his mind was for the moment clear, and he lay and considered. The ship was no more than four miles away. He could see it quite distinctly when he rubbed the mists out of his eyes, and he could see the white sail of a small boat cutting the water of the shining sea. But he could never crawl those four miles. He knew that, and was very calm in the knowledge. He knew that he could not crawl half a mile. And yet he wanted to live. It was unreasonable that he should die after all he had undergone. Fate asked too much of him. And, dying, he declined to die. It was stark madness, perhaps, but in the very grip of Death he defied Death and refused to die.

He closed his eyes and composed himself with infinite precaution. He steeled himself to keep above the suffocating languor that lapped like a rising tide through all the wells of his being. It was very like a sea, this deadly languor, that rose and rose and drowned his consciousness bit by bit. Sometimes he was all but submerged, swimming through oblivion with a faltering stroke; and again, by some strange alchemy of the soul, he would find another shred of will and strike out more strongly.

Without movement he lay on his back, and he could hear, slowly drawing near and nearer, the wheezing intake and output of the sick wolf's breath. It drew closer, ever closer, through an infinitude of time, and he did not move. It was at his ear. The harsh dry tongue grated like sandpaper against his cheek. His hands shot out—or at least he willed them to shoot out. The fingers were curved like talons, but they closed on empty air. Swiftness and certitude require strength, and the man had not this strength.

The patience of the wolf was terrible. The man's patience was no less terrible. For half a day he lay motionless, fighting off unconsciousness and waiting for the thing that was to feed upon him and upon which he wished to feed. Sometimes the languid sea rose over him and he dreamed long dreams; but ever through it all, waking and dreaming, he waited for the wheezing breath and the harsh caress of the tongue.

He did not hear the breath, and he slipped slowly from some dream to the feel of the tongue along his hand. He waited. The fangs pressed softly; the pressure increased; the wolf was exerting its last strength in an effort to sink teeth in the food for which it had waited so long. But the man had waited long, and the lacerated hand closed on the jaw. Slowly, while the wolf struggled feebly and the hand clutched feebly, the other hand crept across to a grip. Five minutes later the whole weight of the man's body was on top of the wolf. The hands had not sufficient strength to choke the wolf, but the face of the man was pressed close to the throat of the wolf and the mouth of the man was full of hair. At the end of half an hour the man was aware of a warm trickle in his throat. It was not pleasant. It was like molten lead being forced into his stomach, and it was forced by his will alone. Later the man rolled over on his back and slept.

There were some members of a scientific expedition on the whaleship *Bedford.* From the deck they remarked a strange object on the shore. It was moving down the beach toward the water. They were unable to classify it, and, being scientific men, they climbed into the whaleboat alongside and went ashore to see. And they saw something that was alive but which could hardly be called a man. It was blind, unconscious. It squirmed along the ground like some monstrous worm. Most of its efforts were ineffectual, but it was persistent, and it writhed and twisted and went ahead perhaps a score of feet an hour.

Three weeks afterward the man lay in a bunk on the whaleship *Bedford,* and with tears streaming down his wasted cheeks told who he was and what he had undergone. He also babbled incoherently of his mother, of sunny Southern California, and a home among the orange groves and flowers.

The days were not many after that when he sat at table with the scientific men and ship's officers. He gloated over the spectacle of so much food, watching it anxiously as it went into the mouths of others. With the disappearance of each mouthful an expression of deep regret came into his eyes. He was quite sane, yet he hated those men at mealtime. He was haunted by a fear that the food would not last. He inquired of the cook, the cabin boy, the captain, concerning the food stores. They reassured him countless times; but he could not believe them, and pried cunningly about the lazaretto to see with his own eyes.

It was noticed that the man was getting fat. He grew stouter with each day. The scientific men shook their heads and theorized. They limited the man at his meals, but still his girth increased and he swelled prodigiously under his shirt.

The sailors grinned. They knew. And when the scientific men set a watch on the man, they knew too. They saw him slouch for'ard after a breakfast, and, like a mendicant, with outstretched palm, accost a sailor. The sailor grinned and passed him a fragment of sea biscuit. He clutched it avariciously, looked at it as a miser looks at gold, and thrust it into his shirt bosom. Similar were the donations from other grinning sailors.

The scientific men were discreet. They let him alone. But they privily examined his bunk. It was lined with hardtack; the mattress was stuffed with hardtack; every nook and cranny was filled with hardtack. Yet he was sane. He was taking precautions against another possible famine—that was all. He would recover from it, the scientific men said; and he did, ere the *Bedford's* anchor rumbled down in San Francisco Bay.

Theme

When theme, or purpose, dominates a story, it means that an author is so convinced of his idea that he is willing to subordinate virtually everything else to this one point. If the author is particularly gifted, like Conrad, he develops his theme in several different ways: through counterpointing of characters and ideas, through the strategic placement of images and symbols, through clever and functional description. When the author is somewhat less talented but is obsessed by a particular attitude or idea—as Jack London was by Naturalism—he drives the story toward its goal with a minimum of side effects.

"Love of Life" accordingly lacks the dimensions of many other stories in which theme dominates, but in its own way it does make effective reading. The chief idea comes from Naturalism. Man is in a constant life-and-death struggle against the forces of the universe, whatever form they may take. As soon as man shows any weakness—whether of character or performance

—the forces operating against him have an advantage and will, like Furies, pursue him to his destruction. Stripped bare in this way, Naturalism would appear to be very simple, even naïve, but in the hands of a great writer, like Émile Zola or Theodore Dreiser, it can rise into a vast vision of human life.

London is not a great writer. His vision is not complex in either design or execution. But he does remind us again and again that civilization is often just a superficial covering of the savage and primitive forces lying beneath human nature. London's great achievement is to show that when his existence is at stake, man is capable of fighting for his life like an animal.

In this story, nearly every description and element of characterization, virtually every comment, is directed toward an analysis of man's relationship to primitive forces.

1 Explain the following descriptions in London's terms:

a "Near the horizon the sun was smoldering dimly, almost obscured by formless mists and vapors, which gave an impression of mass and density without outline or tangibility."
b "He cowered in the midst of the milky water, as though the vastness were pressing in upon him with overwhelming force, brutally crushing him with its complacent awfulness."

2 What does London mean by the phrase "complacent awfulness"?
3 Later, London comments on the element of fear: "He, too, growled, savagely, terribly, voicing the fear that is to life germane and that lies twisted about life's deepest roots." How does "fear" contribute to London's purpose? Or, put another way, why does London stress fear to such an extent?
4 Do you believe that fear is germane to life, as London says it is? Do you feel that the human being could live much better if all fear were somehow eliminated, or does fear give a piquancy to life that makes its presence invaluable?
5 Are we aware of fear most of the time?
6 Now that you recognize London's purpose in the story, explain in some detail the sequence between the sick wolf and the sick man.
7 Why does London make both the wolf and the man "sick" (lame, hungry, physically ill, desperate)?
8 How is it that the man triumphs? Is it because of superior strength? Compare this scene with the one with the bear.
9 What does this scene (with the wolf) indicate of London's

values? Are you sure you understood that the man drinks the wolf's blood after killing it? What is the meaning of this, beyond the man's obvious hunger?

Characterization

1 Did you notice that the chief character has no name? Why do you think London kept him unnamed? Does the story sacrifice its realism because of that?

2 What do we know of this man who becomes the sole focus of our attention? Reconstruct his background as far as you can? Why does London avoid any direct narration of the character's background, even of the relationship with his friend Bill? Does the story lose credibility because of this omission? Does it gain?

3 Did the character sometimes make you feel squeamish: for example, when he ate the newly hatched ptarmigan chicks? Mention some other places where you felt uneasy. Were you supposed to feel that way?

DEAR ALEXANDROS

John Updike

Translation of a letter written by Alexandros Koundouriotis, Needy Child No. 6,511 in the records of Hope, Incorporated, an international charity with headquarters in New York.

July 1959

Dear Mr. and Mrs. Bentley:

Dear American Parents, first of all I want to inquire about your good health, and then, if you ask me, tell you that I am keeping well, for which I thank God, and hope that it is the same with you. May God keep you always well, and grant you every happiness and joy. With great eagerness I was looking forward again this month to receiving a letter from you, but unfortunately, I have again not received one. So I am worried about you, for I am longing to hear about you, dear American Parents. You show such a great interest in me, and every month I receive your help. Over here it is very hot at this time of the year, for we are in the heart of the summer. The work out in the fields is very tiring, as I hear the older people saying. As for me, when I have no work at home I go down to the sea for a swim, and enjoy the sea with my friends. For at this time of the year the sea is lovely. So much for my news. Vacations continue, until it is time for the schools to reopen, when with new strength and joy we shall begin our lessons again. Today that I am writing to you I received again the $8.00 that you sent me, for the month of July, and I thank you very much. With this money I shall buy whatever I need, and we shall also buy some flour for our bread. In closing, I send you greetings from my granny and my sister, and hope that my letter finds you in good health and joy. I shall be looking forward to receiving a letter from you, to hear about you and how you are spending your summer. I greet you with much affection.

Your son,
Alexandros

Reply from Kenneth Bentley, American Parent No. 4,638.

September 25

Dear Alexandros:

We are all sorry that you should worry about us because you

have not received a letter from us. I fear we are not as regular in writing as you are, but the pretentiously named organization which delivers our letters seems to be very slow, they take about three months as far as I can tell. Perhaps they send them by way of China.

You describe the Greek summer very beautifully. It is autumn now in New York City. The sad little trees along the somewhat sad little street where I live now are turning yellow, the ones that are not already dead. The pretty girls that walk along the main streets are putting on hats again. In New York the main streets run north and south so that there is usually a sunny side and a shady side and now people cross the street to be on the sunny side because the sun is no longer too warm. The sky is very blue and some evenings after I eat in a luncheonette or restaurant I walk a few blocks over to the East River to watch the boats and look at Brooklyn, which is another section of this immense city.

Mrs. Bentley and I no longer live together. I had not intended to tell you this but now the sentence is typed and I see no harm in it. Perhaps already you were wondering why I am writing from New York City instead of from Greenwich. Mrs. Bentley and little Amanda and Richard all still live in our nice home in Greenwich and the last time I saw them looked very well. Amanda now is starting kindergarten and was very excited and will never wear dungarees or overalls any more but insists on wearing dresses because that is what makes little girls look nice, she thinks. This makes her mother rather angry, especially on Saturdays and Sundays when Amanda plays mostly in the dirt with the neighbor children. Richard walks very well now and does not like his sister teasing him. As who does? I go to see them once a week and pick up my mail and your last letter was one of the letters I picked up and was delighted to read. Mrs. Bentley asked me to answer it, which I was delighted to do, because she had written you the last time. In fact I do not think she did, but writing letters was one thing she was not good at, although it was her idea for us to subscribe to Hope, Incorporated, and I know she loves you very much, and was especially happy to learn that you plan to begin school with "new strength and joy."

There has been much excitement in the United States over the visit of the head of Soviet Russia, Mr. Khrushchev. He is a very talkative and self-confident man and in meeting some of our own talkative and self-confident politicians there has been some friction, much of it right on television where everybody could see. My main worry was that he would be shot but I don't think he will be shot any more. His being in the country has been a funny feeling, as if you have swallowed a penny, but the American people are so anxious for peace that they will put up with small discomforts if there is any chance it will do any good. The United States, as perhaps you will learn in school, was for many years an isolated country and there still is a perhaps childish wish that other nations, even though we are a great power, just let us alone, and then the sun will shine.

That was not a very good paragraph and perhaps the man or woman who kindly translates these letters for us will kindly omit it. I have a cold in my chest that mixes with a great deal of cigarette smoke and makes me very confused, especially after I have been sitting still for a while.

I am troubled because I imagine I hear you asking, "Then were Mr. and Mrs. Bentley, who sent me such happy letters from America, and photographs of their children, and a sweater and a jackknife at Christmas, telling lies? Why do they not live together any more?" I do not wish you to worry. Perhaps in your own village you have husbands and wives who quarrel. Perhaps they quarrel but continue to live together but in America where we have so much plumbing and fast automobiles and rapid highways we have forgotten how to live with inconveniences, although I admit that my present mode of life is something of an inconvenience to me. Or perhaps in your schooling, if you keep at it, and I hope you will, the priests or nuns will have you read the very great Greek poem The Iliad, in which the poet Homer tells of Helen who left her husband to live with Paris among the Trojans. It is something like that with the Bentleys, except that I, a man, have gone to live among the Trojans, leaving my wife at home. I do not know if the Iliad is a part of your schooling, and would be curious to know. Your nation should be very proud of producing masterpieces which the whole world can enjoy. In the United States the great writers produce works which people do not enjoy, because they are so depressing to read.

But we were not telling lies. Mrs. Bentley and Amanda and Richard and I were very happy and to a degree are yet. Please continue to send us your wonderful letters, they will go to Greenwich, and we will all enjoy them. We will continue to send you the money for which you say you are grateful, though the money we give you this way is not a fourth of the money we used to spend for alcoholic drinks. Not that Mrs. Bentley and I drank all these alcoholic drinks. We had many friends who helped us, most of them very tedious people, although perhaps you would like them more than I do. Certainly they would like you more than they liked me.

I am so happy that you live near the sea where you can swim and relax from the tiring work of the fields. I was born far inland in America, a thousand miles from any ocean, and did not come to love the sea until I was grown up and married. So in that sense you are luckier than I. Certainly to be near the sea is a great blessing and I remember often thinking how nice it was that my own children should know what it was to run on the sand of the pretty though not large beach at Greenwich, and to have that great calm horizon over their shoulders.

Now I must end, for I have agreed to take a young woman out to dinner, a young woman who, you will be interested to hear, is herself Greek in origin, though born an American, and who has much of the beauty of your race. But I have already cruelly burdened our translator. My best wishes to your granny, who has taken such good care of you since your mother died, and to your sister, whose welfare and good health is such a large concern in your heart.

Sincerely,
Kenneth Bentley

P.S.: In looking back at the beginning of my letter I see with regret that I have been unkind to the excellent organization which has made possible our friendship with you, which has produced your fine letters, which we are always happy to receive and which we read and reread. If we have not written as often as we should have it is our fault and we ask you to forgive us.

Theme

The effectiveness of this story more than most stories depends upon the acceptance of its theme, or underlying purpose. Since the progression of the story depends on letters—and only two of these—most of the other ingredients of a short story are lacking: plot, narrative, character development, mood, atmosphere. Even setting may appear to be missing, although it is of importance in contributing to the theme.

The evident theme is the contrast between two different ways of life, between the Greece of Alexandros and the America of Kenneth Bentley. In contrasting the two, Updike is implying a criticism of at least one of them. In any event, he is underlining the differences.

1 What do you learn of Alexandros' Greece? Try to characterize life there as you see it through his letter. Does it seem attractive?

2 Does Alexandros appear to be very worried about his future? Is his letter subservient to the people who are "keeping" him? Do you expect it to be?

3 How would you characterize Alexandros? Does he seem to be a sympathetic young man? How does he differ, if at all, from an American young man of about the same age?

4 Do you think that Alexandros will grow up to understand and admire Mr. Bentley?

5 Now on the other side, what do you learn of Kenneth Bentley's America from his letter?

6 Is it the America that Alexandros thinks he knows? What makes it so different? Which is preferable?

7 Mr. Bentley is the benefactor, and Alexandros is the recipient; yet the American seems almost ashamed of himself when he writes to the boy. Why does Mr. Bentley sound so defensive in his remarks, whereas Alexandros seems so sure of himself?

8 Do you accept the picture of America that Mr. Bentley draws? Do you think it is too narrow?

9 Do you accept the picture of Greece that Alexandros draws? Or do you think it is overdone, possibly sentimentalized?

10 Why is Updike so harsh with Mr. Bentley, or don't you feel that he is? Put another way, do you think that the tone of the story makes us sympathetic to one party over the other? Where are Updike's sympathies, and if he had to choose, which way of life would he choose? Which would you choose?

11 What is the purpose of Mr. Bentley's reference to Homer, particularly to the episode concerning Helen and Paris? Do you see any ironic parallels with his own fate? Why doesn't he draw on something closer to present-day life?

12 Do you feel that Mr. Bentley is condescending toward the Greek boy, or does he confront him man to man? Why does he mention the young woman of Greek origin whom he is taking out that evening?

13 What is the purpose of the P.S.? Do you sense any change in tone on Mr. Bentley's part?

14 Who needs the help, Alexandros or Mr. Bentley?

THE BOILER-ROOM

William Sansom

On the day this happened Piesse arrived at the boiler-house feeling bad in his marrow. All through him, in the inside of his bones, under his muscles, in his brain under its heavy skull he felt bluish and soured, not because he was cold, not even ill, but because for some reason a disgust filled him, so that he shivered against the sight of everything, men and things, with considered hatred and some sort of a remote contempt.

He could not have said exactly why his lips pursed—as if he had licked a sharp lemon—when he saw the blackened brick wall of the school to which the boiler was attached; nor why he turned away his head quickly as a boy, pale and smiling, nodded from across the street; nor why he raised his boot to kick at a pile of refuse upon which some cats were crawling, lowering the boot then and not kicking only from weariness and a foreboding that his action would only disturb things and make things move, and that then they would be even harder to endure.

He stared hard at the daily paraphernalia of the schoolyard—the swings, the stone steps and the tiled washhouse—but his head was bent a little forward, as though even in this deliberate self-assertion of his contempt he was afraid of some power behind or above him. Yet the air above was anything but oppressive, it was fresh and light—the white wintry sun shining low had made one pale golden sheet of high clouds—and a dry, brisk morning echoed with invigorating sounds, tram-bells, the barking of frisky dogs, a sudden peal of treble laughter from one of the classrooms above. Once, looking up at the black branches of a tree veined delicately against the pale sky, Piesse began to wonder why he felt so bad on a morning like this; but while he was still looking at these branches, he wondered instantly why he had ever felt good about things at all, on any morning, anywhere, ever.

Some boys were leaning out of an upstairs window, fluttering an overcoat and a piece of ragged cloth. Piesse stared at them, not understanding, vaguely knowing only that they were playing some game of absurd importance to them. He frowned, resenting, feeling that their action was a personal affront. Then a little girl in a red cap ran out of the school door singing. She ran past him, a small ball of clothes on white legs, and disappeared suddenly, hopping round the corner of the gate. He stopped and stared after her, grunting out a noise of contempt, and then turned again towards the boiler-house.

Sailor was already there, squatting in his blue overalls on one of the iron rails, and intent on a part of his forearm bared of the sleeve. Some long hairs had furred over a tattoo pattern. He was cutting these with an old razor-blade, and at the same time hummed a tune right back in his teeth, so that the sound hissed out like a whistle. Without really raising his head he nodded good morning to Piesse, who felt immediately a new accession of disgust, resenting instantly this new proximity. Though the two of them had worked together closely and amicably in the lonely boiler-room throughout the year, today Piesse just stared hard at the black eyebrows jutting out over Sailor's two little deep-set eyes—as though he now saw them for the first time. Fat, piggish Piesse walked over to the shovels, crushing the coke-grit under his iron-shod boots. "Eight-thirty," he said.

Not hurrying, they began their work. They took the various jobs slowly, often pausing, wandering over to the doorway, smoking cigarettes. Occasionally the sailor made a remark, or grumbled out a joke, or even asked Piesse a question. Piesse never answered, only grunted acknowledgment, keeping his eyes down at his job, or anywhere away from the old sailor's boiler-suit and from his face, and sometimes he pressed his lips together tighter and made no answer at all. But this hardly mattered, for Sailor's questions were not framed to be answered—they were facts believed by Sailor, merely stated as questions; for he was a close man, needing neither the acclamation nor the opinions of others. He was proof against Piesse's mood. He shoveled coke for himself, he talked for himself. When he was resting he seemed always to be adjusting something about his person, setting himself independently shipshape. In the afternoons he would spend long periods sewing, or washing out a shirt, or gathering together old scraps and junk—wood, dustbin iron, even rags—to take home and make into something. Piesse was irritated that the sailor remained unaffected by his silence. He thought darkly of this as an insult. Yet if the sailor had criticized his mood, or, worse, had tried to cheer him, his insides would have been seized with rage. He resented Sailor's presence, either way. He avoided meeting his eyes, straining to do this. But whenever the sailor's face had turned away, when the coast was clear, he glanced quickly over at him, letting his eyes rest for a moment on those overalls, savoring a swelling resentment. Then, as Sailor moved again, he flicked his eyes down instantly.

At all costs he wanted to avoid the sailor's eye. And when he was looking down, hard, so that his throbbing neck arteries darkened the room around and above him, he became terrified that perhaps the sailor would quietly be watching him. He was afraid then that the sailor would question him, cajole him into speaking. Furiously, sweating with both fear and attack, he polished the brass of the big thermometer. He felt he would burst.

The two big boilers stood side by side, separated by a few feet and a protective railing. Their massive round iron sides were rusted brown and then grayed over with dust, but the railings encircling them had been painted bright green, so that in their rough-cast heavy skins the two boilers looked like huge dormant pachyderms enclosed by a bright fence, truncated featureless monsters, but alive. They never moved, never quivered, made no sound. Yet they seemed to live. Of huge weight, they enclosed within their bellies a tremendous sleeping power, hundreds of compressed degrees of heat, piled-up energy bursting to split free.

Sometimes Piesse or Sailor would open the mouth-doors and then the red middles could be seen. Inside—one could not see too far, not all the secret by any means—a mass of red coke nuggets burnt beneath slight, slow-licking flames like the little devil flames in an old picture of hell. As the door opened a fiercely singeing breath would blow out, fanning into the air already dry and hot. It would perhaps be Piesse's job to shovel coke into this inferno, or to rake out with his long iron the golden clinkers.

Their jobs were various. Coke lay piled in two hills, one reaching to the ceiling in an alcove by the door and the other, smaller, hill ranged opposite the boilers. They had to shovel coke from the big pile to the lesser pile, wheeling a light iron wheelbarrow in between. From the smaller hill they fed the boilers. Then they had to rake the boilers, to clean the thermometers and pressure-gauges, to polish a little brasswork, to adjust the valves round the school-buildings, to inspect the safety steam-escape, and many similar tasks. But their main work was below in the boiler-house, shoveling.

They had worked together for a long time. It was a slow, lonely job, in a colorless place, a cell segregated from the rest of life and from all the soft textures—but they had always managed well with each other. The alienation of the place had brought them together, so that their confidence was close. They knew and respected each other's fancies and small habits, they shared the two pictures of each other's homes and wives and children. Sometimes they took a drink together at dinnertime, and once Piesse had spent a Sunday at the sailor's house. But on the whole, although their companionship in the boiler-house had become very close indeed, they kept their home lives apart. They quarreled seldom, and then on trivial matters that were adjusted without malice and soon forgotten.

But today, like a pile of coke suddenly falling, Piesse's equanimity had collapsed and in the void a venomous worm pullulated at every moment more viciously.

Towards eleven o'clock he was shoveling from the small stoke-hill straight into the furnace. The light, dried slag scooped easily into his shovel. It was no effort to lift this stuff, light as pumice and holed like dry lava, and so Piesse went on thinking. His resentment festered and seemed to go on swelling inside him—yet he was not an unself-conscious man, so that even in the course of his rising hatred there came to him sudden flashes of tranquillity and extraordinary calm query. At these moments he forgot the sailor and wondered what could be the cause of his mood, abruptly surprised at himself. Why should he behave so oddly on this ordinary morning? What was this dry hate corroding him? How should the people and the things about seem suddenly so difficult to endure, so worthless? He noticed that he found them worthless; that was because the people themselves seemed to attach to their actions such vital importance.

He looked back on the morning and remembered that until he had left the house his mood had been normally cheerful. Then, as he thought, he recalled certain distressing emotions. A cab-driver had shouted at him when he had crossed the road, and standing on the opposite curb a man in a black hat had laughed. Something about the hat, which was broadbrimmed and clamped down over the man's ears—something there had irritated him. At least he recollected a distaste when now he thought back on the episode. Perhaps it had been the man's face, with yellow carious teeth smirking at him from a hard gray stubble on the lip above? And then the post office had refused to meet an order for money, questioning his identity so that he had begun to believe that he was not perhaps himself after all, and would never again be able to prove this. That had made him furious, and perhaps had frightened him, too; although, of course, he had realized even at that time that the notion was ridiculous. Apart from these two mishaps, he could recollect nothing unpleasant about his walk to the school, except that the latter part of the journey had seemed to grow duller and duller, and that his breakfast had returned upon him. Something had upset his digestion. Now he felt blown-out inside, too unwieldy for his frame. But, he argued to the gray nuggets of coke, it was absurd to think that two such insignificant troubles could have affected him so deeply. Things like that happened every day. Although it was not to be doubted that his depression had overtaken him only during his walk. Or had it? What about the previous night, or had it been the night before . . . hadn't he been dreaming of something that he could scarcely now remember, but something certainly disturbing? His mind drifted back, settling upon this or that experience of the previous days, remembering, accepting, rejecting, even inventing things that possibly had never happened. He jabbed viciously at the coke and it grated dryly on his iron shovel. The moment of detachment passed. Again the atmosphere closed in darkly around him, he felt himself redden, and suddenly he wanted to sob. Everything became dull, unendurably dull again, so pointless as to seem almost aggressive. He flung the last shovelful deep into the boiler and slammed the door shut.

As he bent upwards, by chance he came face to face with Sailor for the first time. Sailor had just turned from polishing a strip of brass on the second boiler. They had been roughly back to back, and now suddenly they had both turned, and they were standing face to face.

Piesse was short, so that now he found himself staring a few inches away from the V in Sailor's blue overalls, a V crested by a dark shag of hair and a roll of woolen undervest. In that second, with Sailor perhaps still moving, he raised his eyes slowly, as though drawn by an exterior will to do so; he felt even then a perilous seizure slowly looking up the sailor's neck to his chin, nose, eyes.

The sailor was a lofty man, lank, thin and still gawkish in his heavy bones. Piesse had to look up at him and felt instantly aggressive, wishing to cut down this disadvantage. For a moment neither of them moved. They were shocked at seeing each other so closely so suddenly, surprised by the coincidence of turning together. They were shocked then to a standstill before the laugh that should have brought relief. In that moment Piesse studied very carefully each feature of the face above him.

He saw the sailor's skin, sallow and even purple beneath the eyes. He saw thin, hard lips and a patch of black stubble where the razor must have slipped. Further up, on the sailor's high, starved cheekbones, several long single hairs straggled from black pocks in his oily, open-pored skin. Then—the eyes, small and deep-set like a monkey's eyes. They were pale gray eyes, ringed with tiny black lashes. All around them the flesh was colored an ill lilac, shadowing the little eyes more deeply, and from the corner of each there stretched beneath the flesh a purple swelling, like a teardrop bruised in the blood itself. Close down above these eyes jutted a bony brow, overhanging them with two thick bursts of bristling hair. So that beneath these and among the black lashes the eyes appeared like little old things, childish and simian, weak and secretly crying. Piesse shuddered.

All at once the lips split open and the sailor smiled, showing suddenly two rows of large, perfectly white teeth, false, and shocking bright, like enameled tin against his sallow lips. Piesse shuddered again. With horror he realized that the smile was meant for him—the first direct act of the sailor towards him that morning. His jaw set like sudden ice. Then, somehow, the shovel seemed to fall forward from his hand, perhaps clumsily pushed forward as his hands lost their feeling of things, perhaps pushed by an automatic intention far, it seemed, from Piesse's brain—yet somehow pushed forward hard and quick, so that the handle struck Sailor in the crotch, bending him over abruptly in sudden pain.

The sailor grunted redly, with his hand to the soft part, and then still grimacing raised his face, stretched with pain, and swore. He swore at Piesse's clumsiness right into Piesse's face, spitting the words out through his clownish teeth: "You bitch! You f——g . . . bad-tempered . . . awkward . . . sod!"

Bad-tempered. The word bolted through Piesse's mind and stuck, shutting out everything else. So all the time Sailor had known it! The bugger had known it and nursed it up to himself! Superior? Smirking over the tattoo mark, all to himself?

Piesse clenched his knuckles into a ram of bone—and smacked hard into the sailor's teeth. He heard the teeth crack before he felt the pain in his knuckles. He saw one white tinny tooth slide out on to Sailor's lip and fall. Then the sailor spat and coughed—the fractured denture and perhaps more teeth must have caught in his throat.

The face opposite Piesse underwent a sharp series of change, as though its muscles were directed by external strings. The changes were each absolute and different, jolted with kaleidoscopic clarity.

A face of disgust, screwed up by the pain and the things he was spitting out.

Then abruptly a new face—as his eyes flickered up to Piesse

—and the whole expression slackened to something idiotic and quite surprised.

This passed as the black brows darkened and Sailor's face set stiff in fury. He clutched up the shovel in his long hands and swung it high above his head, rising again to his full height, poising on his toes, glaring madly before he brought it scything down at Piesse's head.

Piesse crouched back, suddenly terrified. But not at the sight of the shovel about to strike him. Rather he was appalled at the thought of what he himself had done. Like a child he covered his mouth with his hand, as though he had said something wrong. He was ordinarily a passive man. The extent of his sudden action shocked him. This violent broken moment brought him suddenly back to a normal sense of values; he saw now clearly the relationship of himself to others and how he had so violently acted in what seemed now a very distant dream of madness.

But in a rapid instant this terror of what he had done passed and he was assessing the danger of the oncoming shovel. Though a passive man, he came from a boyhood on the street where boys fought. He recognized the moment before the hard knocks came, so that now he was able to rouse himself. He never could have felt the disadvantage of being in the wrong. Fighting was ingrained too naturally in his muscles. Now he was quick with anger and resource, and still crouching he stretched out his hand, grasped the long clinker-iron, and not pausing to weigh it or first draw it back, he lunged it with all his stocky force hard into the sailor's stomach.

Just then, from above, a bell rang. Instantly the air was full of the sound of running feet and the chattering of children's voices swelling out all over the playground as they ran out for their morning break. It was a crystal sound, echoing shrilly, but in some way pure and excited, like the sighing and shattering of windglass.

Piesse fell forward on his lunge. The iron squashed into the sailor's stomach, but never penetrated, blunted off by the resilient overalls. Yet it threw him off his balance, so that he keeled over on one leg, bringing the shovel down clear of Piesse's head, but heavily onto one boot, cutting through the leather and smashing the toe-bones beneath. Piesse gave one high, quick grunt as the pain shot right up and through all his body —yet agile and crazy for survival he leapt instantly upright again and faced the sailor afresh, now with the clinker-iron back across his shoulder to swing it against the second shovel-blow.

The sailor held that shovel now like a bayonet and on a level with Piesse's face.

Then they were at it.

In that muffled dry air the iron cracked heavily, not ringing, but dull and hard. Coke-dust gritted beneath their boots and was flung up in a choking cloud round them. Against this fierce motion the walls and coke-piles and the boilers waited. The walls there were whitewashed, streaked with gray dust, bare but for picks and irons hung in the corner. So that the room was all gray and white, with only the green rail to color it. The massive iron boilers slept their tremendous sleep; the gray slag-piles rustled sometimes and fell, but for the most seemed to wait. White bricks, gray coke and heavy iron made up the big bare cell. The air was dry and stifling, clean in the media of dust and grit, radiating arid heat. From the ceiling hung one yellow electric-bulb, weakly charging the air with ceaseless night, slow-ticking nightmare night, bare and vigilant as the air of a fever ward by night-light. This was made more dismal by the doorway, through which could be seen the white day.

The moving shadows of the two men flickered with a greater urgency against other still-cut shadows. Both men moved awkwardly, yet with swift surprising strength. The bony sailor looked too thin to support his shovel, his knees knocked together; he was all bone, long, and his elbows jutted heavily and at precarious angles from a narrow tubular chest. And Piesse—with his fat round belly and splayed feet—was too comfortable a man to have a clinker-iron in his hands. Piesse was piggishly comfortable, with a sand-haired piggish-pink face, prominent teeth, naked near-set eyes—and his big feet splayed out, giving him a loutish but innocent waddle, like a fat boy anxious for a game. He lifted these feet quickly, yet by nature still planted them flatly and at absurd angles. He moved them now with ferocious agility, and from his flabby body there emerged a secret and horrible strength, as unforeseen as the surprising force knitted from the sailor's complexity of bones. Both men were badly developed—in no sense the picture of two fine males fighting. But despite their deformity they had lived hard lives of manual work, and curiously from their warped bodies there emerged this ungainly strength.

For a few seconds, no more, they sliced and parried with the two brutish tools, circling each other, but never hitting through. The shovel and the iron were both too clumsy to be driven with dexterity through the opposite guard. It was easier to parry than to strike through, though Piesse with his iron could hardly sustain the full smashing weight of the shovel.

Then, suddenly, the shovel swung the sailor off his balance. Piesse saw his chance, drove the iron straight for Sailor's eyes. But the eyes moved and the end of the iron caught instead the flesh beneath Sailor's ear, tearing it and blackening the blood that now suddenly started out. The handle of the shovel caught Piesse's knuckles, numbing all the fingers. He dropped the iron, caught it again with his well hand, swung it up again—this time above his head, one-handed, like a man with a lasso.

His mind was swimming with the pressure of his effort—and also with the chattering of the children playing, above, which seemed to grow louder and more confused. It was like the murmur that rings in the ears before fainting, as confused and as suffocating, yet now much louder. Piesse could not shake off this sound. He was, then, still self-conscious, he had not excluded completely the outer world beyond his effort. Rage should have reddened out all these other things—but perhaps Piesse had remained after all conscious of his first act, of himself in the wrong. He had been able to fight, but nevertheless deeply inside him he felt the blame. The external world of criticism had remained.

With the iron above his head and the sailor stumbling still off his balance, he thought in that fractional second of the children, who suddenly reminded him of little froglike vermin, untold numbers of small, busy white frogs, each with two legs and two clutching hands, squeaking and preying and eating. Their faces were old, yet small and bright with predatory vigor. He did not quite see their faces, yet that was his blurred feeling about them. And still the chattering screamed louder in his ears, fearful music, the windglass in a gale.

One voice above the others suddenly emerged, as a child ran shouting by the door of the boiler-house like a gull swooping and disappearing, then, instantly on the trail of its own lonely shriek.

Piesse brought the iron down. But once again the sailor parried, catching some of the blow on his tattooed arm. The flat of the shovel slammed across Piesse's chest. Piesse struck again—and then abruptly grew afraid. He backed away, then raised his long, hooked iron again, trying to fight the fear. But it persisted. He was afraid not of his enemy, nor of pain, nor of death. He never thought of death. He was afraid instead of being afraid, of the act of retreat, and in a flood his self-criticism took charge of him, blaming him for that first blow at Sailor's teeth, and now merging into a fear of all criticism, of running away and the odor that would follow him. He gripped his iron and swung it—while, above, the lonely voice passed again.

But now the child was screaming louder, in greater excitement, and was suddenly joined by two others. They all screamed close by the door, whooping with glee, stamping and in joyful panic screaming, higher and higher. . . .

It seemed that another voice joined even these—as in the same sudden second—and that this last voice would even scream higher in the end than the others, for it seemed to have a greater force beneath it, and to be piping louder and higher, hissing its cry venomously, as if the child were screaming as a snake might scream, ejecting its cry swiftly, a screaming sound that blew out like a knife . . . the top of the boiler-thermometer had blown off.

Both men recognized it at once and turned dazed to see the steam pouring from this deafening new whistle.

Number two boiler had been overstoked; the furious heat still rising inside had forced the thermometer up and over the danger line, had blown the cap and actuated the warning-whistle; something had blocked the escape-valves outside; it was only seconds before the big boiler would burst. And as these seconds ticked, the boiler still slept, with murder breaking inside it, crouched for the spring beneath its hood of sleep, while on its side a little panicked brass whistle hooted louder, screaming out the danger call like a furious elfin parasite.

Piesse felt a great lightness flood his mind. The boiler was going to blow, but the warning-whistle sounded to him more like a siren for freedom. The sailor had turned his shovel on the boiler-door, which now swung open, blowing out its hot wind and bringing a fierce muttering from the overstacked coke inside.

Even during his sensation of relief Piesse's mind managed to flash for an instant back to the child, to the earlier morning, to the group of boys hanging out of an upstairs window overlooking the schoolyard. Automatically, beneath his relief, he swore. He swore at himself for a fool. How could he not have taken in what they were doing? Had he been mad? For now he saw quite plainly that what they had been doing was this: they had been dressing up the boiler escape-pipe, using it as a prop for a stuffed effigy, perhaps of one of the masters, binding the clothes firmly over the steam escape-pipe, clogging and stuffing this firmly with cloth.

Piesse had not stopped moving and, now shouldered up against the sailor, lunged into the furnace with his iron, scooped out the first red coke. It fell glowing over his boots. Before he kicked it aside he had brought out another rakeful. The sailor was raking too. They went at it hard, crouching back a little against the heat—with the idea that they could protect themselves by those pathetic inches from the coming jet of scalding water.

They raked and sweated. The ear-splitting whistle never ceased. It blinded the room with sound, urging them like a single long stroke of the goad. The steam came down off the ceiling and clouded them, so that now they were alone with the red mouth and this new gray blanket of steam obscuring everything else. The air was wet with it, the sweat poured off their faces close to the furnace-heat, the monotonous shriek enclosed them. They worked shoulder to shoulder, in absolute concord. The sailor's bleeding ear bent near Piesse's face, the furnace glare showed on Piesse's ripped knuckles. But neither noticed these things. There was only one thought between them—to save themselves, to rake out the fire, if possible, before number two should burst.

Theme

This short story interfuses character and theme, but Sansom seems more intent on establishing his idea than on drawing out his characters. Especially toward the end of the story, he concentrates almost solely on the idea and its progression, while submerging his two characters to the needs of the theme.

As is the case with most modern short stories, the theme is developed indirectly. See, for example, the remarks on Lawrence's "The Horse Dealer's Daughter."

1 Almost as significant as the two men are the two boilers. Does Sansom make you think about a boiler for the first time and realize its tremendous energy behind the dull exterior? Do the men and the boilers have any qualities in common which contribute to the overall theme?

2 Pick out the adjectives that Sansom uses to describe the boiler and then the adjectives describing the men. Are there any similarities?

3 What analogy to the boiler does Sansom draw? Carry this analogy as far as you can—to people, events, world situations.
4 What is the point of having the boilers in the basement of a school? Why not a factory, or a ship, or an apartment house?
5 What function does the school serve in terms of the theme? Does Sansom contrast the two boilermen below with the children above? Is there any contrast between above and below, as though between earth and hell?
6 Consider the way the two men fight with each other. Each seems armed with a weapon of war—the shovel is held "now like a bayonet" by Sailor, and Piesse's iron is used like a spear. What is the significance of this struggle? What are they fighting for? What are the issues.
7 Consider further that Piesse's name can be pronounced Peace. Does this point have any relevance?
8 Whoever wins here ultimately loses later. There can be no winner. And yet they struggle to win. Why?
9 When the boiler is ready to blow, they put down their arms. Is Sansom's point that they would join forces to save the boiler valid? What point is Sansom making about them? Do they act to save themselves or the children?
10 The ending is inconclusive. The boiler may blow, or the men may save it. Does the inconclusiveness destroy any of the effectiveness of the story? Do you want to know what happened? Does it matter?

Characterization

The chief character, Piesse, is a man whose past is shadowy, whose position in life is not too interesting, and whose motivation is hardly suggested. Yet he fills the canvas, and his fortunes engage us. This can only be by virtue of the author's art; else we would be uninterested.

1 What initially engages us and holds us throughout is the murderous rage that Piesse feels. Sansom gives Piesse little motivation—beyond two minor incidents that would hardly account for his attitude. His emotions must go far deeper, reaching down into an overriding sense of frustration that makes him feel murderous. We saw a similar frustration in Farrington in Joyce's "Counterparts." Try, if you can, to reconstruct some of the frustration that led to Piesse's desire to break out, if necessary by murder.

2 What effect would the boilers have upon Piesse? What about Sailor, his mentality, his appearance, his self-enclosed attitude —how would all these factors weigh upon Piesse?

3 What about the daily routine? the heat, the dirt, the hard labor? the children? Would these affect him?

4 Further, do people really need much specific provocation to fall into murderous behavior? Possibly Sansom, like London, is suggesting that the human being is merely a facade for the animal that lurks beneath, that man's irrational desires are more powerful than his reason. Does Piesse strike a note of truth in you?

5 Piesse knows it was wrong to strike Sailor, and this knowledge almost weakens him in his fight. What does this aspect of the story mean? Should Piesse have forgotten who was right and who was wrong and simply have fought as well as he could? What point is Sansom suggesting here?

6 If we saw the struggle from Sailor's point of view, what would we learn about Piesse? about the situation?

Mood and Atmosphere

1 Obviously the mood and atmosphere of the story are generated by the presence of the boiler, the boiler-room, and the two boilermen. Try to convey what the atmosphere is like. Is it something, perhaps, like the "dry September" described by Faulkner?

2 Consider what place boredom has in this setting. How much of Piesse's rage is boredom?

IMPULSE

Conrad Aiken

Michael Lowes hummed as he shaved, amused by the face he saw—the pallid, asymmetrical face, with the right eye so much higher than the left, and its eyebrow so peculiarly arched, like a "v" turned upside down. Perhaps this day wouldn't be as bad as the last. In fact, he knew it wouldn't be, and that was why he hummed. This was the bi-weekly day of escape, when he would stay out for the evening, and play bridge with Hurwitz, Bryant, and Smith. Should he tell Dora at the breakfast table? No, better not. Particularly in view of last night's row about unpaid bills. And there would be more of them, probably, beside his plate. The rent. The coal. The doctor who had attended to the children. Jeez, what a life. Maybe it was time to do a new jump. And Dora was beginning to get restless again—

But he hummed, thinking of the bridge game. Not that he liked Hurwitz or Bryant or Smith—cheap fellows, really—mere pick-up acquaintances. But what could you do about making friends, when you were always hopping about from one place to another, looking for a living, and fate always against you! They were all right enough. Good enough for a little escape, a little party—and Hurwitz always provided good alcohol. Dinner at the Greek's, and then to Smith's room—yes. He would wait till late in the afternoon, and then telephone to Dora as if it had all come up suddenly. Hello, Dora—is that you, old girl? Yes, this is Michael—Smith has asked me to drop in for a hand of bridge—you know—so I'll just have a little snack in town. Home by the last car as usual. Yes. . . . Good-bye! . . .

And it all went off perfectly, too. Dora was quiet, at breakfast, but not hostile. The pile of bills was there, to be sure, but nothing was said about them. And while Dora was busy getting the kids ready for school, he managed to slip out, pretending that he thought it was later than it really was. Pretty neat, that! He hummed again, as he waited for the train. Telooralooraloo. Let the bills wait, damn them! A man couldn't do everything at once, could he, when bad luck hounded him everywhere? And if he could just get a little night off, now and then, a rest and change, a little diversion, what was the harm in that?

At half-past four he rang up Dora and broke the news to her. He wouldn't be home till late.

"Are you sure you'll be home at all?" she said, coolly.

That was Dora's idea of a joke. But if he could have foreseen—!

He met the others at the Greek restaurant, began with a couple of *araks,* which warmed him, then went on to red wine, bad olives, *pilaf,* and other obscure foods; and considerably later they all walked along Boylston Street to Smith's room. It was a cold night, the temperature below twenty, with a fine dry snow sifting the streets. But Smith's room was comfortably warm, he trotted out some gin and the Porto Rican cigars, showed them a new snapshot of Squiggles (his Revere Beach sweetheart), and then they settled down to a nice long cozy game of bridge.

It was during an intermission, when they all got up to stretch their legs and renew their drinks, that the talk started—Michael never could remember which one of them it was who had put in the first oar—about impulse. It might have been Hurwitz, who was in many ways the only intellectual one of the three, though hardly what you might call a highbrow. He had his queer curiosities, however, and the idea was just such as might occur to him. At any rate, it was he who developed the idea, and with gusto.

"Sure," he said, "anybody might do it. Have you got impulses? Of course, you got impulses. How many times you think —suppose I do that? And you don't do it, because you know damn well if you do it you'll get arrested. You meet a man you despise—you want to spit in his eye. You see a girl you'd like to kiss—you want to kiss her. Or maybe just to squeeze her arm when she stands beside you in the street car. You know what I mean."

"Do I know what you mean!" sighed Smith. "I'll tell the world. I'll tell the cock-eyed world! . . ."

"You would," said Bryant. "And so would I."

"It would be easy," said Hurwitz, "to give in to it. You know what I mean? So simple. Temptation is too close. That girl you see is too damn good-looking—she stands too near you—you just put out your hand it touches her arm—maybe her leg—why worry? And you think, maybe if she don't like it I can make believe I didn't mean it. . . ."

"Like these fellows that slash fur coats with razor blades," said Michael. "Just impulse, in the beginning, and only later a habit."

"Sure. . . . And like these fellows that cut off braids of hair with scissors. They just feel like it and do it. . . . Or stealing."

"Stealing?" said Bryant.

"Sure. Why, I often feel like it. . . . I see a nice little thing right in front of me on a counter—you know, a nice little knife, or necktie, or a box of candy—quick, you put it in your pocket, and then go to the other counter, or the soda fountain for a drink. What would be more human? We all want things. Why not take them? Why not do them? And civilization is only skin-deep. . . ."

"That's right. Skin-deep," said Bryant.

"But if you were caught, by God!" said Smith, opening his eyes wide.

"*Who's* talking about getting caught? . . . *Who's* talking about doing it. It isn't that we do it, it's only that we *want* to do it. Why, Christ, there's been times when I thought to hell with everything, I'll kiss that woman if it's the last thing I do."

"It might be," said Bryant.

Michael was astonished at this turn of the talk. He had often felt both these impulses. To know that this was a kind of universal human inclination came over him with something like relief.

"Of *course*, everybody has those feelings," he said smiling. "I have them myself. . . . But suppose you *did* yield to them?"

"Well, we don't," said Hurwitz.

"I know—but suppose you did?"

Hurwitz shrugged his fat shoulders, indifferently.

"Oh, well," he said, "it would be bad business."

"Jesus, yes," said Smith, shuffling the cards.

"Oy," said Bryant.

The game was resumed, the glasses were refilled, pipes were lit, watches were looked at. Michael had to think of the last car from Sullivan Square, at eleven-fifty. But also he could not stop thinking of this strange idea. It was amusing. It was fascinating. Here was everyone wanting to steal—toothbrushes, or books—or to caress some fascinating stranger of a female in a subway train—the impulse everywhere—why not be a Columbus of the moral world and really do it? . . . He remembered stealing a conchshell from the drawing room of a neighbor when he was ten—it had been one of the thrills of his life. He had popped it into his sailor blouse and borne it away with perfect aplomb. When, later, suspicion had been cast upon him, he had smashed the shell in his back yard. And often, when he had been looking at Parker's collection of stamps—the early Americans—

The game interrupted his recollections, and presently it was time for the usual night-cap. Bryant drove them to Park Street. Michael was a trifle tight, but not enough to be unsteady on his feet. He waved a cheery hand at Bryant and Hurwitz and began to trudge through the snow to the subway entrance. The lights on the snow were very beautiful. The Park Street Church was ringing, with its queer, soft quarter-bells, the half-hour. Plenty of time. Plenty of time. Time enough for a visit to the drugstore, and a hot chocolate—he could see the warm lights of the windows falling on the snowed sidewalk. He zigzagged across the street and entered.

And at once he was seized with a conviction that his real reason for entering the drugstore was not to get a hot chocolate—not at all! He was going to steal something. He was going to put the impulse to the test, and see whether (*one*) he could manage it with sufficient skill, and (*two*) whether theft gave him any real satisfaction. The drugstore was crowded with people who had just come from the theatre next door. They pushed three deep round the soda fountain, and the cashier's cage. At the back of the store, in the toilet and prescription department, there were not so many, but nevertheless enough to give him a fair chance. All the clerks were busy. His hands were in the side pockets of his overcoat—they were deep wide pockets and would serve admirably. A quick gesture over a table or counter, the object dropped in—

Oddly enough, he was not in the least excited: perhaps that was because of the gin. On the contrary, he was intensely amused; not to say delighted. He was smiling, as he walked slowly along the right-hand side of the store toward the back; edging his way amongst the people, with first one shoulder forward and then the other, while with a critical and appraising eye he examined the wares piled on the counters and on the stands in the middle of the floor. There were some extremely attractive scent-sprays or atomizers—but the dangling bulbs might be troublesome. There were stacks of boxed letter-paper. A basket full of clothes-brushes. Green hot-water bottles. Percolators—too large, and out of the question. A tray of multicolored toothbrushes, bottles of cologne, fountain pens—and then he experienced love at first sight. There could be no question that he had found his chosen victim. He gazed, fascinated, at the delicious object—a *de luxe* safety-razor set, of heavy gold, in a snakeskin box which was lined with red plush. . . .

It wouldn't do, however, to stare at it too long—one of the

clerks might notice. He observed quickly the exact position of the box—which was close to the edge of the glass counter—and prefigured with a quite precise mental picture the gesture with which he would simultaneously close it and remove it. Forefinger at the back—thumb in front—the box drawn forward and then slipped down toward the pocket—as he thought it out, the muscles in his forearm pleasurably contracted. He continued his slow progress round the store, past the prescription counter, past the candy counter; examined with some show of attention the display of cigarette lighters and blade sharpeners; and then with a quick turn, went leisurely back to his victim. Everything was propitious. The whole section of counter was clear for the moment—there were neither customers nor clerks. He approached the counter, leaned over it as if to examine some little filigreed "compacts" at the back of the showcase, picking up one of them with his left hand, as he did so. He was thus leaning directly over the box; and it was the simplest thing in the world to clasp it as planned between thumb and forefinger of his other hand, to shut it softly and to slide it downward to his pocket. It was over in an instant. He continued then for a moment to turn the compact case this way and that in the light, as if to see it sparkle. It sparkled very nicely. Then he put it back on the little pile of cases, turned, and approached the soda fountain—just as Hurwitz had suggested.

He was in the act of pressing forward in the crowd to ask for his hot chocolate when he felt a firm hand close round his elbow. He turned, and looked at a man in a slouch hat and dirty raincoat, with the collar turned up. The man was smiling in a very offensive way.

"I guess you thought that was pretty slick," he said in a low voice which nevertheless managed to convey the very essence of venom and hostility. "You come along with me, mister!"

Michael returned the smile amiably, but was a little frightened. His heart began to beat.

"I don't know what you're talking about," he said, still smiling.

"No, of course not!"

The man was walking toward the rear of the store, and was pulling Michael along with him, keeping a paralyzingly tight grip on his elbow. Michael was beginning to be angry, but also to be horrified. He thought of wrenching his arm free, but feared it would make a scene. Better not. He permitted himself to be urged ignominiously along the shop, through a gate in the rear counter, and into a small room at the back where a clerk was measuring a yellow liquid into a bottle.

"Will you be so kind as to explain to me what this is all about?" he then said, with what frigidity of manner he could muster. But his voice shook a little. The man in the slouch hat paid no attention. He addressed the clerk instead, giving his head a quick backward jerk as he spoke.

"Get the manager in here," he said.

He smiled at Michael, with narrowed eyes, and Michael, hating him, but panic-stricken, smiled foolishly back at him.

"Now, look here—" he said.

But the manager had appeared, and the clerk; and events then happened with revolting and nauseating speed. Michael's hand was yanked violently from his pocket, the fatal snakeskin box was pulled out by the detective, and identified by the manager and the clerk. They both looked at Michael with a queer expression, in which astonishment, shame, and contempt were mixed with vague curiosity.

"Sure that's ours," said the manager, looking slowly at Michael.

"I saw him pinch it," said the detective. "What about it?" He again smiled offensively at Michael. "Anything to say?"

"It was all a joke," said Michael, his face feeling very hot and flushed. "I made a kind of bet with some friends. . . . I can prove it. I can call them up for you."

The three men looked at him in silence, all three of them just faintly smiling, as if incredulously.

"Sure you can," said the detective, urbanely. "You can prove it in court. . . . Now come along with me, mister."

Michael was astounded at this appalling turn of events, but his brain still worked. Perhaps if he were to put it to this fellow as man to man, when they got outside? As he was thinking this, he was firmly conducted through a back door into a dark alley at the rear of the store. It had stopped snowing. A cold wind was blowing. But the world, which had looked so beautiful fifteen minutes before, had now lost its charm. They walked together down the alley in six inches of powdery snow, the detective holding Michael's arm with affectionate firmness.

"No use calling the wagon," he said. "We'll walk. It ain't far."

They walked along Tremont Street. And Michael couldn't help, even then, thinking what an extraordinary thing this was! Here were all these good people passing them, and little knowing that he, Michael Lowes, was a thief, a thief by accident, on his way to jail. It seemed so absurd as hardly to be worth speaking of! And suppose they shouldn't believe him? This notion made him shiver. But it wasn't possible—no, it wasn't possible. As soon as he had told his story, and called up Hurwitz and Bryant and Smith, it would all be laughed off. Yes, laughed off.

He began telling the detective about it: how they had discussed such impulses over a game of bridge. Just a friendly game, and they had joked about it and then, just to see what would happen, he had done it. What was it that made his voice sound so insincere, so hollow? The detective neither slackened his pace nor turned his head. His business-like grimness was alarming. Michael felt that he was paying no attention at all; and, moreover, it occurred to him that this kind of lowbrow official might not even understand such a thing. . . . He decided to try the sentimental.

"And good Lord, man, there's my wife waiting for me—!"

"Oh, sure, and the kids too."

"Yes, and the kids!"

The detective gave a quick leer over the collar of his dirty raincoat.

"And no Santy Claus *this* year," he said.

Michael saw that it was hopeless. He was wasting his time.

"I can see it's no use talking to you," he said stiffly. "You're so used to dealing with criminals that you think all mankind is criminal, *ex post facto.*"

"Sure."

Arrived at the station, and presented without decorum to the lieutenant at the desk, Michael tried again. Something in the faces of the lieutenant and the sergeant, as he told his story, made it at once apparent that there was going to be trouble. They obviously didn't believe him—not for a moment. But after consultation, they agreed to call up Bryant and Hurwitz and Smith, and to make inquiries. The sergeant went off to do this, while Michael sat on a wooden bench. Fifteen minutes passed, during which the clock ticked and the lieutenant wrote slowly in a book, using a blotter very frequently. A clerk had been dispatched, also, to look up Michael's record, if any. This gentleman came back first, and reported that there was nothing. The lieutenant scarcely looked up from his book, and went on writing. The first serious blow then fell. The sergeant, reporting, said that he hadn't been able to get Smith (of course—Michael thought—he's off somewhere with Squiggles) but had got

Hurwitz and Bryant. Both of them denied that there had been any bet. They both seemed nervous, as far as he could make out over the phone. They said they didn't know Lowes well, were acquaintances of his, and made it clear that they didn't want to be mixed up in anything. Hurwitz had added that he knew Lowes was hard up.

At this, Michael jumped to his feet, feeling as if the blood would burst out of his face.

"The damned liars!" he shouted. "The bloody liars! By God—!"

"Take him away," said the lieutenant, lifting his eyebrows, and making a motion with his pen.

Michael lay awake all night in his cell, after talking for five minutes with Dora on the telephone. Something in Dora's cool voice had frightened him more than anything else.

And when Dora came to talk to him the next morning at nine o'clock, his alarm proved to be well-founded. Dora was cold, detached, deliberate. She was not at all what he had hoped she might be—sympathetic and helpful. She didn't volunteer to get a lawyer, or in fact to do anything—and when she listened quietly to his story, it seemed to him that she had the appearance of a person listening to a very improbable lie. Again, as he narrated the perfectly simple episode—the discussion of "impulse" at the bridge game, the drinks, and the absurd tipsy desire to try a harmless little experiment—again, as when he talked to the store detective, he heard his own voice becoming hollow and insincere. It was exactly as if he knew himself to be guilty. His throat grew dry, he began to falter, to lose his thread, to use the wrong words. When he stopped speaking finally, Dora was silent.

"Well, say something!" he said angrily, after a moment. "Don't just stare at me. I'm not a criminal!"

"I'll get a lawyer for you," she answered, "but that's all I can do."

"Look here, Dora—you don't mean you—"

He looked at her incredulously. It wasn't possible that she really thought him a thief? And suddenly, as he looked at her, he realized how long it was since he had really known this woman. They had drifted apart. She was embittered, that was it—embittered by his non-success. All this time she had slowly been laying up a reserve of resentment. She had resented his inability to make money for the children, the little dishonesties they had had to commit in the matter of unpaid bills, the humiliations of duns, the too-frequent removals from town to town—she had more than once said to him, it was true, that because of all this she had never had any friends—and she had resented, he knew, his gay little parties with Hurwitz and Bryant and Smith, implying a little that they were an extravagance which was to say the least inconsiderate. Perhaps they *had* been. But was a man to have no indulgences? . . .

"Perhaps we had better not go into that," she said.

"Good Lord—you don't believe me!"

"I'll get the lawyer—though I don't know where the fees are to come from. Our bank account is down to seventy-seven dollars. The rent is due a week from today. You've got some salary coming, of course, but I don't want to touch my own savings, naturally, because the children and I may need them."

To be sure. Perfectly just. Women and children first. Michael thought these things bitterly, but refrained from saying them. He gazed at this queer cold little female with intense curiosity. It was simply extraordinary—simply astonishing. Here she was, seven years his wife, he thought he knew her inside and out, every quirk of her handwriting, inflection of voice; her passion for strawberries, her ridiculous way of singing; the brown moles on her shoulder, the extreme smallness of her feet and toes, her dislike of silk underwear. Her special voice at the telephone, too—that rather chilly abruptness, which had always surprised him, as if she might be a much harder woman than he thought her to be. And the queer sinuous cat-like rhythm with which she always combed her hair before the mirror at night, before going to bed—with her head tossing to one side, and one knee advanced to touch the chest of drawers. He knew all these things, which nobody else knew, and nevertheless, now, they amounted to nothing. The woman herself stood before him as opaque as a wall.

"Of course," he said, "you'd better keep your own savings." His voice was dull. "And you'll, of course, look up Hurwitz and the others? They'll appear, I'm sure, and it will be the most important evidence. In fact, *the* evidence."

"I'll ring them up, Michael," was all she said, and with that she turned quickly on her heel and went away. . . .

Michael felt doom closing in upon him; his wits went round in circles; he was in a constant sweat. It wasn't possible that he was going to be betrayed? It wasn't possible! He assured himself of this. He walked back and forth, rubbing his hands together; he kept pulling out his watch to see what time it was. Five minutes gone. Another five minutes gone. Damnation, if this lasted too long, this confounded business, he'd lose his job. If it got into the papers, he might lose it anyway. And suppose it was true that Hurwitz and Bryant had said what they said—maybe they were afraid of losing their jobs too. Maybe that was it! Good God. . . .

This suspicion was confirmed, when, hours later, the lawyer came to see him. He reported that Hurwitz, Bryant and Smith had all three refused flatly to be mixed up in the business. They were all afraid of the effects of the publicity. If subpoenaed, they said, they would state that they had known Lowes only a short time, had thought him a little eccentric, and knew him to be hard up. Obviously—and the little lawyer picked his teeth with the point of his pencil—they could not be summoned. It would be fatal.

The Judge, not unnaturally perhaps, decided that there was a perfectly clear case. There couldn't be the shadow of a doubt that this man had deliberately stolen an article from the counter of So-and-so's drugstore. The prisoner had stubbornly maintained that it was the result of a kind of bet with some friends, but these friends had refused to give testimony in his behalf. Even his wife's testimony—that he had never done such a thing before—had seemed rather half-hearted; and she had admitted, moreover, that Lowes was unsteady, and that they were always living in a state of something like poverty. Prisoner, further, had once or twice jumped his rent and had left behind him in Somerville unpaid debts of considerable size. He was a college man, a man of exceptional education and origin, and ought to have known better. His general character might be good enough, but as against all this, here was a perfectly clear case of theft, and a perfectly clear motive. The prisoner was sentenced to three months in the house of correction.

By this time, Michael was in a state of complete stupor. He sat in the box and stared blankly at Dora who sat very quietly in the second row, as if she were a stranger. She was looking back at him, with her white face turned a little to one side, as if she too had never seen him before, and were wondering what sort of people criminals might be. Human? Sub-human? She lowered her eyes after a moment, and before she had looked up again, Michael had been touched on the arm and led stumbling out of the courtroom. He thought she would of course come to say goodbye to him, but even in this he was mistaken; she left without a word.

And when he did finally hear from her, after a week, it was in a very brief note.

"Michael," it said, "I'm sorry, but I can't bring up the children with a criminal for a father, so I'm taking proceedings for a divorce. This is the last straw. It was bad enough to have you always out of work and to have to slave night and day to keep bread in the children's mouths. But this is too much, to have disgrace into the bargain. As it is, we'll have to move right away, for the schoolchildren have sent Dolly and Mary home crying three times already. I'm sorry, and you know how fond I was of you at the beginning, but you've had your chance. You won't hear from me again. You've always been a good sport, and generous, and I hope you'll make this occasion no exception, and refrain from contesting the divorce. Goodbye—Dora."

Michael held the letter in his hands, unseeing, and tears came into his eyes. He dropped his face against the sheet of notepaper, and rubbed his forehead to and fro across it . . . Little Dolly! . . . Little Mary! . . . Of course. This was what life was. It was just as meaningless and ridiculous as this; a monstrous joke; a huge injustice. You couldn't trust anybody, not even your wife, not even your best friends. You went on a little lark, and they sent you to prison for it, and your friends lied about you, and your wife left you. . . .

Contest it? Should he contest the divorce? What was the use? There was the plain fact: that he had been convicted for stealing. No one had believed his story of doing it in fun, after a few drinks; the divorce court would be no exception. He dropped the letter to the floor and turned his heel on it, slowly and bitterly. Good riddance—good riddance! Let them all go to hell. He would show them. He would go west, when he came out—get rich, clear his name somehow. . . . But how?

He sat down on the edge of his bed and thought of Chicago. He thought of his childhood there, the Lake Shore Drive, Winnetka, the trip to Niagara Falls with his mother. He could hear the Falls now. He remembered the Fourth of July on the boat; the crowded examination room at college; the time he had broken his leg in baseball, when he was fourteen; and the stamp collection which he had lost at school. He remembered his mother always saying, "Michael, you *must* learn to be orderly"; and the little boy who had died of scarlet fever next door; and the pink conch-shell smashed in the back yard. His whole life seemed to be composed of such trivial and infinitely charming little episodes as these; and as he thought of them, affectionately and with wonder, he assured himself once more that he had really been a good man. And now, had it all come to an end? It had all come foolishly to an end.

Theme

When we speak of an impulse, we usually mean an act that is generally out of keeping with our normal behavior. An impulse is unplanned, unmotivated, something extraordinary and eccentric. We are all capable of impulses, or impulsive acts, and we are often very surprised by their nature. That is, we suddenly discover aspects of our behavior that astonish us, and we wonder—if we think about such acts at all—what makes us capable of such irrational behavior. We find, accordingly, that under certain circumstances and conditions we are capable of nearly anything.

In this story, Aiken is concerned with showing the kind of impulses which lie under our usually normal behavior. If you can answer the following series of questions, you can perhaps see where Aiken is trying to lead us.

1 What do we know of Michael Lowes's early life? List as many details as you can. What kind of life do these details add up to?

2 What has Michael's married life been like? Are the failures his, or are they shared with his wife?

3 Can you characterize Michael as a man? How does Aiken wish us to see him?

4 Is Michael's desire to "get away" to play bridge understandable, given the nature of his married life?

5 Why should Hurwitz's idea of impulsive behavior attract Michael? Do you believe this part of the story is convincing? That is, do you think Michael should be susceptible to Hurwitz's theoretical argument? Has Aiken prepared the character sufficiently for his acceptance?

6 Is the impulsive act itself much different from what millions of people do when they steal in a supermarket, take pennies or nickels when they are children, cheat on tests and examinations in school, or deceive the state or federal government by evading taxes? How does Michael's action differ?

7 Is Michael's action possibly uncontrollable? That is, is he simply waiting for some new course of action—here Hurwitz's suggestion—in order to find a way out of his life? Briefly, does Aiken suggest that Michael is seeking a disaster in order to extricate himself from a marital situation that has become impossible? Keep in mind, if you try to argue this point, that the course Michael follows would never be consciously clear to him; he would never feel that he was choosing prison over marriage.

8 Does Aiken gain our sympathy for Michael when he is caught and turned over to the authorities? Do we feel that he should be excused? Is it necessary that we should feel sorry for Michael? Or does Aiken create the opposite effect, and make Michael's punishment seem perfectly suitable?

9 Once things begin to happen to Michael, they follow a strict pattern of entrapment; he falls ever deeper. How does the matter-of-fact style help contribute to this sense of doom?

10 Does the character of Michael Lowes possess any significance beyond his impulsive act, or does the act sufficiently define him? Ask yourself why Aiken makes Michael a man possessed by impulses virtually from the beginning of the story. This may give you valuable clues to his nature.

11 Does the story frighten you with the possibility of self-destruction through the commission of some act outside of your control? Or do you feel that you are so well controlled that you could suppress any potentially destructive act? Keep in mind that you will never know whether or not the act is really destructive. It may satisfy some momentary need or seem superficially beneficial. What, then, is Aiken suggesting about human behavior? The answer to this question is really the theme of the story. The final words are "It had all come foolishly to an end." What had come to an end? What does Aiken suggest about Michael? About people in general?

THE WELL

Hugh Nissenson

Sunday. It's ten-year-old Micah, Aviva's kid, waiting in front of the dining-hall just before lunch, who brings us the news: One of the Bedouin camels from Ahmad's camp two kilometers south of the *kibbutz* has strayed into our date grove to give birth. "Come and thee! Come and thee!" Micah cried. Buck-toothed, and with ugly brick-red hair like his mother, he speaks with a lisp, spraying a fine mist of spit into the air that gives me the fantastic notion that he has somehow boiled over from the heat. "Juth for a minute," he insists.

Grossman the mechanic is with me, pale and drawn from his morning's work in the machine shop and his attack of *shil-shul*, the chronic dysentery from which he has suffered the last two days. "Pleath," the boy pleads, but bathed in sweat, and absent-mindedly chewing on the ragged end of his drooping mustache, Grossman refuses with a shake of his head, and goes inside, slamming the screen door behind him, and stirring up the flies. The boy takes hold of my hand.

"It'll only take a minute."

"Where's your mother?"

A hubbub around us, as more and more of the *chaverim*—the comrades, members of the collective settlement—arrive at the dining-hall from the work shops and the fields. They are in much the same state as Grossman and myself, and do not care who knows it; sullen, completely exhausted by the heat, and oppressed by the prospect of a meager meal and an afternoon's work still to be done.

"Oh pleath. Pleath," the boy begs, with the rising inflection, the sad whine of the ugly child who has already learned that he cannot command attention any other way. "You don't underthand."

"Maybe after lunch."

"But that'll be too late. He'th going to kill it."

"Kill what? Who?"

"Oh hurry!"

It's too much of an effort for me to argue or try to understand, and he knows it. Hand in mine, he leads me away, past the deserted machine shop and the cow shed where, attracted by the feed, literally hundreds of twittering sparrows are perched on the corrugated tin roof—the only life, it seems, besides ourselves, abroad on the desert at this hour of the day.

Just noon. At the date grove, row on row of the broad dusty leaves cast no shadow, offer no refuge from the terrific glare of the sun.

"Look!" says the boy.

"Where?"

I shield my eyes with my hand, and there, in the direction that he points, just beyond the line of trees to the south, is the camel with her colt that couldn't have been born more than an hour before. Beside them, on the ground and swarming with flies, is the bloody sac. A wonderful sight, I must admit. The colt, waist high, as yet with only a rudimentary hump, all knees and huge splayed toes, jerks its head convulsively as it sucks at the pendulous swollen udders of the mare.

"Promith me!"

"What?"

"You won't let him kill it, will you?"

"Who, Micah, what are you talking about?"

This time, he only has to turn his head. To my left, not ten feet away, and apparently watching us all the while, is a young Bedouin with a rifle, squatting on his hams against one of the trees.

"*Shalom.*"

"And peace; peace unto you," he replies, speaking Hebrew with a thick Arabic accent. Under the *kafiyah* that shadows his eyes, a rather handsome, intelligent face; high cheekbones, a hooked nose, and a thick black mustache that droops down to the corners of his mouth.

"Ask him yourself. He says he'th going to kill it. Why?" says the boy, and the Bedouin, for an answer, glances up to indicate—what? In the torpor engendered by the heat, it takes me a moment to understand fully. I too, as though compelled, look up at the cloudless sky from which the sun has bleached all the color, leaving a white, translucent haze that dazzles the eyes.

"Tell me why!"

It's the drought, of course. I try to explain to the boy. Now the middle of November, what little autumnal rains the Bedouins depend on to water their herds is more than six weeks overdue.

"But what about their well?"

"Ah, now that's just the trouble. Their well has all gone dry. The colt has to be killed so that their children will have the milk to drink. You wouldn't want the children to die of thirst, would you?"

"I don't care."

"Micah!"

"Is our well dry too?"

"Not yet; no."

"Why not?"

"It's deeper."

While we have been talking, the Bedouin has opened the bolt of his rifle—an old Lee Enfield .303, and inserted a cartridge with a click that rivets our attention to the oiled barrel gleaming in the sun. When he stands up in his soiled, billowing pantaloons, the boy cannot suppress a shout that makes the mare swivel her head in our direction. She apparently has just become aware of us, and with a kind of comical, bewildered ferocity, lets hang her protruding underlip, and bares her teeth. The startled colt has stopped sucking, and skitters backwards, with its shaky forelegs locked together, and the back spread awkwardly apart. For the first time, I catch a glimpse of its bitten cord, already withering from its belly like a dead vine.

"*Chaver!* . . . But comrade," the boy shouts.

"Micah, come here. Come away."

"Comrade, don't."

"Come away, I tell you. It's none of our business."

"You promithed."

"No. There's nothing I can do."

I catch him by the hand and drag him away. At the cowshed, the echoing crack of the shot rouses the sparrows who rise in a dark twittering mass, circle the silo twice, and begin once again to settle on the sloping tin roof.

Grossman is still in the dining-hall when I get back, sitting alone at a corner table.

"Where's the kid?" he asks.

"I left him at the nursery."

"Aviva was looking for him."

"I know. I saw her. How's the stomach?"

"Okay."

"Really better?"

Obviously forcing himself to keep up his strength, he is eating a plate of white goat's cheese and chopped cucumbers, washing down mouthfuls of the stuff with sips from a cup of cold water.

"The water'll give you cramps."

"No," he says, "I really feel better. . . . So the Bedouins are beginning to slaughter their herds."

"You heard the shot. . . . The kid was terribly upset."

"It's a shame."

"I read in yesterday's paper that the government says if the drought keeps up, they'll try and relocate the tribes to better grazing land up north."

"The government," he grimaces. A stomach spasm? It's hard to tell. With a sour expression on his face, wiping off his mustache, he pushes away the plate of food. "Who was doing the shooting?"

"One of the younger men. Good-looking. He speaks a little Hebrew, I think."

"Don't tell me. Not Ali?"

"Which one is Ali? . . . Oh." I remember, Ali, Sheik Ahmad's oldest son, with whom Grossman had struck up a friendship two years before, when for a season both of them were shepherds, pasturing their herds together some thirty kilometers or so north of here.

"Ah," he goes on. "It's a damn shame. By the time the government decides to do anything for them, it'll be too late."

"Not necessarily."

"You know it as well as I do. What's the use? By the time it goes through all the official channels to provide relief, they'll have slaughtered all their young animals. What'll they do come spring?"

"They'll manage."

"They'll starve. That's what."

Then absorbed in thought, he is silent. All around us, like insects in amber, each sound in the room seems embedded and preserved in the thick air, yellowed by the sunlight streaming through the windows; the clatter of tin forks, scrape of plates, murmur of the comrades' voices, and pervading all else the buzz of the flies that are so fat and lazy when they alight you can squash them with a finger.

"Ali, eh?" he asks. "I haven't seen him in over a year. What do you think? Maybe I ought to go over and have a talk with him."

"What you ought to do is go back to your room and lie down."

He gives me an ironic glance and is partly right. It's not his health alone that concerns me, but my reluctance, as elected secretary, more or less a kind of first among equals, general manager of the settlement, to allow the *kibbutz* to become officially involved in Bedouin affairs at all.

"No," I tell him.

"Why not? We were friends."

"You asked my advice and I'm telling you. If they really would like us to help them, let them take the initiative for once—just for once, and come to us."

"I can't see any harm in just talking to Ali."

But there is. That's the trouble, and Grossman knows it as well as I, in spite of any personal relationship he may have cultivated with the Sheik's son. For eleven years now, since the establishment of our settlement in the desert by force of arms, we have lived in a state of truce with Ahmad's tribe, no more and no less. Time and time again, experience has taught us that when we so much as offer them any material assistance, much less demonstrate a willingness for a real peace, it is refused, and taken for nothing but a display of weakness on our part, a loss of face as far as we are concerned.

"No," I continue, "I . . ." But Grossman interrupts by standing up.

"No matter. It was just a thought."

He leaves, but all afternoon in the secretary's office—a desk, two rattan chairs, and a metal filing cabinet—I can think of nothing else while I should be at work checking a list of supplies to be bought tomorrow in Beersheba.

. . . One hundred kilos baking soda, one hundred salt . . .

Impossible to keep my mind on it. The office, adjacent to the radio shack, stands on a little rise behind the dining-hall, commanding a view of the desert to the south. Broken up by a network of wadis running east to west—dry water courses eroded by flash floods—the landscape always gives me the impression that it has been raked by the talons of some gigantic beast. Here and there, glaring in the sun, are white outcroppings of rock; ribs and spines and shoulder blades, only partly buried by the cracked earth. Yes. It is exactly as though some unimaginable animal has dug at the earth to bury the bones of its prey.

. . . Salt, one hundred kilos sugar, tea . . .

Again and again my gaze returns to the window, but at this distance, the black wool tents of the Bedouin encampment are indistinguishable in the chaotic pattern of the shadow cast by the afternoon sun on the broken ground. Once, and only for a moment, one of their camels is to be seen, silhouetted against the sky, and again—or is it my imagination?—I can hear the faint echo of a rifle shot borne on the rising wind.

Four-thirty. Finished by now with his work at the machine shop, Grossman is there, I am sure of it, but to speak with Ali means nothing. That's the whole point. It is Ahmad himself who has always been responsible for most of the difficulties that exist between us. The absolute ruler of the tribe for over twenty years, he is terrified—and with some justification—that even the minimal communication between the two communities will undermine his feudal authority. I have seen him only once or twice, at the Kassid or Morris, cafés in Beersheba; a great hulk of a man, not without dignity, who wears a pointed little beard, and whose dark, unhealthy-looking skin reminds me, for some reason, of the color of a slice of apple left exposed to the air. Purportedly still possessed of a harem of twenty women or more, his licentiousness is legendary. One story has it that one day, long ago, at the height of his powers, he came upon a beautiful fourteen-year-old Bedouin girl drawing water from a desert well, and unable to resist making overtures—pleading, threatening, promising her anything to get her to join his harem—he reduced the child to tears.

"Let me go," she begged. "If you don't let me go, I'll tell tell my father."

"And just who is that?" Ahmad wanted to know.

"A sheik. A very powerful sheik who'd have you gelded like a horse."

"Who?" he laughed.

"Ahmad. Do you realize that? Sheik Ahmad," was the reply.

Five-fifteen. Sure enough, Grossman shows up at the office, looking even worse than before; completely drained, with livid lips and feverish eyes.

"So you went."

"Yes . . ." We walk back to his room and he talks. "Things are terrible there, worse than I imagined. Their well has been dry since the day before yesterday. What water they have will only last them to the end of the week, if they're lucky . . . less . . . They've made up their minds to slaughter most of their herds by then, sell the meat for what they can get in Beersheba, and maybe buy enough water to last them until the rains come."

"Did you speak to Ali?"

"I was right. It was he that you saw. He agrees with me

absolutely. If and when the government acts to help them, it'll be too late."

The evening breeze is blowing from the southwest, drying the sweat from our bodies with a chill, and whipping the sand across the ground with a rasping noise that sets the teeth on edge. We pause in front of the row of attached wooden shacks that serve as the bachelor quarters of the settlement.

"So Ali really was willing to speak with you."

"Of course. One must be willing simply to . . . make the effort."

"And Ahmad?"

Grossman laughs. "The old dog . . . would you believe it? Ali told me he's developed a taste for European women in his old age. He's actually gone so far as to place advertisements in three or four papers on the Continent for a new concubine . . . preferably young, fat, and blonde."

"But you didn't speak with him."

"It wasn't necessary."

"He refused to see you."

"Yes, but it doesn't make any difference. He'll soon be dead. Ali will be Sheik. He has most of the authority right now. . . . I tell you, this is something new. Times have changed."

"I see. And just what did Ali propose?"

"Nothing. He just told me what was happening. Of course, I could see it all with my own eyes. They're desperate. He . . . No. He didn't propose anything."

"But you did."

"No . . . That is, I suggested . . . Actually, I wanted to speak with you first."

We go inside his room that resembles nothing so much as a cell with its iron cot and tiled floor. Grossman insists on making coffee, squatting on his hams in front of the kerosene burner in the same posture as Ali against the date palm. Interesting, the similarities between them. It is never so apparent to me as now. Both of them, Arab and Jew, born in the country, reared here, feeling completely a part of it, even resemble each other physically, affecting the same drooping mustache that is probably Turkish in origin, signifying virility. The water begins to boil on the blue flame.

"Yes," repeats Grossman. "You'll see for yourself. Times have changed."

Does he really believe it? I don't know. Maybe it's so. In any case, what I as a European immigrant can never fully comprehend is the significance of that mustache or peculiar crouch; the sense of utterly belonging in this country of his birth. Whatever the truth concerning the Bedouins may be, it is that which is at the heart of Grossman's passionate desire to effect a rapprochement with the tribe. Knowing no other home, he appreciates and respects the Arab's sense of possession for a land that he loves as well. More, actually speaking fluent Arabic from his childhood, he can remember a time in the not too distant past, when the two populations lived side by side with no more than the usual conflicts that divide one man from another. The fact that he has fought them, has in fact, within my earliest memory of arriving here, fought bravely against Ahmad himself who attacked the settlement on the first night of its establishment, seems to him essentially beside the point. Being young, it is the present that counts for him—this moment alone, and the future, when the development of the land that he loves will depend first and foremost on peace.

"Sugar?"

"No thanks."

He hands me a cup, and sits on the cot which squeaks.

"You realize this is the chance we've been waiting for."

"Maybe."

"But I told you," he says. "Ali will soon be Sheik. If we can just establish good relations with him now . . ."

"But it isn't as if we haven't tried before. What about the drought four years ago? It was the same thing. They refused any help, and then—when was it? You remember. That little girl with appendicitis."

He remembers, nodding his head sadly in the diminishing light. Two summers ago, rather than trust us to take one of their children into Beersheba for an operation, they apparently preferred to see her die.

"Still, this is different," he insists. "Ali is different from the old man. He spent almost a year in Tel Aviv, did you know that? Working at the port. With Jews. That's where he learned to speak some Hebrew. For the first time, they're more than willing to accept our help."

"What exactly do you suggest?"

"What about our own well?"

"All right, so far as I understand."

"That's what I thought. We've probably more than enough water to see us all through."

"That I couldn't say."

"Well, enough for at least a week, surely, if we're careful. The rains will surely be here by then."

"Then what you want is to have us share our water."

"Exactly."

"That's, of course, a decision that neither of us can make alone."

"I realize that," he tells me. "The whole *kibbutz* will have to decide. That's why I wanted to speak with you. We'll hold a meeting."

"When?"

"You should have seen the camp. They're rationing what water they have, and the kids have sores on their lips . . . the corners of their mouths. . . . They surrounded me with tin cans, begging for water, as one would beg for alms."

He has neglected to light a lamp. In the gathering dark, his face is almost invisible, and his momentary anguish is communicated only by the timbre of his voice.

"When do you want me to call a meeting?"

"What? . . . Right away. The sooner the better. Tonight, if you can. Right after supper."

"I'll see what I can do."

"Wonderful. Oh. I almost forgot. Tell the night watch to let Ali through, will you?"

"You asked him to come here tonight?"

Under his mustache, his teeth gleam faintly as he grimaces with a stomach pang or smiles to himself in the dark.

"Yes," he tells me, "of course. About ten."

The meeting, held in the dining-hall, and attended by about sixty adult members of the settlement, is over by nine-forty-five. Grossman's motion is carried by almost two to one after Lev, the engineer who dug our artesian well four years ago, assures us that in all probability there will be enough water to supply the two communities for at least the next week if we are careful.

It's agreed that the Bedouins are to be permitted to take as much as they need every morning without charge—on one condition imposed by Zvika, who holds forth from his bench for more than five minutes, his round face shining with sweat, and his eyes bloodshot from the cigarette smoke that hangs in the air. He is a tractor driver, a man of about twenty-eight, completely bald, and intensely self-conscious about it, so that even indoors, his head is always covered by an army fatigue cap, with its peak turned up. A particularly doctrinaire and pedantic Socialist, and an author to boot, he has recently published a book comparing the life of the modern *kibbutz* to the ancient Hebrew Essenic and early Christian communes. His high-pitched voice drones on. Now, to illustrate some point he is making, he is actually quoting by heart from Philo—the Alexandrian writer of antiquity—describing the life of the Essenic communes near the Dead Sea that were so much like our own.

"For none of them wishes to have any property of his own, but rather by joining together everything without exception, they all have a common profit from it."

Grossman, glancing at his wrist watch, interrupts him impatiently:

"Philo! Who's Philo? What's this Philo got to do with it?"

"I'm discussing the principles upon which this *kibbutz* has been founded. Principles which . . ."

"But there's a motion on the floor. What's all this have to do with sharing the water with the Bedouins?"

"That's it. Aha! Exactly. Sharing . . . You are evidently proposing an equitable distribution of the water. All well and good, and in accordance with our principles. But we are dealing here with a feudal lord—a Sheik, don't forget that. What's there to guarantee that Ahmad will distribute our water fairly among his own people? How can we be absolutely sure, for example, that it's not his harem alone, or his relations—who knows—who are going to benefit. Do I have to tell you . . ."

"I've already explained," says Grossman. "Ali . . ."

"What do I care about Ali? Ahmad. Ahmad is still Sheik, and whether you remember it or not, it was Ahmad who . . ." His shrill voice breaks off, but the rest of the sentence hangs over us as tangibly as the blue smoke. It was Ahmad who ordered the surprise attack on the settlement eleven years ago, and who was responsible for the murder and mutilation of Zvika's first wife, a girl of seventeen. "As a matter of fact . . ." he resumes.

"I guarantee it," says Grossman.

"How?"

"You have my word. I guarantee a fair distribution of the water. I'll supervise myself."

Zvika shrugs. Aviva rises, yawning behind her hand, and suggests that such a guarantee be amended to the original motion. She is exhausted from working all day in the communal laundry, and wants only to be able to go to bed.

"Well?"

A show of hands, throwing a forest of shadows resembling

pruned trees against the wall. The amended motion is carried unanimously, and we adjourn.

"Congratulations," I tell Grossman.

"Thanks. Yes. It's a beginning, at least. A step in the right direction."

Outside, the wind is blowing from a blue-black sky that is ablaze with the innumerable stars of the desert night. Grossman shivers as we walk back to his room. The cold is intense. It is as if the sun today had burned away the atmosphere of the earth, exposing us to a chill from outer space itself.

"Ali ought to be here by now. Would you like to come in for a cup of coffee?"

"No thanks. I'm tired. Bed for me."

A little later, while brushing my teeth at the pump outside the row of shacks, I catch a glimpse of them both through the window of Grossman's room. They are standing in the corner, by the orange crate that serves as a bookcase, talking together with cups of coffee in their hands. Once again, their physical resemblance is striking. They are even the same height and, but for the slightly darker cast of the Bedouin's skin, might be taken for blood relatives, cousins, or even brothers perhaps, with their high cheekbones, and long mustaches that emphasize their thin lips. Are they speaking Arabic or Hebrew? I am too far away to tell. The Bedouin suddenly laughs, touching Grossman on the upper arm. It is not hard to imagine that they are recalling the memories they have of shepherding together, near Halutza. Now Grossman is laughing too, holding his nose. I was right. They are talking about shepherding—the stench of the long-haired sheep, the lonely hours spent under the shade of the cypress tree, with the shared, stale loaf of bread on the grass between them and the goat skin water bag passed from hand to hand.

Monday, just after dawn, it begins. For almost four hours now, patiently queued in the blazing sun, a long line of Bedouin women—perhaps a hundred of them or more, dressed entirely in flowing robes of black wool, with only their eyes showing, and strings of Turkish coins sewed onto their veils—draw water from the spigot outside of the cow shed. There is no sound but the twittering of the sparrows and the tinkle of coins as one by one, they bend down and fill the tin cans they have brought with them. The silence is uncanny. Occasionally, on their arms, a naked infant, covered with flies, is to be seen, but it too, as though enjoined by some mysterious command, makes no noise, but only gazes about with solemn, feverish eyes.

Grossman and I are supervising. Just from the look of him, he feels no better, worse perhaps, than last night. The exhilaration of getting his motion passed and making arrangements with Ali has worn off. Periodically, he must excuse himself to go to the latrine, and when he returns with an embarrassed smile on his ravaged face, I plead with him to go back to his room and lie down.

"No, no, it's all right. I promised . . ."

He dozes a little, stretched out in the bar of shadow cast by the overhanging roof, while the black-robed women shuffle by. In the shed, a cow lows. I too began to fall asleep, only to be abruptly awakened by a confused babble of voices, and a piercing shriek.

"What is it? What's happened?" Grossman rubs his eyes.

At the spigot, two of the women have gotten into a row. For some reason, one of them, holding up the line, evidently cannot make up her mind whether to fill up her rusty can or not. With her hands at her side, clenching and unclenching one fist, she stares at the stream of water that splashes over the hem of her robe and bare feet, while now four or five of the others flap their arms and rage about her. Then, with another shriek, she is shoved aside, stumbling against Grossman who has come up to them, shouting in Arabic at the top of his voice. Silence again, sudden and complete, broken only by the wail of an infant from somewhere in the crowd.

"What's the trouble?" I ask.

"Turn off the water. . . . Just a minute," he tells me, and then, in Arabic, speaks to the woman who has been thrown against him. In a huddle on the ground, apparently mortified by her physical contact with a strange man, she buries her veiled face in her hands and emits nothing but a high-pitched, quavering wail. It is more than a minute before he can get her to answer. Then, listening attentively, with a puzzled expression on his face, he turns to me.

"I don't understand."

"What does she say?"

"It just doesn't make sense. She says that she and her husband are very poor. They will starve because they own only two milch goats that will die of thirst unless they can get water."

"Then why doesn't she take it?"

"That's what's so confusing. She says she can't afford it."

"Are you sure?"

"Positive."

"But tell her it's free. She can take as much as she needs without charge. Didn't you explain that to Ali?"

"Of course."

"Well, didn't he tell them?"

Again, Grossman questions her, but this time she refuses to answer altogether. It is impossible to determine her age, or even the shape of her body underneath that robe. Only her eyes are visible, yellowed and contracted in the glare of sun.

"Useless . . ." Grossman straightens up. The other women have fallen back in a silent semicircle around us. "I just don't get it. There's obviously been a misunderstanding of some kind."

"What are you going to do?"

"I don't know. Ask Ali, I guess."

"Now?"

"I suppose so."

"Wait here, I'll bring the jeep and go with you."

"No, no, there's no need."

"Do as I say. You're in no condition to drive."

With one hand to his head, he closes his eyes and makes a gesture as if to shake off the weakness that has hold of him.

"I don't know," he says. "Maybe we ought to wait."

"For what?"

"They really can't afford it."

"Afford what? What are you talking about?"

"If we drive over to the camp now, we'll be considered guests. You know their laws of hospitality. They'll feel obliged to slaughter a sheep for a meal."

"You wait here."

The communal jeep is kept in the machine shop, but it takes me over twenty minutes to locate Chaim who has charge of the keys. He is working in the shack that houses our electric generator, repairing a worn fan belt. I could have spared myself the effort. By the time I drive back to the cow shed, Ali is there. He had apparently just ridden over from the encampment on a small white mare that one of the women holds by the bridle as he dismounts and shakes hands with Grossman who begins talking to him at once, in a low, anxious voice. They are speaking in Hebrew as I come up, each with his forehead almost touching that of the other, and their hands clasped behind them.

"Then you did tell them," Grossman is saying. The Bedouin nods.

"But I still don't understand. If they know we're not charging them anything, why does the woman say she can't afford it?"

"It's nothing."

"There must be a reason."

"She's talking about the tax."

"What tax?"

"A half a pound."

"For what? Whose?"

"My father's. For the use of the water."

Ali is smiling. He is having difficulty in speaking Hebrew so quickly. Now, very slowly, searching for each word, he says, "You mustn't bother yourself."

"Do you mean to tell me that your father is taxing them a half a pound per person for the use of water from our well?"

"But of course."

Grossman is silent. Behind us, an infant gives a stifled cry, and the mare tosses her head and chomps at her bit.

"Let me get this straight. . . ."

"But I have already explained," says Ali. "There's no need to concern yourself. This is—" He completes the sentence in Arabic.

" 'Our affair entirely.' "

"Yes, that's it. It's the law. The tribe must always pay the Sheik for the right to draw water from the well."

"But the water is ours."

The Bedouin gives a barely perceptible shrug.

"Don't you understand?" says Grossman. "It's impossible. It . . . what we want . . . what I promised . . . I gave my word. . . . The whole point is for us to share with all of your people fairly . . . an equal distribution."

Again, the Bedouin apparently cannot get the drift of the Hebrew. Grossman must translate.

"Equal?"

"Yes," says Grossman. "That woman, for example. What about those who can't afford it?"

"Equal?" the Bedouin repeats, and then, giving up, he lapses entirely into Arabic.

"What's he saying?" I ask Grossman.

"He says it's the law. It's always been the law. He says

it's . . . the lord's . . . his father's right as Sheik to tax them, just as it was his father's before him, and before that, long before. . . ."

"Before what?"

"He didn't say."

I glance at the Bedouin who is looking beyond me, beyond the sloping tin roof of the cow shed and the date grove, toward the desert where the shadows are diminishing as the sun slowly ascends toward noon. . . . Before. Before us, is of course what he means; long before our possession of the land, our settlement and government, when free, or at least subject only to his own law, the Bedouin roamed the desert that belonged to him alone.

"No," says Grossman. "It's out of the question. At the meeting, I promised . . ." and then, in a final effort to make himself understood, he too continues in Arabic.

Before he has finished, the sun has reached its zenith. His eyes are glazed, his face streaked with sweat. The Bedouin says nothing until, with a hopeless gesture, one palm upraised, he abruptly turns on his naked heel and walks with dignity toward the waiting mare. The little horse takes a mincing step as he swings himself into the wooden saddle, and shouts a word of command to the waiting women, one of whom catches his reins as he leads them away. For almost a minute after they are out of sight, their dust hangs in the air. Grossman coughs, and with averted eyes and saying nothing, goes down on one knee to the spigot, where he catches a few drops of water that cling to the spout, and moistens his parched lips.

Tuesday and Wednesday. Not a cloud. No sign of rain. The colorless sky is empty but for the flocks of ravens that wheel in gigantic circles above the Bedouin camp. From morning to night they are to be seen like spots before the eyes, the symptom of some madness induced by the heat of the sun. Now there can be no doubt of it; without water, the Bedouins are slaughtering the remainder of their herds.

Although I am sure he is aware of what is happening, Grossman makes no mention of it. All day Tuesday he is too sick even to get out of bed. Some of the women take turns bringing him tea and toast, and emptying his bedpan, and for the rest of the time, he lies perfectly still, with his face to the wall. Then, as is sometimes the case, on Thursday morning, although greatly weakened, his stomach spasms have subsided sufficiently for him to get up. Restless and inordinately thirsty, he haunts my office where I am busy writing a letter to *Tnuva,* the co-operative marketing organization of the *kibbutzim* that is negotiating with us for the export of our dates overseas. For what seems to be an hour, he sits by the window facing south, sucking on an orange and brushing away the flies that settle on his face and arms.

"What do you think?" he asks at last. "I suppose it's really Ahmad's fault."

I put down my pen. "I guess so."

"Still, it's a shame. There must be something that can be done."

Then, for a while longer, he is silent again. A ray of sunlight, riddled with dust, illuminates his face. In the past few days he has lost weight and looks somehow five years younger and more vulnerable than he really is—twenty-six or twenty-seven at the most. The drooping mustache seems more of an affectation than ever, a pretense of manhood pasted on by a kid.

"I don't suppose Ali was here while I was sick."

"No."

"No, I didn't think so. He'll never come back now. Strange. How well it was going that night when he and I had coffee in my room. Ai, if you only knew how sick of it all I am!"

"Of what?"

"This . . . hatred. Did you know that eleven years ago, the night of the attack, I was the one who found Chava?"

"Chava?"

"You remember. Zvika's wife."

"Chava. Yes."

"She was sleeping in her tent when they came. They went at her with their knives when she was still alive. I've never told Zvika, of course, but she was still alive when I found her. Sometimes, you know, I still . . . have dreams."

"But you don't hate them."

"The Bedouins? I did. Oh, how I did. It's just—how can I possibly explain it? I told you. It makes me sick. All these years, one thing bringing another . . . endless."

More silence. He rises abruptly from his chair.

"Who can say? I wonder if it'll do any good now."

"What's that?" I ask.

"It couldn't do any harm."

"What?"

"It might still help. You never know."

"I see. You want to go to their camp and try to speak with Ali again."

"Yes."

Now it is my turn to say nothing. He shreds the pulp from the orange rind with his teeth.

"It'll be unofficial, of course. No one here will ever know, except you and me."

"Then why tell me?"

"Because I thought you understood. Don't you see? It's better than not doing anything . . . letting it go on and on. What is there to lose?"

"I don't know."

"Nothing, I tell you. Come with me," he says. "You'll see."

I screw on the top of the fountain pen. My sweating wrist has smudged the ink on the letter. It will have to be done over again. "If that's what you really want."

"Yes."

We take the jeep. South of the settlement, there is only a narrow dirt track that eventually leads to the Egyptian border, just north of Nitzana. Surrounded by the white rocks, we are in the valley of the bones, but even here, in the mouths of the wadis, there is still some scrub vegetation left alive, a gray-green stubble incrusted by the white shells of countless snails. Not a tree is to be seen.

"How far now?"

"A half a kilometer. Less," Grossman shouts. Ahead of us, and to the left, where the track intersects with still another narrower path that leads between the rocks, he slows down.

"Their well."

It takes me a moment to be able to distinguish the ruin as a ring of man-raised stones, about knee-high and plastered together with sun-baked mud. He shrugs and drives on, now off the track itself, and up the floor of a huge wadi that runs parallel to the path among the rocks. When he stops, only one black tent can be seen to our right. The rest are apparently hidden around the bend of the wadi walls that are over ten feet tall.

"Where is everybody?"

"Hiding," Grossman explains.

"Are they afraid?"

"It's just the way they are with strangers."

"Well, there's Ali, at any rate."

"Where?"

He is standing with another man in the shadow of a huge boulder about fifty yards away, near the half-skinned carcasses of four or five freshly-slaughtered sheep that lie on the ground covered by a cloud of flies. The blood and flies, the cry of the ravens whose shadows flit across the ground, even the untended fire of dried camel dung smoking in front of the tent give the impression that some kind of sudden catastrophe has overwhelmed the camp. The naked child completes the picture. A little boy, perhaps six years old, with a swollen belly and shaved skull, emerges from the tent at our approach with a tin can in his hands. "Brandied Apricots"—printed in English, coming from God knows where—part of the label is clearly visible as he thrusts it before us, begging for water without a sound.

"Give him your canteen," whispers Grossman, "and wait here."

He starts forward. The child, for some reason, refuses to drink from the canteen itself. I must pour the water into the rusty can, but there is too much of it, and it spills to the ground.

"Wait!" I cry, but it is too late. He has already turned and disappeared once more into the tent. Now Grossman is talking, rapidly and in an undertone to Ali, in Arabic, standing with the bloody carcass of the sheep on the ground between them. The second Bedouin has taken a little step to the left, and for the first time, I can see him clearly.

It's the old man himself, Ahmad, the Sheik, fatter and older than I remember him, with a fuller beard that has turned completely gray. Still, unmistakably, it is he; carrying himself erect, with his shoulders back, and one hand playing with the hilt of a silver dagger stuck in the yellow sash around his waist. Ali has begun to talk too, for the first time, in a loud, clear voice. The old man glances at him, and either because the sun is in his eyes, or because something his son has said amuses him, he screws up his face and shows his teeth in a grimace that could be taken for a smile.

Behind me, the child, or someone, stirs in the tent, and when again, I look around, what happens next, happens so quickly that it is only later, in retrospect, that I can visualize it all as a piece. Ali is talking, gesturing with his hands, and suddenly, without warning, Grossman has lunged at him, slipping on the bloody ground, so that he is only able to give the Bedouin a glancing blow on the right cheek with his fist. They are down, the both of them, and for the moment, incredulous, neither I nor the old man can make a move. He is still grimacing, the smile frozen on his face, his fingers spread on the hilt of the knife. A moment more, and both of us still remain where we are. Grossman is the first to get to his feet, staring stupidly down at the Bedouin who holds his hand to his cheek and rocks his head slightly from side to side. When I come up, the old man retreats another step to the left.

"What's happened?" I ask.

No answer. "What is it?" Still no response. With his mouth open and the same stupefied expression on his face, Grossman reaches out his hand with the evident intention of helping Ali to his feet. "Tell me," I repeat. The hand smeared with sheep's blood, is still extended, but now the Bedouin drags himself back on his elbows and spits on the ground with disgust.

"He blames us for everything," says Grossman, getting behind the wheel of the jeep. "The fact that they've lost their herds . . . this morning, a child died . . . everything. There was nothing I could say. He says his father is right. We've taken their land, and now deny them water."

He tries to turn on the ignition but fumbles with the keys. His hand is trembling. I glance up. The two Bedouins are standing in front of the tent. Something apparently has struck them as funny. The old man, at least, is laughing deep in his throat, with his head thrown back and his hand still on the hilt of his dagger.

"Why did you hit him?" I ask.

The engine starts with a roar. I have to repeat the question.

"Ah, dog," Grossman replies, looking away. "What else could I do? He called me a dog of a Jew."

Theme or Purpose

In the notes, we have stressed that the author of a short story makes his point through several techniques. In a good short story, the author usually does not state his main theme directly but dramatizes it. His dramatization can take many forms. He may present a brief image or picture, a fleeting scene, a minor conflict, the juxtaposition of two things that seem dissimilar, a seemingly irrelevant event, etc. Every short story writer uses some or all of these techniques. Often, these devices indicate to the reader *how* he should read the story. Often, they replace direct statement so that if the reader misses these guides, he may well miss the full significance of the story. In "The Well," some of these devices are:

1 Ali's shooting of the colt
2 Micah's sympathy for the colt
3 The oppressive heat, the overpowering silence
4 Grossman's cramps and dysentery
5 The drought itself
6 The incident of the beautiful fourteen-year-old Bedouin girl
7 Grossman's physical similarity to an Arab, mentioned twice
8 Ahmad's use of the tax
9 The dried-up Arab well, the plentiful Israeli well
10 Grossman's memory of the mutilated Chava, Zvika's first wife
11 The naked child, with swollen stomach, holding a tin can marked "Brandied Apricots"

All these touches are important, but let us take one, the description of Grossman, and examine its application to the theme. First, let us list some of Grossman's qualities:

a His name
b His way of crouching
c His mustache
d His fluency in Arabic
e His passionate love for the land and his kind of life
f His recognition of his enemy's point of view
g His skin color, height, general physical appearance

In all these qualities, Grossman and Ali are never far apart. The two should rightfully share what they have because they are almost brothers. Yet despite their similarities and physical resemblance, their interests cannot merge. Like Cain and Abel, they must remain enemies. This is, of course, their common tragedy.

Thus, the description of Grossman—the carefully selected details—indicates the theme of the story: that men who are so close are nevertheless separated by racial or nationalistic origin; that the Jew and the Arab, with so much in common, will remain apart as enemies at least until the two cultures are brought together in attitudes.

Now apply to the theme of the story some of the details listed above. Ask yourself how they enrich the story and give it thickness and substance. In particular, relate to the theme the incident of the young Bedouin girl, and take note of the experience of Micah with the camel. These two incidents are almost short-short stories in themselves, and yet they are not irrelevant; they help to bring out the theme. Also, how does the tax that Ahmad levies indicate a great deal about the Arab mentality? Finally, what is suggested by the contrast between the condition of the Israeli well and the condition of the Arab well?

Characterization

1 The characters in a story are not separate from the theme of that story. Frequently, a theme is stated *through the characters themselves;* that is, the author will suggest the point of his story through the presence, the frame of mind, or sometimes the gestures, of a character. How is this done with Ali, Grossman, and Ahmad?

2 Very often what the character *is* also relates to the theme. For instance, Ahmad is a domineering, patriarchal figure in contrast to Grossman, who is egalitarian. What does this tell us about the theme of the story?

Further Aspects

1 Think about the theme in terms of a conflict between the old and the new, the superstitious and the "progressive," the autocratic and the free, the familiar and the foreign. In this conflict, where do the author's sympathies lie? Are they clearly in one area only?

2 Does Nissenson's sympathy, in your opinion, distort the reality of the story's conflict as you have understood it from your past reading experience or from your actual direct experience with it?

3 One critic, Bernard Bergonzi, says of this story: "[It] pins down in a single incident the whole tragedy of present-day Arab-Israeli relations." Do you agree with this evaluation?

SIX

STYLE AND POINT OF VIEW

Style is surely the most elusive of all qualities, and therefore we have kept it for the last. It is difficult to justify the inclusion of some writers in a category called style while excluding others, since all writers obviously have a style. Whether good or bad, a writer's style is his own.

All writers, then, have their verbal mannerisms, their technical devices, their gestures and hints, their reliance on certain kinds of detail. But some writers flaunt them, as it were. Consider, for example, Dylan Thomas's deliberate use of a hazy screen around his material, Henry James's conscious disguise of essentially commonplace material to make it appear mysterious, or James Purdy's considered flattening out of his prose, a studied avoidance of image and metaphor to create a sense of aridity and absence of feeling.

Many writers whom we have included in other categories are also stylists in a similar sense and might have been considered here—for instance, Vladimir Nabokov, Graham Greene, Ernest Hemingway, Katherine Anne Porter, William Faulkner. These writers are stylists of great note, but other qualities in their work appear more essential, and therefore we say that style is subordinate rather than predominant. In their stories, frequently, style creates atmosphere; at best, the two elements are difficult to separate.

The two extremes of stylists are always easy to recognize. There are those who are deliberate stylists like Henry James, Joseph Conrad, or Dylan Thomas and those whose styles are commonplace, like Jack London, Sherwood Anderson, Ambrose Bierce, and Liam O'Flaherty. It is the writers who fall in between who create the difficulties. What makes them stylists?

Here are some helpful questions to keep in mind as you read:

1 What function does the author's particular style serve in conveying his theme (or what you think his theme is)? This is of course the most important question we can ask, since style is functional. If it is simply decorative, the work usually suffers.
2 Is the author's choice of a style appropriate to the material? That is, would another type of style—ornate instead of simple, flat instead of rich—have served as well, or better?

3 Exactly what constitutes that particular author's style? How does he achieve whatever you feel he has gained? Some elements for consideration are: sentence structure (long, short, simple, complex), adjectives and adverbs (abundant, spare), use of figurative language, especially metaphor, imagery (the amount, the type), recurring patterns of words and phrases, type of vocabulary, economy or waste in language, sense impressions, verbs (active, passive, loud, soft). Once you have determined some of these qualities, you might consider how they relate to character and theme.

4 How does the author use dialogue? Is dialogue a considerable factor, or does he avoid it? Do his people speak naturally or artificially (that is, in a stylized fashion)? How is dialogue related to character and atmosphere?

5 How does the author convey his tone? That is, how does he make you feel the way you do about his characters and ideas? Does he keep a distance between himself and them, between himself and you? Or do you sense his presence at every moment?

Another aspect of fiction, often treated separately in some critical texts, is *point of view*. Stated simply, it is a term for who tells the story and how the story gets told. Because it is bound up with who tells the story, point of view could have been considered in the section on character—obviously, the nature and personality of the narrator will determine in part what is seen and how it is seen. But because it also is bound up with how the story gets told, point of view is intimately connected with style. It is in this section that we think it should be examined, for ultimately the "how" of a story seems to us more important than the "what," though it would be better not to separate the two sides of the same coin.

If we think of style as the sound of the author's voice (that is, as the mode of utterance rather than the tone), point of view may be likened to the author's vision, that is, the angle from which the events are seen or narrated—from the outside, from the inside, from above or below. And the specific relationship between voice and vision is this: whatever the particular voice may be—tenor or bass, light or dark, gentle or tough—the vision should suit the voice. The questions on point of view after each story in this section should clarify this principle.

Before turning to these stories, you should familiarize yourself with the four basic "angles of vision," or points of view. They will help you in appreciating and evaluating what a writer is trying to do.

Of the four, the most commonly used is the *omniscient* point of view, in which the author himself tells the story in the third person. As the name implies, the narrator knows everything about everyone in the story and can bring into play as much of that knowledge as he chooses—he may tell almost all or almost nothing. He may, at will, move in and out of the minds and hearts of his creations. He may make asides, interpret behavior, comment on the action, even address the reader directly. Perhaps this technique is the most "natural" of the four since it is an outgrowth of the anecdotal manner. Which stories that you have read so far are narrated from the omniscient point of view?

The second most commonly used is the *first-person* point of view. If a writer chooses this angle of vision, he must decide whether the "I" is to be a major or minor character, protagonist or observer, or someone merely repeating a narrative he has heard at second hand. If the "I" is a main character, we are likely to identify with him or at least take interest in his fate. This technique is likely to leave very little inert; the sense of immediacy, of something happening of a personal nature, gives this technique a dramatic quality that third-person narrative derives from dialogue. The author also has the advantage of being able to reveal character through dialect, special idiom, or characteristic rhythms rather than describing it discursively and directly, as the omniscient method so often demands. Of course, the reader must be alert to the narrator's limitations and prejudices and must sometimes reinterpret his version of people and events or fill in where there have been significant omissions. If the "I" is a minor character who merely observes or repeats, he is likely to be more objective, more clear-sighted, and more ironic than the central character who is speaking in his own person. Of course, what is presented will depend upon the degree of distance possible to the narrator: the closer he is to the chief character, the less objective he is going to be; the further away, the more objective, although not necessarily the more perceptive.

Shadings and variations of these points of view have developed as the story has become more sophisticated. In a modification of the omniscient point of view, there is the narrative related from the vision of a single character used by the author as a central observer or central intelligence through whom anything is cleared. We might call this the *observer's* point of view, though other labels would do as well. All events and people are filtered through the sensibility of this central observer, and we are allowed to know no more than he can see or sense. He is in a position to tell the reader what he himself thinks or feels about himself or about anything or anyone else, but not what other characters feel or think unless they reveal their thinking or feeling to him through deed or dialogue. This technique, because it arises from the experience of one individual, creates at its best a sense of unity and realism that other techniques rarely approach; at the same time, the limitations of the individual experience reduce the field of vision and do not allow the character at sometimes vital junctures of the story to tell us what we may want to know about the responses of the other characters.

Finally, there is what is known as the *objective* point of view. Though it too is third-person narrative like the omniscient point of view, the author using this technique refrains from making asides, commenting on the action, or addressing the reader. The author becomes a seeing eye that reports but does not interpret. It is as though the action moved through a vacuum. It is up to the reader to infer the "meaning" of the events reported. This method forces the reader to participate more actively in the story than other techniques do because he is not told what he might think or feel, but instead, must derive his conclusions from the action itself or the dialogue itself. For introspective characters or for stories with little movement, obviously this method is not the most suitable. It works best where speed and tautness are needed, such as for example, in the stories of Ernest Hemingway or Jack London.

Each method has its advantages and shortcomings. The angle of vision an author strikes should depend upon such factors as the imperatives of setting, mood, plot, character, and theme. In the end, the success of a given story depends upon how craftily these elements have been welded together into a coherent unit.

IL PLOE:R DA MO KOE:R

Hortense Calisher

I was taught to speak French *with* tears. It was not I who wept, or the other girls in my high-school class, but the poet Verlaine—the one who wrote "Il plœ:r dã mõ kœ:r." Inside forty slack American mouths, he wept phonetically for almost a semester. During this time, we were not taught a word of French grammar or meaning—only the International Phonetic Alphabet, the sounds the symbols stood for, and Verlaine translated into them. We could not even pick up the celebrated pen of our aunt. But by the time Verlaine and our teacher Mlle. Girard had finished with us, we were indeed ready to pick it up, and in the most classically passionate accents this side of the Comédie Française.

Mlle. Girard achieved her feat in this way. On the very first morning, she explained to us that French could never be spoken properly by us Anglo-Saxons unless we learned to reanimate those muscles of the face, throat, *poitrine* that we possessed—even as the French—but did not use. Ours, she said, was a speech almost without lilt, spoken on a dead level of intonation, "like a sobway train."

"Like this," she said, letting her jaw loll idiotically and choosing the most American subject she could find: "Ay wahnt sahm ay-iss cream." French, on the other hand, was a language *passionné* and *spirituel,* of vowels struck without pedal, of "l"s made with a sprightly tongue tip—a sound altogether unlike our "l," which we made with our tongues plopping in our mouths. By her manner, she implied that all sorts of national differences might be assumed from this, although she could not take the time to pursue them.

She placed a wiry thumb and forefinger, gray with chalk dust, on either side of her mouth. "It is these muscles 'ere I shall teach you to use," she said. (If that early we had been trained to think in phonetic symbols, we would have known that what she had actually said was "mœsl̩z.") When she removed her hand, we saw that she had two little, active, wrinkling pouches, one on either side of her mouth. In the ensuing weeks I often wondered whether all French people had them, and we would get them, too. Perhaps only youthful body tone saved us, as, morning after morning, she went among us pinching and poking our lips into grimaces and compelling sudden ventriloquisms from our astonished sinuses.

As a final coup, she taught us the classic "r." "Demoiselles," she said, "this is an *élégance* almost impossible for Americans, but you are a special class—I think you may do it." By this time, I think she had almost convinced herself that she had effected somatic changes in our Anglo-Saxonism. *"C'est produit,"* she said, imparting the knowledge to us in a whisper, "by vibr-rating the uvula!"

During the next week, we sat there, like forty purring Renaults, vibrating our uvulas.

Enfin came Verlaine, with his tears. As a supreme exercise, we were to learn to declaim a poem by one of the famous harmonists of France, and we were to do it entirely by ear. (At this time, we knew the meaning of not one word except *"ici!"* with which, carefully admonished to chirp "œp, not down!" we had been taught to answer the roll.) Years later, when I could *read* French, I came upon the poem in its natural state. To my surprise, it looked like this:

Il pleure dans mon coeur
Comme il pleut sur la ville.
Quelle est cette langueur
Qui pénètre mon coeur?

O bruit doux de la pluie
Par terre . . .

And so on. But the way it is engraved on my heart, my ear, and my uvula is something else again. As hour after hour, palm to breast, wrist to brow, we moaned like a bevy of Ulalumes, making the exquisite distinction between *"pleure"* and *"pleut,"* sounding our "r" like cat women, and dropping "l"'s liquid as bulbuls, what we saw in our mind's eye was this:

il plœ:rə dɑ̃ mɔ̃ kœ:r
kɔm il plø syr lɑ vil
kɛl ɛ sɛtə lɑ̃gœ:r
ki penɛtrə mɔ̃ kœ:r

o bryi du də lɑ plyi
pɑr te:r . . .

And so on.

Late in the term, Mme. Cécile Sorel paid New York a visit, and Mlle. Girard took us to see her in *La Dame aux Camélias.*

Sorel's tea gowns and our own romantic sensibilities helped us to get some of her phthisic story. But what we marvelled at most was that she sounded exactly like us.

L'envoi comes somewhat late—twenty years later—but, like the tragic flaw of the Greeks, what Mlle. G. had planted so irrevocably was bound to show up in a last act somewhere. I went to France.

During the interim, I had resigned myself to the fact that although I had "had" French so intensively—for Mlle. G. had continued to be just as exacting all the way through grammar, *dictée,* and the rest of it—I still did not seem to "have" it. In college, my accent had earned me a brief eminence, but, of course, we did not spend much time *speaking* French, this being regarded as a frivolous addiction, the pursuit of which had best be left to the Berlitz people, or to tacky parlor groups presided over by stranded foreign widows in need of funds. As for vocabulary or idiom, I stood with Racine on my right hand and Rimbaud on my left—a *cordon-bleu* cook who had never been taught how to boil an egg. Across the water, there was presumably a nation, *obscurcie de miasmes humains,* that used its own speech for purposes of asking the way to the bathroom, paying off porters, and going shopping, but for me the language remained the vehicle of de Vigny, Lamartine, and Hugo, and France a murmurous orchestral country where the *cieux* were full of *clarté,* the oceans sunk in *ombres profondes,* and where the most useful verbs were *souffler* and *gémir.*

On my occasional encounters with French visitors, I would apologize, in a few choicely carved phrases that always brought compliments, for being out of practice, after which I retired—into English if *they* had *it,* into the next room if they hadn't. Still, when I sailed, it was with hope—based on the famous accent—that in France I would somehow speak French. If I had only known, it would have been far better to go, as an underprivileged friend of mine did, armed with the one phrase her husband had taught her—*"Au secours!"*

Arriving at my small hotel in Paris, I was met by the owner, M. Lampacher, who addressed me in arrogantly correct English. When we had finished our arrangements in that language, I took the plunge. *"Merci!"* I said. It came out just lovely, the "r" like treacle, the *"ci"* not down but up.

"Ah, Madame!" he said. "You speak French."

I gave him the visitors' routine.

"You mock, Madame. You have the accent *absolument pur.*"

The next morning, I left the hotel early for a walk around Paris. I had not been able to understand the boy who brought me breakfast, but no doubt he was from the provinces. Hoping that I would not encounter too many people from the provinces, I set out. I tramped for miles, afloat upon the first beatific daze of tourism. One by one, to sounds as of northern lights popping and sunken cathedrals emerging, all the postcards were coming true, and it was not until I was returning on the bus from Chaillot that, blinking, I listened for the first time that day.

Two women opposite me were talking; from their glances, directed at my plastic rain boots, they were talking about me. I was piqued at their apparent assumption that I would not understand them. A moment later, listening with closed eyes, I was glad that they could not be aware of the very odd way in which I was not understanding them. For what I was hearing went something like this: "rəgɑrd lɑmerikɛn se kautʃu sɛkõvnɑbl sɑ nɛspɑ purlɑ̃sɑbl õ pøvwɑrlesulje"

"ɑ ɛl nəsõpɑvremɑ̃ ʃik lezɑmerikɛn ʃɑkynrəsɑ̃blɑlotr"

"ɑ wi [Pause] tykonɛ mɑri lɑ fijœl də mõ dəmi frɛr ɑ̃dre səlwi [or sɛl] ɑvɛk ləbuk tylɑrɑ̃kõtre ʃemwɑ ɑlo:r lœdi swɑ:r ɛl [or il] ɑ fɛt yn foskuʃ"

Hours later, in my room, with the help of the dictionary and Mlle. G.'s training in *dictée,* I pieced together what they had said. It seemed to have been roughly this: "*Regarde, l'Américaine, ses caoutchoucs. C'est convenable, ça, n'est-ce-pas, pour l'ensemble. On peut voir les souliers.*"

"*Ah, elles ne sont pas vraiment chics, les Américaines. Chacune ressemble à l'autre.*"

"*Ah, oui.* [Pause] *Tu connais Marie, la filleule de mon demi-frère André—celui* [*or celle*] *avec le bouc. Tu l'as rencontré chez moi. Alors, lundi soir, elle* [or *il*] *a fait une fausse couche!*"

One of them, then, had thought my boots convenient for the ensemble, since one could see the shoes; the other had commented on the lack of real chic among American women, who all resembled one another. Digressing, they had gone on to speak of Marie, the goddaughter of a stepbrother, "the one with the *bouc.* You have met him [or her, since one could not tell from the construction] at my house." Either he or Marie had made a false couch, whatever that was.

The latter I could not find in the dictionary at all. "*Bouc*" I had at first recalled as "*banc*"—either André or Marie had some kind of bench, then, or pew. I had just about decided that André had a seat in the Chamber of Deputies and had made some kind of political mistake, when it occurred to me that the word had been "*bouc*"—goatee—which almost certainly meant André. What had he done? Or Marie? What the hell did it mean "to make a false couch"?

I sat for the good part of an hour, freely associating—really, now, the goddaughter of a stepbrother! When I could bear it no longer, I rang up an American friend who had lived in Paris for some years, with whom I was to lunch the next day.

"Oh, yes, how are you?" said Ann.

"Dead tired, actually," I said, "and I've had a slight shock. Listen, it seems I can't speak French after all. Will you translate something?"

"Sure."

"What does to '*faire une fausse couche*' mean?"

"Honey!" said Ann.

"What?"

"Where are you, dear?" she said, in a low voice. "At a doctor's?"

"No, for God's sake, I'm at the hotel. What's the matter with you? You're as bad as the dictionary."

"Nothing's the matter with *me,*" said Ann. "The phrase just means 'to have a miscarriage,' that's all."

"Ohhhh," I said. "Then it was Marie after all. Poor Marie."

"*Are* you all right?"

"Oh, I'm fine," I said. "Just fine. And thanks. I'll see you tomorrow."

I went to bed early, assuring myself that what I had was merely disembarkation jitters (what would the psychologists call it—transliteration syndrome?), which would disappear overnight. Otherwise it was going to be very troublesome having to retire from every conversation to work it out in symbols.

A month went by, and the syndrome had not disappeared. Now and then, it was true, the more familiar nouns and verbs did make their way straight to my brain, bypassing the tangled intermediaries of my ear and the International Phonetic Alphabet. Occasionally, I was able to pick up an unpoetically useful phrase: to buy a brassière you asked for "something to hold up the gorge with"; the French said "Couci-couça" (never

"*Comme ci, comme ça*") and, when they wanted to say "I don't know," turned up their palms and said "Schpuh." But meanwhile, my accent, fed by the lilt of true French, altogether outsoared the shadow of my night. When I did dare the phrases prepared carefully in my room for the eventualities of the day, they fell so superbly that any French vis-à-vis immediately dropped all thought of giving me a handicap and addressed me in the native argot, at the native rate—leaving me struck dumb.

New Year's Eve was my last night in Paris. I had planned to fly to London to start the new year with telephones, parties, the wireless, conversation, in a wild blaze of unrestricted communication. But the airport had informed me that no planes were flying the Channel, or perhaps anywhere, for the next twenty-four hours, New Year's Eve being the one night on which the pilots were traditionally "allowed" to get drunk. At least it *seemed* to me that I had been so informed, but perhaps I libel, for by now my passion for accurately understanding what was said to me was dead. All my pockets and purses were full of paper scraps of decoding, set down in vowel-hallucinated corners while my lips moved grotesquely, and it seemed to me that, if left alone here any longer, I would end by having composed at random a phonetic variorum for France.

In a small, family-run café around the corner from my hotel, where I had often eaten alone, I ordered dinner, successive *cafés filtrés,* and repeated doses of marc. Tonight, at the elegiac opening of the new year, it was "allowed"—for pilots and warped failures of educational snobbism—to get drunk. Outside, it was raining, or weeping; in my heart, it was doing both.

Presently, I was the only customer at any of the zinc tables. Opposite, in a corner, the *grand-père* of the family of owners lit a Gauloise and regarded me with the privileged stare of the elderly. He was the only one there who seemed aware that I existed; for the others I had the invisibility of the foreigner who cannot "speak"—next door to that of a child, I mused, except for the adult password of money in the pocket. The old man's daughter, or daughter-in-law, a dark woman with a gall-bladder complexion and temperament, had served me obliquely, and retired to the kitchen, from which she emerged now and then to speak sourly to her husband, a capped man, better-looking than she, who ignored her, lounging at the bar like a customer, I should have liked to know whether her sourness was in her words as well as her manner, and whether his lordliness was something personal between them or only the authority of the French male, but their harsh gutterals, so far from the sugarplum sounds I had been trained to that they did not even dissolve into phonetics, went by me like the crude blue smoke of the Gauloise. A girl of about fourteen—their daughter, I thought—was tending bar and deflecting the remarks of the customers with a petted, precocious insouciance. Now and then, her parents addressed remarks, either to her or to the men at the bar, that seemed to have the sharpness of reprimand, but I could not be sure; to my eye the gaiety of the men toward the young girl had a certain avuncular decorum that made the scene pleasant and tender to watch. In my own country, I loved to listen at bars, where the human scene was often arrested as it is in those genre paintings whose deceptively simple contours must be approached with all one's knowledge of the period, and it saddened me not to be able to savor those nuances here.

I lit a Gauloise, too, with a flourish that the old man, who nodded stiffly, must have taken for a salute. And why not? Pantomime was all that was left to me. Or money. To hell with my perfectionist urge to understand; I must resign myself to being no different from those summer thousands who jammed the ocean every June, to whom Europe was merely a montage of their own sensations, a glamourous old phoenix that rose seasonally, just for them. On impulse, I mimed an invitation to the old man to join me in a marc. On second thought, I signalled for marc for everybody in the house.

"To the new year!" I said, in French, waving my glass at the old man. Inside my brain, my monitor tapped his worried finger —did "*nouvelle*" come before or after "*année*" in such cases, and wasn't the accent a little "ice cream"? I drowned him, in another marc.

Across the room from me, the old man's smile faded in and out like the Cheshire cat's; I was not at all surprised when it spoke, in words I seemed to understand, inquiring politely as to my purpose in Paris. I was here on a scholarship, I replied. I was a writer. ("*Ecrivain? Romancier?*" asked my monitor faintly.)

"Ah," said the old man. "I am familiar with one of your writers. Père Le Buc."

"Père Le Buc?" I shook my head sadly. "I regret, but it is not known to me, the work of the Father Le Buc."

"Pas un homme!" he said. *"Une femme! Une femme qui s'appelle Père Le Buc!"*

My monitor raised his head for one last time. "Pɛrləbyk!" he chirped desperately. "Pɛrləbyk!"

I listened. "Oh, my God," I said then. "Of course. That is how it would be. Pearl Buck!"

"*Mais oui,*" said the old man, beaming and raising his glass. "Pɛrləbyk!"

At the bar, the loungers, thinking we were exchanging some toast, raised their own glasses in courteous imitation. "Pɛrləbyk!" they said politely. "Pɛrləbyk!"

I raised mine. "*Il pleure,*" I began, "*il pleure dans mon coeur comme il pleut. . . .*"

Before the evening was over, I had given them quite a selection: from Verlaine, from Heredia's "Les Trophées," from Baudelaire's poem on a painting by Delacroix, from de Musset's "R-r-ra-ppelle-toi!" As a final tribute, I gave them certain stanzas from Hugo's "L'Expiation"—the ones that begin "*Waterloo! Waterloo! Waterloo! Morne plaine!*" And in between, raised or lowered by a new faith that was not all brandy, into an air freed of cuneiform at last—I spoke French.

Making my way home afterward, along the dark stretches of the Rue du Bac, I reflected that to learn a language outside its native habitat you must really believe that the other country exists—in its humdrum, its winter self. Could I remember to stay there now—down in that lower-case world in which stairs creaked, cops yelled, in which women bought brassières and sometimes made the false couch?

The door of my hotel was locked. I rang, and M. Lampacher admitted me. He snapped on the stair light, economically timed to go out again in a matter of seconds, and watched me as I mounted the stairs with the aid of the banister.

"Off bright and early, hmm?" he said sleepily, in French. "Well, good night, Madame. Hope you had a good time here."

I turned, wanting to answer him properly, to answer them all. At that moment, the light went off, perhaps to reinforce forever my faith in the mundanity of France.

"*Ah, ça va, ça va!*" I said strongly, into the dark. "Couci-couça. Schpuh."

Style

As we have seen in the remarks on the stories by Thomas, James, Purdy, and Powers, style can be many different things. Chiefly, however, it is an accumulation of elements which gives an author his distinctive voice. For Thomas, style meant a certain haziness in which elements blended in a semireal, semiunreal, world; for James, style was the product of indirection, of verbal involutions, of ironic comments; for Purdy, style resulted from a seemingly casual stripping bare of both prose and human souls.

Hortense Calisher's style is possibly less dramatic, perhaps less distinctive. But the humorous nature of her material should not blind us to her stylistic felicities. Through an examination of her verbal devices, we can discover her style.

1 Explain the wit of the very first line. Why is "with" italicized? List words and phrases within the first paragraph that sustain the style.

2 Go through the story and find examples of verbal wit that constitute the style of the piece. Define the following words as part of the witty pattern: *poitrine,* uvula, bulbuls, *L'envoi,* tacky, *cordon-bleu, souffler* and *gémir,* phthisic, *au secours,* treacle, transliteration syndrome, phonetic variorum, avuncular decorum, cuneiform.

3 One reason for the success of the story lies in its sophisticated presentation of frustration, particularly in an area where everyone has been assured he can be competent if only he tries. Where is the wit within that situation? On whom is the joke? Is the narrator of the story capable of self-criticism? How does that add to the wit?

4 Why should difficulties with a foreign language strike so deeply within our psyche? What is there about a foreign tongue that is perhaps more maddening than any other phenomenon, with the possible exclusion of marriage?

5 What usually happens when an American vibrates his uvula? Is the French "r" the epitome of elegance, or are only the French convinced of that?

6 Does Miss Calisher condemn the whole system of language teaching in the United States? Does she offer a better system? What is she making fun of? Have all of us been victimized at one time or another?

7 Do you agree or disagree that an excellent accent on a few words is preferable to a poor accent on many words which no one will understand? Is any moral issue involved here?

8 Put yourself in the position of a Frenchman listening to an American murdering his language and how would you feel? Would you even think of universal brotherhood?

9 What kind of narrator does the style indicate? Is she sympathetic? If so, how does Miss Calisher make her sympathetic?

10 What does the narrator mean when she says that to learn a language you must really believe that the other country exists? Can the other country exist before you learn its language?

11 Does the fact that the narrator is a woman make any difference?

12 The story is narrated in the first person. Which elements in it would have been dissipated if the author had used the omniscient point of view? the objective?

13 Does the sex of the narrator make any difference in your reaction to the story? How do you generally feel about first-person narratives by women?

14 Do you feel you know more than the narrator at many points in this story? Does the author want you to know more? For what reason?

THE EYE

J. F. Powers

All them that dropped in at Bullen's last night was talking about the terrible accident that almost happened to Clara Beck—that's Clyde Bullen's best girl. I am in complete charge of the pool tables and cigar counter, including the punchboards, but I am not at my regular spot in front, on account of Clyde has got a hot game of rotation going at the new table, and I am the only one he will leave chalk his cue. While I chalk it and collect for games and rack the balls I am hearing from everybody how Clara got pulled out of the river by Sleep Bailey.

He is not one of the boys, Sleep, but just a nigger that's deef and lives over in jigtown and plays the piano for dances at the Louisiana Social Parlor. They say he can't hear nothing but music. Spends the day loafing and fishing. He's fishing—is the story—when he seed Clara in the river below the Ludlow road bridge, and he swum out and saved her. Had to knock her out to do it, she put up such a fight. Anyways he saved her from drownding. That was the story everybody was telling.

Clyde has got the idee of taking up a collection for Sleep, as it was a brave deed he done and he don't have nothing to his name but a tub of fishing worms. On the other hand, he don't need nothing, being a nigger, not needing nothing. But Clara is Clyde's girl and it is Clyde's idee and so it is going over pretty big as most of the boys is trying to stay in with Clyde and the rest is owing him money and can't help themselves. I chipped in two bits myself.

Clyde is just fixing to shoot when Skeeter Bird comes in and says, "Little cold for swimming, ain't it, Clyde?"

It upsets Clyde and he has to line up the thirteen ball again. I remember it is the thirteen 'cause they ain't nobody round here that's got the eye Clyde has got for them big balls and that thirteen is his special favor-ite, says it's lucky—it and the nine. I tell you this on account of Clyde misses his shot. Looked to me and anybody else that knowed Clyde's game that what Skeeter said upset his aim.

"What's eating you?" Clyde says to Skeeter, plenty riled. I can see he don't feel so bad about the thirteen getting away as he might of, as he has left it sewed up for Ace Haskins, that claims he once took a game from the great Ralph Greenleaf. "You got something to say?" Clyde says.

"No," Skeeter says, "only—"

"Only what?" Clyde wants to know.

"Only that Bailey nigger got hisself scratched up nice, Clyde."

"So I am taking up a little collection for him," Clyde says. "Pass the plate to Brother Bird, boys."

But Skeeter, he don't move a finger, just says, "Clara got banged up some, too, Clyde. Nigger must of socked her good."

None of us knowed what Skeeter was getting at, except maybe Clyde, that once took a course in mind reading, but we don't like it. And Clyde, I can tell, don't like it. The cue stick is shaking a little in his hand like he wants to use it on Skeeter and he don't shoot right away. He straightens up and says, "Well, he hadda keep her from strangling him while he was rescuing her, didn't he? It was for her own good."

"Yeah, guess so," Skeeter says. "But they both looked like they been in a mean scrap."

"That so?" Clyde says. "Was you there?"

"No, but I heard," Skeeter says.

"You heard," Clyde says. He gets ready to drop the fifteen.

"Yeah," Skeeter says. "You know, Clyde, that Bailey nigger is a funny nigger."

"How's that?" Clyde says, watching Skeeter close. "What's wrong with him?" Clyde holds up his shot and looks right at Skeeter. "Come on, out with it."

"Oh, I don't know as they's a lot wrong with him," Skeeter says. "I guess he's all right. Lazy damn nigger is all. Won't keep a job—just wants to play on the piano and fish."

"Never would of rescued Clara if he didn't," Clyde says. "And besides what kind of job you holding down?"

Now that gets Skeeter where it hurts on account of he don't work hisself, unless you call selling rubbers work or peddling art studies work. Yeah, that's what he calls them. Art studies. Shows a girl that ain't got no clothes on, except maybe her garters, and down below it says "Pensive" or "Evening in Paris." Skeeter sells them to artists, he says—he'll tell you that to your face—but he's always got a few left over for the boys at Bullen's.

Well, Skeeter goes on up front and starts in to study the slot machines. He don't never play them, just studies them. Somebody said he's writing a book about how to beat them, but I don't think he's got the mind for it, is my opinion.

Clyde is halfway into the next game when Skeeter comes back again. He has some of the boys with him now.

"All right, all right," Clyde says, stopping his game.

"You tell him, Skeeter," the boys says.

"Yeah, Skeeter, you tell me," Clyde says.

"Oh," Skeeter says, "it's just something some of them is saying, Clyde, is all."

"Who's saying?" Clyde says. "Who's saying what?"

"Some of them," Skeeter says, "over at the Arcade."

The Arcade, in case you don't know, is the other poolhall in town. Bullen's and the Arcade don't mix, and I guess Skeeter is about the only one that shows up regular in both places, on account of he's got customers in both places. I'd personally like to keep Skeeter out of Bullen's, but Clyde buys a lot of art studies off him and I can't say nothing.

After a spell of thinking Clyde says to Skeeter, "Spill it."

"May not be a word of truth to it, Clyde," Skeeter says. "You know how folks talk. And all I know is what I hear. Course I knowed a long time that Bailey nigger is a damn funny nigger. Nobody never did find out where he came from—St. Louis, Chicago, New York, for all anybody knowed. And if he's stone deef how can he hear to play the piano?"

"Damn the nigger," Clyde says. "What is they saying, them Arcade bastards!"

"Oh, not all of them is saying it, Clyde. Just some of them is saying it. Red Hynes, that tends bar at the El Paso, and them. Saying maybe the nigger didn't get them scratches on his face for nothing. Saying maybe he was trying something funny. That's a damn funny nigger, Clyde, I don't care what you say. And when you get right down to it, Clyde, kind of stuck up like. Anyways some of them at the Arcade is saying maybe the nigger throwed Clara in the river and then fished her out just to cover up. Niggers is awful good at covering up, Clyde."

Clyde don't say nothing to this, but I can tell he is thinking plenty and getting mad at what he's thinking—plenty. It's real quiet at Bullen's now.

"Maybe," Clyde says, "maybe they is saying what he was covering up from?"

"Yeah, Clyde," Skeeter says. "Matter of fact, they is. Yeah, some of them is saying maybe the nigger *raped* her!"

Bang! Clyde cracks the table with his cue stick. It takes a piece of pearl inlay right out of the apron board of the good, new table. Nobody says nothing. Clyde just stares at all the chalk dust he raised.

Then Skeeter says, "Raped her first, rescued her later, is what they is saying."

"What are you going to do, Clyde?" Banjo Wheeler says.

"Clyde is thinking!" I say. "Leave him think!" But personally I never seed Clyde take that long just to think.

"Move," Clyde says.

The boys give Clyde plenty of room. He goes over to the rack and tips a little talcum in his hands. The boys is all watching him good. Then Clyde spits. I am right by the cuspidor and can see Clyde's spit floating on the water inside. Nobody says nothing. Clyde's spit is going around in the water and I am listening to hear what he is going to do. He takes the chalk out of my hand. He still don't say nothing. It is the first time he ever chalks his cue with me around to do it.

Then he says, "What kind of nigger is this Bailey nigger, Roy?"

Roy—that's me.

"Oh, just a no-good nigger, Clyde," I said. "Plays the piano at the Louisiana Social Parlor—*some* social parlor, Clyde—is about all I know, or anybody. Fishes quite a bit—just a lazy, funny, no-good nigger . . ."

"But he ain't no *bad* nigger, Roy?"

"Naw, he ain't *that*, Clyde," I say. "We ain't got none of them kind left in town."

"Well," Clyde says, "just so's he ain't no *bad* nigger."

Then, not saying no more, Clyde shoots and makes the ten ball in the side pocket. I don't have to tell you the boys is all pretty disappointed in Clyde. I have to admit I never knowed no other white man but Clyde to act like that. But maybe Clyde has his reasons, I say to myself, and wait.

Well, sir, that was right before the news came from the hospital. Ace is friendly with a nurse there is how we come to get it. He calls her on the phone to find out how Clara is. She is unconscious and ain't able to talk yet, but that ain't what makes all hell break loose at Bullen's. It's—un-mis-tak-able ev-i-dence of preg-nan-cy!

Get it? Means she was knocked up. Whoa! I don't have to tell you how that hits the boys at Bullen's. Some said they admired Clyde for not flying off the handle in the first place and some said they didn't, but all of them said they had let their good natures run away with their better judgments. They was right.

I goes to Ace, that's holding the kitty we took up for the nigger, and gets my quarter back. I have a little trouble at first as some of the boys has got there in front of me and collected more than they put in—or else Ace is holding out.

All this time Clyde is in the washroom. I try to hurry him up, but he don't hurry none. Soon as he unlocks the door and comes out we all give him the news.

I got to say this is the first time I ever seed Clyde act the way he do now. I hate to say it, but—I will. Clyde, he don't act much like a man. No, he don't, not a bit. He just reaches his cue down and hands it to me.

"Chalk it," he says. "Chalk it," is all he says. Damn if I don't almost hand it back to him.

I chalk his cue. But the boys, they can't stand no more.

Ace says he is going to call the hospital again.

"Damn it, Clyde," Banjo says. "We got to do something. Else they ain't going to be no white woman safe in the streets. What they going to think of you at the Arcade? I can hear Red Hynes and them laughing."

That is the way the boys is all feeling at Bullen's, and they say so. I am waiting with the rest for Clyde to hurry up and do something, or else explain hisself. But he just goes on, like nothing is the matter, and starts up a new game. It's awful quiet. Clyde gets the nine ball on the break. It hung on the lip of the pocket like it didn't want to, but it did.

"You sure like that old nine ball, Clyde," I say, trying to make Clyde feel easy and maybe come to his senses. I rack the nine for him. My hand is wet and hot and the yellow nine feels like butter to me.

"Must be the color of the nine is what he like," Banjo says.

Whew! I thought that would be all for Banjo, but no sir, Clyde goes right on with the game, like it's a compliment.

A couple of guys is whistling soft at what Banjo got away with. Me, I guess Clyde feels sorry for Banjo, on account of they is both fighters. Clyde was a contender for the state heavy title three years back, fighting under the name of Big Boy Bullen, weighing in at two thirty-three. Poor old Banjo is a broken-down carnival bum, and when he's drinking too heavy, like last night and every night, he forgets how old and beat up he is and don't know no better than to run against Clyde, that's a former contender and was rated in *Collyer's Eye*. Banjo never was no better than a welter when he was fighting and don't tip more than a hundred fifty-five right now. What with the drink and quail he don't amount to much no more.

And then Ace comes back from calling up the hospital and says, "No change; Clara's still unconscious."

"Combination," Clyde says. "Twelve ball in the corner pocket."

That's all Clyde has got to say. We all want to do something, but Banjo wants to do it the worst and he says, "No change, still unconscious. Knocked out and knocked up—by a nigger! Combination—twelve ball in the corner pocket!"

"Dummy up!" Clyde says. He slugs the table again and ruins a cube of chalk. He don't even look at Banjo or none of us. I take the whisk broom and brush the chalk away the best I could, without asking Clyde to move.

"Thanks," Clyde says, still not seeing nobody.

I feel kind of funny on account of Clyde never says thanks for nothing before. I wonder is it the old Clyde or is he feeling sick. Then, so help me, Clyde runs the table, thirteen balls. Ace don't even get a shot that game.

But, like you guessed, the boys won't hold still for it no more and is all waiting for Clyde to do something. And Clyde don't have to be no mind reader to know it. He gets a peculiar look in his eye that I seed once or twice before and goes over to Banjo—to—guess what?—shake his hand. Yes sir, Clyde has got his hand out and is smiling—smiling at Banjo that said what he said.

Banjo just stands there with a dumb look on his face, not knowing what Clyde is all about, and they shake.

"So I'm yella, huh, Banjo?" That's what Clyde says to Banjo.

I don't know if Banjo means to do it, or can't help it, but he burps right in Clyde's face.

Boom! Clyde hits Banjo twice in the chin and mouth quick and drops him like a handkerchief. Banjo is all over the floor and his mouth is hanging open like a spring is busted and blood is leaking out the one side and he has got some bridgework loose.

"Hand me the nine, Roy," Clyde says to me. I get the nine ball and give it to Clyde. He shoves it way into Banjo's mouth that is hanging open and bleeding good.

Then Clyde lets him have one more across the jaw and you can hear the nine ball rattle inside Banjo's mouth.

Clyde says, "Now some of you boys been itching for action all night. Well, I'm here to tell you I'm just the boy to hand it out. Tonight I just feel like stringing me up a black nigger by the light of the silvery moon! Let's get gaiting!"

Now that was the old Clyde for you. A couple of guys reaches fast for cue sticks, but I am in charge of them and the tables, and I say, "Lay off them cue sticks! Get some two by fours outside!"

So we leaves old Banjo sucking on the nine ball and piles into all the cars we can get and heads down for the Louisiana Social Parlor. I am sitting next to Clyde in his car.

On the way Ace tells us when he called the hospital the second time he got connected with some doctor fella. Ace said this doctor was sore on account of Ace's girl, that's the nurse, give out information about Clara that she wasn't supposed to. But the doctor said as long as we all knowed so much about the case already he thought we ought to know it was of some month's standing, Clara's condition. Ace said he could tell from the way the doctor was saying it over and over that he was worried about what we was planning to do to the coon. Ace's girl must of copped out to him. But Ace said he thanked the doc kindly for his trouble and hung up and wouldn't give his right name when the doc wanted to know. We all knowed about the doctor all right—only one of them young intern fellas from Memphis or some place—and as for the some months' standing part we all knowed in our own minds what nigger bucks is like and him maybe burning with strong drink on top of it. Ace said he hoped the nurse wouldn't go and lose her job on account of the favor she done for us.

The only thing we seed when we gets to the Louisiana is one old coon by the name of Old Ivy. He is locking up. We asks him about Sleep Bailey, but Old Ivy is playing dumb and all he says is, "Suh? Suh?" like he don't know what we mean.

"Turn on them there lights," we says, "so's we can see."

Old Ivy turns them on.

"Where's the crowd," we says, "that's always around?"

"Done went," Old Ivy says.

"So they's done went," Skeeter says. "Well, if they's trying to steal that piano-playing nigger away they won't get very far."

"No, they won't get very far with that," Clyde says. "Hey, just seeing all them bottles is got me feeling kind of dry-like."

So we gets Old Ivy to put all the liquor on the bar and us boys refreshes ourselves. Skeeter tells Old Ivy to put some beer out for chasers.

Old Ivy says they is fresh out of cold beer.

"It don't have to be cold," Skeeter says. "We ain't proud."

Old Ivy drags all the bottled beer out on the bar with the other. Then he goes back into the kitchen behind the bar and we don't see him no more for a little.

"Hey, old nigger," Skeeter says. "Don't try and sneak out the back way."

"No, suh," Old Ivy says.

"Hey, Old Ivy," Clyde says. "You got something to eat back there?"

"Suh?" He just gives us that old *suh*. "Suh?"

"You heard him," Skeeter says.

"No, suh," Old Ivy says, and we seed him in the service window.

"Guess maybe he's deef," Skeeter says. "You old coon, I hope you ain't blind!" And Skeeter grabs a bottle of beer and lams it at Old Ivy's head. Old Ivy ducks and the big end of the bottle sticks in the wall and don't break. It is just beaverboard, the wall.

All us boys gets the same idee and we starts heaving the beer bottles through the window where Old Ivy was standing, but ain't no more.

"Hit the nigger baby!"

"Nigger in the fence!"

We keeps this up until we done run out of bottles, all except Skeeter that's been saving one. "Hey, wait," he says. "It's all right now, Grampaw. Come on, old boy, you can come out now."

But Old Ivy don't show hisself. I am wondering if he got hit on a rebound.

"Damn it, boy," Skeeter says. "Bring us some food. Or you want us to come back in there?"

"Suh?" It's that old *suh* again. "Yes, suh," Old Ivy says in the kitchen, but we don't see him.

Then we do. And Skeeter, he lets go the last bottle with all he's got. It hits Old Ivy right in the head. That was a mean thing Skeeter done, I think, but then I see it's only the cook's hat Old Ivy's got in his hand that got hit. He was holding it up like his head is inside, but it ain't.

The boys all laughs when they seed what Old Ivy done to fool Skeeter.

"Like in war when you fool the enemy," Clyde says.

"That's a smart nigger," I say.

"So that's a smart nigger, huh?" Skeeter says. "I'll take and show you what I do to smart niggers that gets smart with me!"

"Cut it out," Clyde says. "Leave him alone. He ain't hurting nothing. You just leave that old coon be." That is Clyde for you, always sticking up for somebody, even a nigger.

Clyde and me goes into the next room looking for a place to heave, as Clyde has got to. It is awful dark, but pretty soon our eyes gets used to it, and we can see some tables and chairs and a juke box and some beer signs on the walls. It must be where they do their dancing. I am just standing there ready to hold Clyde's head, as he is easing hisself, when I begins to hear a piano like a radio is on low. I can just barely pick it out, a couple a notes at a time, sad music, blues music, nigger music.

It ain't no radio. It is a piano on the other side of the room. I am going to go and look into it when Clyde says, "It ain't nothing." Ain't nothing! Sometimes I can't understand Clyde for the life of me. But I already got my own idee about the piano.

About then Skeeter and Ace comes in the room yelling for Clyde in the dark, saying the boys out front is moving on to the next place. We hear a hell of a racket out by the bar, like they broke the mirror, and then it's pretty still and we know they is almost all left.

Skeeter gives us one more yell and Ace says, "Hey, Clyde, you fall in?" They is about to leave when Skeeter, I guess it is, hears the piano just like we been hearing it. All this time Clyde has got his hand over my mouth like he don't want me to say we is there.

Skeeter calls Old Ivy and says he should turn on the lights, and when Old Ivy starts that *suh* business again Skeeter lays one on him that I can hear in the dark.

So Old Ivy turns on the lights, a lot of creepy greens, reds, and blues. Then Clyde and me both seed what I already guessed—it's the Bailey nigger playing the piano—and Skeeter and Ace seed it is him and we all seed each other.

And right then, damn if the nigger don't start in to sing a song. Like he didn't know what was what! Like he didn't know what we come for ! That's what I call a foxy nigger.

Skeeter yells at him to stop singing and to come away from the piano. He stops singing, but he don't move. So we all goes over to the piano.

"What's your name, nigger?" Skeeter says.

"Bailey," Sleep says, reading Skeeter's lips.

Old Ivy comes over and he is saying a lot of stuff like, "That boy's just a borned fool. Just seem like he got to put his foot in it some kind of way."

Sleep hits a couple a notes light on the piano that sounds nice and pretty.

"You know what we come for?" Skeeter says.

Sleep hits them same two notes again, nice and pretty, and shakes his head.

"Sure you don't know, boy?" Clyde says.

Sleep is just about to play them notes again when Skeeter hits him across the paws with a fungo bat. Then Sleep says, "I spect you after on account of that Miss Beck I fish out of the river."

"That's right," Skeeter says. "You spect right."

"You know what they is saying uptown, Sleep?" I say.

"I heard," Sleep says.

"They is saying," I say, "you raped Clara and throwed her in the river to cover up."

"That's just a lie," Sleep says.

"Who says it's a lie?" Clyde says.

"That's just a white-folks lie," Sleep says. "It's God's truth."

"How you going to prove it?" Clyde says.

"Yeah," I say. "How you going to prove it?"

"How you going to prove it to them, son?" Old Ivy says.

"Here, ain't I?" Sleep says.

"Yeah, you's here all right, nigger," Skeeter says, "but don't you wish you wasn't!"

"If I'm here I guess I got no call to be scared," Sleep says. "Don't it prove nothing if I'm here, if I didn't run away? Don't that prove nothing?"

"Naw," Skeeter says. "It don't prove nothing. It's just a smart nigger trick."

"Wait till Miss Beck come to and talk," Sleep says. "I ain't scared."

"No," Old Ivy says, "you ain't scared. He sure ain't scared a bit, is he, Mr. Bullen? That's a good sign he ain't done nothing bad, ain't it, Mr. Bullen?"

"Well," Clyde says. "I don't know about that. . . ."

Skeeter says, "You sure you feel all right, Clyde?"

"What you mean you don't know, Clyde?" Ace says. "Clara is knocked up and this is the bastard done it!"

"Who the hell else, Clyde?" I say. I wonder is Clyde dreaming or what.

"He ain't a bad boy like that, Mr. Bullen," Old Ivy says, working on Clyde.

"I tell you what," Clyde says.

"Aw, stop it, Clyde," Skeeter and Ace both says. "We got enough!"

"Shut up!" Clyde says and he says it like he mean it.

"Listen to what Mr. Bullen got to say," Old Ivy says.

"This is the way I seed it," Clyde says. "This ain't no open-and-shut case of rape—leastways not yet it ain't. Now the law—"

Skeeter cuts in and says, "Well, Clyde, I'll see you the first of the week." He acts like he is going to leave.

"Come back here," Clyde says. "You ain't going to tell no mob nothing till I got this Bailey boy locked up safe in the county jail waiting judgment."

"O.K., Clyde," Skeeter says. "That's different. I thought you was going to let him get away."

"Hell, no!" Clyde says. "We got to see justice did, ain't we?"

"Sure do, Clyde," Skeeter says.

Ace says, "He'll be nice and safe in jail in case we got to take up anything with him."

I knowed what they mean and so do Old Ivy. He says, "Better let him go right now, Mr. Bullen. Let him run for it. This other way they just going to bust in the jailhouse and take him out and hang him to a tree."

"The way I seed it," Clyde says, "this case has got to be handled according to the law. I don't want this boy's blood on my hands. If he ain't to blame, I mean."

"That's just what he ain't, Mr. Bullen," Old Ivy says. "But it ain't going to do no good to put him in that old jailhouse."

"We'll see about that," Clyde says.

"Oh, sure. Hell, yes!" Skeeter says. "We don't want to take the law in our own hands. That ain't our way, huh, Ace?"

"Cut it out," Clyde says.

"Maybe Miss Beck feel all right in the morning, son, and it going to be all right for you," Old Ivy says to Sleep. The old coon is crying.

So we takes Sleep in Clyde's car to the county jail. We makes him get down on the floor so's we can put our feet on him and guard him better. He starts to act up once on the way, but

Skeeter persuades him with the fungo bat in the right place, *conk*, and he is pretty quiet then.

Right after we get him behind bars it happens.

Like I say, Clyde is acting mighty peculiar all night, but now he blows his top for real. That's what he does all right—plumb blows it. It is all over in a second. He swings three times—one, two, three—and Skeeter and Ace is out cold as Christmas, and I am holding this fat eye. Beats me! And I don't mind telling you I laid down quick with Skeeter and Ace, like I was out, till Clyde went away. Now you figure it out.

But I ain't preferring no charges on Clyde. Not me, that's his best friend, even if he did give me this eye, and Skeeter ain't, that needs Bullen's for his business, or Ace.

What happens to who? To the jig that said he pulled Clara out of the river?

You know that big old slippery elm by the Crossing? That's the one. But that ain't how I got the eye.

Style

Style, here, stands for the combination of effects which Powers is trying to achieve. Through language, characterization, and a sense of place, he is attempting to illustrate what occurs in a small Southern town when Negro-white relationships are disturbed. To some extent, this story is similar to Faulkner's "Dry September." But the differences, which are great, concern us here. Powers tells the story "humorously," despite the enormity of the theme, whereas Faulkner recreates in most serious terms the full tragic horror of what he is relating. Faulkner depicts characters who assume large significance; Powers, by blunting characterization to gain humor, stylizes the story; that is, he produces effects that are dependent on no single element.

Language more than any other element seems to bring about the stylization. Perhaps people speak like this, perhaps they don't; it is not important. But their dialogue rings true as a re-creation of their lives and thoughts. Notice the first paragraph—the poor grammar, the poverty of vocabulary, the innocence of statement. All these come together to sustain the style of the place, the style of the narrator, Roy, and ultimately the style of the entire story.

1 Pick out instances of such grammar and vocabulary from the first page or so. What overall effect do they have? Does the story flow or is it slowed down?

2 What kind of people are behind this type of language? What is the overall as well as the specific impression?

3 How does Powers convey the sense of brutality that is embodied in the story? What physical facts appear to build up an image of Clyde as a brute, a sadist, a powerful egoist? How does Roy's worshipful attitude toward Clyde help build the latter's image in our minds and make it quite different from the image in Roy's?

4 How does the setting in a billiard parlor somewhere in Louisiana contribute to the overall style of the story? Powers gives instance after instance of pool playing—for what reason? For what effect? In fact, the reader must know something of the game in order to understand the language—to rack up a ball, to chalk the cue stick, to line up a ball, to make a ball in the side pocket, to get a ball on the break, and so on.

5 How does the use of such terms and the play itself operate in the story, besides producing simple effects of atmosphere and mood?

6 Why are the hangers-on so anxious to make Clyde move against Sleep Bailey? What is their interest in the lynching? Is it boredom here, like the heat in "Dry September," which causes man's inhumanity? Or is it something more?

7 Why should they concoct the rape story against Bailey? What do they gain by frightening and then murdering an innocent Negro?

8 Does Powers ask us to face some of these questions, or is everything so inconclusive that perhaps you missed the fact that the Negro was taken from the jail and lynched by the "Crossing"?

9 When you consider Clyde, you should ask yourself why he appears so reluctant to take action against Bailey. Is it that he is devoted to justice and wishes to give every man a chance before condemning him? Is Clyde hiding anything?

10 Would the story have been a better one if Powers had used either the objective or omniscient point of view? Is anything gained by the first-person narrative? Is anything gained by keeping the narrator an observer rather than a participant?

11 What does the title tell us about Powers' preference in point of view? Does the narrator indeed have a good "eye"? What does he omit that you would include if you were the narrator and not from the same part of the country?

Plot and Plot Structure

1 In this kind of story, where the action is telescoped by a narrator, the plot or plot structure is suggested rather than stated. This is, of course, a typical modern literary device and one particularly suited to the short story, which must be short. Telescoping, elision, obliqueness—all these suggest a plot that is somewhere in the careful reader's mind, but not directly stated in the story. In this connection, reconstruct what actually happens. Do not fill in every detail, but consider the main lines of development of the story. What is the sequence?

2 Fill in some of the inconclusive elements: the girl's pregnancy, the guilt or innocence of the Negro, what really occurred in the water, what finally happened to the Negro, the role of Clyde on the final page. Some of this is speculative, certainly, but Powers drops enough hints through tone or attitude to give you a fairly good idea of what occurred.

Characterization

The characters in this story are not sharply distinguished from each other, since they all share more or less the same ideals. Roy, for example, is simply an appendage of Clyde's, without having any real will of his own. This is, possibly, part of Powers' purpose—to show how little distinction there is between characters with regard to intention and belief. Thus, to discuss one is to discuss all.

1 Clyde is what kind of person? What are his ideals? What does he represent, in the story and to you?

2 Can anything change him? Do you feel his willingness to take up a collection for Bailey is an indication of his goodwill?

3 Why does Powers make him a former contender for the state heavyweight title? Does that have any bearing on our view of Clyde, or is it an extraneous fact?

4 Do you feel gratified when Clyde jams the nine ball into Banjo's mouth and then strikes him hard? Do you feel that Clyde would behave differently if he were not egged on by the others? Why does he let himself be influenced by their taunts?

5 What is so depressing about the characters in this story? What is the rather horrifying point that Powers is making?

PASTE

Henry James

"I've found a lot more things," her cousin said to her the day after the second funeral; "they're up in her room—but they're things I wish *you'd* look at."

The pair of mourners, sufficiently stricken, were in the garden of the vicarage together, before luncheon, waiting to be summoned to that meal, and Arthur Prime had still in his face the intention, she was moved to call it rather than the expression, of feeling something or other. Some such appearance was in itself of course natural within a week of his stepmother's death, within three of his father's; but what was most present to the girl, herself sensitive and shrewd, was that he seemed somehow to brood without sorrow, to suffer without what she in her own case would have called pain. He turned away from her after this last speech—it was a good deal his habit to drop an observation and leave her to pick it up without assistance. If the vicar's widow, now in her turn finally translated, had not really belonged to him it was not for want of her giving herself, so far as he ever would take her; and she had lain for three days all alone at the end of the passage, in the great cold chamber of hospitality, the dampish, greenish room where visitors slept and where several of the ladies of the parish had, without effect, offered, in pairs and successions, piously to watch with her. His personal connection with the parish was now slighter than ever, and he had really not waited for this opportunity to show the ladies what he thought of them. She felt that she herself had, during her doleful month's leave from Bleet, where she was governess, rather taken her place in the same snubbed order; but it was presently, none the less, with a better little hope of coming in for some remembrance, some relic, that she went up to look at the things he had spoken of, the identity of which, as a confused cluster of bright objects on a table in the darkened room, shimmered at her as soon as she had opened the door.

They met her eyes for the first time, but in a moment, before touching them, she knew them as things of the theatre, as very much too fine to have been, with any verisimilitude, things of the vicarage. They were too dreadfully good to be true, for her aunt had had no jewels to speak of, and these were coronets and girdles, diamonds, rubies, and sapphires. Flagrant tinsel and glass, they looked strangely vulgar, but if, after the first queer shock of them, she found herself taking them up, it was for the very proof, never yet so distinct to her, of a far-off faded story. An honest widowed cleric with a small son and a large sense of Shakespeare had, on a brave latitude of habit as well as of taste—since it implied his having in very fact dropped deep into the "pit"—conceived for an obscure actress, several years older than himself, an admiration of which the prompt offer of his reverend name and hortatory hand was the sufficiently candid sign. The response had perhaps, in those dim years, in the way of eccentricity, even bettered the proposal, and Charlotte, turning the tale over, had long since drawn from it a measure of the career renounced by the undistinguished *comédienne*—doubtless also tragic, or perhaps pantomimic, at a pinch—of her late uncle's dreams. This career couldn't have been eminent and must much more probably have been comfortless.

"You see what it is—old stuff of the time she never liked to mention."

Our young woman gave a start; her companion had, after all, rejoined her and had apparently watched a moment her slightly scared recognition. "So I said to myself," she replied. Then, to show intelligence, yet keep clear of twaddle: "How peculiar they look!"

"They look awful," said Arthur Prime. "Cheap gilt, diamonds as big as potatoes. These are trappings of a ruder age than ours. Actors do themselves better now."

"Oh, now," said Charlotte, not to be less knowing, "actresses have real diamonds."

"Some of them." Arthur spoke dryly.

"I mean the bad ones—the nobodies too."

"Oh, some of the nobodies have the biggest. But mamma wasn't of that sort."

"A nobody?" Charlotte risked.

"Not a nobody to whom somebody—well, not a nobody with diamonds. It isn't all worth, this trash, five pounds."

There was something in the old gewgaws that spoke to her, and she continued to turn them over. "They're relics. I think they have their melancholy and even their dignity."

Arthur observed another pause. "Do you care for them?" he then asked. "I mean," he promptly added, "as a souvenir."

"Of you?" Charlotte threw off.

"Of me? What have I to do with it? Of your poor dead aunt who was so kind to you," he said with virtuous sternness.

"Well, I would rather have them than nothing."

"Then please take them," he returned in a tone of relief which expressed somehow more of the eager than of the gracious.

"Thank you." Charlotte lifted two or three objects up and set them down again. Though they were lighter than the materials they imitated they were so much more extravagant that they struck her in truth as rather an awkward heritage, to which she might have preferred even a matchbox or a pen-wiper. They were indeed shameless pinchbeck. "Had you any idea she had kept them?"

"I don't at all believe she *had* kept them or knew they were there, and I'm very sure my father didn't. They had quite equally worked off any tenderness for the connection. These odds and ends, which she thought had been given away or destroyed, had simply got thrust into a dark corner and been forgotten."

Charlotte wondered. "Where then did you find them?"

"In that old tin box"—and the young man pointed to the receptacle from which he had dislodged them and which stood on a neighbouring chair. "It's rather a good box still, but I'm afraid I can't give you *that.*"

The girl took no heed of the box; she continued only to look at the trinkets. "What corner had she found?"

"She hadn't 'found' it," her companion sharply insisted; "she had simply lost it. The whole thing had passed from her mind. The box was on the top shelf of the old schoolroom closet, which, until one put one's head into it from a step-ladder, looked, from below, quite cleared out. The door's narrow and the part of the closet to the left goes well into the wall. The box had stuck there for years."

Charlotte was conscious of a mind divided and a vision vaguely troubled, and once more she took up two or three of the subjects of this revelation; a big bracelet in the form of a gilt serpent with many twists and beady eyes, a brazen belt studded with emeralds and rubies, a chain, of flamboyant architecture, to which, at the Theatre Royal, Little Peddlington, Hamlet's mother must have been concerned to attach the portrait of the successor to Hamlet's father. "Are you very sure they're not really worth something? Their mere weight alone—!" she vaguely observed, balancing a moment a royal diadem that might have crowned one of the creations of the famous Mrs. Jarley.

But Arthur Prime, it was clear, had already thought the question over and found the answer easy. "If they had been worth anything to speak of she would long ago have sold them. My father and she had unfortunately never been in a position to keep any considerable value locked up.'' And while his companion took in the obvious force of this he went on with a flourish just marked enough not to escape her: ''If they're worth anything at all—why, you're only the more welcome to them.''

Charlotte had now in her hand a small bag of faded figured silk—one of those antique conveniences that speak to us, in the terms of evaporated camphor and lavender, of the part they have played in some personal history; but, though she had for the first time drawn the string, she looked much more at the young man than at the questionable treasure it appeared to contain. ''I shall like them. They're all I have.''

''All you have—?''

''That belonged to her.''

He swelled a little, then looked about him as if to appeal—as against her avidity—to the whole poor place. ''Well, what else do you want?''

''Nothing. Thank you very much.'' With which she bent her eyes on the article wrapped, and now only exposed, in her superannuated satchel—a string of large pearls, such a shining circle as might once have graced the neck of a provincial Ophelia and borne company to a flaxen wig. ''This perhaps *is* worth something. Feel it.'' And she passed him the necklace, the weight of which she had gathered for a moment into her hand.

He measured it in the same way with his own, but remained quite detached. ''Worth at most thirty shillings.''

''Not more?''

''Surely not if it's paste?''

''But *is* it paste?''

He gave a small sniff of impatience. ''Pearls nearly as big as filberts?''

''But they're heavy,'' Charlotte declared.

''No heavier than anything else.'' And he gave them back with an allowance for her simplicity. ''Do you imagine for a moment they're real?''

She studied them a little, feeling them, turning them round. ''Mightn't they possibly be?''

''Of that size—stuck away with that trash?''

''I admit it isn't likely,'' Charlotte presently said. ''And pearls are so easily imitated.''

''That's just what—to a person who knows—they're not. These have no lustre, no play.''

"No, they *are* dull. They're opaque."

"Besides," he lucidly inquired, "how could she ever have come by them?"

"Mightn't they have been a present?"

Arthur stared at the question as if it were almost improper. "Because actresses are exposed—?" He pulled up, however, not saying to what, and before she could supply the deficiency had, with the sharp ejaculation of "No, they mightn't!" turned his back on her and walked away. His manner made her feel that she had probably been wanting in tact, and before he returned to the subject, the last thing that evening, she had satisfied herself of the ground of his resentment. They had been talking of her departure the next morning, the hour of her train and the fly that would come for her, and it was precisely these things that gave him his effective chance. "I really can't allow you to leave the house under the impression that my stepmother was at *any* time of her life the sort of person to allow herself to be approached—"

"With pearl necklaces and that sort of thing?" Arthur had made for her somehow the difficulty that she couldn't show him she understood him without seeming pert.

It at any rate only added to his own gravity. "That sort of thing, exactly."

"I didn't think when I spoke this morning—but I see what you mean."

"I mean that she was beyond reproach," said Arthur Prime.

"A hundred times yes."

"Therefore if she couldn't, out of her slender gains, ever have paid for a row of pearls—"

"She couldn't, in that atmosphere, ever properly have had one? Of course she couldn't. I've seen perfectly since our talk," Charlotte went on, "that that string of beads isn't even, as an imitation, very good. The little clasp itself doesn't seem even gold. With false pearls, I suppose," the girl mused, "it naturally wouldn't be."

"The whole thing's rotten paste," her companion returned as if to have done with it. "If it were *not*, and she had kept it all these years hidden—"

"Yes?" Charlotte sounded as he paused.

"Why, I shouldn't know what to think!"

"Oh, I see." She had met him with a certain blankness, but adequately enough, it seemed, for him to regard the subject as dismissed; and there was no reversion to it between them before, on the morrow, when she had with difficulty made a place for them in her trunk, she carried off these florid survivals.

At Bleet she found small occasion to revert to them and, in an air charged with such quite other references, even felt, after she had laid them away, much enshrouded, beneath various piles of clothing, as if they formed a collection not wholly without its note of the ridiculous. Yet she was never, for the joke, tempted to show them to her pupils, though Gwendolen and Blanche, in particular, always wanted, on her return, to know what she had brought back; so that without an accident by which the case was quite changed they might have appeared to enter on a new phase of interment. The essence of the accident was the sudden illness, at the last moment, of Lady Bobby, whose advent had been so much counted on to spice the five days' feast laid out for the coming of age of the eldest son of the house; and its equally marked effect was the despatch of a pressing message, in quite another direction, to Mrs. Guy, who, could she by a miracle be secured—she was always engaged ten parties deep—might be trusted to supply, it was believed, an element of exuberance scarcely less active. Mrs. Guy was already known to several of the visitors already on the scene, but she wasn't yet known to our young lady, who found her, after many wires and counter-wires had at last determined the triumph of her arrival, a strange, charming little red-haired, black-dressed woman, with the face of a baby and the authority of a commodore. She took on the spot the discreet, the exceptional young governess into the confidence of her designs and, still more, of her doubts; intimating that it was a policy she almost always promptly pursued.

"Tomorrow and Thursday are all right," she said frankly to Charlotte on the second day, "but I'm not half-satisfied with Friday."

"What improvement then do you suggest?"

"Well, my strong point, you know, is *tableaux vivants.*"

"Charming. And what is your favourite character?"

"Boss!" said Mrs. Guy with decision; and it was very markedly under that ensign that she had, within a few hours, completely planned her campaign and recruited her troop. Every word she uttered was to the point, but none more so than, after a general survey of their equipment, her final inquiry of Charlotte. She had been looking about, but half appeased, at the muster of decoration and drapery. "We shall be dull. We shall want more colour. You've nothing else?"

Charlotte had a thought. "No—I've *some* things."

"Then why don't you bring them?"

The girl weighed it. "Would you come to my room?"

"No," said Mrs. Guy—"bring them tonight to mine." So Charlotte, at the evening's end, after candlesticks had flickered through brown old passages bedward, arrived at her friend's door with the burden of her aunt's relics. But she promptly expressed a fear. "Are they too garish?"

When she had poured them out on the sofa Mrs. Guy was but a minute, before the glass, in clapping on the diadem. "Awfully jolly—we can do Ivanhoe!"

"But they're only glass and tin."

"Larger than life they are, *rather!*—which is exactly what's wanted for tableaux. *Our* jewels, for historic scenes, don't tell—the real thing falls short. Rowena must have rubies as big as eggs. Leave them with me," Mrs. Guy continued—"they'll inspire me. Good-night."

The next morning she was in fact—yet very strangely—inspired. "Yes, *I'll* do Rowena. But I don't, my dear, understand."

"Understand what?"

Mrs. Guy gave a very lighted stare. "How you come to have such things."

Poor Charlotte smiled. "By inheritance."

"Family jewels?"

"They belonged to my aunt, who died some months ago. She was on the stage a few years in early life, and these are a part of her trappings."

"She left them to you?"

"No; my cousin, her stepson, who naturally has no use for them, gave them to me for remembrance of her. She was a dear kind thing, always so nice to me, and I was fond of her."

Mrs. Guy had listened with frank interest. "But it's *he* who must be a dear kind thing!"

Charlotte wondered. "You think so?"

"Is *he,*" her friend went on, "also 'always so nice' to you?"

The girl, at this, face to face there with the brilliant visitor in the deserted breakfast-room, took a deeper sounding. "What is it?"

"Don't you know?"

Something came over her. "The pearls—?" But the question fainted on her lips.

"Doesn't *he* know?"

Charlotte found herself flushing. "They're *not* paste?"

"Haven't you looked at them?"

She was conscious of two kinds of embarrassment. "*You* have?"

"Very carefully."

"And they're real?"

Mrs. Guy became slightly mystifying and returned for all answer: "Come again, when you've done with the children, to my room."

Our young woman found she had done with the children that morning so promptly as to reveal to them a new joy, and when she reappeared before Mrs. Guy this lady had already encircled a plump white throat with the only ornament, surely, in all the late Mrs. Prime's—the effaced Miss Bradshaw's—collection, in the least qualified to raise a question. If Charlotte had never yet once, before the glass, tied the string of pearls about her own neck, this was because she had been capable of no such condescension to approved "imitation"; but she had now only to look at Mrs. Guy to see that, so disposed, the ambiguous objects might have passed for frank originals. "What in the world have you done to them?"

"Only handled them, understood them, admired them, and put them on. That's what pearls want; they want to be worn—it wakes them up. They're alive, don't you see? How *have* these been treated? They must have been buried, ignored, despised. They were half-dead. Don't you *know* about pearls?" Mrs. Guy threw off as she fondly fingered the necklace.

"How *should* I? Do *you?*"

"Everything. These were simply asleep, and from the moment I really touched them—well," said their wearer lovingly, "it only took one's eye!"

"It took more than mine—though I did just wonder; and then Arthur's," Charlotte brooded. She found herself almost panting. "Then their value—?"

"Oh, their value's excellent."

The girl, for a deep moment, took another plunge into the wonder, the beauty and mystery, of them. "Are you *sure?*"

Her companion wheeled round for impatience. "Sure? For what kind of an idiot, my dear, do you take me?"

It was beyond Charlotte Prime to say. "For the same kind as Arthur—and as myself," she could only suggest. "But my cousin didn't know. He thinks they're worthless."

"Because of the rest of the lot? Then your cousin's an ass. But what—if, as I understood you, he gave them to you—has he to do with it?"

"Why, if he gave them to me as worthless and they turn out precious—"

"You must give them back? I don't see that—if he was such a noodle. He took the risk."

Charlotte fed, in fancy, on the pearls, which, decidedly, were exquisite, but which at the present moment somehow presented themselves much more as Mrs. Guy's than either as Arthur's or as her own. "Yes—he did take it; even after I had distinctly hinted to him that they looked to me different from the other pieces."

"Well, then!" said Mrs. Guy with something more than triumph—with a positive odd relief.

But it had the effect of making our young woman think with more intensity. "Ah, you see he thought they couldn't be different, because—so peculiarly—they shouldn't be."

"Shouldn't? I don't understand."

"Why, how would she have got them?"—so Charlotte candidly put it.

"She? Who?" There was a capacity in Mrs. Guy's tone for a sinking of persons—!

"Why, the person I told you of: his stepmother, my uncle's wife—among whose poor old things, extraordinarily thrust away and out of sight, he happened to find them."

Mrs. Guy came a step nearer to the effaced Miss Bradshaw. "Do you mean she may have stolen them?"

"No. But she had been an actress."

"Oh, well then," cried Mrs. Guy, "wouldn't that be just how?"

"Yes, except that she wasn't at all a brilliant one, nor in receipt of large pay." The girl even threw off a nervous joke. "I'm afraid she couldn't have been our Rowena."

Mrs. Guy took it up. "Was she very ugly?"

"No. She may very well, when young, have looked rather nice."

"Well, then!" was Mrs. Guy's sharp comment and fresh triumph.

"You mean it was a present? That's just what he so dislikes the idea of her having received—a present from an admirer capable of going such lengths."

"Because she wouldn't have taken it for nothing? *Speriamo*—

that she wasn't a brute. The 'length' her admirer went was the length of a whole row. Let us hope she was just a little kind!"

"Well," Charlotte went on, "that she was 'kind' might seem to be shown by the fact that neither her husband, nor his son, nor I, his niece, knew or dreamed of her possessing anything so precious; by her having kept the gift all the rest of her life beyond discovery—out of sight and protected from suspicion."

"As if, you mean"—Mrs. Guy was quick—"she had been wedded to it and yet was ashamed of it? Fancy," she laughed while she manipulated the rare beads, "being ashamed of *these!*"

"But you see she had married a clergyman."

"Yes, she must have been 'rum.' But at any rate he had married *her*. What did he suppose?"

"Why, that she had never been the sort by whom such offerings are encouraged."

"Ah, my dear, the sort by whom they are *not*—!" But Mrs. Guy caught herself up. "And her stepson thought the same?"

"Overwhelmingly."

"Was he, then, if only her stepson—"

"So fond of her as that comes to? Yes; he had never known, consciously, his real mother, and, without children of her own, she was very patient and nice with him. And *I* liked her so," the girl pursued, "that at the end of ten years, in *so* strange a manner, to 'give her away'—"

"Is impossible to you? Then don't!" said Mrs. Guy with decision.

"Ah, but if they're real I can't keep them!" Charlotte, with her eyes on them, moaned in her impatience. "It's too difficult."

"Where's the difficulty, if he has such sentiments that he would rather sacrifice the necklace than admit it, with the presumption it carries with it, to be genuine? You've only to be silent."

"And keep it? How can *I* ever wear it?"

"You'd have to hide it, like your aunt?" Mrs. Guy was amused. "You can easily sell it."

Her companion walked round her for a look at the affair from behind. The clasp was certainly, doubtless intentionally, misleading, but everything else was indeed lovely. "Well, I must think. Why didn't *she* sell them?" Charlotte broke out in her trouble.

Mrs. Guy had an instant answer. "Doesn't that prove what

they secretly recalled to her? You've only to be silent!" she ardently repeated.

"I must think—I must think!"

Mrs. Guy stood with her hands attached but motionless.

"Then you want them back?"

As if with the dread of touching them Charlotte retreated to the door. "I'll tell you tonight."

"But may I wear them?"

"Meanwhile?"

"This evening—at dinner."

It was the sharp, selfish pressure of this that really, on the spot, determined the girl; but for the moment, before closing the door on the question, she only said: "As you like!"

They were busy much of the day with preparation and rehearsal, and at dinner, that evening, the concourse of guests was such that a place among them for Miss Prime failed to find itself marked. At the time the company rose she was therefore alone in the schoolroom, where, towards eleven o'clock, she received a visit from Mrs. Guy. This lady's white shoulders heaved, under the pearls, with an emotion that the very red lips which formed, as if for the full effect, the happiest opposition of colour, were not slow to translate. "My dear, you should have seen the sensation—they've had a success!"

Charlotte, dumb a moment, took it all in. "It *is* as if they knew it—they're more and more alive. But so much the worse for both of us! I can't," she brought out with an effort, "be silent."

"You mean to return them?"

"If I don't I'm a thief."

Mrs. Guy gave her a long, hard look: what was decidedly not of the baby in Mrs. Guy's face was a certain air of established habit in the eyes. Then, with a sharp little jerk of her head and a backward reach of her bare beautiful arms, she undid the clasp and, taking off the necklace, laid it on the table. "If you do, you're a goose."

"Well, of the two—" said our young lady, gathering it up with a sigh. And as if to get it, for the pang it gave, out of sight as soon as possible, she shut it up, clicking the lock, in the drawer of her own little table; after which, when she turned again, her companion looked naked and plain without it. "But what will you say?" it then occurred to her to demand.

"Downstairs—to explain?" Mrs. Guy was, after all, trying at least to keep her temper. "Oh, I'll put on something else and say the clasp is broken. And you won't of course name *me* to him," she added.

"As having undeceived me? No—I'll say that, looking at the thing more carefully, it's my own private idea."

"And does he know how little you really know?"

"As an expert—surely. And he has always much the conceit of his own opinion."

"Then he won't believe you—as he so hates to. He'll stick to his judgment and maintain his gift, and we shall have the darlings back!" With which reviving assurance Mrs. Guy kissed her young friend for good-night.

She was not, however, to be gratified or justified by any prompt event, for, whether or no paste entered into the composition of the ornament in question, Charlotte shrank from the temerity of despatching it to town by post. Mrs. Guy was thus disappointed of the hope of seeing the business settled—"by return," she had seemed to expect—before the end of the revels. The revels, moreover, rising to a frantic pitch, pressed for all her attention, and it was at last only in the general confusion of leave-taking that she made, parenthetically, a dash at the person in the whole company with whom her contact had been most interesting.

"Come, what will you take for them?"

"The pearls? Ah, you'll have to treat with my cousin."

Mrs. Guy, with quick intensity, lent herself. "Where then does he live?"

"In chambers in the Temple. You can find him."

"But what's the use, if *you* do neither one thing nor the other?"

"Oh, I *shall* do the 'other,'" Charlotte said; "I'm only waiting till I go up. You want them so awfully?" She curiously, solemnly again, sounded her.

"I'm dying for them. There's a special charm in them—I don't know what it is: they tell so their history."

"But what do you know of that?"

"Just what they themselves say. It's all *in* them—and it comes out. They breathe a tenderness—they have the white glow of it. My dear," hissed Mrs. Guy in supreme confidence and as she buttoned her glove—"they're things of love!"

"Oh!" our young woman vaguely exclaimed.

"They're things of passion!"

"Mercy!" she gasped, turning short off. But these words

remained, though indeed their help was scarce needed, Charlotte being in private face to face with a new light, as she by this time felt she must call it, on the dear dead kind colourless lady whose career had turned so sharp a corner in the middle. The pearls had quite taken their place as a revelation. She might have received them for nothing—admit that; but she couldn't have kept them so long and so unprofitably hidden, couldn't have enjoyed them only in secret, for nothing; and she had mixed them in her reliquary with false things, in order to put curiosity and detection off the scent. Over this strange fact poor Charlotte interminably mused: it became more touching, more attaching for her than she could now confide to any ear. How bad or how happy—in the sophisticated sense of Mrs. Guy and the young man at the Temple—the effaced Miss Bradshaw must have been to have had to be so mute! The little governess at Bleet put on the necklace now in secret sessions; she wore it sometimes under her dress; she came to feel verily a haunting passion for it. Yet in her penniless state she would have parted with it for money; she gave herself also to dreams of what in this direction it would do for her. The sophistry of her so often saying to herself that Arthur had after all definitely pronounced her welcome to any gain from his gift that might accrue—this trick remained innocent, as she perfectly knew it for what it was. Then there was always the possibility of his—as she could only picture it—rising to the occasion. Mightn't he have a grand magnanimous moment?—mightn't he just say: "Oh, of course I couldn't have afforded to let you have it if I had known; but since you *have* got it, and have made out the truth by your own wit, I really can't screw myself down to the shabbiness of taking it back"?

She had, as it proved, to wait a long time—to wait till, at the end of several months, the great house of Bleet had, with due deliberation, for the season, transferred itself to town; after which, however, she fairly snatched at her first freedom to knock, dressed in her best and armed with her disclosure, at the door of her doubting kinsman. It was still with doubt and not quite with the face she had hoped that he listened to her story. He had turned pale, she thought, as she produced the necklace, and he appeared, above all, disagreeably affected. Well, perhaps there was reason, she more than ever remembered; but what on earth was one, in close touch with the fact, to do? She had laid the pearls on his table, where, without his having at first put so much as a finger to them, they met his hard, cold stare.

"I don't believe in them," he simply said at last.

"That's exactly, then," she returned with some spirit, "what I wanted to hear!"

She fancied that at this his colour changed; it was indeed vivid to her afterwards—for she was to have a long recall of the scene—that she had made him quite angrily flush. "It's a beastly unpleasant imputation, you know!"—and he walked away from her as he had always walked at the vicarage.

"It's none of *my* making, I'm sure," said Charlotte Prime. "If you're afraid to believe they're real—"

"Well?"—and he turned, across the room, sharp round at her.

"Why, it's not my fault."

He said nothing more, for a moment, on this; he only came back to the table. "They're what I originally said they were. They're rotten paste."

"Then I may keep them?"

"No. I want a better opinion."

"Than your own?"

"Than *your* own." He dropped on the pearls another queer stare, then, after a moment, bringing himself to touch them, did exactly what she had herself done in the presence of Mrs. Guy at Bleet—gathered them together, marched off with them to a drawer, put them in and clicked the key. "You say I'm afraid," he went on as he again met her; "but I shan't be afraid to take them to Bond Street."

"And if the people say they're real—?"

He had a pause and then his strangest manner. "They won't say it! They shan't!"

There was something in the way he brought it out that deprived poor Charlotte, as she was perfectly aware, of any manner at all. "Oh!" she simply sounded, as she had sounded for her last word to Mrs. Guy; and, within a minute, without more conversation, she had taken her departure.

A fortnight later she received a communication from him, and towards the end of the season one of the entertainments in Eaton Square was graced by the presence of Mrs. Guy. Charlotte was not at dinner, but she came down afterwards, and this guest, on seeing her, abandoned a very beautiful young man on purpose to cross and speak to her. The guest displayed a lovely necklace and had apparently not lost her habit of overflowing with the pride of such ornaments.

"Do you see?" She was in high joy.

They were indeed splendid pearls—so far as poor Charlotte could feel that she knew, after what had come and gone, about such mysteries. The poor girl had a sickly smile. "They're almost as fine as Arthur's."

"Almost? Where, my dear, are your eyes? They *are* 'Arthur's'!" After which, to meet the flood of crimson that accompanied her young friend's start: "I tracked them—after your folly, and, by miraculous luck, recognised them in the Bond Street window to which he had disposed of them."

"*Disposed* of them?" the girl gasped. "He wrote me that I had insulted his mother and that the people had shown him he was right—had pronounced them utter paste."

Mrs. Guy gave a stare. "Ah, I told you he wouldn't bear it! No. But I had, I assure you," she wound up, "to drive my bargain!"

Charlotte scarce heard or saw; she was full of her private wrong. "He wrote me," she panted, "that he had smashed them."

Mrs. Guy could only wonder and pity. "He's really morbid!" But it wasn't quite clear which of the pair she pitied; though the young person felt really morbid too after they had separated and she found herself full of thought. She even went the length of asking herself what sort of a bargain Mrs. Guy had driven and whether the marvel of the recognition in Bond Street had been a veracious account of the matter. Hadn't she perhaps in truth dealt with Arthur directly? It came back to Charlotte almost luridly that she had had his address.

Style

We say that a story like "Paste" is stylized because its manner of expression is more important than the development of the narrative, the characters, or any other single aspect. In brief, manner is the story.

1 The second paragraph is a good example of stylization. All the information in this paragraph—and the amount is considerable—is presented obliquely, indirectly, as if from an angle. Try to thread your way through the prose and find out exactly what James presents here. Your understanding of the story depends to a large extent on your ability to disentangle the various characters and elements right here. If you read ahead hoping for clues, you will not find them.

2 Go on to the third paragraph and try to glean the narrative line. Who is the "honest widowed cleric"? Who is the "obscure actress"? What is the "response" that James speaks of here? What does he mean by his "reverend name and hortatory hand"?

3 The question that naturally comes to mind is: Why does James present his material so indirectly? Why doesn't he go straight to the heart of the problem and state it? The answer lies in the nature of the material itself. Is James making a "straight point"? Is there a heart to the problem? Why must he deal with nuances and hints? Is there in any sense of the word a real story or narrative line here? If James went to the so-called heart of the problem, what would he have?

4 What are some of the atmospheric effects that James is able to create through his style?

5 What type of person does Arthur Prime appear to be? How does the author's style make something of Prime, when actually James divulges very little to us?

6 Usually a tale of jewels involves a common twist: false jewels turn out to be real, and someone benefits, possibly while another loses. James forsakes this type of plot in favor of a completely different point of view. What do we understand of Arthur Prime's attitude toward the jewels? Why does he choose to lose their considerable value? What is he hiding or trying to hide?

7 Where does James himself stand in all this? Does he accept Arthur's decision to brand the necklace as paste? Or does he stand above Arthur and create another dimension?

8 This is, as you may not have realized on first reading, a very witty story. As with so many of James's tales, it is witty in an ironical sense—that is, several elements operate below the surface of the stated word and situation. One reason James could not relate this tale in a straightforward way is that the subsurface nature of his material is only capable of indirect treatment. He gains dimensions this way that he could not gain, let us say, with Jack London's method of narration, where only externals count. Can you find instances of wit where forces are operating that are unknown to the characters? Very often irony works best when you, the reader, know things that the characters are ignorant of. How does that work here? What are some of the assump-

tions you can make about Arthur Prime which seem unknown even to him? About Charlotte?

9 How does Mrs. Guy function as a witty character? Why does James make her such a self-possessed woman?

10 The end is full of ironical possibilities in which all the characters are involved in some kind of deception, deceiving either themselves or the others. Try to straighten out what actually happens—remember that everything is speculative, everything being part of the wit, of the stylization.

11 What does the last line mean? Why does James use the curious adjective "luridly" in a tale which is hardly lurid, not even close to lurid? Does the word have any connection to another strange word in this context, "morbid," which occurs twice in the final paragraph?

12 How would you characterize the point of view? Does it seem suitable to the effect James is after? Would such a point of view work in a story like "The Eye" or "Il Plœ:r Dã Mõ Kœ:r"? Give your reasons.

13 Can you see any way in which point of view (how the author feels about his material, how he chooses to present it) and stylization are connected? From this style, what generalizations can you make about James's outlook on literature, people, life itself? Who else in this volume seems closest to him? Who seems furthest from him in outlook and style?

DON'T CALL ME BY MY RIGHT NAME

James Purdy

Her new name was Mrs. Klein. There was something in the meaning that irritated her. She liked everything about her husband except his name and that had never pleased her. She had fallen in love with him before she found out what his name was. Once she knew he was Klein, her disappointment had been strong. Names do make a great difference, and after six months of marriage she found herself still not liking her name. She began using more and more her maiden name. Then she always called herself on her letters Lois McBane. Her husband seldom saw the mail arrive so perhaps he did not know, and had he known she went by her old name he might not have cared enough to feel any particular hurt.

Lois Klein, she often thought as she lay next to her husband in bed. It is not the name of a woman like myself. It does not reflect my character.

One evening at a party when there had been more drinking for her than usual, she said offhand to him in the midst of some revelry: "I would like you to change your name."

He did not understand. He thought that it was a remark she was making in drink which did not refer to anything concrete, just as once she had said to him, "I want you to begin by taking your head off regularly." The remark had meant nothing, and he let it pass.

"Frank," she said, "you must change your name, do you hear? I cannot go on being Mrs. Klein."

Several people heard what it was she said, and they laughed loudly so that Lois and Frank would hear them appreciating the remark.

"If you were all called Mrs. Klein," she said turning to the men who were laughing, "you would not like to be Mrs. Klein either."

Being all men, they laughed harder.

"Well, you married him, didn't you," a man said, "and we guess you will have to keep his name."

"If he changed his name," another of the men said, "what name would you have him change it to?"

Frank put his hand on her glass, as though to tell her they

must go home, but she seized the glass with his hand on it and drank quickly out of it.

"I hadn't thought what name I did want," she said, puzzled.

"Well, you aren't going to change your name," Frank said. "The gentlemen know that."

"The gentlemen do?" she asked him. "Well, I don't know what name I would like it changed to," she admitted to the men.

"You don't look much like Mrs. Klein," one of the men said and began to laugh again.

"You're not friends!" she called back at them.

"What are we, then?" they asked.

"Why don't I look like Mrs. Klein?" she wanted to know.

"Don't you ever look in the mirror?" one of the men replied.

"We ought to go, Lois," her husband said.

She sat there as though she had heard the last of the many possible truths she could hear about herself.

"I wonder how I will get out of here, Frank," she said.

"Out of where, dear?" he wondered. He was suddenly sad enough himself to be dead, but he managed to say something to her at this point.

"Out of where I seem to have got into," she told him.

The men had moved off now and were laughing among themselves. Frank and Lois did not notice this laughter.

"I'm not going to change my name," he said, as though to himself. Then turning to her: "I know it's supposed to be wrong to tell people when they're drunk the insane whim they're having is insane, but I am telling you now and I may tell the whole room of men."

"I have to have my name changed, Frank," she said. "You know I can't stand to be tortured. It is too painful and I am not young anymore. I am getting old and fat."

"No wife of mine would ever be old or fat," he said.

"I just cannot be Mrs. Klein and face the world."

"Anytime you want me to pull out is all right," he said. "Do you want me to pull out?"

"What are you saying?" she wanted to know. "What did you say about pulling out?"

"I don't want any more talk about your changing your name or I intend to pull up stakes."

"I don't know what you're talking about. You know you

can't leave me. What would I do, Frank, at my age?"

"I told you no wife of mine is old."

"I couldn't find anybody now, Frank, if you went."

"Then quit talking about changing our name."

"*Our* name? I don't know what you mean by *our* name."

He took her drink out of her hand and when she coaxed and whined he struck her not too gently over the mouth.

"What was the meaning of that?" she wanted to know.

"Are you coming home, Mrs. Klein?" he said, and he hit her again. Her lip was cut against her teeth so that you could see it beginning to bleed.

"Frank, you're abusing me," she said, white and wide-eyed now, and as though tasting the blood slightly with the gin and soda mix.

"Mrs. Klein," he said idiotically.

It was one of those fake dead long parties where nobody actually knows anybody and where people could be pushed out of windows without anybody's being sure until the morrow.

"I'm not going home as Mrs. Klein," she said.

He hit her again.

"Frank, you have no right to hit me just because I hate your name."

"If you hate my name what do you feel then for me? Are you going to act like my wife or not?"

"I don't want to have babies, Frank. I will not go through that at my age. Categorically not."

He hit her again so that she fell on the floor, but this did not seem to surprise either her or him because they both continued the conversation.

"I can't make up my mind what to do," she said, weeping a little. "I know of course what the safe thing is to do."

"Either you come out of here with me as Mrs. Klein, or I go to a hotel room alone. Here's the key to the house," he said, and he threw it on the floor at her.

Several of the men at the party had begun to notice what was really going on now. They thought that it was married clowning at first and they began to gather around in a circle, but what they saw had something empty and stiff about it that did not interest and yet kept one somehow watching. For one thing, Mrs. Klein's dress had come up and exposed her legs, which were not beautiful.

"I can't decide if I can go on with his name," she explained from the floor position to the men.

"Well, it's a little late, isn't it, Mrs. Klein," one of the men said in a sleepy voice.

"It's never too late, I don't suppose, is it?" she inquired. "Oh, I can't believe it is even though I feel old."

"Well, you're not young," the same man ventured. "You're too old to be lying there."

"My husband can't see my point of view," she explained. "And that is why he can't understand why his name doesn't fit me. I was unmarried too long, I suppose, to suddenly surrender my own name. I have always been known professionally and socially under my own name and it is hard to change now, I can tell you. I don't think I can go home with him unless he lets me change my name."

"I will give you just two minutes," Mr. Klein said.

"For what? Only two minutes for what?" she cried.

"To make up your mind what name you are going out of here with."

"I know, men," she said, "what the sensible decision is, and tomorrow, of course, when I'm sober I will wish I had taken it."

Turning to Frank Klein, she said simply, "You will have to go your way without me."

He looked hurriedly around as though looking for an exit to leave by, and then he looked back to her on the floor as though he could not come to a decision.

"Come to your senses," Frank Klein said unemphatically.

"There were hundreds of Kleins in the telephone directory," she went on, "but when people used to come to my name they recognized at once that I was the only woman going under my own special name."

"For Jesus Christ's sake, Lois," he said, turning a peculiar green color.

"I can't go with you as Mrs. Klein," she said.

"Well, let me help you up," he said.

She managed to let him help her up.

"I'm not going home with you, but I will send you in a cab," he informed her.

"Are you leaving me?" she wanted to know.

He did not know what to say. He felt anything he said might destroy his mind. He stood there with an insane emptiness on his eyes and lips.

Everyone had moved off from them. There was a silence from the phonograph and from the TV set which had both been going at the same time. The party was over and people were calling down to cabs from all the windows.

"Why won't you come home with me?" she said in a whisper.

Suddenly he hurried out the door without waiting for her.

"Frank!" she called after him, and a few of the men from the earlier group came over and joked with her.

"He went out just like a boy, without any sense of responsibility," she said to them without any expression in her voice.

She hurried on out too, not waiting to put her coat on straight.

She stood outside in the fall cold and shivered. Some children went by dressed in Hallowe'en costumes.

"Is she dressed as anybody?" one of the children said pointlessly.

"Frank!" she began calling. "I don't know what is happening really," she said to herself.

Suddenly he came up to her from behind a hedge next to where she was standing.

"I couldn't quite bring myself to go off," he said.

She thought for a minute of hitting him with her purse which she had remembered to bring, but she did nothing now but watch him.

"Will you change your name?" she said.

"We will live together the way we have been," he said, not looking at her.

"We can't be married, Frank, with that name between us."

Suddenly he hit her and knocked her down to the pavement.

She lay there for a minute before anything was said.

"Are you conscious?" he said crouching down beside her. "Tell me if you are suffering," he wanted to know.

"You have hurt something in my head, I think," she said, getting up slightly on one elbow.

"You have nearly driven me out of my mind," he said, and he was making funny sounds in his mouth. "You don't know what it means to have one's name held up to ridicule like this. You are such a cruel person, Lois."

"We will both change our names, if you like," she said.

"Why do you torture me?" he said. "Why is it you can't control your power to torture?"

"Then we won't think about it, we will go home," she said, in a cold comforting voice. "Only I think I am going to be sick," she warned.

"We will go home," he said in a stupid voice.

"I will let you call me Mrs. Klein this one evening, then tomorrow we will have a good talk." At the same moment she fell back on the walk.

Some young men from the delicatessen who had been doing inventory came by and asked if there was anything they could do.

"My wife fell on the walk," he said. "I thought she was all right. She was talking to me just a moment ago."

"Was it your wife, did you say?" the younger man leaned down to look at her.

"Mrs. Klein," Frank replied.

"You are Mr. Klein, then?"

"I don't understand," the older of the two young men said. "You don't look somehow like her husband."

"We have been married six months."

"I think you ought to call a doctor," the younger man said. "She is bleeding at the mouth."

"I hit her at a party," Frank said.

"What did you say your name was?" the older man asked.

"Mr. Klein. She is Mrs. Klein," Frank told them.

The two men from the delicatessen exchanged looks.

"Did you push her?" the one man asked.

"Yes," Frank said. "I hit her. She didn't want to be Mrs. Klein."

"You're drunk," the one man ventured an opinion.

Lois suddenly came to. "Frank, you will have to take me home," she said. "There is something wrong with my head. My God," she began to scream, "I am in awful pain."

Frank helped her up again.

"Is this your husband?" the one man asked.

She nodded.

"What is your name?" he wanted to know.

"It's none of your business," she said.

"Are you Mrs. Klein?" he asked.

"No," Lois replied, "I don't happen to be Mrs. Klein."

"Come on, J. D., we can't get mixed up in this," the younger man said. "Whatever the hell their names are."

"Well, I'm not Mrs. Klein, whoever you are," she said.

Immediately then she struck Frank with the purse and he fell back in surprise against the building wall.

"Call me a cab, you cheap son of a bitch," she said. "Can't you see I'm bleeding?"

Style

Style, we repeat, can mean many things. To Katherine Mansfield, it meant the placement of small details; to Hemingway, a skeletal narrative with short, jolting dialogue; to Conrad, an elaboration and embroidery that makes the reader enter a labyrinthine world. It is through his style that an author expresses his originality, his vision of the word and the world.

Like the above writers, James Purdy has forged a particular style, one that is unique in its bitter wit and off-key situations and confrontations. "Don't Call Me by My Right Name" is witty; that is, not funny in any broad sense but cutting and biting in a cynical, sarcastic manner.

1 Purdy's prose itself is witty, although it lacks verbal humor. Why are the following three lines witty?

"'We will both change our names, if you like,' she said."

"'I'm not going home as Mrs. Klein,' she said."

"I told you no wife of mine is old."

2 What qualities does the prose have? At first sight, it may not appear to be very distinguished. But reread the story, and you will become aware of the great pains the author has taken.

3 What effect does this studied prose and the eccentric wit of the situation have upon you?

4 What kind of characters are created by Purdy's style?

5 What happens to setting, characterizations, plot in this story?

6 Does it serve Purdy any purpose to have the characters half drunk (or more)? Why?

7 The name "Klein" is German for "little." Do you think this may be behind Mrs. Klein's objection to the name?

8 What is there about the style that makes this a "modern" story in the sense that the stories by O'Flaherty, London, and even Willa Cather are not modern?

9 Why is the objective point of view best suited to the theme of this story?

10 How much of the wit would be lost if either Mr. Klein or Mrs. Klein were telling the story? Where, specifically, would the witty thrusts become awkward if the angle of vision were changed?

11 What are the limitations of this point of view in dealing with the material? Do you see anything potential that is never realized because the style of narration is "objective"?

Theme or Purpose

Although style appears to predominate, there is also a very strong theme, or sense of purpose, behind the story. Much of this purpose is connected with the relationship between the sexes.

1 From this story, what would you think Purdy's views are? What is behind Mrs. Klein's rejection of her husband's name? Why is he so angry that he repeatedly strikes her?

2 Are there racial overtones to her rejection, or is the reason for her rejection something else?

3 Is there any purpose in having Mr. and Mrs. Klein marry late? Neither is young, and they have been married for only six months. Is there anything particularly vicious operating here?

Characterization

1 Are these characters recognizable? Real? In what sense? What makes them appear odd and stilted?

2 How can Purdy build a story around characters who are hardly sympathetic?

Mood as Atmosphere

We accept the significance of this story—if we accept it at all—at a level quite separate from its surface. Things fall together beneath the narrative line—somewhere in a world of bleakness and horror. Somehow Purdy can make the flesh creep in a way that a writer of detective fiction may fail to do. How does Purdy convey this feeling of horror, or remorselessness? What, ultimately, is his view of people, of their relationship, of the world?

ONE WARM SATURDAY

Dylan Thomas

The young man in a sailor's jersey, sitting near the summer huts to see the brown and white women coming out and the groups of pretty-faced girls with pale vees and scorched backs who picked their way delicately on ugly, red-toed feet over the sharp stones to the sea, drew on the sand a large, indented woman's figure; and a naked child, just out of the sea, ran over it and shook water, marking on the figure two wide wet eyes and a hole in the footprinted middle. He rubbed the woman away and drew a paunched man: the child ran over it, tossing her hair, and shook a row of buttons down its belly and a line of drops, like piddle in a child's drawing, between the long legs stuck with shells.

In a huddle of picnicking women and their children, stretched out limp and damp in the sweltering sun or fussing over paper carriers or building castles that were at once destroyed by the tattered march of other picnickers to different pieces of the beach, among the ice-cream cries, the angrily happy shouts of boys playing ball, and the screams of girls as the sea rose to their waists, the young man sat alone with the shadows of his failure at his side. Some silent husbands, with rolled up trousers and suspenders dangling, paddled slowly on the border of the sea, paddling women, in thick, black picnic dresses, laughed at their own legs, dogs chased stones, and one proud boy rode the water on a rubber seal. The young man, in his wilderness, saw the holiday Saturday set down before him, false and pretty, as a flat picture under the vulgar sun; the disporting families with paper bags, buckets and spades, parasols and bottles, the happy, hot, and aching girls with sunburn liniments in their bags, the bronzed young men with chests, and the envious, white young men in waistcoats, the thin, pale, hairy, pathetic legs of the husbands silently walking through the water, the plump and curly, shaven-headed and bowed-backed children up to no sense with unrepeatable delight in the dirty sand, moved him, he thought dramatically in his isolation, to an old shame and pity; outside all holiday, like a young man doomed for ever to the company of his maggots, beyond the high and ordinary, sweating, sun-awakened power and stupidity of the summer flesh on a day and a world out, he caught the ball that a small boy had whacked into the air with a tiny tray, and rose to throw it back.

The boy invited him to play. A friendly family stood waiting some way off, the tousled women with their dresses tucked in their knickers, the bare-footed men in shirtsleeves, a number of children in slips and cut-down underwear. He bowled bitterly to a father standing with a tray before a wicket of hats. 'The lone wolf playing ball,' he said to himself as the tray whirled. Chasing the ball towards the sea, passing undressing women with a rush and a wink, tripping over a castle into a coil of wet girls lying like snakes, soaking his shoes as he grabbed the ball off a wave, he felt his happiness return in a boast of the body, and, 'Look out, Duckworth, here's a fast one coming,' he cried to the mother behind the hats. The ball bounced on a boy's head. In and out of the scattered families, among the sandwiches and clothes, uncles and mothers fielded the bouncing ball. A bald man, with his shirt hanging out, returned it in the wrong direction, and a collie carried it into the sea. Now it was mother's turn with the tray. Tray and ball together flew over her head. An uncle in a panama smacked the ball to the dog, who swam with it out of reach. They offered the young man egg-and-cress sandwiches and warm stout, and he and an uncle and a father sat down on the *Evening Post* until the sea touched their feet.

Alone again, hot and unhappy, for the boasting minute when he ran among the unknown people lying and running loudly at peace was struck away, like a ball, he said, into the sea, he walked to a space on the beach where a hell-fire preacher on a box marked 'Mr. Matthews' was talking to a congregation of expressionless women. Boys with peashooters sat quietly near him. A ragged man collected nothing in a cap. Mr. Matthews shook his cold hands, stormed at the holiday, and cursed the summer from his shivering box. He cried for a new warmth. The strong sun shone into his bones, and he buttoned his coat collar. Valley children, with sunken, impudent eyes, quick tongues and singing voices, chest thin as shells, gathered round the Punch and Judy and the Stop Me tricycles, and he denied them all. He contradicted the girls in their underclothes combing and powdering, and the modest girls cleverly dressing under tents of towels.

As Mr. Matthews cast down the scarlet town, drove out the

bare-bellied boys who danced around the ice-cream man, and wound the girls' sunburnt thighs about with his black overcoat—'Down! down!' he cried, 'the night is upon us'—the young man in dejection stood, with a shadow at his shoulder, and thought of Porthcawl's Coney Beach, where his friends were rocking with girls on the Giant Racer or tearing in the Ghost Train down the skeletons' tunnel. Leslie Bird would have his arms full of coconuts. Brenda was with Herbert at the rifle-range. Gil Morris was buying Molly a cocktail with a cherry at the 'Esplanade.' Here he stood, listening to Mr. Matthews, the retired drinker, crying darkness on the evening sands, with money hot in his pocket and Saturday burning away.

In his loneliness he had refused their invitations. Herbert, in his low, red sports car, G. B. at the back, a sea-blown nymph on the radiator, called at his father's house, but he said: 'I'm not in the mood, old man. I'm going to spend a quiet day. Enjoy yourselves. Don't take too much pop.' Only waiting for the sun to set, he stood in the sad circle with the pleasureless women who were staring at a point in the sky behind their prophet, and wished the morning back. Oh, boy! to be wasting his money now on the rings and ranges of the fair, to be sitting in the chromium lounge with a short worth one and six and a Turkish cigarette, telling the latest one to the girls, seeing the sun, through the palms in the lounge window, sink over the promenade, over the Bath chairs, the cripples and widows, the beach-trousered, kerchiefed, week-end wives, the smart, kiss-curled girls with plain and spectacled girl friends, the innocent, swaggering, loud bad boys, and the poms at the ankles, and the cycling sweetmen. Ronald had sailed to Ilfracombe on the *Lady Moira,* and, in the thick saloon, with a party from Brynhyfryd, he'd be knocking back nips without a thought that on the sands at home his friend was alone and pussyfoot at six o'clock, and the evening dull as a chapel. All his friends had vanished into their pleasures.

He thought: Poets live and walk with their poems; a man with visions needs no other company; Saturday is a crude day; I must go home and sit in my bedroom by the boiler. But he was not a poet living and walking, he was a young man in a sea town on a warm bank holiday, with two pounds to spend; he had no visions, only two pounds and a small body with its feet on the littered sand; serenity was for old men; and he moved away, over the railway points, on to the tramlined road.

He snarled at the flower clock in Victoria Gardens.

'And what shall a prig do now?' he said aloud, causing a

young woman on a bench opposite the white-tiled urinal to smile and put her novel down.

She had chestnut hair arranged high on her head in an old-fashioned way, in loose coils and a bun, and a Woolworth's white rose grew out of it and drooped to touch her ear. She wore a white frock with a red paper flower pinned on the breast, and rings and bracelets that came from a fun-fair stall. Her eyes were small and quite green.

He marked, carefully and coldly in one glance, all the unusual details of her appearance; it was the calm, unstartled certainty of her bearing before his glance from head to foot, the innocent knowledge, in her smile and the set of her head, that she was defended by her gentleness and accessible strangeness against all rude encounters and picking looks, that made his fingers tremble. Though her frock was long and the collar high, she could as well be naked there on the blistered bench. Her smile confessed her body bare and spotless and willing and warm under the cotton, and she waited without guilt.

How beautiful she is, he thought, with his mind on words and his eyes on her hair and red and white skin, how beautifully she waits for me, though she does not know she is waiting and I can never tell her.

He had stopped and was staring. Like a confident girl before a camera, she sat smiling, her hands folded, her head slightly to one side so that the rose brushed her neck. She accepted his admiration. The girl in a million took his long look to herself, and cherished his stupid love.

Midges flew into his mouth. He hurried on shamefully. At the gates of the Gardens he turned to see her for the last time on earth. She had lost her calm with his abrupt and awkward going, and stared in confusion after him. One hand was raised as though to beckon him back. If he waited, she would call him. He walked round the corner and heard her voice, a hundred voices, and all hers, calling his name, and a hundred names that were all his, over the bushy walls.

And what shall the terrified prig of a love-mad young man do next? he asked his reflection silently in the distorting mirror of the empty 'Victoria' saloon. His ape-like, hanging face, with 'Bass' across the forehead, gave back a cracked sneer.

If Venus came in on a plate, said the two red, melon-slice lips, I would ask for vinegar to put on her.

She could drive my guilt out; she could smooth away my shame; why didn't I stop to talk to her? he asked.

You saw a queer tart in a park, his reflection answered, she was a child of nature, oh my! oh my! Did you see the dewdrops in her hair? Stop talking to the mirror like a man in a magazine, I know you too well.

A new head, swollen and lop-jawed, wagged behind his shoulder. He spun round, to hear the barman say:

'Has the one and only let you down? You look like death warmed up. Have this one on the house. Free beer to-day. Free X's.' He pulled the beer handle. 'Only the best served here. Straight from the rust. You do look queer,' he said, 'the only one saved from the wreck and the only wreck saved. Here's looking at you!' He drank the beer he had drawn.

'May I have a glass of beer, please?'

'What do you think this is, a public house?'

On the polished table in the middle of the saloon the young man drew, with a finger dipped in strong, the round head of a girl and piled a yellow froth of hair upon it.

'Ah! dirty, dirty!' said the barman, running round from behind the counter and rubbing the head away with a dry cloth.

Shielding the dirtiness with his hat, the young man wrote his name on the edge of the table and watched the letters dry and fade.

Through the open bay-window, across the useless railway covered with sand, he saw the black dots of bathers, the stunted huts, the jumping dwarfs round the Punch and Judy, and the tiny religious circle. Since he had walked and played down there in the crowded wilderness, excusing his despair, searching for company though he refused it, he had found his own true happiness and lost her all in one bewildering and clumsy half a minute by the 'Gentlemen' and the flower clock. Older and wiser and no better, he would have looked in the mirror to see if his discovery and loss had marked themselves upon his face in shadows under the eyes or lines about the mouth, were it not for the answer he knew he would receive from the distorted reflection.

The barman came to sit near him, and said in a false voice: 'Now you tell me all about it, I'm a regular storehouse of secrets.'

'There isn't anything to tell. I saw a girl in Victoria Gardens and I was too shy to speak to her. She was a piece of God help us all right.'

Ashamed of his wish to be companionable, even in the depth of love and distress, with her calm face before his eyes and her smile reproving and forgiving him as he spoke, the young man defiled his girl on the bench, dragged her down into the spit and sawdust and dolled her up to make the barman say:

'I like them big myself. Once round Bessy, once round the gasworks. I missed the chance of a lifetime, too. Fifty lovelies in the rude and I'd left my Bunsen burner home.'

'Give me the same, please.'

'You mean similar.'

The barman drew a glass of beer, drank it, and drew another.

'I always have one with the customers,' he said, 'it puts us on even terms. Now we're just two heart-broken bachelors together.' He sat down again.

'You can't tell me anything I don't know,' he said. 'I've seen over twenty chorines from the Empire in this bar, drunk as printers. Oh, les girls! les limbs!'

'Will they be in to-night?'

'There's only a fellow sawing a woman in half this week.'

'Keep a half for me.'

A drunk man walked in on an invisible white line, and the barman, reeling in sympathy across the room, served him with a pint. 'Free beer to-day,' he said. 'Free X's. You've been out in the sun.'

'I've been out in the sun all day,' said the man.

'I thought you looked sunburnt.'

'That's drink,' said the man. 'I've been drinking.'

'The holiday is drawing to an end,' the young man whispered into his glass. Bye-bye blackbird, the moment is lost, he thought, examining, with an interest he could not forgive, the comic coloured postcards of mountain-buttocked women on the beach and hen-pecked, pin-legged men with telescopes, pasted on the wall beneath the picture of a terrier drinking stout; and now, with a jolly barman and a drunk in a crushed cap, he was mopping the failing day down. He tipped his hat over his forehead, and a lock of hair that fell below the hat tickled his eyelid. He saw, with a stranger's darting eye that missed no single subtlety of the wry grin or the faintest gesture drawing the shape of his death on the air, an unruly-haired young man who coughed into his hand in the corner of a rotting room and puffed the smoke of his doped Weight.

But as the drunk man weaved towards him on wilful feet, carrying his dignity as a man might carry a full glass around a quaking ship, as the barman behind the counter clattered and whistled and dipped to drink, he shook off the truthless, secret tragedy with a sneer and a blush, straightened his melancholy him like another flesh, he sat sad and content in the plain room of the undistinguished hotel at the sea-end of the shabby, spreading town where everything was happening. He had no need of the dark interior world when Tawe pressed in upon him and the eccentric ordinary people came bursting and crawling, with noise and colours, out of their houses, out of the graceless buildings, the factories and avenues, the shining shops and blaspheming chapels, the terminuses and the meeting-halls, the falling alleys and brick lanes, from the arches and shelters and holes behind the hoardings, out of the common, wild intelligence of the town.

At last the drunk man had reached him. 'Put your hand here,' he said, and turned about and tapped himself on the bottom.

The barman whistled and rose from his drink to see the young man touch the drunk man on the seat of the trousers.

'What can you feel there?'

'Nothing.'

'That's right. Nothing. Nothing. There's nothing there to feel.'

'How can you sit down then?' asked the barman.

'I just sit down on what the doctor left,' the man said angrily. 'I had as good a bottom as you've got once. I was working underground in Dowlais, and the end of the world came down on me. Do you know what I got for losing my bottom? Four and three! Two and three ha'pence a cheek. That's cheaper than a pig.'

The girl from Victoria Gardens came into the bar with two friends: a blonde young girl almost as beautiful as she was, and a middle-aged woman dressed and made up to look young. The three of them sat at the table. The girl he loved ordered three ports and gins.

'Isn't it delicious weather?' said the middle-aged woman.

The barman said: 'Plenty of sky about.' With many bows and smiles he placed their drinks in front of them. 'I thought the princesses had gone to a better pub,' he said.

'What's a better pub without you, handsome?' said the blonde girl.

'This is the "Ritz" and the "Savoy," isn't it, *garçon* darling?' the girl from the Gardens said, and kissed her hand to him.

The young man in the window seat, still bewildered by the first sudden sight of her entering the darkening room, caught the kiss to himself and blushed. He thought to run out of the room and through the miracle-making Gardens, to rush into his house and hide his head in the bed-clothes and lie all night there, dressed and trembling, her voice in his ears, her green eyes wide awake under his closed eyelids. But only a sick boy with tossed blood would run from his proper love into a dream, lie down in a bedroom that was full of his shames, and sob against the feathery, fat breast and face on the damp pillow. He remembered his age and poems, and would not move.

'Tanks a million, Lou,' said the barman.

Her name was Lou, Louise, Louisa. She must be Spanish or French or a gipsy, but he could tell the street that her voice came from; he knew where her friends lived by the rise and fall of their sharp voices, and the name of the middle-aged woman was Mrs. Emerald Franklin. She was to be seen every night in the 'Jew's Harp,' sipping and spying and watching the clock.

'We've been listening to Matthews Hellfire on the sands. Down with this and down with that, and he used to drink a pint of biddy before his breakfast,' Mrs. Franklin said. 'Oh, there's a nerve!'

'And his eye on the fluff all the time,' said the blonde girl. 'I wouldn't trust him any further than Ramon Navarro behind the counter.'

'Whoops! I've gone up in the world. Last week I was Charley Chase,' said the barman.

Mrs. Franklin raised her empty glass in a gloved hand and shook it like a bell. 'Men are deceivers ever,' she said. 'And a drop of mother's ruin right around.'

'Especially Mr. Franklin,' said the barman.

'But there's a lot in what the preacher says, mind,' Mrs. Franklin said, 'about the carrying on. If you go for a constitutional after stop-tap along the sands you might as well be in Sodom and Gomorrah.'

The blonde girl laughed. 'Hark to Mrs. Grundy! I see her with a black man last Wednesday, round by the museum.'

'He was an Indian,' said Mrs. Franklin, 'from the university college, and I'd thank you to remember it. Every one's brothers under the skin, but there's no tarbrush in my family.'

'Oh, dear! oh, dear!' said Lou. 'Lay off it, there's loves. This is my birthday. It's a holiday. Put a bit of fun in it. Miaow! miaow! Marjorie, kiss Emerald and be friends.' She smiled and laughed at them both. She winked at the barman, who was filling their glasses to the top. 'Here's to your blue eyes, *garçon!*' She had not noticed the young man in the corner. 'And one for granddad there,' she said, smiling at the swaying, drunk man. 'He's twenty-one to-day. There! I've made him smile.'

The drunk man made a deep, dangerous bow, lifted his hat, stumbled against the mantelpiece, and his full pint in his free hand was steady as a rock. 'The prettiest girl in Carmarthenshire,' he said.

'This is Glamorganshire, dad,' she said, 'where's your geography? Look at him waltzing! mind your glasses! He's got that Kruschen feeling. Come on, faster! give us the Charleston.'

The drunk man, with his pint held high, danced until he fell, and all the time he never spilt a drop. He lay at Lou's feet on the dusty floor and grinned up at her in confidence and affection. 'I fell,' he said. 'I could dance like a trooper when I had a beatyem.'

'He lost his bottom at the last trump,' the barman explained.

'When did he lose his bottom?' said Mrs. Franklin.

'When Gabriel blew his whistle down in Dowlais.'

'You're pulling my leg.'

'It's a pleasure, Mrs. Em. Hoi, you! get up from the vomitorium.'

The man wagged his end like a tail, and growled at Lou's feet.

'Put your head on my foot. Be comfy. Let him lie there,' she said.

He went to sleep at once.

'I can't have drunks on the premises.'

'You know where to go then.'

'Cru-el Mrs. Franklin!'

'Go on, attend to your business. Serve the young man in the corner, his tongue's hanging out.'

'Cru-el lady!'

As Mrs. Franklin called attention to the young man, Lou peered shortsightedly across the saloon and saw him sitting with his back to the window.

'I'll have to get glasses,' she said.

'You'll have plenty of glasses before the night's out.'

'No, honest, Marjorie, I didn't know any one was there. I do beg your pardon, you in the corner,' she said.

The barman switched on the light. 'A bit of *lux in tenebris.*'

'Oh!' said Lou.

The young man dared not move for fear that he might break the long light of her scrutiny, the enchantment shining like a single line of light between them, or startle her into speaking;

and he did not conceal the love in his eyes, for she could pierce through to it as easily as she could turn his heart in his chest and make it beat above the noises of the two friends' hurried conversation, the rattle of glasses behind the counter where the barman spat and polished and missed nothing, and the snores of the comfortable sleeper. Nothing can hurt me. Let the barman jeer. Giggle in your glass, our Em. I'm telling the world, I'm walking in clover, I'm staring at Lou like a fool, she's my girl, she's my lily. O love! O love! She's no lady, with her sing-song Tontine voice, she drinks like a deep-sea diver; but Lou, I'm yours, and Lou, you're mine. He refused to meditate on her calmness now and twist her beauty into words. She was nothing under the sun or moon but his. Unashamed and certain, he smiled at her: and, though he was prepared for all, her answering smile made his fingers tremble again, as they had trembled in the Gardens, and reddened his cheeks and drove his heart to a gallop.

'Harold, fill the young man's glass up,' Mrs. Franklin said.

The barman stood still, a duster in one hand and a dripping glass in the other.

'Have you got water in your ears? Fill the young man's glass!'

The barman put the duster to his eyes. He sobbed. He wiped away the mock tears.

'I thought I was attending a *première* and this was the royal box,' he said.

'He's got water on the brain, not in his earhole,' said Marjorie.

'I dreamt it was a beautiful tragi-comedy entitled "Love at First Sight, or, Another Good Man gone wrong." Act one in a boozer by the sea.'

The two women tapped their foreheads.

Lou said, still smiling: 'Where was the second act?'

Her voice was as gentle as he had imagined it to be before her gay and nervous playing with the over-familiar barman and the inferior women. He saw her as a wise, soft girl whom no hard company could spoil, for her soft self, bare to the heart, broke through every defence of her sensual falsifiers. As he thought this, phrasing her gentleness, faithlessly running to words away from the real room and his love in the middle, he woke with a start and saw her lively body six steps from him, no calm heart dressed in a sentence, but a pretty girl, to be got and kept. He must catch hold of her fast. He got up to cross to her.

'I woke before the second act came on,' said the barman. 'I'd sell my dear old mother to see that. Dim light. Purple couches. Ecstatic bliss. Là, là chérie!'

The young man sat down at the table, next to her.

Harold, the barman, leaned over the counter and cupped his hand to his ear.

The man on the floor rolled in his sleep, and his head lay in the spittoon.

'You should have come and sat here a long time ago,' Lou whispered. 'You should have stopped to talk to me in the Gardens. Were you shy?'

'I was too shy,' the young man whispered.

'Whispering isn't manners. I can't hear a word,' said the barman.

At a sign from the young man, a flick of the fingers that sent the waiters in evening dress bustling with oysters about the immense room, the barman filled the glasses with port, gin, and Nutbrown.

'We never drink with strangers,' Mrs. Franklin said, laughing.

'He isn't a stranger,' said Lou, 'are you, Jack?'

He threw a pound note on the table: 'Take the damage.'

The evening that had been over before it began raced along among the laughter of the charming women sharp as knives, and the stories of the barman, who should be on the stage, and Lou's delighted smiles and silences at his side. Now she is safe and sure, he thought, after her walking like my doubtful walking, around the lonely distances of the holiday. In the warm, spinning middle they were close and alike. The town and the sea and the last pleasure-makers drifted into the dark that had nothing to do with them, and left this one room burning.

One by one, some lost men from the dark shuffled into the bar, drank sadly, and went out. Mrs. Franklin, flushed and dribbling, waved her glass at their departures. Harold winked behind their backs. Marjorie showed them her long, white legs.

'Nobody loves us except ourselves,' said Harold. 'Shall I shut the bar and keep the riff-raff out?'

'Lou is expecting Mr. O'Brien, but don't let that stop you,' Marjorie said. 'He's her sugar daddy from old Ireland.'

'Do you love Mr. O'Brien?' the young man whispered.

'How could I, Jack?'

He could see Mr. O'Brien as a witty, tall fellow of middle age, with waved greying hair and a clipped bit of dirt on his upper lip, a flash ring on his marriage finger, a pouched, knowing eye, dummy dressed with a whaleboned waist, a broth of a man about Cardiff, Lou's horrible lover tearing towards her now down the airless streets in the firm's car. The young man clenched his hand on the table covered with dead, and sheltered her in the warm strength of his fist. 'My round, my round,' he said, 'up again, plenty! Doubles, trebles, Mrs. Franklin is a jibber.'

'My mother never had a jibber.'

'Oh, Lou!' he said, 'I am more than happy with you.'

'Coo! coo! hear the turtle doves.'

'Let them coo,' said Marjorie. 'I could coo, too.'

The barman looked around him in surprise. He raised his hands, palms up, and cocked his head.

'The bar is full of birds,' he said.

'Emerald's laying an egg,' he said, as Mrs. Franklin rocked in her chair.

Soon the bar was full of customers. The drunk man woke up and ran out, leaving his cap in a brown pool. Sawdust dropped from his hair. A small, old, round, red-faced, cheery man sat facing the young man and Lou, who held hands under the table and rubbed their legs against each other.

'What a night for love!' said the old man. 'On such a night as this did Jessica steal from the wealthy Jew. Do you know where that comes from?'

'*The Merchant of Venice,*' Lou said. 'But you're an Irishman, Mr. O'Brien.'

'I could have sworn you were a tall man with a little tish,' said the young man gravely.

'What's the weapons, Mr. O'Brien?'

'Brandies at dawn, I should think, Mrs. Franklin.'

'I never described Mr. O'Brien to you at all. You're dreaming!' Lou whispered. 'I wish this night could go on for ever.'

'But not here. Not in the bar. In a room with a big bed.'

'A bed in a bar,' said the old man, 'if you'll pardon me hearing you, that's what I've always wanted. Think of it, Mrs. Franklin.'

The barman bobbed up from behind the counter.

'Time, gentlemen and others!'

The sober strangers departed to Mrs. Franklin's laughter.

The lights went out.

'Lou, don't you lose me.'

'I've got your hand.'

'Press it hard, hurt it.'

'Break his bloody neck,' Mrs. Franklin said in the dark. 'No offence meant.'

'Marjorie smack hand,' said Marjorie. 'Let's get out of the dark. Harold's a rover in the dark.'

'And the girl guides.'

'Let's take a bottle each and go down to Lou's,' she said.

'I'll buy the bottles,' said Mr. O'Brien.

'It's you don't lose me now,' Lou whispered. 'Hold on to me, Jack. The others won't stay long. Oh, Mr. Christ, I wish it was just you and me!'

'Will it be just you and me?'

'You and me and Mr. Moon.'

Mr. O'Brien opened the saloon door. 'Pile into the Rolls, you ladies. The gentlemen are going to see to the medicine.'

The young man felt Lou's quick kiss on his mouth before she followed Marjorie and Mrs. Franklin out.

'What do you say we split the drinks?' said Mr. O'Brien.

'Look what I found in the lavatory,' said the barman, 'he was singing on the seat.' He appeared behind the counter with the drunk man leaning on his arm.

They all climbed into the car.

'First stop, Lou's.'

The young man, on Lou's knee, saw the town in a daze spin by them, the funnelled and masted smoke-blue outline of the still, droning docks, the lightning lines of the poor streets growing longer, and the winking shops that were snapped out one by one. The car smelt of scent and powder and flesh. He struck with his elbow, by accident, Mrs. Franklin's upholstered breast. Her thighs, like cushions, bore the drunk man's rolling weight. He was bumped and tossed on a lump of women. Breasts, legs, bellies, hands, touched, warmed, and smothered him. On through the night, towards Lou's bed, towards the unbelievable end of the dying holiday, they tore past black houses and bridges, a station in a smoke cloud, and drove up a steep side street with one weak lamp in a circle of railings at the top, and swerved into a space where a tall tenement house stood surrounded by cranes, standing ladders, poles and girders, barrows, brick-heaps.

They climbed to Lou's room up many flights of dark, perilous stairs. Washing hung on the rails outside closed doors. Mrs. Franklin, fumbling alone with the drunk man, behind the others, trod in a bucket, and a lucky black cat ran over her foot. Lou led the young man by the hand through a passage marked with names and doors, lit a match, and whispered: 'It won't be very long. Be good and patient with Mr. O'Brien. Here it is. Come in first. Welcome to you, Jack!' She kissed him again at the door of her room.

She turned on the light, and he walked with her proudly into her own room, into the room that he could come to know, and saw a wide bed, a gramophone on a chair, a wash-basin half-hidden in a corner, a gas fire and a cooking ring, a closed cupboard, and her photograph in a cardboard frame on the chest of drawers with no handles. Here she slept and ate. In the double bed she lay all night, pale and curled, sleeping on her left side. When he lived with her always, he would not allow her to dream. No other men must lie and love in her head. He spread his fingers on her pillow.

'Why do you live at the top of the Eiffel Tower?' said the barman, coming in.

'What a climb!' said Mr. O'Brien. 'But it's very nice and private when you get here.'

'If you get here!' said Mrs. Franklin. 'I'm dead beat. This old nuisance weighs a ton. Lie down, lie down on the floor and go to sleep. The old nuisance!' she said fondly. 'What's your name?'

'Ernie,' the drunk man said, raising his arm to shield his face.

'Nobody's going to bite you, Ernie. Here, give him a nip of whisky. Careful! Don't pour it on your waistcoat; you'll be squeezing your waistcoat in the morning. Pull the curtains, Lou, I can see the wicked old moon,' she said.

'Does it put ideas in your head?'

'I love the moon,' said Lou.

'There never was a young lover who didn't love the moon.' Mr. O'Brien gave the young man a cheery smile, and patted his hand. His own hand was red and hairy. 'I could see at the flash of a glance that Lou and this nice young fellow were made for each other. I could see it in their eyes. Dear me, no! I'm not so old and blind I can't see love in front of my nose. Couldn't you see it, Mrs. Franklin? Couldn't you see it, Marjorie?'

In the long silence, Lou collected glasses from the cupboard as though she had not heard Mr. O'Brien speak. She drew the curtains, shut out the moon, sat on the edge of her bed with her feet tucked under her, looked at her photograph as at a stranger, folded her hands as she had folded them, on the first meeting, before the young man's worship in the Gardens.

'A host of angels must be passing by,' said Mr. O'Brien. 'What a silence there is! Have I said anything out of place? Drink and be merry, to-morrow we die. What do you think I bought these lovely shining bottles for?'

The bottles were opened. The dead were lined on the mantelpiece. The whisky went down. Harold the barman and Marjorie, her dress lifted, sat in the one arm-chair together. Mrs. Franklin, with Ernie's head on her lap, sang in a sweet, trained contralto voice *The Shepherd's Lass*. Mr. O'Brien kept rhythm with his foot.

I want Lou in my arms, the young man said to himself, watching Mr. O'Brien tap and smile and the barman draw Marjorie down deep. Mrs. Franklin's voice sang sweetly in the small bedroom where he and Lou should be lying in the white bed without any smiling company to see them drown. He and Lou could go down together, one cool body weighted with a boiling stone, on to the falling, blank white, entirely empty sea, and never rise. Sitting on their bridal bed, near enough to hear his breath, she was farther from him than before they met. Then he had everything but her body; now she had given him two kisses, and everything had vanished but that beginning. He must be good and patient with Mr. O'Brien. He could wipe away the embracing, old smile with the iron back of his hand. Sink lower, lower, Harold and Marjorie, tumble like whales at Mr. O'Brien's feet.

He wished that the light would fail. In the darkness he and Lou could creep beneath the clothes and imitate the dead. Who would look for them there, if they were dead still and soundless? The others would shout to them down the dizzy stairs or rummage in the silence about the narrow, obstacled corridors or stumble out into the night to search for them among the cranes and ladders in the desolation of the detroyed houses. He could hear, in the made-up dark, Mr. O'Brien's voice cry, 'Lou, where are you? Answer! answer!' the hollow answer of the echo, 'answer!' and hear her lips in the cool pit of the bed secretly move around another name, and feel them move.

'A fine piece of singing, Emerald, and very naughty words. That was a shepherd, that was,' Mr. O'Brien said.

Ernie, on the floor, began to sing in a thick, sulking voice but Mrs. Franklin placed her hand over his mouth and he sucked and nuzzled it.

'What about this young shepherd?' said Mr. O'Brien, pointing his glass at the young man. 'Can he sing as well as make love? You ask him kindly, girlie,' he said to Lou, 'and he'll give us a song like a nightingale.'

'Can you sing, Jack?'

'Like a crow, Lou.'

'Can't he even talk poetry? What a young man to have who can't spout the poets to his lady!' Mr. O'Brien said.

From the cupboard Lou brought out a red-bound book and gave it to the young man, saying: 'Can you read us a piece out of here? The second volume's in the hatbox. Read us a dreamy piece, Jack. It's nearly midnight.'

'Only a love poem, no other kind,' said Mr. O'Brien. 'I won't hear anything but a love poem.'

'Soft and sweet,' Mrs. Franklin said. She took her hand away from Ernie's mouth and looked at the ceiling.

The young man read, but not aloud, lingering on her name, the inscription on the fly-leaf of the first volume of the collected poems of Tennyson: 'To Louisa, from her Sunday School teacher, Miss Gwyneth Forbes. God's in His Heaven, all's right with the world.'

'Make it a love poem, don't forget.'

The young man read aloud, closing one eye to steady the dancing print, *Come into the Garden, Maud.* And when he reached the beginning of the fourth verse his voice grew louder:

'I said to the lily, "There is but one
With whom she has heart to be gay.
When will the dancers leave her alone?
She is weary of dance and play."
Now half to the setting moon are gone,
And half to the rising day;
Low on the sand and loud on the stone
The last wheel echoes away.
'I said to the rose, "The brief night goes
In babble and revel and wine.
O young lord-lover, what sighs are those,
For one that will never be thine?
But mine, but mine," so I sware to the rose,
"For ever and ever, mine." '

At the end of the poem, Harold said, suddenly, his head hanging over the arm of the chair, his hair made wild, and his mouth red with lipstick: 'My grandfather remembers seeing Lord Tennyson, he was a little man with a hump.'

'No,' said the young man, 'he was tall and he had long hair and a beard.'

'Did you ever see him?'

'I wasn't born then.'

'My grandfather saw him. He had a hump.'

'Not Alfred Tennyson.'

'Lord Alfred Tennyson was a little man with a hump.'

'It couldn't have been the same Tennyson.'

'You've got the wrong Tennyson, this was the famous poet with a hump.'

Lou, on the wonderful bed, waiting for him alone of all the men, ugly or handsome, old or young, in the wide town and the small world that would be bound to fall, lowered her head and kissed her hand to him and held her hand in the river of light on the counterpane. The hand, to him, became transparent, and the light on the counterpane glowed up steadily through it in the thin shape of her palm and fingers.

'Ask Mr. O'Brien what Lord Tennyson was like,' said Mrs. Franklin. 'We appeal to you, Mr. O'Brien, did he have a hump or not?'

Nobody but the young man, for whom she lived and waited now, noticed Lou's little loving movements. She put her glowing hand to her left breast. She made a sign of secrecy on her lips.

'It depends,' Mr. O'Brien said.

The young man closed one eye again, for the bed was pitching like a ship: a sickening, hot storm out of a cigarette cloud unsettled cupboard and chest. The motions of the sea-going bedroom were calmed with the cunning closing of his eye, but he longed for night air. On sailor's legs he walked to the door.

'You'll find the House of Commons on the second floor at the end of the passage,' said Mr. O'Brien.

At the door, he turned to Lou and smiled with all his love, declaring it to the faces of the company and making her, before Mr. O'Brien's envious regard, smile back and say: 'Don't be long, Jack. Please! You mustn't be long.'

Now every one knew. Love had grown up in an evening.

'One minute, my darling,' he said. 'I'll be here.'

The door closed behind him. He walked into the wall of the passage. He lit a match. He had three left. Down the stairs, clinging to the sticky, shaking rails, rocking on seesaw floorboards, bruising his shin on a bucket, past the noises of secret lives behind doors he slid and stumbled and swore and heard Lou's voice in a fresh fever drive him on, call him to return, speak to him with such passion and abandonment that even in the darkness and the pain of his haste he was dazzled and struck still. She spoke, there on the rotting stairs in the middle of the poor house, a frightening rush of love words; from her mouth, at his ear, endearments were burned out. Hurry! hurry! Every moment is being killed. Love, adored, dear, run back and whistle to me, open the door, shout my name, lay me down. Mr. O'Brien has his hands on my side.

He ran into a cavern. A draught blew out his matches. He lurched into a room where two figures on a black heap on the floor lay whispering, and ran from there in a panic. He made water at the dead end of the passage and hurried back towards Lou's room, finding himself at last on a silent patch of stairway at the top of the house: he put out his hand, but the rail was broken and nothing there prevented a long drop to the ground down a twisted shaft that would echo and double his cry, bring out from their holes in the wall the sleeping or stirring families, the whispering figures, the blind startled turners of night into day. Lost in a tunnel near the roof, he fingered the damp walls for a door; he found a handle and gripped it hard, but it came off in his hand. Lou had led him down a longer passage than this. He remembered the number of doors: there were three on each side. He ran down the broken-railed flight into another passage and dragged his hand along the wall. Three doors, he counted. He opened the third door, walked into darkness, and groped for the switch on the left. He saw, in the sudden light, a bed and a cupboard and a chest of drawers with no handles, a gas fire, a wash-basin in the corner. No bottles. No glasses. No photograph of Lou. The red counterpane on the bed was smooth. He could not remember the colour of Lou's counterpane.

He left the light burning and opened the second door, but a strange woman's voice cried, half-asleep: 'Who is there? Is it you, Tom? Tom, put the light on.' He looked for a line of light at the foot of the next door, and stopped to listen for voices. The woman was still calling in the second room.

'Lou, where are you?' he cried. 'Answer! answer!'

'Lou, what Lou? There's no Lou here,' said a man's voice through the open door of the first dark room at the entrance to the passage.

He scampered down another flight and counted few doors with his scratched hand. One door opened and a woman in a nightdress put out her head. A child's head appeared below her.

'Where does Lou live? Do you know where Lou lives?'

The woman and child stared without speaking.

'Lou! Lou! her name is Lou!' he heard himself shout. 'She lives here, in this house! Do you know where she lives?'

The woman caught the child by the hair and pulled her into the room. He clung to the edge of her door. The woman thrust her arm round the edge and brought down a bunch of keys sharply on his hands. The door slammed.

A young woman with a baby in a shawl stood at an open door on the opposite side of the passage, and caught his sleeve as he ran by. 'Lou who? You woke my baby.'

'I don't know her other name. She's with Mrs. Franklin and Mr. O'Brien.'

'You woke my baby.'

'Come in and find her in the bed,' a voice said from the darkness behind the young woman.

'He's woken up the baby.'

He ran down the passage, holding his wet hand to his mouth. He fell against the rails of the last flight of stairs. He heard Lou's voice in his head once more whisper to him to return as the ground floor rose, like a lift full of dead, towards the rails. Hurry! hurry! I can't, I won't wait, the bridal night is being killed.

Up the rotten, bruising, mountainous stairs he climbed, in his sickness, to the passage where he had left the one light burning in an end room. The light was out. He tapped all the doors and whispered her name. He beat on the doors and shouted, and a woman, dressed in a vest and a hat, drove him out of the passage with a walking-stick.

For a long time he waited on the stairs, though there was no love now to wait for and no bed but his own too many miles away to lie in, and only the approaching day to remember his discovery. All around him the disturbed inhabitants of the house were falling back into sleep. Then he walked out of the house on to the waste space and under the leaning cranes and ladders. The light of the one weak lamp in a rusty circle fell across the brick-heaps and the broken wood and the dust that had been houses once, where the small and hardly known and never-to-be-forgotten people of the dirty town had lived and loved and died and, always, lost.

Style

The substance of "One Warm Saturday" comes to us through a kind of fog, virtually a drunken haze of distortion, geniality, and fleeting images such as one finds in dreams. The movement is swift, the characters indeterminate, the speech fantastic. The overall effect is that of a magical, fairy-tale world in which recognizable objects appear in new shapes. This vision of his material constitutes Thomas's style. It is obviously much more mannered and bizarre than the style of Henry James's "Paste" or J. F. Powers' "The Eye."

1 Can you pick out specific instances of Thomas's style which create distortion and weird scenic effects? One good example comes in the first paragraph, where the young man draws in the sand only to have a naked child run over it. The overall result is of the sea running over the figure, washing it out, changing it into something else. This image—of ever-changing quantities—characterizes much of the story. Find as many other types of this image as you can.

2 The humor of the story is apparent, but only infrequently is it verbal humor, that is, humor that derives from a witty remark or a pun. More often it is situational humor, the kind we are familiar with from old silent motion pictures, those of Chaplin, the Keystone comedies, Laurel and Hardy. What situations does Thomas create that are capable of this broad treatment? Try to find as many examples of such humor as you can.

3 How does the scene of ball playing on the beach contribute to the overall atmosphere?

4 Can you figure out where the story takes place? Does it have any special atmosphere? Does the background of the story, the geographical setting, help contribute to the magical effect?

5 Compare the long scene in the bar with the bar scenes of Joyce's "Counterparts." What is the difference in tone? How would you characterize each writer just from these scenes? What different literary effects is each striving to attain? A good approach is to compare and contrast the language each author uses.

6 Explain the title, "One Warm Saturday." What are some of the meanings implicit in it? Cite some descriptive words that back up the title.

7 Does the style of the story change toward the end, when the young man cannot find his way back to Lou? Or does Thomas continue in the same vein? Do you find that the slight shifts in tone, here and elsewhere, take away from the unity of the story?

8 What is your final impression of the story? Does the humor somehow become poignant; do the zany situations somehow take on meaning and form? What is Thomas's view of the world? Is it possible to derive a viewpoint from such a stylized story?

Characterization

1 Try to characterize Thomas's young man. What are some of the attitudes that Thomas gives him? Does he fit into the world which Thomas builds around him?

2 One question that might arise from such a stylized approach to the material is whether anything in the story really exists. Did the young man dream that Lou entered the café and then brought him to her room? What qualities in his mind does the young woman have? What qualities in actuality? The young man himself—what do you know about him that would cause him to romanticize his situation?

Theme

1 The ostensible theme is one of lost, impossible love. Is such a theme capable of realistic treatment at the present time? Would it sink into bathos and sentimentality without the humorous edge that Thomas gives it?

2 What does such a theme indicate about Thomas's chief character? Why is his love lost and impossible? Does it fit into a "warm Saturday"?

3 Does such a theme become sad despite its beery and humorous presentation?

4 How does "atmosphere" contribute to the theme?

5 When Thomas makes you question the reality of the young man's vision, what point do you think he is making? Is it all a joke on the young man and on us?

THE MOUSE

Saki

Theodoric Voler had been brought up, from infancy to the confines of middle age, by a fond mother whose chief solicitude had been to keep him screened from what she called the coarser realities of life. When she died she left Theodoric alone in a world that was as real as ever, and a good deal coarser than he considered it had any need to be. To a man of his temperament and upbringing even a simple railway journey was crammed with petty annoyances and minor discords, and as he settled himself down in a second-class compartment one September morning he was conscious of ruffled feelings and general mental discomposure. He had been staying at a country vicarage, the inmates of which had been certainly neither brutal nor bacchanalian, but their supervision of the domestic establishment had been of that lax order which invites disaster. The pony carriage that was to take him to the station had never been properly ordered, and when the moment for his departure drew near the handyman who should have produced the required article was nowhere to be found. In this emergency Theodoric, to his mute but very intense disgust, found himself obliged to collaborate with the vicar's daughter in the task of harnessing the pony, which necessitated groping about in an ill-lighted outhouse called a stable, and smelling very like one—except in patches where it smelt of mice. Without being actually afraid of mice, Theodoric classed them among the coarser incidents of life, and considered that Providence, with a little exercise of moral courage, might long ago have recognized that they were not indispensable, and have withdrawn them from circulation. As the train glided out of the station Theodoric's nervous imagination accused himself of exhaling a weak odour of stableyard, and possibly of displaying a mouldy straw or two on his usually well-brushed garments. Fortunately the only other occupant of the compartment, a lady of about the same age as himself, seemed inclined for slumber rather than scrutiny; the train was not due to stop till the terminus was reached, in about an hour's time, and the carriage was of the old-fashioned sort, that held no communication with a corridor, therefore no further travelling companions were likely to intrude on Theodoric's semi-privacy. And yet the train had scarcely attained its normal speed before he became reluctantly but vividly aware that he was not alone with the slumbering lady; he was not even alone in his own clothes. A warm, creeping movement over his flesh betrayed the unwelcome and highly resented presence, unseen but poignant, of a strayed mouse, that had evidently dashed into its present retreat during the episode of the pony harnessing. Furtive stamps and shakes and wildly directed pinches failed to dislodge the intruder, whose motto, indeed, seemed to be Excelsior; and the lawful occupant of the clothes lay back against the cushions and endeavoured rapidly to evolve some means for putting an end to the dual ownership. It was unthinkable that he should continue for the space of a whole hour in the horrible position of a Rowton House for vagrant mice (already his imagination had at least doubled the numbers of the alien invasion). On the other hand, nothing less drastic than partial disrobing would ease him of his tormentor, and to undress in the presence of a lady, even for so laudable a purpose, was an idea that made his eartips tingle in a blush of abject shame. He had never been able to bring himself even to the mild exposure of open-work socks in the presence of the fair sex. And yet—the lady in this case was to all appearances soundly and securely asleep; the mouse, on the other hand, seemed to be trying to crowd a Wanderjahr into a few strenuous minutes. If there is any truth in the theory of transmigration, this particular mouse must certainly have been in a former state a member of the Alpine Club. Sometimes in its eagerness it lost its footing and slipped for half an inch or so; and then, in fright, or more probably temper, it bit. Theodoric was goaded into the most audacious undertaking of his life. Crimsoning to the hue of a beetroot and keeping an agonized watch on his slumbering fellow-traveller, he swiftly and noiselessly secured the ends of his railway-rug to the racks on either side of the carriage, so that a substantial curtain hung athwart the compartment. In the narrow dressing-room that he had thus improvised he proceeded with violent haste to extricate himself partially and the mouse entirely from the surrounding casings of tweed and half-wool. As the unravelled mouse gave a wild leap to the floor, the rug, slipping its fastening at either end, also came down with a heart-curdling flop, and almost simultaneously the awakened sleeper opened her eyes. With a movement almost quicker than the mouse's, Theodoric pounced on the rug, and hauled its ample folds chin-high over his dismantled person as he collapsed into the further corner of the carriage. The blood raced and beat in the veins of his neck and forehead, while he waited dumbly for the communication-cord to be pulled. The lady, however, contented herself with a silent stare at her strangely muffled companion. How much had she seen, Theodoric queried to himself, and in any case what on earth must she think of his present posture?

"I think I have caught a chill," he ventured desperately.

"Really, I'm sorry," she replied. "I was just going to ask you if you would open this window."

"I fancy it's malaria," he added, his teeth chattering slightly, as much from fright as from a desire to support his theory.

"I've got some brandy in my hold-all, if you'll kindly reach it down for me," said his companion.

"Not for worlds—I mean, I never take anything for it," he assured her earnestly.

"I suppose you caught it in the Tropics?"

Theodoric, whose acquaintance with the Tropics was limited to an annual present of a chest of tea from an uncle in Ceylon, felt that even the malaria was slipping from him. Would it be possible, he wondered, to disclose the real state of affairs to her in small instalments?

"Are you afraid of mice?" he ventured, growing, if possible, more scarlet in the face.

"Not unless they came in quantities, like those that ate up Bishop Hatto. Why do you ask?"

"I had one crawling inside my clothes just now," said Theodoric in a voice that hardly seemed his own. "It was a most awkward situation."

"It must have been, if you wear your clothes at all tight," she observed; "but mice have strange ideas of comfort."

"I had to get rid of it while you were asleep," he continued; then, with a gulp, he added, "it was getting rid of it that brought me to—to this."

"Surely leaving off one small mouse wouldn't bring on a chill," she exclaimed, with a levity that Theodoric accounted abominable.

Evidently she had detected something of his predicament, and was enjoying his confusion. All the blood in his body seemed to have mobilized in one concentrated blush, and an agony of abasement, worse than a myriad mice, crept up and down over his soul. And then, as reflection began to assert itself, sheer terror took the place of humiliation. With every minute that passed the train was rushing nearer to the crowded and bustling terminus where dozens of prying eyes would be exchanged for the one hat into a hard-brimmed trilby, dismissed the affected stranger. In the safe centre of his own identity, the familiar world about paralyzing pair that watched him from the further corner of the carriage. There was one slender despairing chance, which the next few minutes must decide. His fellow-traveller might relapse into a blessed slumber. But as the minutes throbbed by that chance ebbed away. The furtive glance which Theodoric stole at her from time to time disclosed only an unwinking wakefulness.

"I think we must be getting near now," she presently observed.

Theodoric had already noted with growing terror the recurring stacks of small, ugly dwellings that heralded the journey's end. The words acted as a signal. Like a hunted beast breaking cover and dashing madly towards some other haven of momentary safety he threw aside his rug, and struggled frantically into his dishevelled garments. He was conscious of dull suburban stations racing past the window, of a choking, hammering sensation in his throat and heart, and of an icy silence in that corner towards which he dared not look. Then as he sank back in his seat, clothed and almost delirious, the train slowed down to a final crawl, and the woman spoke.

"Would you be so kind," she asked, "as to get me a porter to put me into a car? It's a shame to trouble you when you're feeling unwell, but being blind makes one so helpless at a railway station."

Style and Point of View

1 The author may choose his point of view mainly to conceal certain information until the end of the story and thus to create suspense or surprise. Jack London's point of view in "Love of Life" contributes to the sense of suspense throughout the story (how?). Does Saki's point of view seem imperative for his effect, or is it part of a trick to mislead the reader? Often the "surprise" ending depends upon tricking the reader. Do you think the end justifies the means?

2 What would be lost if Theodoric Voler were to tell the story in his own person? Would the style, which is witty, urbane, and sophisticated, have to be altered? Why?

3 Would the whole episode seem more convincing if it were told from the objective point of view? What would be lost if it were?

For instance, could lines like this remain: "The mouse . . . seemed to be trying to crowd a Wanderjahr into a few strenuous minutes" or "the task of harnessing the pony . . . necessitated groping about in an ill-lighted outhouse called a stable" or "wildly direct pinches failed to dislodge the intruder, whose motto, indeed, seemed to be Excelsior"?

4 What is the main difference between Saki's humor and Purdy's wit? What specific matters of style lead you into this difference?

BIOGRAPHICAL NOTES

Conrad Aiken (1889–   )

Born in Savannah, Georgia, educated at Harvard, Conrad Potter Aiken spent most of his mature years in England. Though he received the Pulitzer Prize for poetry in 1930 and is best known as a poet, his fiction has brought him increasingly before the general public. A number of his short stories in *Costumes by Eros* (1928) and such novels as *The Blue Voyage* (1927) and *King Coffin* (1935) are typical of his sensitive and exciting studies in mental pathology. He is also a respected critic and a master of the short novel. His style has been influenced by William James and Edgar Allan Poe, and his deep interest in music and psychoanalysis is revealed in both his prose and poetry.

Sherwood Anderson (1876–1941)

Born in Camden, Ohio, the son of a shiftless improvident wanderer, Anderson had little formal education. After serving in the Spanish-American War, he managed a paint factory in Elmyra, Ohio, then wrote advertising copy in Chicago, where he became part of the Chicago "circle." *Winesburg, Ohio* (1919), a collection of stories, established him as a major craftsman in this form, and *The Triumph of the Egg* (1921) consolidated his reputation. He is also the author of novels, autobiography, memoirs, verse, and essays. Most of his fiction deals with the pathos of lives trapped by conventionality and commercialism, the adolescent yearning to know and the despair at discovery. The scene of his stories is almost always the Midwest.

Saul Bellow (1915–   )

Born in Lachine, Canada, Saul Bellow was educated at Chicago, Northwestern, and Wisconsin Universities. While working for the editorial department of the Encyclopedia Britannica, he published his first novel, *Dangling Man.* This was followed in 1947 by another novel, *The Victim,* whose theme is the persecuted Jew. For his third novel, *The Adventures of Augie March,* he won the National Book Award of 1953. Since then, other novels such as *Seize the Day* (1956), *Henderson the Rain-King*

(1959), and *Herzog* (1964), and a play, *The Last Analysis* (1965), have added to his already great stature. He has taught at a number of leading American universities, including the University of Chicago, in the city in which he prefers to live.

Ambrose Bierce (1842–1914?)

Born in Ohio, the son of a poor farmer whom he came to despise, Bierce left Kentucky Military Institute to become a drummer boy in the Civil War. He was wounded twice and left the Union Army as a brevet major. Later, refusing a large sum in back army pay, he said, "When I hired out as an assassin for my country, that wasn't part of the contract."

He went to San Francisco and took up journalism; soon his stories distinguished him among the literary circle of Joaquin Miller, Bret Harte, and Mark Twain. After marrying the daughter of a wealthy silver miner, he lived in England for a while, then in Washington, D.C. In 1904 he divorced his wife and left his family; in 1913, disappointed and bitter, he disappeared into Mexico. His fame rests on three volumes: *In the Midst of Life* (1891), a collection of short stories; *Can Such Things Be?* (1893), a group of bizarre tales; and *The Devil's Dictionary* (1906). He is often regarded as one of the forerunners of realism in American fiction.

Kay Boyle (1903–)

Kay Boyle was born in St. Paul, Minnesota, but has spent most of her adult life in Europe, particularly France. Associated with "small magazines" early in her career, she has become one of the foremost women writers in America through such volumes as *Wedding Day* (1931), *The White Horses of Vienna and Other Stories* (1936), *The Crazy Hunter* (1940), *His Human Majesty* (1949), *The Seagull on the Step* (1955), *Generation without Farewell* (1959), and *Nothing Ever Breaks except the Heart* (1966). She is known for her polished style and her interest in the psychological motives of her characters. She teaches creative writing at San Francisco State College.

Hortense Calisher (1911–)

Hortense Calisher was born in New York and educated at Barnard College, where she later lectured for a year. She also taught at the State University of Iowa, Stanford University, and Sarah Lawrence College. She was awarded a Guggenheim Fellowship in 1952 and again in 1955, and received an American Specialist's grant from the Department of State to visit south-east Asia in 1958. She has also lived in Iran with her husband, a college professor.

Her polished and sophisticated short stories appear in such collections as *In the Absence of Angels* (1951), *Tale for the Mirror* (1962), and *Extreme Magic* (1964), from which "Il Ploeur" is taken. The novel *False Entry* (1961) was such a fine performance that it made her next one, *Journal from Ellipsia* (1965), seem disappointing. Recently, she published *The Railway Police and the Trolley Car* (1966).

Willa Cather (1876–1947)

When Willa Cather was nine, her father brought his family from Virginia to a ranch near Red Cloud, Nebraska. There she grew up among pioneer Scandinavians and Germans struggling against the hardships of frontier living. In 1906 she became the managing editor of *McClure's Magazine,* a position she held until she resigned in 1912 to devote all her energies to writing. She wrote three excellent novels dealing with the lives of immigrant settlers: *O Pioneers* (1913), *The Song of the Lark* (1915), and *My Antonia* (1918). With *The Professor's House* (1925) and *Death Comes for the Archbishop* (1927) Miss Cather turned to the Southwest, and her concern with Catholicism, revealed in the latter book, continued in a novel about eighteenth-century Quebec, *Shadows on the Rock* (1931). She was awarded the Pulitzer Prize in 1932 for her novel *One of Ours*. She remained to the day of her death "a defender of the spiritual graces in the midst of an increasingly materialistic culture."

Joseph Conrad (1857–1924)

Joseph Conrad was born in Berdiczew, Poland, Dec. 3, 1857, and died in England Aug. 3, 1924. Trained as a seaman, he was encouraged to turn to fiction by Edward Garnett, then an editor. Once he gave up thoughts of returning to the sea, Conrad, starting in 1895, rapidly published a large number of novels and stories which brought him critical acclaim, although popular success was not to come until later with the publication of *Chance* (1914) and *Victory* (1915). The turning point in his career came with the writing of *The Nigger of the "Narcissus"* (1897), which indicated a marked development in his fiction. In the next ten or so years, he wrote most of his major works: *Heart of Darkness* (1899), *Lord Jim* (1900), *Nostromo* (1904), *The Secret Agent* (1907), and *Under Western Eyes* (1911). One of his least known stories, "Il Conde" (1908)" reveals Conrad as the master of swift characterization and haunting mood.

Stephen Crane (1871–1900)

Stephen Crane was born in Newark of an old New Jersey family of Revolutionary descent. He financed his college education by acting as a correspondent for the New York *Tribune.* Afterward, he lived in New York and wrote his first book, *Maggie: A Girl of the Streets* (1893). *The Red Badge of Courage* (1895) eventually ensured his fame, but like *Maggie,* earned him almost no money. In 1898, he went to London, married Cora Taylor, and settled in Oxted, Surrey, where he became friendly with Joseph Conrad. While reporting the Spanish-American War, he was troubled by failing health and was rushed to Badenweiler, Germany, where he died. Crane is often regarded as precursor of American naturalism in the novel. His short story "The Open Boat" (1898) is a classic example of men pitted against nature.

His style is marked by great understatement and economy, so that his stories carry more significance and weight than their slight plots would seem to indicate.

William Faulkner (1897–1962)

William Faulkner spent most of his life in his native Mississippi. The town of Jefferson in his work is a fictional replica of Oxford, where he made his permanent home. After graduating from the local high school, he enlisted in the Canadian Air Force during World War I. After a short stay at the University of Mississippi, he worked at odd jobs and began to write poetry, but he soon turned to writing fiction with such works as *These Thirteen* (1931), *Doctor Martino* (1934), two collections of stories; *Soldier's Pay* (1925), *Mosquitoes* (1927), and *Sartoris* (1929). His *The Sound and the Fury* (1929), *Absalom, Absalom* (1936), and *Light in August* (1932) are considered by many critics among the best novels in American literature. He received the Nobel Prize for Literature and in 1955 the Pulitzer Prize for *A Fable* (1954) and the National Book Award.

Graham Greene (1904–)

Graham Greene's early years outwardly showed little of the violence and furious bursts of belief and unbelief that mark his serious work, although his inner life, we learn from his essays, was tumultuous. Born in Hertfordshire, England, the son of a headmaster, Greene attended Oxford University and then took up newspaper work. In the 1930s he began to write what he called "entertainments," but his first major work, *Brighton Rock,* was not to appear until 1938. Then followed a series of artistic successes: *The Power and the Glory* (1940), *The Heart of the Matter* (1948), *The End of the Affair* (1951), as well as several short stories and numerous reviews. Two recent plays brought his name to Broadway, *The Potting Shed* and *The Complaisant Lover.* A novel that many critics have acclaimed as his masterpiece, *Burnt-out Case* (1961), and *The Comedians* (1966) remind us that his creative energies show few signs of flagging.

Nathaniel Hawthorne (1804–1864)

Nathaniel Hawthorne was born in Salem, Massachusetts. After winning notice with his short stories, collected in *Twice-told Tales* (1837), he entered the Brook Farm Institute, the famous Utopian literary and economic community. There he came to know Emerson, Thoreau, Margaret Fuller, and other transcendentalists who were shaping New England's intellectual life. *The Scarlet Letter* (1850) was the first of the somber novels on which Hawthorne's reputation rests: *The House of the Seven Gables* (1851); *The Blithedale Romance* (1852), which gives a picture of the Brook Farm experiment, and *The Marble Faun* (1860). Hawthorne is regarded as one of the greatest American literary figures of the nineteenth century.

Lafcadio Hearn (1850–1904)

Lafcadio Patricio Tessima Carlos Hearn was born in the Ionian Islands of Greek and English-Irish parentage. When he was seven, he was sent to Dublin to live with an aunt. He lost the sight of his left eye while playing a game at school, and the added strain on his right eye caused it to become enlarged to twice its natural size. The effect was to make him morbidly shy and self-conscious. At the age of nineteen, he moved to New York, and for twenty years pursued a sometimes precarious career in journalism, working chiefly in Cincinnati, New Orleans, New York, and the West Indies.

After some early translations of stories by Theophile Gautier, Hearn earned a reputation as a regional novelist of Louisiana and the Caribbean. *Chita* (1887) and *Youma* (1890) are his most successful stories.

His search for the exotic led him to Japan in 1890, where he spent the rest of his life teaching and interpreting Japanese culture to the West in such works as *Kokoro* (1896), *In Ghostly*

Japan (1899), and his best work, *Glimpses of Unfamiliar Japan* (1894). He became a Japanese citizen under the name of Koizumi Yakumo.

Ernest Hemingway (1898–1961)

The son of a physician who committed suicide, Ernest Hemingway enjoyed an adventurous and distinguished career before taking his own life. Born in Illinois, he served on the Italian front in World War I and then settled in Paris to become a writer. *The Sun Also Rises* (1926), *Farewell to Arms* (1929), and *A Moveable Feast* (1964) grew out of these experiences. In 1922, he reported the Turkish massacres of the Armenians and Greeks for a Canadian newspaper and developed a sense of compassion for the oppressed and powerless underdog. The terse vigorous technique of understatement in his stories and novels established him as a major stylist of the thirties. In 1937, his early dissociation from political questions gave way to a position of greater involvement in *To Have and Have Not.* That same year, moved by the Loyalist cause, he went to Spain as a war correspondent during the Civil War. Out of this experience came *For Whom the Bell Tolls* (1940), the best piece of fiction to come out of that war. The novel reveals his deep sympathy for the plight of the Spanish peasant, just as "The Capital of the World" in this volume, one of the finest of his many distinguished short stories, reflects his feeling for the aspirations and tragedies of Spanish youth.

Henry James (1843–1916)

Henry James spent most of his adult life attempting to perfect the novel as an art form, a devotion that extended until the year of his death. As a novelist and as a critic of the novel, he has exerted great influence on the entire course of twentieth-century American and English fiction, although he received little more than sporadic critical acclaim during his lifetime. His most famous novels include *The American* (1876), *The Europeans* (1878), *Daisy Miller* (1878), *The Portrait of a Lady* (1880), *The Princess Casmassima* (1885), *The Wings of the Dove* (1902), *The Ambassadors* (1903), and *The Golden Bowl* (1904). His short stories, which were written mainly during his middle years (1877–1909), combined the famed Jamesian sensibility with a crispness of pace often lacking in the longer, more leisurely fiction.

James Joyce (1882–1941)

James Joyce was born in Dublin, the city that, although he spent most of his adult years as a voluntary exile from his homeland, was to occupy his thoughts until his death in 1941. Dublin is interwoven into the fabric of his short stories, *Dubliners* (1914), into his first novel, *A Portrait of the Artist as a Young Man* (1916), and into the two long works that became the keystones of his career: *Ulysses* (1922) and *Finnegans Wake* (1939). Joyce's work has continued to tower over other twentieth-century English novels. His original techniques and genius with language have as yet found no equal. "Counterparts," one of his most widely admired stories, is from *Dubliners*. Recently, *Ulysses* was made into a film and *Finnegan* into a play.

D. H. Lawrence (1885–1930)

Like Conrad, Lawrence started out in a profession which ultimately he was to forsake, in this case, schoolteaching. Born in Eastwood, near Nottingham, Lawrence re-created the atmosphere and some of the facts of his early home life in his third novel, *Sons and Lovers* (1913). Lawrence was dissatisfied with this novel, however, and subsequently turned to a more poetic vision of life in *The Rainbow* (1915) and *Women in Love* (1920), two of the novels on which his reputation rests. These two long works seem to indicate his general direction, for in the next ten years there appeared *Aaron's Rod* (1922), *St. Mawr* (1925), *The Plumed Serpent* (1926), *Lady Chatterley's Lover* (1928), and *The Man Who Died* (1929). Though more than fifteen million copies of *Lady Chatterley's Lover* have been sold, Lawrence died a poor man, a victim of Victorian censorship. "The Horse Dealer's Daughter" first appeared in *England, My England* (1922).

Jack London (1876–1916)

Born in San Francisco, the illegitimate son of an itinerant Irish astrologer, Jack London by the age of twenty had already been a tramp, a sailor, and a Klondike gold prospector. His Alaskan experiences provided him with the material of his first collection of stories, *The Son of the Wolf* (1900), and for his two most popular novels, *The Call of the Wild* (1903) and its sequel, *White Fang* (1905). *The Sea Wolf* (1904), based upon his sailor's life, is an attempt to portray the Nietzschean superman. *The Iron Heel* (1907) reveals the influence of Marx on his thought, and *Martin Eden* (1909) is an autobiographical novel in which the hero commits suicide just as the author was to do seven years later. London's emphasis upon the primitive, the cruel, and the realistic, combined with his gift for adventure tales of great power, made him for a time the highest-paid and best-known writer in America.

Norman Mailer (1923–   )

Norman Mailer, born in Long Branch, New Jersey, was raised and educated in Brooklyn. After graduating from Harvard in 1943, he served with the combat forces in the Pacific. *The Naked and the Dead* (1948), one of the most impressive novels to emerge from World War II, is based on this experience. Subsequently he wrote *Barbary Shore* (1951), *The Deer Park* (1955), and *An American Dream* (1965), part of which first appeared in *Advertisement for Myself* (1959). Mailer's self-avowed purpose in writing is to "serve as the gadfly to complacency, institution, and the dead weight of public taste." To that end, he has become a controversial public figure.

Bernard Malamud (1914–   )

Bernard Malamud was born in Brooklyn of immigrant Russian parents. He was graduated from the City College of New York, and thereafter worked at various jobs while teaching evenings at a local high school. After taking his M.A. at Columbia, he taught English at Oregon State University (1949–1961) and at Bennington. His novels include *The Natural* (1952), *The Assistant* (1957), and *A New Life* (1961). His short stories collected in *The Magic Barrel* (1958) and *Idiots First* (1963) are marked by compassion and wry humor, usually dealing with the unhappy plight of Jewish life. *The Fixer* (1966) deals with a "simple Jewish man" living in the Russia of Nicholas II, who somehow steps into history more deeply than others. Along with Philip Roth, Saul Bellow, and Norman Mailer, Malamud has been in the forefront of the recent "Jewish Renaissance" in American letters.

Vladimir Nabokov (1899–   )

Novelist, poet, and memoirist, Nabokov was born of Russian nobility in St. Petersburg. He attended the Prince Tenishev Gymnasium there and then specialized in Romance and Slavic languages at Cambridge. Between 1922 and 1940, he lived in Germany and France, devoting himself chiefly to writing. In 1949, he came to the United States, teaching (Stanford, Wellesley, Cornell) and writing. His most controversial work is his satirical novel *Lolita* (1955). His other works include *Pnin* (1957), a partly autobiographical novel about a bumbling university professor of languages, *Nabokov's Dozen* (1958), a collection of stories, and translations of Pushkin and Lermontov. Though all of his early writing is in Russian, his English style is rich and lucid, and he is now regarded as the major émigré Russian writer of our time. At present, he is living in Switzerland.

Hugh Nissenson (1933–)

A relatively little known but promising young writer, Hugh Nissenson was born in New York City and educated at Swarthmore. After graduation, he lived in Israel for a year, some of the time on a *kibbutzim* in the Negev and some near the Syrian border, and covered the Eichmann Trial for *Commentary*. Later, he attended Stanford University on a writing fellowship. He has written screenplays, has published a collection of short stories called *A Pile of Stones* (1965), and is working on a novel.

Flannery O'Connor (1925–1964)

Born in Savannah, Georgia, Miss O'Connor uses Southern settings for the background of her stories. Her first novel, *Wise Blood* (1952), received acclaim for its freshness of view and starkness of power. *The Violent Bear It Away* (1960) has the quasi-comic grotesquery that characterizes many of the stories in the two collections which ensure her reputation in this form: *A Good Man Is Hard to Find* (1955), and *Everything That Rises Must Converge* (1964). Before her career was cut short at the age of thirty-nine, she was one of the most promising younger contemporary writers.

Frank O'Connor—Michael O'Donovan (1903–)

Born in Cork, Frank O'Connor attended the Christian Brothers school there, then worked as a librarian. It was in this profession that he was able to educate himself and to develop as a writer. Like some of his early prose and poetry, his first volume of stories, *Guests of the Nation* (1931), was written in Gaelic. *Dutch Interior* (1940) is a collection of stories that paints a discouraging picture of Irish life, but the comic mood takes over in such collections as *More Stories* (1954) and *Domestic Relations* (1957). Though he directed the Abbey Theatre for a time and has translated Gaelic poetry, his forte is the short story.

Yeats once remarked that O'Connor was "doing for Ireland what Chekov did for Russia." His stories are noted for their sense of humor, realism, and richness of characterization.

Liam O'Flaherty (1896–   )

One of Ireland's great modern writers, O'Flaherty was born in the Aran Islands. He studied for the priesthood in Tipperary and Dublin, but feeling no call to the religious life, he took up secular studies at University College in Dublin. During World War I, he joined the Irish Guards in the British Army, saw action in France, and was discharged, a victim of shell shock, in 1917. Subsequently, he traveled widely, working as a seaman, laborer, and lumberjack. Upon returning to Ireland, he fought with the Irish Republican Army in the insurrection of 1922. After the Irish Free State was established, he turned to writing. His most famous novel, *The Informer* (1925), was made into a memorable motion picture. His other works include *Spring Sowing* (1926), *Famine* (1937), and *Two Lovely Beasts and Other Stories* (1948). He also wrote several "melodramas of the soul," novels which, like Graham Greene's, combine elements of the thriller and the psychoanalytic case history.

Edgar Allan Poe (1809–1849)

Born in Boston of itinerant actors and orphaned at an early age, Poe was reared by John Allan, a foster parent. When, in 1826, Allan refused to support him at the University of Virginia, Poe tried to live by gambling and writing. He joined the army but was expelled from West Point for negligence. About the same time he published *Poems* (1831), which marked the beginning of his literary career. Thereafter he was associated with various publications as editor and contributor of fiction that dealt with abnormal states, with murder or suicide, or with mystery-suspense. He also wrote poetry and criticism, both of which were regarded as important contributions to American literature. Poe literally drank himself to death, the end coming in Baltimore.

His present fame rests more on his short stories than on any of the other forms he practiced with the highest skill. Among his classics of the grotesque and arabesque are "The Tell-tale Heart," "The Pit and the Pendulum," "The Fall of the House of Usher," and "Berenice" (c. 1840).

Katherine Anne Porter (1890–   )

Born at Indian Creek, Texas, into a family with a long Southern heritage, Katherine Anne Porter was raised in Texas and

Louisiana and educated in convent and private schools. She later traveled widely, living in Mexico, Germany, and France. In 1931 she received a Guggenheim Fellowship to study abroad. She married Eugene Pressly, a member of the American consular staff in Paris. After divorce, she married Albert Russel Erskine, a professor of English. The settings for her fiction are drawn from her travels and her Southern background. Her principal works are *Flowering Judas* (1930), *Hacienda* (1934), *Noon Wine* (1937), *Pale Horse, Pale Rider* (1939), *No Safe Harbor* (1942), *The Leaning Tower* (1944), and *Ship of Fools* (1962), a novel that took twenty years to write.

Her style is marked by purity and precision; at the same time, it is delicate, supple, and lucid.

J. F. Powers (1917–)

Born in Jacksonville, Illinois, James F. Powers attended local schools and received his secondary education from Franciscan friars. Before succeeding as a writer, he attended Northwestern University and worked in bookstores in Chicago and as an editor of the *Historical Records Survey.* In 1948, he received a Guggenheim Fellowship in Creative Writing and a grant from the National Institute of Arts and Letters after completing his book *Prince of Darkness and Other Stories* (1947). He taught writing courses at Marquette University in Milwaukee for two years, but then devoted his full time to writing fiction about Catholic clergymen whose contact with the world creates spiritual dilemmas. His stories have been widely praised, particularly *The Presence of Grace* (1956), and his novel *Mort d'Urban* (1962) won the National Book Award.

James Purdy (1923–)

James Purdy was born in rural Ohio and educated in the Midwest. He received his master's degree from the University of Chicago and then studied at the University of Madrid. *Don't Call Me by My Right Name,* a collection of short stories, and *63: Dream Palace,* a novella, were privately published in 1956. Recognizing his talent, a commercial publisher combined their contents and issued them under the title *The Color of Darkness* (1957). His first novel, *Malcolm* (1959), adapted to the stage by Edward Albee, is a satiric commentary on the lack of values in American life. *The Nephew* (1960), set in an area reminiscent of rural Ohio, examines the empty life of a retired schoolteacher mourning the death of her nephew, and the novel *Cabot Wright Begins* (1964) is a satire about a rapist educated at Yale.

Florence Randall (1917–)

Born in the Flatbush section of Brooklyn, Mrs. Randall attended Erasmus Hall High School and sold her first story at the age of eighteen while taking courses at New York University. The demands of raising three children and keeping home in Great Neck, Long Island, did not permit her to take up serious writing again until 1961. Since then, her crisp and polished short stories have appeared in a number of familiar publications including *Harper's* (from which "The Watchers" comes), *Redbook,* and *Seventeen.* Her first novel *Hedgerow,* appeared in 1967, and she is completing her second.

Saki—H. H. Munro (1870–1916)

The son of an army officer, H. H. Munro was born in Burma. He was educated in English public schools and by private tutors. He returned to Burma in 1893 to join the military police, but illness forced him back to England after thirteen months. During this illness he turned to writing. From 1902 until his return to London in 1908, he was a newspaper correspondent in the Balkans, Russia, and Paris, but found time to publish his first volume of stories, *Reginald* (1904). When World War I broke out, he enlisted in the British army and was killed on the Western front. "The Mouse" is taken from *Reginald in Russia* (1910), one of the volumes in *The Complete Short Stories of Saki* (1930). His stories are humorous, ironic, and sometimes macabre visions of a stupid and conventional adult world.

William Sansom (1912–)

Born in England and educated there and on the continent, William Sansom has spent most of his life writing. Through more than a dozen books of fiction, he has developed a wide following and a major reputation. He writes sinister Kafkaesque works such as *The Body* (1945), a novel about a paranoid delusion narrated by its victim, but his true milieu is the short story of stunning impact. Many such stories grace the pages of such collections as *Fireman Flower* (1944), *The Face of Innocence* (1951), *Something Terrible, Something Lovely* (1954), and *A Bed of Roses* (1954). His collection *The Ulcerated Milkman* (1966) deals with moments when people feel their worlds to be suddenly and magically illuminated.

Irwin Shaw (1913–)

Irwin Shaw was born in Brooklyn and took his B.A. at Brooklyn College. While writing radio serials and dramatizations, he achieved Broadway prominence with his Play *Bury the Dead* (1936). Subsequently he wrote screenplays and scenarios for Hollywood and many books of fiction. His finest novel, *The Young Lions* (1948), is based on his military service in World War II. His other novels include *The Troubled Air* (1951), *Lucy Crown* (1956), *Two Weeks in Another Town* (1960), and *Voices of a Summer Day* (1965). They are noted for their dramatic intensity and social awareness. As a writer of short stories, Shaw belongs to the Hemingway school of tough understatement. Among his well-known collections are *Sailor off the Bremen* (1939), *Welcome to the City* (1942), and *Tip on a Dead Jockey and Other Stories* (1957). He and his wife live in both the United States and Europe.

Jesse Stuart (1907–)

Jesse Hilton Stuart was born in the eastern hill country of Kentucky, the locale of his fiction, and was educated at Lincoln Memorial and Vanderbilt Universities in Tennessee. While teaching school, an experience recounted in *The Thread That Runs So True* (1949), he published a volume of poems, *Man with a Bull-tongue Plow* (1934), that launched his career of writing. He has become better known as a novelist and short story writer, with such works as *Head O' W-Hollow* (1936), *Men of the Mountain* (1941), *Taps for Private Tussie* (1943), *Hie to the Hunter* (1950), and *The Good Spirit of Laurel Ridge* (1953), solidifying his reputation. His recent collection of short stories, *My Land Has a Voice* (1966), suggests that he has not forgotten how to blend folk poetry with dog lore.

Dylan Thomas (1914–1953)

Dylan Thomas was the son of a Swansea schoolmaster with poetic ambitions. Not a particularly brilliant schoolboy, he did very well at English, and first became known as a poet through his contributions to *The Sunday Referee,* which backed the publication of his first volume, *Eighteen Poems* (1943). During World War II, he worked for the BBC, and in the forties published two volumes of poetry, *New Poems* and *Deaths and Entrances,* that brought him notice. Soon he developed into the most original poet of his day and a brilliant reader of his own work.

Chiefly a poet, Thomas also wrote a kind of poetic prose that has almost no equal in English. Like his poetry, it is full of lyrical power, surrealism, and vivid metaphors. His earliest stories were not published until 1955 when they appeared as *Adventures in the Skin Trade.* "One Warm Saturday" comes from *Portrait of the Artist as a Young Dog* (1940), a title which reflects his admiration for James Joyce.

John Updike (1932–)

John Updike was born in Pennsylvania and educated at Harvard and Oxford. After working for *The New Yorker* from 1955 to 1957, he published his first novel, *The Poorhouse Fair* (1959). His next works were *Rabbit, Run* (1960) and *The Centaur* (1963). His short stories include a collection in *The Same Door* (1960) and *Pigeon Feathers* (1961). He writes mainly of the lives of ordinary people in small town Pennsylvania settings. Volumes of light verse include *The Carpentered Hen and Other Tame Creatures* (1958) and *Telephone Poles* (1963). He has also published *Assorted Prose* (1965). Among his most recent works is *The Music School* (1966), a collection of short stories.

John Updike is considered one of the most gifted of contemporary novelists, a writer to whom "character is drama, a thought is an act as specific as a gunshot."

Robert Penn Warren (1905–)

Robert Penn Warren has made his impact upon American letters as poet, novelist, short story writer, critic, editor, and teacher. Born in Kentucky, he was educated at Vanderbilt University, where he became a member of the Fugitive Group, which was devoted to agrarian and "Southern" themes in poetry. He was also founder and managing editor of the *Southern Review* and has taught at several universities, including Louisiana State, Minnesota, and Yale. He received the 1947 Pulitzer Prize for his portrait of a southern demagogue, *All the King's Men* (1946), and won a wide audience with other novels: *Night Rider* (1939), *At Heaven's Gate* (1943), and *World Enough and Time* (1950). His poetry, noted for its vivid metaphor, gained him a second Pulitzer Prize for Literature in 1957. Warren is equally distinguished as a critic and short story writer. "The Unvexed Isles" comes from *The Circus in the Attic and Other Stories* (1947).

H. G. Wells (1866–1946)

The first great writer of science fiction, Herbert George Wells was born in Bromley, Kent, and educated at the Royal College of

Science at South Kensington. He began his career as a teacher, but achieved world fame with the publication of his novel *Tono-Bungay* (1909). An indefatigable writer who once said he hoped to be remembered as a journalist, Wells produced many best-selling novels and stories, among them *The Time Machine* (1896), *The Invisible Man* (1897), *The War of the Worlds* (1901), *Ann Veronica* (1909), *The History of Mr. Polly* (1910), *Mr. Britling Sees It Through* (1916), and *The Bulpington of Blup* (1933). His *Outline of History* (1920) is still enormously popular, and his *Experiment in Autobiography* (1934) has just been reissued. Though he turned out books on almost every conceivable theme and current issue, his early stories, fantastic, imaginative, often set centuries in the future or in invented lands, will probably be remembered longest. Of these, "The Country of the Blind," from a 1911 collection of tales with the same title, is a noteworthy instance of his ability to weave together the fantastic and the philosophical.

Eudora Welty (1909–)

Eudora Welty was educated at Mississippi State College for Women, the University of Wisconsin, and Columbia University. Her first collection of stories, *A Curtain of Green* (1941), brought her immediate acclaim for its sensitive, compassionate handling of small town life in the Deep South. *The Wide Net* (1943) and *The Golden Apples* (1949) added to her reputation as a master of the short story, and *Delta Wedding* (1946) and *The Ponder Heart* (1956) established her as a novelist with an ear for the colloquial and an eye for the little tragedies in the lives of ordinary folk.

AUTHOR INDEX

TITLE INDEX